HIDDEN San Francisco and Northern California

"Captures the mystique of the locale. Locals will find it refreshing; vacationers should find it very worthwhile."

—*Los Angeles Times*

"An excellent guide. Riegert seems to have gotten everywhere there is to get and seen everything there is to see."

—*Honolulu Advertiser*

"As complete as a guide can be, and written for the traveler who wants new discoveries"

—*San Antonio Express-News*

"Leads the traveler into some fascinating byways to enrich the journey."

—*San Diego Tribune*

"Whether you're a mountain climber or a shopper, an architecture buff or a whale watcher, this book will be a fine tour guide. The book is packed with inside information."

—*Travel Agent magazine*

"A great guidebook for those who will be traveling in and around the city."

—*Out & About*

HIDDEN San Francisco and Northern California

Ray Riegert

SEVENTH EDITION

Ulysses Press
BERKELEY, CALIFORNIA

Published by:
Ulysses Press
P.O. Box 3440
Berkeley, CA 94703-3440

Library of Congress Catalog Card Number 96-60084
ISBN 1-56975-007-6

20 19 18 17 16 15

Editorial Director: Leslie Henriques
Managing Editor: Claire Chun
Project Director: Lee Micheaux
Update Author: Judy Jacobs
Copy Editor: David Sweet
Editorial Associates: Deema Khorsheed, Kenya Ratcliff, Lily Chou, Toby Bielawski, Mark Rosen
Cartographers: Rob March Harper, Claire Chun
Cover Design: Sarah Levin
Indexer: Sayre Van Young
Cover Photography: Front: Jim Lundgren
Circle and back: Robert Holmes
Back (hikers): Larry Ulrich
Illustrator: Rob March Harper

Distributed in the United States by Publishers Group West, in Canada by Raincoast Books, and in Great Britain and Europe by World Leisure Marketing

To Leslie,

for the wonderful years behind us and the many ahead

Acknowledgments

As soon as I finish a book, everyone who worked on it applies for an unlisted phone number. The zany pace and fatal deadlines cost me colleagues, friends, even relatives. A few stalwart souls stick it out, and to them I feel a tremendous sense of gratitude.

Foremost is my wife Leslie, who contributed to every aspect of the project. She served as researcher, designer, writer, editor, proofreader, and in countless other roles, working impossible hours under incredible pressure. She gave inspiration to the author and life to the book.

Claire Chun added her many abilities, helping to research, copy edit, and typeset the material. Judy Jacobs contributed her talents to this revised edition, assisting with the research and writing alike. I have to give special thank yous to Lee Micheaux, the project director for this edition; Bryce Willett, who added his research and writing abilities; and David Sweet for his editing work.

Sayre Van Young once again lent her ample talents as indexer. Sarah Levin provided a wonderful blend of talent and aesthetics designing the cover. Deema Khorsheed, Kenya Ratcliff, Lily Chou, Toby Bielawski, and Mark Rosen also assisted with the revision of the current edition.

What's Hidden?

At different points throughout this book, you'll find special listings marked with a hidden symbol:

◄ HIDDEN

This means that you have come upon a place off the beaten tourist track, a spot that will carry you a step closer to the local people and natural environment of San Francisco and Northern California.

The goal of this guide is to lead you beyond the realm of everyday tourist facilities. While we include traditional sightseeing listings and popular attractions, we also offer alternative sights and adventure activities. Instead of filling this guide with reviews of standard hotels and chain restaurants, we concentrate on one-of-a-kind places and locally owned establishments.

Our authors seek out locales that are popular with residents but usually overlooked by visitors. Some are more hidden than others (and are marked accordingly), but all the listings in this book are intended to help you discover the true nature of San Francisco and Northern California and put you on the path of adventure.

Write to us!

If in your travels you discover a spot that captures the spirit of San Francisco and Northern California, or if you live in the region and have a favorite place to share, or if you just feel like expressing your views, write to us and we'll pass your note along to the author.

We can't guarantee that the author will add your personal find to the next edition, but if the writer does use the suggestion, we'll acknowledge you in the credits and send you a free autographed copy of the new edition.

ULYSSES PRESS
3286 Adeline Street, Suite 1
Berkeley, CA 94703
E-mail: ulypress@aol.com

Contents

Maps

Special Features

OUTDOOR ADVENTURE SYMBOLS

The following symbols accompany national, state, and regional park listings, as well as beach descriptions throughout the text.

- Camping
- Hiking 
- Biking 
- Horseback Riding 
- Downhill Skiing 
- Cross-country Skiing 
- Swimming 
- Snorkeling or Scuba Diving 
- Surfing 
- Waterskiing 
- Windsurfing
- Canoeing or Kayaking 
- Boating 
- Boat Ramps 
- Fishing

ONE

California Dreaming

Travelers today possess an awareness and imagination lacking in their outlandish predecessors. Vacations were once escapes from routine. People charted two weeks a year as an island-in-time where they changed from wool suits to bathing suits. In desperate attempts to forget office hours and car payments, they gravitated to overcrowded tourist areas where life proved as frenzied as back home.

Now travel is becoming a personal art form. A destination no longer serves simply as a place to relax: it's also a point of encounter, where experience runs feverish and reality unravels. To many, this new wave in travel customs is labeled "adventure travel" and involves trekking glaciers or dusting granite walls in a hang glider; to others, it connotes nothing more daring than a restful spell at a hidden country inn. Actually, it's a state of mind, a willingness not only to accept but seek out the uncommon and unique.

This book is written for those taking up the challenge of this freewheeling style. It's intended not for tourists but travelers—people who are equally at ease on a mountain trail or a city boulevard. As a guide, it leads you through San Francisco, then combs the Bay Area and beyond in search of adventure.

Many traditional tourist spots are described, but I have tried to take you a step further. In San Francisco, for instance, you'll visit ever-popular Chinatown, but after walking the crowded blocks of Grant Avenue, the tour leads down an alleyway to a fortune cookie factory. I've listed well-known restaurants and also uncovered the tradition of dim sum dining. In North Beach, the walking tour carries you from Broadway's neon strip to a silent street lined with wooden sidewalks and flowering gardens. At Fisherman's Wharf, you skirt the tacky tourist section and wander the barnacle-caked waterfront, where Italian fishermen still ply an ancient trade.

Then head for The Neighborhoods, far from the Gray Line crowds, to discover the soul of the city. Union Street is a strange mix of historic Victorian homes and swinging singles bars; Russian Hill contains pocket parks and hills so steep that steps replace sidewalks; Haight-Ashbury is celebrating a comeback; the lively Mission District is a fascinating neighborhood with its colorful murals and authentic mariachi bands. San Francisco's gay neighborhoods, particularly Castro and Polk streets, are fully described.

You can explore Golden Gate Park, the West Coast answer to New York's Central Park. Farther afield lies the Golden Gate National Recreation Area with its joggers and hang gliders; the Presidio, a spacious forest in the midst of a major city; and Land's End, where San Francisco marks its finale in a wild tangle of fractured cliffs and untracked coastline.

For the Bay Area, there are descriptions of Sausalito's unique houseboat community and the secluded country towns of Port Costa and Benicia. In Berkeley, you'll learn how the '60s revolution surrendered to a revolution in the kitchen. During the '70s and '80s "California cuisine" seized the time and created some of the nation's finest restaurants. There are bayside parks galore, plus a look at the hills and dales of Silicon Valley.

The tourism industry has a knack for transforming everyday life into a spectacle and making tourists feel like visitors to a huge, outdoor human zoo. The result is a kind of Heisenberg-uncertainty-principle-of-tourism whereby the mere presence of outsiders changes the human landscape forever. Local residents become actors, historic places are transformed into theme parks, and visitors see something which more nearly reflects themselves than the indigenous culture.

Like Heisenberg's dilemma, the phenomenon is unavoidable. But given the sensitivity and circumspection contemporary travelers are demonstrating, it is possible to gaze into America's cultural kaleidoscope without greatly disturbing the glass pieces.

In the following pages, I've provided a quiet and intimate approach to Northern California, taking you beyond the surface and into the heart of the place. Visiting the Wine Country, for instance, the book explores the burgeoning winegrowing regions of Sonoma and Napa valleys, stopping at tiny wineries where quality is a matter of family pride. Then it rolls west through the Russian River resort area, a getaway destination for gay men and lesbians. Families also vacation here because of the numerous outdoor opportunities.

Along the magnificent California coast, you'll range from Big Sur to Oregon, stopping at quaint bed and breakfast inns and tiny restaurants. The book describes picnics amid the redwoods, hiking trails high above the Pacific, nude beaches, and twisting country roads.

Then it heads for California's golden hills, the Sierra Nevada. Climbing through the Gold Country, where the ghosts of '49ers still wander falsefront towns, it leads to Lake Tahoe and Yosemite. Traditional tourist places are examined in detail, but the important moment is when the tour leaves the beaten track to include hideaway hotels, cozy nightspots, and remote campgrounds.

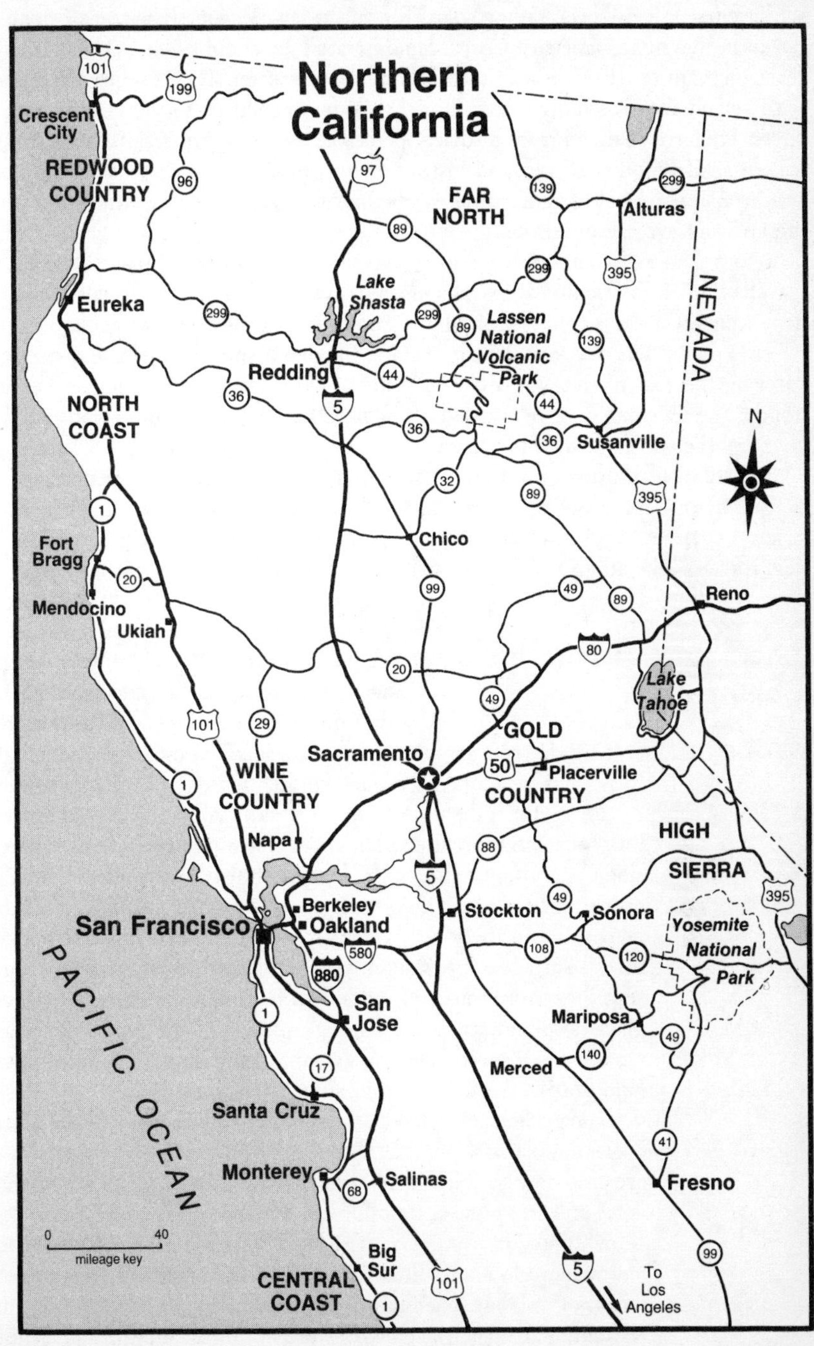

Northern California
Crescent City
REDWOOD COUNTRY
FAR NORTH
Alturas
NEVADA
Lake Shasta
Eureka
Lassen National Volcanic Park
Redding
NORTH COAST
Susanville
N
Chico
Fort Bragg
Mendocino
Ukiah
Reno
Lake Tahoe
GOLD
Sacramento
WINE COUNTRY
Placerville
COUNTRY
Napa
HIGH SIERRA
Berkeley
Oakland
San Francisco
Stockton
Sonora
Yosemite National Park
San Jose
Mariposa
Merced
PACIFIC OCEAN
Santa Cruz
Monterey
Salinas
Fresno
0
40
mileage key
Big Sur
CENTRAL COAST
To Los Angeles

While this fresh style of travel appeals to people ranging in age from sprout to senior citizen, it has been taking shape for only a few decades. The transformation began in the '60s. The Peace Corps demonstrated we could swim freely in foreign seas; Vietnam taught us not to thrash about in the water. Then the preoccupation with self in the '70s, narcissistic though it was, opened us to unmapped experiences. We have changed from a society perceived as "ugly Americans" to a people in search of unique cultures and history. Better informed, more sensitive and adventurous, we travel for education as much as enjoyment. Rather than proclaiming answers, we ask questions.

More than anywhere in the country, Northern California is a place for creative travelers. It's a multicultural extravaganza as well as a region of exceptional natural beauty. Continents have drifted into San Francisco Bay in ways geologists will never explain. Asia overlaps the entire state, Mexico is shifting north, and tides are carrying the rest of the world closer. Chinese are moving into Italian neighborhoods, French vintners have invaded the Wine Country, and Scandinavians are discovering the snows of the High Sierra.

Northern California is a destination best suited to a particular pattern of exploration, one requiring an open spirit and unquenchable curiosity. It's a place where experience and adventure form a pattern of overlapping layers which the new traveler, like an archaeologist, will personally uncover.

The Story of Northern California

GEOLOGY

For billions of years, natural forces have carved the geology of California, creating a land as grand as it is beautiful. Bounded to the west by the cold waters of the Pacific and on the east by sharp mountain ranges and dense forests, Northern California has developed a diverse landscape rich in geologic history.

As a whole, the interior of Northern California can be divided into four natural regions. The first is the Sierra Nevada, the largest single mountain range in the United States. It's a solitary block of earth, tilted and uplifted, 430 miles long and 80 miles wide. A mere child in the long count of geologic history, it rose from the earth's surface a few million years back and did not reach its present form until 750,000 years ago. During the Pleistocene epoch, glaciers spread across the land, grinding and cutting at the mountains. They carved river valleys and deep canyons, and sculpted bald domes, fluted cliffs, and stone towers.

The glaciers left a landscape dominated by ragged peaks where lakes number in the hundreds and canyons plunge 5000 feet. There are cliffs sheer as glass that compete with the sky for dominance. It is, as an early pioneer described it, a "land of fire and ice."

Millions of years ago, the Klamath region separated from the Sierra Nevada and drifted 60 miles to the northwest. Composed of rocky uplands extending as high as 7000 feet in elevation, the Klamaths are deeply etched by the Smith, Klamath, and Trinity rivers. Heavy precipitation and fog have created dense coniferous forests which now dominate the landscape.

To the east of the Klamaths is the third natural region, which encompasses the southern extension of the volcanic Cascade Range and includes Mount Shasta and Lassen Peak. Mt. Shasta, rising over 14,000 feet, is lord of the land, a white-domed figure brooding above a forested realm. Lassen Peak, its infernal cousin, is an active volcano which last erupted in 1921. Composed of andesite volcanic rock and dated at several million years of age, the Cascade Range developed as a result of the process of subduction.

The fourth natural region consists of the Coast Ranges, which extend up the San Francisco peninsula, through Northern California to Oregon. Built of shale, sandstone, and other sedimentary rocks, the Coast Ranges are a product of pressure from the Pacific Plate beneath the western border of North America. These peaks include the Santa Cruz Mountains, which rise to the west and south of San Francisco Bay; on the other side of the Bay are the East Bay Hills and the Diablo Range; to the north looms Mt. Tamalpais. At the mouth of the Bay is the Golden Gate, a rocky conduit through which California's major drainage system empties into the Pacific.

The California coast is lined with softly rolling hills and bounded by a pacific sea. The shoreline is actually a head-on collision between the edge of the ocean and the rim of North America. Two tectonic plates, those rafts of land that float upon the earth's core, meet in California. Here the North American Plate and the Pacific Plate push against each other in a kind of international arm wrestle. Between them, and under colossal pressure from both sides, lies the San Andreas fault. Villain of the 1906 San Francisco earthquake, it is subject at any moment to catastrophic forces.

Things were not always as they are. About 150 million years ago, the California coast rested where the Sierra Nevada mountains reside today. Then the North American Plate shifted west, riding roughshod over the Pacific Plate, compressing and folding the earth upward to create the Coast Ranges, and moving the continent 100 miles westward.

A FLOODED CANYON

According to geologists, San Francisco Bay is a drowned river valley. Glaciers melting 10,000 years ago created it by raising sea levels and causing the ocean to flood a canyon carved earlier by the Sacramento and San Joaquin rivers.

Today the San Andreas fault starts at the coast just south of San Francisco, then cuts north through Stinson Beach, Bodega Bay, and Point Arena, before heading seaward from Shelter Cove. Meanwhile the Pacific Plate, carrying Los Angeles, is shifting north along the North American Plate, which holds San Francisco, at a pace that should position the rival cities next to each other in about ten million years. Anyone planning to hitch a ride north should pack extra sandwiches and prepare for a long wait at the side of the road.

FLORA

From dark redwood forests to sunny alpine meadows to a coastline colored by wildflowers, California's habitats are heaven to natural history lovers. Radical climatic differences within the state are largely responsible for creating this unique diversity.

Heavy precipitation and cold temperatures in the Sierra Nevada create the perfect environment for dense coniferous forests of Ponderosa pine, white fir, and red fir. Higher up, the sugar pines and Sierra redwoods tower over manzanita, deer brush, and Sierra gooseberry. Also included in this high-altitude habitat is California's own giant sequoia, which is the pride of Sequoia and Kings Canyon national parks.

In the riparian woodlands of the Sierra Nevada, smaller trees and larger shrubs including willows, cottonwoods, white alders, and dogwoods thrive. Often bounded by lodgepole forests, Sierra meadows are home to an array of springtime wildflowers—phloxes, paintbrushes, lupines, elephants head, and the brilliant scarlet gilia.

More than 30 percent of the plant species in California are endemic.

In the Far North region of the Klamath mountains, abundant rainfall and moderate temperatures combine to create a dense forest similar to that of the Alaskan coast. Species include Alaskan cedar, Douglas fir, and silver fir. At higher elevations, wind-eroded foxtail pine, a close relative of the ancient bristlecone pine of Southern California, survive. The lower slopes along the coast are host to Pacific madrone, tan oak, and California laurel, while different species of shrubby willow trees are found from Humboldt County to Del Norte County.

East of the Klamaths, the volcanic soils of the Cascades support a unique conifer known as the Baker cypress, which flourishes despite the area's cold weather conditions. In the lowlands, rainfall and fog have created forests dotted with ponderosa and Jeffrey pine.

From the rim of the sea to the peaks of surrounding mountains, the coastline is covered with a complex variety of plant life. Several plant communities flourish along the shore, each clinging to a particular niche in the environment. Blessed with a cooler, more moderate climate near the ocean, they are continually misted by sea spray and must contend with more salt in their veins.

On the beaches and along the dunes are the herbs, vines, and low shrubs of the coastal strand community. Among their numbers are beach primrose, sand verbena, beach morning-glory, and sea figs, those tenacious succulents that run along the ground sprouting magenta flowers and literally carpeting the coast. Characterized by leathery leaves that retain large quantities of water, they are the plant world's answer to the camel.

Around the mud flats and river mouths grow rushes, pickleweed, tules, cord grass, and other members of the salt marsh community. Low, shrubby plants growing in clumps, these hearty fellows are inundated by tides and able to withstand tremendous concentrations of salt.

Coastal sage scrub inhabits a broad swath from above the waterline to about the 3000-foot elevation. White and black sage, wild buckwheat, and California sagebrush belong to this community of short, tough plants.

Along the northern coastal ranges, cold ocean waters create heavy fog, an essential nutrient for the eerily beautiful coastal redwoods. The fabled Monterey cypress inhabits a picturesque region along the Monterey coast, the only place in the world it is found. Closed-cone pines including the Monterey, Bishop, and knobcone skirt the shoreline. Shrubs in the northern coastal ranges include brown dogwood, Western rose-bay, and bunchberry. Scattered along the rolling hills of the coastal interior are the dignified, gnarled oak trees while the coastal woodlands are also sown with drought-tolerant species of dry grasses and assorted wildflowers including the California poppy, the state flower.

FAUNA

From the black bears of Yosemite Valley to the black-tailed deer of the East Bay hills, Northern California is home to a variety of wildlife. This is true despite the environmental stress of humans on the state's wilderness areas, which has caused the extinction of many species. The California grizzly bear, for instance, is no longer found in the Sierra Nevada; and because of the damming of rivers and streams, salmon spawning has become a rare phenomenon. Conservation efforts have increased in the past few years, and many species are now under governmental protection. For example, attempts to preserve the habitat of the bighorn sheep have been so intense that a marked increase in their population occurred for several years. Debates continually rage over the status of mountain lions and coyotes.

The rich habitat of the High Sierra is home to a variety of species including ground squirrels, yellow-bellied marmots, pikas, gophers, jack rabbits, hares, snakes, lizards, golden trout, salamanders, bighorn sheep, and great gray owls. In the lower fields of the Sierra riparian woodlands, multicolored butterflies, and a diverse selection of birds such as starlings, sparrows, blackbirds,

American dipper, and the belter kingfisher make their homes. Lower yet, the cavities in oak trees provide shelter for gray squirrels, owls, woodpeckers, and bluebirds.

The moist forests of the Klamath region are a fertile backdrop for a wide array of wildlife. There are approximately 15 colorful species of salamanders in these northern forests, including the cave-dwelling Shasta salamander and the water-loving Olympic salamander. Colorful hummingbirds, bald eagles, pileated woodpeckers, elusive spotted owls, and the marbled murrelet dart around the forests. Other critters include chipmunks, porcupines, raccoons, weasels, river otters, and Roosevelt elk.

Six species of seals and sea lions inhabit the coast, together with sea otters, those playful creatures that delight visitors and bedevil fishermen.

In the northern Coast Ranges, the insects can be as interesting as reptiles and amphibians. The monarch butterfly migrates between Canada and Central Mexico, stopping off in Pacific Grove every year. The Western pond turtle is found along the coast, while alligator lizards inhabit the coastal interior. The scrub jay helps create oak forests by storing hundreds of acorns underground. Another acorn-loving species is the acorn woodpecker, which stores its provisions in the cavities of oak trees.

Somehow the mud flats of San Francisco Bay are the last place you may think to go sightseeing, particularly at high tide, after the flood has stirred the ooze. But it is at such times that birders gather to view flocks of as many as 60,000 birds.

The California shore is one of the richest bird habitats anywhere in North America. Over 500 species are found across the state, many along the coast and its offshore islands. There are near-shore birds like loons, grebes, cormorants, and scoters, that inhabit the shallow waters of bays and beaches. Others birds are situated offshore; these include shearwaters, which feed several miles off the coast; and pelagic or open-ocean species like albatross and Arctic terns, which fly miles from land and live for up to 20 or 30 years.

Joining the shore birds along California's beaches are ducks, geese, and other waterfowl. Both waterfowl and near-shore birds flee the scene each year, flying north in spring to Canada and Alaska or south during autumn to Mexico and Central America, following the Pacific flyway, that great migratory route spanning the western United States.

The peregrine falcon nests on rock ledges and is capable of diving at 200 miles an hour to prey on ducks, coots, and terns. Among the most beautiful birds are the egrets and herons. Tall, slender, elegant birds, they live from January until July in Bolinas and other coastal towns. Together with sea gulls, sandpipers, and pelicans, they tend to turn travelers into birdwatchers and make inconvenient times, like the edge of dawn, and unusual places, like swamps, among the most intriguing possibilities Northern California has to offer.

California's marine mammals inspire great myth and magic. Foremost are the ocean-going animals like whales, dolphins, and porpoises, members of that unique Cetacean order that left the land 30 million years ago for the alien world of the sea.

While dolphins and porpoises range far offshore, the region's most common whale is a regular coastal visitor. Migrating 12,000 miles every year between the Bering Sea and Baja Peninsula, the California gray whale cruises the shoreline each winter. Measuring 50 feet and weighing 40 tons, these distinguished animals live to 50 years of age and communicate with sophisticated signaling systems.

When to Go

SEASONS

Northern California stretches over 400 miles from Big Sur to Oregon and almost 200 miles from east to west. Within that broad expanse lies the Pacific coastline, a broad interior valley, the lofty Sierra Nevada, and a weather pattern that varies as dramatically as the terrain.

Generally, there are three different climatic zones. San Francisco and the rest of the Pacific shore enjoy mild temperatures year-round, since the coastal fog creates a natural form of air conditioning and insulation. The mercury rarely drops below 40° or rises above 70°, with September and October being the hottest months, and December and January the coolest.

Spring and particularly autumn are the ideal times to visit. During winter, the rainy season brings overcast days and frequent showers. Summer is San Francisco's peak tourist season, when large crowds can present problems. It's also a period of frequent fog; especially in the morning and evening, fog banks from offshore blanket the city and head inland through the Golden Gate.

The seasons vary much more in the interior valleys, creating a second climatic zone. In the Wine Country, Delta, and Gold Country, summer temperatures often top 90°. There's less humidity, winters are cooler, and the higher elevations receive occasional snowfall. Like the coast, this piedmont region experiences most of its rain during winter months.

The Sierra Nevada and Cascade Ranges experience Northern California's most dramatic weather. During summer, the days are warm, the nights cool. Spring and autumn bring crisp temperatures and colorful foliage changes (which the coastline, with its unvarying seasons, rarely undergoes). Then in winter, the thermometer plummets and snow falls so heavily as to make these mountain chains spectacular ski areas.

CALENDAR OF EVENTS

JANUARY

San Francisco During late January or in February, the **Chinese New Year** features an extravagant parade with colorful dragons, dancers, marching bands, and fireworks.

Central Coast The **AT&T at Pebble Beach Pro-Am Golf Championship** swings into action.

FEBRUARY

North Coast The **World Championship Crab Races and Crab Feed** takes place in Crescent City; if you forgot to bring your own, you can rent a racing crab. Who said California lacks culture?

Far North Mount Shasta celebrates a **Winter Carnival** with a downhill ski torchlight parade, chocolate fest, and snow sculpture contests.

MARCH

San Francisco Bands, politicians, and assorted revelers parade through the city on the Sunday closest to March 17, marking **St. Patrick's Day**.

North Coast Mendocino and Fort Bragg celebrate a **Whale Festival** with whale-watching cruises, art shows, and winetasting.

High Sierra The **Snowfest and Winter Carnival** in Truckee and along Lake Tahoe's North Shore is a spectacular celebration with ski races, dancing, and concerts.

Central Coast Monterey presents the **California Wine Festival**, with winetasting, gourmet food stands, and cooking demonstrations.

APRIL

San Francisco Japantown's **Cherry Blossom Festival** features parades, tea ceremonies, theatrical performances, and martial arts displays. **Opening Day on the Bay** launches the yachting season with a blessing of the fleet and a parade of decorated boats. The **San Francisco International Film Festival** offers a wide selection of cinematic events.

Wine Country The entire town of Sebastopol turns out for an **Apple Blossom Festival**, staging exhibits, parades, and pageants.

MAY

San Francisco Over 100,000 hearty souls (soles?) run the **Bay to Breakers Foot Race**, many covering the 7.5-mile course in costumes. San Francisco celebrates **Cinco de Mayo** in the Mission.

Bay Area San Jose marks **Cinco de Mayo** with fiestas, parades, and costumed dancers.

Wine Country Winetasting becomes serious sport at the **Russian River Wine Festival** in Healdsburg.

Gold Country Musicians from around the globe jam at Sacramento's **Dixieland Jazz Jubilee**, the largest such festival in the world. Up in Angels Camp, the **Calaveras County Fair and Jumping Frog Jubilee**, immortalized by Mark Twain, includes not only frog-jumping contests, but a carnival, air show, rodeo, and county fair as well.

JUNE

San Francisco The **Gay Freedom Day Parade**, with its colorful floats and imaginative costumes, marches from the Embarcadero to the Civic Center. The two-month-long **Stern Grove Midsummer Music Festival** begins in June.
Bay Area Artists throughout the East Bay display their work during **Pro Arts Open Studios**. The **Festival at the Lake** brings many folks to Lake Merritt for live music, dance performances, arts and crafts displays, and food.

JULY

San Francisco Here, at Fisherman's Wharf and throughout Northern California, firework displays commemorate the **Fourth of July**. The **San Francisco Marathon** begins in Golden Gate Park, then winds for 26.2 miles to the Civic Center.
Central Coast Gilroy celebrates its favorite crop with a **Garlic Festival** featuring gourmet chefs. The **California Rodeo** in Salinas ranges from horse races to trick riders to clown acts.

AUGUST

San Francisco The **County Fair Flower Show**, at the Hall of Flowers in Golden Gate Park, features thousands of blooms.
Bay Area On Saturdays throughout the month, jazz and blues groups perform in downtown Berkeley during **Jupiter Jam**.
Central Coast Santa Cruz hosts the **International Calamari Festival**, Salinas celebrates its **Steinbeck Festival**, and Pebble Beach sponsors the **Concours d'Élégance**, a classic auto show.
Gold Country The capital city of Sacramento hosts the **California State Fair**.

SEPTEMBER

San Francisco This month for music is marked by the opening of the **San Francisco Opera** and the **San Francisco Symphony**, as well as the annual **Blues Festival** and **Opera in the Park**.
Bay Area The **Renaissance Pleasure Faire** opens in Novato. This celebration of 16th-century life includes music, dancing, jousting, and parades. San Jose sponsors the **Tapestry into Talent Festival of Art**, one of the nation's largest sidewalk art displays.
Central Coast It's also the magic month for the internationally renowned **Monterey Jazz Festival**. Over in Castroville, they stage an **Artichoke Festival**.
Gold Country The **Gold Country Fair** in Auburn features a harvest festival, livestock auction, plenty of food, and country music.

OCTOBER

San Francisco **Columbus Day** is marked by a parade, bocce ball tournament, and the annual blessing of the fishing fleet. Cowboys do their celebrating at the **Grand National Livestock Exposition, Rodeo, and Horse Show**.

Central Coast The **Art and Pumpkin Festival** in Half Moon Bay features food booths, crafts exhibits, and pie-eating contests.

NOVEMBER **San Francisco** The **San Francisco Bay Area Book Festival** is the place to go to meet local publishers and hear author readings. Several fairs and festivals kick off the holiday season. Among them is the **Harvest Festival & Christmas Crafts Market.**

North Coast Mendocino hosts a **Thanksgiving Festival** complete with musical performances and crafts exhibits.

DECEMBER **San Francisco** The **Dickens Christmas Fair**, which goes from Thanksgiving to Christmas, and **Sing-It-Yourself Messiah** commemorate the holiday season. There are also **Christmas Parades** in towns throughout Northern California.

Bay Area Locals head to Oakland's Jack London Square to view the annual **Lighted Yacht Parade.**

Before You Go

VISITORS CENTERS

Several agencies provide free information to travelers. The **California Office of Tourism** will help guide you to areas throughout the state. ~ 801 K Street, Suite 1600, Sacramento, CA 95812; 800-862-2543.

For information on the North Coast counties between San Francisco and Oregon, contact the **Redwood Empire Association.** ~ 2801 Leavenworth Street, San Francisco, CA 94133; 415-543-8334.

The **San Francisco Visitors Information Center** is another excellent resource. ~ Hallidie Plaza, Lower Level, Powell and Market streets; 900 Market Street, San Francisco, CA 94102; 415-391-2000.

Also consult local chambers of commerce and information centers, which are mentioned in the various area chapters.

PACKING There are two important guidelines when deciding what to take on a trip. The first is as true for San Francisco and Northern California as anywhere in the world—pack light. Dress styles here are relatively informal and laundromats or dry cleaners are frequent. The airlines allow two suitcases and a carry-on bag; try to take one suitcase and perhaps a small accessory case.

The second rule is to prepare for cool weather, even if the closest you'll come to the mountains is the top of Nob Hill. "The coldest winter I ever spent," Mark Twain remarked, "was a summer in San Francisco." While the city's climate is temperate, temperatures sometimes descend below 50°. Even that might not seem chilly until the fog rolls in and the ocean breeze picks up. A warm sweater and jacket are absolute necessities. In addition to everyday garments, pack shorts for the autumn or to travel around the interior valleys, bring a raincoat between November and March, and carry cold weather clothing for the high mountains in winter.

LODGING

Overnight accommodations in Northern California are as varied as the region itself. They range from high-rise hotels and neon motels to hostels and bed and breakfast inns. One guideline to follow with all is to reserve well in advance. This is an extremely popular area, particularly in summer, and facilities fill up quickly.

Throughout the book hotel facilities are organized geographically. Check through the various regional sections of each chapter and you're bound to find something to fit your budget and personal taste.

The neon motels offer bland facilities at low prices and are excellent if you're economizing or don't plan to spend much time in the room. Larger hotels often lack intimacy, but provide such conveniences as restaurants and shops in the lobby. My personal preference is for historic hotels, those slightly faded classics which offer charm and tradition at moderate cost. Bed and breakfast inns present an opportunity to stay in a home-like setting. Like hostels, they are an excellent way to meet fellow travelers; unlike hostels, Northern California's country inns are quite expensive.

To help you decide on a place to stay, I've described the accommodations not only by area but also according to price (prices listed are for the high season; prices may decrease in low season). *Budget* hotels are generally less than $50 per night for two people; the rooms are clean and comfortable, but lack luxury. The *moderately* priced hotels run $50 to $90, and provide larger rooms, plusher furniture, and more attractive surroundings. At *deluxe*-priced accommodations you can expect to spend between $90 and $130 for a homey bed and breakfast or a double in a hotel or resort. You'll check into a spacious, well-appointed room with all modern facilities; downstairs the lobby will be a fashionable affair, and you'll usually see a restaurant, lounge, and a cluster of shops. If you want to spend your time (and money) in the city's very finest hotels, try an *ultra-deluxe* facility, which will include all the amenities and price above $130.

DINING

It seems as if Northern California has more restaurants than people. Particularly in San Francisco, they line the streets; vendor stands and lunch wagons line the curbs as well. To establish a pattern for this parade of dining places, I've described not only the cuisine but also the ambience and general price structure of each establishment. Restaurants listed offer lunch and dinner unless otherwise noted.

Within a particular chapter, the restaurants are categorized geographically, with each restaurant entry describing the establishment as budget, moderate, deluxe, or ultra-deluxe in price. Dinner entrées at *budget* restaurants usually cost $8 or less. The ambience is informal café-style and the crowd is often a local one. *Moderately* priced restaurants range between $8 and $16 at dinner and offer pleasant surroundings, a more varied menu, and a slower pace. *Deluxe* establishments tab their entrées above $16, featuring sophisticated cuisines, plush decor, and more personalized service. *Ultra-deluxe* dining rooms, where $24 will only get you started, are gourmet gathering places where the cooking (hopefully) is a fine art form and service is a way of life.

Breakfast and lunch menus vary less in price from restaurant to restaurant. Even deluxe-priced kitchens usually offer light breakfasts and lunch sandwiches which place them within a few dollars of their budget-minded competitors. These early meals can be a good time to test expensive restaurants.

TRAVELING WITH CHILDREN

Visiting Northern California with kids can be a real adventure, and if properly planned, a truly enjoyable one. To ensure that your trip will feature the joy, rather than the strain, of parenthood, remember a few important guidelines.

Use a travel agent to help with arrangements; they can reserve spacious bulkhead seats. Also plan to bring everything you need on board—diapers, food, toys, and extra clothes for kids and parents alike. If the trip to Northern California involves a long journey, plan to relax and do very little during the first few days.

Always allow extra time for getting places. Book reservations well in advance and make sure the hotel has the extra crib, cot, or bed you require. It's smart to ask for a room at the end of the hall to cut down on noise. Also keep in mind that many bed and breakfast inns do not allow children.

The California redwood, the state tree, is the tallest living thing in the world.

Most towns have stores that carry diapers, food, and other essentials; in cities and larger towns, **7-11** stores are open all night (check the Yellow Pages for addresses). In San Francisco, **Cala Foods** has several large groceries, including locations at 6333 Geary Boulevard, 4201 18th Street, and California and Hyde streets, which are open 24 hours a day.

Hotels often provide access to babysitters or you can check the Yellow Pages for state licensed and bonded babysitting agencies.

A first-aid kit is always a good idea. Also, check with your pediatrician for special medicines and dosages for colds and diarrhea. Finding activities to interest children in Northern California could not be easier. Especially helpful in deciding on the day's outing are *Places to Go with Children in Northern California* (Chronicle Books) and the "Datebook" or "pink section" of the Sunday *San Francisco Examiner and Chronicle.*

WOMEN TRAVELING ALONE

It is sad commentary on life in the United States, but women traveling alone must take precautions. It's entirely unwise to hitchhike and probably best to avoid inexpensive accommodations on the outskirts of town; the money saved does not outweigh the risk. Bed and breakfasts, youth hostels, college dorms and YWCAs are generally your safest bet for lodging.

If you are hassled or threatened in some way, never be afraid to scream for assistance. It's a good idea to carry change for a phone call and to know the number to call in case of emergency.

Bay Area Women Against Rape operates a 24-hour crisis line. ~ 415-647-7273, 510-845-7273.

GAY & LESBIAN TRAVELERS

Without doubt, San Francisco is one of the premier gay and lesbian vacation spots in the country. The Castro Street and Polk Street neighborhoods, as well as the South of Market district, are all major gay areas. Each offers gay-owned and gay-friendly lodging, restaurants, and nightspots. (See the "Gay Neighborhoods" and "South of Market" sections in Chapter Two, and "gay and lesbian travelers" in the index.) In many ways, the entire city is a gay-friendly enclave. Gays and lesbians constitute a powerful voting block in local politics, and three gays currently serve on the Board of Supervisors.

San Francisco AIDS Foundation Hotline is the area's best resource for counseling and referrals. ~ 415-863-2437. The **AIDS Nightline** staffs operators from 5 p.m. to 5 a.m. ~ 415-434-2437. **Community United Against Violence Hotline** is available 24 hours a day to assist gay, lesbian, and bisexual people who have been physically assaulted. ~ 415-333-4357.

Despite its name, **The Women's Building** is a community center with bulletin boards loaded with information for gays, lesbians, and bisexuals. ~ 3543 18th Street, San Francisco; 415-431-1180. Medical attention for lesbian and transgender women can be had (by appointment only) at the **Lyon-Martin Women's Clinic.** ~ 1748 Market Street, Suite 201, San Francisco; 415-565-7667. **The Pacific Center** offers low-cost counseling, peer-support groups, job listings, and housing bulletins, as well as an information referral line for anything that is pertinent to the gay-lesbian-bisexual-transgender community. ~ 2712 Telegraph Avenue, Berkeley; 510-548-8283, referral line 510-841-6224.

For weekly updates on the gay community, pick up a *Bay Area Reporter*, which focuses on local news and arts and entertainment. ~ 415-861-5019. *Odyssey* hits the stands twice a week and gives the lowdown on happening nightspots for gays and lesbians. ~ 415-621-6514. *Frontiers* is also biweekly, publishing feature and news articles of interest to the gay community. ~ 415-487-6000. The bi-monthly *San Francisco Bay Times* deals with gay issues and doubles as a resource guide as well. ~ 415-227-0800. *Icon*, a monthly lesbian newspaper, features a calendar of events, a resource guide, interviews, and news articles. ~ 415-282-0942.

The Russian River area, located an hour north of the city, is another key gay and lesbian resort area. (See the "Russian River" section in Chapter Four, and "gay and lesbian travelers" in the index.) For travelers in the Russian River area, the **Amita Center** runs a 24-hour phone line and offers gay and lesbian counseling and education. ~ 707-523-2940. **Legacy of Sonoma County** is a traveler-friendly phone line that provides information and referrals about lodging, dining, and nightlife in the area. ~ 707-526-0442. The local gay and lesbian newspaper is *We the People*, which comes out once a month and is available throughout the Wine Country and the Russian River region.

SENIOR TRAVELERS

Northern California is an ideal spot for older vacationers. The mild climate makes traveling in the off-season possible, helping to cut down on expenses. Many museums, theaters, restaurants, and hotels offer discounts to seniors (requiring a driver's license, Medicare card, or other age-identifying card). Be sure to ask your travel agent when booking reservations.

The **American Association of Retired Persons**, or AARP, offers members travel discounts and provides escorted tours. ~ 3200 East Carson Street, Lakewood, CA 90712; 310-496-2277.

For those 55 or over, **Elderhostel** offers educational programs in California. ~ 75 Federal Street, Boston, MA 02110; 617-426-7788.

Be extra careful about health matters. Bring any medications you use, along with the prescriptions. Consider carrying a medical record with you—including your current medical status, and medical history, as well as your doctor's name, phone number, and address. Also be sure to confirm that your insurance covers you away from home.

DISABLED TRAVELERS

California stands at the forefront of social reform for persons with disabilities. During the past decade, the state has responded to the needs of the blind, wheelchair-bound, and others with a series of progressive legislative measures.

The **Department of Motor Vehicles** provides special parking permits for the disabled. Many local bus lines and other public transit facilities are wheelchair accessible. ~ 1377 Fell Street, San Francisco; 415-557-1191.

There are also agencies in Northern California assisting travelers with disabilities. For tips and information about the San Francisco Bay Area, contact the **Center for Independent Living**, a self-help group that has led the way in reforming access laws in California. ~ 2539 Telegraph Avenue, Berkeley; 510-841-4776.

Water Safety

For swimming, surfing, and skindiving, few places match the California Coast. With endless miles of white sand beach, it attracts aquatic enthusiasts from all over the world. Many water lovers, however, never realize how awesome the sea can be. Particularly in California, where waves can reach significant heights and currents often flow unobstructed, the ocean is sometimes as treacherous as it is spectacular. People drown every year on California beaches, others are dragged from the surf with serious injuries, and countless numbers sustain minor cuts and bruises.

These accidents can be entirely avoided if you relate to the ocean with a respect for its power as well as an appreciation of its beauty. All you have to do is heed a few simple guidelines. First, never turn your back on the sea. Waves come in sets: one group may be small and quite harmless, but the next set could be large enough to sweep you out to sea. Never swim alone.

Don't try to surf, or bodysurf, until you're familiar with the sports' techniques and precautionary measures. Be extremely careful when the surf is high.

If you do get caught in a rip current, do not swim *against* it: swim *across* it, parallel to the shore. These currents, running from the shoreline out to sea, can often be spotted by their ragged-looking surface water and foamy edges.

Around rocks and reefs, wear something to protect your feet. If you sustain a coral cut, clean it with hydrogen peroxide, then apply an antiseptic or antibiotic substance. This is also a good procedure for octopus bites.

When stung by a jellyfish, mix unseasoned meat tenderizer with alcohol, leave it on the sting for ten or twenty minutes, then rinse it off with alcohol. The old Hawaiian remedies, which are reputedly quite effective, involve applying urine or green papaya. If you step on the sharp, painful spines of a sea urchin, soak the affected area in very hot water for fifteen to ninety minutes. Another remedy calls for applying urine or undiluted vinegar. If any of these preliminary treatments do not work, consult a doctor.

Oh, one last thing. The chances of encountering a shark are about as likely as sighting a UFO. But should you meet one of these ominous creatures, stay calm. He'll be no happier to see you than you are to confront him. Simply swim quietly to shore. By the time you make it back to terra firma, you'll have one hell of a story to tell.

There are many organizations offering general information. Among these are:

The **Society for the Advancement of Travel for the Handicapped.** ~ 347 5th Avenue, #610, New York, NY 10016; 212-447-7284, fax 212-725-8253.

The **Travel Information Center.** ~ Corman Building, 12th Street and Tabor Road, Philadelphia, PA 19141; 215-456-9603.

Mobility International USA. ~ P.O. Box 10767, Eugene, OR 97440; 503-343-1284.

Flying Wheels Travel. ~ P.O. Box 382, Owatonna, MN 55060; 800-535-6790.

Travelin' Talk, a network of people and organizations, also provides assistance. ~ P.O. Box 3534, Clarkville, TN 37043; 615-552-6670.

Or consult the comprehensive guidebook, *Access to the World—A Travel Guide for the Handicapped*, by Louise Weiss (Holt, Rinehart & Winston).

Be sure to check in advance when making room reservations. Many hotels and motels feature facilities for those in wheelchairs.

FOREIGN TRAVELERS

Passports and Visas Most foreign visitors are required to obtain a passport and tourist visa to enter the United States. Contact your nearest United States Embassy or Consulate well in advance to obtain a visa and to check on any other entry requirements.

Customs Requirements Foreign travelers are allowed to bring in the following: 200 cigarettes (1 carton), 50 cigars, or 2 kilograms (4.4 pounds) of smoking tobacco; one liter of alcohol for personal use only (you must be 21 years of age to bring in alcohol); and US$100 worth of duty free gifts that can include an additional 100 cigars. You may bring in any amount of currency, but must fill out a form if you bring in over US$10,000. Carry any prescription drugs in clearly marked containers. You may have to produce a written prescription or doctor's statement for the customs officers. Meat or meat products, seeds, plants, fruits, and narcotics are not allowed to be brought into the United States. Contact the **United States Customs Service** for further information. ~ 1301 Constitution Avenue NW, Washington, DC 20229; 202-927-6724.

Driving If you plan to rent a car, an international driver's license should be obtained prior to arrival. Some rental car companies require both a foreign license and an international driver's license along with a major credit card and require that the lessee be at least 25 years of age.

Currency American money is based on the dollar. Bills in the United States come in six denominations: $1, $5, $10, $20, $50, and $100. Every dollar is divided into 100 cents. Coins are the penny (1 cent), nickel (5 cents), dime (10 cents), and quarter (25 cents). You may not use foreign currency to purchase goods and services in the United States. Consider buying traveler's checks in dollar amounts. You may also use credit cards affiliated with an American company such as Interbank, Barclay Card, VISA, and American Express.

Electricity and Electronics Electric outlets use currents of 110 volts, 60 cycles. For appliances made for other electrical systems, you need a transformer or other adapter. Travelers who use laptop computers for telecommunication should be aware that modem configurations for U.S. telephone systems may be different from their European counterparts. Similarly, the U.S. format for videotapes is different from that in Europe; National Park Service visitors centers and other stores that sell souvenir videos often have them available in European format on request.

Weights and Measurements The United States uses the English system of weights and measures. American units and their metric equivalents are as follows: 1 inch = 2.5 centimeters; 1 foot (12 inches) = 0.3 meter; 1 yard (3 feet) = 0.9 meter; 1 mile (5280 feet) = 1.6 kilometers; 1 ounce = 28 grams; 1 pound (16 ounces) = 0.45 kilogram; 1 quart (liquid) = 0.9 liter.

Outdoor Adventures

CAMPING

The state oversees more than 260 camping facilities. Amenities at each campground vary; for a complete listing of all state-run campgrounds, send $2 for the *Guide to California State Parks* to the **California Department of Parks and Recreation.** ~ P.O. Box 942896, Sacramento, CA 94296; 916-653-6995. Reservations for campgrounds may be made by calling 800-444-7275.

For general information on federal campgrounds, contact the **National Park Service.** ~ Western Information Center, Fort Mason, Building 201, San Francisco, CA 94123; 415-556-4122. To reserve specific campsites call **DESTINET.** ~ 800-436-7275 for Yosemite National Park, 800-365-2267 for all others.

For maps and information, contact the **U.S. Forest Service.** ~ 630 Sansome Street, San Francisco, CA 94111; 415-705-2874. Campsites must be booked through **National Forest Recreation Reservations.** ~ 800-280-2267. A fee is charged at these facilities and the length of stay varies from park to park. It's best to reserve in advance, though many parks keep some sites open to be filled daily on a first-come, first-serve basis.

In addition to state and national campgrounds, Northern California offers numerous municipal, county, and private facilities. See the "Beaches & Parks" sections in each chapter for the locations of these campgrounds.

PERMITS

Wilderness Permits For camping and hiking in the wilderness and primitive areas of national forests, a wilderness permit is required. Permits are free and are issued for a specific period of time, which varies according to the wilderness area. You can obtain permits from ranger stations and regional information centers, as described in the "Beaches & Parks" sections in each chapter. Information is available through the **U.S. Forest Service.** ~ 630 Sansome Street, San Francisco, CA 94111; 415-705-2874.

Fishing Licenses For current information on the fishing season and state license fees, contact the **Department of Fish and Game.** ~ 3211 S Street, Sacramento, CA 95816; 916-227-2244.

TWO

San Francisco

It is a city poised at the end of the continent, civilization's last fling before the land plunges into the Pacific. Perhaps this is why visitors demand something memorable from San Francisco. People expect the city to resonate along a personal wavelength, speak to them, fulfill some ineffable desire at the center of the soul. There is a terrible beauty at the edge of America: the dream begins here, or ends. The Golden Gate Bridge, that arching portal to infinite horizons, is also a suicide gangplank for hundreds of ill-starred dreamers. Throughout American history, those who crossed the country in search of destiny ultimately found it here or turned back to the continent and their own past.

Yet San Francisco is only a city, a steel-and-glass metropolis mounted on a series of hills. With a population of about 768,000, it covers 47 square miles at the tip of a peninsula bounded by the Pacific Ocean and San Francisco Bay. A gateway to Asia, San Francisco supports a multicultural population with large concentrations of Chinese, Latinos, African Americans, Italian, Filipinos, and Japanese. Adding to the cosmopolitan atmosphere is a gay population constituting perhaps 25 percent of the city's residents.

The myth of San Francisco originates not only from its geography, but its history as well. If, as early Christians believed, the world was created in 4004 B.C., then the history of San Francisco began on January 28, 1848. That day a hired hand named James Marshall discovered gold in California. Year One is 1849, a time etched in the psyche of an entire nation. The people swept along by the mania of that momentous time have been known forever since as "'49ers." They crossed the Rockies in covered wagons, trekked the jungles of Panama, and challenged the treacherous seas around Cape Horn, all because of a shiny yellow metal.

Gold in California was the quintessence of the American Dream. For anyone with courage and ambition, it represented a chance to blaze trails, expand a young nation, and become rich in the flash of a fortuitous find.

God granted Divine Right to Britain, creating a kingdom that ruled the oceans. To America, God gave Manifest Destiny, a hunger for territory which drove an entire nation west like a fever through the body. Gold was the currency of Manifest Destiny, a myth that lured 100,000 people across an implacable land, and created a civilization on the fringes of a continent.

San Francisco became the capital of that civilization. The peaceful hamlet was transmogrified into a hellbent city, a place to make the Wild West look tame. Its population exploded from 900 to 25,000 in two years; by 1890 it numbered 300,000.

During the Gold Rush, a Barbary Coast ghetto grew along the Bay. Over 500 businesses sold liquor; gambling, drugs, and prostitution were rampant; gangs roamed the boomtown and iron-fisted vigilance committees enforced law and order. Sailors were shanghaied and failed prospectors committed suicide at the rate of 1000 per year.

By 1850, about 500 ships, whose crews had deserted for the gold fields, lay abandoned in San Francisco Bay. Some were used as stores, hotels, even lunatic asylums; others became landfill. Speculators wildly divided the city into tiny plots.

Amid all the chaos, San Francisco grew into an international city. Ambitious Americans, displaced Mexicans, indentured Chinese, itinerant Australians, and Chilean immigrants crowded its muddy streets. The populace soon boasted over a dozen newspapers, published in a variety of languages. Because of its multicultural population, and in spite of periodic racial problems, San Francisco developed a strong liberal tradition, an openness to the unusual and unexpected, which prevails today.

Long before Americans discovered gold in the Sierra Nevada foothills, Spaniards spoke of a mythical land filled with gems and precious metal. A 16th-century Spanish novel described it as an island called California, inhabited by beautiful amazons. San Francisco lay near the northern tip of the colony which the Spanish eventually named after that fabled land.

In 1769 an expedition led by Gaspar de Portolá, intent on expanding Spanish control in California, marched up the San Francisco peninsula and discovered the Golden Gate. Then in 1776, while the American Revolution raged on the East Coast, Captain Juan Bautista de Anza established a mission and presidio near San Francisco Bay.

Of course, the Costanoan Indians had been occupying the area for thousands of years, migrating between the hills, marshes, forests, and meadows. They hunted deer, elk, and grizzly bears, ground acorns to make meal, dug roots, and caught shellfish off the coast. After the conquistadors arrived, the Costanoans built churches. In ever-imperious fashion, the Spanish "civilized" the American Indians, forcibly removing them from ancestral homes, crowding the Indians into dingy quarters, and teaching them the glories of Christianity.

Using slave labor and fortifying a chain of 21 missions, the Spanish eventually colonized the coast from San Diego to San Francisco to Sonoma. When Mexico gained independence from Spain in 1821, this colonial prize became Mexican territory. At the same time, San Francisco and environs began attracting American whalers, Russian seal hunters, French adventurers, and British entrepreneurs.

Finally, in 1846, American settlers, with assistance from the United States government, fomented the Bear Flag Revolt. Seizing California from Mexico, they created an independent republic which soon became part of the United States. Just two years before gold would be found in Spain's mythic land of amazons, the stars and stripes flew over San Francisco.

The funeral of "Emperor Norton," a Gold Rush–era character, drew 10,000 mourners.

The Gold Rush not only lured prospectors to the pulsing young city: many of America's finest writers were soon mining literary material. Mark Twain, fresh from the gold fields, took in the scene during the 1860s, as did local colorist Bret Harte. Ambrose Bierce excoriated everyone and everything in his column for William Randolph Hearst's *Examiner*. In 1879, Henry George published a book in San Francisco called *Progress and Poverty*, which propounded a revolutionary system of taxation. Robert Louis Stevenson explored the Bay Area a few years later, and Jack London used it as a setting for his adventure tales.

With characters like Joshua Abraham Norton roaming the streets, San Francisco was a natural place for storytellers. A riches-to-rags victim, Norton made and lost a fortune within a few years of the Gold Rush, then, unhinged by the ordeal, declared himself the emperor of the United States. Rather than committing the crackbrain, San Francisco welcomed him and made "Emperor Norton" a municipal mascot.

Even a society willing to accept eccentrics can sometimes turn upon itself, bitterly excluding part of its populace. There is a dark side of the dream which blackens the fate of some and casts a shadow upon all. During the 1860s, Chinese immigrants were brought in to build the transcontinental railroad. When they completed it in 1869, San Francisco was linked with the rest of the United States and railroad owners like the Big Four (Mark Hopkins, Leland Stanford, Collis Huntington, and Charles Crocker) were fabulously wealthy. Chinese labor helped stimulate the boom which made San Francisco a city of cable cars and stately Victorians by the end of the century. Regardless, the Chinese were victims of vitriolic racism. "Yellow Peril" hysteria was rampant in San Francisco during the 1880s, and led to beatings, murder, and a ban on Asian immigration to the United States.

Social upheaval gave way to devastating convulsions of the earth on April 18, 1906. Dream turned to nightmare at 5:12 that morning as a horrendous earthquake, 8.3 on the Richter scale, rocked and buckled the land. Actually, the infamous San Francisco earthquake owed its destructive ferocity more to the subsequent fires than the seismic disturbance. One of the few people killed by the earthquake itself was the city's fire chief. Gas mains across the city broke and water pipes lay shattered. Within hours, 50 separate fires ignited, merged, and by nightfall created firestorms that tore across the city. Three-quarters of San Francisco's houses were destroyed in the three-day holocaust, 452 people died, and 250,000 were left homeless.

The city whose municipal symbol is a phoenix rising from the ashes quickly rebuilt. City Hall and the Civic Center became part of a resurrected San Francisco. The Golden Gate and Bay bridges were completed in the 1930s, and during World War II the port became a major embarkation point for men and materiel. A city of international importance, San Francisco was the site for the signing of the United Nations charter in June 1945.

Text continued on page 26.

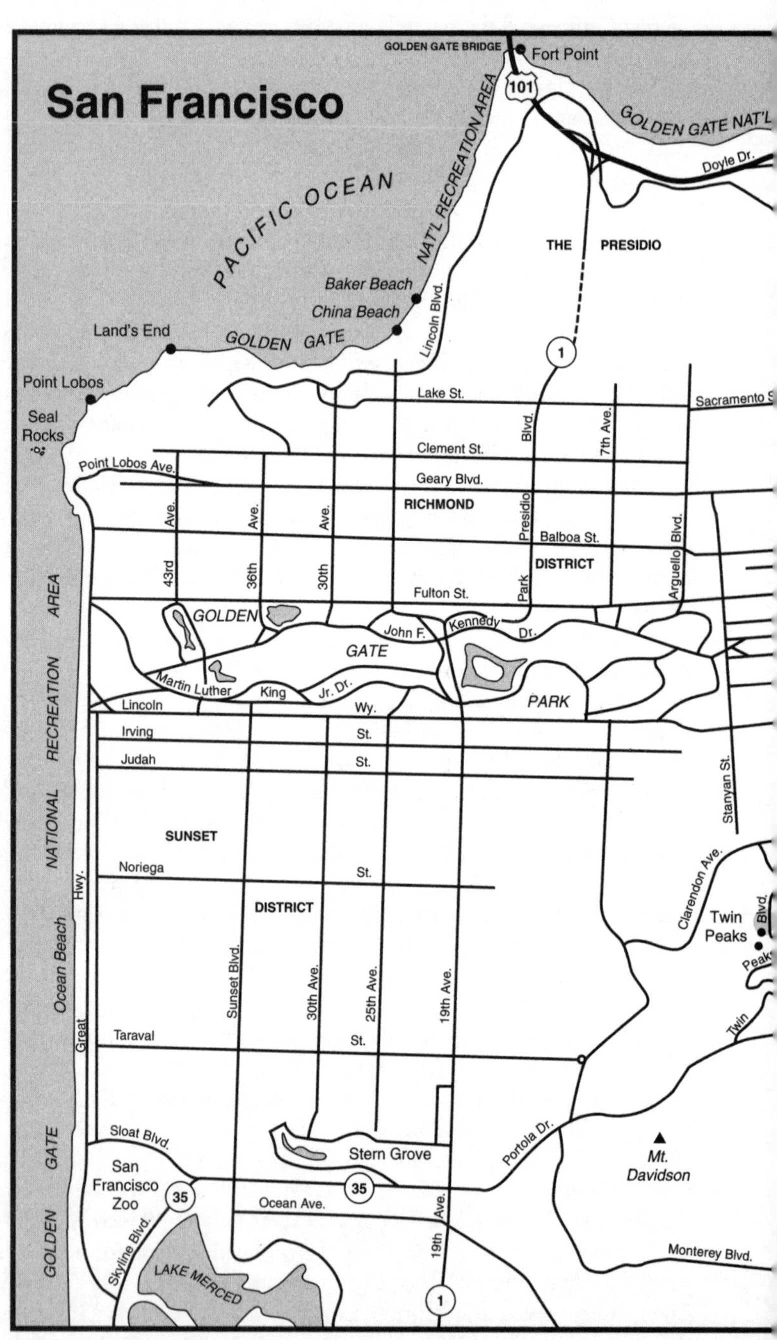

San Francisco
GOLDEN GATE BRIDGE
Fort Point
101
GOLDEN GATE NAT'L
Doyle Dr.
PACIFIC OCEAN
NAT'L RECREATION AREA
THE PRESIDIO
Baker Beach
China Beach
Lincoln Blvd.
Land's End
GOLDEN GATE
Point Lobos
Seal Rocks
Lake St.
Sacramento S
Presidio Blvd.
7th Ave.
Clement St.
Point Lobos Ave.
Geary Blvd.
RICHMOND
DISTRICT
Balboa St.
43rd Ave.
36th Ave.
30th Ave.
Park
Arguello Blvd.
Fulton St.
GOLDEN
GATE
PARK
John F. Kennedy Dr.
Martin Luther King Jr. Dr.
Lincoln Wy.
Irving St.
Judah St.
Stanyan St.
SUNSET
DISTRICT
Noriega St.
Clarendon Ave.
Twin Peaks
Blvd.
Peaks
Twin
Sunset Blvd.
30th Ave.
25th Ave.
19th Ave.
Taraval St.
Great Hwy.
Ocean Beach
GOLDEN GATE NATIONAL RECREATION AREA
Sloat Blvd.
Stern Grove
Portola Dr.
Mt. Davidson
San Francisco Zoo
35
Ocean Ave.
Skyline Blvd.
Monterey Blvd.
LAKE MERCED
1

FISHERMAN'S WHARF
REC. AREA
Marina Blvd.
Aquatic Park
Fort Mason
MARINA DISTRICT
Bay St.
THE EMBARCADERO
Coit Tower
Columbus Ave.
SAN FRANCISCO BAY
N
Lombard St.
101
Union St.
NORTH BEACH
PACIFIC HEIGHTS
Broadway
CHINATOWN
Sacramento St.
FINANCIAL DISTRICT
Divisadero St.
Fillmore St.
Gough St.
Van Ness Ave.
Polk St.
Union Square
Post St.
Geary St.
JAPANTOWN
DOWNTOWN
Market St.
Steuart St.
Main St.
1st St.
2nd St.
3rd St.
4th St.
5th St.
6th St.
7th St.
8th St.
9th St.
10th St.
11th St.
BAY BRIDGE
80
Turk St.
Golden Gate Ave.
Fulton St.
Hayes St.
Fell St.
Oak St.
Haight St.
HAIGHT-ASHBURY
Brannan St.
SOUTH OF MARKET
Howard St.
Buena Vista Park
Ashbury St.
Market St.
Mission St.
MISSION DISTRICT
280
Dolores Park
20th St.
Castro St.
Church St.
Dolores St.
South Van Ness Ave.
3rd St.
Army St.
Diamond Hts. Blvd.
Glen Canyon Park
Mission St.
San Jose Ave.
Bosworth St.
0
1 mile

It entered the post–World War II era at the vanguard of American society. San Francisco's hallmark is cultural innovation. This city at continent's edge boasts a society at the edge of thought. During the 1950s it became the Beat capital of the world. Allen Ginsberg, Jack Kerouac, Gary Snyder, and other Beat poets began haunting places like the Caffe Trieste and the Co-Existence Bagel Shop. The Beats blew cool jazz, intoned free form poems, and extolled the virtues of nothingness.

Lawrence Ferlinghetti opened City Lights Bookstore in 1953. Two years later Ginsberg publicly read a poem called "Howl" which redefined the American dream and outraged the Eisenhower society. In 1957, Jack Kerouac, ricocheting between San Francisco and the East Coast like some kind of human missile, defined the generation in *On the Road*. Later he would pen his finest book, *The Dharma Bums*, using Northern California settings and characters.

Not even Kerouac was prepared for San Francisco's next wave of cultural immigrants. This mecca for the misplaced became a mystical gathering place for myriads of hippies. The Haight-Ashbury neighborhood was the staging area for a movement intent on revolutionizing American consciousness.

Ken Kesey and his Merry Pranksters created the Trips Festival in 1966, combining dynamic light shows and massive doses of LSD in a grand effort to entertain while enlightening. The Jefferson Airplane, Big Brother and the Holding Company, and the Grateful Dead blew minds with an electric sound called acid rock. Then, in January 1967, about 20,000 people gathered in Golden Gate Park for a "Human Be-In." Ginsberg chanted, the Hells Angels blasted through on Harleys, and Tim Leary advised the assembled to "Turn on, tune in, and drop out." It was a happening of colossal proportions, leading to the fabled "Summer of Love" when hippies from around the world set out to make San Francisco the center of cosmic consciousness.

By the 1970s San Francisco was becoming home to a vital and creative minority, gay men and women. The city's gay population had increased steadily for decades; then, suddenly, San Francisco's open society and freewheeling lifestyle brought an amazing influx of gays. In 1977, Supervisor Harvey Milk became the nation's first outfront gay to be elected to a major municipal post. That same year the city passed a landmark gay rights ordinance. With an advancing population which today numbers perhaps 200,000, gays became a powerful social and political force.

Then the dark face of the dream appeared once again. Over 900 members of the People's Temple, one of the countless sects headquartered in San Francisco, committed mass suicide at their outpost in Guyana. Shortly afterwards, on November 27, 1978, in an unrelated incident, Supervisor Dan White assassinated fellow supervisor Harvey Milk and San Francisco Mayor George Moscone.

The dual murder stunned the world and outraged the gay community. When White received a relatively mild sentence the next year, a night of rioting swept the Civic Center, with damages totaling $300,000. And then, within a few years, the AIDS epidemic swept the gay community.

Throughout the 1980s and into the 1990s, San Francisco has retained a gay supervisor whose constituency remains an integral part of the city's life. A multicultural society from its early days, San Francisco remains a city at the edge, open to experiment and experience. The national media still portray the region as a kind of open ward, home to flakes and weirdos. They point to events like the mayoral election in which a character named Jello Biafra, then a singer for a punk band called the Dead Kennedys, polled over three percent of the vote.

The city does sometimes seem to contain as many cults as people, but it also boasts more than its share of artists. The national ecology movement, which began in this area with the pioneering work of John Muir, also flourishes here. This is headquarters for dozens of concerned organizations.

There are problems: during the last few decades, San Francisco's skyline has been Manhattanized, crowded with clusters of dark skyscrapers. The AIDS epidemic has taken a terrible toll, particularly among the area's gay population. And the city has allowed its port to decline. Most cargo ships travel across the Bay to Oakland, while San Francisco's once great waterfront is being converted into gourmet restaurants and chic shopping malls. It is a city in love with itself, trading the mundane business of shipping for the glamorous, profitable tourist industry.

In October 1989 San Francisco once again demonstrated its unsettling ability to combine good fortune with terrible tragedy. As the nation's television viewers settled in to see the third game of the World Series, being played in Candlestick Park between the San Francisco Giants and neighboring Oakland Athletics, they found themselves watching a 7.1-level earthquake. The temblor rocked the stadium and rolled through Northern California, leaving 67 dead, and causing more than $10 billion in damage. After the dust cleared, and despite weeks of startling media reports, new residents continued streaming into California.

Perhaps Rudyard Kipling was right. He once called the place "a mad city—inhabited for the most part by perfectly insane people." William Saroyan saw it as "a city that invites the heart to come to life . . . an experiment in living." The two thoughts do not contradict: San Francisco is madly beautiful, a marvelous and zany place. Its contribution to the world is its lifestyle.

The people who gravitate here become models—some exemplary, others tragic—for their entire generation. Every decade San Francisco moves further out along the edge, maintaining a tradition for the avant-garde and iconoclastic that dates back to the Gold Rush days. The city is a jigsaw puzzle that will never be completed. Its residents, and those who come to love the place, are parts from that puzzle, pieces which never quite fit, but rather stand out, unique edges exposed, from all the rest.

Downtown

Visit any city in the world and the sightseeing tour will begin in a vital but nebulous area called "Downtown." San Francisco is no different. Here, Downtown is spelled Union Square (Geary and Stockton streets), a tree-dotted plot in the heart of the city's hotel and shopping district. Lofty buildings bordering the area house major department stores while the network of surrounding streets features many of the city's poshest shops and plushest hotels.

SIGHTS

Union Square's most intriguing role is as San Francisco's freeform entertainment center. On any day you may see a brass band high-stepping through, a school choir singing the world's praises, or a gathering of motley but talented musicians passing the hat for bus fare home.

Cable cars from the nearby turnaround station at Powell and Market streets clang past en route to Nob Hill and Fisherman's Wharf. So pull up a patch of lawn and watch the world work through its paces, or just browse the Square's hedgerows and flower gardens.

Then you can head off toward the city's high voltage Financial District. Appropriately enough, the route to this pinstriped realm leads down **Maiden Lane**, headiest of the city's high-heeled shopping areas. Back in Barbary Coast days, when San Francisco was a dirty word, this two-block-long alleyway was wall-to-wall with bawdy houses. But today it's been transformed from red light district to ultra chic mall. Of particular interest among the galleries and boutiques lining this pedestrian-only thoroughfare is the building at **140 Maiden Lane**. Designed by Frank Lloyd Wright in 1948, its circular interior stairway and other unique elements foreshadow the motifs he later used for the famous Guggenheim Museum.

LODGING

BUDGET LODGING The cheapest accommodations in town are found in the city's Tenderloin district. Situated between Union Square and the Civic Center, this area is an easy walk from restaurants and points of cultural interest. The Tenderloin is a sleazy neighborhood filled with interesting if sometimes menacing characters, the kind of place you stay because of the low rents rather than the inherent charm. Still, if the spirit is willing, the purse will certainly be appreciative.

Rooms at the **Youth Hostel Centrale** are very basic. Although they lack any decorations or private baths, the rooms are clean and feature wall-to-wall carpeting and televisions. You get, as they say, what you pay for. In this case, you pay very very little and get a tidy, immaculate environment. With its 18 rooms, the hostel is a wayfarer's oasis. ~ 116 Turk Street; 415-346-7835.

There are two sister hotels within two blocks of one another. The **James Court** features 36 beige-colored rooms, 10 with private baths. Coffee and donuts included. ~ 1353 Bush Street; 415-771-2409. **Nob Hill Pensione** offers simple, no-frill rooms that have a double bed, bureau, desk, chair, and television. Rooms with kitchenettes and weekly rates are available. Continental breakfast included. ~ 835 Hyde Street; 415-885-2987, fax 415-921-1648.

The **American Youth Hostel—Union Square** is *the* place if you're looking for budget accommodations in the heart of the city. Rooms are shared (two to five bunks per room) and a kitchen is available for guests to use. ~ 312 Mason Street; 415-788-5604, fax 415-788-3023.

For native funk at rock bottom rates consider the **Adelaide Inn.** Billed as "San Francisco's unique European pensione," it is an 18-room, family-operated establishment. There is a small lobby plus a coffee room and kitchen for the guests. The room prices, with continental breakfast included, are friendly to the pocketbook. Rooms are small, tidy, and plainly furnished; each is equipped with a sink and television; bathrooms are shared. Most important, the inn is located in a prime downtown location, not in the Tenderloin. ~ 5 Isadora Duncan Place; 415-441-2261.

Also away from the Tenderloin, the **Grant Hotel** is basic and clean. The furniture in the guest rooms doesn't exactly match, and the color scheme is not especially coordinated, but the price is right, and a friendly, helpful staff makes this 76-room hotel a pleasant place to stay. There's a lobby sitting room with a large-screen television and a coffeepot brewing throughout the day. ~ 753 Bush Street; 415-421-7540, 800-522-0979, fax 415-989-7719.

Another budgeteer's resting place is **Temple Hotel.** Located near the Financial District, it features a small, stylish lobby highlighted with one of those old-time iron elevators. For a budget price you can stay in a well-kept room with shag carpeting and a shared bath. Or you can rent a room with a private bath in this colorful hotel. ~ 469 Pine Street; 415-781-2565.

Allison Hotel, a few strides away from Union Square, rounds out the Downtown area's budget hotels. The decor in some rooms here is Early Mismatch, but the place is clean, cute, and cheap. Given the location, not to mention the deco ambience, it's a bargain. ~ 417 Stockton Street; 415-986-8737, 800-628-6456, fax 415-392-0850.

Union Square is a scene—where the rich and powerful come to view the merely talented, where panhandlers sometimes seem as plentiful as pigeons.

MODERATE LODGING In my opinion the best hotel buys in San Francisco are the middle range accommodations. These usually offer good location, comfortable surroundings, and reasonable service at a cost that does not leave your pocketbook empty. Happily, the city possesses a substantial number of these facilities, the best of which are listed below.

Somehow the **Commodore International Hotel** does not quite live up to its baronial name. The place does feature a spacious lobby with bas-relief work along the walls, and there is a coffee shop and a cocktail lounge attached. But the rooms are undistinguished. Unambitiously decorated with sketches of San Francisco, they include wall-to-wall carpeting, televisions, shower-tub combos, and the usual creature comforts. Rooms vary in price, depending on "newness" and location. Recommended as a backup hotel, the Commodore International is a fair buy, but does not match other hotels in its class. ~ 825 Sutter Street; 415-885-2464, 800-338-6848, fax 415-923-6804.

The **Sheehan Hotel** was once the YWCA, which means it offers facilities not usually found in a moderately priced hotel, like a swimming pool and exercise rooms. But it's definitely not the Y anymore. The rooms have been nicely decorated with prints on the walls and antique-looking lamps, and the bathrooms are large. Guests can enjoy a complimentary continental breakfast in the lobby tearoom. ~ 620 Sutter Street; 415-775-6500, 800-848-1529, fax 415-775-3271.

Hotel David sits smack-dab in the center of the theater district, but even more important, it is located over David's Delicatessen, one of the best delis in town. The lobby is nearly nonexistent, but the rooms are attractively done in modern deco style, with warm woods, red bedspreads, and a print of a cobbler over each bed bringing a smile to those who enter the room. This hotel is immaculately clean, and anyone would be hard-pressed to find a speck of dust anywhere. The room rate includes an all-you-can-eat breakfast from the deli menu. This place is a true original. ~ 480 Geary Street; 415-771-1600, 800-524-1888, fax 415-931-5442.

DELUXE LODGING If your wallet is willing, the city's deluxe-priced hotels are waiting. Among them are several that I suggest you consider.

European elegance at low cost: that's what the **Beresford Hotel** has offered its clientele for years. You'll sense a touch of class immediately upon treading the lobby's red carpet and settling into a plump armchair. There's a historical flair about the place, highpointed by the adjoining White Horse Tavern and Restaurant, with its Olde England ambience. Upstairs the rooms are outstanding—shag carpets, wooden headboards, original paintings, comfortable furnishings, small refrigerators, and a marble-top vanity in the bathroom. All this, just two blocks from Union Square. If you can beat it, let me know how. ~ 635 Sutter Street; 415-673-9900, 800-533-6533, fax 415-474-0449.

The **Beresford Arms** is a sister hotel to the Beresford in more than name. Featuring a similar antique lobby, the Beresford Arms has gracefully decorated its public area with a crystal chandelier, leather-tooled tables, stuffed armchairs, and an old grandfather clock. Casting that same European aura, rooms often feature mahogany dressers and headboards as well as the expected amenities like wall-to-wall carpeting, tile tubs, and spacious closets. All at the same moderate prices as the Beresford. Both hotels also have rooms with jacuzzis, kitchenettes, and wet bars. ~ 701 Post Street; 415-673-2600, 800-533-6533, fax 415-474-0449.

A sparkling, well-run hotel in one of the best shopping blocks in town is always worth checking out—or checking into. The 114-room **Cartwright Hotel** offers seven floors of accommodations individually decorated in personally selected antiques. The attention to detail shows in touches such as plump reading pillows. ~ 524 Sutter Street; 415-421-2865, 800-227-3844, fax 415-398-6345.

The **Hotel Carlton** features a rich lobby with marble floors, brass wall sconces, and a fireplace. The rooms have been decorated subtly and with great care and are reasonably priced. Complimentary wine is served from 6 to 7 p.m. in the lobby. Though located about a half-mile from Union Square, the Carlton is highly recommended. ~ 1075 Sutter Street; 415-673-0242, 800-227-4496, fax 415-673-4904.

Elegance at a deluxe to ultra-deluxe price. That could well be the motto at **The Orchard Hotel**. The first thing to catch the eye here is the lobby, a marble and crystal affair with an adjoining bar. The private rooms are small, but each is tastefully furnished with rosewood pieces and decorated with artworks. There are mini-bars and tiled baths in each room; room service is available. ~ 562 Sutter Street; 415-433-4434, 800-433-4434, fax 415-441-2700.

The brilliant polished wood facade of the **Savoy Hotel** provides only a hint of its luxurious interior. The lobby is the first word in elegance with black and white marble floors, brass fixtures, and dark woods. The rooms at this lavish but affordable hotel second the invitation of the lobby. Sporting a French-country motif, they blend floral prints with attractive wood furniture. Continental breakfast and an afternoon tea-and-sherry hour are included. Add a tile bath-shower, goosedown featherbeds, color television, plus plenty of space, and you have one very noteworthy hotel. ~ 580 Geary Street; 415-441-2700, 800-227-4223, fax 415-441-2700.

Following the lead of European hotels is **The Raphael Hotel**, a 151-room affair set at the heart of the theater district. An international staff sets the tone here and claims to represent "San Francisco's little elegant hotel." The lobby fills a small area adorned with high-back chairs, wooden antiques, and Italian paintings. The true elegance lies upstairs in the private rooms. Softly carpeted and decorated with an aesthetic eye, they are warm and commodious. Nevertheless, the wise will pay a few dollars more for a "deluxe room" which includes a sitting room complete with game table. Room and nightly turndown services are added features at this lovely hotel. ~ 386 Geary Street; 415-986-2000, 800-821-5343, fax 415-392-2447.

Hotel Bedford is another European-style hotel. The lobby here is a fresh, bright place hung with crystal and dotted about with potted plants. Upstairs the private rooms are brilliantly coordinated and possess an air of artistry with their gallery prints, floral drapes, and white furniture. ~ 761 Post Street; 415-673-6040, 800-227-5642, fax 415-563-6739.

Another upscale establishment is the **Hotel Union Square**. Built early in the century to accommodate visitors to the Panama–

Pacific International Exposition, this 131-plus room hotel has been exquisitely decorated. Mystery writer Dashiell Hammett and playwright Lillian Hellman, who reportedly once frequented the place, might recognize it even today. The lobby still possesses an art deco ambience with its mosaic murals. The old speakeasy is reputed to have included a secret "chute entrance" from Ellis Street. Walls upstairs have been sandblasted to expose original brick and the rooms are decorated in quiet hues and floral prints. ~ 114 Powell Street; 415-397-3000, 800-553-1900, fax 415-885-3268.

Or if you prefer an English theme, try the **King George Hotel**. The lobby at this tasteful establishment is done in pastel peach decor and hung with brass chandeliers. A marble staircase ascends to the "Bread and Honey Tea Room." Convenient in price and location both, featuring comfortable, spiffy rooms, the King George is a noteworthy competitor in its class. ~ 334 Mason Street; 415-781-5050, 800-288-6005, fax 415-391-6976.

When a travel writer is reduced to writing about a hotel's hallways, the establishment is either problematic or exceptional. Corridors at **The Inn at Union Square** are fashionably done along their entire length with mirrors and brass wall sconces, and most rooms leading off the halls are equipped with a brass lion-head door knocker. All that brass is a polisher's nightmare, but adds immeasurably to the charm of this pocket hotel. The entire inn numbers only 30 rooms, so intimacy is a primary consideration here. There is a small lobby with a fireplace on each floor where continental breakfast, afternoon tea and evening hors d'oeuvres are served. Rooms are plush and cozy with quilted bedspreads, wooden headboards, and antique Georgian furnishings. In sum, a marvelous establishment, one of the city's finest bed and breakfasts. ~ 440 Post Street; 415-397-3510, 800-288-4346, fax 415-989-0529.

Up on Cathedral Hill, a mile or two from the Downtown district, stands **The Majestic**. As a hotel this five-story structure dates from 1902 when The Majestic opened as one of the city's first

NOTHING STAID IN THIS HOTEL

From the wild and crazy lobby with its dervish chairs to the sapphire theater curtains in all 140 rooms, the **Hotel Triton** is a place with a sense of humor. If you are seeking a hotel with a fantasy mural, furniture that appears to undulate, iridescent throw pillows, starburst light fixtures, and room service from two trendy restaurants, look no further. An added plus is its proximity to Chinatown. ~ 342 Grant Avenue; 415-394-0500, 800-443-6611, fax 415-394-0555. DELUXE TO ULTRA-DELUXE.

grand hotels. It underwent several incarnations before finally being reincarnated as The Majestic. The current 57-room establishment features a restaurant, bar, and attractive lobby. Some rooms are strikingly appointed with canopied beds, European antiques, and marble bathrooms. Rates start in the deluxe range. ~ 1500 Sutter Street; 415-441-1100, 800-869-8966, fax 415-673-7331.

ULTRA-DELUXE LODGING Elegance and style? That would be the **White Swan Inn.** A six-story, English-style building with curved bay windows, the White Swan was originally built in 1908 as a small hotel. Today it is a fashionable bed and breakfast with a living room, library, solarium, and small courtyard. The decorative theme, reflected in the garden, wallpapers, and art prints, is English. Each room contains a fireplace, television, telephone, wet bar, and private bath. Like the public rooms, they are all beautifully appointed. ~ 845 Bush Street; 415-775-1755, 800-999-9570, fax 415-775-5717.

Accommodations at the 25-story **Hotel Nikko** exude *shibui*, a Japanese word that expresses elegant simplicity. Smooth-edged contemporary furnishings in pearl gray are offset by soft pinks and mauve in carpeting and upholstery. Rates include access to business services and fitness facilities, including a glass-enclosed rooftop swimming pool. ~ 222 Mason Street; 415-394-1111, 800-645-5687, fax 415-394-1106.

It's a one-class-fits-all establishment. Of course, at the 17-story **Campton Place Hotel,** the class is definitely first: 117 luxurious rooms and suites are outfitted with sinfully comfortable beds, Henredon armoires, writing desks, limited edition art, and marble baths. Innumerable services are available around the clock. Located half a block from Union Square, this is the place to stay when you can afford to pay ultra-deluxe prices. ~ 340 Stockton Street; 415-781-5555, 800-235-4300, fax 415-955-5536.

Once inside the 21-story **Pan Pacific San Francisco,** some guests simply cannot believe there are 330 rooms and suites here; the ambience is more like that of an intimate small hotel. Guest rooms have fine furnishings, custom cabinetry, and distinctive arched windows. Despite their size, they feel cozy, almost too much so. Oversized marble baths and attentive valet service are extra indulgences at this ultra-deluxe-priced hotel one block west of Union Square. ~ 500 Post Street; 415-771-8600, 800-533-6465, fax 415-398-0267.

Home to Wolfgang Puck's Postrio eatery, the **Prescott Hotel** is more famous for its restaurant than its rooms. It shouldn't be, for the accommodations are equally as outstanding, from the early California living room warmed by a big stone hearth to 166 rooms and suites beautifully arranged with Empire and Neo-classical furnishings. Cherry armoires, silk wallpapers, and nightstands inlaid with black granite are embellished by rich tones of purple and gold and hunter green. There's complimentary coffee and tea in the mornings, and wine and cheese in the afternoons. And if you don't feel like going out for dinner, you can always order room service from Postrio. ~ 545 Post Street; 415-563-0303, 800-283-7322.

DINING

What can you say about a cozy restaurant that's always packed with diners? In the case of **Nhu's Vietnamese Cuisine,** you can say it passes the ultimate test of ethnic restaurants by attracting ethnics. Not only Vietnamese are drawn to this unassuming café; the menu offers something for everyone. There are steamed rice dishes with spicy chicken, Vietnamese pork kebab, or lemon-grass beef, plus beefball soup, sautéed vegetables, imperial rolls, chicken salad, and prawns. Closed Sunday. ~ 581 Eddy Street; 415-474-6487. BUDGET.

Whoever coined the slogan "Eat at Joe's" surely had San Francisco in mind. The city sports a dizzying number of restaurants named after the omnipresent Joseph. But down along Taylor Street rests the **Original Joe's.** It's one of those cafés where the waiters don tuxes and the prices never compete with the quality of the food. A San Francisco institution for over 50 years, Original Joe's features a steak-and-chop menu which also includes Italian and fresh seafood dinners. Open for any meal. ~ 144 Taylor Street; 415-775-4877. MODERATE.

Whether they are hungry or not, Dashiell Hammett fans always track down **John's Grill.** It's the restaurant that detective Sam Spade popped into during a tense scene in *The Maltese Falcon.* Today the wood-paneled walls, adorned with memorabilia and old photos, still breathe of bygone eras. Waiters dress formally, the bartender gossips about local politicians, and the customers sink onto bar stools. The menu features broiler and seafood dishes as well as a nostalgic platter of chops, baked potato, and sliced tomato (what Spade wolfed down on that fateful day). Closed Sunday for lunch. ~ 63 Ellis Street; 415-986-3274. MODERATE TO DELUXE.

A chain restaurant that calls itself "San Francisco's International Gourmet Soup, Salad, Sandwich & Quiche Restaurant" sounds like a place to be avoided. But **Salmagundi** happens to serve delicious soup. On a given day, they might feature Boston clam chowder or vegetable soup, not to mention salads, sandwiches, cheeses, quiche dishes, and fresh desserts, as well as beer and wine. Set in the midst of the theater district, this deli is particularly popular late in the evening. ~ 442 Geary Street; 415-441-0894. BUDGET TO MODERATE.

Sushi Man is a matchbox sushi bar with matchless style. If that's not evident from the plastic sushi displays in the window,

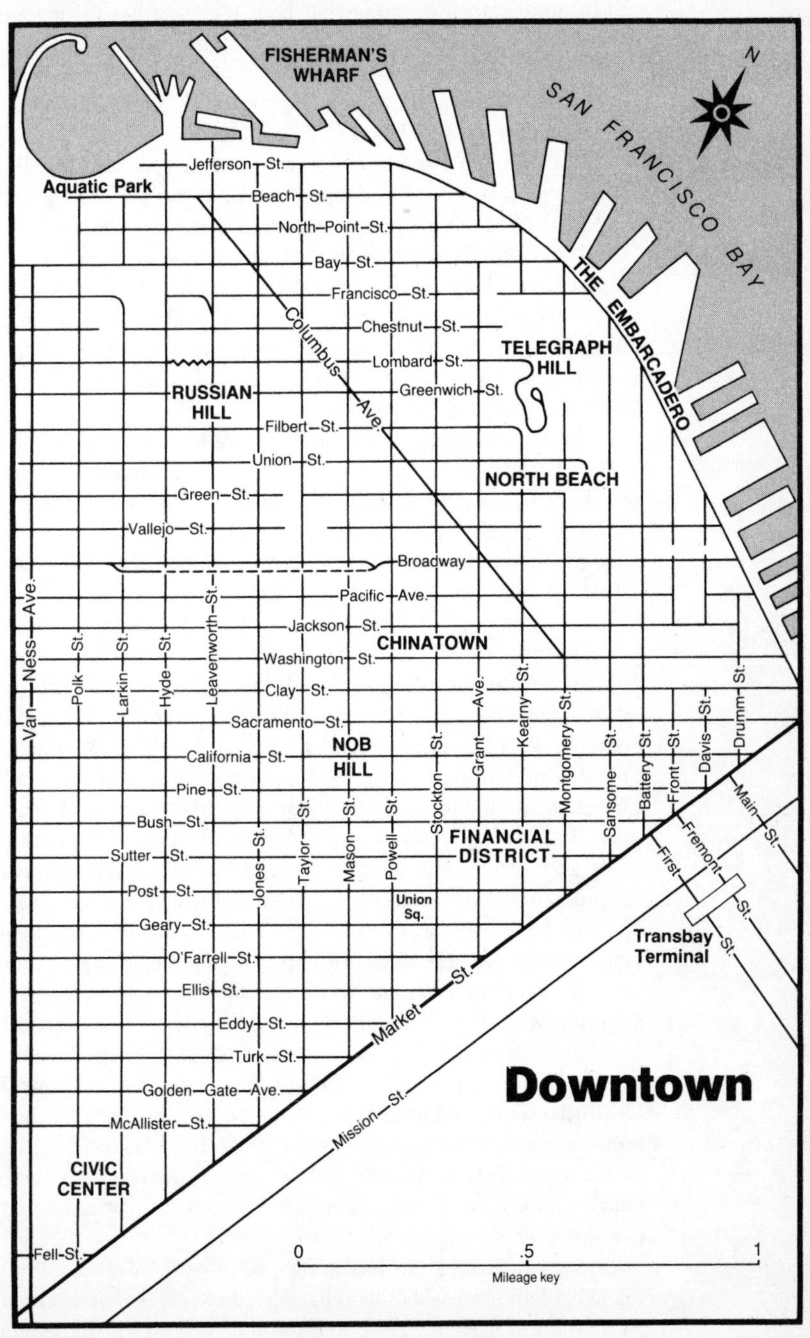
FISHERMAN'S WHARF
SAN FRANCISCO BAY
N
Aquatic Park
Jefferson St.
Beach St.
North Point St.
Bay St.
Francisco St.
Chestnut St.
Lombard St.
Greenwich St.
Filbert St.
Union St.
Green St.
Vallejo St.
Broadway
Pacific Ave.
Jackson St.
Washington St.
Clay St.
Sacramento St.
California St.
Pine St.
Bush St.
Sutter St.
Post St.
Geary St.
O'Farrell St.
Ellis St.
Eddy St.
Turk St.
Golden Gate Ave.
McAllister St.
Fell St.
Columbus Ave.
THE EMBARCADERO
TELEGRAPH HILL
RUSSIAN HILL
NORTH BEACH
CHINATOWN
NOB HILL
FINANCIAL DISTRICT
Union Sq.
CIVIC CENTER
Van Ness Ave.
Polk St.
Larkin St.
Hyde St.
Leavenworth St.
Jones St.
Taylor St.
Mason St.
Powell St.
Stockton St.
Grant Ave.
Kearny St.
Montgomery St.
Sansome St.
Battery St.
Front St.
Davis St.
Drumm St.
Main St.
Fremont St.
First St.
Transbay Terminal
Market St.
Mission St.
Downtown
0
.5
1
Mileage key

then step inside. The tiny wooden bar is decorated with serene silk screens and fresh flowers. Owner Ryo Yoshioka has earned a deserved reputation for his sushi creations. There's *sake* (smoked salmon), *mirugai* (clam), as well as sashimi. Dinner only. Closed Sunday. ~ 731 Bush Street; 415-981-1313. MODERATE.

Stuck for a place to dine—there are more than 3000 restaurants in this city of 768,000.

Maiden Lane used to be a perfect spot for slumming; today it's a fashionable shopping district. But there's one place along the high-priced strip that brings back the easy days. **Nosheria** is an unassuming deli serving an array of sandwiches, salads, and mouth-watering pastries. Dine alfresco at one of the tables out front or pull up a chair inside this brick-walled establishment. At lunch there will likely be a line extending out the door. Also open for breakfast. Closed Sunday. ~ 69 Maiden Lane; 415-398-3557. BUDGET.

What do you get when you cross an American restaurant with a French fad? A pastrami croissant. At **Franciscan Croissants** you'll get many other strange combinations, like smoked turkey, ham, and cheese, or prosciutto croissants. Things are more subdued at breakfast, when they feature apple and berry croissants. These are not ordinary pastries, but colossal croissants served fresh and steaming. *Pourquoi pas?* ~ 301 Sutter Street; 415-398-8276. BUDGET.

Travelers and locals alike wait in line to devour Swedish pancakes, sourdough French toast, and other specialties at **Sears Fine Foods,** a popular local breakfast spot since 1938. Breakfast is served until 3:30 p.m. when the restaurant closes, and there's also a lunch menu that includes meat loaf, Swedish meatballs, and a variety of sandwiches. ~ 439 Powell Street; 415-986-1160. BUDGET.

It is the rare restaurateur who can please both Los Angeles and San Francisco, but that's exactly what Wolfgang Puck has done in bringing his talents north to **Postrio.** Puck's innovative food pairings, such as Chinese duck with spicy mango sauce and sautéed salmon with plum glaze and wasabi mashed potatoes, compete for attention with a stunning dining room. Reserve far in advance. ~ 545 Post Street; 415-776-7825. ULTRA-DELUXE.

Chef Barbara Tropp has created a unique blend of Chinese and California foods at **China Moon Café**. Few of the dishes could be found elsewhere: spring rolls with chiles, fresh water chestnuts, and a pot-browned noodle pillow served with spicy chicken. Dinner only. ~ 639 Post Street; 415-775-4789. MODERATE TO DELUXE.

HIDDEN ►

Indonesia Restaurant has developed a loyal following among the many San Franciscans who have lived or traveled in Indonesia. And for good reason. The complex and diverse flavors in this tiny, crowded hole-in-the-wall establishment tantalize the taste buds.

Such favorite dishes as *gado-gado*, *soto ayam*, beef curry, *mie goreng*, *rendang*, and *sate* are included on the menu, as well as many others. ~ 678 Post Street; 415-474-4026. BUDGET.

San Francisco offers several European-style gourmet restaurants. Most are located in major hotels and feature exquisite surroundings as well as fine cuisine. Others are dotted about town in small, intimate locales. The tab at these exclusive addresses is in the ultra-deluxe range. Two of the very best are listed below. Remember, they usually serve dinner only, require guests to be well-dressed, and recommend advance reservations.

Campton Place Restaurant transforms the freshest all-American ingredients into haute cuisine, all in a blush-pink room where the candlelight is reflected in silver, crystal, and Wedgwood china. Breakfast is worth a special trip for items like whole-wheat apple-walnut pancakes with cinnamon creme. At lunch and dinner, seafood, steaks, and oxtail share the menu with entrées such as grilled duck breast with turnips and kumquats in a lime-leaf sauce and steamed salmon with Vietnamese herbs and pea sprouts. ~ 340 Stockton Street in the Campton Place Hotel; 415-781-5555. ULTRA-DELUXE.

Another small and romantic dining room, **Masa's**, is one of my favorite San Francisco restaurants. Elite yet understated, the decor is a mix of dark woods, softly colored upholstered chairs, and floral arrangements. What makes Masa's famous, however, is not the dining room but the kitchen. Changing daily, the contemporary French menu might include filet mignon with foie gras mousse and black truffles, roasted squab with wild rice risotto, or sautéed medallions of fallow deer with caramelized apples and zinfandel sauce, and lobster with shrimp quenelles. There are soufflés, sorbets, and mousses for dessert. But inventorying the menu can never do justice to this splendid place. You have to experience it yourself. Dinner only. Closed Sunday and Monday. ~ 648 Bush Street; 415-989-7154. ULTRA-DELUXE.

SHOPPING

Union Square quite simply is *the* center for shopping in San Francisco. First of all, this grass-and-hedgerow park (located between Post and Geary, Stockton and Powell streets) is surrounded by department stores. **Macy's** is along one border. ~ 170 O'Farrell Street; 415-397-3333. **Saks Fifth Avenue** guards another. ~ 384 Post Street; 415-986-4300. **Neiman-Marcus**, the Texas-bred emporium, claims one corner. ~ 150 Stockton Street; 415-362-3900. An elite men's clothing shop named **Bullock & Jones** is also situated in this well-heeled neighborhood. ~ 340 Post Street; 415-392-4243. Once the haven of European specialty boutiques, Union Square is becoming a hot address among sport-shoes shops, entertainment-company merchandising centers, and mass-appeal clothing stores.

Of course, that's just on the square. Beyond the plaza are scads of stores. Along Stockton, one of the streets radiating out from the square, you'll find a number of prestigious shops.

Then if you follow Post, another bordering street, there's **Gump's**, which features fine imported decorations for the home. If you get bored looking through the antiques, china pieces, and oriental art, you can always adjourn to the Jade or Crystal Room or the gourmet shop. ~ 135 Post Street; 415-982-1616.

For a vicarious "rich and famous" experience, take a stroll through **Giorgio Armani** at Union Square. This boutique is one of only seven American stores carrying the designer's premier Black Label line. Formalwear and sportswear are elegantly displayed under the tutelage of attentive salespeople, who discreetly disclose the cost of the apparel. ~ 278 Post Street; 415-434-2500.

The streets all around host a further array of stores. You'll encounter jewelers, dress designers, boutiques, furniture stores, tailor shops, and more. So take a gander—there's everything out there from the unexpected to the bizarre.

A shop fitting the former category is **Victoria's Secret**. Of course, it's rarely spoken of. Whispered perhaps among intimates. Victoria, it seems, sells white lace and paper-thin teddies. At scandalous prices, no less. But such a variety and so soft. Lingerie like you never dreamed of. ~ 335 Powell Street; 415-433-9671.

The Galleria is a glass-domed promenade lined with fashionable shops. A center for well-heeled business crowds, the mall showcases designer fashions and elegant gifts. ~ 50 Post Street; 415-956-2846.

Braunstein/Quay Gallery is an outstanding place to view the work of local artists. As the catalog claims, owner Ruth Braunstein "embodies the brash, irreverent, and irrepressible energy of the San Francisco art world." This contemporary gallery also exhibits works from other parts of the world. ~ 250 Sutter Street; 415-392-5532.

Tillman Place Bookshop is a postage stamp–sized store tucked into an alleyway. Within, however, you'll find a tasteful collection of coffee-table books, paperback classics and travel guides, all contained in a Victorian setting. ~ 8 Tillman Place; 415-392-4668.

The Candy Jar is a chocoholic's heaven. This designer candy store is stacked with shiny gold boxes of sinful Godiva chocolate. For the unrepentant, they also offer homemade truffles. ~ 210 Grant Avenue; 415-391-5508.

For toys, there's no place like **FAO Schwarz**. A branch of New York's famous Fifth Avenue emporium, it includes three huge floors dripping with spectacular kites, oversized tinkertoys, and monstrous stuffed animals. There's everything from model Lego cities and designer doll dresses to the latest computer toys. A wonderland for all ages. ~ 48 Stockton Street; 415-394-8700.

When looking for maps and travel guides, try **Thomas Brothers Maps**. This company actually produces many of the maps it sells and has gained renown for its excellent city maps. ~ 550 Jackson Street; 415-981-7520.

Also consider the **Rand McNally Map & Travel Store**. Here is everything the wanderer could conceivably desire: guidebooks, maps, globes, language tapes, and geography games for kids. ~ 595 Market Street; 415-777-3131.

B. Dalton's Bookseller, a link in a national chain, features two floors of books. ~ 200 Kearny Street; 415-956-2850. Just steps from Union Square, you'll find **Borders Books & Music**, with four floors of books, CDs, and tapes, and chairs for serious reading. Stop by the Cafe Espresso for a cup of coffee, an Italian soda, or a snack. ~ 400 Post Street; 415-399-0522.

For used books and magazines, try **McDonald's Bookshop** in the Tenderloin. This musty warren of crowded aisles could keep one browsing for hours. This bookstore boasts more than a million books and a vast array of magazines that date back to the 1920s, including a complete selection of *Life*, which began publication in 1936. There are also hundreds of old photos and a collection of James Dean pictures and books. ~ 48 Turk Street; 415-673-2235.

Harold's Hometown News is a shop specializing in "hometown newspapers." There are dailies from all over the world. For homesick travelers, or those just interested in a little local news, it's a godsend. ~ 524 Geary Street; 415-441-2665.

Located in the Monadnock Building, one of downtown San Francisco's finest historic office complexes, **American Indian Contemporary Arts** is the place to go for traditional and contemporary works. Squash blossom jewelry, mask art, and moccasins are exhibited along with mixed media and acrylic paintings. Also found here are books, posters, and videos focusing on American Indians. The Monadnock's sculpture garden makes a great place to enjoy lunch. ~ 685 Market Street, #250; 415-495-7600.

A nine-story vertical mall at 5th and Market streets, the **San Francisco Shopping Centre** sports six stacked spiral escalators that ascend through an oval-shaped, marble-and-granite atrium toward the retractable skylight. The mall includes nearly 90 upscale shops selling everything from men's and women's sportswear to jewelry and unique gifts. The center is all crowned by a five-floor **Nordstrom**, the high-quality fashion department store. ~ 415-243-8500.

NIGHTLIFE

Since its rowdy Gold Rush days, San Francisco has been renowned as a wide-open town, hard-drinking and easygoing. Today there are over 2000 places around the city to order a drink, including saloons, restaurants, cabarets, boats, private clubs, and even a couple hospitals. There's a bar for every mood and each occasion.

When looking for nightlife, it is advisable to consult the "Datebook," commonly called the "pink section," in the Sunday *San Francisco Examiner and Chronicle* for current shows and performers. However you decide to spend the evening, you'll find plenty of possibilities in this city by the Bay.

San Francisco's answer to a Scottish pub is **Edinburgh Castle**, a cavernous bar complete with dart board. There's a beamed ceiling, heavy wooden furniture, and convivial crowd—Scotland incarnate. ~ 950 Geary Street; 415-885-4074.

Then at **S. Holmes, Esq.**, you'll encounter a pub for the upper crust. Located on the top floor of the Holiday Inn–Union Square, it beautifully re-creates the Baker Street detective's digs. You'll find calabash pipes, period pieces, and various Sherlockian effects placed around this intriguing bar. ~ 480 Sutter Street; 415-398-8900.

Then, for key-plunking saloon music, there's **Lefty O'Doul's**. Friendly, informal, and filled with baseball memorabilia, the place is named for an old-time local ballplayer. ~ 333 Geary Street; 415-982-8900.

Located atop the Westin St. Francis Hotel, **Club Oz** is favored by many for its disco dancing. The place is nicely appointed with marble bar and draws a well-heeled crowd. The deejay sounds include "international pop," while the visual display is provided by video and fiberoptics. Cover; dress code. ~ 335 Powell Street; 415-774-0116.

The **Warfield Theatre**, owned by the late rock impresario Bill Graham's company, brings in top groups from around the country. Bill Graham Productions produces other shows regularly throughout the Bay Area. ~ 982 Market Street; 415-775-7722.

The **Plush Room** in the York Hotel caters to an upscale clientele and draws big name cabaret acts. It's a lovely setting. Cover. ~ 940 Sutter Street; 415-885-6800.

A favored relaxing place for the rich is the **Redwood Room** in the Clift Hotel. With art deco lamps, marble tables, and burnished redwood paneling, it is nothing less than sumptuous. Men will feel more comfortable wearing coats and ties, women dresses. ~ Geary and Taylor streets; 415-775-4700.

The "On Broadway" theater scene in San Francisco is on Geary Street, near Union Square; while the "Off Broadway," or avant-garde drama, is scattered around the city.

The **American Conservatory Theater**, or ACT, is the biggest show in town. It's also one of the nation's largest resident companies. The season runs from October to June, and the repertory is traditional, ranging from Shakespeare to French comedy to 20th-century drama. ~ 415 Geary Street; 415-749-2228.

The **Curran Theatre** brings Broadway musicals to town. ~ 445 Geary Street; 415-474-3800. **Golden Gate Theatre** also attracts major shows and national companies. Built in 1922, the theater is a grand affair with marble floors and rococo ceilings. ~ 1 Taylor Street, at the corner of 6th and Market streets; 415-474-3800. Among the city's other playhouses is the **Marine's Memorial Theatre.** ~ 609 Sutter Street; 415-771-6900. **Theatre on the Square** is right on Union Square. ~ 450 Post Street; 415-433-9500. Close to the Civic Center is the **Orpheum Theatre.** ~ 1192 Market Street; 415-474-3800. Experimental theater is the specialty of **Cable Car Theatre.** ~ 430 Mason Street; 415-403-7340.

Many local radio stations sponsor event hotlines. There's the KKSF **Bayline**, with information on theater, comedy, live music, and other activities in the city. ~ 415-357-1037. Live 105's **The What Line** provides details on concerts, comedy clubs, and the dance club scene. ~ 415-357-9428. Or check KFOG's **Entertainment Line** for local goings-on. ~ 415-777-1045.

Civic Center

On the other side of the Downtown district, to the southwest, rises the Civic Center, architectural pride of the city. The prettiest pathway through this municipal meeting ground begins in United Nations Plaza at Fulton and Market streets.

SIGHTS

HIDDEN

Every Wednesday and Sunday this promenade is home to the **Heart of the City Farmers' Market**, an open-air produce fair that draws farmers from all over Northern California.

To experience one of the country's most modern information centers, saunter on over to the main branch of the **San Francisco Public Library** in its $104.5 million headquarters that opened in the spring of 1996. Exemplifying the fact that libraries are not just about books anymore, the main branch's facilities include 400 electronic workstations with free connection to the Internet. Among the library's 11 special-interest research centers are the San Francisco History Center, the Gay and Lesbian Center, and the Art and Music Center. ~ 100 Larkin Street; 415-557-4400.

With its bird-whitened statues and gray-columned buildings, the Civic Center is the domain of powerbrokers and political leaders; ironically, its grassy plots and park benches also make it the haunt of the city's homeless. As you pass the reflecting pool and formal gardens, then ascend the steps of **City Hall** (Polk and Grove streets), you'll see how both halves live.

Modeled after the national capitol, this granite and marble edifice sports a dome that is actually higher than the one in Washington. The rotunda is a dizzying sandstone and marble affair encrusted with statuary and encircled by a wrought-iron balcony. French Renaissance in style, City Hall is the centerpiece of the Civic Center, which in turn is the ultimate expression of the "City Beautiful" philosophy that inspired the rebuilders of post-earthquake San Francisco to design one of the country's most splendid civic centers.

Beauty seems ineluctably to have its dark side; here it can be found by climbing the grand staircase to Room 200, the Mayor's office. That is the place former San Francisco Supervisor Dan White headed on November 27, 1978. An ultra-conservative, ex-cop, and Vietnam veteran, White was bitterly fighting Mayor George Moscone over retention of his supervisorial seat. On that chilling winter day, White pumped four bullets into the Mayor, crossed City Hall, and gunned down Harvey Milk, the country's first openly gay supervisor. White's dual murder left the entire city outraged, and for a time turned these elegant corridors of power into hallways of horror.

As you step out the back of City Hall on to Van Ness Avenue, you'll be standing face to facade with the center of San Francisco culture. To the right rises the Veterans' Building, which formerly housed the San Francisco Museum of Modern Art. Centerstage is the **War Memorial Opera House**, home of one of the world's finest opera companies. The opera house is closed for renovation; it will reopen in September 1997. ~ Van Ness Avenue and Grove Street.

To the left, that ultramodern glass-and-granite building is the **Louise M. Davies Symphony Hall**, home of the San Francisco Symphony. Through the semi-circle of green-tinted glass, you can peer into one of the city's newest and most glamorous buildings. Or if you'd prefer to be on the inside gazing out, there are tours of the hall and its cultural cousins next door. Admission. ~ Van Ness Avenue and Grove Street; information, 415-552-8338.

✔ CHECK THESE OUT—UNIQUE SIGHTS

- Bring your laptop computer to the main **San Francisco Public Library**, where you can access electronic information just as easily as the 1.5 million books. *page 41*
- Wander Chinatown's **Waverly Place**, an alley-like street where mystery writer Dashiell Hammett led readers in *Dead Yellow Women*. *page 57*
- Browse through the shelves of **City Lights Bookstore**, a Beat-era haunt established by poet Lawrence Ferlinghetti. *page 63*
- Step back to the days of the Spanish empire at Mission San Francisco de Asis, better known as **Mission Dolores**, one of 21 missions built along the California coast. *page 114*

One of the best places in town to appreciate the city's rich cultural tradition is the **San Francisco Performing Arts Library and Museum.** The collection covers San Francisco's musical, theatrical, and literary heritage with photos, programs, books, and costumes. The exhibits cover everything from Jean Cocteau to the local symphony association. Closed Sunday and Monday. ~ 399 Grove Street; 415-255-4800.

LODGING

For fans of the opera (or the symphony or the ballet), the **Inn at the Opera** is heaven on earth. Located virtually within earshot of the major performing arts houses, it plays the ham with concierge services (especially helpful for last-minute tickets) and little touches (such as sheet-music drawer liners) in the 30 rooms and 18 suites. Rooms have tasteful furnishings, along with wet bars and mini-fridges. ~ 333 Fulton Street; 415-863-8400, 800-325-2708, fax 415-861-0821. ULTRA-DELUXE.

A two-story motor court flanking a pool courtyard, spacious rooms and suites with a soft tropical motif, a Caribbean-style restaurant . . . can this be the heart of San Francisco? It is, and it's the **Phoenix Hotel**, just a block from Civic Center. Concierge services, in-room screenings of locally filmed movies and the patronage of music-business mavens may make the Phoenix the hippest inn in town. ~ 601 Eddy Street; 415-776-1380, 800-248-9466, fax 415-875-3109. DELUXE. ◄ HIDDEN

Located on the border between the city's stately Civic Center and unwashed Tenderloin district, **San Francisco Central YMCA** has singles, doubles and triples with shared baths. A private bath will cost slightly more. In traditional Y-style, the rooms are as clean as they are sterile; they are scantily furnished and tend to be cramped. But for those prices—which include a continental breakfast and free use of the sunroof, pool, sauna, steam room, weight room, television, laundry, aerobics area, and basketball and racquetball courts—who's complaining? ~ 220 Golden Gate Avenue; 415-885-0460. BUDGET.

Located right on the edge of the Civic Center, the **Hotel Renoir** is one of the more economical. The lobby is lined with Renoir prints and decorated in gold and soft peach colors. There's a lounge and a friendly ambience about the place. The only detraction is its location on busy Market Street and proximity to the city's Tenderloin district; but the moderate room tabs make it worth the price. Rooms are small but reasonably well furnished. The accommodations I saw featured wall-to-wall carpeting, color television, steam heat, plush furniture, and a tile bathroom with shower-tub combination. ~ 45 McAllister Street; 415-626-5200, 800-576-3388, fax 415-626-5581. MODERATE.

DINING

This area spotlights several outstanding dining rooms. One of the best in my opinion is **Hayes Street Grill**, a chic establishment situated within strolling distance of the opera and symphony. Specializing in mesquite-grilled entrées, it features fresh fish dishes, dry-aged steak, and chicken breast. Excellent food. No lunch on the weekend. ~ 320 Hayes Street; 415-863-5545. DELUXE.

Few, if any, places in the Hayes Valley gourmet ghetto are more popular than **Caffe Delle Stelle**. Cans of tomatoes stacked in pyramids grace the windows, and wreaths of dried red peppers adorn the walls of this quirky, cute Tuscan tratoria. Conversation buzzes, but it's not too loud to enjoy an intimate discussion of your own. The cuisine is Italian country cooking, and meals begin with fresh bread and a bowl of *pansanela*, a dip made from olive oil, bread, tomato juice, and spices. Entrées include a selection of pastas, baked chicken, roasted salmon fillet, and daily specials like ravioli barbarossa stuffed with arugula, ricotta, and walnuts in a basil sauce. ~ 395 Hayes; 415-252-1110. MODERATE.

No place is a better example of the eccentric establishments for which San Francisco is famous than **Mad Magda's Russian Tea Room & Cafe**. You can enjoy a cup of smoked Russian tea or a bowl of homemade borsch, while getting tarot cards, tea leaves, or your palm read by the resident psychic. The sandwiches are named after famous Russians. Catherine the Great is tuna with cheese; Tolstoy, a long sandwich with ham, turkey, and several cheeses; and Rasputin, prosciutto, Brie, sundried tomatoes, and balsamic vinaigrette on a baguette. ~ 579 Hayes Street; 864-7654. BUDGET.

HIDDEN ►

Vicolo Pizzeria may be a bit hard to find, but the reward is gourmet pizza different than any you may have tasted before. The restaurant's decor, marked by corrugated steel hanging from the walls, acts as a reminder that the building was formerly an auto mechanic's shop. Served primarily by the slice, Vicolo's pizza is

CLASSROOM CUISINE

With two restaurants and a deli, the **California Culinary Academy** offers everything from a half pint of delicious potato salad to a classical European buffet. Here students under faculty supervision hone their talents. Located in a skylit Neo-classic hall, the Careme Room serves three-course lunches and dinners as well as buffets. Downstairs, the Academy Grill serves à la carte specialties such as eggplant parmigiana and cider-glazed roast pork loin. With the exception of the deluxe-priced buffets, all restaurant meals are moderately priced. The budget take-out fare at The Culinary Shoppe is ideal for a picnic. Closed Saturday and Sunday. ~ 625 Polk Street; 415-771-3500. BUDGET TO DELUXE.

characterized by its distinctive cornmeal crust. Sausage, four cheese, and two vegetarian varieties are the standards, with other choices changing regularly. ~ 201 Ivy Street; 415-863-2382. BUDGET.

Stars earned its stripes from day one with the stylish cuisine of Jeremiah Tower, a highly celebrated chef in the California cuisine constellation. Seafood, warm salads and French-inspired chicken entrées shine especially bright here. No lunch on the weekend. ~ 150 Redwood Alley; 415-861-7827. DELUXE.

Max's Opera Café serves a variety of fare ranging from smoked barbecued ribs to California cuisine, but the standouts are the thick pastrami, corned beef, and turkey breast sandwiches accompanied by tangy coleslaw and potato salad. A lively bar area features occasional impromptu entertainment by the staff, some of whom are budding tenors and sopranos. ~ 601 Van Ness Avenue; 415-771-7301. MODERATE.

A café setting that features brass fixtures, pastel walls, bentwood furniture, and Asian artwork make **Thepin** an inviting Thai establishment. The fare, ranging from red curry duck to marinated prawns and chicken breast, is also a winner. Specialties include sliced chicken and shrimp with spinach in peanut sauce, marinated filet of salmon in curry sauce, and sliced green papaya salad with tomatoes and chili pepper. No lunch on the weekend. ~ 298 Gough Street; 415-863-9335. MODERATE.

SHOPPING

Hayes Valley lies directly west of the Civic Center and has as its focus the block bounded by Hayes, Franklin, Grove, and Gough streets. Of particular importance here is the **Vorpal Gallery**. One of the city's finest galleries, it features works by Jesse Allen, Ken Matsumoto, and other contemporary artists. There are also paintings and prints by such 20th-century masters as Pablo Picasso and M. C. Escher. ~ 393 Grove Street; 415-397-9200.

The **San Francisco Women Artists Gallery** across the street features artworks by Bay Area women. The variety of arts and crafts is impressive and the pieces are quite good. Several other galleries are located in the immediate neighborhood, making the Hayes Street corridor an artists' enclave. ~ 370 Hayes Street; 415-552-7392.

F. Dorian specializes in crafts from all over the world including ethnic and contemporary items. The company also sells antique furniture from the Philippines, Indian oil lamps, Indonesian diary boxes, and exotic jewelry. ~ 388 Hayes Street; 415-861-3191.

Just a few blocks away lies **Opera Plaza** (Van Ness and Golden Gate avenues), an atrium mall with shops, restaurants, and a movie theater collected around a courtyard and fountain. It's a pretty place to sit and enjoy the day. For booklovers there's an excellent bookstore here: **A Clean Well-Lighted Place For Books.** ~ 601 Van Ness Avenue; 415-441-6670.

NIGHTLIFE San Francisco is rich culturally in its opera, symphony, and ballet, located in the Civic Center area. Since tickets to major theatrical and other cultural events are expensive, consider buying day-of-performance tickets from San Francisco Ticket Box Office Service (TIX) on Stockton Street between Post and Geary streets. Open from 11 a.m. until just before showtime, they sell tickets at half-price on the day of the show and full price for future events. ~ 415-433-7827.

San Francisco takes nothing quite so seriously as its opera. **The San Francisco Opera** is world class in stature and invites operatic greats from around the world to perform. As a result, tickets are very difficult to obtain. The international season begins in mid-September and runs for 13 weeks. The Opera House is currently closed for renovation; performances will take place at the Bill Graham Civic Auditorium and at the Orpheum Theater. ~ 415-864-3330.

Guided tours of the Civic Center begin at the San Francisco Public Library (call 415-557-4266 for information on tours).

The **San Francisco Symphony** stands nearly as tall on the world stage. The season extends from September until June, with a series of special concerts year-round. Michael Tilson Thomas conducts, and guest soloists have included Jessie Norman and Itzhak Perlman. ~ Davies Hall, Van Ness Avenue and Grove Street; 415-431-5400.

The **San Francisco Ballet**, performing for more than a half-century, is the nation's oldest permanent ballet, and one of the finest. Featuring *The Nutcracker* during Christmas, the company's official season runs from February until June. In addition to original works, they perform classic ballets. While the Opera House is closed, performances will run at the Center for the Arts at Yerba Buena Gardens and the Palace of Fine Arts. ~ 415-703-9400.

Over at the **Great American Music Hall**, a vintage 1907 building has been splendidly converted to a nightclub featuring a variety of entertainers. Included in the lineup are musical greats like Hoyt Axton, Etta James, and Queen Ida. ~ 859 O'Farrell Street; 415-885-0750.

Financial District

Beyond the Downtown district, as Maiden Lane debouches into a complex of streets, you'll come upon the "Wall Street of the West," Montgomery Street, locus of the Financial District. The center of Pacific commerce and trade, this is the roosting place for San Francisco's skyscrapers. Here you'll encounter windswept canyons of glass and steel inhabited by exotic birds dressed in three-piece suits or tailor-trim skirts.

SIGHTS Behind the granite and marble along Montgomery are more banks than one could imagine. **A. P. Giannini Plaza**, between Pine and California streets, a combination mall and office building, memorializes the brilliant Italian banker who developed an upstart savings company into one of the world's largest financial institutions, the Bank of America.

Another bank at 420 Montgomery hosts the **Wells Fargo History Museum.** In addition to glistening gold specimens and postal artifacts, there are photos recapturing the raffish days of the Old West. Central to the entire exhibit is an 18-passenger stagecoach reconditioned to sparkle like this year's model. (Remember, this pocket museum is open during banker's hours only.) Closed Saturday and Sunday. ~ 415-396-2619.

Or consider the Bank of Canton of California, which has reconstructed a 19th-century federal mint and incorporated it into the **Pacific Heritage Museum.** The rest of the facility features rotating exhibitions on the art and culture of the Pacific Basin. Closed Saturday and Sunday. ~ 608 Commercial Street; 415-399-1123.

The history-minded will also keep a sharp eye for the bronze markers spotted here and there along this fabled street. Montgomery has always been a center for San Francisco financial adventures. One plaque near 505 Montgomery commemorates the **Hudson's Bay Company headquarters.** It seems that in 1841 the British-owned company set up shop here, sending shivers through the American traders who were beginning to consider California their own preserve. On the side of the California National Bank at Montgomery and Clay streets rests a marker noting the spot where the first pony express rider arrived in 1860 after the dangerously harrowing relay from St. Joseph, Missouri.

That bizarrely shaped edifice between Clay and Washington streets is none other than the **Transamerica Building.** Designed like a pyramid that's been put through a wringer, it is the most striking feature along San Francisco's skyline. Situated on the east side of the building is a pocket park—a significant attraction in itself. It features metal sculptures, a fountain, and a dwarf's eye view of the stone needle rising straight above. ~ 415-983-4100.

The 700 block of Montgomery contains a cluster of buildings dating back to 1850. They are part of the **Jackson Square** area, a misnomered enclave extending from Washington to Pacific streets and from Columbus Avenue to Sansome Street. There is no "square" here, but you will find an official historic district sprinkled with brickface buildings and interior courtyards. During the 1850s, this represented the black heart of the Barbary Coast. Prospectors on the make and convicts on the lam haunted its gambling dens and flophouses. The local denizens' penchant for kidnapping drunken sailors gave rise to the word "shanghaied."

As with Downtown's Maiden Lane, a mixture of time and irony has transformed the area. Fashionable galleries and other upscale emporia have replaced the brothels and dives. Though prices here are as staggering as the neighboring skyscrapers, you might want to browse the shops, which include some of the city's finest antique stores.

DINING

Sam's Grill, established in 1867, is a classic San Francisco businessperson's restaurant. With a new menu printed every day, it features fresh fish, shellfish from surrounding waters, charcoal-broiled steaks and chops, plus seafood casseroles. The menu is the same at lunch or dinner, and you can order a martini anytime from 11 a.m. on. There are diner car booths, waiters in bow ties and tuxedos, a friendly bar, and white walls adorned with hunting scenes. Closed Saturday and Sunday. ~ 374 Bush Street; 415-421-0594. MODERATE.

No, you're not at a Paris metro station, even though the designer of **Cafe Bastille** would like to make you think so. This popular bistro boasts a basement dining room, with floors done in multicolored marble, walls painted with steel girders, and a giant Metro Bastille sign. You can also dine on the ground floor, by the bar, or at umbrella-covered tables in the front alleyway. The daily menu is written on a blackboard and includes crêpes, sandwiches, quiche, and such entrées as roasted chicken breast. ~ 22 Belden Place; 415-986-5673. BUDGET.

Known to local folks as the "Pyramid building," the Transamerica Building is a 48-story structure that rises 853 feet above the city pavement.

Tadich Grill means wood-paneled walls, tile floor, and art deco light fixtures. It also means a counter running the length of the grill, white linen–covered tables, and wooden booths. The history of the place is so rich it consumes the first page of the menu. It all began during that gilded year, 1849, and has continued as a businessperson's restaurant in the heart of the Financial District. A new menu is printed daily, though on any given day, lunch and dinner remain the same. The specialty is seafood (sole, salmon, snapper, swordfish, shrimp, and scallops), but charcoal-broiled steak, chops, and chicken are also available. Proud in tradition and cuisine, this San Francisco institution remains topflight all the way. Closed Sunday. ~ 240 California Street; 415-391-2373. MODERATE TO DELUXE.

There are only about 25 tables, but **Sai's Restaurant** packs in the Financial District lunch crowds, who wait in line to enjoy Vietnamese food at this popular family-run establishment. The decor is simple, with a few paintings on the wall, but the food has a devoted following. Favorite dishes include lemongrass chicken, eggplant with garlic sauce, Sai's special chow mein, and coconut curries. ~ 505 Washington Street; 415-362-3689. BUDGET.

San Francisco is so rich in independently owned restaurants that there is little reason to even consider the city's hotel dining rooms. **Silks**, the Mandarin Oriental's signature restaurant, is a noteworthy exception. Decorated in a blend of soft reds and golds, and highlighted with luminary sculptures and contemporary artwork, it's elegantly understated. The menu combines California with Asia, featuring seared striped bass, roasted squab, and filet mignon, all prepared in a cross-cultural fashion. ~ 222 Sansome Street; 415-885-0999. ULTRA-DELUXE.

London Wine Bar is a rare vintage indeed. Established in 1974, it claims to be "America's first wine bar." Fittingly, there is an impressive and fashionable list of California and imported wines, many sold by the glass. To quench the appetite, they serve lunch and evening hors d'oeuvres like salmon, pâtés, cheeses, and quesadillas. A fashionable treat. Closed Saturday and Sunday. ~ 415 Sansome Street; 415-788-4811. MODERATE.

Dim sum is the Chinese tradition of selecting dishes from trays that are continuously wheeled about the dining room. At **Yank Sing**, you'll discover designer dim sum, a restaurant that has elevated the tea house idea to a culinary art. While tea houses are usually like cafeterias, Yank Sing provides a serene setting with white linen, fresh flowers, and cane-back chairs. Simple but suave, the restaurant offers dim sum delights like stuffed snow crab claws, seafood stuffed green peppers, and rabbit-shaped shrimp dumplings. Open only for lunch, it represents an important dining innovation. ~ 427 Battery Street; 415-362-1640. MODERATE TO DELUXE.

Chic, moderne, and popular is the best way to describe **MacArthur Park**. Particularly favored by the pin-stripe crowd, this brick-wall dining room serves dishes specially prepared in an oakwood smoker and a mesquite grill. There are baby back ribs, live Maine lobster, lamb chops, dry-aged steak, homemade sausage, and fresh fish. The decor is casual but self-conscious: blackwood and Matisse prints and padded park benches, track lights and a skylight, as well as a marble bar with mirrors and wine racks. No lunch on Saturday and Sunday. ~ 607 Front Street; 415-398-5700. MODERATE TO DELUXE.

NIGHTLIFE

A favorite bar in this world of finance is the **Carnelian Room** atop the Bank of America. Perched on the 52nd floor, this luxurious lounge has the best views of all, sweeping from little old San Francisco Bay out across the boundless deep. Dress code. ~ 555 California Street; 415-433-7500.

The comedy scene has been ripping through San Francisco since the early days of Lenny Bruce and Mort Sahl. Today the city has more stand-up comedians than cab drivers. **The Punch Line** books a wide variety of acts from around the country. ~ 444 Battery Street; 415-397-7573.

Embarcadero

Below the Financial District, where the city's skyscrapers meet the Bay, is located the Embarcadero. This waterfront promenade has become increasingly appealing since the 1989 earthquake, which resulted in the dismantling of a freeway that once ran along the bayfront. Today the vistas are unobstructed and the strip is wide open for wandering.

Back in Gold Rush days, before the pernicious advent of landfill, the entire area sat beneath fathoms of water and went by the name of Yerba Buena Cove. Matter of fact, the hundreds of tall-masted ships abandoned here by crews deserting for the gold fields eventually became part of the landfill.

Nature is rarely a match for the shovel. The Bay was pressed back from around Montgomery Street to its present perimeter. As you head down from the Financial District, walk softly; the world may be four billion years old, but the earth you're treading has been around little more than a century.

SIGHTS

Fittingly enough, the first place encountered is **Embarcadero Center**, a skein of five skyscrapers rising sharp and slender along Sacramento Street to the foot of Market Street. This $645 million complex, oft tagged "Rockefeller Center West," features a three-tiered pedestrian mall that links the buildings together in a labyrinth of shops, restaurants, fountains, and gardens.

Embarcadero Five is the **Hyatt Regency**, on the corner of Market and California streets. It's one of the few hotels you'll ever find detailed as a sightseeing feature. The reason is the lobby, a towering atrium that rises 170 feet. It's a triangular affair lined with a succession of interior balconies that rise to a skylighted roof. Along one side, plants cascade in a 20-story hanging garden, while another wall is designed in a zigzag shape which gives the sensation of being inside a pyramid. With fountains and flowering plants all about, glass capsule elevators scaling the walls, and sun flecks splashing in through the roof, the place surely is a 21st-century pyramid.

The Rincon Annex is a restored 1930s post office with magnificent WPA murals glorifying science and technology.

Speaking of the future, that blocky complex of cement pipes from which water pours in every direction is not an erector set run amok. It's **Vaillancourt Fountain**, situated smack in the Hyatt's front yard. The patchwork of grass and pavement surrounding is **Justin Herman Plaza**, a perfect place for a promenade or picnic. Craft vendors with engraved brass belt buckles, silver jewelry, and beanbag chairs have made the plaza their storefront.

Just across the road, where Market Street encounters the Embarcadero, rises San Francisco's answer to the Statue of Liberty. Or what was the city's answer at the turn of the century, when the clock tower of the **Ferry Building** was as well-known a landmark as the Golden Gate Bridge is today. Back then there were no bridges, and 100,000 ferryboat commuters a day poured through the portals of the world's second busiest passenger terminal. Built in 1896, the old landmark is making a comeback. Sleek, jet-powered ferries stream into refashioned slips, and plans are afloat to space age the entire complex with the help of noted architect I. M. Pei.

You might want to walk the ramp that leads up to the **World Trade Center**, on Embarcadero at the foot of Market Street. It's lined with Covarrubias' murals that were preserved from the 1939 Golden Gate International Exposition. They look like those maps in your old sixth grade social studies book; one vividly depicts "the people of the Pacific" with aborigines sprouting up from the Australian land mass and seraped Indians guarding the South American coast. Another pictorial geography lesson features the Pacific economy with salmon swimming off the North American shore and rice bowls growing in China.

One positive result of the horrendous 1989 Loma Prieta earthquake was the demolition of the Embarcadero Freeway, a longtime eyesore that ran like a concrete scar through the waterfront area. Now that the freeway is gone, there is a lighter and brighter look to the area, with palm trees planted along the Embarcadero and more expansive views of the Bay Bridge and Treasure Island. In 1996, the city named the pedestrian promenade that parallels the boulevard Herb Caen Way, in honor of San Francisco's famous gossip columnist. At the same time, a new neighborhood is fast growing up around and to the south of lower Market Street with apartments, restaurants, nightspots, and a Saturday morning farmers' market. A poplar gathering spot for locals, especially at noontime, is the **Rincon Center**, which features a cluster of eateries offering everything from Korean noodles to Indian curries. The eateries surround a central indoor courtyard dining area and spectacular, rainfall-like fountain. ~ 101 Spear Street; 415-777-4100.

Stretching from either side of the Ferry Building are the rows of **shipping piers** that once made San Francisco a fabulous harbor. Today much of the commerce has sailed across the Bay to the Port of Oakland. To recapture San Francisco's maritime era, head north on Embarcadero from the Ferry Building along the odd-numbered piers. The city looms to your left and the Bay heaves and glistens before you. This is a world of seaweed and fog horns where proverbial old salts still ply their trade. Blunt-nosed tugboats tie up next to rusting relics from Guadalcanal. There are modern jet ferries, displaying the latest aeronautical curves and appearing ready at any moment to depart from the water for open sky. The old, big-girthed ferries have been stripped of barnacles, painted nursery colors, and leased out as office space; they are floating condominiums.

Along this parade of piers you'll see cavernous concrete wharves astir with forklifts and dockhands. Locomotives shunt with a clatter, trucks jockey for an inside post, and container cranes sweep the air. Other piers have fallen into desuetude, rust-caked wharves propped on water-rotted pilings. The only common denominators in this odd arithmetic progression of piers are the seagulls and pelicans whitening the pylons.

Across from Pier 23, **Levi's Plaza** features a grassy park ideal for picnicking; just beyond Pier 35 there's a waterfront park with a wonderful vantage for spying on the ships that sail the Bay. ~ 1155 Battery Street.

LODGING

Just one block from the Embarcadero and convenient to the Financial District, the **Hotel Griffon** offers 62 attractive rooms appointed with modern art, window seats, oversized mirrors, and, in a few cases, bay views. A cozy lobby features a library and fireplace, and there's an adjacent fitness center. ~ 155 Steuart Street; 415-495-2100, 800-321-2201, fax 415-495-3522. ULTRA-DELUXE.

On the same block is **Harbor Court Hotel** where some of the 131 rooms and suites also offer marine views. Guest accommodations are small but attractively appointed with nautical prints, big mirrors, canopied beds, and brass sconces. The lobby is large, comfortable, and ideal for leisurely afternoons. You can also relax at the health club and indoor pool adjacent to the hotel. ~ 165 Steuart Street; 415-882-1300, 800-846-0555, fax 415-882-1313. ULTRA-DELUXE.

DINING

San Francisco's modern version of camp is **Fog City Diner**. It is the most upscale diner you've ever seen. Check out the exterior with its art deco curves, neon lights, and checkerboard tile. Then step into a wood-and-brass paneled restaurant that has the feel of a club car on the Orient Express. Featuring California cuisine, the menu changes seasonally, though on a given day it will be the same for both lunch and dinner. The season I was there they were offering "small plates" of garlic custard with mushrooms, quesadilla with peppers and almonds, and crabcakes. The "large plates" included skirt steak with Japanese-style sauce, roasted quail, pork chops with ginger applesauce, pot roast, and calf's liver. Everything is à la carte, including the Fog City T-shirts. What can I tell you except to book a reservation well in advance. ~ 1300 Battery Street; 415-982-2000. MODERATE.

One of San Francisco's finest and most authentic Hong Kong–style restaurants is not located in Chinatown, but is tucked into a corner of the Embarcadero Center. **Harbor Village** serves exquisite Cantonese dishes such as crisp, juicy roast chicken, steamed catfish, and shark's fin soup in an elegant setting of Chinese antiques and teak furnishings. At lunchtime, its dim sum selections are among the best in the city. ~ 4 Embarcadero Center; 415-781-8833. MODERATE.

Walking into **Harry Denton's Bar & Grill** is like entering a turn-of-the-century San Francisco saloon. Ruby red drapes adorn the windows and a baby grand piano and antique mahogany bar decorate the lounge. Diners can enjoy a meal on the mezzanine level and observe the chefs at work in the exhibition kitchen, or be seated in the main dining room and savor spectacular views of the bay. The chefs prepare such favorites as oak-roasted free-range chicken and Peking duck, pot roast with buttermilk mashed potatoes, and cioppino. Desserts include crème brulée and Almost Better Than Sex cake. From Thursday through Saturday, the main dining room turns into a dance club at 10:30 p.m. ~ 161 Steuart Street; 415-882-1333. MODERATE.

◄ HIDDEN

Head on down to **Pier 23 Cafe**, a little shack between Fisherman's Wharf and downtown, for unique waterfront dining. The place is funky but nice, with white tablecloths and linen napkins on the tables. Dine inside or on the huge back patio overlooking the bay. This restaurant specializes in seafood and offers six or seven fish specials daily. The deep-fried calamari appetizer and the oven-roasted crab with garlic, parsley, and butter dipping sauce are two of the most popular items on the menu. ~ Pier 23; 415-362-5125. MODERATE.

SHOPPING

Shoppers along the Embarcadero head for the **Embarcadero Center**, located on Sacramento Street near the foot of Market Street. It's a vaulting glass-and-concrete "town" inhabited by stores and restaurants. This multifaceted mall consists of the lower three levels of five consecutive skyscrapers. You pass from one building to the next along corridors that open onto a galaxy of shops. Verily, what Disneyland is for kids, Embarcadero Center is to shoppers. The place possesses positively everything. There are bookstores, bakeries, jewelry stores, gift bazaars, newsstands, and camera shops. There's even a "general store," plus dozens of restaurants, cocktail lounges, and espresso bars, a luggage shop, a store devoted entirely to nature, and on and on and on in labyrinthine fashion.

NIGHTLIFE

The Holding Company is crowded with young professionals on the make. Closed Saturday and Sunday. ~ 2 Embarcadero Center; 415-986-0797.

Over at the Hyatt Regency, there's a revolving rooftop bar, **The Equinox.** A glass-encased elevator whisks you to this aerie, where you can pull up a window seat and watch the world spin. ~ 5 Embarcadero Center; 415-788-1234.

Pier 23 is a funky roadhouse that happens to sit next to the San Francisco waterfront. The sounds emanating from this saloon are live jazz, reggae, salsa, and blues. Highly recommended to those searching for the simple rhythms of life. There's music every day except Monday and it starts at 4 p.m. Cover. ~ Embarcadero and Pier 23; 415-362-5125.

It's hard to escape tourists along the San Francisco waterfront. Best bet is **Peer Inn**, a bubble-top bar near Pier 33. Passenger liners still embark from a nearby wharf, adding local color to this neighborhood lounge. ~ Bay Street and Embarcadero; 415-788-1411.

Chinatown

It's the largest Chinatown outside Asia, a spot that older Chinese know as *dai fao*, Big City. San Francisco's Chinatown also ranks as the city's most densely populated neighborhood. Home to 40,000 of the city's 150,000 Chinese, this enclave has been an Asian stronghold since the 1850s. Originally a ghetto where Chinese people were segregated from San Francisco society, the neighborhood today opens its arms to burgeoning numbers of immigrants from a host of Asian nations.

On the surface, this pulsing, noisy, chaotically colorful 70-square-block stretch projects the aura of a tourist's dream—gold and crimson pagodas, stores brimming with exquisite silks and multicolored dragons, more restaurants per square foot than could be imagined, roast ducks strung up in shop windows next door to Buddhist temples and fortune cookie factories.

But Chinatown is far more than a tourist mecca. This crowded neighborhood is peopled with families, powerful political groups, small merchants, poor working immigrants and rising entrepreneurs molding a more prosperous future. Although the "city within a city" that Chinatown once symbolized now encompasses only a quarter of San Francisco's Chinese people, it's still a center of Chinese history, culture, arts, and traditions that have lived for thousands of years.

In appropriately dramatic fashion, you enter Chinatown through an arching gateway bedecked with dragons. Stone lions guard either side of this portal at Grant Avenue and Bush Street.

It was during the Gold Rush that "Celestials" sporting queues and exotic costumes arrived en masse in California. Often forced into indentured servitude, they worked the gold fields and later helped build the transcontinental railroad. During the 1870s and 1880s these proud people, who had arrived in San Francisco with visions of the "Great City on the Golden Hill," became victims of the "yellow peril" mentality sweeping the nation. They were beaten and lynched, their homes torched. Racist whites, eyeing the prime real estate upon which the Chinatown ghetto had grown, tried to run the entire population out of town.

It took an earthquake to uproot them. The calamity of 1906 devastated Chinatown, leaving countless dead and homeless. When the smoke and rubble were cleared, a new Chinatown arose; gone were the opium dens and houses of prostitution for which the old ghetto was notorious; in their stead grew a neighborhood that became modern-day Chinatown.

SIGHTS

To stroll the eight-block length of Chinatown's **Grant Avenue** is to walk along San Francisco's oldest street. Today it's an ultramodern thoroughfare lined with Chinese arts and crafts shops, restaurants, and Asian markets. It's also one of the most crowded streets you'll ever squeeze your way through. Immortalized in a song from the musical *Flower Drum Song*, Grant Avenue, San Francisco, California, U.S.A., is a commotion, clatter, a clash of cultures. At any moment, a rickety truck may pull up beside you, heave open its doors, and reveal its contents—a cargo of chinaware, fresh produce, or perhaps flattened pig carcasses. Elderly Chinese men lean along doorways smoking fat cigars, and Chinatown's younger generation sets off down the street clad in leather jackets.

At the corner of California Street, where cable cars clang across Grant Avenue, rises the lovely brick structure of **Old St. Mary's Church**. Dating to 1854, this splendid cathedral was originally built of stone quarried in China. Just across the way in **St. Mary's Square**, there's a statue of the father of the Chinese Republic, Dr. Sun Yat Sen, crafted by San Francisco's foremost sculptor, Beniamino Bufano. You might take a hint from the crowds of businesspeople from the nearby financial center who bring their picnic lunches to this tree-shaded plaza.

Next you'll encounter **Mam Kue School**. With an iron fence, mullioned doors, and pagoda-like facade, it's an architectural beauty ironically backdropped by a glass-and-concrete skyscraper. ~ 755 Sacramento Street.

As you walk along Grant Avenue, with its swirling roof lines and flashing signs, peek down **Commercial Way**. This curious brick-paved street permits a glimpse into "hidden" Chinatown. Lined with everything from a noodle company to a ginseng shop,

CHINATOWN—A DIFFERENT PERSPECTIVE

Near Commercial Way, you'll happen upon a hole-in-the-wall museum that will open wide your perspective on Chinatown's history. The **Chinese Historical Society of America** graphically presents the history of San Francisco's Chinese population. In the museum is a magnificent collection of photos and artifacts re-creating the Chinese experience from the days of pig-tailed "coolies" to the recent advent of ethnic consciousness. Small in size but wide in scope, the museum is a tiny treasure house with a helpful and congenial staff. Open Tuesday and Friday, noon until 4 p.m. or by appointment. ~ 650 Commercial Street; 415-391-1188.

this tightly packed street also houses the **Mow Lee Company**, Chinatown's second oldest establishment. ~ 774 Commercial Way.

After you've immersed yourself in Chinese history, head down to **Portsmouth Square** (Kearny and Washington streets) for a lesson in the history of all San Francisco. Formerly the city's central plaza, it was here in 1846 that Yankees first raised the Stars and Stripes. Two years later, the California gold discovery was announced to the world from this square. Rudyard Kipling, Jack London, and Robert Louis Stevenson once wandered the grounds. At one corner of the park you'll find the bronze statue of a galleon celebrating the ocean-going Stevenson. Today this gracious park is a gathering place for old Chinese men playing mah-jongg and practicing tai chi. From the center of the plaza, a walkway arches directly into the **Chinese Culture Center**, with its displays of Asian art. Closed Monday. ~ 750 Kearny Street; 415-986-1822.

Now that you've experienced the traditional tour, you might want to explore the hidden heart of Chinatown. First take a stroll along **Stockton Street**, which runs parallel to, and one block above, Grant Avenue. It is here, not along touristy Grant Avenue, that the Chinese shop.

The street vibrates with the crazy commotion of Chinatown. Open stalls tumbling with vegetables cover the sidewalk, and crates of fresh fish are stacked along the curb. Through this maze of merchandise, shoppers press past one another. In store windows hang Peking ducks, and on the counters are displayed pigs' heads and snapping turtles. Rare herbs, healing teas, and chrysanthemum crystals crowd the shelves.

The local community's artwork is displayed in a fantastic **mural** that covers a half-block between Pacific and Jackson streets.

To further explore the interior life of Chinatown, turn down Sacramento Street from Stockton Street, then take a quick left into Hang Ah Street. This is the first in a series of alleyways leading for three blocks from Sacramento Street to Jackson Street. When you get to the end of each block, simply jog over to the next alley.

HIDDEN ►

A universe unto themselves, these **alleyways of Chinatown** are where the secret business of the community goes on, as it has for over a century. Each door is a barrier beyond which you can hear the rattle of mah jongg tiles and the sounds of women bent to their tasks in laundries and sewing factories.

Along Hang Ah Street, timeworn buildings are draped with fire escapes and colored with the images of fading signs. As you cross Clay Street, at the end of Hang Ah Street, be sure to press your nose against the glass at **Grand Century Enterprise**. Here the ginseng and other precious roots sell for hundreds of dollars a pound. ~ 858 Clay Street.

The next alley, **Spofford Lane**, is a corridor of painted doorways and brick facades humming with the strains of Chinese melodies. It ends at Washington Street where you can zigzag over to **Ross Alley**. This is the home of the **Golden Gate Fortune Cookie Factory**. At this small family establishment you can watch your fortune being made. ~ 56 Ross Alley; 415-781-3956.

The last segment in this intriguing tour will take you back to **Waverly Place**, a two-block stretch leading from Washington Street to Sacramento Street. Readers of Dashiell Hammett's mystery story, *Dead Yellow Women*, will recall this spot. It's an enchanting thoroughfare, more alley than street. At first glance, the wrought-iron balconies draped along either side of Waverly evoke images of New Orleans. But not even the French Quarter can boast the beauty contained in those Chinese cornices and pagoda swirl roof lines.

Prize jewel in this architectural crown is **Tian Hou Temple**. Here Buddhists and Taoists worship in a tiny temple overhung with fiery red lanterns. There are statues portraying battlefields and country landscapes; incense smolders from several altars. From the pictures along the wall, Buddha smiles out upon the believers. They in turn gaze down from the balcony onto Chinatown's most magical street. ~ 125 Waverly Place.

Just uphill from Chinatown stands the **Cable Car Museum**, a brick goliath which houses the city's cable cars. The museum here provides a great opportunity to see how these wood-and-steel masterpieces operate. The system's powerhouse, repair, and storage facilities are here, as are the 14-foot diameter sheaves which neatly wind the cable into figure-eight patterns. The museum also has on display three antique cable cars, including the first one ever built. ~ 1201 Mason Street; 415-474-1887.

LODGING

Though you'll notice doors and stairways throughout Chinatown advertising hotel accommodations, these are usually residential buildings serving the local Chinese community. Look for the permanent "no vacancy" signs that accompany many of the hotel in-

✔ CHECK THESE OUT—UNIQUE LODGING

- *Budget:* Check into downtown's **Adelaide Inn**, San Francisco's funky but tidy "unique European pensione." *page 29*
- *Moderate to deluxe:* Quietly step into **The Bed and Breakfast Inn**—two ivy-covered Victorians resting apart from the bustling city noise. *page 78*
- *Deluxe:* Unpack your bags at one of the hippest spots in town, **The Phoenix Hotel**, a block from Civic Center. *page 43*
- *Ultra-deluxe:* Settle down and indulge in a bit of sumptuous 19th-century living at the **Sherman House**. *page 78*

Budget: under $50 Moderate: $50–$90 Deluxe: $90–$120 Ultra-deluxe: over $120

signia and you'll realize that these facilities are Asian boarding houses, closed to the general public. There are, however, two hotels and a YMCA providing adequate accommodations for budget travelers. Any of them will give you a chance to fully experience this amazing neighborhood.

If you're after a real budget find, the **Chinatown YMCA** has rooms with shared or private bath facilities. The rooms are devoid of decoration and furnished in spartan fashion with bed, dresser, and table. If your room depresses you, though, you can escape to the pool, gym, or weight room, all free of charge to guests. ~ 855 Sacramento Street; 415-982-4412, fax 415-982-0117. BUDGET.

Situated smack on Broadway along the border of Chinatown and North Beach is **Sam Wong Hotel**. About half the guests here are permanent Chinese boarders, but the rest of the rooms are available to visitors. Accommodations range from sterile to funky—the rooms are matchbox affairs with plaster walls, steam heat, wall-to-wall carpeting, and tacky furniture. But the hotel provides an excellent opportunity to encounter local Chinese, and the prices are definitely competitive—in the budget category for a standard room, and even less for a room with a half-bath (i.e., the shower is down the hall). The lobby alone, with its time-faded photographs and Chinese prints, is worth the price of admission. ~ 615 Broadway; 415-781-6836. BUDGET.

Immediately up from the Grant Avenue gateway to Chinatown you'll encounter **Grant Plaza Hotel**. Staff and management here are quite hospitable and the security buzzer system makes this a safe hotel for women. The place features a small, tastefully decorated lobby and a selection of remodeled rooms. They feature plush carpeting, telephones, color televisions, and private baths. The hotel's location right on Grant Avenue has the advantage of being at the very heart of the district and the disadvantage of being noisy. ~ 465 Grant Avenue; 415-434-3883, 800-472-6899, fax 415-434-3886. BUDGET TO MODERATE.

DINING

Vegetarians favor **Lotus Garden**, a lovely restaurant that includes a Taoist temple on its upper floor. With Asian murals and ornamented altars, the temple provides a calming retreat from bustling Chinatown. The restaurant itself is equally mellow. In addition to standard Chinese vegetarian fare, it serves up exotic dishes like sweet corn and snow fungus soup, plus bitter melon with sliced gluten puff. Closed Monday. ~ 532 Grant Avenue; 415-397-0707. BUDGET.

Among budget restaurants, **Sam Wo** is a San Francisco classic. Dining in this jook house is a rare adventure. The entrance is also the kitchen, and the kitchen is just a corridor filled with pots, stovepipes, cooks, and steamy smells. Sam Wo's menu is extensive and the food is quite good for the price. ~ 813 Washington Street; 415-982-0596. BUDGET.

For luxurious dining in the heart of Chinatown, no place matches the **Empress of China.** Set on the top floor of the China Trade Center, with nothing between you and heaven, it is a culinary temple. Dining rooms are adorned with carved antiques and the maitre'd dons a tuxedo. Lunch at this roof garden restaurant begins with appetizers like Shanghai dumplings and barbecued quail, then graduates to lichee chicken and Manchurian beef. Dinner is the true extravagance. The menu includes a royal variety of chicken, duck, lamb, shellfish, pork, and beef dishes. There are also unique selections like hundred blossom lamb, prepared with sweet and sour ginger; lobster *see jup* in black bean sauce; and phoenix dragon, a medley of shrimp, chicken, and onions sautéed in wine. ~ 838 Grant Avenue; 415-434-1345. DELUXE TO ULTRA-DELUXE.

Of course, the ultimate Chinatown experience is to dine dim sum style. Rather than choosing from a menu, you select dishes from trundle carts laden with steaming delicacies. A never-ending convoy of waitresses wheels past your table, offering plates piled with won tons, pork tidbits, and Chinese meatballs. It's up to you to create a meal (traditionally breakfast or lunch) from this succession of finger-size morsels.

Many dim sum establishments are cavernous restaurants, sparsely decorated like cafeterias. But each has a particular personality and generates warmth from the crowds passing through. Don't be fooled by the neon facades, for an Asian adventure waits within these dining palaces. You should be careful about prices, however: most dim sum courses cost only two or three dollars, but it's easy to lose count as you devour dish after dish. Figure that the restaurants noted below will be moderate in price, unless you become a dim sum addict.

My favorite dim sum restaurant is tucked away in an alley above Grant Avenue. Personalized but unpretentious, more cozy than cavernous, **Hang Ah Tea House** is a rare find. Enter the dining room with its Chinese wood carvings and fiberglass tables. Serving a full Mandarin cuisine as well as dim sum portions, it warrants an exploratory mission into the alleys of Chinatown. ~ 1 Hang Ah Street; 415-982-5686. MODERATE. ◄ HIDDEN

Featuring one of the largest dim sum menus in the city, **J&J Restaurant** is a favorite of the Asian community. And why not? From shark's fin dumpling to crispy taro turnover, there's something for everyone. Feast on spring rolls, barbecued pork buns, fun roll with chicken, and a wide array of desserts. With a decor that ranges from chandeliers to track lighting, the family oriented dining room is appointed with Chinese watercolors. Lunch only. ~ 615 Jackson Street; 415-981-7308. BUDGET TO MODERATE.

At **Royal Jade** you can take a seat at a spacious table upstairs and dine on white linen. The dim sum menu includes nearly 40 items like steamed dumpling with scallops, baked barbecue pork puff, spareribs, stuffed bell pepper, egg custard bun, and noodle crêpe with shrimp. ~ 675 Jackson Street; 415-392-2929. BUDGET TO MODERATE.

Overlooking Portsmouth Square on the second story of a nondescript building, the **Oriental Pearl** serves sophisticated, gourmet dim sum, a step above the usual Chinatown teahouse. Here dim sum is ordered from a menu, allowing diners to concentrate on conversation and cuisine, rather than being distracted by the contents of passing carts. Such treats as shrimp and scallop dumplings, pork buns, and chicken meatballs emerge hot and fresh from the kitchen. White tablecloths, mahogany chairs, and classical Chinese music make this a quiet oasis from the busy streets of Chinatown below. ~ 760–778 Clay Street; 415-433-1817. BUDGET.

SHOPPING

Shopping in Chinatown brings you into immediate contact with both the common and the unique. If you can slip past the souvenir shops, many of which specialize in American-made "Chinese products," you'll eventually discover the real thing—Chinese arts and crafts as well as Asian antiques.

Grant Avenue is the neighborhood's shopping center, but local Chinese favor Stockton Street. My advice is to browse both streets as well as the side streets between. Some of the city's best bargains are right here in Chinatown.

After this soft-spoken introduction, continue on to that buzzing, clanging commercial strip called Grant Avenue. Sensory overload and crazed consumerism are facts of life along this neon thoroughfare. But don't be discouraged by the painted face: beneath that garish exterior Grant Avenue reveals its own particular culture.

The soul of the place resides somewhere between the Hong Kong souvenirs and the antique tapestries. While there is a lot of gimcrackery sold here, many specialty shops provide a sense of the richness of Chinese arts and crafts. Slip into one of the district's silk stores to admire the kimonos, or drop by a tea shop and sample one of the hundreds of varieties of teas.

First stop along Grant Avenue is a mandatory one: **Canton Bazaar.** This four-story emporium is a browser's warehouse. Six-foot-high wooden statues and laughing Buddhas surround the entrance, drawing in the canny and unwary alike. From the ceramic pieces to the gold and jade jewelry, the shelves are laden with exceptionally tasteful goods. The bottom floor is filled with clothing while the new top floor is devoted to furniture. Among the antiques are Buddhist religious paintings, raw-silk wallhangings, and intricately carved statues. ~ 616 Grant Avenue; 415-362-5750.

As you continue down Grant Avenue, several specialty shops are worth noting. The **Chinatown Kite Shop** is hung with dragonfly and box kites. ~ 717 Grant Avenue; 415-391-8217.

The **Wok Shop** sells every kind of wok imaginable—carbon steel, cast iron, Teflon, and electric—as well as all the accessories to cook up a tantalizing stir-fry, succulent roasted chicken, or savory *shiu mai*. There are also towels and a wonderful selection of aprons. ~ 718 Grant Street; 415-982-2299.

Nearby the **Far East Flea Market** you'll find everything from clothing to birdcages. Also available at this Asian emporium are fans and decorative boxes from mainland China. ~ 729 Grant Avenue; 415-989-8588.

At the New China Trade Center there's a store, **Chong Imports**, which seems to offer every item found anywhere else on Grant Avenue. There are bright kites, paper flowers, lacy cut-outs, and China teapots. The prices at this multitiered wonderland are as alluring as the merchandise. ~ 838 Grant Avenue; 415-982-1434.

◄ HIDDEN

For books and periodicals, be sure to peek into **New China Bookstore**. Opened by Mr. Jimmy Lee in 1970, the shop has an exciting collection of books for adults and children alike. The kids' volumes are illustrated with monkeys and dragons and alive with wisdom. Mr. Lee goes out of his way to answer questions and offer gift suggestions. His shop—which is a Chinese-version general store with its shelves of knickknacks, tea boxes, toys, and cutouts—is a bilingual, bicultural center. And a magical place as well. ~ 642 Pacific Avenue; 415-956-0752.

NIGHTLIFE

The best bar in Chinatown, **Li Po**, is complete with incense, lanterns, and carved statuary, plus an incongruous jukebox featuring Caucasian favorites. The potions they mix here are powerful and exotic; the place has an air of intimacy. ~ 916 Grant Avenue; 415-982-0072.

North Beach

It's a region of contrasts, a neighborhood in transition. North Beach combines the sex scene of neon-lit Broadway with the brooding intellect and Beat heritage of Grant Avenue and Columbus Street. Traditionally an Italian stronghold, North Beach still retains its fabulous pasta palaces and bocce ball courts, but it's not making way for a growing influx of Chinese residents.

Introductions to places should be made gradually, so the visitor comes slowly but certainly to know and love the area. In touring North Beach, that is no longer possible, because the logical spot to begin a tour is the corner of Broadway and Montgomery streets, at night when the neon arabesque of Broadway is in full glare.

SIGHTS

Broadway, you see, has long been San Francisco's answer to Times Square, a tawdry avenue that traffics in sex. While the neighborhood is steadily changing, it still features strip joints, peekaramas, and X, Y, Z-rated theaters—a modern-day Barbary Coast.

After you've dispensed with North Beach's sex scene, your love affair with the neighborhood can begin. Start at **City Lights Bookstore.** Established in 1953 by poet Lawrence Ferlinghetti, City Lights is the old hangout of the Beat poets. Back in the heady days of the '50s, a host of "angels"—Allen Ginsberg, Jack Kerouac, Gary Snyder, and Neal Cassady among them—haunted its book-lined rooms and creaking staircase. Today the place remains a vital cultural scene and gathering point. It's a people's bookstore where you're invited to browse, carouse, or even plop into a chair and read awhile. You might also check out the paintings and old photos, or perhaps the window display. Thirty years after the Beats, the inventory here still represents a who's who in avant-garde literature. ~ 261 Columbus Avenue; 415-362-8193.

Some of the nation's most outstanding WPA murals decorate Coit Tower's interior. Done as frescoes by New Deal artists, they sensitively depict the lives of California laborers.

Vesuvio Café next door was another hallowed Bohemian retreat. ~ 255 Columbus Avenue; 415-362-3370. Then head up nearby Grant Avenue to the **Caffe Trieste**, at the corner of Vallejo Street. With its water-spotted photos and funky espresso bar, the place has changed little since the days when bearded bards discussed cool jazz and Eisenhower politics. ~ 415-392-6739.

You're on "upper Grant," heart of the old Beat stomping grounds and still a major artery in the city's Italian enclave. Chinatown is at your back now, several blocks behind, but you'll see from the Oriental script adorning many shops that the Asian neighborhood is sprawling into the Italian. Still remaining, however, are the cafés and delicatessens that have lent this area its Mediterranean flair since the Italians moved in during the late 19th-century.

Beyond Filbert Street, as Grant Avenue continues along the side of Telegraph Hill, the shops give way to Italian residences and Victorian houses. When you arrive at Lombard Street, look to your left and you'll see the sinuous reason why Lombard is labeled "The Crookedest Street in the World." Then turn right as Lombard carries you up to the breeze-battered vistas of Telegraph Hill.

Named for the semaphore station located on its height during the 1850s, **Telegraph Hill** was a Bohemian haunt during the 1920s and 1930s. Money moved the artists out; today, this hillside real estate is about the most desirable, and most expensive, in the city.

Poking through the top of Telegraph Hill is the 180-foot-high **Coit Tower** (admission for elevator to observation platform). Built in 1934, this fluted structure was named for Lillie Hitchcock Coit, a bizarre character who chased fire engines and became a fire company mascot during the 1850s. Lillie's love for firemen gave rise to stories that the phallic tower was modeled after a fire hose nozzle. Architectural critics scoff at the notion.

Upstaging these marvelous artworks is the view from the summit. All San Francisco spreads before you. That sinewy structure to the right is the **Bay Bridge**, which stretches for eight-and-one-quarter miles, the world's longest steel bridge. It is interrupted in its arching course by **Yerba Buena Island** and its manmade extension, **Treasure Island**, created for the 1939 Golden Gate International Exposition. The Bay Bridge's gilded companion to the left is the **Golden Gate Bridge**. Between them lies San Francisco Bay. Tugs and freighters slide past in search of mooring. Fog horns groan. From this aerie the distant sloops and ketches look like children's toys blown astray in a pond puffed with wind.

The island moored directly offshore is **Alcatraz**, named for the pelicans which still inhabit it, but known for the notorious prisoners who have long since departed its rocky terrain. Looming behind America's own Devil's Island is **Angel Island**. That high point on the horizon, between the Golden Gate and Angel Island, is **Mt. Tamalpais**, crown jewel in Marin County's tiara. Across the water, where the Bay Bridge meets terra firma, are the East Bay cities of **Berkeley** and **Oakland**. Behind you, past the high-rise cityscape, the hills and streets of San Francisco sweep out toward the sea.

Now that all San Francisco has been spread before you like a tableau, it's time to descend into the hidden crannies of the city. Unlike Coit Tower, there will be no elevator to assist on the way down, but then again there won't be any tourists either.

After exiting Coit Tower, turn right, cross the street, and make your way down the brick-lined staircase. In the middle of San Francisco, with wharves and factories far below, you have just entered a countrified environment. Ferns and ivy riot on either side of the **Greenwich Steps**, while vines and conifers climb overhead. ◄ HIDDEN

At the bottom of the steps, turn right, walk a short distance along Montgomery Street, then head left down the **Filbert Steps**. ◄ HIDDEN Festooned with flowers and sprinkled with baby tears, the steps carry you into a fantasy realm inhabited by stray cats and framed with clapboard houses. Among the older homes are several that date to the 1870s; if you follow the Napier Lane Boardwalk that extends from the steps, there are falsefront buildings from which sailors reportedly once were shanghaied.

Retracing your tracks back up the steps, then descending the other side of Filbert Street, you'll arrive at **Washington Square**, between Filbert and Stockton streets in the heart of North Beach. Nestled between Russian and Telegraph hills, this is the gathering place for San Francisco's "Little Italy." In the square, old Italian men and women seek out wooden benches where they can watch the "young people" carrying on. From the surrounding delis and cafés you might put together a picnic lunch, plant yourself on the lawn, and catch this daily parade.

St. Peter & Paul Catholic Church anchors one side of the square. Its twin steeples dominate the North Beach skyline. The facade is unforgettable, an ornate affair upon which eagles rest in the company of angels. The interior is a wilderness of vaulting arches hung with lamps and decorated in gilt bas-relief. Tourists proclaim its beauty. For my taste, the place is overdone; it drips with architectural jewelry. Everything is decoration, an artistic happening; there is no tranquility, no silent spot for the eye to rest. ~ Filbert and Stockton streets; 415-421-0809.

North Beach Museum, housed inside Eureka Bank, presents a history in black-and-white. There are sepia photos of Sicilian fishermen, pictures of the terrible quake, and other images of the people who make this neighborhood such an intriguing place to visit. Closed Saturday and Sunday. ~ 1435 Stockton Street; 415-626-7070.

LODGING

As a nighttime visit to North Beach will clearly indicate, this neighborhood was not made for sleeping. The "love acts" and encounter parlors along Broadway draw rude, boisterous crowds until the wee hours.

But if noise and neon have a soporific effect upon you, or if you have some bizarre and arcane need to know what sleeping on the old Barbary Coast was like, check out **Europa Hotel**. The price is certainly right, and you get a clean, carpeted room and shared bath. ~ 310 Columbus Avenue; 415-391-5779. BUDGET.

HIDDEN ► Or better yet, retreat a little farther from Broadway to the **Hotel Bohème** and take a step back into North Beach history. This European pensione–style hotel has been decorated to reflect the beat-generation era, complete with a black-and-white photo retrospective. Poet Allen Ginsberg has even stayed here. Rooms feature antique wardrobes, tile bathrooms, and black iron beds. Ask for one of the rooms in the back, which are quieter than those along busy Columbus Avenue. ~ 444 Columbus Avenue; 415-433-9111, fax 415-362-6292. DELUXE.

DINING

Dining at **Helmand** is like visiting the home of an upper-class Afghani family. Lush handmade Afghan carpets, beautiful chandeliers, and paintings add a touch of elegance, and the food is first-rate. You can feast on grilled rack of lamb, roasted chicken, and many vegetarian dishes. *Aushak*, Afghan ravioli stuffed with leeks and topped with ground beef marinated in yogurt, can be habit-forming. A true find among the sleazy strip joints of Broadway. ~ 430 Broadway; 415-362-0641. MODERATE.

At **Little Joe's and Baby Joe's** the food is outstanding and it's prepared before your eyes by some of the city's great showmen. Working a row of oversized frying pans, these jugglers rarely touch a spatula. Rather, with a snap of the wrist, they flip sizzling veal, steak, or calamari skyward, then nonchalantly catch it on the way down. This restaurant also serves delicious fish, roast chicken, and sausage dishes, each accompanied by pasta and fried vegetables. Very crowded, especially on weekends. ~ 523 Broadway; 415-982-7639. MODERATE.

Some of the best pizza in town is served at **Tommaso's Neapolitan Restaurant** where the chefs bake in an oak-fired oven. The creations they prepare have resulted in this tiny restaurant being written up in national magazines. As soon as you walk in you'll realize it's the food, not the surroundings, that draws the attention. Entering the place is like stepping down into a grotto. The walls are lined with booths and covered by murals; it's dark, steamy, and filled with inviting smells. Filmmaker Francis Ford Coppola drops by occasionally, as should every pizza and pasta lover. Dinner only. Closed Monday. ~ 1042 Kearny Street; 415-398-9696. DELUXE.

At least once during a North Beach visit, you should dine at a family-style Italian restaurant. Dotted all around the neighborhood, these establishments have a local flavor unmatched by the area's chic new restaurants. A good choice is **Capp's Corner**, a local landmark adorned with celebrity photos, more celebrity photos, and a few photos of celebrities. The prix-fixe dinner includes soup, salad, pasta, entrée, and dessert—more food than anyone could consume in a day, much less a sitting. Among the entrées are chicken cacciatore, osso buco, fettuccine with rock shrimp, lamb shanks, and other choices. No lunch on the weekend. ~ 1600 Powell Street; 415-989-2589. MODERATE.

If there is any place in San Francisco that elevates dining to the level of high adventure, it is **Caffe Sport**. First, the place introduces itself a block before you arrive; if you're not buried beneath the waves of garlic it wafts along Green Street, you'll be visually assaulted by the garish orange facade. Once inside, you'll discover a baroque nightmare; the place is chockablock with bric-a-brac—faded photos, tacky candelabra and antiques circa 1972. Besides that, it's hot, steamy, unbelievably crowded, and the waiters are rude. What more can I say, except that you'll love the place. Known for its pasta, this is also *the* spot for Italian-style seafood. They prepare calamari several different ways, and do magical things with lobster, crab, scallops, prawns, and clams. Reservations are recommended. Closed Monday and Tuesday. ~ 574 Green Street; 415-981-1251. DELUXE.

Why anyone would want to dine in a place frequented by writers is beyond me, but if the spirit moves you, and your stomach agrees, head over to the **Washington Square Bar & Grill**. This literary gathering spot is often elbow-to-elbow with such questionable characters as local novelists, newspaper reporters, and aspiring word merchants. They come to gossip and to engage in that vaunted avocation of scribblers everywhere, the imbibing of spirits. Occasionally they wander from the brass-rail bar to the dining area, where the lunch and dinner menu changes daily. The focus here is on pasta, veal, and seafood dishes. It's actually an excellent restaurant, and an even better place to drink. ~ 1707 Powell Street; 415-982-8123. MODERATE TO DELUXE.

For traditional Basque cuisine, consider **Des Alpes Restaurant**. An oilcloth restaurant with a small bar out front, it serves full-course dinners. Menu selections are limited to a few entrées each night, so call ahead for the day's menu. On a typical evening, they'll be serving chicken with rice, roast lamb, roast beef, or sliced filet mignon; dinner also includes soup, salad, coffee, and dessert. A good spot for a family-style meal. Closed Monday. ~ 732 Broadway; 415-391-4249. MODERATE.

Dessert in North Beach means Italian ice cream, and few places make it better than **Gelato Classico**. Creamy and thick, Italian ice cream is made without air, so it's denser and more delicious than other ice cream. At Gelato they also use fresh fruit and other natural ingredients to guarantee great taste. If you try it in summer, you can have fresh strawberry, blueberry, burgundy cherry, or raspberry. During the rest of the year, they serve a host of flavors ranging from coppa mista and banana to good old chocolate and vanilla (made, of course, from vanilla beans). *Viva Italia!* ~ 576 Union Street; 415-391-6667.

The heart of North Beach beats in its cafés. Gathering places for local Italians, the neighborhood's coffee houses are also literary scenes. Step into any of the numerous cafés dotting the district and you're liable to hear an elderly Italian singing opera or see an aspiring writer with notebook in one hand and espresso cup in the other.

✔ CHECK THESE OUT—UNIQUE DINING

- *Budget:* Have your palm read by the resident psychic at **Mad Magda's Russian Tea Room & Café** after enjoying a bowl of homemade borsch. *page 44*
- *Moderate:* Inhale the Caribbean essence of **Cha Cha Cha**, where the food and music carries you away to the islands. *page 97*
- *Moderate to deluxe:* Join the throngs who fill **Restaurant Lulu** for lunch and dinner, an eatery noted for its brick rotisserie. *page 119*
- *Ultra-deluxe:* Experience a culinary treat at **Silks**, where East encounters West in understated elegance. *page 49*

Budget: under $8   Moderate: $8–$16   Deluxe: $16–$24   Ultra-deluxe: over $24

The best North Beach breakfasts are the continental-style meals served in these cafés. But any time of day or night, you can order a croissant and cappuccino, lean back, and take in the human scenery. Foremost among these people-watching posts is **Caffe Trieste**, the old Beatnik rendezvous. ~ 609 Vallejo Street; 415-392-6739. Another prime location is **Caffe Puccini.** ~ 411 Columbus Avenue; 415-989-7033. Right on Washington Square is another popular spot, the **Bohemian Cigar Store.** ~ 566 Columbus Avenue; 415-362-0536.

The *New Yorker* once called **Hunan Restaurant** "the best Chinese restaurant in the world." Those are pretty big words, hard to substantiate this side of Peking. But it's certainly one of the best San Francisco has to offer. Understand now, we're talking cuisine, not ambience. The atmosphere at Hunan is characterized by noise and crowds; there is a bar and a contemporary-style dining room adorned with color photographs. But the food will transport you to another land entirely. It's hot, spicy, and delicious. From the dining room you can watch masterful chefs working the woks, preparing pungent sauces, and serving up bean curds with meat sauce, Hunan scallops, and a host of other delectables. A culinary experience well worth the price. ~ 924 Sansome Street; 415-956-7727. MODERATE.

SHOPPING

Shopping in North Beach is a grand escapade. As you browse the storefronts here, do like the Sicilians and keep an eye out for Italian treasures. Like the hand-painted ceramics and colorful wallhangings still brightening many a home in old Italia.

For the mod mob, there are slick boutiques and avant-garde novelty shops. To start, why not choose a place that stocks both the traditional and the avant-garde—**City Lights Bookstore.** Within the hallowed confines of this oddly shaped store is a treasure trove of magazines on arts and politics, plus books on everything from nirvana to the here and now. Once a roosting place for Beat writers like Allen Ginsberg, Jack Kerouac, and Neal Cassady, it remains a vital gathering point for local artists. The book selection is unique, featuring many contemporary poetry and prose volumes unavailable elsewhere. More important, City Lights is a place where you're welcome to pull up a chair and immerse yourself in conversation or classic literature. ~ 261 Columbus Avenue; 415-362-8193.

There isn't much in **Quantity Postcards** except its namesake. But the array of postcards is staggering. Yes, folks, we're talkin' all kinds: copper cards, roadside postcards from the all 50 states, 3-D cards, movie star postcards, and postcards that squeak when you squeeze them. ~ 1441 Grant Avenue; 415-986-8866.

Biordi Art Imports provides the Italian answer to gourmet living. Specializing in Italian ceramics, the place is loaded with Italian imports. There are hand-painted pitchers from Florence, De Simone folk art from Palermo, and noodle makers. To decorate the home, Biordi's has hand-painted umbrella stands, wall mirrors framed in ceramic fruit, and other high-kitsch items. Walking through this singular shop is like browsing an Italian crafts fair. ~ 412 Columbus Avenue; 415-392-8096.

It's hard to imagine that Washington Square was a tent city back in 1906. The great earthquake and fire totally devastated North Beach, and the park became a refuge for hundreds of homeless.

Head across the street to **Postermat** for movie posters, art prints, and novelty cards. Owner Ben Friedman's store has become a San Francisco institution and a great place to shop for wallhangings and knickknacks. Of particular interest is the outstanding collection of posters from the old Fillmore and Avalon ballrooms. Incorporating psychedelic and collage art at its finest, these posters are 1960s-era collector items. ~ 401 Columbus Avenue; 415-421-5536.

No North Beach shopping spree would be complete without a visit to **A. Cavalli & Company**. Operating since 1880, this family business caters to all sorts of local needs. They offer an assortment of Italian cookbooks as well as records and tapes ranging from Pavarotti to Italian new wave. Cavalli's also stocks Italian travel posters, Puccini opera prints, Italian movies on cassette, and magazines from Rome. ~ 1441 Stockton Street; 415-421-4219.

NIGHTLIFE

North Beach, the old Beatnik quarter, is the area for slumming. It's door-to-door with local bars and nightclubs, not to mention the few topless and bottomless joints that still remain along Broadway.

Vesuvio Café hasn't changed much since the Beat poets haunted the place during the days of Eisenhower. Kerouac, Ginsberg, Corso, and the crew spent their nights here and their days next door at City Lights Books. It's still a major North Beach scene, rich in soul and history. ~ 255 Columbus Avenue; 415-362-3370.

Across the street is **Spec's Museum Café**, another bohemian haunt. There's nary a bald spot on the walls of this literary hangout; they're covered with all manner of mementos from bumperstickers to a "whale's penis bone." A great place to get metaphysical. ~ 12 Saroyan Place; 415-421-4112.

To step uptown, just walk down the hill to the **San Francisco Brewing Company**. Built the year after the 1906 earthquake, it's a mahogany-paneled beauty with glass lamps and punkah wallah fans. Legend tells that Jack Dempsey once worked here as a bouncer. It's also the first pub in San Francisco to brew its own beer on the premises. ~ 155 Columbus Avenue; 415-434-3344.

Bimbo's 365 Club showcases an eclectic mix of live music from jazz and rock to French pop stars. Check out the live mermaid gracefully frolicking in the oversize aquarium. Open weekends. Cover. ~ 1025 Columbus Avenue; 415-474-0365.

There are two theater clubs worthy of note. **Finocchio's** features a succession of screamingly outrageous female impersonators. The costuming is colorful and the acts very bitchy. But the best performance of all is by the audience: the place draws busloads of tourists who figure these wild displays are just another part of the city's notorious lifestyle. Open Thursday through Saturday. Cover. ~ 506 Broadway; 415-982-9388.

Club Fugazi features an equally outlandish musical revue, *Beach Blanket Babylon*, which has been running for years. The scores and choreography are good, but the costumes are great. The hats—elaborate, multilayered confections—make Carmen Miranda's adornments look like Easter bonnets. Shows run Wednesday through Sunday. Cover. ~ 678 Green Street; 415-421-4222.

Fisherman's Wharf

Places have a way of becoming parodies of themselves—particularly if they possess a personal resonance and beauty or have some unique feature to lend the landscape. People, it seems, have an unquenchable need to change them.

Such is the fate of Fisherman's Wharf. Back in the 19th century, a proud fishing fleet berthed in these waters and the shoreline was a quiltwork of brick factories, metal canning sheds, and woodframe warehouses. Genoese fishermen with rope-muscled arms set out in triangular-sailed *feluccas* that were a joke to the west wind. They had captured the waterfront from the Chinese and would be supplanted in turn by Sicilians. They caught sand dabs, sea bass, rock cod, bay shrimp, king salmon, and Dungeness crab. Salt caked their hands, wind and sun gullied their faces.

Today the woodplanked waterfront named for their occupation is hardly a place for fishermen. It has become "Tourist's Wharf," a bizarre assemblage of shopping malls and penny arcades that make Disneyland look like the real world. The old waterfront is an amusement park with a wax gallery, a Ripley's museum, and numerous trinket shops. The architecture subscribes to that modern school which makes everything look like what it's not—there's pseudo-Mission, ready-made antique Victorian, and simulated falsefront.

But salt still stirs the air here and fog fingers through the Bay. There are sights to visit along "the Wharf." It's a matter of recapturing the past while avoiding the plastic-coated present. To do that you need to follow a basic law of the sea—hug the shoreline.

SIGHTS

On the corner of Embarcadero and Beach Street, **Pier 39** itself is an elaborately laid-out shopping mall catering primarily to tourists who spill over from neighboring Fisherman's Wharf. In addition to a plethora of waterfront shops and restaurants, Pier 39 features jugglers, yo-yo champs, and other entertainers who delight the crowd with their sleight of hand.

The central attraction at Pier 39 is the colony of **sea lions** that has taken up residence on the nearby docks. Numbering 400 at times, these thousand-pound pinnipeds are a cross between sea slugs and sumo wrestlers. They began arriving in 1989, taking over a marina, causing a ruckus, and creating the greatest stench this side of a sardine factory. But when Pier 39 attracted over 10 million people the next year, placing it behind Orlando's Disney World and Anaheim's Disneyland as the most popular tourist spot in the country, the local merchants decided to welcome the smelly squatters as permanent residents.

For an up-close look at other residents of the San Francisco Bay, including sharks and fish, go to **Underwater World.** Put on headphones for a 40-minute narrated journey along moving walkways through a 400-foot-long transparent tunnel into two giant two-story tanks. These tanks contain rays, salmon, crabs, jellyfish, eels, and more than 150 examples of the six shark species found in surrounding waters. There's no other aquarium like it in the United States. Admission. ~ Pier 39; 415-623-5300.

Pier 45 is a working wharf, bleached with bird dung and frequented by fishing boats. From here it's a short jog to the docks on Jefferson Street, located between Jones and Taylor streets. The remnants of San Francisco's fishing fleet lies gunnel to gunnel here. The *Nicky-D*, *Saint Teresa*, *Lindy Sue*, *Phu Quy*, *Hai Tai Loc*, and an admiralty of others cast off every morning around 4 a.m. to return in late afternoon. With their brightly painted hulls, Christmas tree rigging, and roughhewn crews, they carry the odor and clamor of the sea.

HIDDEN ►

Fish Alley is another nostalgic nook. Just duck into the narrow corridor next to Castagnola's Restaurant on Jefferson Street and walk out towards Scoma's Restaurant. Those corrugated metal sheds lining the docks are fish-packing operations. The fleet deposits its daily catch here to be processed for delivery to restaurants and markets. This is an area of piers and pilings, hooks and hawsers, flotsam and fish scales, where you pay a price to recapture the past: as you work further into this network of docks, approaching nearer and nearer the old salty truths, you'll also be overwhelmed by the moldering stench of the sea.

For a breather, it's not far to the Hyde Street Pier, where history is less offensive to the nose. Docked along the length of this wharf are the **Historic Ships**. Part of the San Francisco Maritime National Historic Park, they include a wood-hulled, three-masted schooner, *C. A. Thayer*, that once toted lumber along the California coast. You can also board the *Eureka*, an 1890 ferryboat

Cruising the Bay

Pier 41 is the departure point for the Red and White Fleet, which sponsors **Bay cruises,** Alcatraz tours, and ferry service to Angel Island, Sausalito, and Tiburon. ~ 415-546-2810.

The trip to **Alcatraz** is highlighted with a National Park Service tour of the infamous prison. Originally a fort and later a military prison, Alcatraz gained renown as "The Rock" when it became a maximum security prison in 1934. Al Capone, "Machine Gun" Kelly, and Robert "Birdman of Alcatraz" Stroud were among its notorious inmates. On the tour, you'll enter the bowels of the prison, walk the dank corridors, and experience the cage-like cells in which America's most desperate criminals were kept. You can listen to an audio cassette of former guards and prisoners remembering their time at The Rock.

The prison closed in 1963; then in 1969 a group of American Indians occupied the island for almost two years, claiming it as Indian territory. Today Alcatraz is part of the Golden Gate National Recreation Area.

A cruise to **Angel Island State Park** is a different adventure entirely. Unlike "The Rock," this star-shaped island is covered with forest and rolling hills. During previous incarnations it has served as a military installation, quarantine station, immigration center, and prisoner of war camp. Today, the largest true island in San Francisco Bay is a lacework of hiking and biking trails and flowering meadows. For an overview visit the small museum at Ayala Cove. Here you'll find a diorama and map of the island, historical exhibits, and the light fixture from an old lighthouse. You can trek five miles around the island or climb to the top for 360° views of the Bay Area.

Deer graze throughout the area and there are picnic areas galore. It's a perfect spot for a day in the sun. Along the way you can visit the small North Garrison Museum, which is dedicated to the history of the island's early immigration station. Touching photographs document the story of this "West Coast Ellis Island." The buildings on Angel Island are open weekends only April through October. (The day-use fee is included in the ferry price; however, there is a $5 docking fee if you bring your own boat.) ~ 415-435-1915.

which worked the San Francisco–Tiburon run for almost 30 years. To walk this pier is to stride back to San Francisco's waterfront at the turn of the century. Salt-bitten lifeboats, corroded anchors, and old coal engines are scattered hither-thither. The *Eppleton Hall* is an old paddlewheeler and the *Alma* a "scow schooner" with a flat bottom and square beam. A three-masted merchant ship built in Scotland in 1886, the *Balclutha* measures 301 feet. This steel-hulled craft sailed around Cape Horn 17 times in her youth. She loaded rice in Rangoon, guano in Callao, and wool in New Zealand. Today the old ship's cargo consists of a below-deck maritime museum and a hold full of memories. Admission. ~ 415-556-3002.

Together with the nearby **National Maritime Museum**, it's enough to make a sailor of you. The museum, in case you mistook it for a ferryboat run aground, is actually an art deco building designed to resemble the bridge of a passenger liner. Onboard there's a weird collection of body parts from old ships plus models, scrimshaw displays, and a magnificent photo collection. ~ Beach and Polk streets; 415-556-2904.

All these nautical showpieces are anchored in **Aquatic Park**, which sports a lovely lawn that rolls down to one of the Bay's few sandy beaches. A mélange of sounds and spectacles, the park has a bocce ball court where you'll encounter old Italian men exchanging stories and curiously eyeing the tourists. There are street vendors galore. If that's not enough, you can watch the Powell and Hyde Street cable cars being turned around for their steep climb back up Nob Hill. Or catch an eye-boggling glimpse of San Francisco Bay. Alcatraz lies anchored offshore, backdropped by one of the prettiest panoramas in this part of the world.

Since you're in earthquake country why not stop by **The Museum of the City of San Francisco**. Historic photographs, paintings, and artifacts tell the story of that fateful day in 1906 and shed new light on the story of California's greatest natural disaster. Among the notable exhibits is the Goddess of Liberty statue from the old city hall. Closed Monday and Tuesday. ~ In the Cannery, Beach and Leavenworth streets; 415-928-0289.

Of course no tour of Fisherman's Wharf is complete without a stop at **The Cannery**, a shopping center with 40 specialty shops. ~ Jefferson and Leavenworth streets; 415-771-3112. Be sure to stop at **Ghirardelli Square**, an old warehouse that has been converted into an open-air shopping courtyard. ~ 900 North Point Street; 415-775-5500. For more information, see "Shopping" below.

LODGING

Fisherman's Wharf contains more hotels than fishermen. Most facilities here are overpriced and undernourished. I'm only going to mention a few, since I think you'll do much better financially and experience San Francisco more fully in a downtown or neighborhood hotel.

The first is **The Wharf Inn**, a place best described as nondescript. This 51-room motel is a squat four-story affair with purple doors and beige trim. The moderate-size rooms have modern though unimaginative decor. They're carpeted wall-to-wall and feature standard amenities like television and tile bathrooms with stall showers. The ambience is one of naugahyde and simulated wood; the place is clean and bright, offering the same type of facility you could have downtown for moderate cost. In an area of pricey hotels, The Wharf Inn has the best rates around. ~ 2601 Mason Street; 415-673-7411, 800-548-9918, fax 415-776-2181. DELUXE.

Lodging in the **Sheraton at Fisherman's Wharf**, a sprawling 525-room facility, feature spacious rooms tastefully furnished in Sheraton fashion, plus room service and nightly turndown service. The hotel has other alluring features like a brick-paved entranceway, liveried doormen, swimming pool, and attractive gift shops. ~ 2500 Mason Street; 415-362-5500, 800-325-3535, fax 415-956-5275. ULTRA-DELUXE.

The hotel scene around Fisherman's Wharf was enhanced in 1990 when two new hotels opened within a block of each other. One, the **Hyatt at Fisherman's Wharf** is a 313-room luxury retreat that is faced in antique brick and illuminated through skylights. It comes complete with pool, spa, and fitness center. ~ 555 North Point Street; 415-563-1234, 800-233-1234, fax 415-749-6122. ULTRA-DELUXE.

The other newcomer is the **Tuscan Inn**, an Italian-style boutique hotel. Smaller in scale than the Hyatt, the Tuscan is richly decorated and more intimate. ~ 425 North Point Street; 415-561-1100, 800-648-4626, fax 415-561-1199. ULTRA-DELUXE.

DINING

Dining at Fisherman's Wharf usually means spending money at Fisherman's Wharf. The neighborhood's restaurants are overpriced and over-touristed. If you look hard enough, however, it's possible to find a good meal at a fair price in a fashionable restaurant. Of course, the easiest way to dine is right on the street, at one of the **seafood cocktail stands** along Jefferson Street. An old wharf tradition, these curbside vendors began years ago feeding bay

THE SAN FRANCISCO "STAFF OF LIFE"

Another San Francisco favorite, sourdough bread, can be tasted at **Boudin Bakery**. A pungent French bread particularly popular in seafood restaurants, sourdough is the staff of life in these parts. Boudin Bakery, founded in 1849, has had plenty of time to fit its recipe perfectly to the local palate. ~ 156 Jefferson Street; 415-928-1849. BUDGET.

fishermen. Today they provide visitors an opportunity to sample local catches like crab, shrimp, and calamari.

Situated between the Wharf and North Beach, **Café Francisco** enjoys the best of both worlds—it's strolling distance from the water and possesses a bohemian flair. A great place for light and inexpensive meals, this trendy café serves salads and sandwiches for lunch. Breakfast at the espresso bar ranges from a continental repast to bacon and eggs. Decorated with changing exhibits by local artists, it attracts a local crowd. ~ 2161 Powell Street; 415-397-2602. BUDGET.

The **Eagle Café** is another old-timer. It's so much a part of San Francisco that plans to tear the place down years ago occasioned a public outcry. Instead of flattening the old woodframe building, they lifted it—lock, stock, and memories—and moved it to the second floor of the Pier 39 shopping mall. Today it looks like an ostrich at a beauty pageant, a plain café surrounded by glittering tourist shops. The walls are covered with faded black-and-white photos, Eagle baseball caps, and other memorabilia. Actually, the bar is more popular than the restaurant. Who wants to eat when they can drink to old San Francisco? The bar is open all day and into the night, while the restaurant serves only breakfast and lunch. All-American cuisine. ~ Pier 39; 415-433-3689. BUDGET.

HIDDEN ►

Would you believe a hidden restaurant in tourist-mobbed Fisherman's Wharf? **Scoma's** is the place. Seafood is the password to this chummy restaurant. There's *cioppino alla pescatore*, a Sicilian-style broth; *calamone alla anna*, squid prepared "in a totally different manner"; or just plain old sole, snapper, shrimp, or scallops. There's lobster tail, too, and Dungeness crab. ~ Pier 47 near the foot of Jones Street; 415-771-4383. MODERATE TO DELUXE.

For the sights, sounds, and seafood of the San Francisco waterfront, Scoma's is the catch of the day. For spicy food from the subcontinent, everyone's choice is **Gaylord India Restaurant**. From its corner roost in Ghirardelli Square, this fashionable dining emporium enjoys a startling view of San Francisco Bay. It also hosts an extensive menu that varies from tandoori chicken and spiced lamb to meatless entrées such as eggplant baked in a clay oven, creamed lentils, or spiced cauliflower and potatoes. With its unusual artwork, Asian statuary, and potted plants, Gaylord creates a warm ambience into which it introduces a deliciously tangy cuisine. ~ 900 North Point Street; 415-771-8822. MODERATE TO DELUXE.

Crisp, clean, and classy is the way to describe **McCormick & Kuleto's**, a popular seafood restaurant in Ghirardelli Square. Natural woods predominate, white tablecloths adorn the tables, and faux tortoiseshell lamps hang from the high ceilings, but the focus of attention is the incredible view of the bay from the floor-to-ceiling windows. The very extensive menu changes daily depending on what fish is available and includes such specialties as crayfish cakes, seafood pastas, seared ahi, alder-smoked salmon, and mesquite-grilled bass fillet. There's also a very lengthy wine list. ~ 900 North Point Street; 415-929-1730. MODERATE TO DELUXE.

Albona Ristorante Istriano is a high-heeled hole-in-the-wall, a small but fashionable restaurant serving Italian and Central European dishes. The interior is a mélange of beveled mirrors, white linen tablecloths, burgundy banquettes, and fresh flowers. The menu, not to be upstaged, includes sauerkraut braised with prosciutto, pan-fried gnocchi, and exotic entrées like *peppo di pollo* (roast chicken basted with sherry) and *brodetto alla Veniziana* (fish stew or soup). Dinner only. Closed Sunday and Monday. ~ 545 Francisco Street; 415-441-1040. MODERATE.

SHOPPING

Fisherman's Wharf is a shopper's paradise . . . if you know what you're doing. If not, it's a fool's paradise. This heavily touristed district houses a mazelike collection of shops, malls, arcades, and galleries. Most of them specialize in high-priced junk. How someone can arrive in the world's most splendid city and carry away some trashy trinket to commemorate their visit is beyond me. But they do. Since you're certainly not the type searching out an "I Got Crabs at Fisherman's Wharf" T-shirt, the best course is to go where the natives shop.

Though its wooden boardwalks and clapboard buildings look promising, **Pier 39** proves hardly the place for bargains or antiques. It's a haven for tourists and features gift stores that range from cutesy card shops to places selling ceramic unicorns. There are restaurants and stores galore, plus an amusement arcade. Kids often enjoy the carnival atmosphere here. ~ Embarcadero and Beach Street; 415-981-7437.

My main objection is to the ticky-tacky shops. Every year, however, millions of tourists disagree with me. They flock to this two-tiered mall, popping in and out of the more than 100 shops and enjoying the ersatz turn-of-the-century atmosphere.

One noteworthy exception to Pier 39's tourist oriented selection of shops is **The National Park Store**, the only bookshop I know that comes with a view of sea lions basking in the sun. It offers a complete selection of travel, hiking, and wildlife books and also sells educational toys, American Indian arts and crafts, and other gifts. ~ Pier 39; 415-433-7221.

For locally crafted goods, be sure to watch for the **street vendor stalls.** Located along Beach Street between Hyde and Larkin, and on side streets throughout the area, they offer hand-fashioned wares with homemade price tags. You'll find jewelry, leather belts, statuary, framed photos of the bay city, tie-dye shirts, kites, and anything else the local imagination can conjure.

Before people buy anything in the City, they go to **Cost Plus World Market** and see if it's there. If so, it's cheaper; if not, maybe they don't really need it. You'll find jewelry, ceramics, wallhangings, and a host of other items. There are temple rubbings from Thailand, amber jewelry from Egypt, Indian mirrorcloths, scenic San Francisco posters, brassware, household furnishings, clothes, gourmet foods, wine, etc. Everything under the sun, at prices to brighten your day. ~ 2552 Taylor Street; 415-928-6200.

On a given day there might be jugglers, clowns, or other entertainers performing free at Pier 39.

Another popular spot among San Franciscans is the old brick canning factory on Jefferson and Leavenworth streets. Thanks to innovative architects, **The Cannery** has been transformed into a tri-level mall dotted with interesting shops. The central plaza, with its olive trees and potted flowers, contains picnic tables, several cafés, and a snack kiosk. Among the dozens of shops are many selling handcrafted originals. ~ 415-771-3112.

The chocoholics who don't know will be delighted to discover that the home of Ghirardelli chocolate, **Ghirardelli Square**, has been converted into yet another shopping complex. This early 20th-century factory is another example of old industrial architecture being turned to contemporary uses. Around the factory's antique chocolate making machines is located a myriad of shops varying from designer outlets to sundry stores. There are also import stores, boutiques, and so on. ~ 900 North Point Street; 415-775-5500.

One notable Ghirardelli shop is **Folk Art International**, offering antique Guatemalan woven shirts, folk sculptures, baskets, pottery, coconut masks, and other folk crafts from Latin America. Europe and Asia are also represented with antique jewelry from India and gem-quality Baltic amber from Poland and Denmark. ~ Ghirardelli Square, 900 North Point Street; 415-928-3340.

So there you have the secret of shopping Fisherman's Wharf: simply ignore everything else and beeline between the street vendors, Cost Plus, The Cannery, and that brick-red chocolate factory.

NIGHTLIFE

The **Eagle Café**, perched beside Fisherman's Wharf, appears like some strange bird that has landed in the wrong roost. All around lies touristville, polished and preening, while the Eagle remains old and crusty, filled with waterfront characters. Old photos and baseball caps adorn the walls, and in the air hang memories 50 years old. ~ Pier 39; 415-433-3689.

Don't know any local people, but still like to party? Head for **Lou's Pier 47**, have a meal, and dance the afternoon and night away. For eats, there are sandwiches, burgers, pastas, and fried, grilled, or sautéed fish and seafood. The 18 bands that play each week in the glass-enclosed nightclub upstairs range from rhythm-and-blues and Motown to light rock and country-and-western. The music begins at 4 p.m. daily and noon on the weekends. Cover. ~ 300 Jefferson Street; 415-771-0377.

Buena Vista Café, situated near Fisherman's Wharf, is popular with local folks and tourists alike. There's a fine old bar and friendly atmosphere, and the place claims to have introduced America to the Irish coffee. ~ 2765 Hyde Street; 415-474-5044.

Union Street

People go to Union Street for two reasons—shopping and singles bars. Sightseeing is an afterthought. The fact of the matter, however, is that many of the district's trendy shops are housed in magnificent Victorians. So sightseeing can become a case of shopping in architectural wonders.

SIGHTS

Foremost is the **Octagon House**, built in 1861. This eight-sided heirloom is capped with a turret. The National Society of Colonial Dames of America, which runs the old place, opens it to the public on the second and fourth Thursdays and second Sunday of each month (except January) from noon until 3 p.m. Admission. ~ 2645 Gough Street; 415-441-7512.

The park next door, with its easy slope and tall timber, is a lone remnant from the days when Union Street was "Cow Hollow." Thirty dairies once operated from this grassy dale. What is today the sidewalk of Union Street was then the shoreline of "Washerwoman's Lagoon," a small lake where housewives gathered on laundry day.

The structure at 1980 Union Street gained a mark on the map when an eccentric father built this Siamese twin of a house for his two daughters. It seems they were newlyweds needing dowries, who soon found themselves cozily ensconced in these **Twin Wedding Houses.**

Actually, a grander example of the Victorian-in-a-mirror can be seen in the imposing pair of houses across the street at **1923–1929 Union Street.**

Vendanta House is another structural curiosity. No it wasn't levitated here from Moscow. It was built on the spot to celebrate the Hindu religion. At the risk of trying to portray the indescribable, it's a sprawling three-story house, maroon and gray, capped with several towers. One tower sports battlements, another a bulbous dome, and yet another a cluster of cupolas. ~ 2963 Webster Street.

Don't neglect the brick courtyard of **St. Mary's Church**. Graced with a garden and wood-shingled church, St. Mary's also has a fountain. A very special fountain. It's actually a spring where early dairy farmers watered their herds back in Cow Hollow days. ~ Union and Steiner streets.

The **Casebolt House** is the last link in this chain of architectural jewels. With two magnificent palm trees guarding the entranceway and a flanking retinue of willows, it presents an imposing sight. Dating from 1865, it was built in an Italianate style; today the ornate white edifice, set on a rise above the street, is as grand as it was back in California's younger days. ~ 2727 Pierce Street.

LODGING

Amid elegant shops and Victorian homes are some of San Francisco's stateliest bed and breakfast inns.

HIDDEN ►

My personal favorite is **The Bed and Breakfast Inn,** located on a quiet cul de sac. The hotel is set in two ivy-covered Victorians with smiling bay windows. You walk through an entranceway dotted with flowerpots into a highly personalized, very charming setting. Each of the 11 rooms is decorated differently. They range from pension rooms which share a bath and rent for a moderate cost to the deluxe accommodations. There is also a cozy library where guests can relax and chat and an English dining room and garden for continental breakfast. Because of its enchanting atmosphere and outstanding service, the inn is extremely popular, so book reservations several months ahead. ~ 4 Charlton Court; 415-921-9784. MODERATE TO DELUXE.

Union Street Inn is another excellent choice. Again, the emphasis at this six-room hostelry is on personalized service. Guests are often served full breakfast in the garden, an urban oasis of fruit trees and flowering plants. The rooms are quite cozy, grandly decorated, and imaginatively furnished. The Golden Gate Room features a midnight blue and mocha cream decor. Wicker chairs cluster around an oriental rug and the bed is covered with quilted spread and topped by a canopy. The "carriage house," a cottage snugly set in the garden, and one other room feature private jacuzzis. ~ 2229 Union Street; 415-346-0424, fax 415-922-8046. ULTRA-DELUXE.

Antiques, marble fireplaces, and rich fabrics give the 14 accommodations at the **Sherman House** the feeling of 19th-century opulence. Which is as it should be, since this charming Victorian and carriage house were built in 1876 by a devoted opera buff who installed a three-story recital hall for visiting performers. Every room has something extra—a private garden, a view deck. This luxurious hotel has 24-hour room service from the private dining room. ~ 2160 Green Street; 415-563-3600, 800-424-5777, fax 415-563-1882. ULTRA-DELUXE.

"Ours is an attempt to return to the original B & B concept popularized in Britain: a modest room at a practical price." At **Edward II Inn** the proprietors have fully realized their motto. Taking the old Hotel Edward, which provided accommodations for the nearby Panama–Pacific International Exposition of 1915, they transformed it into the 30-room Edward II. In the process they provided an opportunity for guests to enjoy bed-and-breakfast luxury at boarding house cost. The room I saw was English in decor and included such features as quilted bedspread and a dresser with beveled mirror; the bathroom was tiled and trimmed in wood. While I highly recommend this facility, I also advise that you ask for a room in back, away from noisy Lombard Street. ~ 3155 Scott Street; 415-922-3000, 800-473-2846, fax 415-931-5784. MODERATE.

Among the many motels lining busy Lombard Street, only the **Marina Motel** seems to possess character; others are part of the mondo condo world. The Marina is located near a noisy thoroughfare, but most rooms are set back off the street. This 45-unit motel resembles a white adobe structure with the clean and tidy rooms surrounding a courtyard. ~ 2576 Lombard Street; 415-921-9406, fax 415-921-0364. BUDGET TO MODERATE.

DINING

Romantic candlelight and hanging Chianti bottles create an inviting ambience at **Luisa's**. The cuisine is Italian with the accent on dishes such as linguine with calamari and osso buco. There are numerous pasta dishes; Luisa also offers homemade gnocchi and bread. ~ 1851 Union Street; 415-563-4043. MODERATE TO DELUXE.

Joji's House of Teriyaki is a hole in the high-priced wall of Union Street that happens to serve outstanding Japanese and American dishes. In addition to the eponymous teriyaki plates, there's sashimi, pot stickers, and a vegetarian dish. There are also burgers, sandwiches, and salads. For breakfast the ingenious owner serves up "Egg McJoji" on an English muffin with ham and melted cheese, plus numerous omelettes and other egg dishes. A good bet any time of day. ~ 1919 Union Street; 415-563-7808. BUDGET.

With its brass rails and mirrored walls, **Prego** is high tech to the max. The Milanesque interior features a brick oven in which many of the Italian dishes are prepared. There's grilled lamb, veal chops, and fresh fish. The pasta is homemade and the pizza is garnished with everything from prosciutto and artichokes to grilled zucchini and eggplant. *Très chic* and highly recommended. ~ 2000 Union Street; 415-563-3305. MODERATE.

Doidge's is everybody's favorite breakfast spot. I've always thought the place slightly overrated, but I seem to be a minority of one. Its best feature is that it serves breakfast until the middle of the afternoon. So if you're hankering for an omelette, buttermilk pancakes, French toast, or eggs Benedict, say no more. Reservations are required. ~ 2217 Union Street; 415-921-2149. MODERATE.

The history of the **Plump Jack Balboa Café** is almost as rich as its brass, oak, and stained glass interior. In operation since 1914, it specializes in California cuisine. The menu varies from lunch to dinner, and includes fresh fish, pork chops, and fettuccine with smoked salmon. There are appetizers like crab cakes and fried rock shrimp. A splendid restaurant. ~ 3199 Fillmore Street; 415-921-3944. MODERATE.

HIDDEN ►

Over on Chestnut Street, a few blocks from the chic Union Street corridor, you'll find **Judy's Café**. As the local crowds flowing in here every day attest, it's an excellent dining choice. Judy's is small, intimate, and decorated with wicker lamps, linen-covered tables, and potted plants. There's a balcony level where you can enjoy a lunch menu that features sandwiches and omelette specials. Judy also offers breakfast and Sunday brunch. No dinner. ~ 2268 Chestnut Street; 415-922-4588. BUDGET TO MODERATE.

For inexpensive Asian food, try **Yukol Place Thai Cuisine**. At lunch they feature sautéed vegetables, chicken curry, garlic prawns, or Thai fishcake. The dinner menu expands to include fried mussels with chile, ginger chicken, and sautéed pork. It's a comfortable restaurant. Closed Saturday, Sunday, and Monday at lunch. ~ 2380 Lombard Street; 415-922-1599. MODERATE.

In the realm of Japanese restaurants, **Aya** offers a unique diversion. This high-tech dining room, with its modern decor, is highlighted by a Japanese garden. The cuisine varies from teriyaki and sashimi to non-traditional Japanese dishes such as the seasonal butterfish marinated in miso sauce. Closed Monday. ~ 2084 Chestnut Street; 415-929-1670. MODERATE.

Comparable in class, but serving Italian food, is **Ristorante Parma** just a block away. A tiny place with mirror walls and leatherette banquettes, it serves popular Southern European dishes nightly. Offerings range from eggplant scallopine, stuffed veal, and saltimbocca to prawns in garlic and lemon-butter sauce or baked petrale. Closed Sunday. ~ 3314 Steiner Street; 415-567-0500. MODERATE.

One of San Francisco's finest seafood restaurants, **Scott's** should rank high on your dining itinerary. With an oak-paneled

ALL-AMERICAN

The all-American eatery hereabouts is **Mel's Drive In**, a classic '50s-style joint with push-button jukeboxes and posters of vintage cars. I don't have to tell you we're talking burgers, hot dogs, and chili here. For something more substantial, how about meat loaf or a "ground round plate." And don't forget a side of "lumpy mashed potatoes" or "wet fries" (with gravy). ~ 2165 Lombard Street; 415-921-3039. BUDGET.

bar, white tablecloths, and softly lit interior, it provides an inviting atmosphere. The food is simply outstanding. You can sample cracked crab, cioppino, poached salmon, fried calamari, or fisherman's stew. At lunch, the regulars include "soup, steamers, and salads," plus fresh fish dishes. Scott's also serves meat entrées, but to order steak here is to miss the point. ~ 2400 Lombard Street; 415-563-8988. MODERATE TO DELUXE.

Tiny **Bonta** is an intimate, white-walled trattoria with an authentic Italian flair. Housemade pastas, fresh fish, and grilled meats are the mainstays, but some first courses (especially the rice ones) are definitely in order. Closed Monday. ~ 2223 Union Street; 415-929-0407. MODERATE.

Fashionable, French, intimate, and imaginative—**La Folie** combines all the ingredients required of a small San Francisco restaurant. Those heavy French sauces of yore have been replaced with salsas and vegetable purées. The menu includes specialties like roti of quail and squab stuffed with wild mushrooms and wrapped in crispy potato strings, and broiled salmon with horseradish and celery-root crust cooked in wine sauce and served with baby vegetables. Dinner only. Closed Sunday. ~ 2316 Polk Street; 415-776-5577. DELUXE TO ULTRA-DELUXE.

SHOPPING

No doubt about it, Union Street is a budget-busting boulevard. Rich in designer fashions and rare imports, this Victorian street sports some of the finest merchandise and heftiest price tags in town. But as the saying goes, it doesn't cost to look.

Kozo sells sheets of exquisite Japanese handmade paper, beautiful fountain pens, blank books, and handmade photo albums, all excellent examples of one of Japan's many art forms. ~ 1969-A Union Street; 415-351-2114.

Floor-to-ceiling bears and dolls greet shoppers at **Bears & Dolls of Charlton Court**, a tiny store just off Union Street. There are sailor bears, circus bears, patriotic bears, and hundreds of others, ranging in height from 1½ inches to 3 feet. There are also turn-of-the-century antiques, as well as a wide selection of modern dolls. ~ 1957 Union Street; 415-775-3740.

One place where you can look, or more properly gaze, is **Enchanted Crystal**. Aglitter with art glass pieces by about 70 artists, this glass palace is also known for its world-class collection of quartz pieces. The window displays—extravagant, wildly imaginative affairs in rock and glass—are magical. As a matter of fact, in addition to its ordinary clientele, this shop caters to metaphysical covens and others knowledgeable in the mesmerizing powers of crystal. ~ 1895 Union Street; 415-885-1335.

Bay Moon specializes in unusual handcrafted sterling-silver jewelry by California artists. ~ 1832 Union Street; 415-775-7414.

Collectors come from all over the country to purchase the Alaskan Indian art sold at **Images of the North**. This gallery represents more than 100 Inuit artists and sells museum-quality stone sculptures of people, wildlife, and mythological beings carved from soapstone, serpentine, and musk-ox horn, as well as walrus ivory jewelry. Even if you can't afford to buy, it's a great place to look. ~ 1782 Union Street; 415-673-1273.

For rare pieces and exquisite decorative items, consider **Silkroute**. Even if you have no intention of buying, this intriguing locale is worth a browse through. You're bound to find carpets from India and ceremonial masks from Africa. The store specializes in handicrafts from Afghanistan. Among the collectibles are scarves, pillows, jewelry pieces, clothing items, and 500-year-old teapots. ~ 3119 Fillmore Street; 415-563-4936.

NIGHTLIFE This area features bars and clubs where lines of the young and single stretch out the door and down the block. The **Pierce Street Annex** is a throbbing, dimly lit nightspot—pick-up central. There's a dancefloor in back, but the action focuses around any of several bars. On weekends you have to elbow your way in for a drink; during the week you're liable to have the bar to yourself. Loud, hot, and fast. Cover on Thursday, Friday, and Saturday. ~ 3138 Fillmore Street; 415-567-1400.

While in the neighborhood, check out the nearby scene at **Balboa Café**. It's a meat market for the young and upwardly mobile. ~ 3199 Fillmore Street; 415-921-3944.

Mick's Lounge is a warm and friendly San Francisco bar and nightclub. Flying martinis and zooming olives soar across a huge mural of San Francisco that covers one wall. Live bands bring the crowds to the dancefloor six nights a week with rock-and-roll, blues, and funk music. ~ 2513 Van Ness Avenue; 415-928-0404.

For an archetypal San Francisco fern bar, head to **The Royal Oak**. With its plush Victorian parlor couches, its a cozy spot for a nightcap. Be sure to open the drawers of any end tables; you'll find them full of napkins scrawled with poetry. ~ 2201 Polk Street; 415-928-2303.

To take a rest from the crowds, drop into **Perry's**, where you can actually get a seat at the bar on the weekends. It's a friendly spot and reminiscent of San Francisco 20 years ago. ~ 1944 Union Street; 415-922-9022.

Russian Hill

Among the city's better-kept secrets is a tumbling residential area called Russian Hill. According to legend, the neighborhood's vaulting slopes were once the site of a cemetery for Russian seal hunters. The Russians have long since departed, leaving the district to local folks and a few canny travelers.

SIGHTS

There's a single block amid Russian Hill's checkerboard streets which stands out in the public imagination. Located along **Lombard Street** between Hyde and Leavenworth, it has earned for Lombard the sobriquet of "The Crookedest Street in the World." Whether this block represents the planet's most serpentine road remains to be measured; it is certainly the street most congested with shutter-snapping visitors.

Visitors come from around the world to stand astride Lombard's crest and take in the postcard views that stretch in several directions. The western window opens onto the Presidio's wooded expanse; to the north are moored the old ships of Hyde Street Pier and just offshore, Alcatraz Island; eastward rises Telegraph Hill, crowned by Coit Tower and backdropped by Yerba Buena Island. **George Sterling Park**, named for the poet who in turn named San Francisco the "cool grey city of love," stands in the southwest corner of Lombard and Hyde. Its wooded walkways and sunny tennis courts are a cool counterpoint to the surrounding cityscape.

Where Filbert Street plummets from Hyde to Leavenworth is the steepest street in the city.

They're also a prelude to the trip down Lombard Street. This dizzying descent happens to be along a beautifully landscaped street. The brick-paved road winds around hedgerows and banks of hydrangea bushes; at the corners, where zig gives way to zag, trees have been planted. You'll have to see for yourself: it's one of those places so cluttered with tourists you never want to admit visiting, but so beautiful you don't want to miss it.

Afterward you'll be ready for even more ethereal realms. Heaven always seems to evoke images of pearl-encrusted gates and shimmering white boulevards. One hopes the saintly place possesses a few country paths as well. If so, they'll undoubtedly be modeled on **Macondray Lane**. To those who wish a preview of eternal life, Macondray waits off Jones between Green and Union streets. For a solitary block, its cobblestone path leads through a garden, then opens onto a wooden staircase overlooking the Bay. You enter a tunnel of greenery, walled on one side with shingle houses and on the other with an ivy-embowered hillside. It's a realm of flower pots and fluttering birds, one of San Francisco's secret and magical walks.

◄ HIDDEN

Lombard Street represents only one of Russian Hill's two crests. Tourists jam the first, while literary historians know the second. To join the cognoscenti, travel up **Vallejo Street** to the 1000 block. Together with Russian Hill Place and Florence Street, nearby cul-de-sacs, this enclave was a gathering place for 19th-century writers. Ambrose Bierce, Frank Norris, and a sheaf of other California authors were part of the area's famous salon. The beauty they sought can be found among the Mediterranean-style haciendas lining **Russian Hill Place**, and the Pueblo Revival houses that have taken over **Florence Street.**

In 1893, Willis Polk, the master architect for whom Polk Street is named, designed and occupied the gingerbread brown-shingle house at **1013–1019 Vallejo Street**. A few things have been added to the Bay view which Polk enjoyed. Today it sweeps from Fisherman's Wharf to Coit Tower to San Francisco's skyscrapers. Nor did Polk have the steps that lead down Vallejo Street's eastern flank one block to **Ina Coolbrith Park** at Vallejo and Taylor streets. This steep swath of green was named for the Oakland librarian who helped a young fellow named Jack London find his way around the literary world.

Pacific Heights

San Francisco's most prestigious neighborhood resides on a hill looking down upon the Bay. In addition to Rolls-Royces and Mercedes Benzs, Pacific Heights contains some of the city's most outstanding architecture. Stroll the wide streets and you'll encounter straitlaced Tudor homes, Baroque confections, and elaborate Victorians.

SIGHTS

Best place to begin touring this palatial ridgetop is the corner of Franklin and California streets. That twin-turreted structure on the corner is a **Queen Anne–style Victorian**, built for a 19th-century figure who made his fortune in gold and lumber. Its poorer neighbors up the hill are **Italianate-style Victorians,** characterized by slanting edge bay windows; both date to the 1870s.

Head north on Franklin Street to 1735 Franklin, a brick **Georgian-style house** built at the turn of the century for a family of coffee barons. The **Haas-Lilienthal House**, perhaps the grandest of all San Francisco's Victorians, is a gingerbread fantasy adorned with gables and bas-relief figures. Despite the bold tower, ornate design, and sheer size of the place, it cost less than $20,000 to build. Of course, that was back in 1886. Today it's a house museum, operated by the Foundation for San Francisco's Architectural Heritage, open to the public Wednesday and Sunday afternoons. Admission. ~ 2007 Franklin Street; 415-441-3004.

Turn left on Jackson and continue uphill to **Grenlee Terrace** at 1925 Jackson Street. With its white stucco facade and red tile roof, this sophisticated apartment house follows a Mission Revival motif and dates from 1913. The stately brick building across the street at 1950 Jackson Street houses the **Royal Swedish Consulate**. Also nearby is the **Whittier Mansion**, a red sandstone structure built in 1896 and located at 2090 Jackson Street.

Turn right on Laguna, go downhill, then left on Broadway. That stern three-story edifice with lions on either side of the entranceway is the **Hamlin School** (2120 Broadway). Designed as a

Baroque Revival mansion, it was constructed in 1901. James Flood, the man who commissioned the building, also built the white marble **Renaissance-style palazzo** at 2222 Broadway.

Go back a half-block and turn uphill on Webster Street. The **Bourn Mansion** located at 2550 Webster Street is a Georgian townhouse that was built in 1896 by William Bourn, one of California's wealthiest businessmen.

The **Golden Gate Church** at 1901 Franklin Street is a Baroque Revival structure built in 1900 for the Crockers, one of California's most powerful families.

Take a left on Washington Street and continue to **Lafayette Park** between Washington and Laguna streets, a beautiful tree-dotted park with a rolling lawn. Across the street at 2080 Washington Street rises the **Spreckels Mansion**, an ornate edifice with a white limestone surface that is beginning to fall to the forces of San Francisco's wind and weather. There are literally hundreds more houses to visit in this neighborhood. If this thumbnail tour has merely whetted your architectural appetite, you can continue alone, strolling these heights, searching out vestiges of San Francisco's baronial history.

LODGING

For fashionable living, consider **El Drisco Hotel**. This 30-room hotel survived the 1906 earthquake and fire and went on to serve four generations of guests. Located in the city's poshest area, El Drisco has undergone a complete renovation. Both the small standard rooms and the roomier suites combine modern and antique furnishings and offer whirlpool baths. And the place still retains some of its old charms—like the downstairs dining room, the dark wood lobby, and a complimentary continental breakfast. ~ 2901 Pacific Avenue; 415-346-2880, 800-634-7277, fax 415-567-5537. MODERATE TO DELUXE.

If a short spell in a museum intrigues you, there's always **The Mansion Hotel**. Set in a Queen Anne Victorian, this monument to palatial living is chockablock with antique furniture, Bufano statuary, and brilliant wall murals. The first floor, which the public is invited to tour, features a grand, crystal-chandeliered foyer. The parlor incorporates a pig motif, the billiard room contains the original dollhouse set from Edward Albee's *Tiny Alice*, and the music room is a staging area for magic shows. Not your ordinary museum. But who ever heard of a bed and breakfast museum anyway? Perhaps it's the bizarre nature of the beast that attracts guests like comedian Robin Williams. Or maybe it's the individual bedrooms, each dedicated to a historic figure and decorated with a mural depicting that individual's life. For a night in Fantasyland, it could prove worth the investment. ~ 2220 Sacramento Street; 415-929-9444, 800-826-9398, fax 415-567-9391. ULTRA-DELUXE.

DINING While Pacific Heights is primarily residential, you'll find dining rooms in the "Upper Fillmore" area and along Sacramento Street. Both of these gentrified districts features a host of gourmet restaurants. The best way to uncover them is by exploring the area.

Upper Fillmore reaches from Bush Street to Jackson Street, wedged between a proletarian neighborhood and posh Pacific Heights. The accent is on the latter locale, however, and the street is lined with good dining places. Most are restaurants characterized by canvas awnings, hand-lettered signs, brass rails, and ever-changing menus.

My personal favorite is the **Élite Café**, a spiffy establishment with overhead fans and private oak-paneled booths. Open for dinner and Sunday brunch, the Élite specializes in Cajun cuisine. Appetizers include gumbo and Gulf oysters; the main courses vary daily and may feature blackened fish, filet mignon with Cajun butter, housemade chicken sausage and jambalaya, or broiled sea bass with pecan butter. ~ 2049 Fillmore Street; 415-346-8668. MODERATE TO DELUXE.

East meets West in the entrées of **Oritalia**, a tiny storefront restaurant. In accordance with Asian culture, the decor is understated, with white tablecloths, chopsticks on the tables, large flower arrangements scattered about the room, and an exhibition kitchen. The food, however, is an extravagant blend of Asian and European flavors. The chef's "small plates" include smoked chicken *mu shu* with whole-wheat Mandarin pancakes, and tuna tartare with Asian pear, scallions, and sticky rice cakes. Among the pastas is gnocchi with rock shrimp, cilantro, ginger cream, and tobiko caviar, and the "large plates" include miso-poached salmon and grilled flatiron steak with Chinese long beans. ~ 1915 Fillmore Street; 415-346-1333. MODERATE.

SHOPPING Upper Fillmore and Sacramento Street are also convenient shopping districts close to Pacific Heights. "Upper" Fillmore is a double-entendre referring to class as well as altitude. Stretching from Sutter Street to Jackson Street in Pacific Heights, it's a gently sloping boulevard lined with designer shops. Along this seven-block row are galleries, gourmet food outlets, boutiques, and bath accessory stores. *Très chic.*

Doubtless you're in the market for a parrot, finch, or grand cockatoo. On the off chance you're not, stop by **Spectrum Exotic Birds** anyway. They stock a colorful variety of feathered friends. ~ 2011 Fillmore Street; 415-922-7113.

A bit much? Then consider **Seconds To Go**, which has used clothing for guys and gals. ~ 2252 Fillmore Street; 415-563-7806.

There is also a bookstore, **Browser Books**, worthy of note along this strip. ~ 2195 Fillmore Street; 415-567-8027.

One of the streets crossing this upper Fillmore promenade is Sacramento. Follow it several blocks west and you'll discover another fast-growing shoppers' strip. The stores here are not as concentrated, but scattered between Broderick and Spruce streets are a number of fashionable shops.

A real neighborhood shopping area, Sacramento Street combines galleries, boutiques, and antique stores with shops serving the immediate needs of local folks. You can combine your shopping with a tour of this vintage area, which contains a number of impressive Victorian homes.

Between Lyon and Spruce streets, from the 3200 to 3600 blocks, you'll find a bevy of boutiques and trendy shops. **Arts of the Americas**, as stylish as it is pricey, has artwork from the Southwest, American Indian jewelry and rugs, and Mexican silverwork and antiques. By appointment only. ~ 415-346-0180.

The Presidio

What was previously the oldest active military base in the country is now the country's largest urban national park. The Presidio is also a National Historic Landmark. It was established by the Spanish in 1776 and taken over by the United States in 1846. Civil War troops trained here, and the Sixth Army established the base as its headquarters. Even when it was a military base, the Presidio had the feel of a country retreat. Hiking trails snake through the 1400 acres of undulating hills sprinkled with acacia, madrone, pine, and redwood trees, and there are expansive bay views. Although still under development, there are plans for new hiking trails, museums, education centers, and conference facilities.

SIGHTS

The best way to explore the Presidio is by stopping first at the **Visitor Information Center**. The folks here are very knowledgeable; they will provide you with a map and can also arrange guided

THE LAST STAND

The battle lines are drawn at **Lover's Lane**. March, or even stroll, along this narrow pathway, and review these armies of nature. On one side, standing sentinel straight, out-thrust arms shading the lane, are the eucalyptus. Mustered along the other front, clad in darker uniforms, seeming to retreat before the wind, are the conifer trees. Forgetting for a moment these silly games soldiers play, look around. You are standing in an awesome and spectacular spot, one of the last forests in San Francisco. ~ In the southeast corner of the Presidio.

tours with a park ranger. ~ Building 102, Montgomery Street; 415-561-4323.

Make your next stop the **Presidio Army Museum.** This three-story museum was originally a hospital, built in 1857. Faced with pillars and protected by a collection of antique cannons, it's still an imposing sight. The displays inside consist primarily of military uniforms and weapons. Closed Monday and Tuesday. ~ Funston Avenue near Lincoln Boulevard.

The nearby **Officers' Club**, a tile-roof, Spanish-style structure, includes part of the original 1776 Presidio, one of the first buildings ever constructed in San Francisco. ~ Moraga Avenue.

The **National Cemetery**, with rows of tombstones on a grassy knoll overlooking the Golden Gate Bridge, is San Francisco's salute to the nation's war dead. ~ Lincoln Boulevard.

HIDDEN ►

The remainder of our Presidio tour is of a more natural bent. There's **El Polin Spring** where, as the brass plaque proclaims, "the early Spanish garrison attained its water supply." History has rarely been made in a more beautiful spot. The spring is set in a lovely park surrounded by hills upon which eucalyptus trees battle with conifers for strategic ground. Hiking trails lead down and outward from this enchanted glade. ~ Located at the end of MacArthur Avenue.

Mountain Lake Park, stationed along the Presidio's southern flank, is another idyllic locale. With its grassy meadows and wooded walkways, it's a great place to picnic or stroll. The lake itself, a favorite watering hole among ducks visiting from out of town, is skirted with tule reeds and overhung with willows. ~ Lake Street between 8th and Funston avenues.

The base's prettiest walk is actually in civilian territory along the **Presidio Wall** bordering Lyon Street. Starting at the Lombard Street Gate, where two cannons guard the fort's eastern entrance, walk uphill along Lyon Street. That wall of urbanity to the left is the city's chic Union Street district, breeding place for fern bars and antique stores. To the right, beyond the Presidio's stone enclosure, are the tumbling hills and towering trees of the old garrison.

After several blocks, Lyon ceases to be a street and becomes a staircase. The most arduous and rewarding part of the trek begins; you can follow this stairway to heaven, which happens to be Broadway, two heart-pounding blocks above you. Ascend and the city falls away—the Palace of Fine Arts, Alcatraz, the Marina, all become landing points for your vision. Closer to hand are the houses of San Francisco's posh Pacific Heights district, stately structures looming several stories and sprawling across the landscape. When you reach the stone steps at the top of Broadway, they will still rise above, potent and pretentious, hard contrast to the Presidio's leafy acres.

Nob Hill

Perhaps the most famous of all the knolls casting their ever-loving shadows on San Francisco is a prominent prominence called Nob Hill. It is a monument to San Francisco's crusty rich—those old powerbrokers who trace their heritage back to the Big Four. It seems that in the 19th century, Misters Crocker, Huntington, Hopkins, and Stanford—the tycoons who built the transcontinental railroad—chose Nob Hill as the place to honor themselves. They all built estates on top of the 338-foot rise, each more ostentatious than the other. It became, as Robert Louis Stevenson described it, "the Hill of palaces." Until 1906: the fire that followed the great earthquake burned Nob Hill's mansions to the ground.

SIGHTS

All that remains from the robber baron age is the **Pacific Union Club**, a blocky brownstone built in 1855 for a silver king named James Flood. ~ 1000 California Street.

The **Fairmont Hotel** across the street is a partial survivor. Built just prior to 1906, the shell of this grand building endured; the interior was refurbished in time for the hotel to open on the first anniversary of the earthquake. Today the hotel lobby, with its marble columns and gilt bas-relief, evokes memories of the Big Four. ~ 950 Mason Street.

Once the domain of San Francisco's wealthiest families, Nob Hill now is home to the city's finest hotels. Strung like pearls along California Street, a doorman's whistle from the Fairmont, are three luxurious hotels. Fittingly, the **Stanford Court Hotel**, **Mark Hopkins Inter-Continental Hotel**, and the **Huntington Hotel** were built upon the ruins of Big Four mansions. That tree-dotted resting place across the street *naturalement*, **Huntington Park**.

> At Grace Cathedral, there are tiers of stained-glass windows which picture such latter-day luminaries as labor leader John L. Lewis, social worker Jane Addams, and astronaut John Glenn.

The nearby **Grace Cathedral** marks San Francisco's attempt at Gothic architecture. Consecrated in 1964 and constructed of concrete, it's not exactly Notre Dame. But this mammoth, vaulting church does have its charm. Foremost are the doors atop the cathedral steps; they represent Lorenzo Ghiberti's "Doors of Paradise," cast in bronze from the artist's original work in Florence. The church interior is graced with a series of wall murals. In addition to these architectural adornments, the cathedral is filled with objects as dear as they are sacred—a 15th-century carved oak altar piece, 13th-century Spanish crucifix, 16th-century Belgian tapestry, and an organ boasting 7000 pipes. ~ 1051 Taylor Street.

Cathedral, hotels, the park—all are perched in a gilded nest known sarcastically among local folks as "Snob Hill." When you're ready to come down from these heady heights, you might want to decompress slowly by touring some of the area's small townhouses.

You needn't be a millionaire to live along Sacramento Street; you just need a lot of money. Take the sprightly **townhouse** at 1172 Sacramento, for instance. With its mansard roof and cast-iron filigree, it could probably be had for a pittance. The **1200 block of Sacramento** boasts a string of lovely townhouses, including two structures adorned with wrought-iron tracery. At 1298 Sacramento Street, **Chambord Apartments** is a singular Beaux-Arts style building featuring curved balconies and elaborate exterior ornamentation.

Actually it's only the three square blocks at the very top of Nob Hill that possess the pretension of wealth. The neighborhood below, where the hill slopes westward, is rather folksy. One enclave is downright rural. That, of course, is **Priest Street**, which rises from Washington Street between Jones and Leavenworth. Priest is not really a street but a staircase, an ivy-banked country lane in the heart of San Francisco. It requires a bit of imagination to fully experience the place. For one thing you have to always gaze to the right, where slender townhouses are bordered with hedges.

HIDDEN ►

On the left side someone has built an astonishingly hideous apartment house. To add irony to insult, they've barricaded the beast behind a chain-link fence topped with a menacing roll of barbed wire. Follow the trail at the end of the road and emerge on an overgrown hill that looks out upon the city. If you continue on this semi-circular course, you'll come out on **Reed Street**. Like its counterpart, this "street" is a narrow walkway planted with gardens and tucked between clapboard houses. Perhaps we should call Priest and Reed streets, "the Tiny Two," the common folk's answer to Nob Hill's "Big Four." You can take any of the city's three cable car lines to Nob Hill's **Powell–California Street stop**, the only spot in San Francisco where they all intersect.

LODGING

There's an emphasis on style and service at the **Renaissance Stanford Court Hotel**. Its hallmark is the *porte cochère*, illuminated through a leaded-glass dome. The 402 guest rooms combine antiques and modern pieces to create a singular effect. There is one restaurant, a fitness room, several shops and lounges, plus an excellent staff. Of the several well-known hotels that adorn Nob Hill, this is my favorite. Five stars. ~ 905 California Street; 415-989-3500, 800-227-4736, fax 415-391-6513. ULTRA-DELUXE.

Of major Nob Hill hotels, **The Huntington** is no doubt the least known, and it seems to like it that way. Constructed in the 1920s as an apartment house, the building was the first steel-and-brick highrise west of the Mississippi. An aura of understated elegance pervades the hotel and its 140 guest rooms, each individually decorated. The Big Four restaurant, named after the four great railroad magnates—Stanford, Hopkins, Crocker, and Huntington—

is a mini-museum of San Francisco and Western memorabilia and also serves exceptional meals in a comfortable, clublike atmosphere. ~ 1075 California Street; 415-474-5400, 800-227-4683, fax 415-474-6227. ULTRA-DELUXE.

NIGHTLIFE

A poised pianist plays nightly at fashionable **Mason's** on Nob Hill. The sounds will be Porter and Gershwin, the crowd elegant, and the drinks expensive. Dress code. ~ Fairmont Hotel, 950 Mason Street; 415-772-5233.

If San Francisco tourists were given an association test and asked the first thing that came to mind when a "bar with a view" was mentioned, about 101 out of every 100 would list **The Top of the Mark.** With good reason: from its roosting place in Nob Hill's Mark Hopkins Hotel, this venerable lounge enjoys extraordinary vistas of the bay and beyond. There's a live jazz band Wednesday through Saturday. Dress code. Cover. ~ California and Mason streets; 415-392-3434.

Japantown

Center of culture for San Francisco's burgeoning Japanese population is Japantown, a self-contained area bounded by Geary and Post, Laguna and Fillmore streets. This town-within-a-city consists of two sections: the old part, where residential housing is located, and a newer commercial area.

SIGHTS

Japan Center, designed by architect Minoru Yamasaki, is a five-acre monstrosity. Built in 1968, it exemplifies the freeway architecture of the era. There are, nonetheless, fascinating shops and outstanding restaurants located in this Asian mall.

You'll also encounter special features here and there. Like the **Peace Pagoda,** a five-tiered structure designed by world renowned architect Yoshiro Taniguchi as an expression of friendship and goodwill between the people of Japan and America.

During the April Cherry Blossom Festival, August Street Fair, Autumn Bon Dances, and the Aki Matsuri festival in September, Japantown turns out in splendid costumes for musical celebrations. All year round you can enjoy **Nihonmachi Mall** (on Buchanan Street) with its cobblestone pathway and lovely Ruth Asawa origami fountains. There are also park benches featuring bas-reliefs done by local children. Pass through the *torii* gate here, then head up to 1881 Bush Street, and you'll encounter the time-battered **Soto Zen Mission,** a center for the city's ardent *Go* players.

LODGING

Japantown has two excellent hotels which provide a "chance to experience the tranquilities of the East and the amenities of the West."

One of the most reasonable accommodations in the area, the **Miyako Inn** has 125 rooms, some with private steam baths. The lobby is simple but comfortable, featuring mauve sofas and plump armchairs. There is also a restaurant on the premises. ~ 1800 Sutter Street; 415-921-4000, 800-528-1234, fax 415-563-1278. MODERATE TO DELUXE.

Its sibling, and foremost among the city's Asian-style hotels is the **Miyako**. Architecturally the building lacks appeal. The interior is another matter. Pass through the sliding glass doors and you'll enter an oriental milieu. The hotel bar, for instance, is decorated in an Asian motif. The private rooms are adorned with Japanese prints; behind the colorful shoji screens are balconies overlooking a garden. Be sure to ask for a sunken Japanese tub. Some of the special rooms are entirely Japanese in furnishing and decoration with tatami mats, futons (folding beds), and built-in saunas. The Miyako represents one of the city's most exotic hotels. ~ 1625 Post Street; 415-922-3200, 800-333-3333, fax 415-921-0417. DELUXE TO ULTRA-DELUXE.

DINING

The Japan Center Building houses several Japanese restaurants including a *shokuji dokoro*, or traditional bistro called **Koji Osakaya**. Here the atmosphere is mannered and reserved. Japanese tradition at its finest. ~ 1737 Post Street; 415-922-2728. MODERATE.

Tired of humdrum sushi bars? Bored with sea urchin platters? Then **Isobune** is the place for you. Here those raw fish finger foods scud past you on wooden boats along a miniature canal. No joke—we're talking sushi on a stream. You simply sit at the counter and pluck off your favorite cargo as the boat goes by. There are numerous sushi selections, as well as soup and sashimi. ~ 1737 Post Street; 415-563-1030. MODERATE.

Recommended by local residents and gourmets alike, **Sanppo Restaurant** serves excellent food at fair prices. In addition to outstanding sushi, they offer lemon steak, garlic chicken, *chanko nabe* (a fish, chicken, and vegetable dish), tempura, and *donburi* dishes. The interior is unsophisticated café-style, but the cuisine is worthy of a plush establishment. Three stars over Japantown. Closed Monday. ~ 1702 Post Street; 415-346-3486. MODERATE.

AAHHH!!

After a full day sightseeing, you can luxuriate at **Kabuki Hot Spring**. This Japanese-style bathhouse features saunas, steam cabinets, hot tubs, and cold tubs. The resident *massajishi* (masseurs and masseuses) offer shiatsu massage in which muscle and nerve points are kneaded with the fingertips. A Japanese experience without comparison! There is, of course, a fee for all services. ~ 1750 Geary Boulevard; 415-922-6000.

SHOPPING

In this Asian neighborhood, most shopping is done in Japan Center, a modern mall. As you'll discover, most of the listings below are located in this commercial complex.

Shige Nishiguchi Antiques specializes in antique kimonos, those gorgeous heavy silk garments. They also have dolls dressed in kimono miniatures. ~ 1730 Geary Boulevard; 415-346-5567.

Similarly, **Asakichi** features antique furniture as well as Asian arts and crafts. Take special note of those heavy wood antique chests called *tansu*. Cluttered but fascinating, this shop also carries porcelain dinnerware, sake cups, and antique fabrics. ~ 1730 Geary Boulevard, #108; 415-921-2147.

Kinokuniya Bookstore is a warehouse of a store, chockablock with volumes on Japanese language and culture. Among the works in both English and Japanese are books on history, travel, and cooking. ~ 1581 Webster Street; 415-567-7625. The same building houses **Kinokuniya Stationery and Gift**, which stocks Japanese postcards, calendars, and writing supplies. ~ 1581 Webster Street; 415-567-8901.

One of Japan Center's most captivating stores is **Mashiko Folkcraft**, a museum-cum-shop, displaying Japanese folk art. Among the exhibits, you might find an 18th-century tobacco set or a hand-painted papier-mâché pillow. The prices often match the age of these precious objects, but there are affordable items—like ceramic dishes and porcelain chopstick rests. ~ 1581 Webster Street; 415-346-0748.

For gifts at reasonable prices, step over from the Japan Center to **Nichi Bei Bussan**. Here is a collection of Asian wares ranging from standard kimonos to rice paper wallets. There are also a few special treasures, such as batik wallhangings and Japanese shoes. ~ 1715 Buchanan Mall; 415-346-2117.

NIGHTLIFE

Jack's Bar is not at all Japanese, but it does have great live blues and jazz on Thursday, Friday, and Saturday. Big names have played here, including James Cotton, Johnny Lee Hooker, and Greg Allman. Cover. ~ 1601 Fillmore Street; 415-567-3227.

Haight-Ashbury

Places that are part of the cultural mythology have usually gained their prominence centuries before. For Haight-Ashbury that is simply not the case. This neighborhood of quiet streets and Victorian houses blazed across the public consciousness within the past few decades, leaving a vapor trail that may never vanish.

For an entire generation, 1967 was the "Summer of Love," a heady season when psychedelic drugs were food for thought and acid rock was king. On January 14, 1967, about 20,000 enlightened folks streamed through the Haight on the way to a "Human

Be-In—A Gathering of the Tribes," where they tuned in to a succession of speakers, singers, and seers. By that summer, San Francisco had become a mecca for young people seeking religious truth and righteous dope. Haight-Ashbury's streets were thronged with a new breed—clad in motley and carrying bells, feathers, beads, and cymbals. For one brief period it was a kind of dreamland, a creation of the collective imagination. Like all dreams, it was an ephemera, transmogrified into reality by Vietnam and an increasingly repressive society.

SIGHTS

While many of us will carry the memory of those days to the grave, Haight-Ashbury has lost many of its countercultural trappings. As it was before the first hippie floated along its streets, Haight-Ashbury is an upper-middle-class neighborhood resplendent with tree-lined avenues and backyard gardens. Tucked between two of San Francisco's prettiest parks—Golden Gate and Buena Vista—it also sports some of the city's loveliest Victorians. There are Queen Anne styles marked by solitary turrets and boldly painted facades. On **Ashbury Heights**, the hillside overlooking Haight Street, are houses drawn from a gingerbread cakeboard. In the entire neighborhood there are over a thousand Victorians.

Today the Haight is still an area in transition. The district has been partially gentrified but still retains vestiges of its bohemian past. On **Haight Street**, between Masonic and Stanyan streets, the sidewalks are door-to-door with mod shops, trendy bars, antique clothing stores, art galleries, and funky restaurants.

Before strolling this refurbished street, be sure to explore **Buena Vista Park**. Dense with conifers and eucalyptus trees, the park's angling hills offer splendid views of San Francisco from ocean to bay. Buena Vista possesses the beauty of Golden Gate Park but lacks the crowds. ~ Haight and Lyon streets.

Rising like a grand estate and featuring a four-column facade, the house at 2400 Fulton Street served as the original Jefferson Airplane House.

Just off Haight Street are several spots vital to the history of the '60s counterculture. For a vibrant retrospective on psychedelic art, wander past the **mural** that decorates an entire outside wall at 1807 Page Street. Painted in striking colors, it pictures a visionary eye radiating down upon a multiracial band of musicians. Along one side, green hills roll to infinity, while from the other extends the open sea. In the busy but vital style of the era, it is packed with an endless series of images.

To add a ghoulish element to your otherwise pleasant tour, check out the nondescript house at **636 Cole Street.** It served during the "Summer of Love" as home to a man named Charles Manson.

Or, if you like visiting these places-that-are-still-spoken-of-around-town-even-though-they-are-no-longer-what-they-are-known-for, you'll be interested in the pretty Victorian at 710 Ashbury Street. Back in the halcyon days of live music and electric drugs it was the **Dead House**, home to San Francisco's foremost acid rock ensemble, The Grateful Dead.

A rewarding way to discover Haight-Ashbury is by wandering on your own through the neighborhood, seeking out old Victorians and soaking up local ambience. You might also head up to **Corona Heights** for a city view known only to San Franciscans. This six-block uphill walk from Haight Street carries one past some pretty Victorians (take Masonic Street to the end, then continue one-half block after it turns into Roosevelt Avenue). At the top is a rocky, wind-haunted outcropping that commands a sweep of the city from Russian Hill to the Financial District to the southern stretches of the Bay. Backdropped by Twin Peaks, Corona Heights is a lesser promontory, but one that you'll often have to yourself. ◄ HIDDEN

Beauty appears not only in open spaces, but narrow corridors as well. After descending Corona Heights, you might also consider **Edgewood Avenue**. The climb begins on Farnsworth Lane (off Parnassus Avenue, above the University of California Medical Center). Farnsworth is a country lane banked with ivy and trim hedges that someone accidentally placed in the city. It opens on to Edgewood Avenue, a brick-paved street which local resident Else Reisner considers one of San Francisco's prettiest walks. If you ever plan to live in San Francisco, you might as well settle here; you'll never find a more congenial place. The houses on either side are faced with brown shingle or brick; they end at the edge of a forest amid trees heavy with vines. If you're game, a hiking path leads into this primeval wood. ◄ HIDDEN

LODGING

One of San Francisco's most reasonable bed and breakfast hotels can be found right along Haight Street, center of the fabled Summer of Love. **The Red Victorian Inn** evokes a sense of that era. Owner Sami Sunchild promotes an individualistic atmosphere in her 19-room hotel. Each chamber is decorated according to a different theme. The Peacock Room and the Rainbow Room reflect the style of the 1960s. All rooms are nicely appointed with handsome wood tables and chairs, chandeliers, and lacy curtains. The public areas display the owner's colorful artwork as well as historic photos of Golden Gate Park and San Francisco. A continental breakfast is served in the Global Village Room, which also serves as a gathering place for guests. ~ 1665 Haight Street; 415-864-1978, fax 415-863-3293. MODERATE TO DELUXE.

A charming Victorian cottage filled with ethnic dolls, antiques and folk art, **Carl Street Unicorn House** has a strong lesbian following, but also welcomes gay men and straight guests. Accommodations consist of two guest rooms with one shared bath in the downstairs portion of the house. A generous continental breakfast is served and there's a patio for sunbathing. ~ 156 Carl Street; 415-753-5194. BUDGET.

A dozen rooms, convenient to Golden Gate Park, make **Victorian Inn on The Park** a wonderful retreat. The inn's public areas feature a beautiful library and living room, complete with a fainting couch. Each morning you'll enjoy breakfast in the wood-paneled dining room beneath an embossed ceiling and chandelier. Rooms feature brass and canopy beds, fireplaces, and walnut desks. ~ 301 Lyon Street; 415-931-1830, 800-435-1967, fax 415-931-1830. DELUXE TO ULTRA-DELUXE.

DINING

Stepping into **Kan Zaman** is like entering into a dream of Arabian Nights. The lighting is dim, and the walls are covered with desert murals done in relaxing earth tones. Lounge on the big, comfortable cushions set on the floor around low tables and choose from couscous, falafel, grape leaves, and so on. After dinner you may want to indulge in one of the large hookah pipes filled with your choice of apricot, honey, or apple tobacco. No lunch on Monday. ~ 1793 Haight Street; 415-751-9656. MODERATE.

Amid Santería altars and glittering shrines hanging on the black brick walls, **Cha Cha Cha** conjures up a bewitching mix of Latin and Caribbean flavors that can range from Jamaican jerk chicken over white rice to Cajun shrimp in a spicy cream sauce. Fortunately, most menu choices are tapas plates allowing diners to sample a variety of tastes. ~ 1801 Haight Street; 415-386-5758. MODERATE.

SHOPPING

The Haight-Ashbury neighborhood, with its multihued Victorian houses, is slowly undergoing a process of gentrification. Old buildings are being remodeled and chic shops are moving in. As a result, shoppers will find that Haight Street, once a nondescript avenue lined with hardware stores and corner groceries, is becoming a hip, bustling boulevard.

You'll be engulfed in an ethereal aura upon entering **Breath of Heaven** and can take a sample of it home by purchasing some of the creams, candles, lotions, and bath oils sold at this shop. ~ 1715 Haight Street; 415-221-1638.

In addition to an imaginative name, **Off The Wall** has an appealing collection of contemporary poster art and a large line of new rock art. There are assorted eclectic artworks, particularly by ethnic artists. ~ 1669 Haight Street; 415-863-8170.

The Soft Touch, operated by a Bay Area collective of artists, displays sculpture and jewelry. Everything here is original and the store itself totally unique. There are locally designed clothes and ceramics, as well as artwork that twists the word abstract to the breaking point. It is, as the collective explains, a gallery intended "to inspire and amuse ourselves and you." ~ 1580 Haight Street; 415-863-3279.

At **Planet Weaver's Treasure Store** you'll find native people's crafts and clothing, masks, drums, books, cards, music, body products, and hundreds of other items from every corner of the globe. An emphasis on Third World arts and crafts makes this shop full of surprises. ~ 1573 Haight Street; 415-864-4415.

Dress to fit your fantasy at **Piedmont Boutique**. Join the drag queens and strippers who frequent the store for fancy custom-made gowns, boas, baubles, and bangles. You can buy a great outfit for a costume party or something to help you blend into the Haight Street fashion scene. There aren't too many stores like this one. ~ 1452 Haight Street; 415-864-8075.

Gargoyle Beads sells thousands of beads in hundreds of varieties. Just take an ice cube tray and fill it with seed, crystal, ceramic, or whatever other types of beads grab your fancy. Purchase a spool of thread and you'll be ready to create necklaces, earrings, and hanging curtains. ~ 1310 Haight Street; 415-552-4274.

Distractions offers beautiful gay and mixed greeting cards, smoking paraphernalia, and popular items of the hippie era such as bells, incense, jewelry, and tie-dye clothing. In the back is **Euphoria**, a shop that specializes in crafts. ~ 1552 Haight Street; 415-252-8751 (for both stores).

Located a block north of Haight Street, **San Francisco Stained Glass** has stained-glass vases, lamps, clocks, and mirrors. ~ 345 Divisadero Street; 415-626-3592.

NIGHTLIFE

Nightbreak is small, local, and alive with sound and color. Whether the sounds are live or spun by a deejay, the place will be rocking. Cover at times. ~ 1821 Haight Street; 415-221-9008.

The Lower Haight is home to many bars and clubs and on weekends they seem to have a revolving door as people cruise from one to the other and back again. **Mad Dog in the Fog** resembles a British pub and attracts quite a crowd with its dart boards and extensive beer selection (20 on tap plus 30 bottled). Live music Saturday night. ~ 530 Haight Street; 415-626-7279.

A bit more pretentious than Mad Dog is **Noc Noc**, marked by old televisions in the storefront windows. It's quiet enough here to actually have a conversation with your drink. ~ 557 Haight Street; 415-861-5811.

For a game of pool or serious dancing go to **Nickie's Haight Street BBQ**. Open seven nights a week, Nickie's has a different DJ or band each night, playing everything from hip-hop and African to Latin and jazz. Cover. ~ 460 Haight Street; 415-621-6508.

Golden Gate Park

It is the Central Park of the West. Or perhaps we should say that Central Park is New York's answer to Golden Gate Park. It extends from the Haight-Ashbury neighborhood, across nearly half the width of the city, all the way to the ocean. With its folded hills and sloping meadows, its lakes and museums, Golden Gate is everyone's favorite park.

Once an undeveloped region of sand dunes, the park today encompasses over 1000 acres of gardens, lawns, and forests. The transformation from wasteland to wonderland came about during the late-19th and early-20th centuries through the efforts of a mastermind named John McLaren. A gardener by trade, this Scotsman could rightly be called an architect of the earth. Within his lifetime he oversaw the creation of the world's largest human-made park.

What he wrought was a place that has something to suit everyone: there are tennis courts; lawn bowling greens; hiking trails; byways for bicyclers, rollerskaters, skateboarders, even unicyclers; a nine-hole golf course; archery field; flycasting pools; playgrounds; fields for soccer and football; riding stables; even checker pavilions. Facilities for renting bicycles and skates are located just outside the park along Haight and Stanyan streets.

Or, if you'd prefer not to lift a finger, you can always pull up a shade tree and watch the parade. The best day to visit Golden Gate Park is Sunday when many of the roads in the eastern end of the park are closed to cars but open to skaters, jugglers, bicyclers, troubadours, mimes, skateboarders, impromptu theater groups, sun worshippers, and anyone else who feels inspired.

Touring the park should be done on another day, when you can drive freely through the grounds. There are two roads spanning the length of the park. Each begins near Stanyan Street on the east side of Golden Gate Park and runs about four miles westward to the Pacific. The best way to see this area is to travel out along John F. Kennedy Drive and back by Martin Luther King, Jr. Drive, detouring down the side roads that lead into the heart of the park.

SIGHTS

The first stop along John F. Kennedy Drive lies immediately after the entrance. That red-tile building overgrown in ivy is **McLaren Lodge**, park headquarters and home base for maps, brochures, pamphlets, and information. (McLaren Lodge is closed on weekends, but maps are available at the kiosk near the carousel.) ~ Stanyan and Fell streets; 415-666-7200.

The startling glass palace nearby is the **Conservatory**. Built in 1879 and Victorian in style, it's currently being restored after sustaining damage in a 1995 winter storm. Although it's not open to the public, the Conservatory still makes for a stunning photo op.

Just down the street is **Rhododendron Dell**. A lace-work of trails threads through this 20-acre garden; if you're visiting in early spring, when the rose-hued bushes are blooming, the dell is a concert of colors.

Just beyond this garden beats the cultural heart of Golden Gate Park. Located around a tree-studded concourse are the De Young Museum, Academy of Sciences, and Japanese Tea Garden. The **M. H. De Young Memorial Museum**, the city's finest, houses an impressive collection. Exhibits trace the course of American art from colonial times to the mid-20th century. The Art of the Americas gallery features ancient art from Central and South America as well as North American art of the past four hundred years. There's also an intriguing display of works from Africa and Oceania. Closed Monday and Tuesday. Admission. ~ 415-750-3600.

The *pièce de résistance* of this entire complex is the **Asian Art Museum** adjacent to the De Young. Featuring major pieces from China, Tibet, Japan, Korea, Iran, Syria, and throughout the continent, this superlative facility is the largest museum in the country devoted exclusively to Asian art. Some of the pieces date back 6000 years. Closed Monday and Tuesday. Admission. ~ 415-668-8921.

It takes a facility like the **California Academy of Sciences** to even compete with a place like the De Young Museum. Here you'll find a planetarium where the stars rise all day, an array of African animals grouped in jungle settings, and a "roundabout" aquarium in which you stand at the center of a circular glass tank while creatures of the deep swim around you. A tremendous place for kids, this natural history museum also features numerous "hands-on" exhibits. Admission. ~ 415-750-7145.

If you're like me, it won't be more than an hour or two before museum fatigue sets in and dinosaur vertebrae start looking like rock formations. It's time for the **Japanese Tea Garden**. Here you can rest your heavy eyes on carp-filled ponds and handwrought gateways. There are arch footbridges, cherry trees, bonsai gardens, and, of course, a tea house where Japanese women serve jasmine tea and cookies. Admission.

All these cultural gathering places cluster around a **Music Concourse** where concerts are regularly staged.

You can get back on John F. Kennedy Drive and resume your self-guided tour by continuing to **Stow Lake**. This is a donut-shaped body of water with an island as the hole in the middle. From the island's crest you can gaze across San Francisco from Bay to ocean. Or, if an uphill is not in your day's itinerary, there's a footpath around the island perimeter that passes an ornate Chinese pagoda. There are also rowboats, pedalboats, and electric motorboats for rent, and a small snack bar.

Next along John F. Kennedy Drive you'll pass **Rainbow Falls**. That monument at the top, from which this cascade appears to spill, is **Prayerbook Cross**, modeled after an old Celtic cross.

Text continued on page 102.

Clement Street Restaurants

For any city in the country, there's a rule of thumb to good eating: to dine where the locals dine, go where the locals live. In San Francisco that means Clement Street. Paralleling Golden Gate Park and the Presidio and set midway between the two, this friendly street is the center of a multicultural neighborhood. Irish, Russians, Chinese, Japanese, Jews, and others have called the district home for varying periods of time.

The result is a marvelous mix of ethnic restaurants. Stroll Clement Street, from 1st to 12th Avenue or 19th to 26th Avenue, and encounter Italian, Danish, Thai, and Indonesian restaurants. There are Irish bars, French patisseries, bistros, health food stores, open-air vegetable stands, and numerous Asian dining places. The only difficulty you'll encounter is deciding on a particular place. I have a few suggestions, but if they don't fit your fancy, you'll doubtless find a dozen places that do.

There's an outstanding Vietnamese restaurant just off Clement. **New Golden Turtle** might well be the best in the city. This cozy eatery specializes in charcoal-broiled marinated beef. Other delicacies include barbecue pork and a host of finger foods. There's a comfortable atmosphere here with potted plants all around and a rose at each table. *Très bien!* Closed Monday for lunch. ~ 308 5th Avenue; 415-221-5285. BUDGET TO MODERATE.

I also heartily recommend **Mai's**. The dining room is small and informal with a simple decor. Serene and personable, Mai's prepares a host of tempting entrées, among them coconut chicken, lemon-grass barbecued beef, Vietnamese pork shish kebab, as well as several vegetarian dishes. ~ 316 Clement Street; 415-221-3046. BUDGET.

Recent years have brought a new wave of Russian immigrants to the neighborhood. A great choice among their eating places is **Little Russia**, a lively storefront restaurant serving home-style dishes such as dumplings with meat and vegetarian fillings, stuffed cabbage, and a hearty beef stew called *zharkoe*. A truly spectacular appetizer of blini, red caviar, and smoked salmon can be shared by two or more diners. A keyboardist and Russian vocalist perform in the evenings and diners are invited to take to the central dancefloor if the spirit moves them. ~ 5217 Geary Boulevard; 415-751-9661. BUDGET.

The next hardest thing to choosing a restaurant on Clement is selecting a Chinese restaurant. One of the very finest is **Hong Kong Villa**, which offers the chance to feast on a whole Peking duck with steamed buns or fresh Maine lobster at reasonable prices. Dungeness crab, which comes in half a dozen ways, is especially good with fresh ginger and scallions. Spicy Singapore-style noodles, stir-fried prawns with the roe attached, and tender baby ribs in a rich barbecue sauce are also memorable. ~ 2332 Clement Street; 415-752-8833. MODERATE.

The savory tastes of Italy's Emilia-Romagna region have been successfully transferred to **Laghi**, a charming family-run restaurant appointed with cozy window seats and decorated in gold tones. A daily changing menu features housemade pasta dishes such as chestnut fettuccine tossed with roasted duck and porcini mushrooms. Meat selections often include succulent lamb, pork, or veal chops served with polenta. Dinner only. Closed Monday. ~ 1801 Clement Street; 415-386-6266. MODERATE TO DELUXE.

Chandeliers in a hamburger joint? **Bill's Place** ain't just any hamburger joint! Many San Franciscans insist it's a hamburger palace, the best in the city. There's the Dwight Chapin burger (remember Watergate?) with cheese, sprouts, and bacon; the Letterman burger; the Red Skelton burger (garnished like a clown); and so on. If you want to be gauche, you can order a sandwich or hot dog instead. And if you'd rather forego the counter or table service out front, there's an open-air patio in back. Bill's is the place for fast food with a flair. ~ 2315 Clement Street; 415-221-5262. BUDGET.

This is followed close on by a chain of meadows, a kind of rolling green counterpoint to the chain of lakes which lie ahead. **Speedway Meadow** and **Lindley Meadow** offer barbecue pits and picnic tables; both are fabulous areas for sunbathing.

The Buffalo Paddock in Golden Gate Park is where American bison still roam, though within the confines of a barbed wire fence.

Spreckels Lake is home to ducks, seagulls, and model sailboats. Across the road are the **Golden Gate Park Stables**, where you can take riding lessons. ~ John F. Kennedy Drive and 36th Avenue; 415-668-7360.

Immediately beyond is the **Chain of Lakes**, a string of three reservoirs stretching the width of the park, perpendicular to John F. Kennedy Drive. Framed by eucalyptus trees, they offer hiking paths around each shoreline. As you circumnavigate these baby lakes, you'll notice they are freckled with miniature islands. Each lake possesses a singular personality: North Lake is remarkable for its hip-deep swamp cypress; Middle Lake features an island tufted with willows; and South Lake, tiniest of the triplets, sprouts bamboo along its shore.

If these ponds be babies, the great mother of them all rests nearby. Where the road meets the Pacific you'll come upon the **Dutch Windmill**, a regal structure built in 1903. With its wooden struts and scale-like shingles, it stares into the face of the sea's inevitable west winds. The Dutchman's cousin, **Murphy Windmill**, an orphan with broken arms, lives several hundred yards down the coast.

From here at continent's edge, it's a four-mile trip back through the park along Martin Luther King, Jr. Drive. After picking it up at Murphy Windmill, you'll find that this softly curving road passes lakes and forests, meadows and playgrounds. More important, it borders **Strybing Arboretum**, a place specially made for garden lovers. Strybing is a world within itself, a 70-acre flower quilt stitched together by pathways. Over 5000 species peacefully coexist here—dwarf conifers and sprawling magnolias, as well as plants from Asia, the Andes, Australia, and America. There is a "redwood trail" devoted to native California plants, a "garden of fragrance" redolent of flowers, and a Japanese strolling garden. It's a kind of park within a park, a glorious finale for your visit to this park within a city. ~ 415-661-1316.

Gay Neighborhoods

San Francisco's gay neighborhoods center around Castro Street, Polk Street, and in the South of Market area. The city's lesbian community focuses along Valencia Street in the Mission District. With a population that today numbers perhaps 200,000, the community has become a powerful social and political force. In 1977, Supervisor Harvey Milk became the nation's first outfront gay elected to a major municipal post. Since then, despite the AIDS epidemic, San Francisco has retained a gay supervisor and the gay community has remained an integral part of the city's life.

LODGING

Throughout the Castro and Polk districts are numerous hotels catering primarily to gay travelers. Others in these areas serve a wide-ranging clientele, including many gay guests.

There are two hotels located in the center of the action. The first is the **Inn on Castro**, an eight-room bed and breakfast housed in an old Victorian. A class establishment all the way, the inn adds subtle touches like fresh flowers. Each room is decorated in a different fashion, and the house atmosphere is comfortable and personal. The rooms all have private baths. Because of its popularity, the hotel recommends advance reservations. ~ 321 Castro Street; 415-861-0321. DELUXE.

Several blocks from Castro Street is **The Willows Bed and Breakfast Inn**, a beautiful 11-room facility that attracts both gay and straight guests. Each room has been furnished with antique wooden pieces and adorned with French art prints. The trademark of this cozy hostelry, however, is the willow-branch furniture designed expressly for the Inn. It's personal touches like this, as well as breakfast and turndown service with a glass of sherry included, that make it a special place. Shared bath. ~ 710 14th Street; 415-431-4770, fax 415-431-5295. MODERATE.

Nancy's Inn is a friendly, private lesbian home offering sleeping accommodations to women travelers. Located in a quiet residential neighborhood near Twin Peaks, the house is full of women energy and decorated with women's art. There are two bedrooms, and a sliding glass door leads from one bedroom to a deck in the back. The bathroom is shared. ~ 415-239-5692. BUDGET.

Although not just for gay and lesbian travelers, **Dolores Park Inn** sits in a garden behind a wrought-iron fence in the heart of the Castro. This four-guest-room bed-and-breakfast, built in 1874, is filled with antiques, and one room has a four-poster Victorian bed. There are also a formal dining room and a double parlor, both with fireplaces. A full breakfast is served, as is afternoon coffee, wine, and tea. ~ 3641 17th Street; phone/fax 415-621-0482.

The **Inn San Francisco** resides in a 19th-century world. Set in a grand four-story Victorian, this splendid mansion has been furnished entirely with period pieces. There are gilded mirrors and beveled glass in the parlors, wall sconces and marble sinks in many rooms, as well as other antique flourishes. There is a rooftop sundeck, which provides a great view of the city, and an English garden in the back with a gazebo and hot tub. Room prices in this elegant establishment are moderate with shared bath, deluxe with private facilities, or ultra-deluxe with hot tubs or jacuzzis. The clientele is both gay and straight. ~ 943 South Van Ness Avenue; 415-641-0188, 800-359-0913, fax 415-641-1701. MODERATE TO ULTRA-DELUXE.

Midway between Castro Street and the Haight-Ashbury neighborhood is the **Metro Hotel**. Appealing to a mixed clientele, there are 23 rooms, a small lobby, an adjoining café downstairs, and an English garden. The guests rooms are carpeted wall-to-wall, furnished with oak pieces, and decorated with wallhangings. Each has a private bath (shower only) and color television with cable. Set in a white stucco building, it is clean and comfortable. While the location is not ideal, it is close enough to key neighborhoods to make the hotel worth the cost of admission. ~ 319 Divisadero Street; 415-861-5364, fax 415-863-1970. BUDGET TO MODERATE.

The **Hotel Casa Loma** once billed itself as "San Francisco's landmark hotel exclusively for gay men and women." It now caters to a mixed clientele. In addition to serving overnight guests, it functions as a residence club featuring weekly rates. There is a sundeck that attracts both a local and out-of-town crowd. The 48 rooms have either a shared or private bath and are attractively furnished with patterned wallpaper and old-style wallhangings. ~ 610 Fillmore Street; 415-552-7100, fax 415-552-4626. BUDGET.

The **Alamo Square Inn** offers not one but two Victorian mansions, a Queen Anne and a Tudor Revival, both predating the 1906 earthquake by a decade. The bed-and-breakfast hostelry, which welcomes both gays and straights, is just a ten-minute walk from Castro Street and offers a choice of nine individually decorated rooms, a self-contained apartment and three suites, including one with a sunken jacuzzi and private deck. ~ 719 Scott Street; 415-922-2055, 800-345-9888, fax 415-931-1304. MODERATE TO ULTRA-DELUXE.

Those in search of the quintessential "Painted Lady" Victorian will not want to miss **Chateau Tivoli**, a dazzling 1892 mansion resplendent with gold leaf, stained-glass windows, and elaborate iron grillwork. There are even antique pieces that belonged to Sally Stanford, a real painted lady and madam in San Francisco. Accommodations include five rooms, three suites, and one apartment, most with private marble bathrooms and some with canopy beds, fireplaces, and private decks. The clientele is both straight and gay. ~ 1057 Steiner Street; 415-776-5462, 800-228-1647, fax 415-776-0505. DELUXE TO ULTRA-DELUXE.

A European-style boutique hotel, the **Leland Hotel** offers 108 rooms, most with private baths and sunny bay windows, and 16 studio apartments. Most guests are gay men, but women are also welcome. Right in the midst of the Polk Street bar-and-restaurant scene, the hotel bar is a popular gay gathering spot. ~ 1315 Polk Street; 415-441-5141, 800-258-4458, fax 415-441-1449. BUDGET TO MODERATE.

DINING

Over in the Castro Street neighborhood, **Caffe Luna Piena** is a good choice for a casual meal. You can dine indoors or outside on a tree-studded patio. Open all day, they feature a breakfast menu that includes poached eggs, omelettes, and eggs Benedict. Lunch consists of hamburgers, sandwiches, salads, pasta, and quiche. The restaurant serves dinner as well. Closed Monday for dinner only. ~ 558 Castro Street; 415-621-2566. MODERATE.

Anchor Oyster Bar is a hole-in-the-wall café which happens to serve delicious shellfish. There are oysters on the half shell, steamed clams and mussels, seafood cocktails, and various daily specials. Recommended for lunch or dinner. ~ 579 Castro Street; 415-431-3990. MODERATE.

Hot 'N' Hunky, an impeccably designed burger joint, appeals to both gays and lesbians and packs them in from 11 a.m. to midnight (1 a.m. Friday and Saturday). The decor is classic diner with black-and-white tiled floor, formica-topped tables, a jukebox in the center, and pictures of Marilyn Monroe on the walls. Hot "N" Hunky serves 17 kinds of burgers, as well as hot dogs and other sandwiches. ~ 4039 18th Street; 415-621-6365. BUDGET.

For a bite between bar hopping or a quick snack, try **Tom Peasant Pies**. This shop has a few stools and a counter, but the business is mostly carryout. There's a good selection of sweet and savory pies that include clam and tomato, ratatouille and brown rice, leek and red peppers, mushroom and zucchini, almond chocolate, and apple cinnamon. ~ 4117 18th Street; 415-621-3632. BUDGET.

A good place after a late movie at the Castro Theater is **Orphan Andy's**, one of the few San Francisco restaurants open 24 hours. Decorated with a colorful 1950s diner theme with a counter and leatherette booths, Orphan Andy's serves good burgers, sandwiches, omelettes, and other classic coffee-shop fare. ~ 3991 17th Street; 415-864-9795. BUDGET.

Exceptionally popular with the locals, **Cafe Flore** has a partially enclosed outside patio, where diners can watch life in the Castro go by. Inside, the floor is tiled, the atmosphere casual and relaxed. You order at the window from a blackboard menu listing soups, pastas, sandwiches, and burgers. There's also an espresso bar. ~ 2298 Market Street; 415-621-8579. BUDGET.

A gathering spot for casual meals and women's entertainment is **Red Dora's Bearded Lady Women's Café**. Open from morning to early evening, the café offers breakfast specials, salads, and hearty soups. Live music and spoken-word entertainment is often presented on weekends. ~ 485 14th Street; 415-626-2805. BUDGET.

Open for breakfast and lunch, catering to a mixed clientele, and particularly popular with women, is **Just For You**. This diner in the Potrero Hill district has counter service and tables and is decorated with photographs and artwork by local artists. The cuisine is a mix of American and Cajun, with cornmeal pancakes and grits for breakfast, hamburgers and crabcake sandwiches at lunch. ~ 1453 18th Street; 415-647-3033. BUDGET.

Dollar for dollar, the best dining spot along Polk Street is **Swan Oyster Depot**. It's a short-order place serving fresh prawns, crabs, lobster, shrimp, and oysters, all displayed in trays out front. The place consists simply of a counter lined with stools and is always packed. Lunch lingers into late afternoon, but no dinner is served. Closed Sunday. ~ 1517 Polk Street; 415-673-1101. MODERATE.

Running a close second is **The Grubstake**, a brightly painted café adorned with a skylight and exotic murals. The menu consists of hamburgers, sandwiches, salads, and omelettes. At night they serve pork chops, steaks, and a daily fish special. Better yet, it stays open until 4 a.m. Lunch is only served on the weekend. ~ 1525 Pine Street; 415-673-8268. BUDGET TO MODERATE.

HIDDEN ►

There are about a thousand restaurants in San Francisco named Hunan, and the second most popular name seems to be Cordon Bleu. The place claiming to be the original **Cordon Bleu Vietnamese Restaurant** is a simple café-style establishment serving a wide array of Southeast Asian dishes. There are imperial rolls, shishkabobs, beef dishes, and five-spice roast chicken. Closed Monday. ~ 1574 California Street; 415-673-5637. BUDGET.

SHOPPING

The Castro Street shopping district stretches along Castro from 19th Street to Market Street, then continues for several blocks on "Upper Market"; there are also several interesting stores along 18th Street. The entire area is surprisingly compact, but features a variety of shops. Together with Polk Street, it represents the major gay shopping area in San Francisco.

For beads, turquoise and silver jewelry, as well as other bodily adornments, try **The Bead Store**. It's a tiny one-room shop positively crammed with attractive items. ~ 417 Castro Street; 415-861-7332.

Speaking of generic names, how about **Brand X Antiques**? They feature an assortment of antiques and decorative artworks

SHOPPING FOR A GOOD CAUSE

Shopping at **Under One Roof** is like giving to a good cause. This store is underwritten by corporations, so 100 percent of the profits are donated to more than 60 northern California AIDS service organizations. It sells a wide selection of items, including candles, soaps, lotions, coffee, candy, T-shirts, jewelry, and gay and lesbian books. ~ 2362-B Market Street; 415-252-9430.

that are perfect as gifts and souvenirs. Estate jewelry is another very popular part of their line. Silver cigarette cases, glass figurines, Chinese Buddhas, rare porcelain, and objets d'art are among the extraordinary pieces in this fascinating shop. ~ 570 Castro Street; 415-626-8908.

Headlines is San Francisco's answer to a gay department store. Each of these sprawling shops features sections devoted to clothing, novelty buttons, housewares, greeting cards, jewelry, teddy bears, and knickknacks. To shop the Castro Street corridor and bypass Headlines is like window browsing New York and ignoring Bloomingdales. ~ 2301 Chestnut Street, 549 and 557 Castro Street, and 838 Market Street; 415-956-4872.

Along "Upper Market," there's **Image Leather** for black leather. ~ 2199 Market Street; 415-621-7551.

Good Vibrations, a sex toy, book, and video emporium designed in the late 1970s especially for women, has become a San Francisco institution. The store sells erotic literature, self-help sex books, feminist erotica, videos and sex education films, and an unbeatable array of vibrators and electric massagers. A highlight of the store is an antique vibrator museum with some rather unusual items like a cranked version that looks like a rolling pin. ~ 1210 Valencia Street; 415-074-8980.

Polk Street is wall-to-wall with designer fashion shops, boutiques, and all manner of clothing outlets. The central gay area stretches from Post Street to Washington Street, but savvy shoppers will continue on to Union Street, since several intriguing stores lie on the outskirts of the neighborhood.

A wonderfully cluttered antique store called **J. Goldsmith Antiques** has a marvelous collection of miniatures here, as well as old bottles, toys, and jewelry. The perfect place on a leisurely afternoon. ~ 1924 Polk Street; 415-771-4055.

At the **Tibet Shop** are *sili* bangles, painted lanterns, Buddha figurines, prayer beads, and monastic incense. This wonderful little shop also has vests, skirts, dresses, shirts, and jackets made in Nepal and Afghanistan. ~ 1807 Polk Street; 415-982-0326.

Rockstars sells rock and heavy-metal memorabilia, with a good selection of posters, patches, stickers, pins, jewelry, and buttons. ~ 1429 Polk Street; 415-928-7625.

NIGHTLIFE

One example of San Francisco's wide-open tradition is the presence of almost 200 gay bars in the city. There's everything here from rock clubs to piano bars to stylish cabarets. Some are strictly gay, others mix their customers, and some have become so popular that straights have begun to take them over from gays.

There are a dozen or so bars in the Castro Street area, many open from early morning until the wee hours. Among the nicest is

Twin Peaks Tavern with its overhead fans and mirrored bar. ~ 401 Castro Street; 415-864-9470.

Across the street and down a few doors is the disco-blasting **Castro Station.** ~ 456-B Castro Street; 415-626-7220.

Nearby, a large brass rail dominates the window of the **Phoenix.** Weekend cover. ~ 482 Castro Street; 415-552-6827.

A foot-stompin' gay country-and-western dance club in the South of Market area, **Rawhide 2** features music with a deejay every night. Free country-and-western dance classes are offered on week nights. ~ 280 7th Street; 415-621-1197.

Nearby, you'll find **The Stud**, everybody's favorite gay bar. Everybody in this case includes aging hippies, multihued punks, curious straights, and even a gay or two, all packed elbow to armpit into this pulsing club. Cover on most nights. ~ 399 9th Street; 415-863-6623.

The scene is different down the street at the **San Francisco Eagle**, a leather bar. ~ 398 12th Street; 415-626-0880.

San Francisco's lesbian bars are located not only around Valencia Street, but in other parts of the city as well. Catering primarily to women, **The Café San Marcos** is a mirrored club with lots of neon, pool tables, pinball machines, and two full bars. There's DJ music nightly in the lounge. ~ 2367 Market Street; 415-861-3846.

A Bernal Heights bar, **The Wild Side West** operates out of a purple Victorian house. The bar is open to all, but is mainly frequented by women. The red walls and ceiling are adorned with photos and paintings, as well as masks, vintage clothing, and shoes. Guests can play video games, enjoy music from the jukebox, listen to a jug band or even step up to the bongos. ~ 424 Cortland Street; 415-647-3099.

A cabaret offering comedy, theater, and music, **Josie's Cabaret and Juice Joint** produces everything from standup routines to plays on the tragedy of AIDS. Each month the walls of this renovated warehouse are graced with a new art show. ~ 3583 16th Street; 415-861-7933.

For women who are ready to relax after a day of shopping, there's **Osento Bath House**, a quiet and comfortable Japanese-style bath for women. The tiled bath is located in a sunny room; there are also massage and sauna facilities and a deck for lounging. Open from 1 p.m. to 1 a.m. ~ 955 Valencia Street; 415-282-6333.

Club Universe is the hottest gay dance club on Saturday nights. Deejays spin a mix of techno, house, and disco dance music. Cover. ~ 177 Townsend Street; 415-974-6020.

Plays with gay and lesbian themes are the focus of **Theatre Rhinoceros**, an acclaimed company that presents performances at two theaters, Rhino's Mainstage and Rhino's Studio. ~ 2926 16th Street; 415-861-5079.

San Francisco's answer to off-off-Broadway is **The Marsh Theater**, a small, informal theater billed as a "breeding ground for new performers," which offers plays and spoken-word entertainment frequently, but not exclusively, on women's topics. Monday nights are reserved for performers trying out new work. ~ 1062 Valencia Street; 415-641-0235.

Over in the Polk Street neighborhood, the **Polk Gulch Saloon** starts early and parties late. With its raw-wood interior the place has an open air about it. ~ 1100 Polk Street; 415-771-2022. Nicest of all the neighborhood bars, however, is **Kimo's**. With mirrors and potted palms all around, it's a comfortable atmosphere. ~ 1351 Polk Street; 415-885-4535. Another attractively appointed rendezvous is the oak-and-brass **Giraffe.** ~ 1131 Polk Street; 415-474-1702.

The **N'Touch** has a disco dancefloor plus a bank of video monitors. There is always a lively crowd here. With flashing lights and ample sound, it's a good spot for dancing and carousing. Cover on weekends. ~ 1548 Polk Street; 415-441-8413.

For live entertainment, check out **The Q. T.** Open seven nights a week, it has live music Wednesday through Saturday, featuring local bands as well as hot sounds from out of town. ~ 1312 Polk Street; 415-885-1114.

Mission District

Depending on your personal taste or maybe just your mood, you'll come away from the Mission District thinking it either a poem or a ghetto. In truth, it's both. "The Mission," San Francisco's own Spanish barrio, is the vibrant home of the city's Mexican, Colombian, Guatemalan, Nicaraguan, and Salvadoran population. It's a neighborhood where brilliant murals vie with graffiti-scrawled walls, and where children compete with old folks for a seat on the bus or park bench.

Now that Hong Kong investors and bohemian artists have discovered the place, the Mission is becoming even more cosmopolitan. Valencia Street represents the city's main lesbian enclave and 16th Street has become a countercultural center complete with cafés and galleries.

SIGHTS

The *corazón* of the Mission is 24th Street with its outdoor markets and indoor murals. Start your tour at 24th and York streets, about six blocks east of Mission Street.

St. Francis Candies, right on the corner, is a classic. With its cozy booths, old-fashioned fountain, and pink ceiling, the place seems suspended in time since 1955. Actually this after-school ice cream parlor dates from 1918.

Those **murals** in the park across the street are a striking example of *la raza* (the Hispanic people). The artists who worked those walls might be part of the ever-changing exhibits at **Galería de la Raza.** Innovative and provocative, the gallery is as liable to feature a show on the revolutionary movement in El Salvador as a photographic display or artistic exhibit. Closed Sunday and Monday. ~ 2851 24th Street; 415-826-8009.

Another **mural** on the side of 2884 24th Street depicts scenes which also correspond with this theme, and the painting on the facade of **China Books** offers a kaleidoscopic image of village life worldwide. Closed Sunday. ~ 2929 24th Street; 415-282-2994.

Even the alleyways hereabouts are home to art—check out the colorful **children's mural** decorating the Mission Neighborhood Family Center on the corner of 24th Street and Balmy Avenue.

There's more street art just past South Van Ness Avenue—a **wall mural** depicting multihued parrots and thrashing fish. Then, space age counterpoint to this folk art, is the **mural** at 24th and Mission streets, illustrating San Francisco's modernistic BART subways.

If 24th Street is the heart of the barrio, **Mission Street** is its nerve center, a neon ganglia delivering electric charges throughout the community. By day it's a collection of shoe stores, hair salons, and pawn shops. At night, particularly on weekends, the area is transformed into a cruising strip. Although the gaudy, outrageous low-riders have been pushed out of the Mission in recent years, there are still plenty of macho cars competing with spit-shine sleek vans with multicolored designs.

Surprisingly, just one block from this area is **Valencia Street,** center of the city's lesbian community. Along this nondescript thoroughfare are bars, baths, bookstores, and cafés serving the women's community. The **Women's Building** is an important gathering place here. ~ 3543 18th Street; 415-431-1180.

Unless you've sidetracked down Mission or Valencia, you're still on the corner of 24th and Mission, staring at that futuristic mural. Cross Mission and continue along 24th Street uphill several

HIDDEN ►

blocks to **Quane Street.** Walk the three-block length of this alleyway and you'll be convinced the city fathers and mothers meant to name it Quaint Street. It's not much—just picket fences, shade trees, and clapboard houses—but rarely has so little spoken so eloquently.

When this woodframe corridor debouches into 21st Street, turn left, then take a quick right onto Dolores Street. Head down for one block and take a right onto Liberty Street for a view of some magnificent old Victorians. That Italianate-style home at 159 Liberty is the old **Murphy House.** Built in 1878, the place gained notoriety in 1896 when the famous suffragette Susan B. Anthony visited. Five other majestic Victorians, including a turreted Queen Anne–style structure, sit just beyond this fine old home.

Back on **Dolores Street,** you can continue downhill along one of San Francisco's prettiest boulevards. Bordered on either side by bay window homes, Dolores Street's proudest feature is the grassy median planted with stately palm trees. Better still, this marvelous promenade opens onto **Dolores Park**, between Dolores and 20th streets, a rectangle of rolling hills dotted with magnolia and pepper trees. You can follow the sinuous walkways down to the tennis courts or head for the high ground and a luxurious view of the city.

The Mission District is the city's sunniest sector, and there's no better place than Dolores Park for hanging out, people watching, and sunbathing.

Farther downhill, at Dolores and 16th streets, stands the historic building that gave the neighborhood its name. Crown jewel of the city, **Mission San Francisco de Asís**, or Mission Dolores, completed in 1791, was one of the 21 Spanish missions built along the California coast by Franciscans. Its thick adobe walls (and perhaps a few prayers) helped the church survive the earthquake and fire; today it is the city's oldest building. Here you can wander back to the last great days of the Spanish empire: the tabernacle door came from the Philippines, parts of the altar were imported from Mexico, the ceiling design was borrowed from Costanoan Indians—all unfortunate subjects of 18th-century Spain. There's a mini-museum behind the chapel and a massive 20th-century basilica next door, but the most intriguing feature on the mission grounds is the cemetery. Studded with yew trees and tombstones, it is the last resting place of several famous (and infamous) San Francisco figures. Captain Louis Antonio Arguello, California's first Mexican governor, and Father Francisco Palou, the mission's architect, are interred here. So are Charles Cora and James Casey, a notorious pair who died at the hands of San Francisco's Vigilance Committee. Admission. ~ 415-621-8203.

DINING

The blue lilac walls, paintings, and statuary add to the charm of **Bangkok 16**. Thai specialties served at your candlelit table include duck in a spicy lemon sauce, calamari salad, yellow curry, pad Thai noodles, lamb on a skewer served with a peanut sauce, and filet of snapper in a spicy tamarind sauce. Try the fried bananas for dessert. Dinner only. ~ 3214 16th Street; 415-431-5838. BUDGET TO MODERATE.

In Brittany, **Ti-Couz** means The Old House, and worn hardwood floors, blue-and-white-painted walls, and wooden china cabinets give it that homey feeling. But it's the crêpes that draw the crowds. Made from buckwheat flour in the style of Brittany, the crêpes are cooked to order one at a time, filled with cheese, sausage, or smoked salmon, and garnished with crème fraîche. Flavored butters, ice cream, white chocolate, and fruit are folded into the sweet crêpes. Delicious. ~ 3108 16th Street; 415-252-7373. BUDGET.

◄ HIDDEN

It looks and smells like south of the border in **La Cumbre**. By the size of the crowd here, those rumors about the best burritos must be true. For a price comfortable to any budget, you can order pork, tongue, chicken, or steak burritos, as well as tacos and other Mexican finger foods. They also feature vegetarian selections at this simple but special taquería. ~ 515 Valencia Street; 415-863-8205. BUDGET.

HIDDEN ►

The Slanted Door gets rave reviews from Mission residents. This simple storefront done in greens, with green-topped tables and wooden chairs, may be a bit spartan, but the food has an incredible following. Specialties include green papaya salad, chicken and rice in clay pot, and caramelized shrimp. The restaurant also serves a selection of premium teas from China, some of which have medicinal properties. ~ 584 Valencia Street; 415-861-8032. BUDGET.

Entering **Arabian Nights** is like stepping into a Middle Eastern bazaar. Afghan carpets decorate the dimly lit dining room and gold-threaded scarves hang from the ceiling. There's Egyptian music and belly dancing nightly, with male belly dancing on Saturday night. The menu includes shish kabob, roast rack of lamb, stuffed catfish, and a vegetarian plate laden with humus, baba ghanouj, cheese, olives, and grape leaves. ~ 811 Valencia Street; 415-821-9747. MODERATE.

It's Christmas every day at **La Rondalla**. Where else will you encounter gold tinsel decor in the middle of July? Not to mention multihued foil snowflakes and a religious scene illuminated with, you guessed it, Christmas lights. The menu is nearly as unique: those pots on the stove are liable to contain *albóndigas* (meatball soup) or even *birria de chivo* (barbecued goat meat). For the less daring, there are enchiladas, rellenos, *y mucho más*. Closed Monday. ~ 901 Valencia Street; 415-647-7474. BUDGET TO MODERATE.

Esperpento shines among the city's many tapas places, distinguished by its colorful atmosphere. Fans, ceramic plates, shawls, and pictures of bullfights adorn the walls, and the tables are painted with flowers and giant suns. You can linger over plates of paella and tapas of fried fish, garlic shrimp, pork kebab, and salads, while enjoying lively conversation and good Spanish wine. ~ 3295 22nd Street; 415-282-8867. MODERATE.

Over in the Potrero Hill area, about a mile east of the Mission District, is **Garibaldi Café**. Clever decor and excellent value belie the drab look outside. The menu changes daily and encompasses fish, chicken, and few meat dishes. There are specials such as tuna wrapped in grape leaves and salmon with raspberry-brandy sauce (risky, but successful). Closed Sunday. ~ 1600 17th Street; 415-552-3325. MODERATE.

Nearby, the cheery and modest **S. Asimakopoulos Café** is a prime example of San Francisco neighborhood dining. The menu is solidly, but not overbearingly, Greek. There is moussaka, yes, but also a mild lemon chicken, for instance. Tremendous value. ~ 288 Connecticut Street; 415-552-8789. MODERATE.

West of the Mission District in the Noe Valley area, there's an understated Mediterranean restaurant called **Panos'**. It's a neighborhood place nicely decorated with artwork and black marble floors featuring a seafood menu. Among the dinner entrées are grilled ahi tuna, seafood Aegean, and pasta. Carnivores can cut into grilled lamb medallions or herb-roasted half chicken. It's also open for lunch and weekend brunch. ~ 4000 24th Street; 415-824-8000. MODERATE.

SHOPPING

This Latin American neighborhood favors shoe stores, groceries, and novelty shops over boutiques and galleries. There are, however, a few old-timey stores, plus one screamingly modern place. For unusual clothing, how about flesh-tight Highway Patrol pants, a police badge, or Cromwell field boots? These and more at **Caleb Smith Uniforms**. ~ 2298 Mission Street; 415-861-7165.

Then there's **Arik Surplus**, stocking American Army surplus clothing. They also have outdoor wear, boots, camping equipment, and rain gear. ~ 2650 Mission Street; 415-285-4770.

The Mission is known for its secondhand shops, but few beat **Community Thrift Store**. When people donate items to this massive emporium of previously owned furniture, books, posters, records, dishes, and clothes, they designate their favorite charity, which receives the proceeds. Because of the store's policy, it receives better than average donations. ~ 623 Valencia Street; 415-861-4910.

The Mission offers perhaps the richest and most eclectic mix of used and special-interest book stores in the city. An invaluable aid for exploring the district is "The Book Lovers Guide to the Mission," a free map available at various locations in the area, which covers not only book stores but also restaurants, art galleries, special services, and one-of-a-kind shops.

The **Book Building** at 2141 Mission Street offers worthwhile places to browse. Go to **Bolerium Books** for writing on American labor and social history. ~ 415-863-6353. **Meyer Boswell Books** has books on historic and current law. ~ 415-255-6400. **Tall Stories** specializes in 19th- and 20th-century literature, including many first editions. ~ 415-255-1915.

NOE VALLEY

Noe Valley, a district near the Mission, features an opportunity to shop far from the tourist areas. All along 24th Street between Church and Castro streets, small stores line either side of the road. There are bookstores, galleries, handicrafts shops, open-air fruit stalls, and numerous other locally owned establishments. There's a distinctive neighborhood feeling here, which makes shoppers seem more like friends than consumers.

Of all the used bookstores in the Mission, none is more pleasant to browse than **The Abandoned Planet Bookstore.** Neatly arranged books, dark woods, and a red carpet create a used-book lovers' heaven. There are easy chairs for serious readers and a resident cat to pet. ~ 518 Valencia Street; 415-861-4695.

Specializing in books on contemporary culture, feminism, sexuality, and politics is **Modern Times Books**, which also has a multicultural, international selection of children's books. ~ 888 Valencia Street; 415-282-9246.

Captain Jack's is a favorite source of vintage clothing. Here you can find dresses and suits from the 1940s and 1950s, sailor pants, bowling shirts, leather jackets, and velvet goods. ~ 866 Valencia Street; 415-648-1065.

Hocus Pocus is not your average antique store. Far from it. Scores of chairs, lamps, and chandeliers hang from the ceiling. Cases of crystal door knobs and jewelry, and shelves of silver pitchers and candle holders crowd the floor. And endless framed prints and paintings decorate one wall. It may take the help of a magic wand to maneuver through this store, but you're sure to find a hidden treasure. ~ 900 Valencia Street; 415-824-2901.

NIGHTLIFE **Cesar's Latin Palace**, way out in the Mission District, features live music with a salsa beat. The ballroom is as big as a warehouse, with enough tables and dance space to fit a Latin American army. It's hot. Cover Thursday through Sunday. ~ 3140 Mission Street; 415-648-6611.

Many of the city's important experimental theater groups are located in or near the Mission District. Among them is **Theatre Artaud.** ~ 450 Florida Street; 415-621-7797.

This area is also home to many outstanding dance companies. Featuring modern and experimental dance, they include the **Margaret Jenkins Dance Company.** ~ 3973-A 25th Street; 415-863-1173. Also based in the Mission is the **Oberlin Dance Company.** ~ 3153 17th Street; 415-863-6606. **Della Davidson Dance Company** is another leading troupe. ~ 440 16th Street; 415-695-2979.

South of Market

Just 20 years ago, South of Market, popularly known as SOMA, had the reputation as one of the most unattractive and unsafe neighborhoods in the city. Filled with residential hotels, vacant warehouses, and seedy bars, it was ignored by many of the city's residents. This neglect presented an opportunity for those who wanted to be isolated, and in the '70s SOMA became a hub for the gay-bathhouse crowd and the gay-leather crowd.

During the '80s SOMA metamorphosed again. Gay bathhouses were closed in a sweeping move by government officials and replaced by trendy nightclubs; gay-leather bars with names like "The Arena" converted into popular dance clubs with names like the "DNA Lounge."

The underutilized warehouses then brought in a different countercultural crowd—artists. Modeling themselves after the residents of New York City's SOHO (South of Houston) district, Bay Area artists converted SOMA warehouses into combination live/work spaces featuring art galleries, music studios, and performance spaces. Many of San Francisco's most creative people still live and display (or perform) in small galleries and theaters throughout SOMA. Independent retailers also took advantage of the cheap warehouse space by opening large factory outlets and discount stores. These were followed in the '90s by national superstores.

Catering to this modern urban crowd are many restaurants and cafés that offer a true SOMA twist to their atmosphere and menu. Don't be surprised if your café table has a computer hooked up to the Internet or the restaurant you're dining at has decor created during the slow hours before lunch.

SIGHTS

Named for George Moscone, the San Francisco mayor assassinated in 1978, **Moscone Center** is a mammoth convention center which extends across 11 acres. With restaurants, hotels, apartments, and stores encircling it like satellites, the center is the dominant feature in San Francisco's fastest-changing district. ~ Howard Street between 3rd and 4th streets.

An important new addition to the area is **Yerba Buena Gardens**, a project that was 30 years in the making but is proving to be worth the wait by providing a new forum for the visual and performing arts as well as some much needed green space.

One component of the ten-acre complex located on top of the underground Moscone Convention Center is the **Center for the Arts at Yerba Buena Gardens** with two buildings, one designed by the acclaimed Japanese architect, Fumihiko Maki. It includes three galleries devoted primarily to the works of Northern California artists and a screening room for video and film. (Open Tuesday through Sunday from 11 a.m. to 6 p.m.) The other is a 750-seat theater offering a diverse lineup of music, dance, and performance art. Softening the contemporary hard edges of Yerba Buena is a five-and-a-half-acre esplanade of gardens and outdoor public art. Admission. ~ 415-978-2787.

The **San Francisco Museum of Modern Art**'s popularity soared after it moved to its current South of Market location in early 1995, and it is now one of the top-ten most visited museums in the United States. The building, designed by Swiss architect Mario Botta, is a Modernist work of art in itself, distinguished by a tower finished in alternating bands of black and white stone. Inside are three large galleries and more than 20 smaller ones, totaling 50,000 square feet. The first floor displays selections from the museum's permanent collection. The second-floor gallery features photographs and works on paper. The top two gallery floors accommodate special exhibitions and large-scale art from the museum's collection. ~ 151 3rd Street; 415-357-4000.

A focal point of Yerba Buena Gardens is the Martin Luther King Jr. Memorial, a graceful waterfall spilling over Sierra granite.

One of SOMA's more prominent galleries, **The Ansel Adams Center** features five galleries of fine art photography. Four of them have changing exhibits that range from 19th century to contemporary. The fifth and most popular gallery is devoted exclusively to the works of Ansel Adams. Closed Monday. Admission. ~ 250 4th Street; 415-495-7000.

HIDDEN ►

The **Cartoon Art Museum** is also located in the Yerba Buena neighborhood. The museum features rotating exhibits of cartoon art in all its various incarnations: newspaper strips, political cartoons, comic books, and animation are amply represented. Highlights include a children's gallery and an interactive CD-ROM room. One of only three such museums of its kind in the United States, this rare treat should not be missed. Closed Monday and Tuesday. Admission. ~ 814 Mission Street; 415-227-8666.

Tucked into an area between Bryant, Brannan, Second, and Third streets is **South Park**, an oval-shaped park ringed by cafés and artists' studios. The surrounding neighborhood is an industrial district that in recent years has drawn artists and multimedia companies in search of loft space in converted warehouses.

A place to appreciate the urban artistic vitality of the area is **Capp Street Project**, a former warehouse that offers artists both housing and exhibition areas on two floors connected by a central steel staircase. The changing shows concentrate on contemporary "alternative" art by both local and international artists. Closed Sunday and Monday. ~ 525 2nd Street; 415-495-7101.

To see a startling example of the force with which the 1906 earthquake warped and buckled San Francisco buildings, drive down the alleyway between 5th and 6th streets just south of Mission Street to **479 and 483 Tehama Street**. These old warehouses look like the earth collapsed beneath them at the same time a giant hand shoved them backwards.

DINING

Among several trendy restaurants here is the **Cadillac Bar**, a raucous Mexican eatery that may be the noisiest place you've ever entered. The bar itself is *muy grande*, a massive wood structure adorned with sombreros and a wall-length mirror. Cooking is by mesquite grill (what else?). The menu ain't your standard south of the border inventory. We're talking prawns with *aguacate* sauce, red snapper with sautéed chiles, marinated skirt steak, and chicken stuffed with jalapeños and bacon. Warehouse chic. ~ 1 Holland Court; 415-543-8226. MODERATE.

It's not every day you can enjoy a dry martini while seated at a curved pink leatherette bar right out of the '50s and then be treated to a postmodern nouvelle American dinner, but that's the case at **Julie's Supper Club**. Despite the loud music, insist on a table in the front room, to enjoy the passing array of trendy SOMA club-goers. Stick with the imaginative salads for starters, followed by outstanding chicken, lamb, or fish dishes. Closed Sunday. ~ 1123 Folsom Street; 415-861-4084. MODERATE TO DELUXE.

More than just the cuisine is noteworthy at **Eleven**. This Italian restaurant, which features regional dishes from all over Italy, also sports a sophisticated decor. The antiqued walls are painted with grapevines and set off by a loft ceiling, creating an al fresco atmosphere. Closed Sunday. ~ 374 11th Street; 415-431-3337. MODERATE.

A hot spot not far from the new Yerba Buena Gardens complex is **Restaurant Lulu**, a noisy warehouse-sized restaurant that draws in crowds at lunch and dinner for superb meats and chicken prepared on a brick rotisserie. Also noteworthy are the shellfish selections such as iron skillet–roasted mussels and Dungeness crab with garlic. So popular is Lulu that it has spawned one off-shoot at the same location: the more casual **Lulu Café**, open for breakfast, lunch, and dinner and specializing in light antipasto items. At night, Lulu Café offers the option of dining off the regular Lulu menu. ~ 816 Folsom Street; 415-495-5775. MODERATE TO DELUXE.

In the morning **South Park Café** is a casual coffee-and-croissant place for folks who live and work in the area. At lunch and dinner the café, which has only a long bar and a few tables, is a popular gourmet dining spot known for imaginative salads and daily meat and fish specials. In the early evening there's a special tapas menu. Closed Sunday. ~ 108 South Park; 415-495-7275. MODERATE.

Or try **Max's Diner**, the '90s version of a classic old diner. The music is vintage, the menu is meat and potatoes, and the bar is jammed with nostalgic people. ~ 311 3rd Street; 415-546-6297. MODERATE.

If you're looking to nosh on a bagel, pizza, sandwich, or salad while your duds spin around in the suds, drop by **Brain Wash**. This innovative address combines a café with a laundromat. ~ 1122 Folsom Street; 415-861-3663. BUDGET.

Open until the wee hours, **Hamburger Mary's** draws gays and straights alike. When the crowd is not drinking famous daiquiris in Cissy's Saloon, it's gorging on hamburgers, sandwiches, and omelettes. ~ 1582 Folsom Street; 415-626-5767. MODERATE.

A kind of faux Pompeiian eatery, **Café Rustico** offers excellent pizza, panini, calzone, sandwiches, and salads. Homemade soups, quiche, vegetarian lasagna, and tasty tarts are also served in the dining area or at sidewalk tables. Convenient to the South of Market discount outlets, this is the place to refuel on the bargain trail. ~ 300 DeHaro Street; 415-252-0180. BUDGET.

SHOPPING Headquarters for discount shopping in San Francisco is the South of Market area—outlets sell everything from leotards to wedding dresses. The best time to visit is early Saturday morning, before the vanloads of out-of-town shoppers begin arriving. The very nature of off-price boutiques means limited hours and often limited lifespans; always try to call in advance to check hours of operation. Concentrated in the blocks bounded by Market and Townsend, 2nd and 9th streets are a variety of concerns:

Brand-name apparel for the whole family, as well as some jewelry, is discounted as much as 40 to 70 percent at **Six Sixty Center.** Open Sunday from noon until 5 p.m. ~ 660 3rd Street; 415-227-0464.

For terrific bargains on tapes and CDs go to the **Tower Record Outlet.** ~ 660 3rd Street; 415-957-9660.

The highly regarded auction house **Butterfield & Butterfield** has regular sales that are open to the public. ~ 220 San Bruno Avenue; 415-861-7500.

The ultimate cut-rate camping and sports emporium, **North Face** outlet sells tents, clothing, sleeping bags, backpacks, and other equipment, with a continually changing stock in a huge warehouse space. ~ 1325 Howard Street; 415-626-6444.

Also located South of Market is the **Flower Mart,** where dozens of florists offer excellent prices. ~ 6th and Brannan streets.

Walking or driving around will net additional possibilities, from seconds outlets for ceramics to temporary warehouse displays of baskets and wicker furniture.

Slightly farther afield is one of the best outlets in town. The **Esprit Outlet** is a gigantic emporium where most shoppers push grocery carts around to select pants, dresses, blouses, suits, and shoes. ~ 449 Illinois Street; 415-957-2500.

NIGHTLIFE The fanciest club in the hip South-of-Market area is **Club DV8,** with several levels decorated in an eclectic mix ranging from Greco-Roman columns to Keith Haring murals. The music (live and canned) is cutting edge; the crowd is mostly in the 20s-to-30s range with an inclination toward European fashions. Cover. ~ 55 Natoma Street; 415-957-1730.

For some local theater, comedy, improv, or storytelling, check out **Above Brainwash.** There's always something happening on Thursday, Friday, and Saturday night, and also on other nights as well. ~ 1122 Folsom Street; 415-225-4866.

There is only one thing in the world better than a rocking nightclub: three rocking nightclubs. That's what you get over at 3rd and Harrison streets where **The X** (415-979-8686) features modern rock on Friday night. On Saturday **City Nights** (415-979-8686) jumps to the sound of Top-40 hip-hop in the same location. On Thursday, it's gay and lesbian night at **The Box** (415-972-8087). Cover. ~ 715 Harrison Street.

Martini's offers up modern dance music on weekends. Cover on Friday and Saturday. ~ 1015 Folsom Street; 415-431-1200.

Voted Best Brewpub in a local newspaper poll (*Bay Guardian*) two years in a row, **Twenty Tank Brewery** packs in those who prefer a pub to a South of Market club. Formerly a sheet metal shop, this brewery sports 1930s industrial decor and houses brewers who are truly creative, producing such brews as Pollywanna Porter and Kinnikinick Old Scout Stout. While enjoying a beer, you can also throw a few darts, play shuffleboard, watch movies (on Mondays only), or listen to jazz. ~ 316 11th Street; 415-255-9455.

The **DNA Lounge** has lasted much longer than most trendy clubs. The scene is high-decibel with a mixed crowd clearly born to dance. And dance they do, on all sides of an oval bar in the middle of a bare-wood floor. At a quieter upstairs bar you can watch the goings-on. Cover. ~ 375 11th Street; 415-626-1409.

It's a slightly older than usual SOMA crowd that patronizes **Slim's,** possibly because entertainer Boz Scaggs is an owner. Whatever, it's the place where you're most likely to run across a jam session with traveling high-profile musicians. The music may be local bands or legends like Buddy Guy or Bay Area–bred talents such as Huey Lewis. Cover. ~ 333 11th Street; 415-522-0333.

With more than 800 bands performing each year, the **Paradise Lounge** is one of the busiest clubs on the West Coast. Three stages offer as many as five acts nightly. The early-bohemian Above Paradise Room leans toward acoustic performances. In the pumped-up Downstairs Lounge, a kind of 1974 downtown Reno venue, you'll enjoy hard rock and R&B. The Blue Room's main stage is a straight ahead performance space. There's also an elegant turn-of-the-century pool room with walnut wainscotting. ~ 1501 Folsom Street; 415-861-6906.

The San Francisco Mime Troupe has performed musical political satires in the city's parks for a quarter of a century. ~ 855 Treat Avenue; 415-285-1717.

Club TownSend, opened in 1989 in a veritable cavern, that, despite its size, is SRO on weekends. The inevitable doorman picks couples to let in ahead of others from the line outside. Attitude is everything here; those who don't know how to dance to rap music might not fit in. Cover. ~ 177 Townsend Street; 415-974-6020.

With 39 tables, **The Great Entertainer** is one of the largest poolhalls on the West Coast. Located in a former warehouse, this vast establishment also offers snooker tables, shuffleboard, ping pong, darts, and video games. ~ 975 Bryant Street; 415-861-8833.

Located in a renovated licorice factory, **South Beach Billiards** has 35 pool tables as well as a snooker table. This South of Market establishment also has a good sound system. ~ 270 Brannan Street; 415-495-5939.

Waterfront bars are generally attractively appointed and expensive. Not so **Mission Rock Resort**. True, it *is* on San Francisco Bay, but in the South of Market neighborhood, where the specialties are shipyards and factories rather than scenic views. The crowd at the bar is lively, the sundeck warm and inviting, and the drinks are priced to fit small pockets. This is what bars were like back when San Francisco was a sailor's city. ~ 817 China Basin; 415-621-5538.

Golden Gate National Recreation Area

One of San Francisco's most spectacular regions belongs to us all. The Golden Gate National Recreation Area, a 31,000-acre metropolitan park, draws about 25 million visitors annually. A place of natural beauty and historic importance, this magnificent park stretches north from San Francisco throughout much of the Bay Area. In the city itself, the Golden Gate National Recreation Area forms a narrow band around the waterfront. It follows the shoreline of the Bay from Aquatic Park to Fort Mason to the Golden Gate Bridge. On the ocean side it encompasses Land's End, an exotic and untouched preserve, as well as the city's finest beaches.

SIGHTS

The most serene way to begin exploring the Golden Gate National Recreation Area is via the **Golden Gate Promenade**. This three-and-a-half-mile walk will carry you across a swath of heaven that extends from Aquatic Park to the shadows of the Golden Gate Bridge.

Just start in the park and make the short jaunt to the **Municipal Pier**. This hook-shaped cement walkway curls several hundred yards into the Bay. As you follow its curving length a 360° view unfolds—from the Golden Gate to the Bay Bridge, from Mt. Tamalpais to Alcatraz to downtown San Francisco. The pier harbors fisherfolk and seagulls, crabnetters and joggers; few tourists seem to make it out here.

From the pier it's uphill and downstairs to **Fort Mason Center**, a complex of old wharves and tile-roof warehouses that was once a major military embarkation point. Fort Mason today is the cultural heart of avant-garde San Francisco. During the 1970s the warehouses were recycled into offices; over 50 nonprofit organizations subsequently set up shop. ~ Marina Boulevard and Buchanan Street; 415-979-3010.

Nearly all the arts and crafts are represented—several theater groups are home here; there is an on-going series of workshops in dance, creative writing, painting, weaving, printing, sculpture, music, and so on. A number of environmental organizations also have offices in the center. As one brochure describes, "You can see a play, stroll through a museum or gallery, learn how to make poetry films, study yoga, attend a computer seminar, or find out about the rich maritime lore of San Francisco."

At the **San Francisco Craft and Folk Art Museum** exhibitions range from Cook Island quilts to San Simeon architect Julia Morgan's craftware. You'll also want to visit the gift shop where they sell native and tribal goods, as well as a wide variety of jewelry. Admission. ~ Building A; 415-775-0990.

Museo Italo Americano presents samplings of Italian artistry. The museum is dedicated to displaying the works of Italian and Italian-American artists. The permanent collection features the work of several artists, some of whom have made San Francisco their home for years. There are also temporary exhibits ranging from 1930s photos of Italy to a pictorial display of contemporary Italian cinematographers like Francis Ford Coppola, Dino deLaurentiis, Michael Cimino, and Martin Scorcese. Closed Monday and Tuesday. Admission. ~ Building C; 415-673-2200.

For a look at the rich culture of our neighbor to the south, visit the **Mexican Museum.** There are rotating exhibits of pre-Columbian art, Mexican Colonial art, and Mexican-American contemporary art. One outstanding exhibit is the Nelson Rockefeller Collection of Mexican folk art. Closed Monday and Tuesday. Admission. ~ Building D; 415-441-0404.

Permanently docked at one end of Fort Mason is the **S.S. Jeremiah O'Brien,** the only one of 2751 World War II Liberty Ships to remain in original condition. A beamy hulk, the *Jeremiah O'Brien* numbers among its combat ribbons the D-Day invasion of Normandy. Visitors may walk the decks of the old tub, explore the sailors' quarters, and descend into the depths of the engine room. Call ahead for tour information. Admission. ~ 415-441-3101.

Now that you're fully versed in the arts, environment, and World War II history, continue on the shoreline to the **Marina,** along Marina Boulevard. (The remainder of the tour can be completed by car, though walking is definitely the aesthete's and athlete's way.) Some of this sailor-city's spiffiest yachts are docked along the esplanade.

Nearby **Marina Green,** a stretch of park paralleling the Bay, is a landlubber's haven. Bicyclers, joggers, jugglers, soccer players, touch football aficionados, sunbathers, and a world of others inhabit it. The park's most interesting denizens are the kitefliers who fill the blue with a rainbow of soaring colors.

Continue on past a line-up of luxury toys—boats with names like *Haiku*, *Sea Lover*, *Valhalla*, and *Windfall*. When you arrive at the far end of that small green rectangle of park, you'll have to pay special attention to your navigator; you're on Marina Boulevard at the corner of Yacht Road; if going by car, proceed directly ahead through the U.S. Army gate and follow Mason Street, Crissy Field Avenue, and Lincoln Boulevard, paralleling the water, to Fort Point; if on foot, turn right onto Yacht Road, then left at the waterfront, and follow the shoreline toward the Golden Gate Bridge.

Before doing either, you have an alluring detour in store. Turn left at Yacht Road, cross Marina Boulevard, and proceed to that magnificent Beaux-Arts monument looming before you. It's the **Palace of Fine Arts**, a domed edifice built of arches and shadows. Adorned with molded urns and bas-relief figures, it represents the only surviving structure from the 1915 Panama–Pacific International Exposition. Happily, it borders on a sun-shivered pond. The pond in its turn is peopled by mallards and swans, as well as pintails and canvasbacks from out of town. Together, the pool, the pillars, and surrounding park make this one of the city's loveliest spots for sitting and sunning.

But enough for detours; we were embarked on a long march to the bridge. If you cheated and drove, you're already at Fort Point, and we'll catch up with you later; otherwise you're on foot, with the Bay at your side and the Golden Gate dead ahead. This is a land where freighters talk to foghorns, and sloops scud along soundlessly. The waterfront is a sandy beach, a rockpile in seeming upheaval, then beach again, sand dunes, and occasional shade trees. That wooded grove rising to your left is the Presidio; those bald-domed hills across the Bay to the right are the Marin Headlands, and the sharp-rising buildings poking at your back are part of the San Francisco skyline. You'll pass a Coast Guard Station

IT'S HANDS-ON TIME HERE

If education is on your mind, note that the Palace of Fine Arts houses the **Exploratorium.** This "hands-on" museum, with imaginative exhibits demonstrating the principles of optics, sound, animal behavior, etc., was once deemed "the best science museum in the world" by *Scientific American*. It's an intriguing place with constantly changing temporary exhibits and permanent displays that include a "distorted room" lacking right angles and an illusionary mirror into which you seemingly pass. Also check out the Tactile Dome (reservations required), an enclosed crawl-space of textural adventures. Closed Monday. Admission. ~ Marina Boulevard and Lyon Street; 415-561-0360.

and a fishing pier before arriving at the red brick fort that snuggles in the arch of the Golden Gate Bridge.

Modeled on Fort Sumter and completed around the time Confederate forces opened fire on that hapless garrison, **Fort Point National Historic Site** represents the only brick fort west of the Mississippi. With its collection of cannons and Civil War–era exhibits, it's of interest to history buffs. Call for information on guided tours and special programs. ~ End of Marine Drive; 415-556-1693.

From Fort Point, a footpath leads up to the observation area astride the **Golden Gate Bridge**; if driving, take Lincoln Boulevard to the vista point. By whichever route, you'll arrive at "The Bridge at the End of the Continent." Aesthetically, it is considered one of the world's most beautiful spans, a medley of splayed cable and steel struts. Statistically, it represents one of the longest suspension bridges anywhere—6450 feet of suspended concrete and steel, with twin towers the height of 65-story buildings, and cables that support 200 million pounds. It is San Francisco's emblem, an engineering wonder that has come to symbolize an entire metropolis.

If you're game, you can walk across, venturing along a dizzying sidewalk out to one of the most magnificent views you'll ever experience. The Bay from this height is a toy model built to scale; beyond the bridge, San Francisco and Marin, slender arms of land, open onto the boundless Pacific.

The Golden Gate Promenade ends at the bridge, but Lincoln Boulevard continues along the cliffs that mark the ocean side of San Francisco. There are **vista points** overlooking the Pacific and affording startling views back toward the bridge. After about a mile you'll reach **Baker Beach** (off Lincoln Boulevard on Gibson Road), a wide corridor of white sand. Ideal for picnicking and sunbathing, this lovely beach is a favorite among San Franciscans. Adventurers can follow this strand, and the other smaller beaches with which it connects, on a fascinating walk back almost all the way to the Golden Gate Bridge. With the sea unfolding on one side and rocky crags rising along the other, it's definitely worth a little sand in the shoes. As a final reward, there's a **nude beach** on the northern end, just outside the bridge. ◄ HIDDEN

Lincoln Boulevard transforms into El Camino del Mar which winds through Sea Cliff, one of San Francisco's most affluent residential neighborhoods. This exclusive area has something to offer the visitor in addition to its scenic residences—namely **China Beach** (formerly known as James Phelan Beach). More secluded than Baker, this pocket beach is backdropped by a rocky bluff atop which stand the luxurious plate-window homes of Sea Cliff. Named for the Chinese fishermen who camped here in the 19th century, the beach has a dilapidated beach house. (To get there, turn right on 25th Avenue, left on Sea Cliff Avenue, then follow until it dead ends.)

Continuing on El Camino del Mar as it sweeps above the ocean, you'll come upon San Francisco's prettiest museum. With its colonnaded courtyard and arching entranceway, the **Palace of the Legion of Honor** is modeled after a gallery in Paris. Appropriately, it specializes in European art and culture. The exhibits trace European aesthetic achievements from the religious art of the Middle Ages to Renaissance painting, the Baroque and Rococo periods, and the Impressionists of the 19th and 20th centuries. Closed Monday. Admission. ~ 34th Avenue and Clement Street, in Lincoln Park; 415-750-3600.

At Fort Point, if you follow the spiral granite staircase to the roof, you'll stand directly beneath the Golden Gate Bridge and command a sentinel's view out into the Pacific.

After you've drunk in the splendid view of city and Bay from the museum grounds, head downhill on 34th Avenue past the golf course, turn right on Geary Boulevard, which becomes Point Lobos Avenue, then turn right on to El Camino del Mar and follow it to the end. (Yes, this is the same street you were on earlier; no, I'm not leading you in circles. It seems that years ago landslides collapsed the midriff of this highway, leaving among the survivors two dead-end streets known forever by the same name.)

HIDDEN ► This is **Land's End**, a thumb-like appendage of real estate which San Francisco seems to have stolen from the sea. It is the nearest you will ever approach to experiencing San Francisco as the Costanoan Indians knew it. Hike the trails which honeycomb the hillsides hereabout and you'll enter a wild, tumbling region where winds twist cypress trees into the contours of the earth. The rocks offshore are inhabited by slithering sea creatures. The air is loud with the unceasing lash of wave against shoreline. Land's End is San Francisco's grand finale—a line of cliffs poised at the sea's edge and threatening imminently to slide into eternity.

From the parking lot located at the end of El Camino del Mar, walk down the steps that begin at the U.S.S. San Francisco Memorial Flagpole, and head east on the trail to the water. That dirty HIDDEN ► blonde swath of sand is a popular **nude beach**, perfectly situated here in San Francisco's most natural region.

(While hiking the footpaths in the region, beware! Land's End is plagued by landslides and foolish hikers. Remain on the trails. Exercise caution and this exotic area will reward you with eye-boggling views of Marin's wind-chiseled coast.)

Continuing down Point Lobos Avenue, at the corner where the road turns to parallel the Pacific Ocean, rest the ruins of the **Sutro Baths**. From the configuration of the stones, it's a simple trick to envision the foundation of Adolf Sutro's folly; more difficult for the mind's eye is to picture the multitiered confection that the San Francisco philanthropist built upon it in 1896. Sprawling across three oceanfront acres, Sutro's baths could have washed the entire city. There were actually six baths total, Olympian in size, as well as three restaurants and 500 dressing rooms—all contained beneath a stained-glass dome.

Towering above them was the Cliff House, a Gothic castle which survived the earthquake only to be consumed by fire the next year. Following several reincarnations, the **Cliff House**, located at 1090 Point Lobos Avenue, is a rather bland structure housing several restaurants and tourist shops. Most important among its features are the National Park Service information office (415-556-8642) and the view. From this crow's nest you can gaze out over a sweeping expanse of ocean. Just offshore the **Seal Rocks** lie anchored. Don't look for the seals, though. They have all moved to Pier 39.

Below the Cliff House, extending to the very end of vision, is the Great Highway. The salt-and-pepper beach beside it is **Ocean Beach**, a slender ribbon of sand that decorates three miles of San Francisco's western perimeter. Remember, this is San Francisco—land of fog, mist, and west winds—beachwear here more often consists of sweaters than swimsuits. The water, sweeping down from the Arctic, is too cold for mere mortals; only surfers and polar bear swimmers brave it. Nevertheless, to walk this strand is to trek the border of eternity. American Indians called San Francisco's ocean the "sundown sea." If you'll take the time some late afternoon, you'll see that the fiery orb still settles nightly just offshore.

Located on Skyline Boulevard at the far end of Ocean Beach, **Fort Funston** is the prettiest stretch to stroll. The fort itself is little more than a sequence of rusting gun emplacements, but there is a half-mile nature trail here that winds along cliffs overlooking the sea. It's a windblown region of dune grass and leathery succulent plants, with views that span San Francisco and alight on the shore of Marin. Hang gliders dust the cliffs of Fort Funston, adding another dramatic element to this spectacle of sun and wind.

Heading back along the Great Highway, you'll encounter the **San Francisco Zoo.** With over 50 endangered species, plus an excellent gorilla habitat and Primate Discovery Center, it's a great place to visit. Admission. ~ 45th Avenue and Sloat Boulevard; 415-753-7061.

LODGING

Say the word "hostel" and the first pictures to come to mind are spartan accommodations and shabby surroundings. At **Hostelling International—San Francisco—Fort Mason** that simply is not the case. Set in Fort Mason, an old military base that is now part of a magnificent national park, the hostel overlooks San Francisco Bay. In addition to eye-boggling views, the facility is within walking distance of the Marina district and Fisherman's Wharf. The hostel itself is contained in a Civil War–era barracks and features a living room, kitchen, and laundry. The rooms, carpeted and quite clean, are dorm-style with 3 to 16 bunk beds in each. The catch to this otherwise excellent accommodation is that you can't use your room between 11 a.m. and 1 p.m. ~ Fort Mason, Building 240, Bay and Franklin streets; 415-771-7277, 800-444-6111, fax 415-771-1468. BUDGET.

If you're seeking a hotel near the ocean, removed from the hubbub of downtown San Francisco, consider **Seal Rock Inn**. Perched on a bluff overlooking the Pacific, it's located just outside the Golden Gate National Recreation Area, a stone-skip away from Ocean Beach and Golden Gate Park. The 27 guest rooms are very spacious, easily sleeping four people. Furnishings and decor are unimaginative but quite comfortable; the rooms are carpeted wall-to-wall and equipped with televisions and telephones. Also, a godsend in this region of frequent fog, some rooms have fireplaces. These are a little extra, as are rooms featuring mini-kitchenettes and panoramic ocean views. ~ 545 Point Lobos Avenue; 415-752-8000, fax 415-752-6034. MODERATE TO DELUXE.

San Francisco's first motel is a 24-room art deco beauty. Built in 1936, the same year as the Golden Gate Bridge, the **Ocean Park Motel** combines modern furnishings, cedar paneling, and floral wallpapers. In addition to attractive rooms (some with kitchens) and large family suites, it offers guests an outdoor hot tub, courtyard, and small playground. ~ 2690 46th Avenue; 415-566-7020, fax 415-655-8959. MODERATE.

DINING

San Francisco's most popular vegetarian restaurant is incongruously situated in an old waterfront warehouse. With pipes exposed and a metal superstructure supporting the roof, **Greens at Fort Mason** possesses the aura of an upscale airplane hangar. But this outstanding eatery, run by the Zen Center, has been deftly furnished with burlwood tables, and there's a view of the Golden Gate out those warehouse windows. The lunch menu includes vegetable brochettes fired over mesquite charcoal, pita bread stuffed with hummus, grilled tofu, soups, and daily specials. Dinner menu

LAKE MERCED

At the intersection of Skyline and Lake Merced boulevards lies **Lake Merced**, a U-shaped reservoir which has the unusual distinction of once having been salt water. Bounded by the Harding Park golf links and hiking trails, it provides a pretty spot to picnic. If you decide to pass up the hang gliding at Fort Funston, you might rent a rowboat or sailboat at the clubhouse here and try a less nerve-jangling sport.

is à la carte Monday through Friday, pre-set on Saturday. The menu changes daily: a typical multicourse repast would be fougasse with red onions, spinach linguine with artichokes, shiitake mushrooms, pinenuts, rosemary and parmesan, Tunisian salad, eggplant soup, Gruyère tart, lettuce salad, tea, and dessert. Reservations recommended for lunch and dinner. Closed Monday for lunch, open Sunday for brunch only. ~ Fort Mason, Building A; 415-771-6222. DELUXE TO ULTRA-DELUXE.

Try as you might to escape the trodden paths, some places in the world are simply inevitable. Such a one is the Cliff House, a historic structure at the edge of the sea which is positively inundated with tourists. Since there's little else out on the city's ocean side, you'll have to consider one of the three restaurants here. Downstairs at the **Seafood & Beverage Co.** you'll find a trim restaurant overlooking Seal Rocks and serving lunches and dinners of steak, poultry, and seafood; also Sunday brunch. ~ 1090 Point Lobos Avenue; 415-386-3330. MODERATE TO DELUXE.

Upstairs at the Cliff House offers the same view in a café setting. The breakfast and lunch menu boasts 30 kinds of omelettes as well as soups and sandwiches. At dinner there are pasta dishes, several seafood selections, and a few chicken, steak, or veal entrées. ~ 1090 Point Lobos Avenue; 415-386-3330. MODERATE TO DELUXE.

For a tad less expensive meal, head uphill a few steps to **Louis'**, a cliffside café that's been family-owned since 1937. The dinners, served with soup or salad, include New York steak, prawns, scallops, and hamburger steak. Breakfast and lunch are similar all-American affairs. Add a postcard view of the Sutro Baths and Seal Rocks and you have one hell of a bargain. ~ 902 Point Lobos Avenue; 415-387-6330. MODERATE.

Seafood lovers start lining up early at the popular **Pacific Café** in the outer Richmond District where the wait for a table is soothed by a complimentary glass of wine and convivial talk. Then it's time to sink into a high-backed wooden booth and ponder the daily specials, which always include a wide assortment of grilled fresh fish and frequently ahi tuna garnished with wasabe butter, spicy crab cakes, and garlic-infused steamed mussels. ~ 7000 Geary Boulevard; 415-387-7091. MODERATE TO DELUXE.

The Beach House is not really on the water, but once you step into this cozy restaurant ocean views will seem irrelevant anyway. The interior features a comfortable country-style decor with dried wildflower bouquets, decorative dishes, and an antique sideboard. Come prepared to like seafood. The menu is divided into about a dozen categories, all hailing from the ocean. There's sole, snapper, swordfish, calamari, crab, clams, and so on. Dinner only. ~ 4621 Lincoln Way; 415-681-9333. MODERATE.

Out in San Francisco's southwest corner, in Harding Park on the shores of Lake Merced, you'll discover a spiffy dining room, **The Boathouse Sports Bar and Restaurant**. With pretty views, it offers a lunch and dinner menu of steak, seafood, sandwiches, and salad. They take their sports themes seriously. Corridor walls are lined with photos of local athletes and every corner (as in all four) has a television to keep you posted on the latest scores. If you're out here to begin with, it's probably to go golfing, boating, hiking, or hang gliding, so the athletic ambience shouldn't bother you. Saturday and Sunday brunch. ~ 1 Harding Park Road; 415-681-2727. MODERATE.

NIGHTLIFE Where San Francisco meets the Pacific, there's **Phineas T. Barnacle**. Set in the Cliff House, it's heavily touristed and rather pricey, but the views are unmatched: Seal Rocks stand sentinel offshore. ~ 1090 Point Lobos Avenue; 415-386-3330.

The **Magic Theatre** has premiered several plays by Pulitzer Prize–winning dramatist Sam Shepard, who was playwright-in-residence here for several years. ~ Fort Mason, Building D; 415-441-8822.

San Francisco's "Backyard"

There is an area of San Francisco, stretching across the southern sector of the metropolis, which I call the city's "Backyard." Dotted throughout this sprawling residential region are a number of inviting places. Most are unknown to tourists; some remain hidden even to native San Franciscans. To find them you'll require a feel for adventure, a touch of patience, and a good road map. Plus a special desire to uncover secret locales.

SIGHTS Everyone knows about the 1906 quake, just as everyone has heard of Lombard, San Francisco's "crookedest street." Few are aware

HIDDEN ►

of **Vermont Street**, even though it might just be crookeder than the crookedest. That's because it's located out on Potrero Hill, a clapboard neighborhood that has been gentrified by artists, craftspeople, and imaginative others. From a public park at Vermont and 20th streets, there's a back-door view of San Francisco's skyline; in the opposite direction loom Twin Peaks, Mt. Davidson, and a ridgeline of lesser hills. From this coign of vantage, Vermont snakes down to 22nd Street in a mesmerizing series of zigs and zags.

For another splendid view, head to **Bernal Heights**. This working class neighborhood is similar to Potrero Hill, though economically more upscale and geographically a bit upslope. Bernal Heights Boulevard encircles a shale-strewn hill from the top of which the entire Bay Area spreads before you. Just park on the street and climb a short distance uphill. To the north stands the Golden Gate and beyond it the fog-curled mountains of Marin.

Then as the eye moves clockwise, the San Francisco skyline appears in the foreground. The Bay, long and narrow here, draws a line along the eastern perimeter as it ebbs and flows from San Jose. Complete this 360-degree sweep and your eye will hike the ridgeline that protects San Francisco from the rolling fogs of the Pacific Ocean.

Of course, the view of views is from **Twin Peaks** on Twin Peaks Boulevard. Atop these bald knobs the eye traces a circle around the entire Bay. The Golden Gate Bridge becomes a mere corridor that opens onto a mountain range called Marin. The Bay is a pond inhabited by sailboats. The cityscape lies before you, and buildings appear as out of the wrong end of a telescope. Jostled and teeming, civilization stretches to the west, only to pile up at the Pacific's edge. It is a view for travelers who can wander back in the mind to the days before humankind when wind and water were all the land could see.

After leaving the metropolis in the dust, spur your mount toward **Glen Canyon Park**. With its meandering stream, dense underbrush, and twisted geologic formations, there's something about this steep canyon that evokes the Old West. Granted, the sunglinted windows of civilization surround the hillsides, but deep in the heart of this draw are hiking trails that are escapes from urbanity. Like all treasures, Glen Canyon is hard to find and requires a map. Most visitors to the park come along Portola Drive to O'Shaughnessy Boulevard, then down to Elk Street. Turning left onto Elk, there's a ballfield and tennis courts, followed immediately by a road. Turn onto the road as it parallels the courts; it becomes a dirt road that forks into several hiking trails.

Legend has it that rustlers and smugglers hid in one of the caves in Glen Canyon Park, as did a bunch of bootleggers who specialized in a tongue-numbing concoction called "Panther's Piss."

Another wooded retreat rests nearby atop **Mt. Davidson.** A trail from the corner of Myra Way and Sherwood Court climbs sharply to the 938-foot summit of San Francisco's highest peak. The concrete cross at the top measures another 103 feet; for more than 60 years the Council of Churches has celebrated its Easter sunrise services here. If today doesn't happen to be Easter, you can still peer through the eucalyptus forest out over the Pacific.

Stern Grove, at the corner of 19th Avenue and Sloat Boulevard, is known for its summer concerts in the park. Aficionados of jazz and classical music flock every Sunday to this natural amphitheater. (Check newspapers, or call 415-666-7035 for program details.) Regardless of the day or season, the grove offers visitors grassy meadows, shady spots, and a tiny lake encircled by eucalyptus trees and freckled with ducks. It's a beautiful stroll from the gingerbread house (once an infamous gambling den) to the lake, even when there's nary a symphonic sound to be heard.

DINING

Out in the Sunset district, a tiny storefront restaurant that serves some of the most flavorful and authentic Mexican dishes north of Veracruz is **Casa Aguila.** Mini tamales are good for starters. As for the entrées, seafood paella and pork steaks marinated in citrus juices and fresh herbs are standouts; as are chicken *mole* and chile rellenos with pork, dried fruits, marinated vegetables and walnuts. ~ 1240 Noriega Street; 415-661-5593. MODERATE.

Hearty Greek dishes prepared with finesse are the trademark of **Stoyanoff's,** an attractive inner-Sunset restaurant furnished with bleached wood and handwoven rugs from Macedonia. Phyllo-wrapped salmon, moussaka, and roast lamb are specialties, along with an array of hot and cold *mezéthes*—Greek appetizers. The restaurant is also a popular place for an afternoon cappuccino and pastry on the landscaped rooftop patio. Closed Monday. ~ 1240 9th Avenue; 415-664-3664. MODERATE TO DELUXE.

NIGHTLIFE

Trad'r Sam is kind of like Trader Vic's, but it's a lot cheaper and a lot more fun. You sit in booths named Guam, Samoa, and various Hawaiian islands; slowly sip such tropical concoctions as Tahitian deep purples, mai tais, and banana cows; and soak in the 1940s Polynesian atmosphere. This bar is a classic. ~ 6150 Geary Boulevard; 415-221-0773.

Perhaps the closest thing to an authentic Dublin pub in San Francisco is **The Plough and the Stars** with its burnished wood paneling and framed political cartoons hanging on the walls. A stage in the back presents rousing Irish folk bands on most nights. Cover on Friday and Saturday. ~ 116 Clement Street; 415-751-1122.

The **Last Day Saloon** is a neighborhood watering hole that features blues, rock, and Motown groups. It's attractively decorated, yet informal and friendly. ~ 406 Clement Street; 415-387-6343.

An important member of the city's group of small theaters is the **Asian American Theatre Company,** which represents the city's burgeoning Asian community. ~ 403 Arguello Boulevard; 415-751-2600.

Outdoor Adventures

SPORT-FISHING

If you hanker to spend a day deep-sea fishing for rock cod, bass, or salmon, check out **Hot Pursuit Sport Fishing.** ~ 47 Fisherman's Wharf; 415-965-3474. **New Easy Rider Sport Fishing Center** also leads tours. ~ 225 University Avenue; 415-285-2000. **Wacky Jacky** is another charter operation. ~ 473 Bella Vista Way; 415-586-9800. Bring a lunch and dress warmly.

SAILING & NATURE CRUISES

Some of the world's most challenging sailing can be found on San Francisco Bay. To charter boats and captains, contact **A Day on the Bay.** ~ San Francisco Marina; 415-922-0227. Or you can try **Pacific Marine Yacht Charters.** ~ Pier 39; 415-788-9100.

For tours of the Farallon Islands contact the **Oceanic Society**. From the deck of their 63-foot vessel you'll observe harbor seals and sea lions. Puffins, porpoises, and humpback and gray whales also frequent the waters. Tours of the Farallon Islands are offered June through November; whale-watching tours go from December until April. ~ Fort Mason Center, Building E; 415-474-3385.

KITE FLYING

San Francisco has been called the "city of kites." Ocean breezes, mild weather, and lots of open space create perfect conditions for kite flying. Nearly every day, brightly colored streamers litter the sky, swooping and soaring. Popular kite-flying spots include the Marina Green, Golden Gate Park's Polo Field, Lake Merced, and Fort Funston.

Local kite stores sell exotic designs ranging from traditional box kites to tandems, octagons, hexagons, and silk dragons. Try **Kite Flite** for your flyer. ~ Pier 39; 415-956-3181.

HANG GLIDING & PARA-GLIDING

If you'd prefer to soar the skies yourself, try hang gliding. For lessons in paragliding, contact **Airtime of San Francisco.** ~ 3620 Wawona Street; 415-759-1177. For those into hang gliding, there are sites at Fort Funston (Skyline Boulevard at the far end of Ocean Beach) and Westlake (just south of Fort Funston). If you're not ready to test those wings, you'll find it's fun just watching.

ROLLER-BLADING

When Sunday rolls around, several hundred folks are apt to don rollerblades and roller skates and careen along the sidewalks and streets of Golden Gate Park. John F. Kennedy Drive, on the east side of the park, is closed to cars on Sundays and holidays. It's great exercise, and a lot of fun, to boot. Rentals are available outside of the park at **Skates on Haight.** ~ 1818 Haight Street; 415-752-8376. You can also rent on the park's north side from **Golden Gate Park Skate and Bike.** ~ 3038 Fulton Street at 6th Avenue; 415-668-1117.

✔ CHECK THESE OUT—UNIQUE OUTDOOR ADVENTURES

- Go fly a kite, or watch as others circle and swoop their adult toys high above the **Marina Green.** *page 122*
- Soar through the air on a multicolored hang glider as you skirt sand dunes and the Pacific Ocean. *page 132*
- Roll along through **Golden Gate Park,** where they close the streets on Sundays and holidays and everyone is on wheels—skates or bikes, that is. *page 132*
- Spy on the mighty humpback as it travels the Pacific, or observe porpoises, puffins and sea lions on a **nature cruise.** *page 131*

Or, if you want to get downright serious about it, roll over to the **Bladium**. Billed as "inline hockey's premier facility," this popular sports center features a full-size roller-hockey rink as well as an equipment shop, changing rooms, and snack shop. With open rink times and pick-up games every day, it's a great place to enjoy one of the nation's fastest growing sports. ~ 1050 3rd Street; 415-442-5060.

JOGGING

In a city of steep hills, where walking provides more than enough exercise, jogging is nevertheless a favorite pastime. There are actually places to run where the terrain is fairly level and the scenery spectacular. Most popular are the Golden Gate Bridge, the Presidio Highlands, Glen Canyon Park Trail, Ocean Beach, Golden Gate Park, and Angel Island.

Parcourses, combining aerobic exercises with short jogs, are located at Justin Herman Park (the foot of Market Street near the Ferry Building; half course only), Marina Green (along Marina Boulevard near the foot of Fillmore Street), Mountain Lake Park (Lake Street between 8th and Funston avenues), and the Polo Field in Golden Gate Park.

SWIMMING

Although the air temperature remains moderate all year, the ocean and bay around San Francisco stay cold. If you're ready to brave the Arctic current, join the hearty swimmers who make the plunge regularly at Aquatic Park. Many of these brave souls belong to either the **Dolphin Club** or the **South End Rowing Club**. Both clubs are open to the public (on alternating weekdays) and provide saunas and showers for a small fee. ~ Dolphin Club: 502 Jefferson Street; 415-441-9329. South End Rowing Club: 500 Jefferson Street; 415-441-9523.

SURFING

West of Golden Gate Park there are several spots along San Francisco's wide, sandy **Ocean Beach**; however the conditions vary seasonally and because of strong rip currents, this is not a place for beginners. **Fort Point**, located on the bay side of the Golden Gate Bridge's south tower, is another surf break in the city. Fast-flowing currents moving out the Gate make this another spot for experts only.

GOLF

For the earthbound, golf can be a heavenly sport in San Francisco. Several courses are worth checking out, including **Glen Eagles International Golf Club**. This nine-hole course is hilly and narrow. ~ 2100 Sunnydale Avenue; 415-587-2425. **Golden Gate Park Golf Course** is a short but tricky nine-hole course. ~ 47th Avenue and Fulton Street; 415-751-8987. **Harding Park Golf Course** is considered to be one of the finest public courses in the country. ~ Harding Park Road and Skyline Boulevard; 415-664-4690.

TENNIS

With over 150 free public courts, San Francisco could easily be called The City of Nets. **Golden Gate Park** (John F. Kennedy and Middle drives; fee) has 21 courts. In the Marina try the **George Moscone Playground** (Chestnut and Buchanan streets). A popular spot in the Mission is **Mission Dolores Park** (18th and Dolores streets). On Nob Hill the **Alice Marble Memorial Playground** (Greenwich and Hyde streets) is recommended. In Chinatown try the **Chinese Playground** (Sacramento Street and Waverly Plaza). Over in North Beach try the **North Beach Playground** (Lombard and Mason streets). For more information on all city courts call the San Francisco Parks and Recreation Department. ~ 415-753-7032.

BIKING

San Francisco is not a city designed for cyclers. Some of the hills are almost too steep to walk and downtown traffic can be gruelling. There are places, however, that are easy to ride and beautiful as well. **Golden Gate Park**, the **Golden Gate Promenade**, and **Lake Merced** all have excellent bike routes.

Among the city's most dramatic rides is the bicyclists' sidewalk on the **Golden Gate Bridge.** Or, if you're less adventurous, the **Sunset Bikeway** begins at Lake Merced Boulevard, then carries through a residential area and past views of the ocean to the Polo Field in Golden Gate Park.

Bike Rentals To rent a bike in the city, contact **Lincoln Cyclery**, located adjacent to Golden Gate Park. ~ 772 Stanyan Street; 415-221-2415. Right around the corner, you can rent from **Park Cyclery**. ~ 1865 Haight Street at Stanyan Street; 415-221-3777.

Transportation

CAR

The major highways leading into San Francisco are **Route 1**, the picturesque coastal road, **Route 101**, California's main north-south thoroughfare, and **Route 80**, the transcontinental highway that originates on the East Coast.

AIR

San Francisco International Airport, better known as SFO, sits 15 miles south of downtown San Francisco off Routes 101 and 280. A major destination from all points of the globe, the airport is always bustling.

Most domestic airlines fly into SFO, including Alaska Airlines, American Airlines, Continental Airlines, Delta Airlines, Hawaiian Airlines, Southwest Airlines, Trans World Airlines, United Airlines, and USAir.

International carriers are also prominent here: Aeroflot, Air Canada, British Airways, China Airlines, Canadian Airlines International, Japan Airlines, Lufthansa German Airlines, Mexicana Airlines, Philippine Airlines, Qantas Airways, Singapore Airlines, and TACA International Airlines have regular flights into San Francisco's airport.

To travel from the airport to downtown San Francisco, call **San Francisco Airporter** which runs frequently. ~ 415-495-8404. **Supershuttle** provides door-to-door service. ~ 415-871-7800. Or catch a **San Mateo County Transit**, or **SamTrans**, bus (800-660-4287) to the Transbay Terminal (425 Mission Street) or transfer in Colma or Daly City to BART (415-992-2278). Taxi and limo service are also available, or try **Lorrie's Airport Service**. ~ 415-334-9000.

BUS

Greyhound Bus Lines services San Francisco from around the country. ~ 800-231-2222. The Transbay Terminal is located at 425 Mission Street. ~ 415-495-1575.

Also consider the **Green Tortoise**, a New Age company with a fleet of funky buses. Each is equipped with sleeping platforms allowing travelers to rest as they cross the country. The buses stop at interesting sightseeing points en route. The Green Tortoise, an endangered species from the '60s, travels to and from the East Coast, Seattle, Los Angeles, and elsewhere. It provides a mode of transportation as well as an experience in group living. ~ 494 Broadway, San Francisco, CA 94133; 415-821-0803.

TRAIN

For those who prefer to travel by rail, **Amtrak** has train service via the "Coast Starlight," "California Zephyr," and "San Joaquin." These trains arrive and depart the Emeryville train station, with connecting bus service to San Francisco's Ferry Building, where Market Street meets the Embarcadero. ~ 800-872-7245.

CAR RENTALS

The easiest way to explore San Francisco is by foot or public transit. Driving in San Francisco can be a nightmare. Parking spaces are rare, parking lots expensive. Then there are the hills, which require you to navigate along dizzying inclines while dodging cable cars, trollies, pedestrians, and double-parked vehicles. The streets of San Francisco make Mr. Toad's wild ride look tame. If you do decide to rent a car, most major rental agencies have franchises right at the airport. These include **Avis Rent A Car** (415-877-6780, 800-331-1212), **Budget Rent A Car** (415-875-6850, 800-527-0700), **Dollar Rent A Car** (415-244-4130, 800-800-4000), **Hertz Rent A Car** (415-877-1600, 800-654-3131), and **National Interrent** (415-877-4745, 800-227-7368).

For less expensive but also less convenient service, try the agencies that are outside the airport and provide pick-up service: **Ace Rent A Car** (415-771-7711), **California Compacts Rent A Car** (415-871-4421, 800-954-7368), and **Flat Rate Rent A Car** (415-583-9232, 800-433-3058).

PUBLIC TRANSIT

San Francisco is a city where public transit works. To get anywhere in the city, call **San Francisco Muni** and an operator will direct you to the appropriate mode of public transportation. ~ 415-673-6864.

Over 90 bus lines travel around, about, and through the city. Trolley buses, street cars, light-rail subways, and cable cars also crisscross San Francisco. Most lines operate daily (with a modified schedule on weekends and holidays). Free transfers allow a 90-minute stopover or connection to two more lines. Exact fares are required. For complete information on the Muni system, obtain a copy of the "Muni Street and Transit Map" from the Visitors Center (900 Market Street; 415-391-2000), the Information Desk at City Hall, or local bookstores.

Unlike San Francisco's classic cable cars, the **Bay Area Rapid Transit System**, or **BART**, operates streamlined cars that zip beneath the city's streets. This space-age system travels from Downtown to the Mission District, Glen Park, and Colma. It also runs under the San Francisco Bay to the cities of Oakland, Berkeley, and other parts of the East Bay. Trains run every 8 or 20 minutes depending on the time of day. BART opens at 4 a.m. (6 a.m. on Saturday and 8 a.m. on Sunday) and closes at midnight every night. ~ 415-992-2278.

Many surrounding communities feature transportation services to and from San Francisco. To the north, **Golden Gate Transit** provides both bus and ferryboat service. ~ 415-332-6600. South of San Francisco, **San Mateo County Transit**, or **SamTrans**, offers bus service as far south as Palo Alto. ~ 800-660-4287. In addition, **CalTrain** provides daily commuter service from San Jose to San Francisco with stops along the way. ~ 800-660-4287. Across the Bay, **Alameda–Contra Costa Transit**, or **AC Transit**, carries passengers from Oakland, Berkeley, and other East Bay cities to the Transbay Terminal in San Francisco. ~ 510-839-2882.

CABLE CARS

Cable cars, those clanging symbols of San Francisco, are *the* way to see this city of perpendicular hills. This venerable system covers a ten-mile section of downtown San Francisco.

The cable car was invented in 1873 by Andrew Hallidie and works via an underground cable that travels continuously at a speed of nine-and-a-half miles per hour. Three of the system's original twelve lines still operate year-round. The Powell–Mason and Powell–Hyde cars travel from the Downtown district to Fisherman's Wharf; the California Street line runs east to west and passes through Chinatown and Nob Hill.

Built partially of wood and furnished with old-style running boards, these open-air vehicles are slow and stylish. Edging up the city's steep heights, then descending toboggan-run hills to the Bay, they provide many of San Francisco's finest views. Half the joy of riding, however, comes from watching the operators of these antique machines. Each has developed a personal style of gripping, braking, and bell-ringing. In addition to the breathtaking ride, they'll often treat you to a clanging street symphony.

TAXIS

Cabs are plentiful, but flagging them down is a trick—it's best to call by phone. The main companies are **DeSoto Cab Company** (415-673-1414), **Luxor Cabs** (415-282-4141), **Veteran's Taxi Cab Company** (415-552-1300), and **Yellow Cab** (415-626-2345).

WALKING TOURS

San Francisco is a city made for walkers. Appropriately, it offers a number of walking tours which explore various neighborhoods and historical spots.

Chinese Heritage Walks, conducted every Saturday at 2 p.m. by the Chinese Culture Center reveals the true Chinatown. They also offer a **Culinary Walk** which visits markets and herb shops, then stops for lunch in a dim sum restaurant. Fee. ~ Holiday Inn at the corner of Kearny and Washington streets; 415-986-1822.

Wok Wiz Chinatown Walking Tours, led by cookbook author Shirley Fong-Torres, features local markets, pastry shops, private Chinese tea ceremonies, and a dim sum lunch. This three-hour walk is a convenient way to get acquainted with Chinatown's culinary culture. ~ 750 Kearny Street, Suite 800; 415-355-9657.

The **Flower Power Haight-Ashbury Walking Tour** explores the neighborhood made famous during the hippie era of the 1960s. Along with sites from the Summer of Love, the tour takes a longer look back at the area's Victorian architecture stemming from the days when the once-rural Haight was a weekend resort. ~ 520 Shrader Street, #1; 415-221-8442.

The **Dashiell Hammett Walking Tour** is a three-mile search for the old haunts of the mystery writer and his fictional sleuth, Sam Spade. Hammett lived in the bay city from 1921 to 1930, and used it as the setting for numerous short stories and novels, including *The Maltese Falcon*. Following the tracks of Sam Spade, the tour combs the city from the Tenderloin to Nob Hill. The tour is given every Saturday in May, June, July, and August and begins at noon in front of the San Francisco Public Library at Larkin and Grove streets. Fee. ~ P.O. Box 982, Glen Ellen, CA 95442; 707-939-1214.

Folks at the Mexican Museum lead a tour of the **San Francisco City Club**, a turn-of-the-century building that once housed the San Francisco Stock Exchange and features a fresco by Diego Rivera. Fee. ~ Fort Mason, Building D; 415-441-0445. Tours are also given by **Precita Eyes Muralists.** ~ 348 Precita Avenue; 415-285-2287.

City Guides, a volunteer organization sponsored by the Friends of the San Francisco Public Library, offers free tours of various locations throughout the city. They include separate tours of Pacific Heights Victorians, Historic Market Street, North Beach, Nob Hill, Coit Tower, and other points of interest. For information on times and starting places, call 415-557-4266.

THREE

Bay Area

Geologists demythologize even the most romantic places. San Francisco Bay, they state, is a drowned river valley. Glaciers melting 10,000 years ago created it by raising sea levels and causing the ocean to flood a canyon that earlier had been carved by the Sacramento and San Joaquin rivers.

Mountains surround the entire area. The Santa Cruz Mountains rise to the west and south; on the other side are the East Bay Hills and Diablo Range; to the north looms Mt. Tamalpais. At the mouth of the Bay is the Golden Gate, a rocky conduit through which California's major drainage system empties into the Pacific.

Then the geographers take over, explaining that San Francisco Bay covers 900 square miles. It extends 50 miles south from the Golden Gate to San Jose, and ranges east for 30 miles through San Pablo and Suisun bays to the Delta.

Along the west side of the Bay sits the Peninsula. Containing wealthy suburban towns, it reaches to Palo Alto, home of Stanford University. Santa Clara Valley, better known as Silicon Valley, capital of the computer industry, sprawls along the South Bay. San Jose, with a population greater than San Francisco, dominates the area. The East Bay, directly across the water from San Francisco, features Oakland, one of the world's largest container shipping ports, and the dynamic campus town of Berkeley. To the north lies Marin County, a posh enclave highlighted by the town of Sausalito, with its aura of the Mediterranean.(Western Marin, along the Pacific, is covered in Chapter Five.)

That last word is important to meteorologists, who use it to describe the Bay Area climate. With an average temperature of 57°, it resembles sections of southern Europe. Summers are warm and dry and the warm winters bring plentiful rainfall. Though snow is extremely rare, annual precipitation varies from 20 inches in the warm South Bay to 33 inches in cooler Marin. Fog is a fact of life, particularly around the Golden Gate.

Historians perceive the area differently. They begin with the Ohlone Indians, part of the Costanoan language group, who occupied the region perhaps as early as 7000 B.C. In Marin, the Coast Miwok held sway. By the 18th century, on the eve of the white man's appearance, the Indian population numbered about 9000.

The Spanish arrived in 1769. Gaspar de Portolá explored the length of the Peninsula, and was probably the first European to see San Francisco Bay. By 1777, his countrymen founded San Jose, building Mission Santa Clara de Asís and establishing a pueblo with 66 residents. They pressed on to Marin in 1817, creating Mission San Rafael Archangel in the town of San Rafael.

By then the Spanish were already in decline, and San Rafael represents the next-to-last of their 21 California missions. The Bay was becoming a major shipping point for merchants from several countries. Traders bartered sugar, spices, and other goods for cattle hides, better known as "California banknotes."

After the Americans took over California in 1846, the fruit farming industry blossomed in the South Bay and lumbering dominated elsewhere. Timber was stripped from surrounding mountains and shipped through the Golden Gate. Then the Gold Rush brought further prosperity to towns along the Bay and made the Delta a vital corridor for goods shipped upriver to Sacramento and the Gold Country. After Chinese and other workers built a labyrinthine system of levees later in the century, the Delta became the nation's richest agricultural area.

Communities in the East Bay and Marin bloomed after the 1906 earthquake as thousands of refugees sought new homes. When the Golden Gate and Bay bridges opened during the 1930s, another trans-Bay migration occurred.

By the 1950s, the South Bay was moving to center stage. The electronics boom sounded and computer manufacturing replaced fruit farming. Between 1940 and 1980, the population of Santa Clara County increased exponentially from about 300,000 to almost 1,300,000. Today, a staggering percentage of the nation's electronic components originate from this Silicon Valley region.

History in the 1960s was written in red and black. Berkeley became a rallying point, first for the Free Speech Movement in 1964, and later for the anti–Vietnam War mobilization. Its provocative populace set the pace for a nationwide movement that helped force the United States out of Southeast Asia. In 1967, Huey Newton and Bobby Seale founded the Black Panther Party in Oakland. The East Bay was a staging ground for revolution with demonstrations and riots continuing into the early 1970s.

Later in that decade, as the "Me Generation" matured, sybaritic Marin became known for its hot tubs and peacock feather massages. Berkeley politics mellowed and moved from the radical fringes to the liberal center. Oakland expanded its port at the expense of San Francisco's shrinking waterfront, and San Jose overtook San Francisco as the state's third largest city. Meanwhile, the entire Bay Area (including San Francisco) grew to almost six million population.

Rather than visualizing the Bay Area as geologists and historians, it's time to look at the region through the eyes of the traveler. To ease the visitor's entry, this chapter is divided into five sections. Proceeding counterclockwise from San Francisco, they are the Peninsula, South Bay, East Bay, and Marin, followed by a northeastern tangent out into the Delta.

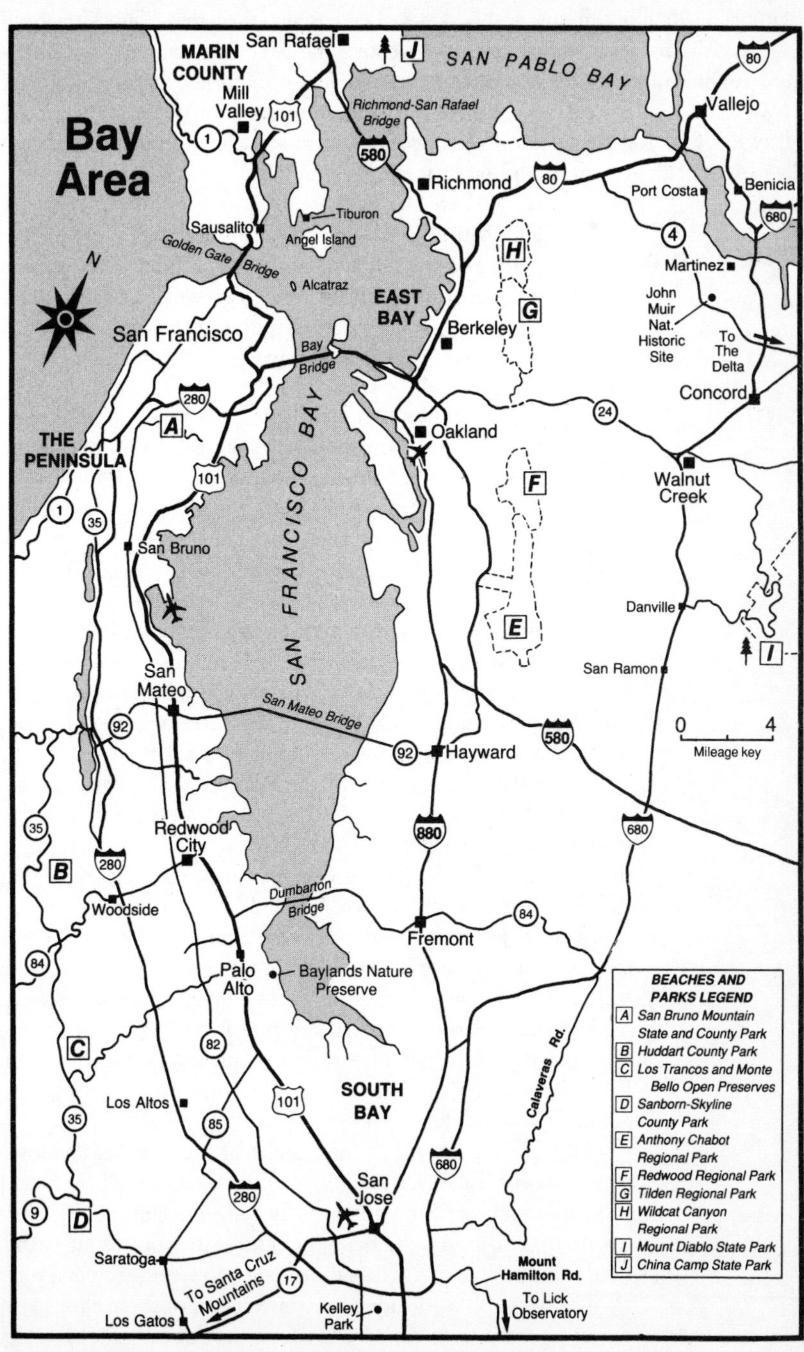
Bay Area
MARIN COUNTY
San Rafael
SAN PABLO BAY
Mill Valley
Richmond-San Rafael Bridge
Vallejo
Richmond
Port Costa
Benicia
Tiburon
Sausalito
Angel Island
Golden Gate Bridge
Alcatraz
EAST BAY
Martinez
John Muir Nat. Historic Site
To The Delta
San Francisco
Berkeley
Bay Bridge
Concord
Oakland
THE PENINSULA
Walnut Creek
SAN FRANCISCO BAY
San Bruno
Danville
San Ramon
San Mateo
San Mateo Bridge
Hayward
0 4
Mileage key
Redwood City
Woodside
Dumbarton Bridge
Fremont
Palo Alto
Baylands Nature Preserve
SOUTH BAY
Calaveras Rd.
Los Altos
San Jose
Saratoga
To Santa Cruz Mountains
Mount Hamilton Rd.
To Lick Observatory
Kelley Park
Los Gatos
BEACHES AND PARKS LEGEND
A San Bruno Mountain State and County Park
B Huddart County Park
C Los Trancos and Monte Bello Open Preserves
D Sanborn-Skyline County Park
E Anthony Chabot Regional Park
F Redwood Regional Park
G Tilden Regional Park
H Wildcat Canyon Regional Park
I Mount Diablo State Park
J China Camp State Park

Within this lazy loop reside two of the nation's finest universities—Stanford, with its 8100-acre campus, and Berkeley. There is also the Santa Clara Valley, where the box-shaped architecture of the electronics industry gives way to fruit orchards and rolling hills. Marin, one of the nation's richest counties, features picturesque towns and opulent estates. The Delta is a dreamy maze of waterways linked by drawbridges. Together these diverse sections form a circle and salient along which lies some of the prettiest land west of the Atlantic.

The Peninsula

The Peninsula of which San Francisco is the tip extends south and encompasses some of the Bay Area's wealthiest bedroom communities. Here you will find Hillsborough, Atherton, and Palo Alto, a series of high-toned towns adorned with wooded realms and prestigious homes.

SIGHTS

The best way to explore an area is to scout it out first. So the initial stop in a Peninsula tour should be **San Bruno Mountain** (Summit Road, Brisbane), a bald-domed rise from which to survey the entire region. With its steep flanks and wooded ravines, this park affords views of all the Bay Area. To get there, take Bayshore Boulevard to Guadalupe Canyon Parkway, which goes through the park to the summit. You'll have to share the heights with radio antennas, but there are nearby hiking trails to escape civilization.

Peer south and the world spreads before you, with the Pacific to the west, San Francisco Bay to the east, and the Santa Cruz Mountains running down the Peninsula like a spine. (The ocean side of the Peninsula is covered in Chapter Six.)

To explore the bay side of the Peninsula, you can choose between three highways. Route 101, closest to the Bay, is a major freeway which streams past San Francisco International Airport, then beelines south. It is quick, painless, and downright ugly. Route 82, or El Camino Real, named for the old royal road, is a commercial highway lined with shopping areas. Passing through the heart of most peninsula towns, it involves a lot of stop-and-go traffic and is largely uninteresting. The third option is Route 280, farther inland. To call a parkway pretty takes gall and imagination, but this high-speed freeway does possess beautiful stretches. It has been nicely landscaped and skirts the eastern fringe of the Santa Cruz Mountains.

All these highways will pass some of the Bay Area's most exclusive towns. Like Marin County to the north, the Peninsula is a suburban enclave filled with wealthy bedroom communities. In the towns of Hillsborough, Belmont, and Atherton, along winding roads above the Bay, are outlandish mansions and secluded estates.

The town of **Woodside** is a rural version of these elite communities. Situated near Route 280 along the Santa Cruz Mountains, its fabulous homes are tucked away in forested heights.

The most splendid of all is **Filoli,** a sumptuous 43-room mansion designed in 1916 by Willis Polk. Built for William Bourn II, whose wealth derived partially from the Empire Mine in Grass Valley, the house features a gilded ballroom. The floors are inlaid with exquisite designs, murals decorate the ballroom, and the marble work is impeccable. The gardens surrounding the house, equally beautiful, once required the maintenance of 18 gardeners. Reservations are required for a two-hour guided tour of the mansion and grounds on Tuesday, Wednesday, and Thursday; on Friday and Saturday visitors may take a self-guided tour with a brochure. Closed Monday and Tuesday. Admission. ~ Canada Road, Woodside; 415-364-2880.

Also of interest is the old **Woodside Store**, a bare wood structure that dates back to 1854. A general store in the days when this region was a lumbering center, the establishment is now a three-room museum containing old tools and other artifacts. Closed Monday, Wednesday, and Friday. ~ Kings Mountain and Tripp roads, Woodside; 415-851-7615.

If you decide to follow Route 280 and visit Woodside, consider getting off the freeway in Hillsborough and taking the small side roads which parallel the main road. Skyline Boulevard (Route 35), Ralston Avenue, and Canada Road link together to form an alternate north-south route between Hillsborough and Woodside. Passing through the **San Francisco State Fish and Game Refuge**, they provide splendid views of Crystal Springs Reservoir and the Santa Cruz Mountains.

Regardless of the highway you take, you will ultimately arrive in Palo Alto, home to one of America's prettiest college campuses. Named for a "tall tree" that served as an early landmark, this wealthy community is still noted for its beautiful arbors. The centerpiece of the town, however, is **Stanford University**, an immense campus

✔ CHECK THESE OUT—UNIQUE SIGHTS

- Take in the Wildlife Habitats exhibit, play a round of golf, or hike one of the many trails at **Coyote Point Park** in San Mateo. *page 147*
- Step back in time to ancient Egypt at San Jose's **Rosicrucian Egyptian Museum,** where you'll discover sphinxes, hieroglyphs, and 3000-year-old mummies. *page 150*
- Explore the plaza where the Free Speech Movement began in 1964 at the **University of California–Berkeley.** *page 157*
- Roam through orchards and a grand Victorian at **John Muir National Historic Site,** home of one the nation's most renowned naturalists. *page 177*

created by railroad baron Leland Stanford during the 1880s. ~ For information on walking tours, call Stanford Visitor Information at 415-723-2560.

The arcade of trees lining the entrance along Palm Drive will provide an idea of Palo Alto's arboreal heritage and of Stanford's magnificent landscaping. You'll also pass the **Stanford University Museum of Art**. Among the pieces in this diverse collection are an Egyptian mummy, California landscape oil paintings, a 19th-century Yurok canoe carved from a redwood log, and the golden spike which marked completion of the transcontinental railroad. At present the museum is still closed because of damage from the 1989 earthquake. They do, however, host ongoing exhibits in the art gallery. Until the museum's scheduled reopening in 1998, the main attraction is the outdoor Rodin sculpture garden, accessible 24 hours a day. ~ Museum Way and Lomita Drive, Palo Alto; 415-723-4177.

The center of campus, the **Quadrangle**, lies at the end of Palm Drive. Built of sandstone and capped with red tile, it's an elegant Spanish-style courtyard. The architecture throughout the university is Romanesque, and the Quad's colonnaded walkways evoke the image of a cloister.

Fittingly, the **Memorial Church** anchors the far edge of the plaza. That tile mosaic facade portraying the Sermon on the Mount was fashioned in Venice, Italy. Inside, the cathedral is a vaulting structure illuminated through stained glass and adorned with stone filigree. Behind the altar, past the candelabra and solitary cross, hangs "The Last Supper," re-created from the Sistine Chapel original with special permission from the Pope.

Just west of the Quad rises **Hoover Tower**, a 285-foot landmark from the top of which you can survey the campus and beyond. Home to the Hoover Institution, a conservative think tank, the tower also houses the memorabilia of Stanford's most famous graduate, President Herbert Hoover. Admission. ~ 415-723-2053.

Ingenuity is the password to the **Museum of American Heritage**. Truly an original, this little showplace traces the history of mechanical and electrical invention with displays of cameras, calculators, cash registers and kitchenware. There is a 1890s-era "stocking knitter," as well as electric trains, antique bicycles, and a working orchestrion, a contraption consisting of eight instruments that play simultaneously. Closed Monday through Thursday. ~ 3401 El Camino Real, Palo Alto; 415-321-1004.

In addition to these historic and academic heights, Palo Alto possesses mucky lowlands along the shores of San Francisco Bay. Though the contrast between the two is startling, both are well

HIDDEN ►

worth exploring. **City of Palo Alto Baylands Nature Preserve** is a land of pickleweed and cord grass, home to the endangered clapper rail and salt marsh harvest mouse. It takes a special person to appreciate the beauty of a salt marsh. For those who don't mind black mud and pungent smells, this preserve offers unique opportunities. There's a small interpretive center here, as well as a boardwalk that leads through the marsh to the edge of the Bay. ~ On the east end of Embarcadero Road, Palo Alto; 415-329-2506.

A major stop along the Pacific Flyway, the marshlands of the City of Palo Alto Baylands Nature Preserve are visited by over one million birds each year.

Most important, the preserve is a birdwatcher's paradise—on a single day, there were once 10,000 western sandpipers in residence. You may see a great egret, four-foot tall great blue heron, northern harrier, canvasback duck, or a burrowing owl.

Also on Embarcadero Road near Baylands is 40-acre **Byxbee Park.** Created on an old landfill site, this waterfront spot features environmental art displays and plenty of room for peacefully contemplating the universe. Mysteriously arranged poles scattered across the moguled landscape make this an intriguing place (as do the wind waves, oyster shell pathways, and industrial flair).

To get in tune for a visit to these mudflats, you can follow a route from Stanford that leads along one of Palo Alto's tree-shaded streets. Most people take University Avenue, the main drag. Instead take Hamilton Avenue, one block to the south, then turn right on Greer Road, and pick up Embarcadero Road to the Bay. Along this **arboreal route** are trees exotic in both name and appearance—Irish yews, sugarplums, bottle-brushes, bunya-bunyas, Australian brush cherries, and monkey puzzle trees.

LODGING

At the **Best Western Grosvenor Hotel** you're just ten minutes from the San Francisco Airport (which is really the only reason to check in to the hotel in the first place). This nine-story facility offers 206 rooms and suites, some with bathtub jet-whirlpools and in-shower saunas. Decorated in mauves and pastels, the rooms feature king-size beds and comfortable sofas. If you like watching planes take off, this is the place for you. Fortunately the rooms are all soundproofed. There's a pool and 24-hour airport shuttle. Continental breakfast is included when your reservations are made through the toll-free number. ~ 380 South Airport Boulevard, South San Francisco; 415-873-3200, 800-722-7141, fax 415-589-3495. MODERATE TO DELUXE.

Just half a mile from the Stanford campus, the European-style **Stanford Park Hotel** offers 162 rooms and eight suites. English yew wood furniture adds to the charm of rooms decorated with landscape paintings. Many offer courtyard views. You can work out in the exercise room and pool. Each afternoon guests gather around the fireplace in the three-story lobby for a hospitality hour.

~ 100 El Camino Real, Menlo Park; 415-322-1234, 800-368-2468, fax 415-322-0975. ULTRA-DELUXE.

DINING

The Castaway provides plate-glass dining on the Bay. Located in a waterfront park, this spiffy establishment specializes in spectacular views. The decor consists of potted plants and high-backed chairs, with a touch of stained glass. Open for lunch, dinner, and weekend brunch, the restaurant has a seafood and steak menu in the evening. Among the entrées are swordfish, lobster tail, filet mignon, and prime rib. At lunch, the choices are similar, the portions smaller. ~ Coyote Point Park, San Mateo; 415-347-1027. MODERATE TO DELUXE.

Nina's Café is a country-style French restaurant with urban elegance. The dinner menu changes every evening, but often includes roasted duckling, sweetbreads flambé, Cajun seafood pasta, and other delicacies. The appetizers alone—escargots, French onion soup, baked brie—could keep a gourmet smiling. Lunch involves crêpes, chicken brochettes, fresh fish, and seafood salad, plus special entrées. This little gem is worth discovering. Closed Sunday. ~ 3525 Alameda de las Pulgas, Menlo Park; 415-854-6386. MODERATE TO DELUXE.

Tresidder Memorial Union on the Stanford University campus has a cafeteria, **Baker Street**, that serves three meals daily. Not exactly gourmet cuisine, the steam-tray food is inexpensive and filling. Sharing the same dining room, the **Corner Pocket** serves student-made pizza, smoothies, ice cream, and "fro-yo." At the **Coffee House** next door, you can order breakfast pastries, or sandwiches and salads at lunch and dinnertime. Each place will be crowded with students. Since the eateries are located near the central quadrangle, they're convenient when touring the campus. ~ 520 Lagunita Drive, Palo Alto; 415-723-5959. BUDGET.

To dine in style while visiting Stanford, I recommend **MacArthur Park**. Located between campus and downtown, it rests in a 1918 building designed by noted Bay Area architect Julia Morgan. Originally serving as a World War I hospitality house, the structure now contains a lovely restaurant specializing in food prepared in an oakwood smoker or mesquite grill, plus a piano bar. There's mesquite chicken breast, famous barbecued baby back ribs, marinated skirt steak, shrimp, sizzling whole catfish, as well as other fresh fish. Vegetarian dishes are also available. The menu is similar at dinner and lunch; they also serve Sunday brunch. ~ 27 University Avenue, Palo Alto; 415-321-9990. MODERATE.

World Wrapps takes the burrito on an international whirlwind tour. Brilliantly decorated in bright Crayola colors of red, yellow, and blue, this popular eatery cooks up such concoctions as mango snapper, Peking duck, and Bombay wraps. For the less adventurous, there's grilled steak and chicken burritos. World Wrapps also specializes in gourmet and health-boosting smoothies, with 14 varieties on the menu. ~ 201 University Avenue, Palo Alto; 415-327-9777. BUDGET.

Way up in the hills above Palo Alto, there's a roadhouse called the **Alpine Inn** that dates back to the 1850s. It's a simple, homey place serving locally famous hamburgers, sandwiches, and other basic fare. The spot is very popular with local folks. You can dine indoors beneath trophy heads or outside at a picnic table. ~ 3915 Alpine Road, Portola Valley; 415-854-4004. BUDGET.

◄ HIDDEN

SHOPPING

The loveliest spot to shop in all California may well be the **Allied Arts Guild**, adjacent to the Stanford campus. Contained in a park-like setting amid fruit trees and flowering gardens, this artists' colony features numerous crafts. Strolling the courtyards of the hacienda, you'll encounter studio-shops devoted to ceramics, candle making, knitting, weaving, woodwork, and needlepoint. ~ 75 Arbor Road, Menlo Park; 415-325-3259.

For detailed maps and cartographic information, it's hard to top the **United States Geological Survey Earth Science Information Center**. In addition to excellent USGS topographic maps, this facility sells thematic maps and various literary works. ~ 345 Middlefield Road, Building 3, Menlo Park; 415-329-4390.

The volumes at USGS are only a sketchy introduction to what you'll find at **Kepler's**. One of the Peninsula's best bookstores, it offers a complete line of paperbacks and hardcovers. ~ 1010 El Camino Real, Menlo Park; 415-324-4321.

If you can't find it here, that elusive volume will doubtless be in one of downtown Palo Alto's many bookstores. This campus town has practically as many bookstores as restaurants. Don't miss **Phileas Fogg's**, a travel bookstore with an excellent selection of guides and maps. ~ 87 Stanford Shopping Center, Palo Alto; 415-327-1754.

To browse shops in downtown Palo Alto, plan to stroll University Avenue from Alma Street to Webster Street, then return along Hamilton Avenue. Like the side streets between, these thoroughfares are door-to-door with boutiques, galleries, and knickknack shops. One of particular interest is the artists' cooperative **Artifactory**, featuring jewelry, pottery, weavings, calligraphy, mask making, and knitting by artists on the premises (classes are also offered here). ~ 226 Hamilton Avenue; 415-853-9685. Also exceptional is the **Gallery House**, which contains striking works of contemporary art and pottery by local artists. ~ 538 Ramona Street; 415-326-1668.

NIGHTLIFE

Night owls flying south from San Francisco will find plenty of diversions along the Peninsula. **Molloy's**, a few miles from the City, is a 100-year-old bar crowded with memories and memorabilia. There's live country, rock, or traditional Irish music every Friday and Saturday. ~ 1655 Old Mission Road, Colma; 415-755-9545.

HIDDEN ►

In an unlikely spot near the San Francisco International Airport, **Caribbean Gardens** bills itself as an international dance club and is undoubtedly one of the peninsula's hottest places to dance to salsa, merengue, reggae, African, and soca music. Cover. ~ 1306 Bayshore Avenue, Burlingame; 415-347-9007.

At **The Castaway**, overlooking San Francisco Bay, you can enjoy a quiet evening and beautiful views along a cozy bar. ~ Coyote Point Park, San Mateo; 415-347-1027.

With a warm atmosphere and 16 microbrewed beers on tap, the **Empire Grill & Tap Room** is a choice spot for a candlelit evening drink. Out back, the spacious patio is complemented by lush greenery and a fountain. Fine cigars are sold and regularly smoked here after dinner. ~ 651 Emerson Street, Palo Alto; 415-321-3030.

St. Michael's Alley is an intimate coffeehouse—a good place to go for a cappuccino, a pastry, and quiet conversation. There's live music (acoustic, blues, reggae, or jazz) Thursday, Friday, and Saturday nights. ~ 806 Emerson Street, Palo Alto; 415-326-2530.

Popular with folks 18 to 21, **The Edge** offers modern deejay rock, dancing, and special events. Cover. ~ 260 California Avenue, Palo Alto; 415-324-1402.

Check the "Once Around the Quad" section of the *Stanford Daily* and other university publications for information about programs on the Stanford campus. You can also call 415-723-0336 for a tape-recorded calendar of events.

BEACHES & PARKS

SAN BRUNO MOUNTAIN STATE AND COUNTY PARK

This 1700-acre facility seems to be perennially under construction. After bitter debates between conservationists and developers, the park was finally established in the late 1970s. Today, it is one of San Francisco's last wild places, harboring six endangered plant species and three endangered butterflies. A spectacular time to visit is during the wildflower season from February through May. Scenically, it provides one of the Bay Area's most spectacular views, a 360° panorama from atop 1314-foot San Bruno Mountain. This hillside park is also a fine place to picnic. There are 12 miles of hiking trails, picnic areas, and toilets. Day-use fee, $3 on the weekend. ~ In Brisbane a few miles south of San Francisco. From 101 South, take the Sierra Point exit to Lagoon Road. Follow through to Bayshore Boulevard and go right. Follow to Guadalupe Canyon Parkway and go left; 415-355-8289.

COYOTE POINT PARK A multi-use facility, this bayshore park contains everything from a museum to a firing range, with stops in between for a marina and four playgrounds. There's a pebble beach for sunbathers, a nearby golf course, and a $3.8 million Wildlife Habitats exhibit occupied by a menagerie of local animals. Because of the proximity to San Francisco Airport, jets pass overhead continually, but there are excellent views of the Bay, and the park is extremely popular with local residents. Facilities include restrooms, picnic areas, a restaurant, and a museum (admission); showers and lifeguard in summer. Day-use fee, $4. ~ Located in San Mateo; from Route 101 south take the Poplar Avenue exit to Coyote Point Drive; 415-573-2592.

HUDDART COUNTY PARK Situated on the Bay side of the Santa Cruz Mountains, this densely forested park provides a touch of the wild within whistling distance of San Francisco. Rising to 2000 feet, it features redwood and mixed evergreen forests. Twenty-five miles of hiking trails crisscross the landscape, and the park is a habitat for blacktail deer, raccoons, coyotes, and an occasional bobcat or gray fox. There are picnic areas (some with shelters and electricity), restrooms, playground, and archery range. Day-use fee, $4. ~ Located in Woodside; take Woodside Road off Route 280, then go three-and-a-half miles west to 1100 Kings Mountain Road; 415-851-0326 or 415-851-1210.

WUNDERLICH PARK Also set along the eastern slopes of the Santa Cruz Mountains, this facility is largely undeveloped. It does have a private stable, however, and is very popular with equestrians. Hikers also favor the 25 miles of trails which wind along mountain streams, across rolling meadows, and through redwood groves. The only facilities here are toilets. ~ Located on Route 84 in Woodside, two miles west of the town center; 415-851-1210.

LOS TRANCOS AND MONTE BELLO OPEN SPACE PRESERVES Together these contiguous parks cover over 3300 acres of rolling countryside. They're located in the hills above Palo Alto and provide sweeping views from San Francisco to Mount Diablo. The terrain varies from grassland to mixed evergreen forest to canyons shaded with oak trees. Most visitors are drawn here by the San Andreas Fault, which bisects Los Trancos and can be explored along one of the area's many hiking trails. From these heights, it's possible to visually follow the fault past San Francisco. The only facilities are toilets at Monte Bello. ~ From Route 280 in Palo Alto, take Page Mill Road seven miles southwest. The entrances to both preserves are along the roadside; 415-691-1200.

▲ Campers can spend the night at the very primitive Black Mountain Backpack Camp, which is a one-and-a-half-mile hike from Page Mill Road. A permit is required for overnight camping.

The South Bay

Located about 50 miles south of San Francisco, the San Jose area is a sprawling collection of cities and towns laid out like Los Angeles. It's one of California's wealthiest and fastest-growing sections, home to the state's vaunted electronics industry. Scattered around this Santa Clara Valley region are several points of interest.

SIGHTS

For sightseeing information, your best resource is the **Tour and Travel Information Center.** Located in downtown San Jose, it is run by the San Jose Convention and Visitors Bureau and can provide details and directions for the entire area. ~ 333 West San Carlos Street; 408-295-9600. For information on San Jose and the Santa Clara Valley in general, contact the **San Jose Metropolitan Chamber of Commerce.** ~ 180 South Market Street, San Jose; 408-291-5250.

Downtown, a billion-dollar renovation has brought a metamorphosis to this formerly rundown area. Center stage stands the 425,000-square-foot **San Jose Convention Center.** Critical raves met this unique soft-peach-colored structure—with its enormous vaulted entranceway highlighted by a porcelain-tile mural, its multilevel glass-enclosed arcade and concourse, and its black-and-white marble terrazzo promenade—upon its completion in 1989. ~ West San Carlos Street between Almaden Boulevard and Market Street, San Jose; 408-277-3900.

High-class hotels, restaurants, shops, and financial centers are also sprouting in the area, where people can now zip along via a modern light-rail system. Landscaping has not been forgotten amid all this glass and concrete. The city has planted 600 sycamore trees to shade the downtown transit mall and has spiffed up **Plaza Park,** a green oasis with palms and acres of grass along Market Street across from the convention center.

The nearby **Children's Discovery Museum** presents an amazing collection of interactive exhibits. Kids can climb on real fire trucks and ambulances, operate traffic lights along simulated roadways, help run the city's water department or contact others using video phones. Your kids can also explore a hands-on art studio and an interactive bubble exhibit. Closed Monday. Admission. ~ 180 Woz Way, San Jose; 408-298-5437.

For larger kids and adults there's the **Tech Museum of Innovation.** Here you'll discover a collection of interactive exhibits in which you can drive a space rover through a Martian landscape, view a tower of 500 telephone books representing the amount of information in a single DNA molecule or have a robot draw a picture of you. Closed on Monday from September to June. Admission. ~ 145 West San Carlos Street, San Jose; 408-279-7150.

The **San Jose Museum of Art**, housed in a century-old Romanesque-style building, is now complemented by a new wing featuring a barrel-vaulted ceiling and two outdoor sculpture courts. Focusing on 20th-century art, the collection includes such contemporary artists as Richard Diebenkorn, Robert Arneson, Rupert Garcia, David Best, and Robert Hudson. Over the next several years the museum will feature exhibitions of American art from the permanent collection of New York's Whitney Museum. Closed Monday. Admission. ~ 110 South Market Street, San Jose; 408-294-2787.

The Tech Museum of Innovation features a World Wide Web exhibit with free access and regular demonstrations.

Not all of the changes that took place in downtown San Jose involved new construction. Two restored historic houses in San Pedro Square, the Fallon House and Peralta Adobe, form a living history museum designed to honor the city's roots. The **Peralta Adobe**, San Jose's only surviving adobe structure, illustrates California pueblo life in both the 1790s and 1840s. The **Fallon House**, an Italianate Victorian mansion built by an early mayor, shows how a prosperous family lived in the 1850s. Tours are given Wednesday through Sunday. ~ 175 West St. John Street, San Jose; 408-993-8182.

Located near the Museum of Art, the **American Museum of Quilts and Textiles** is another recommended stop. Quilts and other textiles from around the world are featured in changing exhibits. Closed Monday. Admission. ~ 60 South Market Street, San Jose; 408-971-0323.

While San Jose likes to bill itself as a high tech capital, you can turn back the clock with a trip on one of the city's **historic trolleys**. Built at the beginning of the century, these refurbished railroad cars depart from the transit mall at 2nd and San Carlos streets on a 20-minute loop. ~ San Jose; 408-321-2300.

Kelley Park contains more than 150 wooded acres with picnic areas and recreation facilities. There's a petting zoo (admission) for children which also contains rides and puppet shows. Next to this playland sits the Japanese Friendship Garden, a serene setting with koi pond, footbridges, and a teahouse. ~ Story and Senter roads, San Jose; 408-277-5254.

Of Kelly Park's several attractions, the highlight is the **San Jose Historical Museum**, an outdoor museum featuring several antique buildings in a plaza setting. Inside the old Pacific Hotel, you'll find displays tracing San Jose's history from the Indians through the trappers, miners, and farmers. The nearby soda fountain, still operating, is definitely the highpoint of any visit. Not far from here rise the old firehouse, a clapboard livery stable complete with rickety wagons, printing office, Gothic-style house from the 1870s, and a 1927 gas station with gravity-feed pumps. Admission. ~ 1600 Senter Road, San Jose; 408-287-2290.

Certainly San Jose's most unique and exotic site is the **Rosicrucian Egyptian Museum**. The landscaping and buildings throughout this elaborate complex (which includes a planetarium and science museum) re-create ancient Egypt. There are sphinxes, tile murals of charioteers, and temples decorated with hieroglyphs. The museum entranceway is lined on either side by stone statues of rams, reproducing an ancient avenue in Thebes. Inside are mummies dating back 3000 years, alabaster urns, bronze pieces portraying lion-headed goddesses, incense burners in the shape of falcon heads, statues of the Nile gods, and mummy shrouds painted with holy insignia. Also featuring Babylonian, Persian, and Assyrian artifacts, it's a place to make you ponder the texture of life and the structure of infinity. Admission. ~ Park and Naglee avenues, San Jose; 408-947-3636.

If the Rosicrucian museum represents humankind's search for universal meaning, the **Winchester Mystery House** is a study in the meaningless lives of the idle rich. Numbering 160 rooms and covering four acres, this Victorian monstrosity is still unfinished. It was built by Sarah Winchester, heiress to the Winchester rifle fortune, who kept adding on rooms for 38 years in the belief that she would live as long as the house continued to grow. Either the carpenters took a day off or Sarah's seeress miscalculated—she died in 1922. Her legacy is an architectural riddle complete with stairways leading nowhere and closets that open onto walls. The interior design is very beautiful, however, and there are ghost stories galore surrounding the house and its unbalanced owner. Admission. ~ 525 South Winchester Boulevard, San Jose; 408-247-2101.

The Winchester house is frivolous, and **Great America** adds fun to the frivolity. A 100-acre theme park, it re-creates New England during the Revolutionary War, New Orleans in the 1850s, the Klondike gold rush, and early 20th-century rural America. There are also movies, theatrical revues, concerts, video galleries, a flight simulator, and white-knuckle rides with menacing names such as Tidal Wave, Demon, Vortex, and The Edge. The newest addition is the Drop Zone, the world's tallest freefall ride. Closed during the winter. Admission. ~ Great America Parkway, Santa Clara; 408-988-1800.

The South Bay's other features are further afield, and far more placid. **Los Gatos**, a wealthy and luxurious town in the foothills of the Santa Cruz Mountains, provides peaceful country lanes and Carpenter Gothic-style homes. **Saratoga** also contains sumptuous hillside homes.

None, however, match the grandeur of **Villa Montalvo**. This Mediterranean-style mansion and surrounding estate was home to

James Phelan, a three-term mayor of San Francisco and former U.S. Senator. Today his 19-room house serves as a cultural center featuring artistic exhibits and events; the luxurious grounds have been converted to an arboretum laced with nature trails. There are gardens, rare plants, creeks, and forests of maple and oak. ~ 15400 Montalvo Road, Saratoga; 408-741-3421.

Hakone Gardens, smaller and more modest, is a lovely Japanese-style retreat with wisteria arbors, dwarf pines, and a wooden footbridge. Irises and rushes border the koi pond and a waterfall spills across the landscape. A perfect place to meditate, or simply soak up the sun, this enchanting garden also contains a house built without nails that serves as a cultural exchange center. On the first Thursday afternoon of each month, a tea ceremony is performed, and on summer weekends docent-led tours of the grounds are available. Admission. ~ 21000 Big Basin Way, Saratoga; 408-741-4994.

◄ HIDDEN

The Santa Clara Valley formerly represented one of the nation's largest fruit-growing regions. Despite the urban sprawl following the electronics revolution, it still boasts **orchards and farms.** Some permit visitors to pick produce directly from the fields. The Small Farms Center at UC Davis can provide a list of farms in the area. A few hours on the farm is a great way to escape the city and capture the region's rural past. ~ 916-757-8910.

The valley still supports numerous wineries, some offering tours and winetasting. **Mirassou Vineyards & Winery** is a sixth-generation family concern producing generic and varietal wines as well as champagne. While the grapes here don't match those of Napa Valley, the winery is well worth a visit. ~ 3000 Aborn Road, San Jose; 408-274-4000.

The 45-minute drive to the **Lick Observatory**, atop 4209-foot Mount Hamilton, will carry you even further from the smoggy center of San Jose. One of the world's largest telescopes, a giant eye 120 inches in diameter, stares heavenward from this lofty perch. In operation for nearly a century, the observatory sponsors guided tours and a visitors center. ~ Mount Hamilton Road, San Jose; 408-274-5061.

Mount Hamilton Road (Route 130) winds over 20 miles past rolling ranch lands, oak groves, and flowering fields en route to the summit. With the white-domed observatory above you and the entire South Bay spread below, there are views no telescope can hope to match.

LODGING

An art deco gem restored to its 1931 grandeur is the **Hotel De Anza**, a 100-room boutique hotel that is a fine component of the impressive urban facelift taking place in downtown San Jose. Rooms are light and airy, decorated with the blond woods and geometric prints reflective of the 1930s. ~ 233 West Santa Clara Street, San

Jose; 408-286-1000, 800-843-3700, fax 408-286-0500. DELUXE TO ULTRA-DELUXE.

Combining easy suburban living with a rustic setting is the **Inn At Saratoga**, a contemporary 46-room hotel. Located in downtown Saratoga, within strolling distance of the town's many shops, the inn is backdropped by a creek and wooded park. Each guest room looks out on a forest of maple, pine, and eucalyptus. The lobby, where guests are served complimentary continental breakfast and afternoon hors d'oeuvres, is decorated in English Country style. Guest rooms are adorned with California artworks, painted in soft pastel colors, and equipped with light wood furniture. A small hotel with a European theme, the inn adds a personal touch to its service. ~ 20645 4th Street, Saratoga; 408-867-5020, 800-543-5020, fax 408-741-0981. ULTRA-DELUXE.

Of Northern California's many hostels, **Sanborn Park Hostel** is among the prettiest. It sits in a striking 1908 building fashioned from redwood logs in the midst of a county park. Dense forest surrounds the place and nearby hiking trails lead up into the Santa Cruz Mountains. There are several bunk rooms, as well as a kitchen, laundry, and living room with stone fireplace. ~ 15808 Sanborn Road, Saratoga; 408-741-9555. BUDGET.

DINING

In downtown San Jose, home of business professionals and urban developers, there's an invitingly informal place called **Eulipia Restaurant and Bar**. With its local crowd and light, airy, bistro-like atmosphere, the place is a prime choice when you're in the mood for charcoal-grilled food. Serving lunch and dinner, they offer an array of fresh fish, chicken, and pasta dishes. Closed Monday; dinner only on weekends. ~ 374 South 1st Street, San Jose; 408-280-6161. MODERATE.

✔ CHECK THESE OUT—UNIQUE LODGING

- *Budget:* Park your bags at the **Sanborn Park Hostel**, tucked away in a 1908 redwood-log building and surrounded by dense forest in Saratoga. *page 152*
- *Moderate:* Check into **Grand Island Inn**, a former speakeasy in Ryde once owned by horror-movie star Lon Chaney, Jr. *page 180*
- *Deluxe to ultra-deluxe:* Slip into one of the nine vessels at **Dockside Boat & Bed** fleet, Oakland's classy collection of moored boats. *page 160*
- *Ultra-deluxe:* Gather around the fireplace in the three-story lobby of the European-style **Stanford Park Hotel** in Menlo Park for an afternoon hospitality hour. *page 143*

Budget: under $50 Moderate: $50–$90 Deluxe: $90–$120 Ultra-deluxe: over $120

For that special occasion there's **Paolo's Restaurant**, a lavishly decorated dining room with a sophisticated Italian cuisine. The menu, which changes seasonally, has more than a dozen pasta dishes as well as such entrées as roast duck, poached striped bass, scampi, and grilled rib eye. ~ 333 West San Carlos Street, San Jose; 408-294-2558. MODERATE TO DELUXE.

Like its sister restaurants in San Diego and San Francisco, **Hamburger Mary's**, next to the Peralta Adobe in San Pedro Square, specializes in custom-made burgers but also serves sandwiches, salads, steaks, mahimahi, and weekend brunch with free champagne. Outside is a secluded courtyard for relaxed dining; inside is a kaleidoscope for the eyes and ears with two video screens and a funky flea market of prints, board games, and antiques stuck to the walls. ~ 170 West St. John Street, San Jose; 408-947-1667. BUDGET.

Part of a whole new infusion of sophisticated bistro-style restaurants in downtown San Jose is **Bella Mia**, which packs in the upwardly mobile at lunch and dinner for flatbread pizzas, pastas, and succulent meat entrées such as spit-roasted duck with raspberry vinegar sauce and grilled pork chops with sour cherries and orange brandy sauce. On the weekend, the restaurant offers dinner theater, and on Sunday morning there's a jazz brunch on the outdoor patio. ~ 58 South 1st Street, San Jose; 408-280-1993. MODERATE.

Bella Saratoga, once the location of the original Bella Mia in San Jose, offers a similar menu in the more laid-back setting of a yellow Victorian house with sunny patio. ~ 14503 Big Basin Way, Saratoga; 408-741-5115. MODERATE.

You'll have to travel many leagues to find a seafood restaurant as good as **Steamer's Fish Again and Pasta Too!** Serving scallops, prawns, shrimp, and crab, they also offer calamari cooked two different ways plus a host of seafood pasta dishes. Attractively paneled in hardwood, the establishment features an oyster bar, dining area, and fashionable saloon. Quite popular with young professionals, this gourmet spot is usually very crowded. ~ 50 University Avenue, Los Gatos; 408-395-2722. MODERATE TO DELUXE.

SHOPPING

Much of San Jose's downtown district is continuing to be refurbished. Already refurbished, amid the stately palms and 1920s houses of San Jose's Willow Glen neighborhood is **Lincoln Avenue**, a street lined with craft and antiques shops, cafés and gourmet delis.

For hours of interesting shopping and some of the best bargains in the South Bay, head for the **San Jose Flea Market**. It has 2700 vendors selling everything from bikes to books and 35 food stalls for a quick order of chow mein or a plate of nachos. You could get lost here. Open Wednesday through Sunday. ~ 1590 Berryessa Road, San Jose; 408-453-1110.

Some of the area's better shops have moved to the suburbs where they cater to Silicon Valley's affluent young executives. Two towns are particularly noteworthy.

The San Jose Flea Market is the largest flea market in the entire country.

Saratoga features an upscale shopping strip in the center of town along **Saratoga Avenue**. There are antique stores and galleries galore, as well as malls with an assortment of shops.

Los Gatos is quite simply a window browser's dream. Along **Santa Cruz Avenue** from Saratoga–Los Gatos Road to Main Street are block on block of posh establishments. There are stores specializing in antique interiors, teddy bears, magic tricks, and travel accessories. You'll find high-fashion boutiques, gourmet food outlets, novelty shops, custom clothiers, and antique garment stores. **Old Town**, a misnomered mall at 50 Universal Avenue, is another prime shopping enclave. Attractively landscaped with flowering gardens, it features a string of stores in a hacienda-style building.

NIGHTLIFE The focus for San Jose high culture is the **Center for the Performing Arts,** located at 255 Almaden Boulevard in the downtown district. The **San Jose Symphony** (408-288-2828) performs here regularly, as does the **San Jose Civic Light Opera** (408-453-7100), and the center presents many other concerts and special events. Also consider the **San Jose Repertory Company** at the Montgomery Theatre, located at West San Carlos and Market streets; 408-291-2255.

Head on over to **Agenda** in SOFA, South of First Street Area, San Jose's SOHO/SOMA/hip and trendy district. This three-level establishment is a dinner club serving California regional cuisine on the ground floor, a lounge with live jazz nightly upstairs, and a speakeasy with jazz in the basement. ~ 399 South 1st Street, San Jose; 408-287-3991.

The Saddlerack is San Jose's answer to Gilley's in Houston. A country-style saloon with enough space to herd cattle, the place has three large dancefloors and two stages for bands. They also bring in top name country rock bands Wednesday through Saturday. ~ 1310 Auzerais Avenue, San Jose; 408-286-3393.

Frederic Remington bronzes of cowboy life, American Indian paintings, and photos of natural areas adorn **Buck's.** This popular bar attracts a gay and lesbian crowd as well as a straight clientele. There's dancing to country and popular deejay-selected tunes. ~ 301 Stockton Street, San Jose; 408-286-1176.

Hamburger Mary's, a gathering place for gay men and women, features two bars, a gameroom, piano lounge, and patio. The deejay dance music varies from Top-40 to country-and-western.

Cover Thursday through Saturday. ~ 170 West St. John Street, San Jose; 408-947-1667.

Mountain Charley's Saloon is a down-home drinking hole with a magnificent old wooden bar that must weigh four tons. The live sounds here include rock of the '80s and '90s; most of the bands hail from the Bay Area. Cover. ~ 15 North Santa Cruz Avenue, Los Gatos; 408-395-8880.

BEACHES & PARKS

SANBORN-SKYLINE COUNTY PARK Rising from the foothills of the Santa Cruz Mountains to 3000 feet, this outstanding facility is covered with Douglas fir and second-growth redwoods. It covers over 6000 acres, spreading across several ecological zones. Along the 20 miles of hiking trails, there are extraordinary views of the Santa Clara Valley; the trails also connect with a network leading all the way to the Pacific. Facilities include restrooms, picnic areas, a science museum, and a hostel. Day-use fee, $3. ~ Located off Route 9 about four miles west of Saratoga, the park is at 16055 Sanborn Road; 408-867-4642.

▲ There are 33 walk-in sites at $6 per night; 15 RV sites with full hookups at $20 per night. Information, 408-358-3751.

The East Bay

Point your compass east from San Francisco, cross the Bay Bridge, and lo and behold, you have arrived in the East Bay. Framed by wooded hills and looking out on the Golden Gate, Oakland and Berkeley are the two key towns in this suburban enclave.

SIGHTS

To tour the former, a city of 386,800 people, pick up the maps and brochures available from the **Oakland Convention and Visitors Authority**. ~ 550 10th, Suite 214, Oakland; 510-839-9000.

Prettiest place in all Oakland is **Lake Merritt**, an unassuming body of water that happens to be the world's biggest saltwater tidal lake located within a city. Now that you've digested another meaningless statistic, you can work it off by joining the legions of joggers and bicyclists who continually circle the lake's three-mile perimeter. Or you can practice lawn bowling, stroll the park's botanical gardens, or rent a sailboat, rowboat, paddle boat, kayak, or canoe. ~ Sailboat House: 568 Bellevue Avenue, Oakland; 510-444-3807. For kids, there are duck feeding areas and a **Children's Fairyland** complete with rides and puppet shows. Closed Monday and Tuesday in the spring and fall; closed Monday through Thursday in winter. Admission. ~ Grand Avenue at Bellevue Avenue, Oakland; 510-452-2259.

Also part of this lakeside complex is the **Camron-Stanford House**, an 1876 Victorian home decorated with furniture from that historic era. Admission. ~ 1418 Lakeside Drive, Oakland; 510-836-1976.

For complete information about Lake Merritt, stop by the **Office of Parks and Recreation.** ~ 1520 Lakeside Drive, Oakland; 510-238-7275.

Located just a few blocks from Lake Merritt sits the **Oakland Museum**, a beautifully landscaped, triple-tiered facility. With its terraced gardens, courtyards, and lily ponds, the place has won international acclaim. The theme here is California—its history, art, and environment. Historical exhibits trace the area's development from early Indian settlements to the present day, artistic works present California artists from the Gold Rush era forward, and the natural science exhibits carry visitors along a simulated exploration route from the Pacific to the Sierra Nevada peaks. ~ 1000 Oak Street, Oakland; 510-238-3401.

HIDDEN ►

Chinatown in Oakland is a miniature neighborhood compared to San Francisco's crowded enclave, but it's still an intriguing area to stroll. Most of the markets and restaurants lie along 8th and 9th streets between Harrison and Franklin streets. Early morning is the time to visit. That's when you'll see live catfish being delivered to local restaurants and shopkeepers shelving daikon roots, Napa cabbage, and other Chinese-style vegetables.

Another area that will be of increasing interest is **Preservation Park** on 9th Street between Broadway and Washington. All around this cluster of old Victorian houses, downtown blocks are being refurbished and developed. Hotels, restaurants, shops, and offices are moving to this formerly rundown section of town and promise to turn it into one of Oakland's spiffiest commercial districts.

Jack London Square is everyone's favorite Oakland sightseeing spot. Today it harbors retail shops, overpriced restaurants, and heavily touristed bars, but the place packs a lot of history. Located on the Alameda estuary and overlooking one of the world's busiest ports, it marks the city's early days. Richard Henry Dana visited the area in 1835 while gathering material for *Two Years Before the Mast*; by 1852 the waterfront boasted a couple of rickety wharves from which the hamlet's oak timber was shipped to San Francisco. ~ At the foot of Broadway, Oakland.

A TOUCH OF CLASS

One of the grandest mansions in the Bay Area, the **Dunsmuir House and Gardens** sits high in the Oakland hills. A redwood paneled game room, turn-of-the-century kitchen, greenhouse, carriage house, and formal gardens make this baronial spot a favorite retreat. The grounds are open to the public at no charge from March through October; there is a fee to tour the house, which is open to the public from April through September. ~ 2960 Peralta Oaks Court; 510-615-5555.

Jack London, who grew up in Oakland, was in turn a sailor and oyster pirate along this hard-bitten waterfront. You can stroll the boardwalks, conjuring visions of the fabled adventure writer, then visit the **Jack London Cabin.** It's a classic log cabin, little more than a dozen feet across, where London lived in 1897 during the Klondike gold rush. Back then it rested along the north fork of Henderson Creek up in the Yukon. Today it sits next to **Heinold's First and Last Chance**, a funky woodframe saloon which London haunted as a young man. They still serve spirits, so you can engage in a little historical research while toasting the writer who made Oakland infamous. ~ 56 Jack London Square, Oakland; 510-839-6761.

From Oakland, Telegraph Avenue beelines to the University of California campus in Berkeley. During the tumultuous '60s and early '70s, "Telegraph" was the battleground for a wave of riots. Demonstrators protesting the Vietnam War spilled out from the campus to confront phalanxes of police and National Guardsmen. Protesters trashed the Bank of America's plate-glass windows so many times the bank finally replaced them with brick. Police brutality ran rampant.

The **mural** at the corner of Telegraph Avenue and Haste Street brilliantly depicts this chaotic era. Tracing the history of the Berkeley movement in overlapping images, it portrays the Free Speech Movement, anti-war protests, flower children, and the battle for People's Park.

In May 1969, a patch of Berkeley ground became a symbol for an entire generation. **People's Park**, a vacant lot owned by the university, was expropriated early in 1969 by radicals and converted to a public facility. The university responded by fencing the area, demonstrators promptly tore down the enclosure, and several days of vicious rioting followed. National Guardsmen and police occupied the town, killing one bystander and blinding another. Today the university has developed the park and installed volleyball courts, though part of it remains a public area planted with flowers and occupied by street people. ~ Bowditch Street between Haste Street and Dwight Way, Berkeley.

One of the nation's finest schools, the **University of California–Berkeley** is home to over 30,000 students. Founded in 1868, it covers over 1200 acres and is easy to tour with a map available at the information center in the Student Union. ~ Telegraph Avenue and Bancroft Way, Berkeley; 510-642-4636.

From here you can stroll across **Sproul Plaza**, site of countless rallies and demonstrations during the Vietnam era. Sproul Hall, the administration building, was the scene of a massive sit-in during the 1964 Free Speech Movement. Led by Mario Savio, over 700 people were dragged from the building, the largest mass arrest in California history.

Centerpiece of the campus is **Sather Tower**, a 307-foot spire modeled after St. Mark's campanile in Venice. A 61-bell carillon tolls from this lofty perch, and an elevator (admission) carries visitors to an observation perch from which there are extraordinary views. Just west of the campanile sits **South Hall**, the oldest and prettiest building on campus, and **Bancroft Library**, which houses the world's finest Western Americana collection.

Among its many features, the university also offers several important museums. The **Phoebe Hearst Museum of Anthropology**, boasting a half-million specimens, has fine collections of American Indian artifacts and archaeological and ethnographic materials from Europe, Asia, Egypt, and the Pacific Islands. Call to find out what is currently on display, as all exhibits are temporary. Admission. ~ Kroeber Hall, UC Berkeley; 510-643-7648.

The **University Art Museum**, with its skylights and spiraling ramps, features a permanent collection of Western and Asian artworks. There are oils by old masters and contemporary artists alike, as well as a sculpture garden on the grounds. Closed Monday and Tuesday. Admission. ~ 2626 Bancroft Way, UC Berkeley; 510-642-0808.

HIDDEN ► Not far from the University, the **Judah L. Magnes Museum** is an important center for Jewish history and art. Occupying a stately 1908 three-story house, its collections include a room dedicated to the Holocaust, works by contemporary artists, and a wealth of rare books, oral histories, and original documents. Closed Friday and Saturday. ~ 2911 Russell Street, Berkeley; 510-849-2710.

En route to the next museum, located in the hills above the Berkeley campus, visit the **Botanical Garden**. One of the finest in the state, it contains over 11,000 species arranged geographically. There are environments planted with African, South American, Himalayan, Asian, European, Australasian, and Californian species, as well as an herb garden, Japanese pool, and palm garden. ~ 200 Centennial Drive, Berkeley; 510-642-3343.

THE WAY IT WAS

Just a minute from the freeway and blissfully behind the times, 205-acre **Ardenwood Historic Farm** is a charming farmstead preserving the region's agrarian tradition. Tour the Queen Anne home, watch a blacksmith at work, enjoy craft and cooking displays, visit the cornfield, and see living history demonstrations. Closed Monday through Wednesday. Admission. ~ 34600 Ardenwood Boulevard, Fremont; 510-796-0663.

Continue uphill to the **Lawrence Hall of Science**, an oddly shaped structure that looks more like a southwestern rock formation than a building. Intended for the eight-to-eighty set, this marvelous place is a hands-on museum with labs where you perform experiments and play computer games. Kids can handle animals in the biology lab, and the planetarium features a series of stellar shows. Admission. ~ Centennial Drive, Berkeley; 510-642-5132.

For a tour of the **Berkeley hills**, follow Centennial Drive up to Grizzly Peak Boulevard and continue north; Euclid Avenue will lead you back down to central Berkeley. All through these magnificent hills are splendid houses of brick and brown shingle; others re-create Spanish styles with red tile roofs and whitewashed facades. The views spread across the Bay to San Francisco and out beyond the Golden Gate.

To experience some of the East Bay's lesser-known locales, head south on Route 880 to the **San Francisco Bay Wildlife Refuge Center**. Within this broad, flat expanse of salt grass and pickleweed you'll find 30 miles of trails and 250 bird species. ~ Near the junction of Route 84 and Thornton Avenue, on Marshland Road, Newark; 510-792-0222.

There's a visitors center to help direct you through this wetland, but the highlight of your explorations will undoubtedly be the tiny ghost town of **Drawbridge**. Back in the late 19th century this remote railroad town, accessible then only by train or boat, sported a couple hotels and a colony of hunters' shacks. Today the track is still in use but the sole signs of human habitation are the old vacation shacks slowly sinking back into the mud. Access is by guided tour from May through November on Saturdays only. ~ 510-792-0222.

◄HIDDEN

From here it's a short drive east on Route 84 to the town of **Niles**. Actually part of Fremont, this falsefront community played an important role in the history of Hollywood. More than 450 one-reel films were shot here after Essanay Studios made it their West Coast headquarters around 1910. Charlie Chaplin's classic *The Tramp* was filmed in town. You can still see a few of the silent stars' cottages on 2nd Street between F and G streets. If you head east into Niles Canyón on Route 84 you'll pass the rolling hills where Bronco Billy filmed his fabled Westerns.

◄HIDDEN

Over the East Bay hills in Danville rests the **Eugene O'Neill National Historic Site**. Here during the 1940s playwright Eugene O'Neill resided in a beautiful home overlooking the Las Trampas Wilderness while writing some of his greatest dramas—*The Iceman Cometh*, *A Moon for the Misbegotten*, and *Long Day's Journey into Night*. Decorated in the fashion of the era, Tao House and its grounds are open to the public. Access is by bus only; arrangements can be made through the National Park Service. Tours are run twice a day, Wednesday through Sunday, at no charge. ~ 510-838-0249.

LODGING

A 1927 art deco beauty, the **Lake Merritt Hotel** has been completely refurbished and brought up to 1990s' standards. Overlooking Lake Merritt, this 51-room hotel has stylish rooms and suites. Most rooms have refrigerators; all suites have kitchenettes. ~ 1800 Madison Street, Oakland; 510-832-2300, 800-933-4683, fax 510-832-7150. DELUXE TO ULTRA-DELUXE.

When you're ready for a nautical experience, why not spend the night on one of the nine vessels in the **Dockside Boat & Bed** fleet. Moored sailboats and power yachts ranging up to 75 feet in length are fully equipped for the night and some even offer whirlpool baths. They are available in both Oakland and San Francisco. Continental breakfast is included. ~ 77 Jack London Square, Oakland; 510-444-5858. DELUXE TO ULTRA-DELUXE.

With each of the four guest rooms named for an architect, **Elmwood House** is a gracious bed-and-breakfast inn located in a classic Berkeley brown-shingle residence built in 1902. The gay-friendly hostelry located four blocks south of the University of California campus offers proximity to the cafés, import shops and gourmet delis of the Elmwood and Rockridge neighborhoods. Continental breakfast. ~ 2609 College Avenue, Berkeley; 510-540-5123, 800-540-3050, fax 510-540-5123. MODERATE.

One of the coziest spots in the Bay Area is **Gramma's Rose Garden Inn**, a 1905 Tudor-style house converted to an inn. The public areas in this homey establishment include several ornately designed sitting rooms as well as a spacious yard and deck. There are 11 guest rooms in the main house plus 29 more in four adjacent buildings. Many are creatively appointed with hand-carved headboards, antique wardrobes, quilts, and plump armchairs, but the primary antiques at Gramma's are the houses themselves. The price includes breakfast, and wine and cheese in the afternoons. Gramma's provides the best of both worlds: a country inn in the city. ~ 2740 Telegraph Avenue, Berkeley; 510-549-2145, fax 510-549-1085. DELUXE.

When looking for a convenient location, it's hard to top the **Hotel Durant**. This 140-room facility sits just one block from the Berkeley campus. Designed for preppies and their parents, it nevertheless possesses charm. The hotel includes a restaurant and pub. The rooms are creatively decorated with photographs from Berkeley's early days, contain hardwood furniture, and feature all the creature comforts from cable television to shower-tub combinations. ~ 2600 Durant Avenue, Berkeley; 510-845-8981, 800-238-7268, fax 510-486-8336. DELUXE.

Right across the street from the Berkeley campus is the **Bancroft Club Hotel**, a 22-room boutique hotel listed on the National Register of Historic Places. A prime example of the Arts and Crafts architecture that once flourished in Berkeley, the 1928 building was designed by Walter T. Steilberg, one of Julia Morgan's associates, as a private clubhouse for the College Women's Club. Many rooms feature large balconies and there's a rooftop garden with panoramic views of San Francisco Bay. Continental breakfast included. ~ 2680 Bancroft Way, Berkeley; 510-549-1000, 800-549-1002, fax 510-549-1070. MODERATE TO DELUXE.

DINING

In Oakland's Chinatown section, there's a restaurant that can compete dish for dish with many of San Francisco's popular Chinese restaurants. **Hunan Restaurant** serves Mandarin-style cuisine with special flair. Among the dozens of dishes are smoked tea duck, Szechuan prawns, Peking spareribs, squid, braised fish, and ginger crab. This family restaurant is highly recommended. ~ 392 11th Street, Oakland; 510-444-1155. MODERATE TO DELUXE.

Jack London Square, a high-rent area situated along the Oakland waterfront, specializes in expensive restaurants. **Il Pescatore**, however, is a reasonably priced place with a view of the marina and estuary. The decorative motif is nautical and the menu follows the theme, specializing in seafood entrées like scampi, calamari, and salmon. There are also numerous Italian-style dishes, including veal scaloppine, chicken cacciatore, and eggplant parmigiana. Closed Monday. ~ 57 Jack London Square, Oakland; 510-465-2188. MODERATE.

✔ CHECK THESE OUT—UNIQUE DINING

- *Budget:* Stop by **Alpine Inn**, a roadhouse in Portola Valley where diners have been pulling in since the 1850s. *page 145*
- *Moderate:* Join Mill Valley locals at **Avenue Grill**, and soak up the warmth of the fiery rotisserie behind the long counter. *page 174*
- *Deluxe:* Dine on "Louisiana Fancyfine" gourmet Creole dishes at **T. J.'s Gingerbread House**, while a gallery of rag dolls watch from the Victorian shelves. *page 162*
- *Ultra-deluxe:* Indulge yourself at **Chez Panisse**, where owner Alice Waters has presented meals to world notables, including President Bill Clinton. *page 164*

Budget: under $8 Moderate: $8–$16 Deluxe: $16–$24 Ultra-deluxe: over $24

The nearby **Oakland Grill** is located away from the water in an old produce-market warehouse. This eatery offers a steak and seafood dinner menu. Lunch consists of sandwiches and salads, and breakfast is served all day. With knotty-pine booths and potted trees, it's an attractive setting. ~ 301 Franklin Street, Oakland; 510-835-1176. MODERATE.

Old town Oakland with its red-brick facades has catered to the new trend in social life, the microbrewery. Down on Washington Street, a block away from the Convention Center, the **Pacific Brewing Company** boasts award-winning homebrew and an elbow-polished hardwood bar where executives battle for the bartender's attention after 5. At lunch, bartenders double as waiters and serve hearty blue-collar fare like bangers and mash or meat pies. The service is notoriously slow, but beer gourmets don't mind. ~ 906 Washington Street, Oakland; 510-836-2739. MODERATE.

T. J.'s Gingerbread House is the place to enjoy "Louisiana Fancyfine" gourmet Creole dishes while a gallery of rag dolls adorning the shelves of a Victorian dining room looks on. This truly enchanted cottage serves up hunks of "sassy" cornbread, heaping bowls of jambalaya and such specialties as whiskey-stuffed lobster and smoked prime rib. There is also a dining annex that looks like a greenhouse and a retail shop selling handicrafts and the restaurant's delicious cookies. Open for lunch and two dinner seatings; reservations are required. ~ 741 5th Street, Oakland; 510-444-7373. DELUXE.

HIDDEN ►

L. J. Quinn's Lighthouse claims to be Oakland's best-kept secret, and it may very well be. Hidden away across from Coast Guard Island along the Oakland/Alameda estuary, the building where Quinn's is located dates to 1903, once served as the Oakland harbor entrance lighthouse, and was moved to its present site in 1965. The main dining room is decorated in nautical motif and has great views of the marina below and downtown Oakland in the distance. An upstairs deck proves a wonderful place to dine on a sunny day. Specialties of the house include salmon Wellington, blackened prawns, and a variety of seafood pastas. On Thursday nights, Sons of the Buccaneers entertains in the upstairs bar, and you can listen to lively sea chanteys, throw peanut shells on the floor, and have a rollicking good time. There are many waterfront restaurants in the Bay Area, but few, if any, rate better than Quinn's. ~ 52 Embarcadero Cove, Oakland; 510-536-2050. MODERATE.

Surprisingly few of Berkeley's fine restaurants are found near the college campus. **Joshu-Ya Japanese Restaurant**, featuring a cozy dining room, is a welcome exception. Sit western-style at a table, and dine on tempura, teriyaki, and sukiyaki dishes, or broiled entrées such as salmon and *yakitori* (skewered chicken and vegetables). There is also a selection of *nigiri* and *maki* sushi. ~ 2441 Dwight Way, Berkeley; 510-848-5260. MODERATE.

The finest hamburgers in the Bay Area are served at **Fatapple's Restaurant and Bakery**. That's a fact known to very few visitors, but everyone in town seems to be aware, so the place is inevitably crowded. Decorated with photos of Jack London, it's a comfortable café which also offers breakfast fare, lasagna, soup, chili, salads, and outrageously delicious pie. ~ 1346 Martin Luther King Jr. Way, Berkeley; 510-526-2260. BUDGET TO MODERATE. ◄ HIDDEN

Located in Berkeley's gourmet ghetto, **Café de la Paz** serves delicious Latin American, vegetarian, and seafood specialties. Ecuador, Venezuela, Brazil and Argentina are among the countries represented on the menu. Mouth-watering tapas include *llapingachos* (potato onion cake stuffed with cheese, plantains, and chile *crema*). For the main course, try *xim xim* (prawns, chicken, and roasted almonds sautéed in coconut milk and chiles). ~ 1600 Shattuck Avenue, Berkeley; 510-843-0662. MODERATE.

Berkeley may be known for California cuisine, but one of the great finds here is an Italian restaurant called **Café Venezia**. The walls in this eatery are decorated with murals portraying an Italian street scene. Adding three-dimensional reality is a clothesline hung with laundry stretched from one wall to another and a fountain. There are pasta dishes like spaghetti carbonara, fettuccine with scallops, and ravioli, plus fresh fish, chicken, and veal dishes. Rate this restaurant with a night sky worth of stars! No lunch on weekends. ~ 1799 University Avenue, Berkeley; 510-849-4681. MODERATE TO DELUXE.

The best way to eat economically on the UC campus is at one of the many vendor stands lining Bancroft Way. They sell sandwiches, smoothies, falafels, Japanese dishes, and an assortment of finger foods.

One of the top lesbian gathering places in the East Bay is **The Brick Hut Café**. This informal spot also attracts a straight crowd with its excellent omelettes and cranberry waffles, outstanding chicken salad sandwiches, and fresh blueberry muffins. Breakfast and lunch served all week; dinner Wednesday through Saturday. ~ 2510 San Pablo Avenue, Berkeley; 510-486-1124. BUDGET TO MODERATE.

SHOPPING

Situated on the Oakland waterfront, **Jack London Square** offers many opportunities for shopping. In addition to several national chains, there are interesting boutiques, gift emporiums, and specialty shops. Every Sunday, locals flock to the **farmers' market** for fresh fruit, produce, bread, and flowers. If you favor a literary respite, **Barnes & Noble**, one of the largest bookstores in northern California, will occupy you for hours. ~ 98 Broadway; 510-272-0120.

Text continued on page 166.

Revolution in the Kitchen

During the past several decades Berkeley has shed its image as a center of revolt and assumed the role of gourmet capital. Turbulence these days occurs not on the campus but in the Cuisinart. The shift in sensibility occurred during those dolorous days in the '70s when Berkeley's affluent graduates traded barricades for bouillabaisse.

Culinary consciousness is a cause célèbre. It means repudiating the fast food–frozen dinner mentality of the older generation and taking up the banner of fresh fruits and vegetables. Preservatives are out, natural foods are in. "Grow your own!" no longer refers to plants that are rolled and smoked.

Several exemplary restaurants were born of this movement. Developing a cooking style termed "California cuisine," they serve select dishes to small groups. All ingredients, from spice to shellfish, are fresh; the focus is on locally produced foods in season. Menus change daily and sometimes include dishes invented that afternoon to be tested on an adventurous clientele.

The vanguard of this culinary revolution is **Chez Panisse**. Set in a modest woodframe building, it hardly looks the part of a world-famous restaurant. But the owner, Alice Waters, has long been the guiding light in Berkeley kitchens. Her reputation is so imposing that President Clinton stopped in for dinner during a Bay Area visit. Dinner is served downstairs in her two-tiered establishment and features a prix-fixe menu nightly. It's a multicourse extravaganza from appetizer to sorbet. A typical evening will include local salmon with herb blossom vinaigrette, grilled lamb with wild mushrooms, grilled pigeon breasts, berry *feuillete* with Sabayon, garden salad and hazelnut *semifreddo*, all for an ultra-deluxe price. Reservations are *de rigueur* and rather difficult to arrange. Upstairs, however, the café offers moderately priced meals in a lively setting. Open for lunch and dinner, it may serve calzone with goat cheese, oysters on the half shell, sorrel soup, plus daily specials such as sautéed sole, fettuccine with sweetbreads, and grilled steak with rosemary butter. If time and budget permit, indulge yourself: this is where it all began. ~ 1517 Shattuck Avenue; dinner reservations 510-548-5525; café information 510-548-5049. MODERATE TO ULTRA-DELUXE.

Another well-known Berkeley restaurant is the **Santa Fe Bar & Grill**. Set in a turn-of-the-century train station, it's decorated with wall-hangings that portray early railroad days. The oak bar at the far end serves potent concoctions and the pianist in the center of the room performs nightly. Evening meals include smoked Petaluma duck, rack of lamb, and mesquite-grilled chicken, plus special entrées like grilled game hen in green peppercorn sauce, bluefin tuna smothered in ginger-cilantro butter, and New York steak. Particularly recommended for lunch or dinner are the fresh fish dishes and ceviche appetizers. ~ 1310 University Avenue; 510-841-4740. MODERATE TO DELUXE.

Berkeley exported the revolution to Oakland's **Bay Wolf Restaurant**. Here, four partners founded a gourmet restaurant in a woodframe house. There are two dining rooms, one decorated with modern art pieces, the other displaying ceramic platters. Run by a friendly staff, the place has the feel of home. Lunch and dinner menus vary weekly. If they're not serving sautéed duck breast or swordfish with braised leeks, the chefs may be preparing roast leg of lamb, fresh pasta with scallops and mushrooms, or pork loin with artichoke purée. In any case, the food is outstanding, the service impeccable, and the ambience soft as candlelight. ~ 3853 Piedmont Avenue; 510-655-6004. DELUXE.

Bon appétit. Don't feel guilty. Ho Chi Minh was once a pastry chef for Escoffier. *Vive la révolution!*

College Avenue is one of the East Bay's major shopping sections. From its starting point at Broadway in north Oakland all the way to Russell Street in Berkeley, this thoroughfare hosts every type of store imaginable, from antique shops to clothing boutiques to children's secondhand stores.

Moe's Books is a prime place to pick up secondhand books at reduced prices.

Shattuck Avenue, a broad boulevard complete with landscaped median, is Berkeley's central district. The street divides into two entirely different sections, with University Avenue as a line of demarcation. To the south, from Durant Avenue to University, lies the city's old downtown section with traditional businesses.

North Berkeley, along Shattuck Avenue north of University Avenue, is far more interesting. This area, nicknamed "the gourmet ghetto" for its specialty food shops, is home to **The Cheese Board.** Run by an eclectic collective, this shop stocks a dizzying inventory of cheeses. With its baguettes, pizzas, and other breads, it's a perfect place to stock up for a picnic. ~ 1504 Shattuck Avenue, Berkeley; 510-549-3183.

You can fill the rest of the basket with fresh flowers and goods from the wine shop, produce store, and pastry store, all of which are within whistling distance. And don't miss **Black Oak Books**, an exceptionally fine bookstore and an important literary gathering place. ~ 1491 Shattuck Avenue, Berkeley; 510-486-0698.

On the road again? Then stop by **Easy Going.** No matter where you're headed, this travel shop can help out with a wide array of guidebooks, maps, and accessories. ~ 1385 Shattuck Avenue, Berkeley; 510-843-3533.

A shopping district of another sort lies along Berkeley's **Telegraph Avenue** between Dwight Way and Bancroft Way. While this campus area is being steadily remodeled and made to conform to the chic standards of the '90s, it still retains the native funk of Berkeley circa 1968. Street vendors line either side of the thoroughfare, selling clothes, metalwork, leather goods, and jewelry. Most of these artisans produce their own handiworks: there are painters, potters, weavers, and woodworkers here, dividing their days between studios at home and this open-air marketplace.

"Telegraph," as it's known locally, also supports enough bookstores to keep even a college town busy. Two of them, located practically next door to one another, are among the best in the country. **Moe's Books**, operated by a cigar-chomping bibliophile named Moe Moskowitz, contains four floors of new and used titles. ~ 2476 Telegraph Avenue, Berkeley; 510-849-2087.

Cody's Books, with its beautiful design and smart layout, features new volumes. The selection here ranges from recondite titles to bestsellers. Don't forget to visit the bargain books section upstairs. ~ 2454 Telegraph Avenue, Berkeley; 510-845-7852.

Decorated with the work of women artists, **Mama Bears Bookstore Coffeehouse,** is a popular meetingplace for women. It serves espresso drinks and munchies, and also features a bookstore specializing in books for women and children. ~ 6536 Telegraph Avenue, Oakland; 510-428-9684.

West Berkeley has become a major center for design stores, art galleries, and discount outlets. Among the renovated warehouses and stores is **Smith and Hawken Outlet Store**, a trendy gardening supply store that also sells sportswear, books, and vases. ~ 1330 10th Street; 510-527-1076. At **Earthworks Ceramics Coop** you'll find several potters creating functional dinnerware and decorative work. ~ 2547 8th Street; 510-841-9810.

Fourth Street, a refurbished warehouse district in West Berkeley, has become ground zero for savvy shoppers. Outlet stores and stylish gift shops abound along this tree-lined street. **The Nature Company** has books, games, toys, and more, all focusing on a single theme—the world of nature. ~ 740 Hearst Avenue; 510-649-5448. At **Hear Music** customers can don headphones and listen to a wide selection of classical and ethnic sounds. ~ 1809-B 4th Street; 510-204-9595. **The Gardener** has rustic home furnishings and upscale gardening supplies. ~ 1836 4th Street; 510-548-4545. A very popular place with the very young crowd, **Hearthsong** sells a vast selection of high-quality children's toys, games, and things for make-believe. ~ 1812 4th Street; 510-849-3956. **AERIAL** is stocked with an eclectic mix of puppets, wind chimes, artsy T-shirts, and Mexican kitsch. ~ 1840 4th Street; 510-644-1566.

NIGHTLIFE

Across the Bay from San Francisco, the evening activities revolve around places of high culture and those specializing in high spirits. From September to December, the **Oakland Ballet**, a nationally acclaimed company, presents dazzling premieres and performs classic ballets. ~ 510-465-6400.

The Oakland Ballet is at home at the **Paramount Theatre.** This fully restored art deco building is a showcase of structural flourishes and decorative details. A kind of architectural museum, the sumptuous theater alone is worth the price of admission. In addition to performing arts events and concerts, the Paramount hosts a series of movie classics. ~ 2025 Broadway; 510-465-6400.

The **Berkeley Repertory Theatre** at 2025 Addison Street in Berkeley (510-845-4700) and the **California Shakespeare Festival** located in Orinda on Gateway Boulevard (510-548-9666) are the most visible examples of Berkeley's rich dramatic tradition.

Also check with **Cal Performances** for a current listing of campus cultural events. They regularly present jazz concerts, chamber music, modern dance companies, ballet performances, and countless other programs. ~ 101 Zellerbach Hall, Companies, UC Berkeley; 510-642-9988.

Pacific Film Archive, also connected with the University, is an extraordinary showcase for early and artistic movies. ~ 2625 Durant Avenue, Berkeley; 510-642-1412.

As for spirits, there's **Heinold's First and Last Chance**, a roisterous little bar once frequented by Jack London. ~ 56 Jack London Square, Oakland; 510-839-6761. While London aficionados crowd this rustic bar, blues enthusiasts head for **Eli's Mile High Club**, the Bay Area's finest blues club. Cover. ~ 3629 Martin Luther King Jr. Way, Oakland; 510-655-6661.

The **Bench & Bar** near the Oakland Museum is popular with gay men and women (particularly men). There is dancing to deejay music nightly as well as strip and drag shows on Thursday and Sunday, respectively. Weekend cover. ~ 120 11th Street, Oakland; 510-444-2266.

Yoshi's Restaurant & Nitespot is where locals go for live jazz and delicious Japanese food. It's an intimate place with lots of wood, stained glass, a balcony, and tables surrounding the stage; there's not a bad seat in the house. Performers vary between locally trained musicians and national and international greats. (Yoshi's will move to Jack London Square in late 1996.) Cover. ~ 6030 Claremont Avenue, Oakland; 510-652-9200.

On the Berkeley waterfront, **Skates on the Bay** provides otherworldly views of the Bay and San Francisco skyline. Just pull up to a plate-glass window, order a cocktail, and watch nature perform. ~ 100 Seawall Drive, Berkeley; 510-549-1900.

Bison Brewery is a popular campus-area bar. Featuring made-on-the-premises brews, Bison offers live music Thursday through Saturday—everything from folk, rock, and country, to bluegrass and blues. Cover for live shows. ~ 2598 Telegraph Avenue, Berkeley; 510-841-7734.

You can sample up to 40 of the best local brews at **Jupiter**. The setting is a turn-of-the-century building that originally housed a lumber merchant, with decor that the owner calls "beer gothic." This popular hangout also serves pizzas, focaccia sandwiches, and salads, and there's jazz several evenings a week in the beer garden in the back. ~ 2181 Shattuck Avenue, Berkeley; 510-843-7625.

Another often-crowded brewery is **Triple Rock Brewery and Ale House**. Choose from a pale ale, an amber, or a porter and relax inside at one of the large wooden tables or outside on the back patio. ~ 1920 Shattuck Avenue, Berkeley; 510-843-2739.

The **Freight and Salvage Coffee House** is a folk and acoustic music venue with national renown. Performers have included bluegrass legend Doc Watson, folksinger Tom Paxton, local star Taj Mahal, and younger acoustic artists such as Michelle Shocked. Local musicians perform here as well, and on Tuesday night the famous (or infamous) open mike is, at $2, a great entertainment deal for the good-humored. ~ 1111 Addison Street, Berkeley; 510-548-1761.

Kimball's East is one of the Bay Area's leading jazz venues. Headliners have included Dizzy Gillespie, Bobbie Blue Bland, Eartha Kitt, and Wynton Marsalis. Modeled after a luxurious 1940s supper club, it has a full restaurant and bar, great acoustics, and an intimate ambience. Cover. ~ 5800 Shellmound, Emeryville; 510-658-2555.

Downstairs from Kimball's East is **Kimball's Carnival**, a culturally diverse club with an eclectic music calendar. During the week there's live jazz and world beat as well as deejay-generated reggae; on the weekends, expect a live salsa band. Cover. ~ 5800 Shellmound, Emeryville; 510-653-5300.

BEACHES & PARKS

ANTHONY CHABOT REGIONAL PARK AND REDWOOD REGIONAL PARK These contiguous facilities spread across nearly 7000 acres in the hills above Oakland. Foremost among their features are Lake Chabot, a haven for anglers and boaters, and the second-growth redwoods in Redwood Park. Chabot Park alternates between grass-covered hills and dense stands of eucalyptus, live oak, and madrone; the forests of Redwood Park are home to deer, raccoons, squirrels, and bobcats. Both parks have restrooms, picnic areas, and hiking trails. Chabot offers a golf course, an equestrian center, and a shooting range. Redwood has an archery range. There's a $3 parking fee at both parks. ~ The parks are located off Route 580 and can be entered from Skyline Boulevard or Redwood Road in Oakland or San Leandro; 510-635-0135.

▲ There are 75 sites (12 with RV hookups) near the lake in Chabot; $13 to $19 per night.

TEMESCAL REGIONAL RECREATIONAL AREA The highlight of this 48-acre park is Lake Temescal, created in 1868 when the Temescal Creek was dammed to supply water to Oakland. But soon larger reservoirs replaced Temescal and in 1936 it opened as one of the first recreational areas in the East Bay. Today this park, enhanced by lush growth of live oak, willow, and laurel, is a favorite spot among locals for swimming, sunbathing, fishing, picnicking, and hiking. In addition to a rose garden, a fishing pier, and both paved and unpaved trails, facilities include a snack bar, picnic areas, restrooms, and showers. Swimming fee, $2.50; fishing permit, $2.50; parking fee, $3. ~ Located at the intersection of Routes 24 and 13 in Oakland. There are entrances from both highways; take the Broadway exit from Route 24, or the Broadway Terrace exit off Route 13; 510-652-1155.

TILDEN REGIONAL PARK AND WILDCAT CANYON REGIONAL PARK These two gems lie side by side in the hills above Berkeley. Tilden, by far the more diverse and popular, is a magnificent park. Stretching over 2000 acres, it features swimming in Lake Anza, a botanical garden that condenses California's

160,000 square miles of plant life into a six-acre preserve, a small environmental museum, and a rolling landscape which varies from volcanic rock to grassy meadows. A wonderland for kids, it also offers an antique merry-go-round with beautiful carved horses, a miniature steam train, pony rides, and a small farm. Wildcat Canyon Park, with its meandering creek and forested arroyos, is a rustic counterpoint to Tilden's crowded acres. Both parks have restrooms, picnic areas, and hiking trails. Tilden also has a snack bar and a golf course. ~ Tilden Park is off Wildcat Canyon Road in the Berkeley hills; Wildcat Canyon Park is reached from McBryde Avenue in Richmond; 510-635-0135.

POINT PINOLE REGIONAL SHORELINE Located along San Pablo Bay, this 2100-acre park offers diverse possibilities. There are salt marshes to explore, as well as eucalyptus groves and open grasslands. Anglers gravitate to the fishing pier, which extends several hundred yards into the Bay. Steelhead, salmon, sturgeon, striped bass, and leopard shark are a few of the game fish swimming these waters. There are also sea cliffs with sweeping vistas and pebble beaches popular among driftwood collectors. Facilities include restrooms, picnic areas, and a basketball court. Parking fee, $3. ~ Located off Route 80 and can be reached by taking Hilltop Drive to San Pablo Avenue to Atlas Road in Richmond; 510-635-0135.

MOUNT DIABLO STATE PARK Rising 3849 feet above sea level, Mount Diablo is the Bay Area's loftiest peak. From this surveyor's vantage point you can gaze east to the Sierra Nevada and west to the Pacific. Americans Indians considered it a place of power, the only point not submerged by the primordial flood. The mountain landscape ranges from shady cottonwood canyons to open woodlands to hillsides carpeted with wildflowers. Golden eagles, red-tailed hawks, and horned larks number among the many birds here. Rabbits, raccoons, coyotes, foxes, blacktail deer, bobcats, and an occasional mountain lion are also seen. In all, the park covers over 22,000 acres. There are restrooms, picnic areas, and over 160 miles of hiking trails. Day-use fee, $5. ~ Located five miles east of Danville off Route 680, the park is reached via Mount Diablo Scenic Boulevard or North Gate Road out of Walnut Creek; 510-837-2525.

▲ There are 55 tent sites; $12 per night.

LAS TRAMPAS REGIONAL WILDERNESS Within this 3400-acre expanse are sheer sandstone cliffs, chaparral-coated hillsides, and grassy meadows. It's a rugged region crossed by two ridges and containing a box canyon. Geologic forces have twisted and uplifted large sections of rock which the wind has sculpted into exotic shapes. Golden eagles are often spotted here and wildlife is plentiful. Hiking trails thread throughout the preserve. The only facilities are picnic areas and restrooms. ~ Located off Route 680 about seven miles northwest of San Ramon, the preserve lies along Bollinger Canyon Road; 510-635-0135.

SUNOL REGIONAL WILDERNESS An area of oak-covered hills and tumbling streams, this preserve stretches across almost 6000 acres. Much of the land is cattle-grazing country, but more remote sections are covered with willows and inhabited by coyotes, mountain lions, and eagles. The foothills rise to almost 2000 feet, forming one of the wildest sections of the Diablo Range. An excellent trail system crosses the park. Facilities include an information center, restrooms, and picnic areas. Day-use fee, $3. ~ Located about eight miles due east of Fremont, the park is just off Geary Road; 510-862-2244.

▲ There are four tent sites; $10 per night; there is also a backpack camp available for $5 per person. Reservations: 510-636-1684.

Marin County

While the Pacific side of Marin County, described in Chapter Five, is known for its wave-lashed shoreline, the San Francisco Bay side of this wealthy region is renowned for posh homes and sleek shopping areas. Towns like Sausalito, Tiburon, and Mill Valley sit on dramatic hillsides and gaze out over the Bay toward the San Francisco skyline.

Once across the Golden Gate Bridge in Sausalito, sightseeing begins on Bridgeway, a sinuous road paralleling the waterfront. I won't even begin to describe the views of Belvedere, Angel Island, and Alcatraz along this esplanade. Suffice it to say that the Sausalito waterfront offers the single element missing from every vista in San Francisco—a full-frame view of the city itself. It is also a perfect introduction to Marin County, a collection of luxurious bedroom communities that comprise one of the wealthiest counties in the nation.

SIGHTS

Sausalito is a shopper's town: galleries, boutiques, and antique stores line Bridgeway, and in several cases have begun creeping uphill along side streets. **Plaza Vina del Mar** (Bridgeway and El Portal), with its elephant statues and dramatic fountain, is a grassy oasis in the midst of the commerce. Several strides seaward of this tree-thatched spot lies **Gabrielson Park**, where you can settle on a bench or plot of grass at water's edge.

Then continue along the piers past chic yachts, delicate sloops, and rows of millionaires' motorboats. To get an idea of the inland pond where the rich sail these toys, check out the U.S. Army Corps of Engineers **San Francisco Bay Model.** Built to scale and housed in a two-acre warehouse, this hydraulic model of San Francisco

Bay is used to simulate currents and tidal flows. An audiotape guided tour leads you around the mini-Bay. When the model actually runs, you can watch the tide surge through the Golden Gate, swirl around Alcatraz, and rise steadily along the Berkeley shore. The tidal cycle of an entire day takes 14 minutes as you witness the natural process from a simulated height of 12,000 feet. Also part of the permanent exhibit is a display portraying Sausalito during World War II, when it was converted into a mammoth shipyard that produced almost 100 vessels in three years. Closed Sunday and Monday; call ahead to make sure the model will be operating (at last report, it was running only on Friday and Saturday). ~ 2100 Bridgeway, Sausalito; 415-332-3870.

Imagine a cluster of seven buildings and more than 100 hands-on activities all devoted to children ages one through ten. Throw in a multimedia center and a miniature model of the ports of San Francisco and what you have is a place called the **Bay Area Discovery Museum**. Closed Monday. Admission. ~ 557 East Fort Baker, Sausalito; 415-487-4398.

I heartily recommend the quarter-mile self-guided tour through the **Richardson Bay Audubon Center and Sanctuary**. It will provide an inkling of what Marin was like before the invention of cars and condominiums. During the winter months harbor seals can be seen in sanctuary waters. You can wander through dells and woodlands, past salt marshes and tidepools. Also contained on the property is **Lyford House**, a magnificent Victorian which commands a strategic spot on the shore of Richardson Bay. On Sunday afternoon from October through April, tours are given of the interior. The sanctuary is closed on Monday and Tuesday. Admission. ~ 376 Greenwood Beach Road, Tiburon; 415-388-2524.

Only 11 of Richardson Bay Audubon Center and Sanctuary's 900 acres are on land!

Another field trip will lead you to a building, constructed of concrete and steel, which nevertheless evokes the rolling golden hills and blue-domed sky of Northern California. Perhaps that is because the **Marin County Civic Center** was designed by Frank Lloyd Wright, an architect with a passion for blending a building to the surrounding landscape. Take Route 101 north to the North San Pedro Road exit in San Rafael; before even leaving the highway you'll see this long, low, graceful building that seems almost a landbridge between the three hills it spans. A self-guided tour will reveal interior corridors brilliantly illuminated by skylights and landscaped with trees and shrubs. A singular structure, it represents the last commission of Frank Lloyd Wright, who died in 1959, several years before the Civic Center's dedication. ~ 3501 Civic Center Drive, San Rafael; 415-499-7407.

LODGING

Casa Madrona Hotel features a New England–style complex of rooms attached to a 19th-century landmark house. You'll find this two-part structure on a Sausalito hillside overlooking San Francisco Bay. The guest rooms have a personal feel and individual names. The "Artist's Loft" is decorated with antique artists' supplies and enjoys a bay view from its large deck, while the "La Posada" is styled after an old Portuguese inn. There are also five private cottages available at this 35-room bed and breakfast. ~ 801 Bridgeway, Sausalito; 415-332-0502, 800-567-9524, fax 415-332-2537. DELUXE TO ULTRA-DELUXE.

If you're longing to get away to a quiet hideaway in a tropical setting reminiscent of Key West (but actually located in a residential Victorian neighborhood), book a room at the **Panama Hotel.** The 13 rooms and two garden cottages are decorated with a hodgepodge of antiques, some with clawfoot tubs and canopied beds. Most have ceiling fans and either a balcony or garden patio. Continental breakfast included. Gay-friendly. ~ 4 Bayview Street; San Rafael; 415-457-3993, 800-899-3993, fax 415-457-6240. BUDGET TO MODERATE.

◄ HIDDEN

Calling the accommodations at **East Brother Light Station** unusual is a slight understatement. Where else can you find a bed and breakfast inn located within a lighthouse on an offshore island? The old beacon was built back in 1873 and operated for almost a century. Today the two-story house and light station feature four bedrooms furnished with period pieces. Guests travel out to this one-acre hideaway by motorboat and enjoy a multi-course dinner as well as breakfast the next morning. Of course, there's a premium on such seclusion: rates run in the ultra-deluxe range and reservations must be made far in advance. Shared and private bathrooms are available. Open Thursday through Sunday, this San Pablo Bay retreat is a unique opportunity to trade the trappings of civilization for your own private island. ~ 117 Park Place, Point Richmond; 510-233-2385. ULTRA-DELUXE.

DINING

You'll know the bill of fare by the name—**Hamburgers**; and you can tell the quality of the food by the line outside. Local folks and out-of-towners alike jam this postage stamp–sized eatery. They come not only for charcoal-broiled burgers, but bratwurst, Italian sausage, and foot-long hot dogs as well. It's tough securing a table, but you can always pull up a bench in the park across the street. ~ 737 Bridgeway, Sausalito; 415-332-9471. BUDGET.

Sausalito sports many seafood restaurants, most of which are overpriced and few of which are good. So it's best to steer a course for **Seven Seas.** It lacks the view of the splashy establishments, but does feature an open-air patio in back. The menu includes scallops, bouillabaisse, and salmon. Landlubbers can choose from several meat platters; at lunch sandwiches are served; also open for breakfast. ~ 682 Bridgeway, Sausalito; 415-332-1304. MODERATE.

If you long for a sea vista and an eyeful of San Francisco skyline, try **Horizons**. Housed in the turn-of-the-century San Francisco Yacht Club, this spiffy seafood restaurant has a wall of windows for those inside looking out, and a porch for those who want to be outside looking further. Then, of course, there's the food: shellfish and other aquatic fare, with chicken, pasta, and steak dishes added for good measure. Some beautiful carpentry went into the design of this place. There's also a popular bar here, making it a choice spot to drink as well as eat. Open for brunch, lunch, and dinner every day. ~ 558 Bridgeway, Sausalito; 415-331-3232. MODERATE TO DELUXE.

If the tide doesn't carry you, current trends may very well deliver you to the door at **Guaymas** in Tiburon. This upscale Mexican restaurant bakes fresh tortillas and tamales daily. Pork, steak, and shrimp dishes are prepared on a mesquite grill; or try the duck with pumpkin seed sauce or the red snapper sautéed with jalapeños and onions. Located next door to the ferry dock, Guaymas rounds out the bill of fare with a bay view. ~ 5 Main Street, Tiburon; 415-435-6300. MODERATE TO DELUXE.

Another bayside spot that's accessible by ferry is **The Marin Brewing Company**. Famous for the beer (the Blueberry Ale has won a gold medal and Mt. Tam Pale Ale is a regional favorite), this popular spot also serves delicious pub grub. Clams, burgers, buffalo wings, and pizzas from the wood-fired oven are all tasty accompaniments to your brew of choice. The 50-foot-long wooden bar is claimed to be the longest in California. ~ 1809 Larkspur Landing Drive, Larkspur; 415-461-5677. BUDGET TO MODERATE.

Bathed in a soft golden light and exuding a faintly nostalgic 1940s atmosphere is **Avenue Grill**, a place where locals go to warm themselves on a winter evening when rain drips from the redwood trees. A fiery rotisserie behind the long counter turns out the premier menu item: juicy herb-basted chicken served with crisp vegetables and garlicky mashed potatoes. A blender wizard at the bar whips up the definitive mango margarita. Open for dinner only. ~ 44 East Blithedale, Mill Valley; 415-388-6003. MODERATE.

SHOPPING

The best shopping spot in all Marin is the town of Sausalito. Here you can stroll the waterfront along Bridgeway and its side streets, visiting gourmet shops, boutiques, and antique stores. One of the Bay Area's wealthiest towns, Sausalito sports few bargains, but it does host an assortment of elegant shops.

In a town known for its galleries, the **Laurel Burch Gallerie** stands out for its uniqueness. Artist Laurel Burch uses the space to display and sell her work, which concentrates on cats, mythological beings, and women spirit themes. There are paintings, prints, tote bags, T-shirts, jewelry, and mugs. ~ 539 Bridgeway, Sausalito; 415-332-7764.

Several shops in the mini-mall at 660 Bridgeway are also worth a browse. Style-savvy women will check out **Georgiou** with its designer line of cotton resort wear. ~ Sausalito; 415-331-0579.

A standout among the art galleries lining Sausalito's streets is **Fine Art Collections**, which eschews tourist landscapes in favor of contemporary art from around the world. Mixed-media sculpture, limited edition serigraphs and fine arts and crafts are among the changing works on display. ~ 686 Bridgeway, Sausalito; 415-499-9300.

The downtown facility most crowded with shops and shoppers is **Village Fair**, a multilevel mall boasting 37 stores. Here are leather shops, jewelers, clothing stores, confectioners, notion shops, crafts galleries, ceramic shops, and so on. ~ 777 Bridgeway, Sausalito; 415-332-1902.

Stretching for a half mile and numbering two dozen stores is the antique shop district of San Anselmo. You can bid on entire estates at spots like the **San Rafael Auction Gallery**. ~ 634 5th Avenue; 415-457-4488. Look for pewter and early American furniture at **Oveda Maurer Antiques**. ~ 34 Greenfield Avenue; 415-454-6439. Or shop for tribal and village rugs and textiles at **Adraskand**. ~ 15 Ross Avenue; 415-459-1711. **Michael Good** specializes in a wide variety of antiquarian books including limited editions, fine art, and California history. ~ 35 San Anselmo Avenue; 415-459-6092. You can pick up a handy map to the area from the **Antique Dealers of San Anselmo**, or one of the other antique stores. ~ 415-454-6439.

Your next trip begins the minute you step in to **Book Passage**. Travel guides, maps, and accessories make this store a favorite among Bay Area travelers. After you've selected the books you need, sit down with an Italian soda in the café and begin plotting your itinerary. ~ 51 Tamal Vista, Corte Madera; 415-927-0960.

NIGHTLIFE

The window simply reads "Bar"; the address is 757 Bridgeway in Sausalito; and the place is famous. Famous for its name, the **no name**, and because it's a favored hangout among young swingers and old salts alike. With an antique bar, piano, and open-air patio, it's a congenial spot to bend an elbow. You'll hear live blues Tuesday through Thursday, live jazz on Friday and Saturday, and Dixieland on Sunday. ~ 415-332-1392.

One of the top repertory theater groups in the Bay Area is the **Marin Theater Company**, which performs classic and contemporary dramatic works in a state-of-the-art playhouse that many other larger troupes would envy. ~ 397 Miller Avenue, Mill Valley; 415-388-5208.

Sweetwater jams every night. Featuring blues and rock sounds, the club often headlines big-name groups. Cover. ~ 153 Throckmorton Avenue, Mill Valley; 415-388-2820.

If you're in the mood for a mellow evening, several popular coffeehouses offer live acoustic music. **Mama's Royal Café** has jazz and folk music every evening, and during the day on weekends. ~ 387 Miller Avenue, Mill Valley; 415-388-3261. **Java Café** serves California cuisine and features jazz and rhythm-and-blues for a cover charge. ~ 320 Magnolia Avenue, Larkspur; 415-927-1502. The cozy **Lansdale Station** entertains with folk and jazz. ~ 1507 San Anselmo Avenue, San Anselmo; 415-453-0624.

BEACHES & PARKS

CHINA CAMP STATE PARK This 1500-acre park, located shoreside along San Pablo Bay, is a perfect picnic spot. Heavily wooded and adorned with several midget islands just offshore, it has a particular lure. Part of the attraction is the old Chinese fishing village, dating to the 1860s. This ghost community of tumbledown houses was home to thousands of Asians who were uprooted by the 1906 San Francisco earthquake and fire. Now it's a peaceful park inhabited by shore birds, anglers, and daytrippers. The park has picnic areas, restrooms, and six miles of hiking trails. Day-use fee, $3. ~ Located along North San Pedro Road about five miles east of San Rafael; 415-456-0766.

▲ There are 30 primitive walk-in sites; $12 to $14 per night. For reservations call DESTINET at 800-444-7275.

The Delta

California's two major rivers, the Sacramento and San Joaquin, flow together around Sacramento, creating the state's fertile delta region. The heart of this bayou country lies about 70 miles northeast of San Francisco. From the city, the fastest way to go is by following Route 80 east to Fairfield, turning right on Route 12 and taking it to Route 160 in Rio Vista. Route 160 leads north through the heart of the Delta.

An alternative course is to take Route 4 instead of Route 12. This will allow you to see a greater stretch of the Delta along Route 160. It will also carry you near two waterfront towns—Port Costa and Benicia—which should not be missed.

SIGHTS

HIDDEN ►

Port Costa enjoyed its heyday early in the century when the town served as a major grain-shipping port. Today it's a lazy community at the end of a country lane. A few sagging stores have been converted to artists' quarters and antique shops, and one of the warehouses has become a cavernous restaurant. Otherwise, the wrinkled hills all around seem like time warps in which this church-steeple village rests suspended. Farmland and forest enclose Port Costa, so finding your way becomes half the enjoyment of exploring the town: Well-marked side roads lead to it from Route 4.

A few miles farther along this highway, past rounded hills tufted with grass, sits the **John Muir National Historic Site.** This grand 17-room Victorian was home to the renowned naturalist for almost a quarter-century until his death in 1914. It was here that Muir wrote voluminously on conservation and became a founder of the Sierra Club. Muir also helped create Yosemite National Park; he personally led Theodore Roosevelt through the Sierra, admonishing him for hunting big game and urging the president to preserve other wilderness areas.

◄ HIDDEN

The countryside that once surrounded the Scottish conservationist's house has given way to suburban plots. But nine acres of the orchards Muir once managed remain. Within the house, many rooms have been restored as they originally appeared. Muir's "scribble den," or study, remains littered with manuscripts and research materials, the family quarters are opulently furnished, and the parlor is filled with Victorian effects. While John Muir's primary love was the wild, a tour of his estate provides a singular glimpse into the life of the man. Open Wednesday through Sunday. Admission. ~ 4202 Alhambra Avenue, Martinez; 510-228-8860.

Across the Carquinez Strait from Port Costa looms **Benicia** (from Route 4 in Martinez continue east a few miles, then take Route 680 north to Route 780), a community whose early dreams proved to be delusions of grandeur. The folks who founded the town foresaw it as the state capital. In 1853 it was actually named the seat of government, but by 1854 dissatisfied legislators had moved their operation to Sacramento. The founding mothers and fathers also pictured Benicia as a magnificent port.

All of which makes it a great place to visit. The **Benicia Capitol** still stands, an imposing brick building marked by twin pillars. True to antiquity, every desk in the Senate chamber is set up to be illuminated by candle and has a spittoon by its side. Admission. ~ West 1st and G streets, Benicia; 707-745-3385.

There are walking tour booklets at the Capitol that will lead you past the other historic sites which make Benicia the little town that couldn't. Tour booklets are also available at the **Benicia Chamber of Commerce.** ~ 601 1st Street, Benicia; 707-745-2120.

On Route 160, you can travel north along the Sacramento River all the way to the state capital. En route is a dreamy land of drawbridges, meandering waterways, and murky mists. This bayou country is as dateless as the Deep South. Sam Goldwyn once claimed that the California Delta "looks more like the Mississippi than the real thing," and chose it as the movie location for *Huckleberry Finn.*

Back in the 1850s, steamboats sidewheeled upriver from San Francisco to the Gold Country outside Sacramento. Residents still tell of the pirates who stretched chains across the river to snag steamboats laden with gold. The area is renowned among anglers for its striped bass, blue gill, sturgeon, and black bass. Waterskiers and other aquatic enthusiasts favor it as well.

The Delta is an endless expanse of orchards and flatlands, levees and dikes. A thousand miles of waterways meander through this mazework. There are channels bearing names like Hog, Whiskey, Disappointment, and Montezuma Slough.

The gateway to this watery world is **Bethel Island**, one of the 55 islands that comprise the Delta. Featuring marinas, motels, restaurants, and boat rentals, it sits a few miles east of the intersection of Routes 4 and 160. Like the rest of the Delta, it is busiest during summer and on weekends. In the winter, many local businesses close for the season, so it's best to check in advance.

Two other points of interest border the southern fringes of the Delta. **Black Diamond Mines Regional Preserve**, a 3900-acre park at the foot of Mt. Diablo, features a 19th-century cemetery complete with cracked tombstones engraved in Welsh. ~ Somersville Road, three miles south of Route 4, Antioch; 510-757-2620. The **Western Railway Museum** features dozens of vintage railroad cars, many of them in working order. Wander this 25-acre, open-air museum and you'll come across an Australian tram, a Gay Nineties streetcar, and the 1931 "Scenic Limited," once used on a whistlestop tour by Franklin D. Roosevelt. Open on the weekends only. Admission. ~ 5848 Route 12, between Suisun City and Rio Vista; 707-374-2978.

HIDDEN ►

The high point of any Delta trip is a visit to **Locke** (population 75; elevation 13 feet), a creaky community of clapboard houses and falsefront stores. This intriguing town, located on Route 160, is the only rural community in the entire country built and occupied by Chinese. Many contemporary residents trace their ancestry back to the pig-tailed Asian immigrants who mined California gold fields and helped build the transcontinental railroad, then moved on to construct the Delta's intricate levee system.

During its heyday in the early 1900s, Locke was a wide-open river town. Chinese and non-Asians alike frequented its gambling parlors, speakeasies, and opium dens. These raffish denizens have long since disappeared, but little else has changed.

Today Locke is like an outdoor museum, an example of what America's small towns would be like if time were measured not in terms of human progress, but in the eternal effects of the elements. You can still stroll along wooden sidewalks, which now slope like the pathways in an amusement park funhouse. Elderly Asians sit in the doorways reading Chinese newspapers.

On either side of the town's block-long Main Street, there are tumble-down two-story buildings with balconies that lean toward the road. Rust streaks the tin roofs, and some structures have sagged so heavily that the doors are rectangular forms collapsing into parallelogram shapes. Some of the outer walls are covered with rose vines, others are buried in an avalanche of honeysuckle. Along the edge of town are the trim orchards and communal gardens which Chinese residents have tended for generations.

Every building has a story to relate. As you wander through town, glance up near the ridgetops of the falsefront buildings. On many you can still discern the outlines of hand-lettered signs proclaiming that once this place was a Chinese "Bakery and Lunch Parlor," the "Star Theatre," or "Waih & Co. Groceries & Dry Goods."

Another Delta adventure lies along the filigree of waterways just behind Locke known as **The Meadows**. The best way to explore the preserve is in a boat. By car, go south from Locke about two hundred yards and turn left on the first paved road (just before the concrete bridge). Proceed about a hundred feet and turn left on the gravel road; a mile in length, it leads into The Meadows. Generally considered the Delta's most picturesque region, The Meadows is like an everglades. Its narrow canals are shaded by oak and walnut trees that droop Spanish moss to the water's edge. Frogs croak in the lily pads. Pheasant, great horned owls, Canada geese, and a variety of ducks inhabit the place, and along the riverbanks you can pick blackberries and grapes.

LODGING

There's a wonderful resting place on the way to the Delta. The **Union Hotel** has been around so long it presents itself as a place where you can "sleep in the 19th century." The building is a white

FUN FOR ALL

Route 80 can stop at **Marine World–Africa USA**, particularly when they have children to entertain. This 160-acre theme park features an aquarium with killer whales and a 55-acre lake. The exhibits and shows, including dolphin, bird, and sea lion shows, are designed around educational themes. At the Elephant Encounter you'll have a chance to ride a variety of Asian and African elephants. Butterfly World features species from all over the world. There are also shows featuring performing vultures, parrots, cockatoos, macaws, and chickens. Many of these performances offer informative commentaries on endangered species. Limited hours in winter; call for schedule. Admission. ~ Marine World Parkway, Vallejo; 707-643-6722.

clapboard structure, three stories tall, with a pretty green awning. Each of its twelve rooms has been decorated in period fashion. One features a canopy bed, another a Chinese Chippendale armoire, marble-top chest, simple rag rug, and so on. To remind you it's really the 20th century, every room has a private bath with jacuzzi. ~ 401 1st Street, Benicia; 707-746-0100, 800-544-2278, fax 707-746-6458. MODERATE TO DELUXE.

Good lodging places are rare around the Delta, but there's one that I highly recommend. **B & W Resort Marina**, set on the Mokelumne River, features a covey of wood-frame cottages scattered across spacious grounds. There's a marina as well as a picnic area and small beach. The units include one-bedroom cottages and two-bedroom duplexes. These are tidy efficiency units with knotty-pine walls, linoleum floors, and no decoration; they include kitchenettes but no utensils. During July and August, peak season, the minimum stay is one week. ~ 964 Brannan Island Road, Isleton; 916-777-6161. MODERATE.

A former speakeasy once owned by Lon Chaney Jr., a star of early Hollywood horror flicks, **Grand Island Inn** retains its art deco charm with 39 period-decorated guest rooms and a restaurant reminiscent of a 1930s supper club complete with arched windows, palms and a grand piano. The restaurant is open April through October. ~ Highway 160 at Highway 220, Ryde; 916-776-1318. MODERATE.

The most adventurous lodging on the Delta is aboard a houseboat. These vessels are quite simple to operate with 45 minutes of instruction and require no captain's license. There's no finer way to experience California's bayou than by spending a few lazy days on the river. Among the many companies renting houseboats are **Herman & Helen's Marina**. ~ At the end of Eight Mile Road, Stockton; 209-951-4634. DELUXE.

DINING

In Benicia, en route to the Delta, **First Street Café** serves standard breakfast fare, soups, salads, and sandwiches for lunch, and seafood, meat, and pasta dishes for dinner. A contemporary café, this popular spot has an espresso machine and offers an assortment of baked desserts. Weekend brunch. No dinner on Monday. ~ 440 1st Street, Benicia; 707-745-1400. BUDGET TO MODERATE.

For a more upscale adventure, stroll down the street and into the dining room at the **Union Hotel**. Dinner at this stained-glass establishment features dishes like New York steak with Jack Daniels sauce, Sonoma rack of lamb, pizzeta, and fresh fish. The lunch menu is equally elegant. ~ 401 1st Street, Benicia; 707-746-0100. MODERATE TO DELUXE.

For local color, nothing compares to **Giusti's**, a reasonably priced seafood and prime rib restaurant. Dating to 1896, it's housed in a wooden building with a timeworn exterior. It's the kind of place where the walls are decorated with autographed photos inscribed to the owner and the ceiling is covered with 1250 baseball caps. At lunch they serve steaks, burgers, pasta, and daily specials; then for dinner, Giusti's features prawns, grilled halibut, veal cutlets, and fresh fish. Closed Monday. ~ Old Walnut Grove Road, Walnut Grove; 916-776-1808. MODERATE.

◄ HIDDEN

The Delta's most bizarre restaurant is **Al's Place**, better known as "Al the Wop's." It may be the strangest joint you've ever entered. The bar out front is a saloon with hunting trophies protruding from the walls and a fading mural of a cowboy challenging a bucking bronco. The high ceiling is plastered with dollar bills (it'll cost you a buck to find out how they got there). Dinner consists primarily of steak and steak. A stack of sliced bread accompanies your slab of meat. At lunch, every table is set with big jars of peanut butter and jelly. The idea is to swab the peanut butter on the bread, add a dollop of jelly, and enjoy it with your steak. Sorry you asked? ~ Main Street, Locke; 916-776-1800. MODERATE.

For riverside dining, head for **The Point** at the Delta Marina Yacht Harbor in Rio Vista. The walls are tastefully sponge-painted in pastel pinks and blues and decorated with local art, and the chef serves up a variety of seafood, pasta, steak, and chicken dishes. You can dine in a cozy booth by the window and watch the Sacramento River scene in the River Room or on an enclosed patio known as the Garden Room. There's live rock-and-roll in the lounge on weekend nights and brunch on Sunday. ~ 120 Marina Drive, Rio Vista; 707-374-5400. MODERATE.

SHOPPING

Historic downtown Benicia is antique store heaven. **Hagen's House of Clocks** features a vast array of timepieces and music boxes. ~ 513 1st Street; 707-745-2643. To discover hidden treasures, head to the **Benicia Antique Shop**, where you'll find silver, glassware, furniture, and jewelry. ~ 305 1st Street; 707-745-0978. **Dials Antiques** offers a variety of decorative furniture. ~ 190 West J Street; 707-745-2552.

In the Delta, try the antique community of Locke, where you can combine shopping with a search for the town's historic roots. **River Road Gallery** is housed in a building that has experienced several incarnations as a grocery, pool hall, and old-style ice cream parlor. Today it contains oil and pastel paintings, ceramics, and wood carvings, all created by local artists. ~ 13944 Main Street, Locke; 916-776-1132.

NIGHTLIFE

By car or boat you can cruise to several spots around the Delta, including the **Grand Island Inn.** This rambling, multistoried affair features a plush bar and an intimate dining room; the bar is open weekends only during winter, but every day in summer. Back in Prohibition days, the hotel was a notorious speakeasy. Today it is one of the hottest nightspots in the Delta. ~ Route 160, Ryde; 916-776-1318.

BEACHES & PARKS

BRANNAN ISLAND STATE RECREATION AREA Located along the Sacramento River, this park sits in the midst of the Delta Country. With sloughs and levees all around, it's a region of willows and cottonwoods. There's a beach for swimmers, picnic tables for daytrippers, and a maze of waterways for anglers. Black bass, sturgeon, catfish, and perch number among the Delta's many gamefish. There are picnic areas, restrooms, and showers; restaurants and groceries are available four miles away in Rio Vista. ~ Located on Route 160 about four miles south of Rio Vista; 916-777-6671.

▲ There are 102 sites; $12 to $14 per night.

Outdoor Adventures

Deep-sea and bay expeditions for salmon, rock cod, halibut, and bass draw countless anglers to the Bay Area.

SPORT-FISHING

THE EAST BAY For charters, contact **Berkeley Marina Sport Center**. Depending on the season, they fish the bay or the ocean. ~ 225 University Avenue, Berkeley; 510-849-2727.

MARIN COUNTY For charters contact **Caruso's Sportfishing Center**. They fish the ocean exclusively for salmon. ~ At the foot of Harbor Drive, Sausalito; 415-332-1015. **Loch Lomond Live Bait House** handles charter reservations. ~ Loch Lomond Marina, San Rafael; 415-456-0321.

THE DELTA Fishing the Delta is another favored sport: try **Crockett Sport Fishing**. ~ At the foot of Port Street, Crockett; 510-787-1047. Contact **Outrigger Marina** for information on companies currently chartering from their docks. ~ Sherman Island Road, Three-Mile Slough; 916-777-6480.

Go out on one of **Fishooker Sport Fishing's** six-hour, 77-mile fishing trips and try your luck at catching a striper or sturgeon. ~ P.O. Box 742, Rio Vista, 94571; 916-777-6498.

SAILING

Nothing is more visually stunning than the sight of the sailboats on a clear, breezy San Francisco morning. Don't miss the experience of capturing the wind and drinking in endless vistas.

THE EAST BAY At the Berkeley Marina, **Cal Adventures** offers lessons and rentals on 15-foot Coronados. ~ U.C. Aquatic Center, foot of University Avenue, Berkeley; 510-642-4000. For lessons and rentals on larger boats, try **Olympic Circle Sailing**, also at the Berkeley Marina. ~ 1 Spinnaker Way, Berkeley; 510-843-4200.

MARIN COUNTY In the North Bay try **Cass' Rental Marina**. In addition to running a sailing school, they rent keel sloops that range in size from 22 to 35 feet. ~ 1702 Bridgeway, Sausalito; 415-332-6789. For charters on San Francisco Bay call **Ocean Voyages**, which has 26 vessels including 40-foot sailboats. ~ 1709 Bridgeway, Sausalito; 415-332-4681.

KAYAKING

Your trip will take on a new dimension as you paddle among seals and seagulls, along the cityfronts and through the harbors of the world's largest landlocked bay. The popularity of kayaking has soared in the past few years, and the Bay Area certainly hasn't missed the boat; there are several small companies that cater to kayakers and would-be kayakers of all physical and financial abilities. While the most convenient place to paddle is on the bay itself, there are also wonderful locations to the north in Marin County.

THE EAST BAY In Oakland, try **California Canoe and Kayak** at Jack London Square, which organizes classes, trips, and rentals. ~ 409 Water Street; 510-893-7833.

MARIN COUNTY To paddle across Richardson Bay under the bright silvery moon, contact **Sea Trek Ocean Kayaking Center**. They also do trips to Angel Island. ~ Schoonmaster Point Marina, Sausalito; 415-488-1000. For kayak rentals call on **Boardsports Marin**. ~ 2233 Larkspur Landing Circle, Larkspur Landing; 415-925-8585.

WIND-SURFING

The surf may not be up on San Francisco Bay, but the wind almost always is! The choice spot to windsurf in the East Bay is the Berkeley Marina. In Marin, everyone goes to Larkspur Landing.

THE EAST BAY For sailboard rentals go to **Berkeley Windsurf and Snowboard**. ~ 1601 University Avenue, Berkeley; 510-843-9283.

MARIN COUNTY For sailboard rentals and classes, try **Boardsports Marin**. ~ 2233 Larkspur Landing Circle, Larkspur Landing; 415-925-8585.

GOLF

It may not be the Monterey Peninsula, but the Bay Area offers many golfing opportunities at challenging, picturesque courses.

THE PENINSULA Duffers and professionals alike tee off at **Crystal Springs Golf Course**. ~ 6650 Golf Course Drive, Burlingame; 415-342-0603.

THE SOUTH BAY **San Jose Municipal Golf Course** is an 18-hole treelined course. ~ 1560 Oakland Road, San Jose; 408-441-4653.

THE EAST BAY With steep rolling hills, **Lake Chabot Golf Course** is quite challenging. ~ Golf Links Road, Oakland; 510-351-5812. Traversed by a creek and dotted with redwood and pine trees, **Tilden Park Golf Course** is a choice spot. ~ Grizzly Peak

Boulevard and Shasta Road, Berkeley; 510-848-7373. Located in a valley surrounded by rolling hills, **Sunol Valley Golf Club** encompasses two full golf courses. ~ Interstate 680 and Andrade Road, Sunol; 510-862-2404.

MARIN COUNTY Situated in a valley surrounded by the China Camp Recreation Area, **Peacock Gap Golf and Country Club** is a relatively flat 18-hole course. ~ 333 Biscayne Drive, San Rafael; 415-453-4940.

TENNIS

The Bay Area is the third most active region in the nation for tennis. Cities all around the Bay have public courts, many lighted for night play.

THE PENINSULA For tennis under the sun, try out the two courts at **Peers Park.** ~ 1899 Park Boulevard, Palo Alto. If you're looking to swing a racket, be sure to check out the eight courts at **Mitchell Park.** ~ 600 East Meadow Park. For more information in Palo Alto, call 415-329-2261.

THE SOUTH BAY In **Wallenberg Park** there are twelve lighted courts for your enjoyment. ~ Corner of Curtner and Hicks avenues, San Jose. Four lighted courts are open to the public at **Paul Moore Park.** ~ Corner of Hillsdale and Cherry avenues, San Jose. For more information on public courts in the South Bay, call 408-277-5556.

THE EAST BAY Perched high in the Berkeley hills, the four courts at the **Rose Garden** are the most picturesque courts in town. ~ 1201 Euclid Avenue. Also located in north Berkeley, the two courts in scenic **Live Oak Park** have night lighting. ~ Walnut and Berryman. The city of Berkeley has courts in eight other locations. Call 510-644-6530 for information.

There are many public courts throughout Oakland. **Chabot** has two tennis courts. ~ Patton Avenue and Broadway. You can play in the evening on one of ten lighted courts at **Laney.** ~ 900 Fallon Street. **Davie Tennis Stadium** features five lighted courts. ~ 198 Oak Road. For more information, call 510-238-3494.

MARIN COUNTY Sausalito has tennis courts in three locations. With a stunning view of the San Francisco Bay and skyline, **South View Park** has one court. ~ North Street. Three lighted courts are open to the public at **Marinship Park.** ~ North end of the San Francisco Bay Model. **M.L.K. Park** has five tennis courts. ~ Coloma Street. For more information call 415-289-4125.

BIKING

With its Mediterranean climate and gentle terrain, the Bay Area is a perfect place to travel by bicycle. Thousands of local folks commute to work on two-wheelers. Bike paths are appearing everywhere and some public transportation systems accommodate passengers with bikes.

THE PENINSULA Cycling is a great way to explore the sights of the Peninsula. There's a beautiful 15-mile loop through **Portola Valley** with an interesting side trip to the quaint town of Woodside. For a journey through a eucalyptus grove, try the four-mile loop in **Coyote Point Park.** To ride through academia, check out the numerous paths at **Stanford University** in Palo Alto.

THE SOUTH BAY If you take your bicycle on a sightseeing tour of the South Bay, **Kelley Park** in San Jose is a great place to begin. There are 150 acres of rolling hills with numerous sights along the way. Another jaunt travels between two stunning garden parks—**Villa Montalvo** and **Hakone Gardens.** More challenging is the steep 24-mile climb up **Mount Hamilton Road** to the Lick Observatory.

THE EAST BAY This area offers diverse routes for two-wheeling sightseers. In Oakland, there's a bike path around **Lake Merritt,** the city's saltwater lake. **Tunnel Road** and **Skyline Boulevard** climb the East Bay hills to several regional parks. Out at **Point Pinole Regional Shoreline,** a path takes cyclists through grassy meadows to the shores of San Pablo Bay.

MARIN COUNTY In Marin, the **Sausalito Bikeway** carries along the shoreline past marshes and houseboats. Another bikeway in Tiburon offers spectacular views of Sausalito and San Francisco.

THE DELTA For a truly enjoyable bike ride past mud flats, ponds, sloughs, rickety towns, country lanes, and levees, take your bike to the **Delta.** The roads are flat, lightly traveled, and offer a chance to experience Huck Finn's Mississippi right here in Northern California.

Bike Rentals For bike rentals on the Peninsula, try **Action Sports.** ~ 401 High Street, Palo Alto, 415-328-3180. **Bicycle Outfitter** is another possibility. ~ 963 Fremont Avenue, Los Altos; 415-948-8092. In the South Bay contact **Action Sports** ~ 1777 Hillsdale Avenue, San Jose; 408-978-8383 or **Stan's Cyclery** ~ 19685 Stevens

✔ CHECK THESE OUT—UNIQUE OUTDOOR ADVENTURES

- Laze the days away in a **houseboat** as you ply the waters of the California Delta, a western version of the Mississippi bayou. *page 180*
- Paddle your away around the seals and seagulls as you **kayak** in the San Francisco Bay, the world's largest landlocked bay. *page 183*
- Grab a sailboard and skim the challenging waters near the **Berkeley Marina.** *page 182*
- Trek the **San Andreas Fault Trail,** a self-guided path along California's infamous earthquake fault. *page 186*

Creek Boulevard, Cupertino; 408-996-1234. In the East Bay, try **Carl's Bikes.** ~ 2416 Telegraph Avenue, Oakland; 510-835-8763. The place to call in Marin is **Wheel Escapes.** ~ 30 Liberty Ship Way, Sausalito; 415-332-0218. The **Angel Island Company** rents bicycles to explore that state park's paved paths. ~ Angel Island; 415-897-0715.

HIKING

Though much of the landscape has been built up to serve growing urban needs, some of the surrounding wilderness regions have been preserved. So the Bay Area still offers diverse terrains for hikers—grassy hillsides, open meadows, stark mountainsides, and meandering creek beds. Where the pavement ends and the pathways begin, you can often find solitude and serenity.

THE PENINSULA Several trails wind through **San Bruno Mountain County Park,** offering spectacular views of the Bay Area. **Summit Loop Trail** (3.1 miles) takes you past mountain springs to views of the bay and the ocean. **Old Guadalupe Trail** (.8 mile) is an easy walk through a "fog forest" of fern-bedecked Monterey cypress and eucalyptus. **Ridge Trail to East Peak Vista** (2.5 miles) offers a hawk's eye perspective on the Bay.

At the **San Francisco State Fish and Game Refuge**, the **Sawyer Camp Historic Trail** (6 miles) provides access to this beautiful preserve in the Santa Cruz Mountains. The road is paved, but open only to hikers, equestrians, and bicycle riders. The trail climbs past San Andreas and Crystal Springs lakes, providing excellent opportunities for birdwatchers and wildflower-gazers.

A fascinating journey through earthquake country is the high point of a trek through **Los Trancos Open Space Reserve**. The **San Andreas Fault Trail** (.6 mile) is a self-guided path along a portion of California's infamous earthquake fault. A brochure points out sag ponds, benches, and scarps near the fault. The **Franciscan–Lost Creek Loop Trail** (4.3 miles) crosses a high meadow, cuts through stands of bay and oak, and crosses Los Trancos Creek. Its final destination is open countryside dotted with wildflowers.

THE EAST BAY **Anthony Chabot Regional Park** teems with wildlife and offers several good hikes. **Hidden Canyon Trail** (1.1 miles), near Anthony Chabot Campground, leads through stands of oak to an amphitheater set in a eucalyptus grove. **East Shore and West Shore Trails** (5.5 miles), bicycle paths with gentle slopes, also make for an enjoyable hike along Lake Chabot. If waterfalls, grass valleys, weeping willows, and wooded hillsides sound inviting, try the **Cascade** and **Columbine Trails** (2 miles). For a trek that covers the length of the park, there's **MacDonald–Brandon Trail** (8.7 miles). It's part of the 31-mile-long Skyline National Recreation Trail that connects Chabot with other regional parks. After the first uphill mile, the hike is fairly easy as it passes ridges and ravines, offering wonderful views to the south.

Tilden Regional Park, the most popular park in the East Bay, is a playground for naturalists. Its trails lead through nature areas, around lakes, and along mountain ridges. Be sure to visit the nature center. **Jewel Lake Trail** (.9 miles) is an easy walk through woods and fields to a marsh pond. Frogs, ducks, and bog vegetation are part of the setting. **Laurel Canyon** and **Wildcat Peak Trails** (3 miles) begin at the Little Farm and present striking views of the park as they carry you through groves of eucalyptus and Monterey pine. Another gentle hike nearby lies along **Sylvan Trail** (.7 mile).

The **Nimitz Way Trail** (3 miles) is also part of the 31-mile-long Skyline National Recreation Trail connecting six Bay Area parks. This section, a paved road, traverses San Pablo ridge.

The granddaddy of East Bay mountains, **Mount Diablo's State Park** is appealing both for its challenges and rewards. **Summit Trail** (7.2 miles) is an uphill climb across stark, rocky terrain, but the views are outstanding; bring water. **Devil's Slide and Oyster Point Trail** (3.8 miles) traverses rolling grasslands and oak forests en route to another stunning vista. **North Peak Trail** (1.4 miles) is a varied hike up steep slopes and down through shady woods. In the end it arrives atop Mount Diablo's second peak and offers marvelous views of the Bay Area.

Hiking through the wild and rugged chaparral country of **Las Trampas Regional Wilderness** evokes dreams of the early West. **Chamis Trail to Las Trampas Ridge Trail** (6 miles round trip) begins in a valley and climbs 1000 feet to an impressive view point. **Creek Trail** (1.5 miles) is an easy, shady trail through hardwood forests and grasslands past Bollinger Creek. **Devil's Hole Trail** (6.6 miles) requires a strenuous 2000-foot climb, both out and back. The rewards include a small creek, fern gorge, and magnificent views. Bring food and water.

Sunol Regional Wilderness offers several pathways through hills and along tumbling creeks. **Flag Hill Trail** (1.3 miles) involves a 1000-foot climb to a grand view of the park. **McCorkle Trail via Cerro Este** (2.9 miles) follows Alameda Creek, then climbs a hill en route to a backpacking camp. To get away from other hikers, try the **Maguire Peaks Loop Trail** (3.9 miles). It carries past oaks, streams, and sage-scented grasslands to a pair of wind-sculpted peaks.

See Chapter Five for descriptions of hiking in Marin.

Transportation

CAR

The Bay Area is a sprawling region threaded with major highways. Along the Peninsula, **Routes 101, 280, and 82** travel north and south. All three lead to the South Bay; from here, **Routes 880** and **80** travel up along the East Bay.

From San Francisco, **Route 101** streams north to Marin, and **Route 80** cuts through the East Bay and connects with other roads leading into the Delta.

AIR

Three major airports service the Bay Area: ***San Francisco International Airport*** (see Chapter Two), San Jose International Airport, and Oakland International Airport. To avoid the crowds and parking problems at San Francisco's mammoth airport, consider landing in Oakland, just across the Bay. If you're interested in touring the South Bay or Central Coast, San Jose is very convenient.

San Jose International Airport: Airlines flying into San Jose include Alaska Airlines, American Airlines, America West Airlines, Continental Airlines, Delta Air Lines, Trans World Airlines, and United Airlines.

Several bus companies provide ground transportation from the San Jose airport. Check with **Greyhound Bus Lines** (800-231-2222) and the **Airport Connection** (408-730-5555) for schedules and destinations. **Santa Clara County Transit** (408-321-2300) provides frequent service to downtown San Jose. Taxi cabs are also available: **Alpha Cab** (408-295-9500) or **Yellow Cab** (408-293-1234).

Oakland International Airport: Oakland's airport is serviced by Alaska Airlines, American Airlines, America West Airlines, Delta Airlines, Southwest Airlines, and United Airlines.

Excellent ground transportation to and from the Oakland airport makes it one of the most convenient terminals in the area. **The Bayporter** (415-467-1800) has regularly scheduled service between the Oakland and San Francisco airports, with a stop at the Parc Oakland Hotel. **Alameda–Contra Costa Transit,** or **AC Transit,** stops regularly at the terminal and transports passengers to downtown Oakland.~ 800-559-4636. For a quick trip to various East Bay points, climb aboard the **Oakland Air-Bart** which connects the airport with the **Bay Area Rapid Transit**, or **BART**, system. ~ 510-465-2278.

Several cab and shuttle companies service the airport as well: try **Friendly Cab** (510-536-3000) or **Yellow Cab** (510-444-1234). For travelers with disabilities, there's the **Oakairporter** (510-568-7433) and **Supershuttle** (510-268-8700).

BUS

Greyhound Bus Lines offers extensive bus service to the Bay Area from around the country. There are stations in Oakland at 2103 San Pablo Avenue and San Jose at 70 Alameda Avenue. ~ 800-231-2222.

Peerless Stages carries passengers from Oakland to San Jose and south. ~ 510-444-2900.

TRAIN

Amtrak has several trains coming into the Bay Area daily. Two cover California routes: the "Coast Starlight" runs from Los Angeles to Seattle with stops in San Jose and Oakland, and the "San Joaquin" covers the San Joaquin Valley, stopping in Oakland. From Chicago, the "San Francisco Zephyr" traverses the western United States to Oakland. ~ 800-872-7245.

CAR RENTALS

Most towns in the Bay Area have car rental agencies; check the yellow pages to find the best bargains. To pick up a car at the San Jose airport, call **Avis Rent A Car** (408-993-2224, 800-331-1212), **Budget Rent A Car** (408-286-7859, 800-527-0700), **Dollar Rent A Car** (408-280-1111, 800-800-4000), **Hertz Rent A Car** (408-437-5700, 800-654-3131), or **National Interrent** (408-295-1344, 800-227-7368).

At the Oakland airport, check with **Avis Rent A Car** (510-562-9000, 800-331-1212), **Budget Rent A Car** (510-568-4771, 800-527-0700), **Dollar Rent A Car** (510-638-2750, 800-800-4000), **Hertz Rent A Car** (510-568-1177, 800-654-3131), or **National Interrent** (510-632-2225, 800-227-7368). Several other companies, listed in the Yellow Pages, offer free pickup and delivery to both airports.

PUBLIC TRANSIT

Most sections of the Bay Area are accessible by some form of public transportation. It may be a bus, subway, or ferry boat, but it will get you to your destination.

On the Peninsula, **San Mateo County Transit**, or **Sam Trans**, carries passengers from San Francisco as far south as Palo Alto. ~ 800-660-4287.

The South Bay is traversed by **Santa Clara County Transit** buses and the **Light-Rail System**, with service extending from Palo Alto through San Jose. ~ 408-321-2300.

A network of bus routes crisscrosses the East Bay. Call **Alameda–Contra Costa County Transit**, or AC Transit, for schedules. ~ 510-839-2882, 800-559-4636. **Peerless Stages** serves the South Bay and East Bay. ~ 510-444-2900, 800-231-2222.

Golden Gate Transit buses can take you from points in San Francisco to locations throughout Marin County (Sausalito, San Rafael, and beyond). ~ 415-453-2100.

Daily commuter trains run the length of the Peninsula from San Francisco to San Jose. Call **CalTrain** for information. ~ 415-508-6200, 800-660-4287.

Bay Area Rapid Transit, or BART, runs from Fremont north to Richmond, stopping in Oakland and Berkeley, and from Colma through San Francisco to Concord. ~ 510-465-2278.

Public transportation from San Francisco to Marin can become a sightseeing adventure when you book passage on a **Golden Gate Transit** ferry boat. Cruises to Sausalito and Larkspur from the Ferry Building in San Francisco are crowded with commuters and vacationers alike. ~ 415-453-2100. The **Red and White Fleet** also operates ferries from San Francisco to Sausalito, Vallejo, and Tiburon. ~ 415-546-2628. The **Alameda/Oakland Ferry** provides service from the East Bay to the Ferry Building and Pier 39 in San Francisco. ~ 510-522-3300.

FOUR

Wine Country

Just one hour from the streets of San Francisco lies an agricultural area which can match for beauty farmlands anywhere in the country. It's a region of tree-tufted mountains and luxurious valleys. Tilled fields create quiltlike patterns across the landscape and country roads wind into its hills.

Despite the grandeur of the place, its visual appeal is only a secondary feature. The lure of the land is its temptation to all the senses, particularly taste and smell. The plants stippling those picturesque fields are grapes and the product is wine, fine vintages which rival even those of France.

Winemaking in California dates back to the 18th century when Spanish padres planted vineyards at the missions. The Franciscans grew black grapes for sacramental wines, crushing them by foot in hide troughs, then fermenting the harvest in leather sacks.

Spanish vineyards spread north to Sonoma where in 1823 church fathers established their last mission. In Napa Valley, across the mountains east of Sonoma, George Yount, the area's original settler, cultivated grapes in 1843. During the next decade numerous Europeans, drawn initially by the Gold Rush, forsook prospecting for planting. A Prussian immigrant named Charles Krug became a pioneer in commercializing Napa wines. He also taught other early vintners like Jacob Beringer and Carl Wente, whose names even today adorn wine bottles.

In 1857, Agoston Haraszthy, a Hungarian count, founded the Buena Vista Winery in Sonoma. Commissioned by the California governor, he traveled through France, Italy, and Germany a few years later, collecting cuttings from 300 grape varieties. Soon thereafter, the University of California perfected fermentation techniques and established a national center for viticulture and oenology at its Davis campus.

California's wine business boomed. Four million gallons were produced in 1869, 28 million in 1900, and by 1911 the total rose to 58 million gallons. Then came Prohibition. From 1920 until 1933, an entire industry withered on the vine. Many wineries shut down; others converted their fields to orchards.

It took nearly 30 years for the industry to recover. Not until the 1960s, as wine became an increasingly popular national drink, did California's vineyards burgeon once more. This long-awaited renaissance proved extraordinary. Within a five-year period, vineyard acreage doubled. Wineries mushroomed in the Napa and Sonoma valleys, along the Russian River, and elsewhere throughout the state. Family-run wineries blossomed, national companies like Coca-Cola and Nestlé moved into the vineyards, and formerly aloof French winemakers, impressed with the quality of the wines, formed partnerships with local growers. Winemaking became a multibillion dollar business, with millions of people touring California's vineyards each year.

The natural elements for this success story have always been present, though only recently did the social factors begin to coalesce. Geography and climate play vital roles in winemaking and combine north of San Francisco to create ideal growing conditions. Here several valleys—Napa, Sonoma, and the Russian River—are protected by mountains from the cold winds and rain along the Pacific coast. They enjoy hot (very hot!) summers and cool, moist winters, ensuring good harvests.

In Napa Valley, sun, low hills, and fog drifting up from San Francisco Bay produce one of the world's finest winegrowing regions. Today, the area has become so well-known and fashionable that it is not only drawing fog from San Francisco. Celebrities and millionaires are moving here faster than new wineries. Gourmet restaurants and country inns have multiplied, and tourists are causing weekend traffic jams in this once rustic realm. Even the health spa at Calistoga has gained such importance that France's Perrier took over the mineral water bottling. It's a far cry from a century ago when a penniless writer named Robert Louis Stevenson explored the isolated farming community.

Sonoma Valley's history traces back further than that of Napa, but lately the "valley of the moon" has been hard-pressed to keep pace with its starstruck neighbor. Resting between the volcanic Sonoma Mountains and the Mayacamas Mountains to the east, it was once inhabited by Coastal Miwok, Pomo, Wappo, and Patwin Indians. They gathered berries and acorns, fished the waters of nearby San Pablo Bay, and stalked the mountains for bear and deer. The advent of the Spanish mission changed their lifestyle unalterably and ushered in an era of international intrigue. During the early 1840s, Mexico's General Mariano Guadalupe Vallejo controlled Sonoma. Then in 1846 a band of roughhewn Americans arrested Vallejo and declared California the Bear Flag Republic. Within weeks the United States took control, eventually converting Sonoma to a military base.

Novelist Jack London settled in the nearby town of Glen Ellen in 1904, living there until his death in 1916. Interested in ranching as well as writing, London chose a region which today is an important dairy farming and sheep ranching area. The Sonoma Valley is also noted for its apple orchards, not to mention many excellent wineries.

Like the Russian River region to the north, it's planted with an extraordinary variety of grapes. Moving in a southerly course from Mendocino County, the Russian River passes Alexander Valley, Dry Creek Valley, and other regions which have greatly contributed to California's wine renaissance. Then, as it turns west toward the sea, it has given birth to a different sort of rebirth, a gay renaissance. Since the 1970s, the area around Guerneville, long popular for its excellent canoeing and

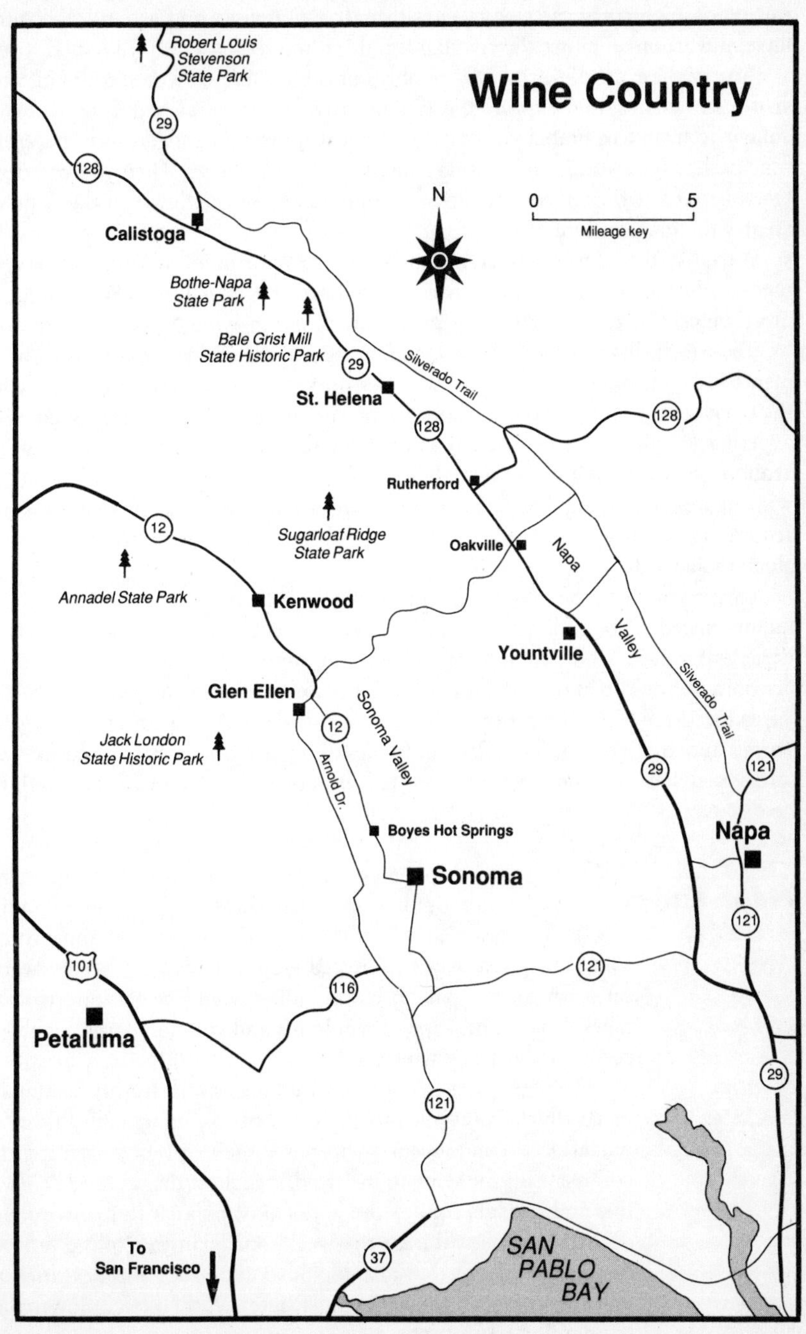
Wine Country
Robert Louis Stevenson State Park
Calistoga
Bothe-Napa State Park
Bale Grist Mill State Historic Park
St. Helena
Silverado Trail
Rutherford
Oakville
Napa Valley
Sugarloaf Ridge State Park
Annadel State Park
Kenwood
Yountville
Glen Ellen
Sonoma Valley
Jack London State Historic Park
Arnold Dr.
Boyes Hot Springs
Sonoma
Napa
Petaluma
To San Francisco
SAN PABLO BAY
N
0 5
Mileage key
29
128
12
121
101
116
37

fishing, has become Northern California's top gay resort. Country inns, restaurants, and nightclubs catering to gays from San Francisco and around the country have mushroomed along the riverbanks and in the region's deep redwood forests.

Any of these areas—providing opportunities to taste fine wines, tour vineyards, visit historic sites, and explore the Russian River—can be visited in the course of a day trip from San Francisco. But you might want to take longer—a week, or lifetime perhaps, to wander California's luscious Wine Country. Then you can decide for yourself whether it's the beauty of the landscape or the flavor of the wine that creates the magical lure of the place.

A tour of the Wine Country will give you an opportunity to sample choice vintages, explore vineyards, and experience the art of winemaking. You'll find that most wineries, large or small, welcome visitors and provide tours and tasting.

To visit the area, pack a picnic lunch, wander through the growing region, and plan to stop at only three or four wineries during the day. Small wineries, where the operation is family run and tours are personalized, create the most memorable experiences. Usually the winemaker or a member of the family will show you around, providing a glimpse into their lives as well as their livelihoods. Since the winemakers will be leaving their normal duties to help you, small wineries usually require advance reservations. It's also a good idea to ask directions to these secluded vineyards.

Large wineries schedule tours and tasting all day and permit you to drop by unannounced. Though impersonal, they're convenient to visit and provide a wider variety of wines. Many are housed in beautiful buildings of historic interest.

Both family-run and multinational wineries are described here, though the vineyards listed are a small fraction of those you can visit. They also represent my favorites and are liable to the follies and foibles of my personal taste. So test for yourself; somewhere out there lies a hidden vineyard or unheralded vintage, waiting to be discovered.

Napa Valley

California's premier winegrowing region is a long, narrow valley, laid out like a checkerboard and stretching 35 miles. Here grape arbors alternate with wild grasses and rich bottom land gives way to forested slopes. If natural beauty were a question for the palate, Napa Valley would be the rarest of vintages. It is a landscape of windmills and wooden barns, clapboard cottages and stone wineries.

The region is also a millionaire's preserve, a freshly fashionable place which draws the most affected people imaginable. There are pinch-faced connoisseurs who purse their lips as they taste, then comment on the wine in mangled French. It draws hordes of visitors and is fast becoming the state's most popular tourist attraction.

So try to visit during the week, and plan to explore not only the main highway, but also the Silverado Trail. An ideal itinerary will carry you up the valley on Route 29, then back down along the parallel roadway.

SIGHTS

The **Napa Valley Conference and Visitors Bureau** is a good place to get started. They will supply you with maps and brochures for the area. ~ 1310 Napa Town Center, Napa; 707-226-7459.

An unusual option for touring the wine country is to climb aboard the **Napa Valley Wine Train**. In 1989 service was restored on the old line between the city of Napa and the vineyards slightly north of St. Helena. Travelers may choose the luncheon, brunch, or dinner trip, each of which takes three hours and smoothly chugs past some of the most scenic parts of the valley. Three lounge cars have been beautifully restored; the dining car is straight out of a romance novel. ~ 1275 McKinstry Street, Napa; 707-253-2111.

If you choose to do it on your own, you'll find one of the area's most interesting wineries right in Napa. Located on the site of the former Christian Brothers' Mont LaSalle winery, the **Hess Collection** is where fine wine meets fine art. The self-guided tour is unique: It is the only winery in the valley that includes two floors displaying some 130 museum-quality artworks by contemporary European and American artists. The Hess Collection also refers to the cabernets and chardonnays that are just being released and are available for sampling (at a small fee) in the ground-floor tasting room. ~ 4411 Redwood Road, Napa; 707-255-1144.

A new winery with an old French name, **Mumm Napa Valley** is a good place to see *methode champenoise* production. Located on an oak-shaded hillside, the pitched-roof winery looks like a redwood barn. In the tasting room you can sample flutes of sparkling wine as well as hors d'oeuvres. ~ 8445 Silverado Trail, Napa; 707-942-3434.

◄ HIDDEN

Mayacamas Vineyards provides a different setting entirely. Located deep in the mountains west of Napa Valley, it sits astride an extinct volcano. The blocks of vineyard appear hewn from surrounding rock walls. Indeed, the fields of chardonnay and cabernet sauvignon rest on terraces along the mountainside. Like the en-

✔ CHECK THESE OUT—UNIQUE SIGHTS

- Board the **Napa Valley Wine Train**, and survey rows on rows of grapevines while enjoying a meal in an elegantly restored dining car. *page 195*
- Contemplate the colorful chapel at the **Sonoma Mission**, the last of the 21 California missions to be built. *page 210*
- Roam the estate of a great novelist at **Jack London State Historic Park**, and peruse the keepsakes from his world adventures. *page 212*
- Take a plunge or launch a canoe at **Johnson's Beach**, on the shoreline of the Russian River. *page 223*

circling hills, the winery is made of stone, built in 1889. Tours of this unique place are by appointment; it lies about ten miles off Route 29 along winding mountain roads. ~ 1155 Lokoya Road, Napa; 707-224-4030.

Located between Sonoma and Napa is Piper Sonoma's sister company, **Carneros Alambic Distillery**. Guests are treated to a tour of the production facility. This culminates in a "sensory evaluation," where guests can sniff the differences in the six separate distilled grape varietals used in the final brandy. ~ 1250 Cuttings Wharf Road, Napa; 707-253-9055.

As you proceed north, the next group of major wineries lie clustered around **Yountville**. Residents of this rural town claim that their town is "where it all began." George Yount, the municipal namesake, was the first American to settle in Napa Valley. Arriving in 1836, he took control of an 11,000-acre land grant and built a Kentucky-style log house.

Domaine Chandon, owned by France's fabled champagne producer, Moët & Chandon, sits on a knoll west of town. Producing some of California's foremost sparkling wines, this winery provides a close look into the production and bottling of the bubbly. It's housed in a modernistic building with barrel-vaulted ceilings and contains a small wine museum as well as a gourmet restaurant. The regularly scheduled tours are free, but there's a charge to taste. ~ 1 California Drive, Yountville; 707-944-2280.

Among the largest in the Napa Valley, **Robert Mondavi Winery** is a Spanish mission–style building offering two informative tours by reservation. Choose between the basic production tour or a three-hour long look at the entire process from vineyard to laboratory to winery (the latter is only offered a few days a week). The chardonnay and fumé blanc are excellent and you can also sample reserve wines by the glass (tasting fee). In addition to visiting the art gallery, you may want to attend summer jazz concerts held on Saturday nights in the courtyard. ~ 7801 St. Helena Highway, Oakville; 707-963-9611.

Continuing along Route 29 you'll drive through the tiny town of Rutherford, passing a patchwork of planted fields. In a valley virtually spilling over with wineries, how does a new one get noticed? In the case of **St. Supéry Vineyards & Winery**, it's by constructing a first-rate gallery with numerous exhibits on Napa Valley winemaking. Three-dimensional displays include a replica of an actual grapevine growing out of deep soil, smell-a-vision (a contraption that enables you to smell four of the aromatic components of wine), and topographical maps that show why the valley is good for grapes. An outdoor tasting area (again, nominal fee) and a restored Victorian add spice to the winery tour. ~ 8440 St. Helena Highway, Rutherford; 707-963-4507.

One of the prettiest wineries in Rutherford is the **Niebaum–Coppola Estate Winery**, where movie great Francis Coppola and his wife Eleanor have been making wine since 1975. In 1995 they purchased the adjacent Inglenook Château and vineyard, unifying the original 1879 estate of winemaker Gustave Niebaum. The ivy-draped château houses the Centennial Museum, where the history of winemaking at the estate is chronicled as is Coppola's career (five of his Oscars along with artifacts from several of his films are displayed). Specialties of the winery include rubicon, chardonnay, cabernet franc, merlot, and zinfandel. Tasting fee. ~ 1991 St. Helena Highway, Rutherford; 707-963-9099.

Capital of the Wine Country is the falsefront town of St. Helena. Surrounded by vineyards, this old farm town still retains much of its early charm. In the Victorian-style downtown area, the brick-and-stone **IOOF Building** at 1352 Main Street looms several stories above the pavement, as it has for a century. The cynosure of St. Helena is the **Ritchie Block** at 1331 Main Street, a stone structure with brick-and-wood facade. Featuring more frills and swirls than a wedding cake, it is a study in ornate architecture.

The town's **Silverado Museum** houses a collection of artifacts from Robert Louis Stevenson's life and his sojourn in the Napa Valley. Having visited Monterey and San Francisco, the Scottish author arrived in Calistoga in 1880. Stevenson was en route to Hawaii and the South Seas, seeking a salubrious environment in which to escape his lifelong illnesses. Among the memorabilia at the museum are manuscripts, letters, photographs, and first editions, as well as personal effects left behind by the globe-girdling Victorian. Closed Monday. ~ 1490 Library Lane, St. Helena; 707-963-3757.

While the way to see Napa wineries is to visit the smaller concerns, big sometimes is better. Take **Beringer Vineyards**, for example. The vintage product here is the Rhine House, a century-old Tudor-style mansion. With its mansard roof and stone inlay, it is a masterwork of spires, turrets, and gables. The interior, complete with tasting room, is illuminated through stained glass and paneled in hand-carved hardwoods. Among the winery's other features are 1000-foot-long tunnels cut into the neighboring hillside by 19th-century Chinese laborers. One of these tunnels has been converted into a tasting room. You can also take a tour, which covers several interesting parts of the operation, including the tunnels. ~ 2000 Main Street, St. Helena; 707-963-7115.

North of St. Helena, **Bale Grist Mill State Historic Park** is a picturesque stop. Sitting beside a tumbling stream, an 1846 waterwheel mill creates a classic scene. It was built for a Napa Valley settler and served as an early gathering place for farmers throughout the area. The mill is now partially restored and functioning, and there are water wheel demonstrations as well as guided tours.

There's a visitors center plus a pair of raw wood buildings which housed the mill and granary. Admission. ~ Route 29, St. Helena; 707-942-4575.

Not far past the old mill stream, a side road leads from Route 29 to **Tudal Winery**. Touted as one of the world's smallest wineries, it consists of a cluster of contemporary buildings surrounded by luxurious grape arbors. Tours and tasting at this family affair are by appointment. A walk around the entire winery will probably take a grand total of ten minutes, after which the owner may regale you for hours with tales of the Wine Country. ~ 1015 Big Tree Road, St. Helena; 707-963-3947.

HIDDEN ►

It's easy to find **Litto Damonte's Hubcap Ranch**. Just take Howell Mountain Road east from the Silverado Trail in St. Helena to the hamlet of Pope Valley. Head north three miles until you see at least a thousand points of light. Those are Damonte's hubcaps, more than two thousand strong, adorning houses, barns, fences, and pastures. Just to make sure you know who's responsible, Damonte has plastered his name on the barn in—what else—hubcaps.

When Robert Louis Stevenson visited the **Schramsberg Vineyards**, he tasted 18 different wines. Today you'll have to settle for a tour (by appointment) of this historic facility. The road up to Schramsberg burrows through a dense forest before arriving at the original owner's home. The winery has added several buildings since Stevenson's day and now specializes in sparkling wine, but the old tunnels and cellars remain. Tasting fee. ~ Schramsberg Road, Calistoga; 707-942-4558.

In the 19th century, roads were unpaved and no modern conveyances transported guests to hillside wineries. All that has changed at **Sterling Vineyards**. Set atop a knoll near the head of Napa Valley, this Greek monastery–style winery is reached via an aerial tramway (fee). The gondolas carry visitors to a multitiered building, painted a brilliant white, which commands sentinel views of the surrounding valley. Once atop this lofty retreat, a self-guided tour leads through various winemaking facilities to an elegant tasting room. It also takes in the spectacular stained-glass windows and 18th-century church bells which add an exotic element to this unusual winery. ~ 1111 Dunaweal Lane, Calistoga; 707-942-3344.

Back on terra firma, you'll arrive in the town of **Calistoga**. Founded in 1859, this well-known health spa owes its origin and name to Sam Brannan. Brannan, of course, is the shrewd Mormon journalist and entrepreneur who first alerted San Francisco to the gold discovery. A decade later he saw liquid gold in Napa Valley's mineral springs and geysers. Determined to create a California version of New York's famous Saratoga spa, he named the region Calistoga. Indeed, its hot springs and underwater reservoirs were perfectly suited to a health resort.

Today Brannan's idea is carried on by numerous spas and health resorts. After imbibing at vineyards throughout the valley, visitors arrive in Calistoga to luxuriate in the region's mineral waters. I highly recommend that you sign up for "the works" at one of the local spas. You'll be submerged in a mud bath, led into a whirlpool bath, then a steam room, wrapped head to toe in a blanket, and finally given a massage. By the end of the treatment, your mind will reside somewhere in the ozone and your body will be completely loose. If you're game, contact **Nance's Hot Springs**, which opened in 1923 and is one of the oldest spas in Calistoga. ~ 1614 Lincoln Avenue, Calistoga; 707-942-6211. **Calistoga Village Inn and Spa** is another possibility. They offer the unique powdered mustard seed bath as well as the more standard steam baths, blanket wraps, and facials. ~ 1880 Lincoln Avenue, Calistoga; 707-942-0991.

About six million years ago, when nearby Mount St. Helena was an active volcano, the magma itself exploded. Evidently, eruptions from this firepit leveled an entire redwood grove, which transformed over the ages into a **Petrified Forest**. Located six miles from Calistoga, this eerie spot contains a succession of fallen giants. Redwoods measuring over 100 feet long and 8 feet in diameter lie along the forest floors, perfectly preserved in stone. Unfortunately, the place has the trappings of a tourist trap. Admission. ~ 4100 Petrified Forest Road, Calistoga; 707-942-6667.

Other Calistoga points of interest are the **Sharpsteen Museum** and adjacent **Sam Brannan Cottage**. Dedicated to the town's original settlers, the museum displays tools from a blacksmith's shop and early California kitchen. Sam Brannan's cottage is furnished in period fashion with Victorian furniture and a glorious old piano. Highlight of the entire display, however, is an elaborate diorama portraying Brannan's health resort in miniature. Representing Calistoga circa 1865, it contains everything from railway station to racetrack, hotel to distillery. ~ 1311 Washington Street, Calistoga; 707-942-5911.

THAR SHE BLOWS

More evidence of Calistoga's infernal geology issues forth from **Old Faithful Geyser**, a subterranean stream heated to 350° that blows skyward every 40 minutes, reaching 60 feet high. This geothermal gusher, a hokey but interesting tourist attraction, is caused when hot magma heats water deep within the earth and intense pressures force it violently to the surface. Admission. ~ 1299 Tubbs Lane, Calistoga; 707-942-6463.

One of the Napa Valley's most intriguing wineries is 160-acre **Château Montelena.** Tours by appointment lead to a castle that overlooks a lake landscaped in classic Chinese manner. Bridges lead out to tiny islands that are ideal for picnicking. Oh, by the way, you'll also find a tasting room known for its chardonnays and cabernets. Tasting fee. ~ 1429 Tubbs Lane, Calistoga; 707-942-5105.

At **Clos Pegase** the tasting room is a post-modern affair designed by architect Michael Graves that features Honduran mahogany flourishes, antique glass decorations, and an art gallery. A glass wall exposes the tank room where vintners make cabernet sauvignons, merlots, and chardonnays. Tasting fee. ~ 1060 Dunaweal Lane, Calistoga; 707-942-4981.

SILVERADO TRAIL As mentioned earlier, there's an alternate route through the valley, an old stagecoach road called the **Silverado Trail.** Fully paved, it parallels Route 29 on the east and links with it via a succession of cross-valley roads. In addition to glimpses of Napa Valley as it was 30 years ago, it's an excellent place to search out small wineries. All along this rural stretch are family-owned vineyards, set on the valley floor or tucked into nearby hills.

Shafer Vineyards lies at the base of a rocky outcropping. Surrounding the woodframe winery are fields of chardonnay, merlot, and cabernet sauvignon grapes. Removed from the road, it's a placid spot with views along owner John Shafer's tilled fields and out across the valley. Tours of the winery, with its oak tanks and aging barrels, are by appointment only, as are tastings. ~ 6154 Silverado Trail, Napa; 707-944-2877.

Caymus Vineyards is run by an old-timer named Charlie Wagner, his wife Lorna and their son Chuck. The winery buildings are simple and unpretentious, because, as Charlie explains, he concentrates on quality, not showmanship. The feisty owner, whose parents were Napa winemakers back in the early 1900s, was a pioneer in the production of Oeil de Perdrix, or Eye of the Partridge, a delicious pinot noir developed in the 1970s. Now the focus is on producing cabernet sauvignon and Conundrum, a proprietary blended white wine. The best part of a winetasting with Charlie arrives when he pours a glass of his premium wine and begins spinning stories about Napa Valley way back when. Tasting fee. ~ 8700 Conn Creek Road, Rutherford; 707-963-4204.

Robert Louis Stevenson wrote sections of *The Silverado Squatters* and studied settings later used in *Treasure Island* at what is now Robert Louis Stevenson State Park.

After arriving in Calistoga, the Silverado Trail trades the warm, level terrain of the valley for the cool, rugged landscape of the mountains. It climbs and winds through thick coniferous forests and past bald rockfaces. In touring Napa, you've undoubtedly noticed the stately mountain that stands sentinel at the north end of the valley. **Mount St. Helena,** named by 19th-century

Russian explorers for their empress, rises 4343 feet, dominating the skyline.

Perched on the side of this mountain is **Robert Louis Stevenson State Park.** The Scottish writer and his wife honeymooned in these parts, camping in the hills and enjoying the recuperative air. Today the Memorial Trail leads through this undeveloped park one mile to an old mine and a monument commemorating the spot where Stevenson spent his honeymoon. Then a fire road continues four more miles to the top of Mount St. Helena. From this impressive aerie the entire Napa Valley lies before you and the views reach from the Sierra Nevada to San Francisco. Admission. ~ Route 29 about eight miles north of Calistoga; 707-942-4575.

LODGING

Moderately priced bed-and-breakfasts are nearly nonexistent in the wine country, with one exception—**Churchill Manor.** Located on an acre of landscaped, flower-filled grounds just south of downtown Napa, the manor, built in 1889, is now a ten-room inn. The rooms are furnished with European antiques, and exquisite redwood columns front the main staircase. The innkeepers serve a full breakfast in the tile-floored sunroom, and on nice mornings you can take it out on the veranda, which surrounds three sides of the home. There are tandem bikes to ride and a sitting room with games and puzzles to enjoy. ~ 485 Brown Street, Napa; 707-253-7733, 800-799-7733, fax 707-253-8836. MODERATE TO DELUXE.

For a dash of history with your evening glass of port, consider the **Maison Fleuris.** A lodging place since 1873, this stone building is currently a fashionable bed and breakfast. There are seven rooms in the old ivy-covered structure and six others in two adjacent buildings, each room crowded with antiques. Quilts and teddy bears adorn the beds, while chandeliers and brass lamps illuminate the historic setting; all have private baths. As a contemporary touch, there is a swimming pool, jacuzzi, and mountain bikes available for guest use. Breakfast is buffet style, and afternoon wine and tea are served daily. ~ 6529 Yount Street, Yountville; 707-944-2056, 800-788-0369; fax 707-944-9342. DELUXE TO ULTRA-DELUXE.

The **Vintage Inn Napa Valley** is ideally located for exploring the Wine Country. Rose gardens and trickling fountains surround smart-looking, two-story villas with brick facades and wood shingles on the roof. Eighty rooms are like mini-suites, adorned with fireplaces and shuttered windows, marble wet bars and baths—all-in-all, some of the most desirable rooms in the valley. The complimentary breakfast buffet is quite extensive. An Olympic-sized pool and tennis courts are here, and Yountville's exclusive shops and eateries are but a short stroll. ~ 6541 Washington Street, Yountville; 707-944-1112, 800-351-1133, fax 707-944-1617. ULTRA-DELUXE.

Perched on a hillside studded with olive trees, **Auberge du Soleil Resort** is a curious blend of adobe-style buildings named after

French winegrowing regions and decorated in a breezy California/Southwest style. Bare Mexican tile floors, louvered doors, fireplaces, and private terraces are a refreshing change from the cluttered feel of older hotels in the valley. A dozen low-rise cottages stagger down the hill, all but one of them contain four rooms. There's also a pool to relax in. ~ 180 Rutherford Hill Road, Rutherford; 707-963-1211, 800-348-5406, fax 707-963-8764. ULTRA-DELUXE.

Crafted from white oak, the Spanish colonial **Rancho Caymus Inn** is a romantic retreat with stained-glass windows, a colonnade, courtyard, and gardens. There is a total of 26 rooms; in the two-level rooms you'll find carved black walnut beds, private balconies, and charming adobe beehive fireplaces. ~ 1140 Rutherford Road, Rutherford; 707-963-1777, 800-845-1777, fax 707-963-5387. ULTRA-DELUXE.

In the center of town, the **Hotel St. Helena** is a traditional false-front building dating to 1881. Entirely refurbished several years ago, it features 18 guest rooms, all but four of which have private baths. Many rooms include such decorative flourishes as caneback chairs, brass beds, antique armoires, marbletop vanities, and bent-willow headboards. Each is painted in warm pastel colors and plushly carpeted. Guests share an indoor reading room and sitting room with fireplace, plus other facilities like the hotel's wine bar. ~ 1309 Main Street, St. Helena; 707-963-4388, fax 707-963-5402. ULTRA-DELUXE.

A gracious Victorian topped with a fanciful cupola affording 360-degree views of the Napa Valley, **Ink House Bed & Breakfast** attracts mostly straight guests but has a strong gay and lesbian following as well. The 1884 house is encircled by a wide veranda with white wicker chairs and offers four antique-filled guest rooms, each with private bath. In addition to a full breakfast, wine and

✔ CHECK THESE OUT—UNIQUE LODGING

- *Budget to moderate:* Soak in the mineral-water pools at **Harbin Hot Springs**, a New Age retreat center in Middletown. *page 204*
- *Moderate to deluxe:* Slip into the **Churchill Manor**, a small inn nestled on an acre of flower-filled countryside just south of downtown Napa. *page 201*
- *Deluxe to ultra-deluxe:* Combine history with comfort at the **Sonoma Hotel**, a hostelry that dates back to 1872. *page 213*
- *Ultra-deluxe:* Luxuriate at **Auberge du Soleil**, where a dozen low-rise cottages decorate the hillside in Rutherford. *page 201*

Budget: under $50 Moderate: $50–$90 Deluxe: $90–$120 Ultra-deluxe: over $120

appetizers are served in the afternoon. ~ 1575 St. Helena Highway, St. Helena; 707-963-3890. ULTRA-DELUXE.

Set in the Mayacamas Mountains, just 12 minutes from Napa's wineries and restaurants, the contemporary-style **Hilltop House** is an excellent place to spot deer, raccoons, rabbits, hawks, and hummingbirds while enjoying the amenities of a 135-acre retreat. The four rooms are furnished with antiques, brass beds, and down comforters, and offer panoramic mountain views. There's a large deck, garden, a hot tub, and a network of nearby hiking trails. Full breakfast is included. ~ 9550 St. Helena Road, St. Helena; 707-944-0880, fax 707-571-0263. DELUXE TO ULTRA-DELUXE.

Spread across 330 acres and claiming to be the oldest resort in California, **White Sulphur Springs** dates to 1852. A deeply shaded creek and several hiking trails run through the property, which also contains a redwood grove and a series of natural sulphur springs and pools. The tiny one-room cabins and lodge-like carriage house possess a rustic charm. The former have private baths, knotty pine walls, kitchenettes, throw rugs, and an ambience that borders between homey and funky. The latter share a bathroom, lounge, and kitchenette. There are also "inn rooms" with private baths available at moderate cost. In the health spa you can treat yourself to a massage, an herbal facial, or a mud wrap. ~ 3100 White Sulphur Springs Road, St. Helena; 707-963-8588, 800-593-8873, fax 707-963-2890. DELUXE TO ULTRA-DELUXE.

◄ HIDDEN

Located at the end of a tree-shaded country road, **Meadowood Resort** is comprised of 95 accommodations, a nine-hole golf course, two croquet lawns, two pools, tennis courts, and a fitness center. Guests may choose to stay in cozy cabins or in the newer Croquet Lodge; either way, they'll have comfortable furnishings and serene views of the grounds. ~ 900 Meadowood Lane, St. Helena; 707-963-3646, 800-458-8080, fax 707-963-3532. ULTRA-DELUXE.

The **Calistoga Inn** has rooms for moderate prices, with a continental breakfast included. This 18-room hostelry sits atop a restaurant and bar which serves Napa Valley Brewing Company beer from the brewery next door. The accommodations are small but tidy, carpeted wall-to-wall, and plainly decorated. The furniture is nicked, baths are shared, and the television room will remind you of a boardinghouse. ~ 1250 Lincoln Avenue, Calistoga; 707-942-4101, fax 707-942-4914. MODERATE.

Several Calistoga spas also provide overnight accommodations. **Indian Springs Hotel Resort**, located on the same grounds as the town's original resort, offers bungalow-style cottages (actually duplexes) with kitchenettes. Guests are welcome to use the spa's 98° mineral pool, tennis courts, and bicycles. Indian Springs also features mud baths, steam baths, massages, and facials, making it an excellent resting place for the health-minded. ~ 1712 Lincoln Avenue, Calistoga; 707-942-4913, fax 707-942-4919. ULTRA-DELUXE.

Built in 1917, the renovated **Mount View Hotel** has the aura and feel of a classic small-town hotel. It's a 30-room affair with dining room and lounge downstairs and Victorian flourishes throughout. The lobby is spacious and homey, featuring a fireplace and plump furnishings. Guest rooms upstairs receive a guarded recommendation: They're nicely decorated in a contemporary style, but plainly furnished. There are also three cottages, each with a private hot tub. Guests are free to use the hotel's pool and spa. ~ 1457 Lincoln Avenue, Calistoga; 707-942-6877, 800-816-6877, fax 707-942-6904. MODERATE TO ULTRA-DELUXE.

Even in the over-touristed Napa Valley, there's a way to leave the crowds behind—head for the hills. Travel several miles upslope from Calistoga and you'll find **Mountain Home Ranch**. Once there, you may never make it back to the wineries. This is a fully equipped resort with a dining room, swimming pools, picnic areas, tennis court, and fishing lake. It rests on 300 acres threaded with hiking trails. Accommodations range from rustic cabins, which are self-maintained and require bedding and towels, to all-weather cabins to rooms in the main lodge. Choose between the American plan or buffet breakfast. ~ 3400 Mountain Home Ranch Road, Calistoga; 707-942-6616, fax 707-942-9091. DELUXE.

Meadowlark Country House is a beautiful 19th-century home with 20 acres of wooded grounds. Out beyond the swimming pool (clothing optional) you can watch horses being trained for jumping events. Each of the seven rooms features contemporary or English country antique furniture, comforters, and a view of forest or meadow. A generous breakfast is served each morning and you'll find the serene veranda a great place to catch up on your reading. ~ 601-605 Petrified Forest Road, Calistoga; 707-942-5651, fax 707-942-5023. ULTRA-DELUXE.

It may not be for everyone, but **Harbin Hot Springs** is a popular place, as witnessed by the crowds on weekends. Seven natural springs feed the warm, hot, and cold mineral-water pools of this New Age retreat center. You may stay in a dormitory, a guest room, or camp out and relax and soak in the clothing-optional pools, hike on trails through the hills, and enjoy quiet conversation with the other guests. There's a café serving meals or you can bring your own vegetarian food to cook in a communal kitchen. ~ Harbin Springs Road, Middletown; 707-987-2477. BUDGET TO MODERATE.

If a room proves hard to reserve, or you need assistance with other bookings, several agencies offer reservation services. These can prove very convenient during peak tourist periods, or any time that you want to reduce long-distance calls. If interested, contact

Bed & Breakfast Exchange. ~ 1047 Main Street, St. Helena; 707-942-5900, fax 707-963-9595.

DINING

Domaine Chandon does more than bottle sparkling wine. This European concern also features a widely acclaimed restaurant at its winery. A multitiered affair with curved ceiling and colorful banners, it serves fine French cuisine. Lunch includes such delicacies as mesquite-grilled asparagus salad, grilled quail, and tuna peppersteak with a mustard sauce. At dinner, the chef prepares special appetizers and entrées. These might include cream of tomato soup in puff pastry, home-smoked salmon carpaccio with onions and chives, and venison tournedos wrapped in pancetta. Little wonder Domaine Chandon has won national awards. ~ California Drive, Yountville; 707-944-2892. DELUXE.

The only thing generic about **The Diner** is its name. This unassuming Yountville eatery, popular with local residents, prepares a mix of Mexican and American dishes. Dinner ranges from burgers and broiled chicken to burritos and quesadillas. Add specialties like fresh seafood dishes; breakfast and lunch vary from Mexican dishes to more standard egg, sandwich, and salad choices. Such a bargain. Closed Monday. ~ 6476 Washington Street, Yountville; 707-944-2626. BUDGET TO MODERATE.

Set in an old building, **The French Laundry** is a family-owned venture featuring contemporary American cuisine with a classic French influence. The food is excellent, the wine list extensive, and the prix-fixe menu changes nightly. It's very popular; reservations are a must. Closed Monday. ~ 6640 Washington Street, Yountville; 707-944-2380. DELUXE.

Mustards Grill is an ultramodern brass-rail restaurant complete with track lighting and contemporary wallhangings. There's an attractive wooden bar and paneled dining room, but the im-

✔ CHECK THESE OUT—UNIQUE DINING

- *Budget:* Chow down on Italian food at **Bosko's**, an informal Calistoga eatery with a sawdust floor and exposed-rafter ceiling. *page 207*
- *Moderate:* Feast on hearty fare at **Southside Saloon and Dining Hall**, where you can choose from a myriad of regional wines. *page 222*
- *Deluxe:* Applaud the superb French cuisine as you sit beneath colorful banners at the multitiered **Domaine Chandon**. *page 205*
- *Deluxe to ultra-deluxe:* Dine on locally grown foods prepared with a flair at **John Ash & Co.**, a fashionable Santa Rosa eatery. *page 221*

Budget: under $8 Moderate: $8–$16 Deluxe: $16–$24 Ultra-deluxe: over $24

portant features are the wood-burning grill and oven. Here the chefs prepare rabbit, smoked pork chops, baby back ribs, and skirt steak. This eatery specializes in fresh grilled fish like sea bass, mako shark, spearfish, and salmon. ~ 7399 St. Helena Highway, Yountville; 707-944-2424. MODERATE TO DELUXE.

Jeremiah Tower, one of the superstar chefs in the Northern California culinary firmament, is the guiding force behind **Stars Oakville Café**, a former filling station magically transformed into a stylish dining room with cathedral ceiling and glassed-in kitchen. The frequently changing menu concentrates on hearty entrées of grilled meat and fish such as rib eye steak accompanied by roasted beets and rock cod dressed with a tangy lemon and caper sauce. Appetizers include house-cured gravlax served with a crunchy potato pancake and warm bitter greens served with duck confit. Closed Tuesday and Wednesday. ~ 7848 St. Helena Highway, Oakville; 707-944-8905. DELUXE.

First and last word in Napa Valley elegance is **Auberge du Soleil**, a hillside dining room overlooking the vineyards. Modern in design, this gourmet hideaway is a curving stucco structure with a wood-shingle roof. The circular lounge is capped by a skylight-cum-cupola and the dining area is an exposed-beam affair with caneback chairs and open fireplace. Even architecture such as this pales in comparison with the menu, which changes seasonally. Lunch might begin with an appetizer of pumpkin ravioli, then move on to caramelized carrot broth or grilled Pacific spearfish. Dinner entrées include pistachio-crusted salmon, garlic-rosemary rack of lamb, and thyme-roasted pheasant. Extensive wine list. ~ 180 Rutherford Hill Road, Rutherford; 707-963-1211. ULTRA-DELUXE.

It's obvious from the schedule that **Spring Street** is a restaurant for local folks rather than out-of-towners: It's open for lunch and dinner daily, brunch on Saturday and Sunday. The sandwiches include "crunchy tuna" (with chutney and almonds) and "Spanish Delight" (broiled cheese with avocado and green chiles). There are also specials like chile relleno casserole and corn chowder, plus an array of salads and wines. ~ 1245 Spring Street, St. Helena; 707-963-5578. MODERATE TO DELUXE.

Tra Vigne can claim the most dramatic interior in the Wine Country. Soaring ceilings, unusual lighting, and festive displays of peppers and garlic make the setting as exciting as the menu. The theme here is Tuscan: chewy breads, bold pizzas, hearty salads, lamb, chicken, and grilled seafood dishes, and a first-rate wine list. ~ 1050 Charter Oak Avenue, St. Helena; 707-963-4444. DELUXE.

HIDDEN ►

Showley's is in downtown St. Helena but a little tough to find, tucked in a darkened corridor near the railroad tracks. Inside the eatery is not the least bit dark, but bright and good-looking, its white walls embellished with chic artwork and flickering sconces, its dining rooms intimate and peopled by a handsome, hip clientele. Outside, a brick courtyard is ruled by a fig tree, and you should eat here in the summer. Lunch and dinner feature such fresh and tasty fare as cold smoked ahi, grilled sea bass over julienne vegetables with a shrimp bechamel, and braised lamb shanks with garlic mashed potatoes and rosemary glaze. ~ 1327 Railroad Avenue, one block east of Main Street, St. Helena; 707-963-1200. MODERATE TO DELUXE.

For southern French and northern Italian–style cooking with a Pacific Rim influence, head to **Restaurant Terra**. Appetizers include fried rock shrimp, crab cabbage egg rolls, and *tataki* of tuna. Salmon with a Thai red curry sauce, broiled sea bass, braised oxtail with wild mushrooms, and osso bucco with risotto milanese are among the most popular entrées. By way of ambience there are stone walls, terra cotta features, and a wooden trim that lends an oriental overtone to this comfortable, Tuscan farmhouse–style dining room. Closed Tuesday. ~ 1345 Railroad Avenue, St. Helena; 707-963-8931. DELUXE.

The setting is informal and the menu Italian: informal as in sawdust floor and exposed-rafter ceiling; Italian as in pasta and pizza. At **Bosko's**, they don't even bother to change the menu from lunch to dinner. Day or night, you'll find fresh pasta dishes like fettuccine marinara, spinach *fusilli* with Italian sausage, and spaghetti with meatballs. Or you can have a meatball, sausage, or Italian ham sandwich. The wine list is actually longer than the menu, but the meals they offer are good and filling. ~ 1364 Lincoln Avenue, Calistoga; 707-942-9088. BUDGET.

SHOPPING

Almost by definition, shopping malls are unattractive. **Vintage 1870** is a rare exception to a modern rule. Housed in the historic Groezinger Winery, a massive brick building smothered in ivy, it contains several dozen fashionable shops. Wooden corridors, designed with an eye to antiquity, lead along two shopping levels. There are clothing stores galore, and several restaurants, as well as specialty shops offering arts and crafts products. ~ 6525 Washington Street, Yountville; 707-944-2451.

Across the street, the **Groezinger Wine Company** features a wine bar. ~ 6528 Washington Street; 707-944-2331.

Oakville Grocery is a prime place to stock up for a picnic. This falsefront country store sells wines and cheeses, fresh fruits, and baked goods, as well as a host of gourmet items. ~ 7856 St. Helena Highway, Oakville; 707-944-8802.

For people living in northern Napa Valley, going on a shopping spree means heading for either St. Helena or Calistoga. Both towns combine local businesses with general merchandise stores. Main Street, St. Helena, is a falsefront boulevard lined with a hardware store, stationery shop, newspaper office, and grocery. Of interest to visitors are the boutiques, bookstore, jewelers, and wine shop.

The **Gallery on Main Street** features works by Napa Valley artists as well as prints, posters, and ceramics. ~ 1359 Main Street, St. Helena; 707-963-3350.

The **Napa Valley Olive Oil Manufacturing Co.** is more than a gourmet shopping spot: It's a sightseeing adventure as well. Housed in a former oil manufacturing plant, it contains the original press and crusher. Railroad tracks run along the cement floor, and posters of old Italia cover the walls. Today this tiny factory sells delicious cheeses and salami, as well as pasta and condiments. ~ 835 Charter Oak Avenue, St. Helena; 707-963-4173.

During the summer months, several Napa Valley wineries sponsor concerts and other special events.

Outside town, **Hurd Beeswax Candles** elevates candle-making to the level of art. The waxworks resemble statues rather than tapers; fashioned on the premises, they are formed into a myriad intricate shapes. In addition to a showroom, the adjacent candle factory provides an opportunity to watch wax being dipped, cut, and rolled. ~ 3020 North St. Helena Highway, St. Helena; 707-963-7211.

Up the road at **Village Outlets of St. Helena** you'll find a shopping mall with clothing stores and an assortment of other shops. ~ 3111 North St. Helena Highway, St. Helena.

Up in Calistoga, shops of general interest are mixed with those catering to local concerns. Along Lincoln Avenue, near the barber shop and town cobbler, are antique stores, clothing shops, and a bookstore. The historic **Calistoga Depot**, located at 1458 Lincoln Avenue, has been converted to a mall. Within this former railway station are assorted stores, including the **Calistoga Wine Stop**, housed in an antique railroad car. ~ 707-942-5556.

NIGHTLIFE

The Napa Valley has yet to learn the fine art of evening entertainment. Perhaps by nightfall visitors are already tipsy from tasting wine all day. In any case, there's not a lot to do; what scene there is centers around the wineries and the hotel and restaurant bars.

An entertainment calendar ranging from comedy shows to rock bands makes **Marlowe's** one of the region's most popular nightspots. Cover. ~ 1637 West Imola Avenue, Napa; 707-224-2700.

Joe Namath, Joey Heatherton, Joe DiMaggio, and Joseph Stalin are just a few of the celebrities represented on the walls of **Joe's Bar**. Located at the Inn at Napa Valley, it also features pool tables and a CD jukebox. ~ 1075 California Boulevard, Napa; 707-253-9540.

The **Mount View Hotel** has an old-time saloon. With a purple ceiling, green beams, wooden booths, and hardwood floors, this bar is certainly original. ~ 1457 Lincoln Avenue, Calistoga; 707-942-6877.

PARKS

BOTHE-NAPA VALLEY STATE PARK Rising from the valley floor to about 2000 feet elevation, this outstanding park is fully developed along one side, wild and rugged on the other. For those seeking to escape the Wine Country crowds, there are ten miles of hiking trails leading along steep hillsides through redwood groves. More than 100 bird species inhabit the area, including hawks, quail, and six types of woodpecker. There are also coyotes, bobcats, deer, and fox here. The park's developed area features spacious picnic groves, campgrounds, a swimming pool, restrooms, and showers; restaurants and groceries are located five miles away in St. Helena and four miles away in Calistoga. Day-use fee, $5. ~ On Route 29 about five miles north of St. Helena; 707-942-4575.

▲ There are 40 tent/RV sites and nine walk-in sites; $16 per night per campsite. Reservations recommended.

CALISTOGA RANCH CAMPGROUND This privately owned facility spreads across 167 acres in Napa Valley's eastern hills. Home to recreational vehicles as well as tent campers, it features hiking trails, picnic areas, a fishing lake, an olympic-sized swimming pool, restrooms, laundry, and a snack bar; restaurants and groceries are four and one-half miles away in Calistoga. ~ Located at 580 Lommel Road, Calistoga, the campground lies off Silverado Trail about four and one-half miles from town; 707-942-6565, 800-847-6272.

▲ Permitted in 144 designated tent/RV sites; $19 for two people per night for tent sites; $25 for full RV hookups.

Sonoma Valley

Touring the wineries of Sonoma provides a perfect excuse not only for tasting California's fine varietals, but also for exploring the state's beautiful interior. Cutting a long, luxurious swath between the ocean and the distant Sierra, this piedmont country divides its terrain between vineyards, ranches, and dense forest.

SIGHTS

The logical place to begin a tour of the valley is in Sonoma, a Spanish-style town of 8200 people. And the spot to begin this tour-within-a-tour is the **Plaza**, bounded by 1st Street East, 1st Street West, Spain, and Napa streets. The center of Sonoma for 150 years, this shady park is an excellent picnic place. The largest plaza in the state, it contains a playground, open-air theater, duck pond, and rose garden. At the **Sonoma Valley Chamber of Commerce** there are maps and brochures of the area. ~ 645 Broadway; 707-996-1033. For information on the outlying areas as well, contact the **Sonoma County Convention & Visitors Bureau.** ~ 5000 Roberts Lake Road, Suite A, Rohnert Park; 707-586-8100. Also located at the Sonoma Country Convention & Visitors Bureau is the **California Welcome Center**, which provides an overview not only of the region's wineries and attractions but also of the winemaking process itself. There is an interactive video program, a demonstration vineyard and winery, a tasting room and over 200 types of local wine for sale. ~ 707-586-3795.

Spanish adobes, stone buildings, and falsefront stores surround the historic square. Mission San Francisco Solano, or **Sonoma Mission**, stands at one corner. Founded in 1823, this was the last and most northerly of the 21 California missions. With its stark white facade, the low-slung adobe houses a small museum. There are dozens of paintings portraying other California missions; the chapel has also been painted brilliant colors and adorned with carved wood statues. ~ 1st Street East and East Spain Street, Sonoma.

The **Sonoma Barracks**, across the street, were built with Indian labor during the 1830s to house the troops of Mexico's General Mariano Guadalupe Vallejo. A two-story adobe with sweeping balconies, it also houses a museum devoted to early California history. ~ 1st Street East and East Spain Street, Sonoma.

Next door, the **Toscano Hotel** is furnished in 19th-century fashion with wood-burning stoves, brocade armchairs, and two gambling tables with poker games in progress. Dating to 1852, this wood-frame structure was built as a general store but later was used to house Italian workers. ~ 20 East Spain Street, Sonoma.

The only remains of General Vallejo's 1840 house, **La Casa Grande** (East Spain Street between 1st Street East and 1st Street West), is the servant's house with its sagging adobe facade. Together with the mission and other antique buildings encircling the plaza, it is part of **Sonoma State Historic Park**; all these noteworthy places can be toured for a single admission price. ~ Sonoma; 707-938-1519.

Just north of the plaza stands the **Depot Park Museum**, where the displays commemorate the Bear Flag uprising when Americans revolted against General Vallejo in 1846. Closed Monday and Tuesday. ~ 270 1st Street West, Sonoma; 707-938-1762.

About one-half mile from the town square, you'll find another antique structure. **Lachryma Montis** was the home General Vallejo built in 1852, after the United States had assumed control of California. Vallejo successfully made the change to American rule, becoming a vintner and writing a five-volume history of early California. Something was lost in the transition, however, and this yellow Victorian house with pretty green shutters fails to evoke images of a Mexican general.

Nevertheless, it's well worth touring. Every room is appointed in 19th-century style, as though Vallejo were expected to arrive any moment. The old pendulum clock still swings and the dinner table is set. Out back, the cookhouse contains personal effects of the Chinese cook and ducks flap around the pond. Part of Sonoma

State Historic Park, it also features a cactus garden, mini-museum, and picnic area. ~ At the end of 3rd Street West; 707-938-1519.

While Vallejo was settling into his American-style home, Count Agoston Haraszthy, a Hungarian aristocrat, moved to Sonoma and founded **Buena Vista Winery** in 1857. Popularly known as the "father of the California wine industry," he eventually imported 100,000 vines from Europe. Today the actual winemaking occurs at the vineyard estate in the Carneros area, but you can taste sample vintages in the old stone winery and take a self-guided tour around the grounds. Now a historical monument, the winery also has picnic tables for the crowds that visit. ~ 18000 Old Winery Road, Sonoma; 707-938-1266.

One of Spain's premier winemaking families began winning awards with their very first vintages from **Gloria Ferrer Champagne Caves**. The Ferrers carved caves (typical in their native country) out of the hillside for storing premium sparkling wines. The wines are available for purchase or for tasting (at a nominal fee) either indoors or on a wide patio with lovely views of the surrounding countryside. ~ 23555 Carneros Highway, Sonoma; 707-996-7256.

Sam Sebastiani, of the famous Sonoma family of vintners, opened his own winery, **Viansa Winery**, in the heart of the prolific Carneros region. A multilevel stucco compound mounted on a hill at the south end of the Sonoma Valley, this Tuscan-style winery offers tours and tastings of premium wines. ~ 25200 Arnold Drive, Sonoma; 707-935-4700.

If the Napa Valley is Stevenson country, Sonoma Valley belongs to Jack London. A world adventurer and self-described "sailor on horseback," London was not the type to settle down. Illegitimate son of an astrologer, he was in turn an oyster pirate, socialist, gold prospector, and internationally renowned author. But settle he did, a few miles northwest of Sonoma in the town of Glen Ellen.

Calling this area "the valley of the moon," London and his wife Charmian acquired a 1400-acre ranch and began construction of the Wolf House, an extraordinary mansion with 26 rooms and nine fireplaces. In 1913, when nearly completed, London's dream house mysteriously burned. Three years later, after produc-

TIME OUT FOR TRAINS

Kids who tire of all the dusty history can be bribed with a visit to **Train Town**. Miniature steam engines chug around a ten-acre park, passing over trestles, through three tunnels, and arriving at a scale-model Western town. Also visit the petting zoo, antique carousel, and cabooses. Admission. ~ 20264 Broadway, Sonoma; 707-938-3912.

ing 51 books and becoming America's first millionaire author, he committed suicide at age 40.

Today, at **Jack London State Historic Park**, you can wander the old estate. At the east end of the park, the House of Happy Walls, occupied by Charmian after her husband's death, is a museum containing first editions and original manuscripts. London's study is adorned with the original artwork for his stories, and many keepsakes from his world adventures are here. At the west end of the park, the cottage where London lived and wrote from 1911 until his death in 1916 still stands. Admission. ~ 2400 London Ranch Road, Glen Ellen; 707-938-5216.

In Jack London State Historic Park, a half-mile path leads past the author's grave, simply marked by a stone boulder, to the tragic ruins of the Wolf House, a monument to a lost dream.

Route 12, the Sonoma Highway, travels north through Sonoma Valley, past miles of vineyard and forest. Numerous small wineries dot this rustic area, including **Kenwood Vineyards**. Backed up against the mountains in a group of redwood buildings, the winery was founded in 1906. The current owners, who took over in 1970, instituted the French style of fermenting small batches of wine individually. You can taste the results of their experiment any day, but tours of the grounds are by appointment. ~ 9592 Sonoma Highway, Kenwood; 707-833-5891.

The strikingly beautiful **Château St. Jean Winery** sits beside a colonnaded mansion built during the 1920s. The winery has added several similar buildings, including one with an observation tower from which to view the surrounding countryside. Wine, not extraordinary vistas, is the business here, and the winery has won several awards for its chardonnays and Johannesberg rieslings. You can taste these and other varietals while taking a self-guided tour of the grounds. ~ 8555 Sonoma Highway, Kenwood; 707-833-4134.

LODGING

The **Sonoma Mission Inn and Spa** lives up to its name, in all three senses of the word. The pale pink stucco facade on this gracious Mission Revival–style hotel harks back to the days when American Indians enjoyed the natural mineral waters of this area. The 168 accommodations are appointed in earthy tones, with wooden shutters and ceiling fans adding a touch of the plantation. A full-service spa, tennis courts, and two swimming pools add up to one of the best retreats in the Wine Country. ~ 18140 Sonoma Highway 12, Boyes Hot Springs; 707-938-9000, 800-862-4945, fax 707-935-1205. ULTRA-DELUXE.

The **Swiss Hotel** is an adobe building dating from 1840. This five-room hostelry features rooms with private baths and a refrigerator. One has a four-poster bed and pine furniture, others have a variety of antique and modern pieces. The hotel rests on the town's central plaza and contains a bar and restaurant downstairs. ~ 18 West Spain Street, Sonoma; 707-938-2884, fax 707-938-3298. DELUXE TO ULTRA-DELUXE.

Sonoma's plaza features another historic hostelry, the **Sonoma Hotel**, which dates to around 1872, is a 17-room facility decorated entirely with antiques. The lobby has a stone fireplace and the adjoining lounge features a hand-carved bar. The rooms (some share a bath) offer such flourishes as marbletop dressers, beveled mirrors, brass beds, and mahogany chests. Combining history with comfort, this vintage hotel is worth a visit. ~ 110 West Spain Street, Sonoma; 707-996-2996. DELUXE TO ULTRA-DELUXE.

The **El Dorado Hotel**, also located on the square, is a small gem. Originally an adobe built in 1843, this refurbished stucco establishment offers 26 small- to moderate-size rooms. Appointed with four poster beds, peach down comforters, Mexican tile floors, and California/Spanish style furniture, each has a private balcony. ~ 405 1st Street West, Sonoma; 707-996-3030, 800-289-3031, fax 707-996-3148. ULTRA-DELUXE.

DINING

The Grille, a handsome Southwestern-inspired dining room, is the best restaurant in the county. Startlingly innovative but not pretentious, the menu features a dozen entrées such as grilled fish and various chicken and lamb dishes, virtually all from local sources. The Grille also offers items for the health conscious—low in calories, cholesterol, and sodium. ~ Sonoma Mission Inn and Spa, 18140 Sonoma Highway 12, Boyes Hot Springs; 707-938-9000. DELUXE.

Sonoma Cheese Factory is *the* spot to stop on the way to the picnic grounds. In addition to a grand assortment of cheeses, it sells wines, sandwiches, and gourmet specialty foods. There's also a small, outdoor patio for diners. In back, where store gives way to factory, you can watch Jack cheese being made. ~ 2 West Spain Street, Sonoma; 707-996-1931. BUDGET.

Savor the flavors of Tuscany at **Lo Spuntino**, a classy Italian deli and marketplace accented with a black-and-white tile floor and marble countertops. A selection of cold pasta salads, rotisserie meats (marinated rabbit, leg of lamb), and Italian specialties (polenta lasagna, grilled torta) can be ordered to go or enjoyed on one of the café tables looking out at the Sonoma Mission. Oenophiles can visit the adjoining wine bar featuring vintages from Viansa Winery. ~ 400 1st Street East, Sonoma; 707-935-5656. BUDGET.

Marioni's Restaurant, located right on the plaza, is an attractive split-level dining room with adjoining bar. Decorated with American Indian rugs and paneled in dark wood, it features a steak and seafood menu. Dinner includes steak and lobster, seafood specials, prime rib, and vegetable casserole. At lunch (not served in the winter) there are sandwiches, soups and salads, plus several egg dishes. Closed Monday. ~ 8 West Spain Street, Sonoma; 707-996-6866. MODERATE TO DELUXE.

Housed in a high-ceilinged Victorian, the decor of **Pasta Nostra** can be described as "pastel Gothic." Fresh pasta is served with either fish, vegetables, poultry, or meat. More than 40 dishes appear on the menu, including linguine Rafael, prepared with eggplant, artichokes, and red peppers; angelhair Thai, a combination of chicken, celery, ginger, peanuts, and scallions; and spinach fettuccine with smoked salmon. No lunch on Monday and Tuesday. ~ 139 East Napa Street, Sonoma; 707-938-4166. MODERATE.

Set in a Victorian building and adorned with stained glass and a garden, **Magliulo's** serves Italian and American dishes. The dining room offers homemade minestrone soup, gnocchi, chicken piccata, and broiled New York steak. ~ 691 Broadway, Sonoma; 707-996-1031. MODERATE.

If you prefer Mexican cuisine, try **La Casa**. Located just off the plaza, this colorful restaurant offers a full menu from south of the border. There are margaritas and other tequila drinks at the bar, plus a bill of fare ranging from snapper with salsa to chile verde to chimichangas. ~ 121 East Spain Street, Sonoma; 707-996-3406. MODERATE.

Jack London Grill sits just down the road from Jack London's estate. The dining room is a plate-glass facility overlooking forest and stream. In addition to views, there are ample lunch and dinner menus at reasonable prices. Entrées include crispy fish, Moroccan-style leg of lamb, and roast duck. Closed Sunday. ~ 13740 Arnold Drive, Glen Ellen; 707-996-4401. MODERATE.

Family owned and operated, **Caffe Citti** is an Italian trattoria set amongst the vineyards of Kenwood and extremely popular with Sonoma Valley locals, who love its casualness and friendly atmosphere. Flowers and candles on the tables add a bit of romance. The Italian chef serves up a variety of pastas; rotisserie chicken stuffed with fresh herbs, garlic, and rosemary; and weekend specials. He also makes his own mozzarella cheese and biscotti. ~ 9049 Sonoma Highway, Kenwood; 707-833-2690. MODERATE.

SHOPPING

The old Spanish town of Sonoma contains a central plaza around which you'll find its best shops. Stroll the square (bounded by 1st Street East, 1st Street West, Spain, and Napa streets) and encounter gourmet stores, boutiques, a designer lingerie company, antique stores, poster galleries, and a brass shop. Many of these establishments are housed in historic Spanish adobes.

One place to consider is the **Arts Guild of Sonoma**, containing works by local artisans. Here are paintings, ceramics, jewelry, and handwoven textiles. ~ 140 East Napa Street, Sonoma; 707-996-3115.

California Winetasting

The Greeks had it all wrong. They fervently believed that the gods drank nectar. Anyone who has explored the vineyards of California knows that wine, not sweet ambrosia, is the drink of the gods. It's also obvious that deciding on the finest wine is as simple as determining the true religion. This is not to say that a tour of the Wine Country is a pilgrimage, though it can have a lifetime effect on the drinking habits of mere mortals.

In order to find that ultimate wine, keep in mind a few principles. The best season to visit the vineyards is during the harvest in late September and early October. The scent of freshly fermenting wine fills the air and the vineyards are colored brilliant red and gold. Winter is the rainy season and a fallow period. It's also less crowded than the rest of the year and allows opportunities for more relaxed and personalized tours, particularly at small wineries. The growing season begins in March when buds appear on previously bare, gnarled vines. By early summer, the buds are miniature grape clusters which ripen during the torrid months of midsummer.

Once the grapes are picked in autumn, the activity shifts from the vineyard to the winery. The berries are crushed; white wines are then filtered or clarified and fermented in temperature-controlled tanks. Red wines are fermented, together with their skins and seeds, at higher temperatures (70 to 90°). Later the wines are racked, or stored, in wooden barrels to add flavor, and then bottled. Requiring two or three years to reach their potential, reds mature more slowly than whites.

There are two basic types of California wine: *varietals*, made primarily from a particular type of grape such as cabernet sauvignon or zinfandel, and lower-quality *generics*, wines generally blended from several different grapes and often named for a European wine region like Burgundy.

The true test, of course, is in the tasting. Unfortunately, winetasting also becomes a test of the taster's wine knowledge. Folks unversed in the liturgy and lexicon of wine sampling can feel mighty uncomfortable. Adding to their consternation are the region's self-styled wine connoisseurs.

Not to worry. It really only requires a sensitive nose, tongue, and eye to master the art of tasting. Just remember a few simple criteria. The look or appearance is important: wine should be clear and brilliant, not cloudy, in the glass. Consider the smell or *nose* of the vintage: this includes *aroma*, or scent of the grapes themselves, and *bouquet*, the smell from fermentation and aging. Of final importance is the taste. Let the wine wash around your mouth a moment and you'll be able to tell if it's sweet or dry, light-bodied (watery) or full-bodied (like milk), rough or mellow.

A nearby mall, **El Paseo de Sonoma**, contains more off-street shops. ~ 414 1st Street East, Sonoma.

The Sign of the Bear, a gourmet cook's general store, pays homage to the California lifestyle. The shop sells everything from nutmeg to napkin rings, gadgets to glassware, cookware to make just about anything and cookbooks to teach you how to do it. ~ 435 1st Street West, Sonoma; 707-996-3722.

Robin's Nest specializes in discount kitchen accessories, tableware, and gifts such as vases and tile pictures. ~ 116 East Napa Street, Sonoma; 707-996-4169.

Slightly west of the square, **Sonoma Country Store** is out-and-out adorable, with a comely collection of glassware, ceramics, decorative items, and paper goods suited to the small-town ambience of the valley. ~ 165 West Napa Street, Sonoma; 707-996-0900.

On the way to Jack London State Historic Park, be sure to stop in at the **Jack London Bookstore**. An important resource center for London scholars and fans, it contains numerous first editions of the author's works. ~ 14300 Arnold Drive, Glen Ellen; 707-996-2888.

NIGHTLIFE

As in the Napa area, Sonoma Valley nightlife revolves around summer events at the wineries. Check local calendars for concerts, theatrical performances, and other special programs. If that seems uninteresting, or it's not summertime, you'll have to rely on hotel and restaurant bars for entertainment. There's a particularly good one at the **Sonoma Hotel Restaurant** on the town plaza. The building is over a century old, and the lounge is filled with antique furnishings and fixtures. ~ 110 West Spain Street, Sonoma; 707-996-2996.

On Thursday and Saturday nights, **Marioni's Restaurant** fills up with a 20-to-30 crowd that comes to enjoy the live blues or rock music. ~ 8 West Spain Street, Sonoma; 707-996-6866.

With old photos adorning its walls, the bar of the historic **Swiss Hotel** is a favorite meetingplace of locals and travelers alike. ~ 18 West Spain Street, Sonoma; 707-938-2884.

London Lodge, out in Jack London country, has a pretty, brick-faced barroom which draws a mixture of locals and visitors. Fashionably decorated with Tiffany-style lamps and old movie posters, it's a good drinking place. ~ 13740 Arnold Drive, Glen Ellen; 707-996-3100.

PARKS

SUGARLOAF RIDGE STATE PARK Within this 2800-acre facility lie two different ecological systems, as well as 25 miles of hiking trails along which to explore them. There are chaparral-coated ridges with views of San Francisco and the Sierra Nevada, plus forests of maple, laurel, madrone, and alder. Sonoma Creek tumbles through the park. Spring brings a profusion of wildflowers, and autumn is another popular season in the park. Facilities include picnic areas and restrooms; restaurants and groceries are a few miles away in the town of Kenwood. Day-use fee, $5. ~ Located off Route 12 between Sonoma and Santa Rosa, the park is at 2605 Adobe Canyon Road in Kenwood; 707-833-5712.

▲ Permitted in 47 sites; $14 per car per night.

Northern Wine Country

Sonoma's vine-rich country continues north of Santa Rosa along Route 101 to Cloverdale, but the secret to touring this region resides along country lanes paralleling the highway. At the center of this area is Healdsburg, a country town centered on a plaza and dating back to 1852.

SIGHTS

Santa Rosa, the largest city in Sonoma County, is perhaps best known as the home of Luther Burbank, the great horticulturist who worked miracles on plantlife, creating the Santa Rosa plum, Shasta daisy and hundreds of other hybrids. His legacy remains in full bloom at the **Luther Burbank Home and Gardens** where visitors can stroll through gardens filled with the descendants of his plant "inventions" and tour the Victorian house where he lived for 50 years. The house is open from April through October. Admission to tour the house. ~ Santa Rosa and Sonoma avenues, Santa Rosa; 707-524-5445.

Housed in a former 1909 post office, the **Sonoma County Museum** provides a historical and cultural perspective on the region with changing exhibits, some of them especially designed for kids. The museum includes the Hart Collection of early California art, the Sonoma County history exhibit, and the Dixon Collection of metal jewelry and sculpture. Closed Monday and Tuesday. Admission. ~ 425 7th Street, Santa Rosa; 707-579-1500.

Up in the mountains outside Santa Rosa, hidden along country lanes, lies **Fisher Vineyards**. Tucked into a fold in the hills and surrounded by redwood forest, this picturesque winery is a family-style operation. The main building, a lofty board-and-batten structure, was built with wood cut and milled on the site. It follows a contemporary California design and overlooks the surrounding vineyards. Planted primarily with cabernet sauvignon, chardonnay, and merlot vines, the winery produces a small but delicious quantity of wine each season. Visiting by appointment only. ~ 6200 St. Helena Road, Santa Rosa; 707-539-7511. ◄ HIDDEN

Just north of Santa Rosa, around the tiny towns of Forestville and Windsor, are numerous family wineries. Without doubt, one of the prettiest vineyard settings in all California belongs to **Iron Horse Vineyards**. The driveway snaking into this hidden spot is ◄ HIDDEN bordered with flowers and palm trees. Hills roll away in every direction, revealing a line of distant mountains. The winery buildings, painted barn-red, follow the classic architecture of American farms. Laid out around them in graceful checkerboard patterns are fields of pinot noir and chardonnay grapes. At harvest time these will be handpicked and then barrel-aged, for the emphasis at this elegant little winery is on personal attention. Open for tastings on Saturday from 10 a.m. to 4 p.m. Appointments are necessary on other days. ~ 9786 Ross Station Road, Sebastopol; 707-887-1507.

In addition to wineries, there are countless orchards around Sebastopol. Known as the Gold Ridge region, it is California's premier apple-producing area. Many farms allow visitors to wander

HIDDEN ►

the orchards and **pick produce**. For details, contact the **Sebastopol Chamber of Commerce** and ask for a Sonoma county farm trails map. It will lead you to farms producing apples, pears, berries, cherries, peaches, and vegetables. ~ 265 South Main Street, Sebastopol; 707-823-3032.

At the **Healdsburg Chamber of Commerce** you can pick up maps, brochures, and other information on the region. ~ 217 Healdsburg Avenue, Healdsburg; 707-433-6935.

Born of an international marriage between Sonoma Vineyards and France's Piper-Heidsieck, **Piper Sonoma** produces California sparkling wines by the classic *méthode champenoise*. On the self-guided tour you can walk around the production facility and go on to a tasting at the winery's tasting room. The entire complex is ultramodern, particularly the central building with its terraced facade. If you long for a taste of the bubbly in elegant surroundings, there's no finer place. ~ 11447 Old Redwood Highway, Healdsburg; 707-433-8843.

Dry Creek Valley, a luxurious landscape of vineyards and forest, stretches to the west of Healdsburg. Two small wineries warrant special attention. **Dry Creek Vineyard** sits in an ivy-covered building surrounded by shade trees. There's tasting every day and the winery provides picnic tables for guests. Among the excellent wines produced are chenin blancs, fumés, cabernets, chardonnays, merlots, and zinfandels. ~ 3770 Lambert Bridge Road, Healdsburg; 707-433-1000.

Along the far rim of Dry Creek Valley rises **A. Rafanelli Winery**, a classic family-style enterprise. David A. Rafanelli, whose roots go far back in the wine industry, owns the place and does much of the work himself along with his wife Patty. Planting primarily zinfandel and cabernet grapes, they produce excellent wines in limited quantities. The winery itself consists of an old barn behind the family home. Backdropped by forested hills, it overlooks the valley and surrounding countryside. Tours and tasting are by appointment. ~ 4685 West Dry Creek Road, Healdsburg; 707-433-1385.

East of Healdsburg lies the Alexander Valley, a region whose wines are gaining an increasingly fine reputation. Because of its warm climate, the valley is sometimes compared with the Bordeaux area of France. Its vintages, however, have a quality all their own.

Jordan Vineyard & Winery is a lavish facility built along the lines of a Bordeaux château, and the winery is housed in a grand building that overlooks the Alexander Valley. Electronic gates protect the grounds, and no signs mark the entranceway. So a tour of the estate is a rare experience, providing a glimpse into a winery whose elegance matches its excellence. Tours are by appointment. ~ 1474 Alexander Valley Road, Healdsburg; 707-431-5250.

A long dirt road leads to an unpainted barn at **Johnson's Alexander Valley Winery**. The slapdash ambience, however, ends at the front door. Within this nondescript tasting room sits a pipe organ used for the winery's occasional concerts. There is also a wealth of modern equipment around the place, which produces fine pinot

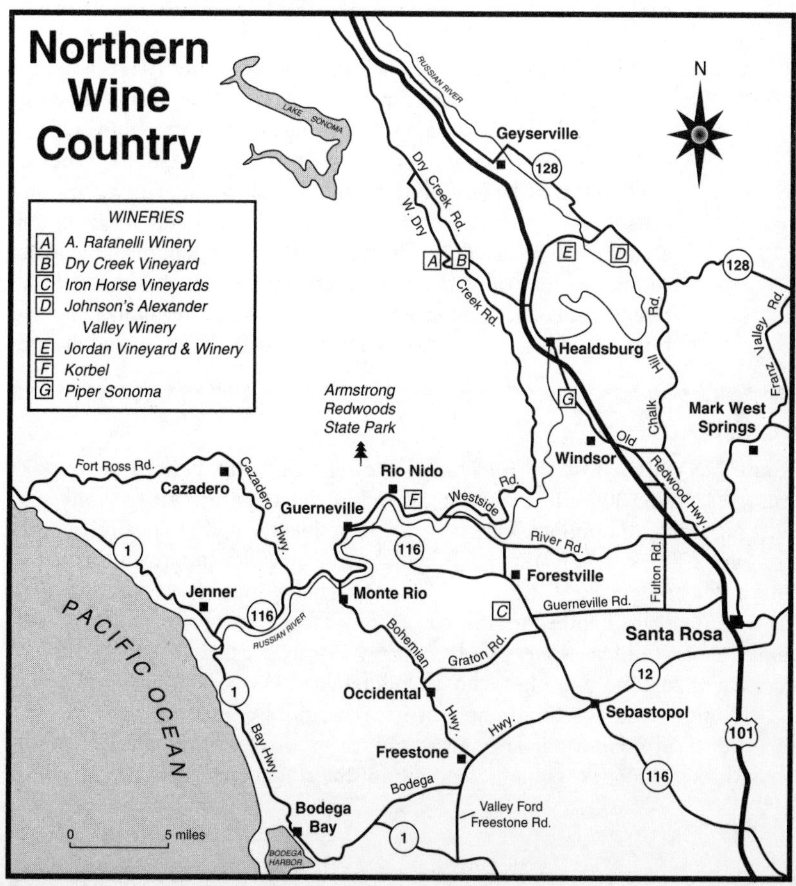

noirs and cabernets. Founded by three brothers, the little winery offers tasting anytime and tours by appointment. ~ 8333 Route 128, Healdsburg; 707-433-2319.

Beyond Cloverdale, Route 101 streams north past Ukiah and several more wineries. A more interesting course lies along Route 128, which leads northwest from Cloverdale through piedmont country. En route, the two-lane road meanders like an old river, bending back upon itself to reveal sloping meadows and tree-tufted glades. It's a beautiful country drive through rolling ranch land. Sheep graze the hills and an occasional farmhouse stands along the roadside, its windows blinking sunlight at solitary cars.

LODGING

Now that the 50 acres of surrounding vineyards have matured, the **Vintners Inn** blends in with the landscape. Huge accommodations are decorated in European country style, with antiques and home-made quilts. Little piazzas and lots of open landscaping between two-story townhouses create a luxurious ambience. ~ 4350 Barnes Road, Santa Rosa; 707-575-7350, 800-421-2584, fax 707-575-1426. ULTRA-DELUXE.

Healdsburg, located farther north along Route 101, is a perfect jumping-off point for visiting the wineries in the area. Numerous country inns dot the area, including the **Haydon Street Inn**, a lovely eight-bedroom bed and breakfast set in a vintage 1912 house. Each room is beautifully appointed with antique furniture and artistic wallhangings. Both the private rooms and the common areas are quite spacious. The tree-shaded lawn, comfortable living room, and luxurious front porch are a perfect expression of Main Street, America. Serving a full breakfast and afternoon wine and hors d'oeuvres, the inn has rooms in the main building and the sep-

"BOONTLING"

As Route 128 rolls down into Anderson Valley, it passes **Boonville**, a farming community of 1000 folks. Back in the 1880s, this town invented a kind of local pig Latin, "boontling," known only to residents. With a vocabulary of over 1000 words, it neatly reflected Anderson Valley life. A photo became a "Charlie Walker" after the Mendocino fellow who took portraits. Because of his handlebar whiskers, "Tom Bacon" lent his name to the moustache. Rail fences were "relfs," heavy storms became "trash-movers," and pastors (those heavenly skypilots) were "skipes." Vestiges of the old lingo remain—restaurants, for instance, still boast of their "bahl gorms," or good food. They also produce good wine in these parts, and several award-winning wineries dot the Anderson Valley.

arate carriage house, all with private baths. ~ 321 Haydon Street, Healdsburg; 707-433-5228. DELUXE TO ULTRA-DELUXE.

Built around the turn of the century as a private summer retreat, the **Madrona Manor Country Inn** is a charming example of Gothic Victorian architecture, complete with a balconied porch, turrets, and gables. The best rooms are in the main house; they are spacious (two upstairs sport private verandas) and furnished in serious antiques, including chaises lounges and armoires. There are an additional 21 accommodations in several outbuildings on an eight-acre site, including a carriage house. Guests enjoy the pool and a breakfast buffet. ~ 1001 Westside Road, Healdsburg; 707-433-4231, 800-258-4003, fax 707-433-0703. ULTRA-DELUXE.

◄ HIDDEN

If you're yearning to retreat back into the '60s, check out **Isis Oasis** a ten-acre hideaway that combines bed-and-breakfast facilities with massage, tarot readings, and past-life experiences. Set in the tiny town of Geyserville, this New Age camp offers an array of accommodations. You can check into a yurt, "tower house lodge," or a three-room honeymoon cottage; wander the Egyptian-style grounds, which include a pyramid and obelisk; and luxuriate in the hot tub, sauna, and swimming pool. There is also a zoo with exotic animals and birds, and an Egyptian meditation temple. ~ 20889 Geyserville Avenue, Geyserville; 707-857-3524, 800-679-7387. MODERATE TO ULTRA-DELUXE.

Up in the Anderson Valley, Mendocino's winegrowing region, there's a two-story bed and breakfast called the **Philo Pottery Inn**. It sits in an 1888 house, an old stagecoach stop, built entirely of redwood. The five bedrooms are high-ceilinged, wood-paneled affairs with such decorative flourishes as oak dressers, patchwork quilts, and brass beds (some rooms share a bath). There's a comfortable living room as well as other lounging areas. The spacious grounds also boast "one of the largest blackberry patches in Mendocino County." A great place for a few days of easy living. ~ 8550 Route 128, Philo; 707-895-3069. MODERATE TO DELUXE.

The **Wine Country Inns of Sonoma County** is a referral service that can help you with local bed and breakfast reservations. ~ 707-433-4667.

DINING

One of the most beloved restaurants in Sonoma County, **John Ash & Co.** resides in an elegant adobe-style building, decorated with local artworks that blend in nicely with vineyards visible through enormous windows. John Ash, known for his devotion to local fish, fowl, and produce prepared with a confident flair, has created a widely varied menu including Dungeness crab cakes, venison, lamb, and filet mignon. ~ 4330 Barnes Road next door to the Vintners Inn, Santa Rosa; 707-527-7687. DELUXE TO ULTRA-DELUXE.

A self-described American bistro serving fresh Sonoma County cuisine, **Mixx** makes good use of the region's agricultural bounty, including 30 wines that can be sampled by the glass. The contemporary dining room with Art Nouveau touches and an elegant mahogany bar imported from Europe is the place to sample such choices as grilled fresh oysters with tomato salsa or duck with a cassis and black currant sauce. ~ 135 4th Street, Santa Rosa; 707-573-1344. MODERATE TO DELUXE.

You'll be able to drink from a huge variety of Sonoma Valley wines and dine on hearty fare in pleasant surroundings at the **Southside Saloon and Dining Hall** located on the south side of the plaza in Healdsburg. High ceilings, hardwood floors, and batik hangings set the scene in the large dining room. Among the menu selections available are turkey schnitzel, smoked chicken fettuccine, deep-fried oysters, salmon, and baby back ribs. Wine is served by the glass and the bottle. ~ 106 Matheson Street, Healdsburg; 707-433-4466. MODERATE.

Up in Anderson Valley, a prime Mendocino County winegrowing region, there are a few cafés and family-style restaurants in the small towns along rural Route 128. When hunger strikes, Boonville presents the best possibilities. Particularly recommended for dinner is the **New Boonville Hotel,** an outstanding California cuisine restaurant with a gourmet menu. ~ Route 128, Boonville; 707-895-2210. DELUXE.

SHOPPING

Winetasting is a much more popular sport in these parts than window-browsing. If intent on shopping, you'll have to skip from town to town searching out a few interesting stores. Starting in Healdsburg and proceeding north, try Geyserville, Cloverdale, and Boonville. The pickings, I'm afraid, will be slim.

NIGHTLIFE

Some of the area wineries feature programs during the summer. Otherwise, there are bars and hotel lounges scattered throughout the area in towns such as Healdsburg, Geyserville, Cloverdale, and Boonville.

PARKS

ANNADEL STATE PARK Also possessing a wealth of possibilities, this 5000-acre facility has 39 miles of trails through meadow and forest. A volcanic mountain flanks one end of the park and a lake provides fishing for black bass and bluegill. There's also a marsh where many of the area's 160 bird species flock. Blacktailed deer and coyotes roam the region. The park has picnic areas and toilets; restaurants and groceries are about five miles away in Santa Rosa. Day-use fee, $2. ~ Located off Route 12 about five miles east of Santa Rosa; 707-539-3911.

Russian River

With its headwaters in Mendocino County, the Russian River rambles south through north central California to Healdsburg. Here it turns west toward the sea, as the surrounding landscape changes from rolling ranch land to dense redwood forest. The area around Guerneville, where the river begins its headlong rush to the Pacific, has enjoyed a rebirth as a gay resort area. Earlier a family vacation spot, the Guerneville–Forestville–Monte Rio area became a raffish home to bikers and hippies during the '50s and '60s. Then in the '70s, gay vacationers from San Francisco began frequenting the region.

Today, the Russian River is San Francisco's answer to Fire Island. There are many gay resorts in and around Guerneville, and almost without exception every establishment in town welcomes gay visitors. The area is also a popular family resort area. This stretch of the river offers prime fishing and canoeing opportunities. As the river rumbles downslope, it provides miles of scenic runs past overhanging forests. Black bass, steelhead, bluegills, and silver salmon swim these waters, and there are numerous beaches for swimming and sunbathing. From Santa Rosa, the winding, two-lane River Road follows the northern edge of the Russian River taking you to the ocean, where it stops at Jenner.

SIGHTS

The **Visitors Information Center** provides maps and brochures on facilities and water sports. ~ 14034 Armstrong Woods Road, Guerneville; 707-869-9212.

Founded in 1882 by three brothers, **Korbel** produces today's most popular sparkling wines. On any day of the week you may taste these award-winning bubblies and sample their still wines and brandies. The tasting room and attached store offer nine different champagnes, some of which are available nowhere else. While guided tours are offered throughout the year, I recommend visiting during spring and summer when the winery's century-old garden is alive with roses, tulips, and daffodils. ~ 13250 River Road, Guerneville; 707-887-2294.

As you first arrive in downtown Guerneville you will come to a stop sign at the intersection of Armstrong Woods Road. Turning north will take you to **Armstrong Redwoods State Reserve** where you undoubtedly will marvel at the grove of ancient redwoods dating back 1400 years and reaching heights of 300 feet. Admission. ~ 17000 Armstrong Woods Road, Guerneville; 707-869-2015.

Of course, Guerneville would never have developed into a resort destination had it not been for the gentle, slow moving waters of the Russian River. The most popular spot around Guerneville to plunge in for a swim or launch a canoe is **Johnson's Beach**. Located just two blocks from the heart of downtown, this sunny waterfront strip is also home to many summer events, including the renowned Russian River Jazz Festival. ~ At the south end of Church Street, Guerneville.

LODGING

Resting on 15 waterfront acres on the edge of downtown Guerneville, **Fifes Resort** is the Russian River's largest gay resort. In addition to a restaurant and a bar, Fifes offers such facilities as a beach, a pool, and volleyball courts. Accommodations are as varied as the sports activities. There are 100 budget-priced campsites as well as moderate-to-deluxe-priced individual cabins which were built in the 1920s and haven't changed much since then. Each is simply furnished with a queen-sized bed and without television or telephone. Some two-room cabins have a wood-burning stove and a sofa bed in one room. ~ 16467 River Road, Guerneville; 707-869-0656, 800-734-3371, fax 707-869-0658. BUDGET TO DELUXE.

Fondly called "triple R," **Russian River Resort** offers 24 cheerfully decorated guest rooms situated around a clothing-optional pool/hot tub area. Whereas most other resorts in the area can be described as rustic, this resort provides more modern, contemporary accommodations; each room is carpeted, has a private bath and a cable TV (several have wood-burning fireplaces as well). Throughout the year, the Russian River Resort organizes 15 to 20 events celebrating major holidays and festivities such as Western Weekend and Women's Weekend. The guests are almost exclusively gay male but lesbians and gay-friendly straights are welcome. ~ 16390 4th Street, Guerneville; 707-869-0691, 800-417-3767, fax 707-869-0698. BUDGET TO DELUXE.

Catering primarily to gays and lesbians, **Highlands Resort** sits on three acres. Accommodations here come in many forms. Some are individual cabins with fireplaces, private baths, and kitchenettes; others are more standard motel-style rooms. The pool suite has a brass bed, TV, refrigerator, and a view of the pool, where sunbathing is *au naturel*. A hot tub, continental breakfast, and a guest lounge with a piano, TV, VCR, and books complete the amenities. There is also space for 20 tents. ~ 1400 Woodland Drive, Guerneville; 707-869-0333, fax 707-869-0370. BUDGET TO DELUXE.

Spread over five wooded acres along the Russian River, **The Willows** is a gay and lesbian guesthouse resort with spots for tent camping and barbecuing on the grounds. The main lodge has 13 bedrooms, most with private baths, and a spacious living room with a stone fireplace, library, and grand piano. The price tag includes breakfast, tea, and coffee served in the morning and afternoon, as well as use of the canoes. ~ 15905 River Road, Guerneville; 707-869-2824, 800-953-2828. MODERATE TO DELUXE.

Fern Grove Inn sits at the foot of a mountain and is a five-minute walk from town. The 20 mustard-colored craftsmen cottages were built in 1926 and are furnished with a mixture of antiques and contemporary styles. Some have canopied beds, and all suites have down comforters and pillows. Guests enjoy breakfast, as well as sherry and port in the evenings. There's a two-night minimum on the weekends. ~ 16650 River Road, Guerneville; 707-869-9083, 800-347-9083, fax 707-869-2948. DELUXE.

Village Inn, a refurbished woodframe complex on the river, draws a mixed clientele. This cozy country inn, set amid redwood trees, has a homey, old-time feel. The lobby's a friendly spot, crowded with plump furniture and potted plants, and you'll also find a good restaurant and bar. Rooms begin in the budget range; deluxe price with river view and private bath; they're trim little units, clean, carpeted, and decorated with an occasional piece of art. ~ 20822 River Boulevard, Monte Rio; 707-865-2304, 800-303-2303. BUDGET TO DELUXE.

Located on the water, **Highland Dell Inn** has long served as an ideal hostelry for enjoying Russian River–style peace and quiet. This three-story turn-of-the-century building features a grand lobby complete with fireplace, cathedral ceiling, and antique candelabra. Take your pick: the five rooms and three suites, some paneled with knotty pine, offer captain's beds, sleigh beds, and brass beds. There's also a pool, or you can swim at Monte Rio beach across the river. A full breakfast is served. ~ 21050 River Boulevard, Monte Rio; 707-865-1759, 800-767-1759, fax 707-865-4128. MODERATE TO ULTRA-DELUXE.

DINING

While even remote Guerneville now offers more than a couple of places to get an espresso, none are better than the **Coffee Bazaar**. Located on Armstrong Woods Road a block off the main strip, this cafe's food and beverages are tasty and affordable. There is a wide range of coffee creations and a generous selection of pastries each morning. Lunch choices include soups, salads, sandwiches, quiche, calzones, and even lasagna. There is plenty of seating inside, but take a sidewalk table to peoplewatch and enjoy the music that's pumped out of the neighboring record store. ~ 14045 Armstrong Woods Road, Guerneville; 707-869-9706. BUDGET.

For a fun and downright funky dinner spot in downtown Guerneville, head over to **Lalita's Mexican Restaurant**. While the address and front door are on Main Street, the restaurant fills the back of The Cactus Club and is more easily reached from 1st Street. The friendly staff serves up large portions of authentic Mexican favorites in an area that's small and dark yet a joy to behold: Mexican crafts adorn the walls, strings of Christmas lights circle the ceiling while large plastic palms and vines add a touch of greenery. The boisterous atmosphere of The Cactus Club spills into Lalita's and rubs off on the diners—perhaps it sneaks in when the waiters open the door between the club and the restaurant on their many round trips to the bar for margaritas. ~ 16225 Main Street, Guerneville; 707-869-3238. BUDGET TO MODERATE.

Also downtown on Main Street, **Sweet's River Grill** is big on atmosphere and satisfying food. Nearly all the seating is on the front patio, which is well-protected from the sun, and is warmed by overhead heaters on chilly evenings. The full menu offers appetizers, salads, soups, and a wide selection of grilled entrées. Gourmet burgers are a specialty; you may consider the Michelangelo burger with melted gorgonzola or the Russian Burger with a sour cream–horseradish sauce. For vegetarians there is a meatless burger. ~ 16251 Main Street, Guerneville; 707-869-3383. MODERATE.

The restaurant at **Fifes** is an intimate dining room with a stone fireplace, pine walls, and an exposed-rafter ceiling. There's also a sundeck for warm-weather dining. Fifes features a sophisticated California-cuisine menu that changes seasonally. Dinner includes scampi, steak, chicken curry, and prosciutto tortellini. For breakfast you'll find eggs Benedict, while lunch combines sandwiches and salads with special entrées. Open for breakfast, lunch, and dinner in the summer; dinner only in the off-season. ~ 16467 River Road, Guerneville; 707-869-0656. MODERATE.

If you're looking to have a cozy dinner away from downtown, head east out of town on River Road to **Burdon's**. Here you will find an elegant dining room with low lighting, white tablecloths, and minimal decor. Chicken, steak, and seafood predominate the menu, although there are a few pasta dishes. Appetizers such as bay shrimp cocktail and escargot regularly appear on the menu, while main courses include filet mignon and filet of sole in a lemon and tartar sauce. Dinner only. Closed Sunday through Wednesday. ~ 15405 River Road, Guerneville; 707-869-2615. MODERATE TO DELUXE.

Just eight miles southeast of Guerneville in downtown Forestville, **Chez Marie** is a quaint lesbian-owned eatery. The country-French cuisine is always prepared and served by the owners themselves. Duck à l'orange, *crab à la creole* (sautéed crab cakes with a creole sauce), and *ris de veau supreme* (veal sweetbreads in a nutmeg cream sauce) are among the recommended offerings. Closed Tuesday and Wednesday in winter. ~ 6675 Front Street, Forestville; 707-887-7503. MODERATE TO DELUXE.

SHOPPING

An excellent bookstore and a true community resource, the **River Reader, Inc.** has a small but strong selection of books, magazines, cards, games, and gifts. Visitors to Guerneville will find plenty of choices for poolside reading in all categories including fiction, spirituality, and regional topics. There is also a good selection of gay reading material including books and magazines. ~ 16355 Main Street, Guerneville; 707-869-2242.

NIGHTLIFE

Fifes, one of the area's first gay resorts, has a beautiful bar area, which spreads through several pine-paneled rooms and extends out to a poolside deck. They offer disco dancing and other live entertainment throughout the week. ~ 16467 River Road, Guerneville; 707-869-0656.

Like Fifes, the **Russian River Resort** invites nonguests to enjoy the facilities and mingle with guests at the bar and around the pool. The bar isn't large but the crowd is friendly and if nothing is jumping in town, there will surely be some people hanging out at the "Triple R." ~ 16390 4th Street, Guerneville; 707-869-0691.

Located in the same building as Lalita's Mexican Restaurant, **The Cactus Club** is a downtown nightspot that attracts a lively crowd of both gays and straights. The same fun and funky atmosphere you'll find at Lalita's exists here. There's live music on most Friday and Saturday nights. ~ 16225 Main Street, Guerneville; 707-869-3238.

Also in the middle of downtown is the **Rainbow Cattle Company**. While it's located just across Main Street from The Cactus Club you will not find the same mixed crowd here. The Rainbow Cattle Company is a true gay bar. Offering nothing more than a couple of pool tables, three pinball machines, bar stools, and long benches, this nightspot doesn't provide much in the way of entertainment, but it's a congenial place for socializing and drinking. ~ 16220 Main Street, Guerneville; 707-869-0206.

A former theater that is unquestionably the biggest and best nightclub space in Guerneville recently metamorphosed from the "Jungle" into the **Stumptown Brewery**. Billing itself as a full bar with loads of microbrews, the Stumptown is still finding an identity and a following but is definitely worth checking out. ~ 16135 Main Street, Guerneville; 707-869-1400.

Molly's Country Club is a local bar with a strong gay clientele. On weekend nights expect a DJ playing a mixture of country and house music. Wednesday nights are open-mike night when people share music and comedy. ~ 14120 Cazadero Road, Guerneville; 707-869-0511.

PARKS

ARMSTRONG REDWOODS STATE RESERVE AND AUSTIN CREEK STATE RECREATION AREA These two parks, lying side by side, are a study in contrasts. Armstrong features a deep, cool forest of redwood trees measuring over 300 feet high and dating back 1400 years. Rare redwood orchids blossom here in spring and there is a 1200-seat amphitheater that was once used for summer concerts. Austin Creek offers sunny meadows and oak forests. Fox, bobcats, deer, wild pigs, and raccoons inhabit the region, and a nearby bullfrog pond is stocked with sunfish and bass. There are 22 miles of trails threading the park. Facilities include picnic areas, restrooms, and a visitors center; restaurants and groceries are a few miles away in Guerneville. Day-use fee, $5. ~ Located at 17000 Armstrong Woods Road, Guerneville; 707-869-2015.

▲ Permitted in Austin Creek and Bullfrog Pond Campground, which has 24 campsites ($10 per night); there are also four hike-in campsites ($7 per night); for restrictions and permit information call 707-869-2015.

Outdoor Adventures

There are many opportunities for boating in the Wine Country, primarily along the Russian River. This river is a Class I from April to October, and during that time canoe and kayak rentals are plentiful. Most folks rent for the day, canoe one way, and are picked up by the outfitter and shuttled back.

WATER SPORTS

SONOMA VALLEY For a relaxing cruise down the Petaluma River, try the **Petaluma Queen.** This facsimile of a Victorian riverboat departs from the Petaluma waterfront on lunch, brunch, dinner-dance, and jazz cruises. ~ 255 Weller Street; 707-762-2100.

RUSSIAN RIVER The Russian River is the place to explore in a canoe or kayak. Several outfits offer everything from one-day excursions to five-day expeditions. The scenery, ranging from rolling ranch land to dense redwood groves, is stunning. The experience of floating timelessly along this magnificent river will long be remembered. If you're ready for the adventure, contact **Burke's Canoe Trips.** They offer a ten-mile day trip to Guerneville. ~ At the north end of Mirabel Road at River Road, Forestville; 707-887-1222. **W. C. "Bob" Trowbridge Canoe Trips** has canoes and kayaks. ~ 20 Healdsburg Avenue, Healdsburg; 707-433-7247. For kayaking lessons and guided trips, call **North Coast Kayaking Company.** ~ 614 Solano Avenue, Sonoma; 707-935-6510.

BALLOON RIDES & GLIDING

All puns aside, no sport in the Wine Country has taken off like hot-air ballooning. Every morning, colorful balloons dot the sky, providing riders with a billowing crow's nest from which to view the sweeping countryside.

NAPA VALLEY For a ride straight from the pages of *Around the World in 80 Days*, call **Balloon Aviation of Napa Valley.** ~ 6525 Washington Street, Yountville; 707-252-7067. **Adventures Aloft** will also get you airborne. ~ 6525 Washington Street, Yountville; 707-255-8688.

SONOMA VALLEY In business for more than 25 years, **Air Flamboyant** soars above Sonoma Valley and afterward treats the riders to a champagne brunch. ~ 250 Pleasant Avenue, Santa Rosa; 707-838-8500.

If you'd prefer to soar silently in a glider, contact **Calistoga Gliders.** ~ 1546 Lincoln Avenue, Calistoga; 707-942-5592.

GOLF

The Wine Country's excellent weather makes golf a popular pastime. This is one of the few places in the world where you can play golf amidst beautiful grape vines.

NAPA VALLEY You can tee off at **Chimney Rock Golf Course.** ~ 5320 Silverado Trail, Napa; 707-255-3363. Also in Napa is the **Napa City Municipal Golf Course.** ~ 2295 Streblow Drive; 707-255-4333. In Calistoga, try **Mount St. Helena Golf Course.** ~ Napa County Fairgrounds, Calistoga; 707-942-9966.

SONOMA VALLEY You'll find greens in Sonoma at **Sonoma Golf Club.** ~ 17700 Arnold Drive, Sonoma; 707-996-0300. **Oakmont Golf Club** is the place to play in Santa Rosa. ~ 7025 Oakmont Drive; 707-539-0415.

RUSSIAN RIVER Around the Russian River, try **Northwood Golf Course.** ~ 19400 Route 116, Monte Rio; 707-865-1116. In Sebastopol, try **Sebastopol Golf Course.** ~ 2881 Scott's Right of Way; 707-823-9852.

RIDING STABLES

The hills and valleys of the Wine Country provide wonderful opportunities for equestrians. Slide into the saddle and saunter through the forest on a guided journey offered by **Wine Country Trail Rides.** They operate horseback-riding trips three times a day all year round at Sugarloaf Ridge State Park in Kenwood and from May through October at Jack London and Bothe–Napa Valley state parks in Napa. A moonlight ride in Sugarloaf four or five days before a full moon is an unforgettable experience. ~ P.O. Box 877, Glen Ellen, CA 95442; 707-996-8566.

BIKING

One of the nicest ways to explore the Wine Country is to bike the backroads, pedaling between wineries, historic sites, and health spas. To see the area by an organized bike tour, contact **Backroads Bicycle Touring Company.** ~ 1516 5th Street, Berkeley; 510-527-1555.

NAPA VALLEY The **Silverado Trail** through Napa Valley is the best road to travel. It's less crowded than Route 29, the main thoroughfare, and is fairly level. Several steep mountain roads lead from Napa Valley across to Sonoma Valley.

SONOMA VALLEY A bike path on the western edge of Sonoma passes numerous sightseeing spots.

At Sugarloaf Ridge, try the seven-mile **Bald Mountain Trail** to Gray Pine and then through the meadow loop. You'll pass open meadows sprinkled with oak trees. On a clear day, from the top of Bald Mountain Trail, you'll see as far as the Golden Gate Bridge and the Sierra Nevada.

RUSSIAN RIVER **River Road,** between Windsor and Guerneville, meanders past rolling hills and rural scenery, but carries a moderate amount of traffic.

Bike Rentals In the Napa area, try **Napa Valley Cyclery**, which also offers guided bike tours of the Napa Valley. ~ 4080 Byway East, Napa; 707-255-3377. For rentals and repairs, check out **St. Helena Cyclery**. ~ 1156 Main Street, St. Helena; 707-963-7736. In the Sonoma area, head to **Dave's Bike Sport**. ~ 353 College Avenue, Santa Rosa; 707-528-3283. **Spoke Folk Cyclery** includes helmets, locks, and backpacks with their rental bikes. ~ 249 Center Street, Healdsburg; 707-433-7171. In the Russian River area, **Mike's Bikes** rents mountain bikes and beach cruisers. ~ 16442 Main Street, Guerneville; 707-869-1106.

HIKING

For backpackers and daytrippers, state parks in the Wine Country offer a chance to escape the crowds while exploring forests, meadows, and mountain ridges.

NAPA VALLEY For those interested in communing with nature amid splendid redwood groves, **Bothe–Napa Valley State Park** has ten miles of hiking trails.

History Trail (1.2 miles) is a fairly strenuous hike which begins at the picnic area and leads past an old pioneer cemetery, the site where an 1853 church once stood, and Mill Creek en route to Old Bale Grist Mill.

Coyote Peak Trail (1.4 miles) heads away from Ritchey Creek, then climbs up to 1170 feet elevation for scenic views of the Napa Valley.

Ritchey Canyon Trail (3.9 miles) starts off on an 1860 roadbed which wanders beside a stream and is shadowed by redwoods and firs. Farther along, the trail leads past a small cascade which flows into a small canyon.

A tranquil hike along Ritchey Creek can also be found on **Redwood Trail** (1 mile). In spring, redwood orchids and trilliums add to the beauty of this tree-shaded pathway.

The **South Fork Trail** (.9 mile) is a moderately strenuous hike that circles across the rim of Ritchey Creek and arrives at a vista point overlooking the canyon.

✔ CHECK THESE OUT—UNIQUE OUTDOOR ADVENTURES

- Float timelessly down the **Russian River** by kayak or canoe. *page 228*
- Soar the skies of **Napa Valley** on a technicolor hot air balloon. *page 228*
- Bike the **Silverado Trail** through Napa Valley, a road less traveled. *page 229*
- Trek past an old pioneer cemetery and other historic sites on the way to Old Bale Grist Mill along **History Trail**. *page 230*

SONOMA VALLEY In addition to views of the Sierra Nevada and San Francisco Bay, the trails at **Sugarloaf Ridge State Park** (707-833-5712) provide opportunities to explore ridges and open fields. Every spring, wildflowers riot throughout the meadows. The park's most popular hike is along **Creekside Nature Trail** (.8 mile). This self-guided walk begins at the day-use picnic area and carries past stands of oak, alder, ash, maple, and Douglas fir. Watch for several species of lichen *and* poison oak! If you're up for a steep climb, try **Bald Mountain Trail** (3 miles), which leads to the top of the mountain. At an elevation of 2700 feet, the summit offers spectacular views of the Sonoma and Napa valleys and, on a clear day, the Sierras and St. Helena. The climb begins at the day-use parking lot near the campground, which is already 1000 feet in elevation.

Once inhabited by Pomo and Wappo Indians, **Annadel State Park** is a mix of forest and meadow laced with 39 miles of hiking paths. ~ 707-539-3911. **Richardson's Trail** (5 miles) loops through a forest of redwood and Douglas fir en route to Lake Ilsanjo. Spring brings redwood orchid blossoms, adding a rare experience to an already splendid hike. For a trek into a Douglas fir forest and through a meadow ringed with oak trees, consider **Louis Trail** (.2 mile) just off Richardson's Trail.

Marsh Trail (3.6 miles) climbs the side of Bennett Mountain and offers grand views of Lake Ilsanjo as well as nearby mountain ranges. For a trip to an old quarry site where cobblestones were once excavated, head down the aptly named **Cobblestone Trail** (2 miles).

Transportation

CAR

The quick, painless, and impersonal way to the Napa Valley is along **Route 80**. From San Francisco, the freeway buzzes northeast to Vallejo, where it connects with **Route 37** and then **Route 29**, the main road through Napa Valley.

An alternative course leads north from San Francisco along **Route 101**. From this freeway you can pick up Route 37, which skirts San Pablo Bay en route to its junction with Route 29.

For the most scenic drive, turn off Route 37 onto **Route 121**. This rural road, which also connects with Route 29, provides a preview of the Wine Country. The curving hills along the way are covered with vineyards, ranches, and sheep farms. Route 121 also connects with **Route 12**, which leads into the Sonoma Valley.

Route 101 runs like a spine through the Russian River region. Vineyards lie in clusters on either side of the highway. Another road, **Route 116**, leaves this freeway and heads to the gay resort area around Guerneville.

BUS

Greyhound Bus Lines has frequent service to the both Napa and Sonoma areas. It also stops in Healdsburg, Geyserville, and points further north. ~ 800-231-2222.

PUBLIC TRANSIT

There is no public transportation system in the Napa Valley. You'll have to take a Greyhound bus to Napa, then fend for yourself.

In Sonoma, **Sonoma County Transit** covers the area from Sonoma to Santa Rosa, stopping in Glen Ellen and Kenwood; it continues from Santa Rosa to Windsor, Healdsburg, and Geyserville. Sonoma County Transit also serves the area between Healdsburg and Guerneville. ~ 707-576-7433.

FIVE

North Coast

When visitors to San Francisco seek a rural retreat, paradise is never far away. It sits just across the Golden Gate Bridge along a coastline stretching almost 400 miles to the Oregon border. Scenically, the North Coast compares in beauty with any spot on earth.

There are the folded hills and curving beaches of Point Reyes, Sonoma's craggy coast and old Russian fort, plus Mendocino with its vintage towns and spuming shoreline. To the far north lies Redwood Country, silent domain of the world's tallest living things.

Along the entire seaboard, there are fewer than a dozen towns with populations over 600 people. Traffic lights are almost as rare as unicorns. Civilization appears in the form of fishing villages and logging towns. Matter of fact, a lot of the prime real estate is saved forever from developers' heavy hands. California's Coastal Commission serves as a watchdog agency protecting the environment.

Much of the coast is also preserved in public playgrounds. Strung like pearls along the Pacific are a series of federal parks—Golden Gate National Recreation Area, Point Reyes National Seashore, and Redwood National Park.

The main highway through this idyllic domain is Route 1. A sinuous road, it snakes along the waterfront, providing the slowest, most scenic route. Paralleling this road and following an inland course is Route 101. This superhighway streaks from San Francisco to Oregon. It is fast, efficient, and boring. In the town of Leggett, Route 1 merges into Route 101, which continues north through Redwood Country.

Route 1 runs through San Francisco into Marin County, passing Sausalito before it branches from Route 101. While the eastern sector of Marin, along San Francisco Bay, is a suburban sprawl, the western region consists of rolling ranch land. Muir Woods is here, featuring 1000-year-old redwoods growing within commuting distance of the city. There is Mt. Tamalpais, a 2600-foot "sleeping maiden" whose recumbent figure has been the subject of numerous poems.

According to some historians, Sir Francis Drake, the Renaissance explorer, landed along the Marin shore in 1579, building a fort and claiming the wild region for dear old England. The Portuguese had first sighted the North Coast in 1543 when they espied Cape Mendocino. Back then Coastal Miwok Indians inhabited Marin, enjoying undisputed possession of the place until the Spanish settled the interior valleys during the early 1800s.

To the north, in Sonoma County, the Miwok shared their domain with the Pomo Indians. After 1812 they were also dividing it with the Russians. The Czar's forces arrived in California from their hunting grounds in Alaska and began taking large numbers of otters from local waters. The Russians built Fort Ross and soon proclaimed the region open only to their shipping. Of course, these imperial designs made the Spanish very nervous. The American response was to proclaim the Monroe Doctrine, warning foreign powers off the continent.

By the 1830s the Russians had decimated the otter population, reducing it from 150,000 to less than 100. They soon lost interest in the area and sold their fort and other holdings to John Sutter, whose name two decades hence would become synonymous with the Gold Rush.

Many of the early towns along the coast were born during the days of the '49ers. Established to serve as pack stations for the mines, the villages soon turned to lumbering and fishing. Today these are still important industries. About seven percent of California's land consists of commercial forest, much of it along the coastal redwood belt. Environmentalists continue to battle with the timber interests as they have since 1918 when the Save-the-Redwoods League was formed.

The natural heritage they protect includes trees which have been growing in California's forests since before the birth of Christ. Elk herds roam these groves, while trout and steelhead swim the nearby rivers. At one time the forest stretched in a 30-mile-wide swath for 450 miles along the coast. But in little more than a century the lumber industry has cut down over 90 percent of the original redwoods. Presently, 155,000 acres of ancient trees remain, half of which are protected in parks.

Another, much younger, cash crop is marijuana. During the '60s and early '70s, Mendocino and Humboldt counties became meccas for counterculturalists intent on getting "back to the land." They established communes, built original-design houses, and plunged into local politics. Some also became green-thumb outlaws, perfecting potent and exotic strains of *sinsemilla* for personal use and black-market sale. They made Northern California marijuana famous and helped boom the local economy.

The North Coast has become home to the country inn as well. All along the Pacific shoreline, bed and breakfasts serve travelers seeking informal and relaxing accommodations. Local artisans have also proliferated while small shops have opened to sell their crafts.

The great lure for travelers is still the environment. This coastal shelf, tucked between the Coast Ranges and the Pacific, has mountains and rivers, forests and ocean. Once the habitat of Yuki, Athabascan, Wiyot, Yurok, and Tolowa Indians, it remains an adventureland for imaginative travelers. Winters are damp, mornings and evenings sometimes foggy, but the weather overall is temperate. It's a place where you can fish for salmon, go crabbing, and scan the sea for migrating whales. Or simply ease back and enjoy scenery that never stops.

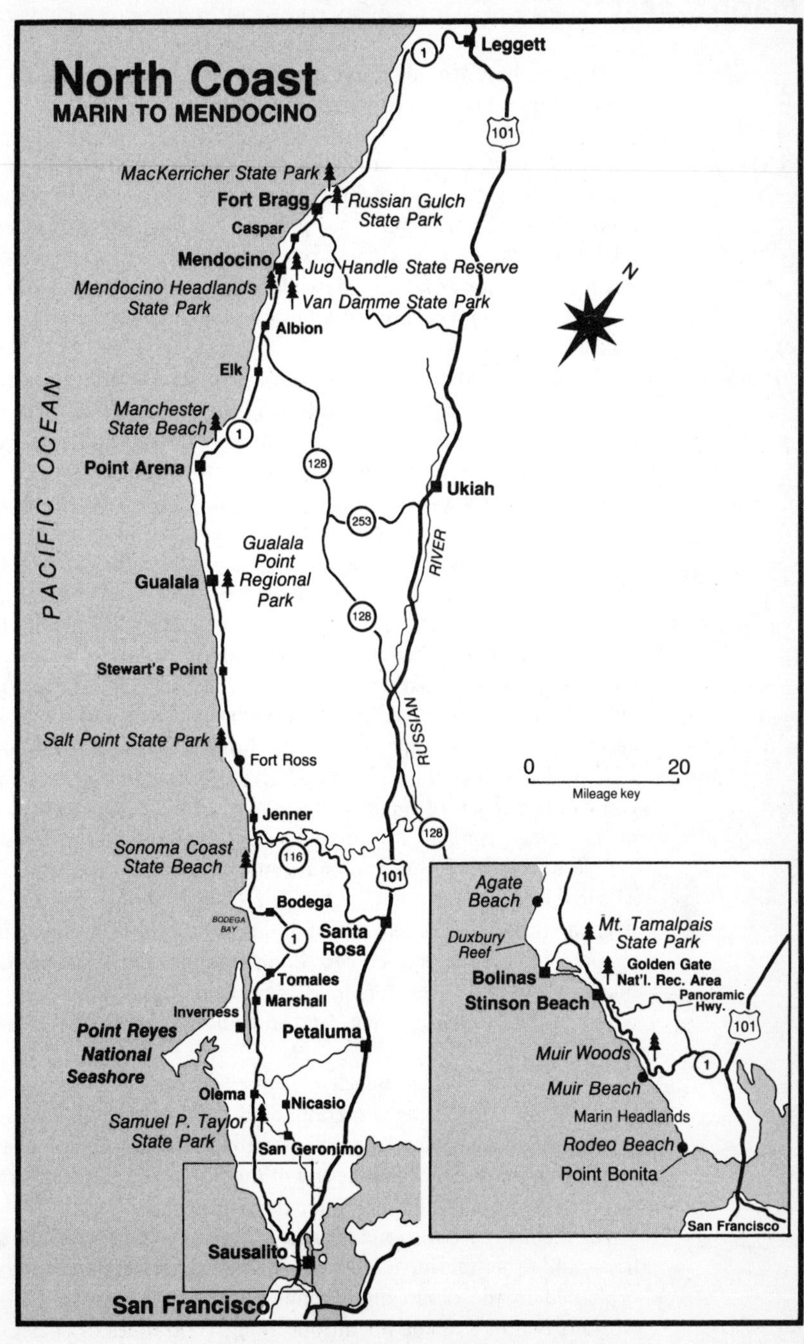
North Coast
MARIN TO MENDOCINO
Leggett
1
101
MacKerricher State Park
Fort Bragg
Russian Gulch State Park
Caspar
Mendocino
Jug Handle State Reserve
Mendocino Headlands State Park
Van Damme State Park
N
Albion
Elk
PACIFIC OCEAN
Manchester State Beach
1
Point Arena
128
Ukiah
253
Gualala Point Regional Park
Gualala
RIVER
128
Stewart's Point
RUSSIAN
Salt Point State Park
Fort Ross
0
20
Mileage key
Jenner
128
Sonoma Coast State Beach
116
101
Bodega
BODEGA BAY
1
Santa Rosa
Tomales
Marshall
Inverness
Point Reyes National Seashore
Petaluma
Olema
Nicasio
Samuel P. Taylor State Park
San Geronimo
Sausalito
San Francisco
Agate Beach
Mt. Tamalpais State Park
Duxbury Reef
Golden Gate Nat'l. Rec. Area
Bolinas
Stinson Beach
Panoramic Hwy.
101
Muir Woods
1
Muir Beach
Marin Headlands
Rodeo Beach
Point Bonita
San Francisco

Marin Coast

As frequently photographed as the Golden Gate Bridge, the coast of Marin County consists of rolling ranch lands and spectacular ocean bluffs. It extends from San Francisco Bay to Tomales Bay, offering groves of redwoods, meadows filled with wildflowers, and miles of winding country roads.

SIGHTS

An exploration of this vaunted region begins immediately upon crossing the Golden Gate Bridge on Route 101. There's a **vista point** at the far north end of the bridge affording marvelous views back toward San Francisco and out upon the Bay. (If some of your party want to start off with an exhilarating walk across the bridge, drop them at the vista point on the city side and pick them up here a little later.)

Once across the bridge, take the first exit, Alexander Avenue; then take an immediate left, following the sign back toward San Francisco. Next, bear right at the sign for Marin Headlands.

For what is literally a **bird's-eye view** of the Golden Gate Bridge, go three-tenths of a mile uphill and stop at the first turnout on the left. From here it's a short stroll out and up, past deserted battery fortifications, to a 360° view point sweeping the Pacific and Bay alike. You'll practically be standing on the bridge, with cars careening below and the tops of the twin towers vaulting above you.

Continue along Conzelman Road and you will pass a series of increasingly spectacular views of San Francisco. Ahead the road will fall away to reveal a tumbling peninsula, furrowed with hills and marked at its distant tip by a lighthouse. That is **Point Bonita,** a salient far outside the Golden Gate. After proceeding to the point, you can peer back through the interstices of the bridge to the city or turn away from civilization and gaze out on a wind-tousled sea.

Nature writes in big letters around these parts. You're in the **Marin Headlands** section of **Golden Gate National Recreation Area,** an otherworldly realm of spuming surf, knife-edge cliffs, and chaparral-coated hillsides. From Point Bonita, follow Field Road, taking a left at the sign for the Marin Headlands Visitors Center, where you can pick up maps and information about the area. ~ 415-331-1540.

Walk along **Rodeo Beach,** a sandy corridor separating the Pacific from a tule-fringed lagoon alive with waterfowl. Miles of hiking trails lace up into the hills (see the "Hiking" section at the end of this chapter). At the far end of the beach you can trek along the cliffs and watch the sea batter the continent.

At the nearby **California Marine Mammal Center** are seals, sea lions, and other marine mammals who have been found injured or orphaned in the ocean and brought here to recuperate. Center workers conduct rescue operations along 1000 miles of coastline, returning the animals to the wild after they have gained sufficient strength. ~ 415-289-7325.

Bunker Road leads through a long tunnel and out of the park. You've completed a lazy loop and will emerge near an entrance to Route 101. Follow this north a few miles, then pick up Route 1. You'll be on the northern leg of one of the most beautiful roads in America. With its wooded sanctuaries and ocean vistas, Route 1 is for many people synonymous with California.

When Route 1 forks after several miles, turn right on Panoramic Highway toward Muir Woods and Mt. Tamalpais; the left fork leads to Stinson Beach, but that comes later. It's uphill and then down to **Muir Woods National Monument**, a 560-acre park inhabited by *Sequoia sempervirens*, the coast redwood. Though these forest giants have been known to live over two millennia, most enjoy a mere four-to-eight-century existence. In Muir Woods they reach 240 feet, while further up the coast they top 350 feet (with roots that go no deeper than six feet!). ~ 415-388-2595.

Facts can't convey the feelings inspired by these trees. You have to move among them, walk through Muir's Cathedral Grove where redwoods form a lofty arcade above the narrow trail. It's a forest primeval, casting the deepest, most restful shade imaginable. Muir Woods has the double-edged quality of being the redwood forest nearest to San Francisco. It can be horribly crowded. Since silence and solitude are vital to experiencing a redwood forest, plan to visit early or late in the day, and allow time to hike the more remote of the park's six miles of trails.

Back up on Panoramic Highway, the road continues through Mt. Tamalpais State Park en route to **Mt. Tamalpais'** 2571-foot peak. Mt. Tam, as it is affectionately known, represents one of the Bay Area's most prominent landmarks. Rising dramatically between the Pacific and the Bay, the site was sacred to Indians. Even today some people see in the sloping silhouette of the mountain the sleeping figure of an Indian maiden. So tread lightly up the short trail that leads to the summit. You'll be rewarded with a full

✔ CHECK THESE OUT—UNIQUE SIGHTS

- Go tidepooling at **Duxbury Reef**, and spot starfish, periwinkles, limpets, and other clinging critters in a remarkable marine preserve. *page 239*
- Stop in at Point Reyes National Seashore's **Miwok Indian Village**, featuring replicas of round-domed shelters. *page 240*
- Hop on board the **Skunk Train**, a logging train dating back to 1885 that takes you through 40 miles of redwood forests. *page 257*
- Step back to the Victorian era when you visit **Ferndale**, a perfectly refurbished town featuring Gothic Revival, Queen Anne, and other "painted ladies." *page 270*

circle view that sweeps across the Bay, along San Francisco's miniature skyline, and out across the Pacific.

Then continue on Panoramic Highway as it corkscrews down to Stinson Beach. Better yet, take the longer but more spectacular route to Stinson: backtrack along Panoramic to where the fork originally separated from Route 1 (Shoreline Highway). Turn right and head north on Route 1.

Contrary to rumor, on a clear day you cannot see forever from Mt. Tam, but you can see north toward Redwood Country and east to the Sierras.

Shortly, a turnoff will lead down to **Green Gulch Farm**, a 115-acre Zen retreat tucked serenely in a coastal valley. Residents here follow a rigorous program of work and meditation. There is a temple on the grounds and guests are welcome to tour the organic farm. Sunday is the best day to visit since a special guest program is offered then. ~ 1601 Shoreline Highway, near Muir Beach; 415-383-3134.

It's not far to **Muir Beach** where you'll find a crescent-shaped cove with sandy beach. Though swimming is not advised, this is a good spot for picnicking. About a mile further up the road, follow the "vista point" sign to **Muir Beach Overlook**. Here you can walk out along a narrow ridge for a view extending from Bolinas to the coastline south of San Francisco. It's an outstanding place for whale watching in winter. Matter of fact, this lookout is so well placed it became a site for World War II gun batteries, whose rusty skeletons remain.

You have entered a realm that might well be called the Land of a Thousand Views. Until the road descends to the flat expanse of Stinson Beach, it follows a tortuous route poised on the edge of oblivion. Below, precipitous cliffs dive to the sea, while above the road, rock walls edge upward toward Mt. Tamalpais. Around every curve another scene opens to view. Before you, Bolinas is a sweep of land, an arm extended seaward. Behind, the San Francisco skyline falls away into the past. If God built highways, they'd look like this.

Stinson Beach, that broad sandy hook at the bottom of the mountain, is one of Northern California's finest strands. Anglers haunt the rocks along one end in pursuit of blenny and lingcod, while birdwatchers are on the lookout for sandpipers, shearwaters, and swallows. Everyone else comes for sand, surf, and sun.

Birdwatchers also flock to **Audubon Canyon Ranch**, located astride Route 1 on Bolinas Lagoon. Open only on weekends and holidays from mid-March to July, the ranch includes four canyons, one of which is famed as a rookery for egrets and herons. From the hiking trails here you can see up to 90 bird species as well as gray fox, deer, badgers, and bobcats. ~ Route 1; 415-868-9244.

Bolinas Lagoon is also a bird sanctuary. Great egrets, ducks, and great blue herons make this one of their migratory stops. A colony of harbor seals lives here permanently and is joined in summer by migrating seals from San Francisco.

To reach the next point of interest you'll have to pay close attention. That's because you're approaching **Bolinas.** To get there from Route 1, watch for the crossroad at the foot of the lagoon; go left, then quickly left again and follow the road along the other side of the lagoon; take another left at the end of the road.

There should be signs to direct you. But there probably won't be. Not because the state neglected them or highway workers forgot to put them up. It seems that local residents subscribe to the self-serving philosophy that since Bolinas is beautiful and they got there first, they should keep everyone else out. They tear down road signs and discourage visitors. The rest of Northern California is fair game, they seem to say, as long as Bolinas is left as some sort of human preserve.

The place they are attempting to hide is a delightful little town which rises from an S-shaped beach to form a lofty mesa. There are country roads along the bluff that overhangs the beach.

Whether you stroll the beach or hike the highlands, you'll discover in the houses here a wild architectural array. There are domes, glass boxes, curved-roof creations, huts, ranch houses, and stately brown-shingle designs.

Bolinas, abutting on the Point Reyes National Seashore, is also a gateway to the natural world. Follow Mesa Road for several miles outside town and you'll encounter the **Point Reyes Bird Observatory**, where scientists at a research station study a bird population of over 200 species.

On the way back to town take a right on Overlook Drive, then a right on Elm Road; follow it to the parking lot at road's end. Hiking trails lead down a sharp 160-foot cliff to **Duxbury Reef**, a mile-long shale reef. Tidepool-watching is great sport here at low tide: starfish, periwinkles, abalone, limpets, and a host of other clinging creatures inhabit the marine preserve. Back in 1971 a huge oil spill endangered this spectacular area, but volunteers from all around the state worked day and night to save the reef and its tenacious inhabitants. Just north of this rocky preserve is **Agate Beach**, an ideal spot to find agates, driftwood, and glass balls (however, no collecting is permitted). ◄ HIDDEN

Back on Route 1, continue north through Olema Valley, a peaceful region of horse ranches fringed by forest. Peaceful, that is, until you realize that the **San Andreas Fault**, the global suture that shook San Francisco back in 1906, cuts through the valley. As a matter of fact, the highway you are traveling parallels the fault line. During the great quake, houses collapsed, trees were uprooted, and fences decided to mark new boundaries.

As you turn off Route 1 onto Sir Francis Drake Boulevard headed for the Point Reyes Peninsula, you'll be passing from the North

American Plate, one of the six tectonic plates on which the entire earth's surface rides, to the Pacific Plate, which extends across the ocean. It is the pressure formed by the collision of these two great land masses that causes earthquakes. No sign will notify you as you cross this troubled geologic border, no guide will direct you along the rift zone. If you're like the people who live hereabouts, within 15 minutes of crossing over you'll have forgotten the fault exists. Especially when you see what is served on the Pacific Plate.

POINT REYES NATIONAL SEASHORE Point Reyes National Seashore is without doubt one of the finest seaside parks on any of the world's six plates. It is a realm of sand dunes and endless beaches, Scottish moors and grassy hillsides, salt marshes and pine forests. Bobcats, mountain lions, fox, and elk inhabit its wrinkled terrain, while harbor seals and gray whales cruise its ragged shoreline. It supports dairies and cattle ranches. In October of 1995, fire ripped through Point Reyes, burning 12,000 acres. To date, a few hiking trails remain closed. However, this should not discourage you from exploring. All trails listed here and in the "Hiking" section are open and additional trails lead through the charred area, giving you a close-up look at the awesome healing power of nature.

The first stage in exploring this multifeatured preserve involves a stop at the **Bear Valley Visitors Center**. Here you can obtain maps, information, and camping permits. ~ Bear Valley Road; 415-663-1092. A short hike from the center will lead you to a **Miwok Indian Village**, where the round-domed shelters and other structures of the area's early inhabitants have been re-created.

Most points of interest lie along Sir Francis Drake Boulevard, which rolls for miles through the park. It will carry you past the tiny town of **Inverness**, with its country inns and ridgetop houses, then out along **Tomales Bay**. Like the Golden Gate, this finger-shaped inlet is a drowned river valley.

Deeper in the park, a side road twists up to Mount Vision Overlook, where vista points sweep the peninsula. At **Johnson's Oyster Company**, along another side road, workers harvest the rich beds of an estuary. The farm is a conglomeration of slapdash buildings, house trailers, and rusty machines. The shoreline is heaped over with oyster shells and the air is filled with pungent odors. Raw oysters are for sale. Even if you don't care for them, you might want to visit anyway. After all, when was the last time you saw an oyster farm? Closed Monday. ~ 17171 Sir Francis Drake Boulevard, Inverness; 415-669-1149.

The main road continues over folded hills that fall away to reveal sharp bluffs. Farm animals graze through fields smothered in wildflowers. There are ocean vistas stretching along miles of headland.

On **Drake's Beach** you can picnic and beachcomb. Or gaze at the surrounding cliffs and wonder whether they truly resemble the

White Cliffs of Dover. In that question resides a story told by one school of historians and vehemently denied by others. It seems that in 1579 the English explorer Sir Francis Drake anchored somewhere along the Northern California coast. But where? Some claim he cast anchor right here in Drake's Bay, others say Bolinas Lagoon, even San Francisco Bay.

A brass plate, purportedly left by Drake, was discovered near San Francisco Bay in 1936; later it was believed that the plate had been first located near Drake's Bay and then moved; finally the plate was deemed a counterfeit.

Point Reyes Beach (also known as "North Beach" and "South Beach"), a windy ten-mile-long strip, is an ideal place for beachcombers and whale-watchers. From there, it's not far to the end of Point Reyes' hammerhead peninsula. At one tip is **Chimney Rock**, a sea stack formed when the ocean eroded away the intervening land mass, leaving this islet just offshore. On the way to Chimney Rock you'll pass an **overlook** that's ideal for watching sea lions; then from Chimney Rock, if the day is clear, you'll see all the way to San Francisco.

At the other tip is **Point Reyes Lighthouse**, an 1870-era beacon located at the foggiest point on the entire Pacific coast. The treacherous waters offshore have witnessed numerous shipwrecks, the first occurring way back in 1595. The original lighthouse, constructed to prevent these calamities, incorporated over a thousand pieces of crystal in its intricate lens. A modern beacon eventually replaced this multifaceted instrument, but the old lighthouse and an accompanying information center are still open to the public Thursday through Monday. ~ 415-669-1534.

From Olema you can continue north on Route 1 or follow a looping 25-mile detour through the region's **pastoral interior**. On the latter, Sir Francis Drake Boulevard leads east past bald-domed hills and isolated farms. Livestock graze at the roadside while overhead hawks work the range. Grassland gives way to dense forest as you enter the realms of **Samuel P. Taylor State Park**. Then the road opens again to reveal a succession of tiny, woodframe towns.

◄ HIDDEN

At San Geronimo, turn left on Nicasio Valley Road. This carries you further into the pastoral region of west Marin, which varies so dramatically from the county's eastside suburban enclaves. Indeed, the inland valleys are reminiscent more of the Old West than the busy Bay Area. At the Nicasio Reservoir, turn left onto Point Reyes–Petaluma Road and follow it to Sir Francis Drake Boulevard, closing the circle of this rural tour.

From Olema, Route 1 continues north along Tomales Bay, the lovely fjord-shaped inlet. Salt marshes stretch along one side of the road; on the other are rumpled hills tufted with grass. The waterfront village of Marshall consists of fishing boats moored offshore and woodframe houses anchored firmly onshore. Then the road turns inland to Tomales, another falsefront town with clapboard church and country homes. It continues past paint-peeled barns and open pastureland before turning seaward at Bodega Bay.

LODGING

Marin Headlands Hostel, also known as Golden Gate Hostel, is ideally located in the spectacular Marin Headlands section of the Golden Gate National Recreation Area. Housed in a historic woodframe building, this hostel's dormitory-style accommodations go for low prices. There are kitchen facilities available, a game room, and a living room. Like most hostels it is closed during the day; you're permitted access only at night and in the morning. Reservations are advised during the summer. ~ Fort Barry, Building 941; 415-331-2777, 800-444-6111. BUDGET.

HIDDEN ►

Green Gulch Farm, a Zen retreat and organic farm, offers a guest residence program. Located on a 115-acre spread in a lovely valley, it's a restful and enchanting stop. Enroll in the Buddhist Practice Retreat Program, stay three days or longer, and you will pay budget rates. The schedule involves meditation, chanting and bowing, as well as manual labor and includes all meals. Or you can simply rent a room by the night (at deluxe prices including meals). With nearby hiking trails and beaches, it's a unique place. ~ 1601 Shoreline Boulevard near Muir Beach; 415-383-3134. BUDGET AND DELUXE.

Most folks grumble when the fog sits heavy along the coast. At **The Pelican Inn**, guests consider fog part of the ambience. Damp air and chill winds add a final element to the Old English atmosphere at this seven-chamber bed and breakfast. Set in a Tudor-style building near Muir Beach, The Pelican Inn re-creates 16th-century England. There's a pub downstairs with a dart board on one wall

✔ CHECK THESE OUT—UNIQUE LODGING

- *Budget:* Withdraw to **Green Gulch Farm**, a Zen retreat and organic farm, where you can enhance your meditation and chanting skills or relax in serenity. *page 242*
- *Moderate:* Spend the night in an art gallery that doubles as a bed and breakfast at **Tomales Country Inn** and listen to the local population of crickets and bullfrogs. *page 245*
- *Moderate to deluxe:* Look out over the Russian River while settling into a cozy room at **Jenner Inn and Cottages.** *page 257*
- *Deluxe to ultra-deluxe:* Relax next to the Eel River at the **Benbow Inn**, one of the finest old lodges in Northern California. *page 275*

Budget: under $50 Moderate: $50–$90 Deluxe: $90–$120 Ultra-deluxe: over $120

and a fox hunting scene facing on another. The dining room serves country fare like meat pies, prime rib, and bangers. Upstairs the bedrooms complete the theme. The room I saw contained time-honored furnishings, a wooden chest that looked to have barely survived its Atlantic crossing, and several other antiques. The bed was canopied and the walls adorned with period prints. Highly recommended; reserve well in advance. ~ Route 1, Muir Beach; 415-383-6000, fax 415-383-3424. ULTRA-DELUXE.

Sandpiper Motel is ideally located just a short stroll away from Stinson Beach, close enough to hear the surf wash the sand. Once rundown, the motel's rooms and cottages have been thoroughly upgraded and redecorated with country-style furnishings, cable TV, VCRs, and fireplaces. A backyard area with barbecues, tables, and umbrellas is available to guests. ~ 1 Marine Way, Stinson Beach; 415-868-1632. MODERATE TO DELUXE.

High on a hill above Stinson Beach is **Casa del Mar**, a lovely peach-colored stucco Mediterranean-style bed-and-breakfast inn surrounded by terraced gardens brimming with succulents, flowers, herbs, and vegetables. Four upstairs guest rooms have French doors opening onto private verandas and are adorned with such touches as paintings by West Marin artists and soft down comforters. ~ 37 Belvedere Avenue, Stinson Beach; 415-868-2124, fax 415-868-2305, 800-552-2124. DELUXE TO ULTRA-DELUXE.

Smiley's Schooner Saloon and Hotel is one of the cheapest deals around. This modest facility, located in the rustic town of Bolinas, has easy access to the beach. Accommodations are clean and nicely refurbished. The rooms are done in a rose color with antiques and have no radio, TV, phones, or other newfangled inventions. Be forewarned, however: one reader wrote to complain that music from a nearby bar kept her awake long into the night! ~ 41 Wharf Road, Bolinas; 415-868-1311, fax 415-868-0502. MODERATE.

There's also **Grand Hotel**, a tiny business where the two units share a bath and a kitchen. The proprietor also serves as a referral service for other places in town, so check with him about local accommodations. ~ 15 Brighton Avenue, Bolinas; 415-868-1757. BUDGET.

As country living goes, it's darn near impossible to find a place as pretty and restful as Point Reyes. People with wander in their hearts and wonder in their minds have been drawn here for years. Not surprisingly, country inns sprang up to cater to star-struck explorers and imaginative travelers. Seven of these small bed and breakfasts, dotted in towns around Point Reyes National Seashore, have joined together to form an information service, **The Inns of Point Reyes**. Contact them for a descriptive brochure. ~ 415-663-1420. Another good source is **Point Reyes Lodging**, which offers 24-hour information on 22 inns and cottages in coastal Marin. ~ 415-663-1872, 800-539-1872.

Coastal Lodging of West Marin is a telephone service providing information on local accommodations. Specializing in cottages, guest homes, and inns, they can help visitors find lodging all around the Point Reyes area. ~ 415-663-1351.

Within Point Reyes National Seashore, consider the **Point Reyes Hostel**, providing low-rent lodging. In addition to dormitory-style accommodations, the hostel has a patio, ranch-style kitchen, and a living room with wood stove. Perfect for explorers, it is situated near several hiking trails. ~ Limantour Road, Point Reyes National Seashore; Box 247, Point Reyes Station, CA 94956; 415-663-8811. BUDGET.

Foremost among this bed and breakfast confederacy is the **Blackthorne Inn**, an architectural extravaganza set in a forest of oak, bay trees, and Douglas fir. The four-level house is expressive of the flamboyant "woodbutcher's art" building style popular in the 1970s. Using recycled materials and heavy doses of imagination, the builders created a maze of skylights, bay windows, and French doors, capped by an octagonal tower. A spiral staircase corkscrews up through this multitiered affair to the top deck, where an outdoor hot tub overlooks the canyon. There are five bedrooms, three with private baths. Each room has been personalized; the most outstanding is the "Eagle's Nest," occupying the glass-encircled octagon at the very top of this Aquarian wedding cake. ~ 266 Vallejo Avenue, Inverness Park; 415-663-8621, fax 415-663-8635. ULTRA-DELUXE.

Nearby in Inverness there's **Inverness Motel**, commanding a location along Tomales Bay that would be the envy of many well-heeled hostelries. Unfortunately the architect who designed it faced the rooms toward the road, not the water. You can, however, enjoy views of the bay in the motel's common room, which features a billiards table, stereo, pinball machine, and wide-screen television. The guest rooms come equipped with color televisions and cable. ~ 12718 Sir Francis Drake Boulevard, Inverness; 415-669-1081. MODERATE.

In a secluded setting on four acres bordering Tomales Bay is **Sandy Cove Inn**, which offers a private world shared with horses, sheep, deer, osprey, egrets, hawks and quail. Within the Cape Cod–style house are three guest rooms, each with a fireplace, private deck and entrance, Turkish kilim rugs, and antique-finished pine furniture. A country breakfast prepared with home-grown ingredients is served either in the privacy of your own room or in a glass solarium overlooking the grounds. No smoking is permitted anywhere. ~ 12990 Sir Francis Drake Boulevard, Inverness; 415-669-2683, 800-759-2683, fax 415-669-7511. ULTRA-DELUXE.

Another favorite bed and breakfast lies along the flagstone path at **Ten Inverness Way**. The place is filled with pleasant surprises, like fruit trees and flowers in the yard, a player piano, and a warm living room with stone fireplace. The five bedrooms are small but cozy, carpeted wall-to-wall, and imaginatively decorated with hand-fashioned quilts; all have private baths. It's a short stroll from the house to the shops and restaurants of Inverness. ~ 10 Inverness Way, Inverness; 415-669-1648, fax 415-669-7403. DELUXE TO ULTRA-DELUXE.

In the town of Tomales consider **Tomales Country Inn**. It's an old Victorian offering spacious rooms with shared or private bath. The rooms are furnished in an imaginatively slapdash fashion and the entire house is decorated with original paintings. That, you see, is because this bed and breakfast doubles as an art gallery. Why not? It also boasts a library and living room for guest use, farmland out back, and a local population of robins, owls, crickets, and bullfrogs. Personally I rate this place with a sky full of stars. ~ 25 Valley Street, Tomales; 707-878-2041. MODERATE. ◄ HIDDEN

DINING

From the Marin Headlands region, the nearest restaurants are in the bayside town of Sausalito. Then, progressing north, you'll find dining spots scattered throughout the towns and villages along the coast.

Stinson Beach sports several restaurants; my favorite is the **Sand Dollar Restaurant**, with facilities for dining indoors or on the patio. At lunch this informal eatery serves hamburgers and sandwiches. At dinner there are fried prawns, scallops, and fresh fish dishes; they also serve meat dishes like chicken parmesan and beef *médallions*. With oilcloths on the table and random artwork on the wall, it is a local gathering point. ~ 3458 Route 1, Stinson Beach; 415-868-0434. MODERATE.

In Bolinas, consider **The Shop**, where you can pull up a table or counter space and order from a soup, salad, and sandwich menu. With its dark pine walls and rustic decor, this café has a singular air. A good spot for a light meal. Closed Monday. ~ 46 Wharf Road, Bolinas; 415-868-9984. MODERATE.

The Station House Café comes highly recommended by several local residents. There is a down-home feel to this wood-paneled restaurant. Maybe it's the artwork along the walls or the garden patio. Regardless, it's really the food that draws folks from the surrounding countryside. The dinner menu includes fresh oysters, plus chicken, steak, and fish dishes. There are also daily chef's specials, such as salmon with a dill-smoked salmon sauce. Dinners are served with soup or salad, and a basket of cornbread and piping hot popovers. The Station House also features a complete breakfast menu; at lunch time there are light crêpe, pasta, and seafood dishes, plus sandwiches and salads. ~ 11180 Main Street, Point Reyes Station; 415-663-1515. MODERATE. ◄ HIDDEN

The Grey Whale, a woodframe café in the center of tiny Inverness, serves delicious pizza and bakery goods as well as soups and salads. The place has a touch of city style in a country setting; there are overhead fans and an espresso machine. ~ 12781 Sir Francis Drake Boulevard, Inverness; 415-669-1244. MODERATE.

Manka's Inverness Lodge is set in a 1917 hunting lodge with open fireplace and American arts and crafts. This white-tablecloth dining room prepares American regional cuisine. Morning dishes include eggs scrambled with local goat cheese, garden herbs and Inverness wild mushrooms. In the evening you can feast on poached salmon, grilled venison, boar, or duck. Open Friday and Saturday in January, Friday through Monday from February to April, and Thursday through Monday from April to December. ~ 30 Callendar Way, Inverness; 415-669-1034. DELUXE.

SHOPPING

Past Sausalito, the shopping scene along the North Coast is concentrated in a few towns. There are small shops scattered about in rural areas, but the best selection of arts and crafts is located around Point Reyes.

During the '60s and '70s many talented people, caught up in the "back to the land" movement, migrated to the state's northern counties. Here they developed their skills and further refined their art. As a result, crafts like pottery, woodworking, weaving, stained-glass manufacturing, jewelry, and fashion designing have flourished.

Stinson Beach Books may be located in a small town, but it handles a large variety of books. Compressed within the confines of the place is an array of travel books, field guides, bestsellers, novels, how-to handbooks, etc. It's a great place to stop before that long, languorous day at the beach. ~ 3455 Shoreline Highway, Stinson Beach; 415-868-0700.

For an idea of the local art scene, you should certainly stop by **Bolinas Gallery**. Judy Molyneux has stocked it with an impressive selection of her work. ~ 52 Wharf Road, Bolinas; 415-868-0782.

HIDDEN ►

Just one mile north of the Bolinas turnoff on Route 1 there are signs for **Dogtown Pottery**. Follow the bumpy road down to this informal establishment and you'll find a building full of ceramics. Combining fine designs and glazes, this gallery features an assortment of decorative and functional items including early European Celtic pieces. ~ 5953 Shoreline Highway; 415-868-1435.

Gallery Route One spotlights sculptures, photographs, and paintings by contemporary artists. ~ 11101 Route 1, Point Reyes Station; 415-663-1347.

Shaker Shops West is a marvelous store specializing in reproductions of Shaker crafts, particularly furniture. In addition to rag rugs, candlesticks, and woven baskets, there are beautifully handcrafted boxes. The Early American household items range from cross-stitch needlepoint to wall clocks. Touring the store is like visiting a mini-museum dedicated to this rare American community. ~ 5 Inverness Way, Inverness; 415-669-7256.

NIGHTLIFE

When the sun goes down in Bolinas, you are left with several options. Sleep, read, curl up with a loved one, fade into unrelieved boredom, or head for **Smiley's Schooner Saloon**. Since local folks often follow the latter course, you're liable to find them parka-to-parka along the bar. They come to shoot pool, listen to weekend live music, and admire the lavish wood-panel bar. Smiley's, after all, is the only show in town. ~ 41 Wharf Road, Bolinas; 415-868-1311.

Local folks in Point Reyes Station ease up to a similar wooden bar at **Old Western Saloon** practically every night of the week. But on Friday and Saturday, when the place features dancing 'til the wee hours, the biggest crowds of all arrive. Occasional cover. ~ 11201 Route 1, Point Reyes Station; 415-663-1661.

BEACHES & PARKS

KIRBY COVE This pocket beach, located at the end of a one-mile trail, nestles in the shadow of the Golden Gate Bridge. The views from beachside are unreal: gaze up at the bridge's steel lacework or out across the gaping mouth of the Gate. When the fog's away, it's a sunbather's paradise; regardless of the weather, this cove is favored by those who like to fish. Facilities include a picnic area and toilets; restaurants and groceries are available several miles away in Sausalito. ~ The beach is located in the Marin Headlands section of the Golden Gate National Recreation Area. Take the first exit, Alexander Avenue, after crossing the Golden Gate Bridge. Then take an immediate left, following the sign back toward San Francisco. Next, bear right at the sign for Marin Headlands. Follow Conzelman Road three-tenths of a mile to a turnout where a sign will mark the trailhead; 415-331-1540.

▲ There are four sites for tents only. The camping is free but a permit is required and can be obtained at the Marin Headlands Visitors Center in Fort Barry (Field and Bunker roads, Sausalito).

◄ HIDDEN

UPPER FISHERMAN'S BEACH This is a long, narrow corridor of sand tucked under the Marin Headlands. With steep hills behind and a grand view of the Golden Gate in front, it's a perfect place for naturists and nature lovers alike. It is a popular beach for nudists, although not officially recognized as such. It cannot be found on maps or atlases, but local folks and savvy travelers know it well (some call it "Black Sands"). There are no facilities here; restaurants and groceries are several miles away in Sausalito. ~ This beach is located in the Marin Headlands section of the Golden Gate National Recreation Area. Follow the directions to Kirby Cove trailhead (see listing above). Continue on Conzelman

Road for two-and-a-third miles. Shortly after passing the steep downhill section of this road, you'll see a parking lot on the left with a trailhead. Follow the trail to the beach.

RODEO BEACH A broad sandy beach, this place is magnificent not only for the surrounding hillsides and nearby cliffs, but also for the quiescent lagoon at its back. It boasts a miniature island offshore, named appropriately for the creatures that turned its surface white—Bird Rock. Given its proximity to San Francisco, Rodeo Beach is a favorite among the natives. The beach has restrooms; restaurants and groceries are several miles away in Sausalito. ~ Located in the Marin Headlands section of the Golden Gate National Recreation Area. After crossing Golden Gate Bridge on Route 101, take the first exit, Alexander Avenue. Then take an immediate left, following the sign back toward San Francisco. Next, bear right at the sign for Marin Headlands. Follow this road to Rodeo Beach; 415-331-1540.

▲ Though not permitted on the beach, camping is available at three campgrounds in the area. They are hike-in campgrounds, ranging from three to six miles. There are five sites at Haypress, three sites at Hawkcamp, and three sites at Bicentennial. These campgrounds are for tents only, all are free, and permits are required. Call the information number above for more details.

MUIR WOODS NATIONAL MONUMENT If it weren't for the crowds, this redwood preserve would rank little short of majestic. Designated a national treasure by President Theodore Roosevelt in 1908, it features stately groves of tall timber. There are six miles of hiking trails, a snack bar, a gift shop, and restrooms. ~ Located off Route 1 on Panoramic Highway about 17 miles north of San Francisco; 415-388-2596.

MT. TAMALPAIS STATE PARK Spectacularly situated between Mt. Tamalpais and the ocean, this 6300-acre park offers everything from mountaintop views to a rocky coastline. Fifty miles of hiking trails wind past stands of cypress, Douglas fir, Monterey pine, and California laurel. The countryside draws nature lovers and sightseers alike. The park's facilities include picnic areas, restrooms, a refreshment stand, and a visitors center (open weekends only); ranger stations are located in various parts of the park. Parking fee, $5. ~ Follow Route 1 north through Mill Valley; turn right on Panoramic Highway, which runs along the park border.

▲ There are 15 sites at Pantoll Park Headquarters (415-388-2070); facilities in this well-shaded spot include picnic areas, restrooms, running water; seven-day limit; $14 per night. There's also camping at Frank Valley Horsecamp (good for people on horseback), located near Muir Beach in the southwest end of the Park. Picnic tables, pit toilet, running water; reservations are required and can be obtained at park headquarters. For information on Steep Ravine Environmental Camp see the listing below. At **West Point Inn** there are rooms, cabins, and kitchen facilities available. Located along Matt Davis Trail, the inn provides a marvelous retreat. Bring a sleeping bag and food. No heat or electricity; very rustic. Advance reservations are required; $29 per person nightly. ~ Junction of Old Railroad Grade and Old Stage Road; 415-388-9955.

MUIR BEACH Because of its proximity to San Francisco, this spot is a favorite among local people. Located at the foot of a coastal valley, Muir forms a semicircular cove. There's a sandy beach and ample opportunity for picnicking. Other than picnic tables the facilities are limited to toilets; restaurants and groceries are located several miles away. ~ Located on Route 1, about 16 miles north of San Francisco; 415-388-2596.

STEEP RAVINE ENVIRONMENTAL CAMP Set on a shelf above the ocean, this outstanding site is bounded on the other side by sharp slopes. Contained within Mt. Tamalpais State Park, it features a small beach and dramatic sea vista. This is a good place for nature study. Restaurants and groceries are located one mile away in Stinson Beach. ~ Located along a paved road off Route 1 about one mile south of Stinson Beach. Turn at the sign; 415-388-2070.

▲ There are six walk-in tent sites ($9 per night) and ten rustic cabins ($30 per night). Reservations are required; call DESTINET at 800-444-7275.

RED ROCK BEACH One of the area's most popular nude beaches, this pocket beach is wall-to-wall with local folks on sunny weekends. Well protected along its flank by steep hillsides, Red Rock is an ideal sunbathers' retreat. There are no facilities here; restaurants and groceries are located one mile away in Stinson Beach. ~ Part of Mt. Tamalpais State Park, Red Rock is located off Route 1 about one mile south of Stinson Beach. Watch for a large (often crowded) parking area on the seaward side of the highway. Follow the steep trail down to the beach. ◄ HIDDEN

STINSON BEACH PARK One of Northern California's finest beaches, this broad, sandy corridor curves for three miles. Backdropped by rolling hills, Stinson also borders beautiful Bolinas Lagoon. Besides being a sunbather's haven, it's a great place for beachcombers and birdwatchers. To escape the crowds congregating here weekends, stroll up to the north end of the beach. You'll find a narrow sand spit looking out on Bolinas. You still won't have the beach entirely to yourself, but a place this beautiful is worth sharing. There are picnic areas, a visitors center (open summers only), a snack bar, and restrooms; lifeguards in summer. Because of currents from Bolinas Lagoon, the water here is a little warmer than elsewhere. If you dare swim anywhere along the North Coast, it might as well be here. ~ Located along Route 1 in the town of Stinson Beach, 23 miles north of San Francisco; 415-868-0942.

BOLINAS LAGOON BEACH Beginning near Bolinas Lagoon and curving around the town perimeter, this salt-and-pepper beach provides ample opportunity for walking. A steep bluff borders the beach. In the narrow mouth of the lagoon you can often see harbor seals and waterfowl. There are no facilities but the town of Bolinas is within walking distance. ~ Located at the end of Wharf Road in Bolinas.

AGATE BEACH AND DUXBURY REEF A prime area for beachcombers, Agate Beach is rich in found objects and objects waiting to be found—(however, collecting is not permitted). At low tide, Duxbury Reef to the south is equally outstanding for tidepool gazing. Both are highly recommended for adventurers, daydreamers, and amateur biologists. There are no facilities but downtown Bolinas is nearby. ~ From Olema–Bolinas Road in Bolinas, go up the hill on Mesa Road, left on Overlook Drive, and right on Elm Road. Follow Elm Road to the parking lot at the end; take the path down to the ocean.

HIDDEN ►

HAGMAIER POND Favored by swimmers and nude sunbathers, this miniature lake offers a variation from nearby ocean beaches. It's fringed with grassland and bounded by forest, making it an idyllic spot within easy reach of the highway. There are no facilities; restaurants and groceries are located several miles away in Bolinas. ~ On Route 1 go three-and-a-half miles north of the Bolinas turnoff (at the foot of Bolinas Lagoon). You'll see a shallow parking lot on the right side of the highway. A dirt road leads uphill several hundred yards to the lake; take the first left fork.

SAMUEL P. TAYLOR STATE PARK Located several miles inland, this redwood facility provides an opportunity to experience the coastal interior. The place is heavily wooded and offers 2900 acres to roam. In addition to the campgrounds, there are hiking trails and a creek. The park has picnic areas, restrooms, and showers; restaurants and groceries are located nearby in several small towns. Day-use fee, $5. ~ Located on Sir Francis Drake Boulevard, east of Route 1 and six miles from Olema; 415-488-9897.

▲ There are 60 sites, 25 for tents only, no hookups; $12 to $16 per night. Reservations are required from Memorial Day through Labor Day; call DESTINET at 800-444-7275.

POINT REYES NATIONAL SEASHORE One of the great natural features of Northern California, this 72,000-acre park contains everything from wind-blown beaches to dense pine forests. No traveler should miss it. The park's facilities include an information center, picnic areas, restrooms, and miles of hiking trails; restaurants and groceries are located in the nearby towns of Inverness and Point Reyes Station. ~ It's off Route 1 about 40 miles north of San Francisco; 415-663-1092.

▲ You may camp in any of four campgrounds, which are all accessible only by hiking trails. Sky Camp, with 12 primitive sites, sits on the side of Mt. Wittenberg, commanding stunning views of Drake's Bay. Coast Camp rests on a bluff above a pretty beach; there are 14 primitive sites. Glen Camp lies in a forested valley and has 12 primitive sites. Wildcat Camp nestles in a meadow near the beach; there are 7 primitive sites. Each camp is equipped with toilets, water, and picnic areas. Wood fires are not allowed; plan to bring alternate campfire materials. Camping is free, but permits are required. You are limited to four nights in the park. Reservations are strongly recommended. Permits can be obtained at Bear Valley Visitors Center. ~ Point Reyes, CA 94956; 415-663-1092.

LIMANTOUR BEACH This white sand beach is actually a spit, a narrow peninsula pressed between Drake's Bay and an estuary. It's an exotic area of sand dunes and sea breezes. Ideal for exploring, the region shelters over 350 bird species. There's good (but cold) swimming and fishing seaside; in the estuary behind the beach you can search for clams, mussels, and crabs as well as seals and stingrays. The only facilities are toilets; restaurants and groceries are nearby in Inverness. ~ Once in Point Reyes National Seashore, follow Limantour Road to the end.

▲ None, but the Point Reyes Youth Hostel is located on the road to Limantour.

TOMALES BAY STATE PARK This delightful park, which abuts on Point Reyes National Seashore, provides a warm, sunny alternative to Point Reyes' frequent fog. The water, too, is warmer here in Tomales Bay, making it a great place for swimming, as well as fishing and boating. Rimming the park are several sandy coves; most accessible of these is Heart's Desire Beach, flanked by bluffs and featuring nearby picnic areas. From Heart's Desire a self-guided nature trail goes northwest to Indian Beach, a long stretch of white sand fringed by trees. Hiking trails around the park lead to other secluded beaches, excellent for picnics and day hikes. The park has picnic areas and restrooms; restaurants and groceries are four miles away in Inverness. Day-use fee, $5. ~ From Route 1 in Olema take Sir Francis Drake Boulevard to Inverness. From Inverness it's another eight miles. When Sir Francis Drake forks, take the right fork, which becomes Pierce Point Road. Then follow Pierce Point Road to the park; 415-669-1140.

▲ There are six sites for tents only; $3 per night per person. Campsites are hike-in or bike-in only.

SHELL BEACH Actually part of Tomales Bay State Park, this pocket beach is several miles from the park entrance. As a result, it is often uncrowded. A patch of white sand bordered by steep hills, Shell Beach is ideal for swimming and picnicking. The only facilities are toilets; restaurants and groceries are located two miles away in Inverness. ~ Once in Point Reyes National Seashore, take Sir Francis Drake Boulevard one mile past Inverness, then turn right at Camino del Mar. The trailhead is located at the end of this street; follow the trail three-tenths of a mile down to the beach.

HIDDEN ►

MARSHALL BEACH This secluded beach on Tomales Bay is a wonderful place to swim and sunbathe, often in complete privacy. The beach is a lengthy strip of white sand fringed by cypress trees. The only facilities are toilets; restaurants and groceries are eight miles away (over hiking trail and roads) in Inverness. ~ Once in Point Reyes National Seashore, take Pierce Point Road. Immediately after passing the entrance to Tomales Bay State Park, turn right onto the paved road. This road travels uphill, turns to gravel and goes two-and-six-tenths miles to a gate. From the gate you hike one-and-a-half miles along the road/trail to the beach.

ABBOTTS LAGOON Because of its rich waterfowl population and beautiful surrounding dunes, this is a favorite place among hikers. From the lagoon it's an easy jaunt over the dunes to Point Reyes Beach. The only facilities are toilets; restaurants and groceries are located six miles away in Inverness. ~ Once in Point Reyes National Seashore, take Pierce Point Road. The trailhead is located along the roadside, two miles past the turnoff for Tomales Bay State Park; follow the trail one mile to the lagoon.

KEHOE BEACH Bounded by cliffs, this strand is actually the northern end of ten-mile-long Point Reyes Beach. It's a lovely place, covered with wildflowers in spring and boasting a seasonal lagoon. The isolation makes it a great spot for explorers. The only facilities are toilets (at the trailhead); restaurants and groceries are eight miles away in Inverness. ~ Once in Point Reyes National Seashore, take Pierce Point Road. The trailhead is along the roadside four miles past the turnoff for Tomales Bay State Park; follow the trail a half-mile to the beach.

MCCLURE'S BEACH Of the many beautiful beaches in Point Reyes National Seashore, this is by far my favorite. It is a white sand beach protected by granite cliffs which stand like bookends on either flank. Tidepool watching is a great sport here; if you arrive during low tide it's possible to skirt the cliffs along the south end and explore a pocket beach next door. But don't let a waxing tide catch you sleeping! Swimming is dangerous here; surf fishing, birdwatching, and driftwood gathering more than make up for it. Quite simply, places like this are the reason folks visit Northern California. The only facilities are toilets (at the trailhead); restaurants and groceries are 12 miles away in Inverness. ~ Located in

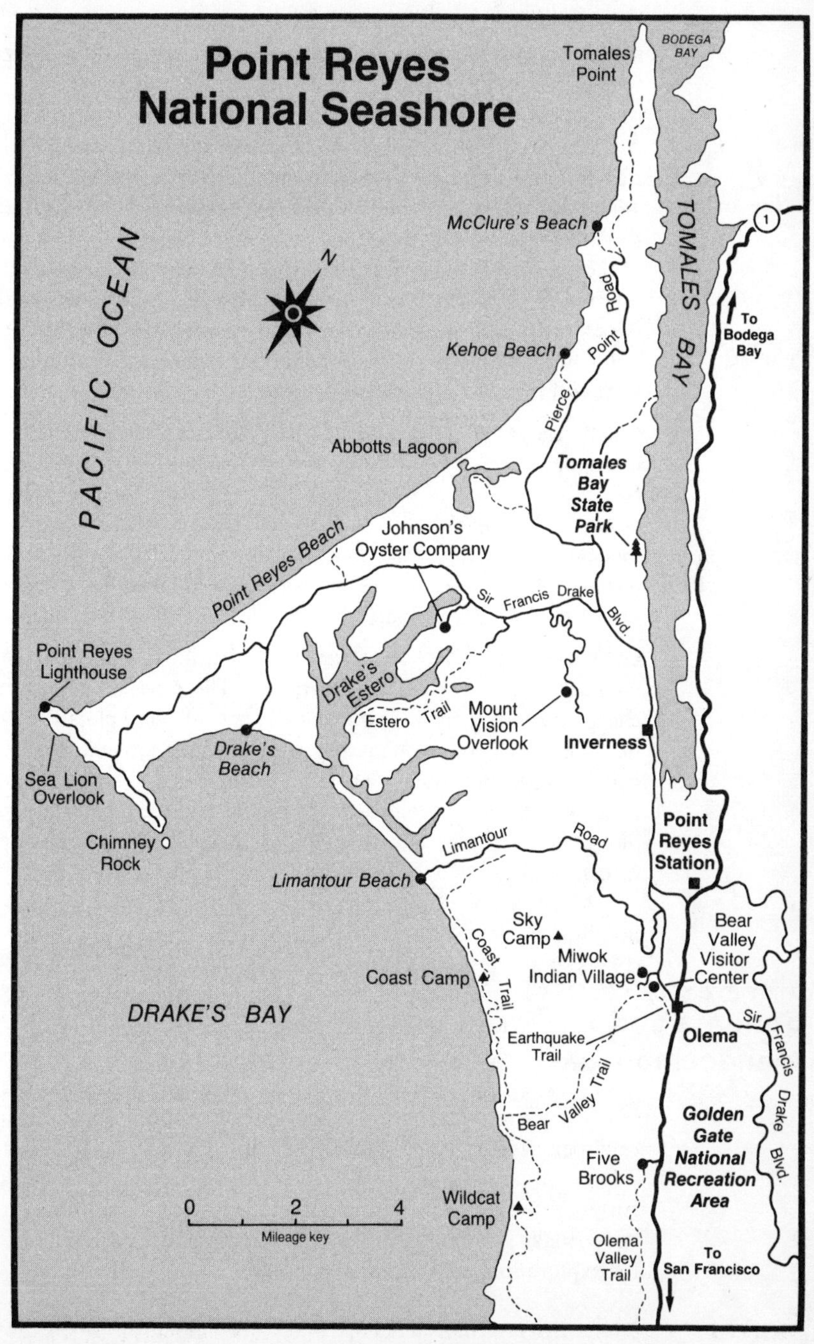
Point Reyes
National Seashore
Tomales Point
BODEGA BAY
TOMALES BAY
To Bodega Bay
1
PACIFIC OCEAN
N
McClure's Beach
Kehoe Beach
Pierce Point Road
Abbotts Lagoon
Tomales Bay State Park
Point Reyes Beach
Johnson's Oyster Company
Sir Francis Drake Blvd.
Point Reyes Lighthouse
Drake's Estero
Estero Trail
Mount Vision Overlook
Inverness
Drake's Beach
Sea Lion Overlook
Chimney Rock
Limantour Road
Point Reyes Station
Limantour Beach
Sky Camp
Bear Valley Visitor Center
Miwok Indian Village
Coast Camp
Coast Trail
Olema
Sir Francis Drake Blvd.
DRAKE'S BAY
Earthquake Trail
Bear Valley Trail
Golden Gate National Recreation Area
Five Brooks
Wildcat Camp
0
2
4
Mileage key
Olema Valley Trail
To San Francisco

Point Reyes National Seashore at the end of Pierce Point Road. A steep trail leads a half-mile down to the beach.

POINT REYES BEACH It will become wonderfully evident why this is nicknamed "Ten Mile Beach" when you cast eyes on this endless sand swath. A great place for whale watching, beachcombing, and fishing, this is not the spot for swimming. Sharks, riptides, and unusual wave patterns make even wading inadvisable. Also the heavy winds along this coastline would chill any swimmer's plans. But that does not detract from the wild beauty of the place, or the fact you can jog for miles along this strand (also referred to as North Beach and South Beach). Restrooms are the park's only facilities; restaurants and groceries are located nine miles away in Inverness. ~ Located off Sir Francis Drake Boulevard about 14 miles from park headquarters.

DRAKE'S BEACH Edged by cliffs, this crescent beach looks out upon the tip of Point Reyes. Since it's well protected by Drake's Bay, this is a good swimming spot. It also provides interesting hikes along the base of the cliffs to the inlet at Drake's Estero. Facilities include picnic areas, restrooms, a visitors center, and a snack bar; restaurants and groceries are ten miles away in Inverness. ~ Located off Sir Francis Drake Boulevard 15 miles from park headquarters.

OLEMA RANCH CAMPGROUND This roadside camping park has facilities for trailers and tent campers. The price however, ain't cheap—$16 for a tent and two people. That will buy a plot of ground in a grassy area. You won't have a sense of wilderness amid the Winnebagos here, but the place is strategically situated along Route 1 near the turnoff for Point Reyes National Seashore. There are picnic areas, restrooms, showers, and a laundromat; restaurants are nearby. ~ Located at 10155 Route 1 in Olema; 415-663-8001.

▲ There are 115 sites for tents and another 91 for RVs (full hookups available); $16 to $24 per night.

Sonoma and Mendocino Coast

Just north of Marin County lie the coastlines of Sonoma and Mendocino, beautiful and still lightly developed areas. Placid rangeland extends inward while along the shoreline, surf boils against angular cliffs. Far below are pocket beaches and coves; offshore rise dozens of tiny rock islands, or sea stacks. The entire coast teems with fish—salmon and steelhead—as well as crabs, clams, and abalone. Rip currents, sneaker waves, and the coldest waters this side of the Arctic make swimming inadvisable. But the landscape is wide open for exploration, enchanting and exotic.

SIGHTS

Jenner, Mendocino, and Fort Bragg are among the small towns along this endless coastline, but the first place you'll come to is a somewhat different type community. In fact the fishing village of

Bodega Bay might look vaguely familiar, for it was the setting of Alfred Hitchcock's eerie film *The Birds*. It's questionable whether any cast members remain among the population of snowy egrets, brown pelicans, and blue herons, but the Bay still supports a variety of winged creatures.

For a rustic detour, follow Coleman Valley Road when it departs from Route 1 north of Bodega Bay. It weaves through farmland and offers great views of ocean and mountains, and leads to the forest-rimmed village of **Occidental.**

Here, at **Lucas Wharf**, and elsewhere along this working waterfront, you can watch fishermen setting off into the fog every morning and hauling in their catch later in the day. ~ Route 1 and Smith Brothers Lane, Bodega Bay.

When Route 1 winds down to the woodframe town of **Jenner** (population 200, elevation 19), where the broad Russian River meets the ocean, you can take Route 116 up the river valley to the fabled Russian River resort area and the town of Guerneville.

The Russians for whom the river is named were explorers and trappers sailing down the Pacific coast from Russian outposts in Alaska. They came in search of sea otters and in hope of opening trade routes with the early Spanish settlers. In 1812 these bold outlanders went so far as to build **Fort Ross**, a wooden fortress overlooking the sea. The old Russian stronghold, 13 miles north of Jenner, is today a state historic park. Touring the reconstructed fort you'll encounter a museum, an old Russian Orthodox chapel, a stockade built of hand-tooled redwood barracks and officers' houses, and two seven-sided blockhouses. Together they provide an insight into an unusual chapter in California history. Admission. ~ 707-847-3286.

From Jenner north through Fort Ross and beyond, Route 1 winds high above the coast. Every curve exposes another awesome view of adze-like cliffs slicing into the sea. Driving this corkscrew route can jangle the nerves, but the vistas are soothing to the soul. With the exception of scattered villages, the coastline remains undeveloped. You'll pass sunbleached wooden buildings in the old town of Stewart Point. Then the road courses through **Sea Ranch,** a development bitterly opposed by environmentalists, which nevertheless displays imaginative contemporary-design houses set against a stark sea.

Just north of Point Arena, a side road from Route 1 leads out to **Point Arena Lighthouse**. The original lighthouse, built in 1870, was destroyed in the 1906 San Francisco earthquake, which struck Point Arena even more fiercely than the bay city. The present beacon, rebuilt shortly afterwards, rises 115 feet from a narrow peninsula. The lighthouse is open for tours. The views, by definition, are outstanding. Open from 11 a.m. to 2:30 p.m. during the week and from 10:30 a.m. to 3:30 p.m. on weekends. Admission. ~ 707-882-2777.

In Mendocino County, the highway passes through tiny seaside villages. Elk, Albion, and Little River gaze down on the ocean from rocky heights. The coastline is an intaglio of river valleys, pocket beaches, and narrow coves. Forested ridges, soft and green in appearance, fall away into dizzying cliffs.

The houses which stand amid this continental turmoil resemble Maine saltboxes and Cape Cod cottages. In the town of Mendocino, which sits on a headland above the sea, you'll discover New England incarnate. Settled in 1852, the town was built largely by Yankees who decorated their village with wooden towers, Victorian homes, and a Gothic Revival Presbyterian church. The town, originally a vital lumber port, has become an artists' colony. With a shoreline honeycombed by beaches and a villagescape capped with a white church steeple, Mendocino is a mighty pretty corner of the continent.

Mendocino Headlands State Park, located atop a sea cliff, offers unmatched views of the town's tumultuous shoreline. From the bluffs you can gaze down at placid tidepools and wave-carved grottoes.

Adjacent to the park is the historic **Ford House**, an 1854 home with a small museum, which also serves as a visitors center for the park. ~ Main Street, Mendocino; 707-937-5397.

The best way to experience this antique town is by stopping at the **Kelly House Museum**. Set in a vintage home dating from 1861, the museum serves as an historical research center and unofficial chamber of commerce. Open daily from 1 to 4 p.m. from June 1 through September; open Friday through Monday from October through May. Admission. ~ 45007 Albion Street, Mendocino; 707-937-5791.

Among Mendocino's intriguing locales are the **Chinese Temple**, a 19th-century religious shrine located on Albion Street; the **Presbyterian Church**, a national historic landmark on Main Street; and the **MacCallum House**, a Gingerbread Victorian on Albion Street, which has been reborn as an inn and restaurant. Another building of note is the **Masonic Hall**, an 1865 structure adorned with a hand-carved redwood statue on the roof. ~ Ukiah Street.

Then after meandering the side streets, stop at the **Mendocino Art Center**. Here exhibits by painters, potters, photographers, textile workers, and others will give an idea of the tremendous talent contained in tiny Mendocino. ~ 45200 Little Lake Street, Mendocino; 707-937-5818.

North of town, on the way to Fort Bragg, stop at **Jug Handle State Reserve**. Here you can climb an ecological stairway which ascends a series of marine terraces. On the various levels you'll encounter the varied coast, dune, and ridge environments that form the area's diverse ecosystem. ~ Along Route 1 about one mile north of Caspar; 707-937-5804.

Near the center of Fort Bragg you can board the **Skunk train** for a half or full-day ride aboard a steam engine or a diesel-powered railcar. Dating from 1885, the Skunk was originally a logging train; today it also carries passengers along a 40-mile route through mountains and redwoods to the inland town of Willits and back. For information, contact California Western Railroad. ~ Fort Bragg; 707-964-6371.

North of Fort Bragg, Route 1 runs past miles of sand dunes and traverses several small towns. Then, after having followed the coast all the way from Southern California, it abruptly turns inland. The reason is the mysterious Lost Coast of California. Due north, where no highway could possibly run, the King Range vaults out of the sea, rising over 4000 feet in less than three miles. It is a wilderness inhabited by black bears and bald eagles, with an abandoned lighthouse and a solitary beach piled with ancient Indian shellmounds.

LODGING

Located a few miles east of Bodega Bay, the **Inn at Occidental** is a charming Victorian homestead encircled by a wide porch bedecked with pots of pink geraniums and white wicker rockers. The eight guest rooms are furnished with antique mahogany and pine beds and display cases of antique glass and pottery from the owner's private collection. ~ 3657 Church Street, Occidental; 707-874-1047, 800-522-6324, fax 707-874-1078. DELUXE TO ULTRA-DELUXE.

A prime Jenner resting spot is **Jenner Inn and Cottages**, a bed and breakfast overlooking the river. Several buildings comprise Murphy's spread: you can rent a room, a suite, even a house. One of the less expensive accommodations, the personalized "Gull Room," features a quilted bed, old oak wardrobe, and a deck overlooking the river. The "Captain Will's Room," a higher-priced suite, adds features like a hand-carved headboard, living room with a wood stove and antique rocker, and a loft for extra guests. ~ 10400 Route 1, Jenner; 707-865-2377, 800-732-2377, fax 707-865-0829. MODERATE TO DELUXE.

A fair bargain can be found along the coast at **Fort Ross Lodge**, two miles north of the old Russian fort. Overlooking the ocean, this 22-unit establishment consists of a cluster of woodframe buildings. The rooms have ocean views; the ceilings are knotty pine, floors are carpeted wall-to-wall, and the varied decor includes everything from wicker to antique furniture. There are TVs, VCRs, and private baths in all rooms, plus a community sauna and hot tub. ~ 20705 Route 1, Jenner; 707-847-3333, fax 707-847-3330. MODERATE TO ULTRA-DELUXE.

Several lodges along the California coast reflect in their architecture the raw energy and naked beauty of the surrounding sea. Such a one is **Timber Cove Inn**. Elemental in style, it is a labyrinth of unfinished woods and bald rocks. The heavy timber lobby is dominated by a walk-in stone fireplace and sits astride a Japanese pond. The 49 guest rooms are finished in redwood with beams and columns exposed. Many are decorated with Ansel Adams prints. Furniture is fashioned from oak and a Japanese motif is reflected in the hot tubs. A bit too stark and unfinished for my taste, the guest rooms nevertheless afford marvelous views of the mountains and open sea. Many have decks, fireplaces, and hot tubs. Timber Cove, fittingly, rests on a cliff directly above the ocean. Restaurant and lounge. ~ 21780 North Route 1, 15 miles north of Jenner; 707-847-3231, fax 707-847-3704. DELUXE TO ULTRA-DELUXE.

Set on a plateau above the ocean, **Stillwater Cove Ranch** is set on lovely grounds and populated with peacocks. Formerly a boys' school, this complex of buildings has been transformed into a restful retreat. Accommodations are varied, from single rooms to a cottage with a fireplace. Even the dairy barn can house guests: it's been converted to a bunkhouse with kitchen. Stillwater Cove is certainly worth checking into. Closed for one week before Christmas. ~ 22555 Route 1, 16 miles north of Jenner; 707-847-3227. BUDGET TO MODERATE.

Accessible via a scenic country lane, **Timberhill Ranch** is as serene and simple a resort as you'll find anywhere in California. Fifteen handmade cedar cabins dot the forested hillside property, each with cozy quilts, fireplaces, and decks where you can enjoy breakfast . . . or share it with the resident ducks. Tennis courts, a pool, and a jacuzzi with a view may be enough to keep guests ranch-bound for days. Rates include breakfast and dinner, the last a multicourse gourmet affair in the main lodge. ~ 35755 Hauser Bridge Road, Cazadero; 707-847-3258, fax 707-847-3342. ULTRA-DELUXE.

Sea Ranch Lodge is the ultimate Sonoma coast retreat. Miles of secluded beaches and hiking trails, fields of wildflowers and beautiful bluffs make this resort a perennial favorite. The lodge, faced with weathered wood siding, offers 20 rooms, all with views. The wood furniture is handmade, as are the luxurious quilts. But the biggest draw is the array of contemporary-style homes, spaced far apart and set amid fields of windblown grasses. Offering sea and mountain views, they constitute the heart and soul of this unique North Coast colony. There are tennis courts, a restaurant, a store, a playground, and a pool (the latter available for guests in the homes, not the main lodge). ~ 60 Sea Walk Drive, Sea Ranch; 707-785-2371, 800-732-7262, fax 707-785-2243. DELUXE TO ULTRA-DELUXE.

Mar Vista Cottages at Anchor Bay is a community of 12 separate cottages scattered around eight acres of oceanview property. Each is an old woodframe affair with a sitting room and kitchen as well as a bedroom. Several are equipped with decks, fireplaces, or wood stoves. A soaking tub and barbecue facility on the property are surrounded by trees; a long path leads across Route 1 to the beach. ~ 35101 South Route 1, Gualala; 707-884-3522. MODERATE TO DELUXE.

Built in 1903, the **Gualala Hotel** is a massive two-story structure. It's an old clapboard affair, fully refurbished, that includes a bar and dining room. The 19 rooms upstairs are rather small, but the wallpaper, decor, and old-time flourishes give the place a comfy traditional feel, making it a rare find on the North Coast. ~ 39301 Route 1, Gualala; 707-884-3441. BUDGET TO MODERATE. ◄ HIDDEN

A short distance north of the Gualala Hotel, but a long step up in price, is the **Old Milano Hotel**. Dating from 1905, it is one of those very special places that people return to year after year. The two-story shiplap house rises between a delicately tended garden and the sea. Anchored just offshore is Castle Rock, a dramatic sea stack. But this pales in comparison to the interior. Each of the six bedrooms upstairs has been furnished and decorated with luxurious antiques: oil paintings, brass lamps, quilts, oak headboards, and plump armchairs. There are two shared baths, and the downstairs master suite has its own bathroom. The "wine parlor" downstairs features a stone fireplace and the music room is decorated with William Morris designs. Little wonder the house is registered as a historic place. There's also a cottage available, as well as an old caboose converted into living quarters. ~ 38300 Route 1, Gualala; 707-884-3256. MODERATE TO ULTRA-DELUXE.

Every one of the sixteen rooms at **Seacliff** stares straight at the Pacific Ocean, and some days you can see whales rubbing their bellies on the sandbar. Accommodations are simple but entirely comfortable, with everything you need for an atmospheric retreat: wood-burning fireplaces, two-person whirlpool tubs with ocean views, downy kingsize beds and plush comforters, coffee makers and refrigerators stocked with complimentary champagne. The staff treats you like family. ~ Route 1, Gualala; 707-884-1213, 800-400-5053. ULTRA-DELUXE.

THE GARDEN BY THE SEA

For a thoroughly delightful stroll to the sea, meander through the **Mendocino Coast Botanical Gardens**. This coastal preserve, with three miles of luxuriant pathways, is "a garden for all seasons" with something always in bloom. The unique Northern California coastal climate is conducive to heathers, perennials, succulents, and rhododendrons, which grow in colorful profusion here. Trails lead past gardens of ivy, ferns, and dwarf conifers to a coastal bluff with vistas up and down the rugged shoreline. Admission. ~ 18220 North Route 1, Fort Bragg; 707-964-4352.

Country inns of this genre are quite abundant farther north. Near the town of Mendocino there are numerous bed and breakfasts, some outstanding. The seaside towns of Elk, Albion, Little River, Mendocino, and Fort Bragg each house several. Prices are generally high, but for intimacy and personal care, Northern California's inns are unparalleled.

Among the more renowned is **Harbor House Inn**. Set on a rise overlooking the ocean, the house is built entirely of redwood. The living room alone, with its fireplace and exposed-beam ceiling, is an architectural feat. The house was modeled on a design exhibited at San Francisco's 1915 Panama–Pacific Exposition. Of the ten bedrooms and cottages, all have fireplaces and patterned wallpaper as well as antique appointments. Rates include breakfast and dinner. ~ 5600 South Route 1, Elk; 707-877-3203. ULTRA-DELUXE.

Heritage House was constructed in 1877 and reflects the New England architecture popular then in Northern California. Baby Face Nelson is reputed to have hidden in the old farmhouse which today serves as the inn's reception and dining area. Most guests are housed in nearby cottages which, like the hideout itself, overlook a rocky cove. Some rooms have jacuzzis and private decks. Rates include breakfast and dinner. Closed from the end of November to early February. ~ 5200 North Route 1, Little River; 707-937-5885, 800-235-5885, fax 707-937-0318. DELUXE TO ULTRA-DELUXE.

The New England–style farmhouse that has become **Glendeven** dates even farther back, to 1867. The theme is country living, with a meadow out back and dramatic headlands nearby. The sitting room is an intimate affair with a baby grand piano and comfortable armchairs set before a brick fireplace. In the rooms you're apt to find a bed with wooden headboard, an antique wardrobe, and perhaps ferns hanging from the ceiling. Glendeven is as charming and intimate as a country inn can be. A light breakfast is complimentary. ~ Route 1, Little River; 707-937-0083, 800-822-4536, fax 707-937-6108. DELUXE TO ULTRA-DELUXE.

The **Little River Inn**, centered in a quaint 1850s-era house, has expanded into a mini-resort with 56 units, a restaurant, tennis courts, a lounge, and a nine-hole golf course. Intimacy was lost along the way, but a host of facilities were added. Rooms at the inn proper, decorated in early-California fashion, are moderately priced. There is also a tastefully done motel wing as well as a series of cottages. The cottages are paneled in wood, furnished in hardwood, and decorated with watercolors. Like most of the other accommodations, they afford grand ocean views. ~ 7751 North Route 1, Little River; 707-937-5942. DELUXE TO ULTRA-DELUXE.

Less expensive accommodations can be found at the **Mendocino Hotel**. Set in a falsefront building which dates to 1878, the 51-room hotel is a wonderful place, larger than other nearby country inns, with a wood-paneled lobby, full dining room, and living quarters adorned with antiques. There are rooms in the hotel with both private and shared baths as well as quarters in the garden cottages out back. ~ 45080 Main Street, Mendocino; 707-937-0511, 800-548-0513, fax 707-937-0513. DELUXE TO ULTRA-DELUXE.

The queen of Mendocino is the **MacCallum House Inn**, a Gingerbread Victorian built in 1882. The place is a treasure trove of antique furnishings, knickknacks, and other memorabilia. Many of the rooms are individually decorated with rocking chairs, quilts, and wood stoves. Positively everything—the carriage house, barn, greenhouse, gazebo, even the water tower—has been converted into a guest room. ~ 45020 Albion Street, Mendocino; 707-937-0289, 800-609-0492. MODERATE TO ULTRA-DELUXE.

Also consider **Mendocino Village Inn**, a vintage 1882 house that has two attic rooms, one with a sea view. A blue-and-white clapboard building with mansard roof, the place offers more spacious accommodations with private baths at higher prices. Full breakfast included. ~ 44860 Main Street, Mendocino; 707-937-0246, 800-882-7029. MODERATE TO ULTRA-DELUXE.

The nearby **Sea Gull Inn** has rooms with ocean views. In a land of pricey hotels, this establishment is a rare discovery. Breakfast is included. ~ 44960 Albion Street, Mendocino; 707-937-5204. BUDGET TO DELUXE.

Set on two landscaped acres overlooking Mendocino village and the coast, the **Joshua Grindle Inn** is a 19th-century New England–style farmhouse with spacious rooms, all with sitting areas, and some with woodburning fireplaces and ocean views. An inviting gathering spot during evening hours, the parlor offers a cheerful fire and an antique pump organ. Full breakfast included. ~ 44800 Little Lake Road, Mendocino; 707-937-4143, 800-474-6353. DELUXE TO ULTRA-DELUXE.

For women guests only, **Sallie & Eileen's Place** offers a studio A-frame cottage and a spacious cabin three miles from Mendocino. The studio has a fireplace, rockers, and a sunken tub, while the cabin, which can sleep up to six, has a loft bedroom, a woodstove, a deck, and a private backyard. ~ Box 409, Mendocino, CA 95460; 707-937-2028. MODERATE.

Behind the picket fence of **Pudding Creek Inn** is a pretty pink and white Victorian with an enclosed garden of ferns and fuchsias where guests can unwind in the late afternoon with complimentary beverages and snacks. There are ten individually decorated rooms offering such touches as a stone fireplace, white wicker sitting area, or built-in captain's bed. The rates include a full breakfast served in a sunny room bedecked with pastel velvet chairs and lace tablecloths. ~ 700 North Main Street, Fort Bragg; 707-964-9529. MODERATE TO DELUXE.

The **Bowen's Pelican Lodge & Inn** is an 1890-vintage hotel that has been converted into a country inn with six guest rooms (two with shared baths). The place sits across the street from the ocean with a path that leads down to a sandy beach. ~ 38921 North Route 1, Westport; 707-964-5588. BUDGET TO MODERATE.

DINING

For the best meal hereabouts (or for that matter, anywhere about), head for **River's End Restaurant**. Situated at that momentous crossroad of the Russian River and Pacific Ocean (and commanding a view of both), this outstanding little place is a restaurant with imagination. How else do you explain a dinner menu that ranges from *médallions* of venison to crisped duckling to coconut-fried shrimp; or a Sunday brunch that includes German glazed apple pancakes and *gravlax* with shrimp and capers? Not to mention good service and a selection of apéritifs. River's End is a great place for ocean lovers and culinary adventurers. Open Friday, Saturday, and Sunday from October through May; open daily from June to September. ~ Route 1, Jenner; 707-865-2484. DELUXE.

The **Salt Point Bar and Grill** features a small restaurant serving breakfast, lunch, and dinner. The menu relies heavily on seafood—halibut, oysters, scallops—but also includes chicken, steak, and prawn dishes. At lunch, enjoy a variety of salads, sandwiches, or seafood selections. ~ 23255 Route 1, 17 miles north of Jenner; 707-847-3234. MODERATE TO DELUXE.

The 93-year-old **Gualala Hotel** has an attractive dining room with a menu that varies from country fried chicken to breaded oysters. Stops along the way include snapper, ravioli, and rib-eye steak. Lunch is served and you can also stop for a hearty breakfast featuring omelettes. What makes dining here really special is the old hotel with its big front porch and antique decor. ~ 39301 Route 1, Gualala; 707-884-3441. BUDGET TO MODERATE.

✔ CHECK THESE OUT—UNIQUE DINING

- *Budget:* Meet Mendocino "society" at **Bay View Café** and savor the fluffy omelettes or spicy burgers. *page 263*
- *Moderate:* Dine on fresh oysters or enjoy piping hot popovers at the **Station House**, a local hangout in Point Reyes Station. *page 245*
- *Deluxe:* Don't miss the gourmet feasts at **River's End Restaurant**, where the Pacific meets the Russian River. *page 262*
- *Ultra-deluxe:* Make believe you're in Russia at **St. Orres**, an exceptional eatery where the architecture summons an image of St. Petersburg. *page 263*

Budget: under $8 Moderate: $8–$16 Deluxe: $16–$24 Ultra-deluxe: over $24

Okay, so **St. Orres** is yet another California cuisine restaurant. But it's the only one you'll see that looks as if it should be in Russia rather than along the California coast. With its dizzying spires, this elegant structure evokes images of Moscow and old St. Petersburg. Serving dinner only, the kitchen provides an everchanging menu of fresh game and fish dishes. The fixed-price menu will include hot and chilled soups, poached salmon, rabbit, rack of lamb, stuffed wild boar, and several seasonal specialties. Even if you're not interested in dining, it might be worth a stop to view this architectural extravaganza. Cash or check only. ~ 36601 Route 1, Gualala; 707-884-3303. ULTRA-DELUXE.

The Galley at Arena Cove looks out on a pier as well as a series of ocean bluffs. With a hand-carved bar and woodplank dining room, it's a local seafood restaurant serving fresh red snapper, sautéed prawns, oysters, and broiled swordfish. If an oyster bar and homemade clam chowder don't interest you, there are steaks and chops at this good ol' style eating place. ~ 790 Port Road, Point Arena; 707-882-2189. MODERATE.

Although the dining room at **Harbor House Inn** mainly serves guests at this bed-and-breakfast, there are at least two extra tables for two people each evening. A fire in the fireplace will keep you warm and cozy on a cold coastal night, and in the summer you can watch the sunset over the ocean out of the huge windows. The chef prepares a set menu, served at 7 p.m., with entrées such as salmon, pork tenderloin, or halibut. A vegetarian meal can also be prepared upon request. Reservations are required. ~ 5600 South Route 1, Elk; 707-877-3203. ULTRA-DELUXE.

The **Albion River Inn**, set high on a hillside above the Albion River and the ocean, is a plate-glass dining spot serving California cuisine, and specializing in otherworldly ocean views. The pasta, seafood, vegetables, and herbs are all fresh. You can also dine on steaks and pasta. Dinner only. ~ 3790 North Route 1, Albion; 707-937-4044. MODERATE TO DELUXE.

I'm told that the **Little River Restaurant** is an absolute must. ◄ HIDDEN It's only open Friday through Monday, just for dinner, and has but a half-dozen tables. The California cuisine includes appetizers of escargot and steamed clams. For entrées there are roast duck with apricot-vermouth sauce, quail in a hazelnut-port sauce, and filet mignon stuffed with prosciutto. ~ 7750 North Route 1, Little River; 707-937-4945. MODERATE TO DELUXE.

A morning ritual for locals and visitors alike is to climb the rough-hewn stairs to the loft-like **Bay View Café** for coffee, French toast, or fluffy omelettes. On sunny afternoons, the deck overlooking Main Street and the coastal headlands makes an ideal lunch spot, especially for fish and chips or a jalapeño chile burger. ~ 45040 Main Street, Mendocino; 707-937-4197. BUDGET.

At the **Mendocino Hotel** you can enjoy California-style cuisine in the main dining room or out in the "garden room." The menu represents a mix of meat and seafood entrées such as filet mignon, smoked duck ragoût, and oysters in puff pastry. The ambience in this 19th-century building evokes Mendocino's early days. ~ 45080 Main Street, Mendocino; 707-937-0511. DELUXE.

Situated in a cozy little house, the **Moosse Café** offers imaginative seasonal dishes. There's wild mushroom lasagna, smoked salmon, and braised lamb shank. For dessert of course you have to sample the moosse puff. ~ 390 Kasten Street, Mendocino; 707-937-4323. MODERATE.

For French and California cuisine, **955 Ukiah Street** is an address worth noting. Candles, fresh flowers, and impressionist prints set the tone here. Serving dinner only, it prepares brandied prawns, red snapper in phyllo pastry, roast duck, and calamari. For the diet-conscious, they also offer lighter dishes. Open Wednesday through Sunday July through October and Thursday through Sunday November through May. ~ 955 Ukiah Street, Mendocino; 707-937-1955. MODERATE TO DELUXE.

Mendocino's best-known dining room is well deserving of its renown. **Café Beaujolais**, situated in a small antique house on the edge of town, serves designer dishes. Dinner, served seven nights a week, is ever changing. Perhaps they'll be serving warm duck salad and Thai rock shrimp salad with entrées like *poulet verjus*, chicken braised with Navarro vineyards Verjus, leg of lamb stuffed with garlic, and steamed salmon with chervil *sabayon* sauce. Excellent cuisine; cash or check only. ~ 961 Ukiah Street, Mendocino; 707-937-5614. MODERATE TO DELUXE.

Fort Bragg's favorite dining spot is easy to remember—**The Restaurant**. Despite the name, this is no generic eating place but a creative kitchen serving excellent dinners. It's decorated with dozens of paintings by contemporary artists, lending a sense of the avant-garde to this informal establishment. The Restaurant's menu offers seasonal entrées like sautéed prawns, salmon, rockfish, and vegetarian selections. Open for Sunday brunch, lunch Thursday and Friday, and dinner every day except Wednesday. ~ 418 North Main Street, Fort Bragg; 707-964-9800. MODERATE TO DELUXE.

SHOPPING

In the New England–style town of Mendocino you'll discover a shopper's paradise. Prices are quite dear, but the window browsing is unparalleled. Housed in the town's old Victorians and Cape Cod cottages is a plethora of shops. There are stores specializing in soap, seashells, candles, and T-shirts; not to mention bookstores, potters, jewelers, art galleries, and antique shops galore. Most are located along the woodframe Main Street, but also search out the side streets and passageways in this vintage town.

One particularly noteworthy gallery is the **William Zimmer Gallery**, which houses an eclectic collection of contemporary and traditional arts and crafts. ~ Kasten and Ukiah streets, Mendocino; 707-937-5121. Be sure to also check out **Highlight Gallery**, featuring displays of handmade furniture, contemporary art, jewelry, and woodwork. ~ 45052 Main Street, Mendocino; 707-937-3132. The **Mendocino Art Center** houses numerous crafts studios as well as two art galleries. ~ 45200 Little Lake Street, Mendocino; 707-937-5818.

Books are the order of the day at the **Gallery Bookshop and Bookwinkle's Children's Books**. ~ Main and Kasten streets, Mendocino; 707-937-2665.

NIGHTLIFE

There's music six nights a week at the **Caspar Inn**. This down-home bar room spotlights local bands as well as groups from outside the area. Hit it on the right night and the joint will be rocking. Cover. ~ 14961 Caspar Road, Caspar; 707-964-5565.

For a night on the town, enjoy a quiet drink at the **Mendocino Hotel**. You can relax at a Victorian-style lounge or in an enclosed garden patio. ~ 45080 Main Street, Mendocino; 707-937-0511.

For a pint of Guinness, a game of backgammon, and a roaring fire slip into **Patterson's Pub**. The pub is small, in keeping with its Irish persona, and furnished in dark wood and brass. There's no live entertainment, but the local characters and friendly chit chat should more than make up for the absence of loud music. ~ 10481 Lansing Street, Mendocino; 707-937-4782.

The Restaurant has live jazz on Friday and Saturday nights, and Sunday brunch. ~ 418 North Main Street, Fort Bragg; 707-964-9800.

BEACHES & PARKS

DILLON BEACH Located at the mouth of Tomales Bay, this beach is popular with boaters and clammers. The surrounding hills are covered with resort cottages, but there are open areas and dunes to explore. There are picnic areas and restrooms, groceries, boat rentals, and fishing charters. Day-use fee, $5. ~ From Route 1 in Tomales take Dillon Beach Road west for four miles; 707-878-2204.

▲ Located nearby, Lawson's Landing (707-878-2443) has open meadow camping for tents and RVs (no hookups); $12 per night. Take note: this campground hosts hundreds of trailers.

DORAN REGIONAL PARK This peninsular park is situated on a sand spit between Bodega Harbor and the ocean. With a broad sand beach and good facilities, it's an excellent spot for daytrippers and campers alike. You can explore the tidal flats or fish up on the jetty. There are picnic areas, restrooms, and showers; restaurants and groceries are nearby in Bodega Bay. Day-use fee, $3. ~ Located off Route 1 in Bodega Bay; 707-875-3540.

▲ There are 134 sites for tents and RVs (no hookups); $12 per night for residents and $14 for nonresidents.

BODEGA HEAD There are pocket beaches here dramatically backdropped by granite cliffs. A good place to picnic and explore, this is also a favored whale-watching site. There are restrooms and showers located in nearby Westside Park (707-875-2640). ~ It's off Route 1 in Bodega Bay along Bay Flat Road.

▲ Westside Park has 47 tent/RV sites (no hookups); $14 a night.

SONOMA COAST STATE BEACH This magnificent park extends for 13 miles between Bodega Head and the Vista Trail. It consists of a number of beaches separated by steep headlands; all are within easy hiking distance of Route 1. The beaches range from sweeping strands to pocket coves and abound with waterfowl and shorebirds, clams, and abalone. The park headquarters and information center is at Salmon Creek Beach, where endless sand dunes backdrop a broad beach. Schoolhouse Beach is a particularly pretty pocket cove bounded by rocky cliffs; Portuguese Beach boasts a wide swath of sand; Blind Beach is rather secluded with a sea arch offshore; and Goat Rock Beach faces the town of Jenner and is decorated with offshore rocks. Pick your poison—hiking, tidepooling, birdwatching, whale watching, camping, picnicking, fishing—and you'll find it waiting along this rugged and hauntingly beautiful coastline. Bodega Dunes, Salmon Creek Beach, Schoolhouse Beach, Goat Rock, Portuguese Beach, and Wrights Beach have restrooms; Bodega Dunes and Wrights Beach also feature picnic areas. The closest restaurants and groceries are either in Bodega Bay or Jenner. Day-use fee for developed campgrounds, $5. ~ It's along Route 1 between Bodega Bay and Jenner; 707-865-2391.

▲ At Bodega Dunes, there are 98 tent/RV sites (no hookups); $14 a night. At Wrights Beach, there are 30 tent/RV sites (no hookups); $19 a night. Reservations are required; call DESTINET at 800-444-7275. At Pono Canyon and Willow Creek there are 31 walk-in primitive sites; $9 per night.

FORT ROSS REEF CAMPGROUND Set in a canyon surrounded by bluffs, this facility is beautifully located and features a redwood grove. At one time it was a private park, but the state took it over. The result is a public facility with spectacular surroundings and gorgeous views. There are picnic areas and restrooms; restaurants and groceries twelve miles away in Jenner; small store and deli four miles away in Fort Ross. Day-use fee, $3. ~ Located at 19005 Route 1, 12 miles north of Jenner; watch for a cluster of white barns on the west side of the highway; 707-847-3286.

▲ There are 20 tent/RV sites (no hookups); $10 per night. Open April to November. Depending on the weather, fires may not be allowed.

STILLWATER COVE REGIONAL PARK Situated amid pine trees on a hillside above the ocean, this is a small park with access to a beach. The canyon trail leads up to the restored (but closed) Fort Ross Schoolhouse. There are picnic areas, restrooms, and showers; restaurants and groceries are located within a few miles. Day-use fee, $3. ~ Located on Route 1, about 16 miles north of Jenner; 707-847-3245.

▲ There are 23 tent/RV sites (no hookups); $14 a night.

OCEAN COVE STORE AND CAMPGROUND This privately owned campground has sites on a bluff above a rocky shoreline. The scenery is mighty attractive, and the campsites are well removed from the road. There are hot showers and toilets. ~ Located on Route 1 about 17 miles north of Jenner; 707-847-3422.

▲ There are 90 tent/RV sites(no hookups); $12 per night. Open from April to November.

SALT POINT STATE PARK Extending from the ocean to over 1000 feet elevation, this 6000-acre spread includes coastline, forests, and open range land. Along the shore are weird honeycomb formations called tafoni, caused by sea erosion on coastal sandstone. Up amid the stands of Douglas fir and Bishop pine there's a pygmy forest, where unfavorable soil conditions have caused fully mature redwoods to reach only a few feet in height. Blacktail deer, black bear, mountain lions, and bobcats roam the area. Miles of hiking trails lace the park, including one through a rhododendron reserve. There are picnic areas and restrooms; restaurants and groceries are available within a few miles. Day-use fee, $5. ~ Located on Route 1 about 20 miles north of Jenner; 707-847-3221.

▲ There are several campgrounds here with sites for tents and RVs (no hookups); $3 to $15 per night. Reservations are required on weekends and from April to October; call DESTINET at 800-444-7275.

GUALALA POINT REGIONAL PARK Located where the Gualala River meets the ocean, this charming place has everything from a sandy beach to redwood groves. There are picnic areas, restrooms, and an information center; restaurants and groceries are located in nearby Gualala. Day-use fee, $3. ~ Located along Route 1 due south of Gualala; 707-785-2377.

▲ There are 19 tent/RV sites (no hookups) and 7 walk-in sites; $14 per night for tent/RV sites, $3 for walk-in sites.

MANCHESTER STATE BEACH This wild, windswept beach extends for miles along the Mendocino coast. Piled deep with driftwood, it's excellent for beachcombing and hiking. There are picnic areas, restrooms, and an information center; restaurants and groceries are about eight miles away in Point Arena. ~ Located along Route 1 about eight miles north of Point Arena; 707-937-5804.

▲ There are 46 tent/RV sites (no hookups) and 10 primitive, hike-in environmental sites; $7 to $9 per night.

VAN DAMME STATE PARK Extending from the beach to an interior forest, this 2069-acre park has several interesting features: a "pygmy forest" where poor soil results in fully mature pine trees reaching heights of only six inches to eight feet; a "fern canyon" smothered in different species of ferns; and a "cabbage patch" filled with that fetid critter with elephant ear leaves—skunk cabbage. This park is also laced with hiking trails and offers excellent beachcombing opportunities. Day-use fee, $5 for the fern canyon. Facilities include a visitors center, picnic areas, restrooms, and showers. ~ On Route 1 about 30 miles north of Point Arena, or three miles south of Mendocino; 707-937-5804.

▲ There are 74 tent/RV sites (no hookups); $12 to $16 per night. For reservations call DESTINET at 800-444-7275.

MENDOCINO HEADLANDS AND BIG RIVER BEACH STATE PARKS These adjoining parks form the seaside border of the town of Mendocino. And quite a border it is. The white sand beaches are only part of the natural splendor. There are also wave tunnels, tidepools, sea arches, lagoons, and 360 vistas that sweep from the surf-trimmed shore to the prim villagescape of Mendocino. The only facilities are restrooms; private canoe rental nearby; restaurants and groceries in Mendocino. ~ Located in the town of Mendocino.

RUSSIAN GULCH STATE PARK Set in a narrow valley with a well-protected beach, this park has numerous features. There are marvelous views from the craggy headlands, a waterfall, and a blowhole that rarely blows. Rainbow and steelhead trout inhabit the creek while hawks and ravens circle the forest. There are picnic areas, restrooms, and showers. Day-use fee, $5. ~ Located along Route 1 two miles north of Mendocino; 707-937-5804.

▲ There are 30 sites for tents and RVs (no hookups); $12 to $16 per night. Reservations can be made through DESTINET at 800-444-7275.

MACKERRICHER STATE PARK Another of the region's outstanding parks, this facility features a crescent of sandy beach, dunes, headlands, a lake, a forest, and wetlands. Harbor seals inhabit the rocks offshore and over 90 bird species frequent the area. The park has picnic areas, restrooms, and showers. ~ Along Route 1 about three miles north of Fort Bragg; 707-937-5804.

▲ There are 142 sites for tents and RVs (no hookups) as well as 11 walk-in sites; $12 to $16 per night. Reservations can be made through DESTINET at 800-444-7275.

Redwood Country

Near the nondescript town of Leggett, Route 1 joins Route 101. Logging trucks, those belching beasts that bear down upon you without mercy, become more frequent. You are entering Redwood Country.

This is the habitat of *Sequoia sempervirens*, the coastal redwood, a tree whose ancestors date to the age of dinosaurs and which happens to be the world's tallest living thing. These "ambassadors from another time," as John Steinbeck called them, inhabit a 30-mile-wide coastal fog belt stretching 450 miles from the Monterey area north to Oregon. Redwoods live five to eight centuries, though some have survived over two millennia, while reaching heights over 350 feet and diameters greater than 20 feet.

There is a sense of solitude here uncapturable anywhere else. The trees form a cathedral overhead, casting a deep shade across the forest floor. Solitary sun shafts, almost palpable, cut through the grove; along the roof of the forest, pieces of light jump across the treetops, poised to fall like rain. Ferns and a few small animals are all that survive here. The silence and stillness are either transcendent or terrifying. It's like being at sea in a small boat.

SIGHTS

The Redwood Highway, Route 101, leads north to the tallest, most dense stands of *Sequoia sempervirens*. At **Richardson Grove State Park** the road barrels through the very center of a magnificent grove. A short nature trail leads through this virgin timber, though the proximity of the road makes communing with nature seem a bit ludicrous.

North of Garberville, follow the **Avenue of the Giants**, a 33-mile alternative route which parallels Route 101. This two-lane road winds along the Eel River south fork, tunneling through dense redwood groves. Much of the road is encompassed by **Humboldt Redwoods State Park**, a 52,000-acre preserve with some of the finest forest land found anywhere. Park headquarters contains a visitors center. ~ 707-946-2409.

Farther along is **Founder's Grove**, where a nature trail loops through a redwood stand. The forest is dedicated to early Save-the-Redwoods League leaders who were instrumental in preserving thousands of redwood acres, particularly in this park. Nearby **Rockefeller Forest** has another short loop trail that winds through a redwood grove. Avenue of the Giants continues through towns that are little more than way stations and then rejoins Route 101, which leads north to Eureka.

There are alternate routes to Eureka, however, leading along the perimeter of California's **Lost Coast** region. One of the state's most remote wilderness areas, it is a tumbling region of extraordinary vistas. Here the King Range, with its sliding talus and impassable cliffs, shoots 4087 feet up from the ocean in less than three miles. No road could ever rest along its shoulder. The place has been left primitive, given over to mink, deer, river otter, and black bear; rare bald eagles and peregrine falcons work its slopes.

HIDDEN ►

The range extends about 35 miles. Along the shore is a wilderness beach from which seals, sea lions, and porpoises, as well as gray and killer whales, can be seen. There's also an abandoned lighthouse and the skeletons of ships wrecked on the rocks.

To reach this remote area, from Route 101 near Redway take Briceland–Thorne Road, which turns into Shelter Cove Road as it winds through the King Range.

Shelter Cove is a tiny bay neatly folded between sea cliffs and headlands. A point of embarkation for people exploring the Lost Coast, it has a few stores, restaurants, and hotels. Stock up here: The rest of this backcountry jaunt promises little more than a couple stores.

Outside Shelter Cove you can pick up Kings Peak Road or Ettersburg–Honeydew Road, which connect with Wilder Ridge Road and lead to the general store town of **Honeydew**. This is a prime marijuana growing region and a colony of hippies is bound to be sitting on the stoop swapping tales.

Mattole Road heads northeast, meandering along the Mattole River, to another forest hamlet, **Petrolia**. Nestled in a river valley and marked by a white-steeple church, the town is a scene straight from a Norman Rockwell painting. Hawks glide overhead. Old men rock on their front porches. The fire tower houses a red bell.

HIDDEN ►

Next, Mattole Road ascends a succession of plateaus to a ranch land of unpainted barns and broad shade trees, then noses down to the coastline and parallels the waves for perhaps five miles. Here the setting is Scottish. Hillsides are grazed by herds of sheep and covered with tenacious grasses that shake in the sea wind. The gray sand beach is covered with driftwood. Along the horizon peaks rise in jagged motions, seemingly thrust upward by the lash of the surf.

It's not far to **Cape Mendocino**, second-most westerly point in the contiguous United States. Here you'll have broad views of the ocean, including the menacing shoals where countless ships have been slapped to timber. Next, the road curves up through forest and sheep-grazing lands before rolling down to the gentle pastureland near the unique town of Ferndale.

A Victorian-style hamlet set in the Eel River valley, **Ferndale** is so perfectly refurbished it seems unreal. Main Street and nearby thoroughfares are lined with Gothic Revival, Queen Anne, East-

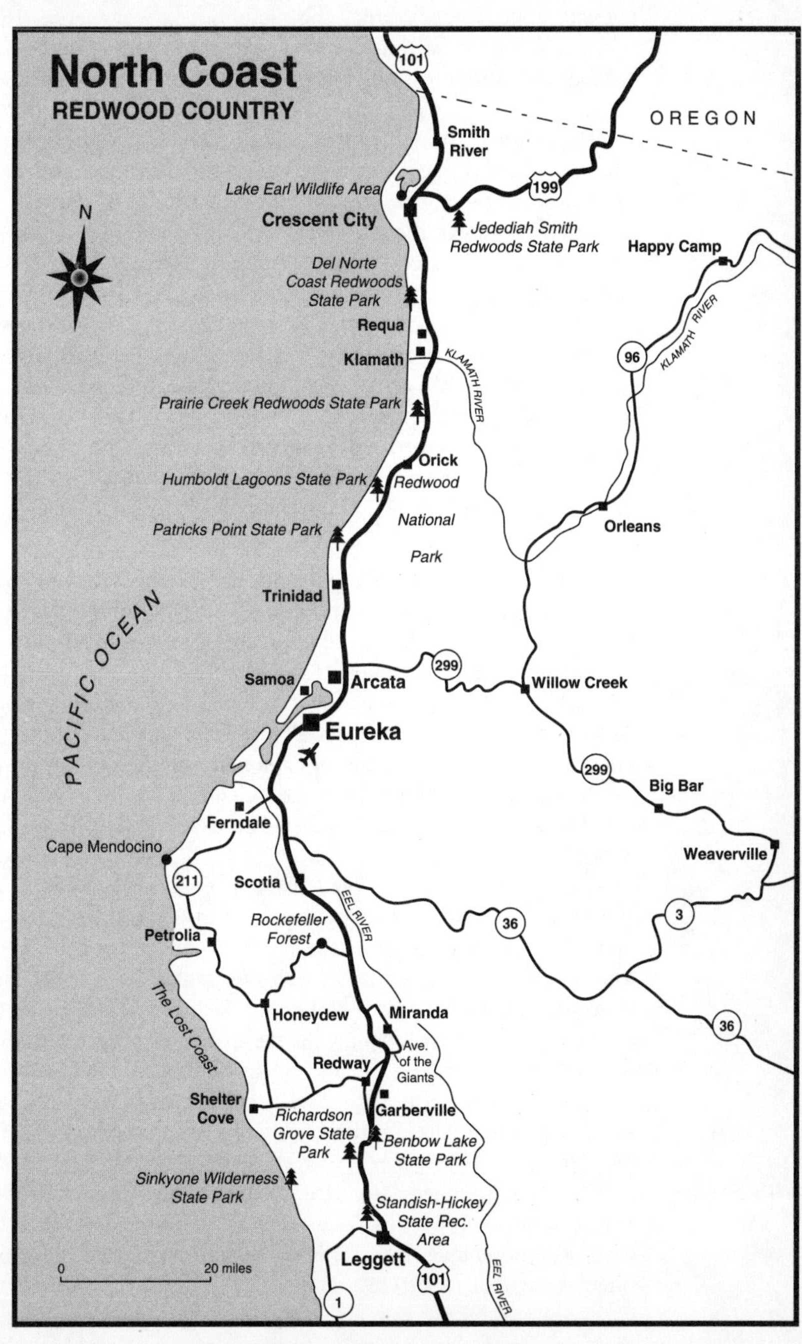
North Coast
REDWOOD COUNTRY
OREGON
N
Smith River
Lake Earl Wildlife Area
Crescent City
Jedediah Smith Redwoods State Park
Happy Camp
Del Norte Coast Redwoods State Park
Requa
Klamath
Klamath River
Prairie Creek Redwoods State Park
Orick
Humboldt Lagoons State Park
Redwood National Park
Patricks Point State Park
Orleans
Trinidad
Pacific Ocean
Samoa
Arcata
Willow Creek
Eureka
Big Bar
Ferndale
Cape Mendocino
Weaverville
Scotia
Eel River
Rockefeller Forest
Petrolia
The Lost Coast
Honeydew
Miranda
Ave. of the Giants
Redway
Shelter Cove
Garberville
Richardson Grove State Park
Benbow Lake State Park
Sinkyone Wilderness State Park
Standish-Hickey State Rec. Area
Leggett
0 20 miles
101
199
96
299
211
36
3
1

lake, and Italianate-style Victorians, brightly painted and blooming with pride. Tragedy struck this picturesque town in April 1992 when a 6.9-level earthquake and several powerful aftershocks rocked the entire area. Since then local residents have devotedly rebuilt the Main Street district and other affected neighborhoods.

The best way to see the town is by stopping first at the **Ferndale Museum**. Here is an ever-changing collection of antiques and memorabilia from the region, plus an old blacksmith shop. There are also maps available for self-guided walking tours of this historic community. It's an architectural wonder that shouldn't be missed. Closed Monday during summer and Monday and Tuesday during winter. Admission. ~ 515 Shaw Avenue, Ferndale; 707-786-4466.

Built in 1866 by Joseph and Zipporah Russ, **Fern Cottage** expanded from 8 to 28 rooms as the family grew. Joseph was a state senator and one of the first settlers of Ferndale. Today you can tour the home and view original furnishings, clothes, and family papers. Open weekends; call in advance if you plan to visit during the week. Admission. ~ 2121 Centerville Road, Ferndale; 707-786-4835.

EUREKA Eureka's 28,600 inhabitants make it the largest town on the Northern California coast. Founded in 1850, the town's first industry was mining; the name "Eureka!" came from an old gold mining exclamation meaning "I found it."

Today fishing and lumbering have replaced more romantic occupations, but much of the region's history is captured in points of interest. Stop at the **Chamber of Commerce** on the way into town for maps, brochures, and information. Closed Saturday and Sunday during winter. ~ 2112 Broadway, Eureka; 707-442-3738, 800-356-6381.

Make certain to ask at the Chamber of Commerce for the **architectural tour** map. Eureka has over 100 glorious Victorian homes ranging from understated designs to the outlandish **Carson Mansion**, a multilayered confection that makes other Gothic architecture seem tame. It was built in the 1880s by William Carson, a wealthy lumber merchant with the same need for ostentation that afflicted the robber barons on San Francisco's Nob Hill. The Carson Mansion is a private residence, but you can drive by and view its distinctive architecture. ~ 2nd and M streets, Eureka; 707-443-5665.

HIDDEN ►

Of a more subdued nature are the **covered bridges** on the southern outskirts of town. To reach them from Route 101, take Elk River Road two miles to Berta Road or three miles to Zanes Road (there is a wooden span covering both). You'll enter a picture of red barns and green pasture framed by cool, lofty forest. The bridges, crossing a small river, evoke Vermont winters and New Hampshire sleigh rides.

Fort Humboldt is also stationed at this end of town. Built in the early 1850s to help settlers war against indigenous tribes of Yurok, Hoopa, and Mattole Indians, it has been partially restored. In addition to re-creating army life (experienced here by a hard-drinking young officer named Ulysses S. Grant), the historic park displays early logging traditions. There's a drafty logger's cabin, a small lumber industry museum, a military museum displaying army artifacts, and a couple of remarkable old steam engines. ~ 3431 Fort Avenue, Eureka; 707-445-6567.

Nearby **Sequoia Park** provides a nifty retreat from urban life. Tucked into its 52-acre preserve is a petting zoo (closed Monday), picnic area, playground, and a thick stand of redwoods. ~ W Street between Glatt and Madrone streets, Eureka.

Then head to **Old Town,** Eureka's answer to the nation's gentrification craze. This neighborhood was formerly the local bowery; the term "skid row" reputedly originated right here. It derived from the bums residing beside the nearby "skid trails," along which redwood logs were transported to the waterfront. Now the ghetto is gilded: old Victorians, woodframe warehouses, brick buildings, and clapboard houses have been rebuilt and painted striking colors. Stylish shops have sprung up and restaurants have opened.

At the foot of C Street in Old Town, where the bowery meets the bay, the **Humboldt Bay Harbor Cruise** departs. For several well-invested dollars, you'll sail past an egret rookery, oyster beds, pelican roosts, ugly pulp mills, and the town's flashy marina. Closed January. ~ Eureka; 707-445-1910.

If you're a landlubber, however, and prefer a shoreside tour of Eureka, you can always take a horse-and-buggy ride around town. The **Old Town Carriage Company** has turn-of-the-century reproduction carriages pulled by massive draft horses. ~ 2nd and F streets at the gazebo, Eureka; 707-442-7264.

Heading north from Eureka there are two towns worth noting. **Arcata,** home of Humboldt State University, is a student town with an outstanding collection of old Victorians. For a self-guided archi-

AMERICAN INDIAN HISTORICAL TREASURES

Don't miss **Clarke Memorial Museum**, with its outstanding collection of California American Indian artifacts. Here are ornate baskets, feather regalia, fur quivers, beaded moccasins, war clubs, and a dugout redwood canoe. It provides a unique insight into this splendid Humboldt Bay region before the age of gold pans and axe handles. There is also the museum's Victorian section, which focuses on more recent history. Closed January. Open Tuesday through Saturday from noon until 4 p.m. ~ 240 E Street, Eureka; 707-443-1947.

tectural tour, obtain a map at the **Chamber of Commerce.** Closed Sunday. ~ 1062 G Street, Eureka; 707-822-3619.

Trinidad, one of the area's oldest towns, perches above a small port. Sea stacks and sailboats lie anchored offshore, watched over by a miniature lighthouse. For a tour of the pocket beaches and rocky shores lining this beautiful waterfront, take a three-mile trip south from town along Scenic Drive.

Next is **Redwood National Park**, a fitting finale to this lengthy coastal journey. Park of parks, it's a necklace strung for over 40 miles along the coast. Among its gems are secluded beaches, elk herds, and the world's tallest tree.

First link in the chain is the **Redwood Information Center.** ~ 119231 Route 101, Orick; 707-464-6101 ext. 5263. In addition to information, the center issues permits for **Tall Trees Grove.** A one-and-one-quarter-mile hike leads to a redwood stand boasting the loftiest of all California's redwoods, including a 367-foot giant which represents the tallest tree in the world. **Lady Bird Johnson Grove**, located off Bald Hill Road on a one-mile trail, represents another magnificent cluster of ancient trees.

Another side road, Davison Road (day-use fee), leads along remote **Gold Bluffs Beach** eight miles to Fern Canyon. Here angular walls 50 feet high are covered with rioting vegetation.

Redwood National Park encompasses three state parks—Prairie Creek Redwoods, Del Norte Redwoods, and Jedediah Smith Redwoods. Just after the main entrance to the first you'll pass **Elk Prairie**, where herds of Roosevelt elk graze across open meadows. Immediately past the entrance, Cal Barrel Road, another short detour, courses through dense redwood forest.

HIDDEN ► Also plan to turn off onto **Coastal Drive**, a gravel road paralleling Route 101. Its numerous turnouts expose extraordinary ocean vistas. The road snakes high above the coast before emptying onto the main highway near the mouth of the Klamath River.

The Del Norte section of the park reveals more startling sea views en route to Crescent City, where the **main park headquarters** is located. ~ 1111 2nd Street, Crescent City; 707-464-6101. There is travel information aplenty at the headquarters and at the **Chamber of Commerce** building just across the street. Open daily from Memorial Day to Labor Day. ~ 1001 Front Street, Crescent City; 707-464-3174.

Perched on a rocky island off Route 101 in Crescent City is **Battery Point Lighthouse**, an 1856 stone and masonry structure that is one of the best preserved original lighthouses on the Pacific Coast. At low tide from April through September visitors can walk across a spit of sand and rock to the lighthouse for tours of the lantern room and a small museum. Closed Monday and Tuesday. Admission. ~ Crescent City; 707-464-3089.

HIDDEN ► Woodlands, wetlands, grasslands—you'll find them all at **Lake Earl Wildlife Area.** This preserve also offers secluded sand dunes and a sufficient number of bird species, 260 at last count, to make it look like it was created by the Audubon Society. One of the finest birdwatching spots on the North Coast, this Pacific Flyway destination is the place to see hawks, falcons, bald eagles, Canada geese, and canvasback ducks. ~ Old Mill Road, three miles north of Crescent City; 707-464-2523.

To get away from it all, head out along the Lost Coast, where the 4000-foot King Range has created a shoreline wilderness. Amenities are rare in these parts but you will find a collection of clapboard cottages back up in the mountains.

Route 101 north to Route 199 leads to the park's Jedediah Smith section with its mountain vistas and thick redwood groves. The Smith River, rich in salmon and steelhead, threads through the region. For further details on this remote area check with the **Hiouchi Information Center**. Open from June 21 through Labor Day. ~ On Route 199, four miles east of Route 101; 707-458-3134.

LODGING

One of Northern California's finest old lodges is the imposing, Tudor-style **Benbow Inn**. Located astride the Eel River, this regal retreat is bounded by lawns, gardens, and umbrella-tabled patios. The structure itself is a bold three-story manor in the English country tradition. The lobby, paneled in carved wood and adorned by ornamental molding, is a sumptuous sitting area with a grand fireplace. Jigsaw puzzles lie scattered on the clawfoot tables and rocking horses decorate the room. The dining area and lounge are equally elegant. Guest quarters offer such flourishes as quilted beds with wooden headboards, hand-painted doors, marble topped period wallprints,nightstands, and complimentary sherry. Visitors also enjoy tea and scones in the afternoon and evening hors d'oeuvres. The inn is closed from January 1 through the middle of April. ~ 445 Lake Benbow Drive, Garberville; 707-923-2124, 800-355-3301, fax 707-923-2122. DELUXE TO ULTRA-DELUXE.

The cheapest lodging I've found in the southern redwoods area is **Johnston's Motel**. Unlike the region's big-tag caravansaries, this 14-unit facility has rooms at budget prices. Don't expect a lot of shine. The plain rooms are small, display scarred furniture, and lack any decoration along the cinderblock walls. But they do have wall-to-wall carpeting and stall showers. ~ 839 Redwood Drive, Garberville; 707-923-3327. BUDGET.

Not that I have anything against Johnston's; it's just that Garberville is not my idea of paradise. For a few well-spent dollars more you can rent a room in any of several motels along redwood-lined Avenue of the Giants. **Miranda Gardens Resort** is a good choice. This 16-unit motel has rooms with kitchens and fully equipped cabins. The place features a heated swimming pool, playground, and market. The facilities are tucked into a redwood grove and the rooms are partially paneled in redwood. ~ 6766 Avenue of the Giants, Miranda; 707-943-3011, fax 707-943-3584. MODERATE.

The predominant business in Redwood Country is the lumber industry, which casts a lengthy shadow in surrounding towns like Scotia. Here the 1920s-era **Scotia Inn** lavishly displays the region's product in a redwood-paneled lobby. Antique furnishings decorate this sprawling hotel, which boasts a fashionable restaurant and lounge. The guest rooms are furnished in oak and adorned with armoires, brass lamps, and silk wallpaper. The bathrooms, not to be upstaged, boast brass fixtures, clawfoot tubs, and medicine cabinets of carved wood. A gem. ~ Main and Mill streets, Scotia; 707-764-5683, fax 707-764-1707. MODERATE TO DELUXE.

HIDDEN ►

Way out in Shelter Cove, at the southern end of California's remote Lost Coast, there's the **Shelter Cove Beachcomber Inn**. A rare find, the inn rests near a bluff overlooking the ocean and consists of two houses with five units. The rooms are stylishly furnished and appointed in smart fashion. Two come with kitchens and woodburning stoves; all seem to be lovingly cared for. All come with barbecue grills and patios. Considering that the price tag on this luxury is reasonable and that Shelter Cove is one of the coast's most secluded hideaways, the Beachcomber Inn is well worth the effort. ~ 7272 Shelter Cove Road, Shelter Cove; 707-986-7733. BUDGET TO MODERATE.

HIDDEN ►

Mattole River Resort offers full-facility cottages complete with kitchenettes. Each is plain but comfortably furnished and features a sitting room and a bedroom. This rustic colony sits amid shade trees and is backdropped by forested hills. ~ 42354 Mattole Road, Petrolia; 707-629-3445, 800-845-4607, fax 707-629-3494. MODERATE.

The cheapest lodging of all is in the neon motels along Route 101 on the outskirts of Eureka. Many advertise room rates on highway signs along the southern entrance to town. **Surf Motel** is typical. These small bland rooms have wood furniture, paintings on the walls, and stall showers, etc. They are clean, carpeted, and equipped with color televisions. ~ 2411 Broadway, Eureka; 707-443-4660. BUDGET.

For country inn sensibility in an urban environment, **Old Town Bed & Breakfast Inn** comes highly recommended. Just a couple blocks from Eureka's fabled Carson Mansion, this seven-bedroom house dates from 1871. It's a Greek Revival structure with a winding staircase and a wealth of antiques. Plushly carpeted and adorned with patterned wallpaper, the house has been beautifully redecorated. The cost includes a hot tub and a full country-style breakfast. ~ 1521 3rd Street, Eureka; 707-445-3951, 800-331-5098, fax 707-445-8346. MODERATE TO ULTRA-DELUXE.

Another of Eureka's spectacular bed and breakfasts is **Carter House**, one of the finest Victorians I've ever seen. This grand old four-story house is painted in light hues and decorated with contemporary artwork, lending an airy quality seldom found in vintage homes. The place, quite simply, is beautiful: light streams through bay windows; Oriental rugs are scattered across hardwood floors; there are sumptuous sitting rooms, and oak banisters that seemingly climb forever. In the seven rooms are antique nightstands and armoires, beds with bold wooden headboards, ceramic pieces, and knickknacks. The price includes a full breakfast, complimentary wine, and cookies before bedtime. ~ 1033 3rd Street, Eureka; 707-445-1390, 800-404-1390, fax 707-444-8067. ULTRA-DELUXE.

Mark and Christi Carter added the 23-room **Hotel Carter** to their lodging empire a few years ago. Its pale pine furniture and peach-colored walls offer a refreshing counterpoint to the Carter House across the street. Accommodations are quite spacious; some have fireplaces and whirlpool baths. Complimentary breakfast is served in the ground floor dining room, where colorful dhurrie rugs and crystal candleholders add an elegant touch. ~ 301 L Street, Eureka; 707-444-8062, 800-404-1390, fax 707-444-8067. DELUXE TO ULTRA-DELUXE.

For traditional and stylish lodging, also consider **Eureka Inn.** Set in an imposing Tudor-gabled building near Eureka's Old Town section, it provides excellent accommodations. There's a wood-beamed lobby with large fireplace and comfortable sitting area, a pool, jacuzzi and sauna, plus a café, gourmet restaurant, and piano bar. Built in 1922 and registered as a National Historic Landmark, this huge hotel has 105 guest rooms. These are well appointed and attractively decorated. ~ 7th and F streets, Eureka; 707-442-6441, 800-862-4906, fax 707-442-0637. DELUXE TO ULTRA-DELUXE.

In 1888, a Eureka newspaper reporter called the newly built mayor's home, **"An Elegant Victorian Mansion,"** now the title of the bed and breakfast that occupies this National Historic Landmark. The lavishly ornate five-room residence is one of the most photographed gingerbread-style houses in Eureka. Lush lawns and colorful flower gardens fill the surrounding property. The interior is furnished with antiques to complete the old Victorian feel. A multicourse French gourmet breakfast is served every morning. An architectural tour of Eureka is gratis as well. ~ 1406 C Street, Eureka; 707-444-3144, fax 707-442-5594. DELUXE TO ULTRA-DELUXE.

For an extra dash of history in your nightly brew, there's the **Shaw House** in nearby Ferndale. It's only fitting to this bed and breakfast that Ferndale is an island in time where the Victorian era still obtains. The Shaw House, it seems, is the oldest home in town. A Carpenter Gothic creation, it was modeled on Hawthorne's *House of the Seven Gables*. A library, two parlors, dining room, and balconies are available to guests, and the home is furnished throughout with precious antiques. All rooms have private baths. ~ 703 Main Street, Ferndale; phone/fax 707-786-9958, 800-557-7429. MODERATE TO DELUXE.

In a town chockablock with precious Victorians, one of the most precious of all is **The Gingerbread Mansion**. Turrets and gables, an intimate garden, interesting antiques, and a delicious homemade breakfast are among the features; but what you'll find particularly special about this bed and breakfast are the bathrooms. One has mirrored ceilings and walls; another, his-and-hers clawfoot tubs set near a tiled gas fireplace. The ten distinct accommodations are comfortably cozy. ~ 400 Berding Street, Ferndale; 707-786-4000, 800-952-4136, fax 707-786-4381. DELUXE TO ULTRA-DELUXE.

Arcata Crew House Hostel provides lodging at inexpensive prices. One of the more commodious hostels, it has several private and double rooms; no room contains more than four sleepers. Varying from similar set-ups, the Crew House permits couples to stay together. Situated in two adjacent houses, the place features a wood-paneled living room with brick fireplace, dining room, yard, and kitchen. Open only in summer (late June to late August). ~ 1390 I Street, Arcata; 707-822-9995. BUDGET.

Set in a quiet residential neighborhood within walking distance of downtown, the **Lady Anne** is Arcata's only bed-and-breakfast. The five rooms of the 1888 Queen Anne–style home are each appointed with antiques. One has a wood-burning stove. You can sit on the porch or in a chair in the front yard and watch the world go by, or play the grand piano and guitars in one of the inn's two parlors. ~ 902 14th Street, Arcata; 707-822-2797. DELUXE.

You will be hard pressed anywhere along the coast to find a view more alluring than that of **Trinidad Bay Bed & Breakfast**. This New England–style shingle house, set in a tiny coastal town, looks across Trinidad Bay, past fishing boats and sea rocks, seals and sandy beaches, to tree-covered headlands. The four country-style rooms are equipped with standard furnishings and painted soft colors. There is a fireplace and a dining room for guests to share. Closed December and January. ~ Corner of Edwards and Trinity streets, Trinidad; 707-677-0840. DELUXE TO ULTRA-DELUXE.

Redwood AYH Hostel, set in an 1890-era ranch house, provides basic accommodations for singles and couples alike. It's across the highway from a beach and features a laundry room, kitchen facilities, and a common room. ~ 14480 Route 101 at Wilson Creek Road, Klamath; 707-482-8265, fax 707-482-4665. BUDGET.

Farther north in Crescent City, along the scimitar strand that gave the town its name, is **Crescent Beach Motel**. This 27-unit motel has plate-glass views of the ocean. Rooms are small, unimaginatively furnished in naugahyde, and lack any decoration. They do have carpets, TVs, and most rooms have those oh-so-priceless sea vistas. ~ 1455 Route 101, Crescent City; 707-464-5436. MODERATE.

DINING

Personally, my favorite dining place in these parts is the **Benbow Inn**. This Tudor lodge serves meals in a glorious wood-paneled dining room that will make you feel as though you're feasting at the estate of a British baron. The sideboards are carved wood with marble tops and the multipane windows look out upon landscaped gardens. Every evening the bill of fare includes rack of lamb, pasta primavera, pork loin, and filet mignon. There is also salmon, duck, curried chicken, and trout amandine. ~ 445 Lake Benbow Drive, Garberville; 707-923-2124. MODERATE TO DELUXE.

In the southern redwoods region you'll be hard pressed to find a better restaurant than **Woodrose Café**. T'aint much on looks—just a counter, a few tables and chairs, and a small patio out back. But the kitchen folk cook up some potent concoctions. That's why the place draws locals in droves. The breakfast menu offers buckwheat pancakes, lox and bagels, and spinach and feta cheese omelettes. At lunch they make homemade soups, organic salads, sandwiches, and tofu burgers; no dinner served. The Woodrose Café is a good reason to visit otherwise drab Garberville. No lunch on Saturday and Sunday. ~ 911 Redwood Drive, Garberville; 707-923-3191. MODERATE.

Proceeding north along the Avenue of the Giants, you'll encounter cafés in tiny towns like Miranda, Myers Flat, Weott, and Pepperwood. Most are tourist-oriented businesses, adequate as way stations, but undistinguished and slightly overpriced.

For a touch of good taste in the heart of Redwood Country try the **Scotia Inn**. The dining room of this revered old hotel is trimly paneled in polished redwood, furnished with captain's chairs, and illuminated by brass chandeliers. It features a menu with fresh fish dishes, tenderloin of elk, pheasant, oysters, prime rib, steak, and special "ethnic theme dishes" on Sundays. No dinner on Monday and Tuesday. ~ Main and Mill streets, Scotia; 707-764-5683. MODERATE TO DELUXE.

The historic Old Town section of Eureka, a refurbished neighborhood of stately Victorians, supports several good restaurants. At **Tomaso's Tomato Pies** they serve pizzas as well as spinach pie and sausage sandwiches. That's at lunch. Come dinner they add calzone, lasagna, ravioli, cannelloni, scampi, grilled halibut, and a host of other Italian dishes. Excellent food. No lunch on Sunday. ~ 216 E Street, Eureka; 707-445-0100. MODERATE.

A meal at the **Sea Grill** is a chance to enjoy fine dining in a historic 1876 storefront. The place has an airy Victorian feel about it, with lots of peachy pastels, fabric drapes, raised wallpaper, and an antique mahogany bar. Oil paintings by local artists add to the atmosphere. Chicken, steak, and seafood dishes are the specialties here. ~ 316 E Street, Eureka; 707-443-7187. MODERATE.

For Asian fare there's **Samurai Restaurant**, a simple dining room appointed with bamboo screens and colorful cloth paintings. It's dinner only, folks, with a menu that includes seafood, standard sukiyaki, tempura, and teriyaki dishes, plus a "Shogun's Feast" featuring marinated shrimp and beef. Closed Sunday and Monday. ~ 621 5th Street, Eureka; 707-442-6802. MODERATE.

For a seafood dinner in a historic setting, one place stands above anything else. **Lazio's**, a sprawling restaurant, has been a Eureka institution for years. It features shrimp, scallops, and oysters prepared in a variety of ways. There's also stuffed halibut, broiled salmon, and grilled rex sole. The meat menu is limited to steak and chicken. But when in Rome . . . do as Italian fishing families like the Lazios do. Closed Sunday for lunch. ~ 327 2nd Street, Eureka; 707-443-9717. MODERATE TO DELUXE.

HIDDEN ►

For a dining experience lumberjack-style, there's **Samoa Cookhouse** just outside Eureka. A local lumber company has opened its chow house to the public, serving three meals daily. Just join the crowd piling into this unassuming eatery, sit down at a school cafeteria–style table and dig in. You'll be served redwood-size portions of soup, salad, meat, potatoes, vegetables, and dessert—you can even ask for seconds. Ask for water and they'll plunk down a pitcher, order coffee and someone will bring a pot. It's noisy, crowded, hectic, and great fun. Reduced rates for children. ~ Samoa Road, Samoa; 707-442-1659. MODERATE.

The **Seascape Restaurant** is small and unassuming. There are only about three dozen tables and booths at this seafood dining room. But the walls of plate glass gaze out upon a rocky headland and expansive bay. Situated at the foot of Trinidad Pier, the local eating spot overlooks the town's tiny fishing fleet. The dishes, many drawn from surrounding waters, include halibut, rock cod, salmon, crab, and shrimp. Landlubbers dine on filet mignon. Lunch and breakfast menus are equally inviting. ~ Trinidad Pier, Trinidad; 707-677-3762. MODERATE.

From Trinidad to the Oregon border the countryside is sparsely populated. Crescent City is the only town of real size, but you'll find nondescript cafés in such places as Orick, Klamath, and Smith River.

Crescent City—like the entire North Coast—is seafood country. Best place around is **Harbor View Grotto**, a family restaurant with an ocean view. This plate-glass eatery features a long inventory of ocean dishes—whole clams, fried prawns or oysters, scallops, red snapper, salmon, cod, halibut, and so on, not to mention the seafood salads and shrimp cocktails. There are also a few meat dishes plus an assortment of sandwiches. Worth a stop. ~ 150 Starfish Way, Crescent City; 707-464-3815. MODERATE.

SHOPPING

In Ferndale, a picturesque Victorian town south of Eureka, there's a covey of intriguing shops. The community has attracted a number of artisans, many of whom display their wares in the 19th- and early-20th-century stores lining Main Street. There are shops selling needlework, stained glass, and kinetic sculptures; others deal in ironwork, used books, and handknits. There are even stores specializing in "paper treasures," boots and saddles, dolls, and "nostalgic gifts." All are contained along a three-block section that more resembles a living museum than a downtown shopping district.

Eureka, too, has been gentrified. Most of the refurbishing has occurred in Old Town, where stately Victorians, falsefront stores, and tumbledown buildings have been transformed into sparkling shops. Window browse down 2nd and 3rd streets from C Street to H Street and you're bound to find several inviting establishments. Of particular interest is **Imperiale Square**, a quaint open-air courtyard housing several shops. ~ 320 2nd Street, Eureka. Be sure to visit **Humboldt Arts Council Gallery**, with its displays of the work of North Coast artists. ~ 214 East Street, Eureka; 707-442-0278.

NIGHTLIFE

The **Benbow Inn** features a fine old lounge with carved walls and an ornate fireplace. A pianist plays on weekends, adding to the intimacy. ~ 445 Lake Benbow Drive, Garberville; 707-923-2124.

For a quiet drink in a traditional setting, consider the **Scotia Inn**, an old country-hotel with a comfortable lounge. The lounge also has live music on the weekend. Occasional cover. ~ Main and Mill streets, Scotia; 707-764-5683.

There's rock, blues, and reggae live at **Jambalaya**. This college town bar has a dancefloor and down-home crowd. The bands are local or national and the scene is loose. Cover. ~ 915 H Street, Arcata; 707-822-4766.

BEACHES & PARKS

HIDDEN

THE "LOST COAST" California's coastal Route 1 is one of the greatest highways in America. Beginning in Southern California, it sweeps north through Big Sur, Carmel, San Francisco, and Mendocino, past ocean scenery indescribably beautiful. Then it disappears. At the foot of Redwood Country, Route 1 quits the coast and turns into Route 101.

The region it never reaches is California's fabled "Lost Coast." Most of the region is now protected as the King Range National Conservation Area. Three major trails traverse it: King Crest Trail, which climbs the main coastal ridge for 16 miles, with views of the ocean and Eel River Valley; the five-mile-long Chemise Mountain trail; and the 26-mile-long Lost Coast Trail along the King Range. There is also hiking along the wilderness beach.

One of the wettest areas along the Pacific Coast, King Range gets about 100 inches of rain a year. The precipitation is particularly heavy from October to April. Summer carries cool coastal fog and some rain. Weather permitting, it's a fascinating region to explore—wild and virgin, with the shellmounds of American Indians who inhabited the area over a century ago still scattered on the beach.

Motels, restaurants, groceries, and boat rentals are available in Shelter Cove, at the south end of the Conservation Area. ~ From Garberville on Route 101, a road leads to nearby Redway and then southwest to Shelter Cove. About 15 miles down this road, Kings Peak Road forks northwest, paralleling the Conservation Area, to Ettersberg and Honeydew. Just before Kings Peak Road, Chemise Mountain Road turns off into Nadelos and Wailaki campgrounds. For information contact the Resource Area Office, U.S. Bureau of Land Management, 1695 Heindon Road, Arcata, CA 95521; 707-825-2300.

▲ There are numerous campgrounds for tents and RVs (most sites have no hookups); fees range from free to $7 per night.

SINKYONE WILDERNESS STATE PARK This 7000-acre park below the southern tip of the King Range is known for the narrow and steep winding roads leading to its interior. For this reason trailers and RVs are prohibited from the park. Featuring old growth redwood groves and clear-cut prairies, the park hugs the southern section of the Lost Coast. The ranch house and visitors center are a mere 200 yards from awe-inspiring bluffs. Other facilities include picnic tables and pit toilets. ~ Located 30 miles west of Redway on Briceland Road or 50 miles north of Fort Bragg on County Road 431; 707-986-7711.

▲ There are 15 drive-in and 17 hike-in sites for tents only; $10 to $11 per night. All of the north end sites are hike-in only.

STANDISH-HICKEY STATE RECREATION AREA Near the southern edge of Redwood Country, this 1500-acre park primarily consists of second-growth trees. The single exception is a 1200-year-old giant named after the Mayflower pilgrim, Captain Miles Standish. The forest here also has Douglas fir, oak, and maple trees. The south fork of the Eel River courses through the area, providing swimming holes and fishing spots. There are picnic areas, restrooms, and showers; restaurants and groceries are two miles away in Leggett. Day-use fee, $5. ~ Located along Route 101 two miles north of Leggett; 707-925-6482.

▲ There are 162 tent/RV sites (no hookups); $12 to $16 per night. Reservations recommended; call DESTINET at 800-444-7275.

RICHARDSON GROVE STATE PARK The first of the virgin redwood parks, this 1500-acre facility features a grove of goliaths. For some bizarre reason the highway builders chose to put the main road through the heart of the forest. This means you won't miss the redwoods, but to really appreciate them you'll have to disappear down one of the numerous hiking trails that loop through the grove. The south fork of the Eel River flows through the park, providing swimming and trout fishing opportunities. The park has an information center, a grocery, snack bar, gift shop, picnic areas, restrooms, and showers. Day-use fee, $5. ~ It's about 18 miles north of Leggett along Route 101; 707-247-3318.

▲ There are 176 sites for tents and RVs (no hookups); $12 to $16 per night.

BENBOW LAKE STATE RECREATION AREA One of the less desirable parks in the area, this facility fronts the Eel River near the dam that creates Benbow Lake. Route 101 streams through the park's center, disrupting an otherwise idyllic scene. Nevertheless, there's good swimming and fishing in the river-lake. Day-use fee, $5. There are picnic areas, restrooms, and showers; groceries and restaurants are in nearby towns. ~ It's about 23 miles north of Leggett along Route 101; 707-247-3318.

▲ There are 75 sites for tents and RVs (no hookups) along the river; $12 to $14 per night.

HUMBOLDT REDWOODS STATE PARK One of the state's great parks, it is set within a 20-million-year-old forest. The park is a tribute to early conservationists who battled lumber interests in an effort to save the area's extraordinary trees. Today 100 miles of hiking trails lead through redwood groves and along the south fork of the Eel River. Within the park's 30-mile length there are also opportunities for swimming, biking, horseback riding, fishing, or tree gazing. Facilities include an information center, picnic areas, restrooms, and showers; restaurants and groceries are in small towns within the park. Day-use fee, $5. ~ Located along the Avenue of the Giants between Miranda and Pepperwood; 707-946-2311

▲ There are three different campgrounds (one in winter) with a total of 249 sites for tents and RVs (no hookups); $12 to $16 per night. There are also five hike-in camps.

CLAM BEACH COUNTY PARK There's a broad expanse of beach here with good views of surrounding headlands, but this place is best known for its clams. Low tides and early mornings bring local people out to dig for razor clams, sweet and fleshy mollusks that can be baked, sautéed, or eaten raw. If interested, you'll need a state license. There's a picnic area and toilets; restaurants and groceries are several miles away in Trinidad. ~ Along Route 101 about 15 miles north of Eureka; 707-445-7652.

▲ There is a number of open ground sites here for tents and RVs (no hookups); $8 per night.

PATRICK'S POINT STATE PARK This 650-acre park is particularly known for Agate Beach, a long crescent backdropped by wooded headlands. Here it's possible to gather not only driftwood but semiprecious agate, jasper, and black jade. There are tidepools to explore, sea lions and seals offshore, and several miles of hiking trails. The facilities include a museum, picnic areas, restrooms, and showers; restaurants and groceries are several miles away in Trinidad. Day-use fee, $5. ~ It's off Route 101 about 25 miles north of Eureka; 707-677-3570.

▲ There are 124 sites for tents and RVs (no hookups); $12 to $16 per night. Reservations are recommended in the summer; call DESTINET at 800-444-7275.

HUMBOLDT LAGOONS STATE PARK A 2000-acre facility, this beach park is full of surprises. The main entrance leads to a sandy beach tucked between rocky outcroppings and heaped with driftwood. Behind the beach an old lagoon has slowly transformed into a salt marsh. Add the two areas together and you come up with a splendid park. Fishing at Stone Lagoon is good for cutthroat trout. Pit toilets are the only facilities; restaurants and groceries seven miles away in Orick. ~ Off Route 101 about 31 miles north of Eureka; 707-488-2041.

▲ There are 12 environmental hike-in and boat-in sites; $7 per night.

REDWOOD NATIONAL AND STATE PARKS Actually four parks in one, this 110,000-acre giant encompasses Prairie Creek Redwoods, Del Norte Coast Redwoods, Jedediah Smith Redwoods state parks and Redwood National Park. Together they stretch over 33 miles along the coast from Orick to the Crescent City region. Within that span, one of California's wettest areas (80 inches of rain yearly in Del Norte), are hidden beaches, ocean cliffs, deep redwood forests, and mile on mile of hiking trails.

Along the coast are wind-scoured bluffs and gently sloping hills. The beaches range from sandy to rocky; because of the rugged terrain in certain areas, some are inaccessible. In addition to beaches, many streams—including Prairie Creek, Redwood Creek, and the Smith River—traverse this series of parks.

Hikers and redwood lovers will find that several spectacular groves lie adjacent to Routes 101 and 199. Others can be reached along uncrowded trails. Tan oak and madrone grow around the redwoods, while farther inland there are Jeffrey pine and Douglas fir.

Birdwatchers will encounter mallards, hawks, owl, shorebirds, quail, and great blue herons. The mammal population ranges from shrews and moles to rabbit and beaver to black-tail deer, Roosevelt elk, and an occasional bear. Along the coast live river otters and harbor seals. These and other features make the parks a natural for swimming, fishing, canoeing, and kayaking.

Facilities include information centers, picnic areas, restrooms, and showers; restaurants and groceries are in the park's small towns. Day-use fee, $5 for campsites. ~ Located along Route 101 between Orick and Crescent City; Jedediah Smith Redwoods State Park is along Route 199 nine miles east of Crescent City. The park headquarters is at 1111 2nd Street, Crescent City; 707-464-6101.

▲ In the national park, there are three hike-in campgrounds: Nickel Creek, with five sites; and Flint Ridge and Demartin, each with ten sites. All are free and completely primitive. The incorporated state parks offer more campgrounds: At **Prairie Creek Redwoods State Park** there are 100 sites for tents and RVs (no hookups); $12 to $16 per night. ~ 707-488-2171. **Jedediah Smith State Redwoods Park** has 108 sites for tents and RVs (no hookups); $12 to $16 per night. ~ 707-464-6101. **Del Norte Redwoods State Park** has 145 sites for tents and RVs (no hookups); $12 to $16 per night. ~ 707-464-6101. In winter, sites are on a first come, first served basis. In summer, call DESTINET for reservations at 800-444-7275.

Outdoor Adventures

FISHING

All along the coast, charter boats depart daily to fish for salmon, Pacific snapper, or whatever else is running. Please note that many fishing companies are seasonal operators.

MARIN COAST If you hanker to try your luck, contact **Caruso's Sportfishing and Seafood.** ~ Harbor Drive, Sausalito; 415-332-1015. **Loch Lomond Live Bait House** sells bait and tackle. ~ Loch Lomond Marina, San Rafael; 415-456-0321.

SONOMA AND MENDOCINO COAST **Bodega Bay Sportfishing** operates three boats, from 49 to 65 feet. Besides salmon charters, they run charters for rock cod and crab. ~ 1500 Bay Flat Road, Bodega Bay; 707-875-3344. In Fort Bragg, try **Noyo Fishing Center.** ~ 32450 North Harbor Drive; 707-964-7609.

REDWOOD COUNTRY In Eureka, try **King Salmon Charters** for deep-sea charters. ~ 3458 Utah Street; 707-442-3474. At the King Salmon Resort, check out **Sailfish.** ~ 1821 Buhne Drive, Eureka; 707-442-6682.

RIVER EXPLORING

With the Eel, Klamath, Smith, and Trinity rivers traversing many of the North Coast's parks, you're never far away from enjoying a stretch of river. In this mysterious fog-filled area, river exploration is a great way to discover natural vegetation and wildlife.

Try **All Outdoors Adventure Trips** for trips down the rivers of Northern California. ~ 1250 Pine Street, Suite 103, Walnut Creek; 510-932-8993. In addition to offering trips on all the major rivers, **Beyond Limits** rents kayaks and canoes. ~ P.O. Box 215, Riverbank, CA 95367; 209-869-6060. Contact the **Electric Rafting Company** for trips on the Trinity, Smith, Klamath, and Eel rivers. ~ 295 Electric Street, Arcata; 707-826-2861.

GOLF

From Marin to the Oregon border you'll find several clubs where it's relatively easy to get tee times.

SONOMA AND MENDOCINO COAST On the Sonoma Coast **Bodega Harbor Golf Links** is an 18-hole course, which is hilly and scenic. Part of the course meanders around a freshwater marsh. ~ 21301 Heron Drive, Bodega Bay; 707-875-3538.

REDWOOD COUNTRY In the home of that lofty tree, I recommend **Eureka Municipal Golf Course,** which has a pro shop and a driving range. ~ 4750 Fairway Drive, Eureka; 707-443-4808. In

Crescent City, be sure to check out **Del Norte Golf Course.** ~ 130 Club Drive; 707-458-3214.

TENNIS

The best bet for finding a court without staying at the most expensive hotels is to call the local parks and recreation department.

REDWOOD COUNTRY In Eureka, you can play at Highland Park. ~ Highland and Glen streets. You can also check out the courts at **Hammond Park.** ~ 14th and E streets; 707-441-4203. For information on courts in Crescent City, call 707-464-7230.

RIDING STABLES & PACK TRIPS

Riding along the hauntingly beautiful North Coast is not an experience easily forgotten. This area also offers opportunities for a more delightfully primitive mode of transport—llama riding.

MARIN COAST There are few prettier places to ride than Point Reyes National Seashore, where you can canter through rolling ranch country and out along sharp sea cliffs. **Five Brooks Stables** conducts mounted tours of this extraordinary area. ~ 8101 Route 1, Olema; 415-663-1570. If you'd rather tour Point Reyes by llama than horse, contact **Sierra Llama Company.** ~ 13325 Peninsula Drive, Auburn; 916-269-2204.

REDWOOD COUNTRY Near Redwood National Park, try **Tall Tree Outfitters.** They offer interpretive tours of the park and have their own riding trails. ~ 1100 Dry Dens Road, Orick Rodeo Grounds, Orick; 707-488-5785.

BIKING

Two-wheeling north of San Francisco is an invigorating sport. Not only is the scenery magnificent, but the accommodations aren't bad either. Many state and national parks sponsor campgrounds where cyclists and hikers can stay for a nominal fee.

Route 1, the coast road, offers a chance to pedal past a spectacular shoreline of hidden coves, broad beaches, and sheer headlands. Unfortunately, the highway is narrow and winding, and therefore recommended for experienced cyclists only.

MARIN COAST Point Reyes National Seashore features miles of bicycling, particularly along Bear Valley Trail.

SONOMA AND MENDOCINO COAST Other popular areas farther north include the towns of Mendocino and where level terrain and beautiful landscape combine to create a cyclist's haven.

Bike Rentals Near Point Reyes National Seashore, **Trail Head Rentals** has bikes, binoculars, and brochures. Closed Wednesday. ~ 88 Bear Valley Road, Olema; 415-663-1958. In Mendocino, try **Catch a Canoe and Bicycles Too!** ~ Coast Highway 1 at Comptche-Ukiah Road; 707-937-0273. Located on the bicycle migration route between Canada and Mexico, **Fort Bragg Cyclery** rents bicycles and does full-service repairs. Closed Sunday. ~ 579 South Franklin Street, Fort Bragg; 707-964-3509.

Whale Watching

It is the world's longest mammal migration: 6000 miles along the Pacific coast from the Bering Sea to Baja California, then back again. The creatures making the journey measure 35 to 50 feet and weigh 40 tons. During the entire course of their incredible voyage they neither eat nor sleep.

Every year from mid-December through early February, the California gray whale cruises southward along the Northern California coast. Traveling in "pods" numbering three to five, these magnificent creatures hug the shoreline en route to their breeding grounds.

Since the whales use local coves and promontories to navigate, they are easy to spot from land. Just watch for the rolling hump, the slapping tail, or a lofty spout of spuming water. Sometimes these huge creatures will breach, leaping 30 feet above the surface, then crashing back with a thunderous splash.

The best crow's nests from which to catch this aquatic parade are Muir Beach Overlook, Chimney Rock at Point Reyes National Seashore, Bodega Head State Park, Sonoma Coast State Beach, Salt Point State Park, Mendocino Headlands State Park, Shelter Cove or Trinidad Head in Humboldt County, and Point St. George up near Crescent City. Visitors to California's Central Coast also enjoy this annual event.

Several outfits sponsor whale-watching cruises. During the winter and early spring, **Oceanic Society Expeditions** offers gray whale migration tours, which are led by qualified naturalists. ~ Fort Mason Center, Building E, San Francisco; 415-474-3385. For a close look at our fellow mammals, contact **New Sea Angler & Jaws**. ~ 1445 Route 1, Bodega Bay; 707-875-3495. For more intimate whale-watching groups of six or less be sure to call **King Salmon Charters**. ~ 3458 Utah Street, Eureka; 707-442-3474.

California gray whales live to 40 or 50 years and have a world population numbering about 21,000. Their only enemies are killer whales and humans. They mate during the southern migration one year, then give birth at the end of the following year's migration. The calves, born in the warm, shallow waters of Baja, weigh a ton and measure about 16 feet. By the time they are weaned seven months later, the young are already 26 feet long.

Blue whales, humpback whales, dolphins, and porpoises also sometimes visit the coast. Gray whales can be seen again from March through mid-May, though farther from shore, during their return migration north. So keep an eye sharply peeled: that rocky headland on which you are standing may be a crow's nest in disguise.

HIKING

To call California's North Coast a hiker's paradise is an understatement. After all, in San Francisco and north of the city is the Golden Gate National Recreation Area. Together with continuous county, state, and national parks it offers over 100,000 acres to be explored.

Within this ambit are trails ranging from trifling nature loops to tough mountain paths. The land varies from tidal areas and seacliffs to ranch country and scenic mountains. In the far north are the giant redwood forests, located within national parks and featuring networks of hiking trails.

MARIN COAST The **Marin Headlands,** a region of bold bluffs and broad seascapes, contains a few hiking paths in its otherwise unpredictable landscape. ~ 415-331-1540.

Kirby Cove Trail (1.5 miles) leads from Conzelman Road down to a narrow beach. The views of San Francisco en route and the caves along the beach's east end provide a lot of adventure for a short hike.

Wolf Ridge Loop (4.5 miles) begins at Rodeo Beach, follows the Pacific Coast Trail and Wolf Ridge Trail, then returns along Miwok Trail. It ascends from a shoreline environment to heights with sweeping views of both San Francisco and Mt. Tamalpais.

Tennessee Valley Trail (2 miles) winds along the valley floor en route to a small beach and cove. The trailhead sits off Route 1 at the end of Tennessee Valley Road.

About 45 miles of trails loop through **Mt. Tamalpais State Park** (415-388-2070). These link to a 200-mile network of hiking paths through Muir Woods National Monument and Golden Gate National Recreation Area. Explorers are rewarded with a diverse terrain, startling views of the entire Bay Area, and a chance to hike within commuting distance of San Francisco. Most trails begin at Pantoll Park Headquarters. Here you can pick up trail maps and descriptions from which to devise your own combination loop trails, or consult with the rangers in planning anything from an easy jaunt to a rugged trek.

Dipsea Trail (6.8 miles) is a favorite path beginning in Mill Valley and heading along rolling hills, past sea vistas, then ending near Stinson Beach. The easiest way to pick up the trail is in Muir Woods, about a mile from the Mill Valley trailhead.

Matt Davis Trail (3.8 miles) descends 1200 feet from Pantoll Park Headquarters to Stinson Beach; you'll encounter deep woods, windswept knolls, and views of San Francisco and Point Reyes.

Steep Ravine Trail (2.8 miles), true to its name, angles sharply downward from Pantoll Park Headquarters through a redwood-studded canyon, then joins the Dipsea Trail.

Redwood Creek Trail (2.5 miles) loops through several remarkable redwood stands. A favorite with tourists, this trail begins near Muir Woods park headquarters and is often crowded. So it's best hiked either early or late in the day.

There are numerous other trails which combined form interesting loop hikes. For instance, from Bootjack picnic area in Mt. Tamalpais State Park, you can follow **Bootjack Trail** down a steep canyon of redwood and Douglas fir to Muir Woods, then take **Ben Johnson Trail** back up to Pantoll Park Headquarters. From there it's a half-mile walk back to Bootjack. This 4.2-mile circle tour carries through relatively isolated sections of Muir Woods.

For a more challenging (7.5 miles) circular trek to the top of Mt. Tamalpais, begin at Mountain Home, an inn located along Panoramic Highway. Follow **Old Railroad Grade.** This will lead to West Point Inn, a cozy lodging place for hikers. From here you climb to the road that goes to East Peak, one of Mt. Tamalpais' three summits. Heading down along **Fern Creek Trail**, you'll encounter Old Railroad Grade once more. En route are flowering meadows, madrone stands, chaparral-cloaked hillsides, and mountaintop views.

POINT REYES NATIONAL SEASHORE Within its spectacular 72,000-acre domain, this park contains over 100 miles of hiking trails plus four hike-in campsites. The trails form a latticework across forests, ranch lands, and secluded beaches and along sea cliffs, brackish inlets, and freshwater lakes. Over 350 bird species inhabit the preserve. Black-tailed deer, Eurasian fallow deer, and spotted axis deer abound. You might also encounter raccoons, weasels, rabbits, badgers, bobcats, even a skunk or two.

Most trailheads begin near **Bear Valley Visitors Center**, Palomarin, Five Brooks, or Estero. For maps and information check with the rangers at the visitors center. ~ 415-663-1092.

Earthquake Trail (0.6 mile) begins from the visitors center and leads along the epicenter of the 1906 earthquake. The ground here shifted over 16 feet during that terrible upheaval.

Nearby **Woodpecker Trail** (.7 mile) is a self-guiding trail with markers explaining the natural environment. The annotated path leads to a horse "museum" set in a barn.

✔ CHECK THESE OUT—UNIQUE OUTDOOR ADVENTURES

- Set up a tent at **Steep Ravine Environmental Camp**, with its dramatic sea views. *page 249*
- Mount your steed and cantor along the rolling ranch lands or sharp sea cliffs of **Marin County**. *page 286*
- Hike along the **Hiouchi Trail** in Del Norte Coast Redwoods State Park, with its huckleberries, trilliums, and rhododendrons. *page 291*
- Pedal **Route 1** past a spectacular shoreline studded with hidden coves, broad beaches, and sheer headlands. *page 286*

Bear Valley Trail (4.1 miles), also beginning near the visitors center, courses through range land and wooded valley to cliffs overlooking the ocean. The park's most popular trail, it is level and may unfortunately be crowded with hikers and bicyclists.

Coast Trail (13.3 miles) runs between Palomarin (near Bolinas) and Limantour Beach. Hugging the shoreline en route, this splendid trail leads past four freshwater lakes and two camping areas, then turns inland to the American Youth Hostel.

Olema Valley Trail (5.2 miles) parallels Route 1 as it tracks a course along the infamous San Andreas Fault. Originating from Five Brooks, it alternates between glades and forest while beating a level path to Dogtown.

Estero Trail (4.4 miles) shadows the shoreline of Drake's Estero and provides opportunities to view local waterfowl as well as harbor seals, sea lions, and bat rays.

REDWOOD COUNTRY There are more than 100 miles of hiking and riding paths within **Humboldt Redwoods State Park**. Many lead through dense redwood stands, others meander along the Eel River, and some lead to the park's hike-in camps. ~ 707-946-2409.

Founders Grove Nature Trail (.5 mile) tunnels through a virgin redwood forest that once boasted the national champion coastal redwood. Though a storm significantly shortened the 362-foot giant, it left standing a cluster of equally impressive neighbors.

Rockefeller Loop Trail (.5 mile) ducks into a magnificent grove of old growth redwoods.

There are also longer trails leading deep into the forest and to the top of 3379-foot Grasshopper Peak.

Comprising three distinct state parks and extending for miles along California's northwestern corner, **Redwood National Park**'s diverse enclave offers adventure aplenty to daytrippers and mountaineers alike. There are over 150 miles of trails threading the parks, leading through dense redwood groves, along open beaches, and atop wind-buffeted bluffs. ~ 707-464-6101.

Yurok Loop Trail (1 mile), with its berry patches and wildflowers, begins near the terminus of Coastal Trail.

Enderts Beach Trail (.5 mile), south of Crescent City, features tidepools, seaside strolling, and primitive camping. It also offers access to the **Coastal Trail** (8.2 miles), an old roadway that cuts through forests of redwood, alder, and spruce and features glorious ocean views.

Within **Prairie Creek Redwoods State Park** there are numerous trails to enjoy.

Redwood Creek Trail (9 miles) leads from a trailhead two miles north of Orick to Tall Trees Grove, home of the world's tallest trees. There is backcountry camping en route; permits available at the trailhead.

Tall Trees Trail (1.6 miles) provides a shorter route to the same destination.

Lady Bird Johnson Grove Nature Loop Trail (1 mile) winds through ancient redwood country.

Rhododendron Trail (7.8 miles) begins at park headquarters and continues along the eastern ridge of the park, which is filled with rhododendrons.

James Irvine Trail (4.3 miles) goes from the Prairie Creek visitors center along a redwood ridge to Fern Canyon. For a longer loop (10.3 miles), hike south on Gold Bluffs Beach, then pick up Miner's Ridge Trail. This last trail follows a corduroy mining road used early in the century.

The **Fern Canyon Trail** (.8 mile) courses along a gulch dripping with vegetation.

Coastal Trail (5 miles) begins at Fern Canyon and parallels Gold Bluffs Beach.

West Ridge Trail (7.1 miles) traces a sharp ridgetop through lovely virgin forest, ending at the Butler Creek backpacking camp.

The **Revelation Trail** (.3 mile), a marvelous innovation, contains handrails and a tape-recorded description of the surroundings for the blind. For those of us gifted with sight, it provides a fuller understanding of the scents, sounds, and textures of a redwood forest.

Cathedral Trees Trail (1.4 miles) heads along streams and meadows to elk country.

Brown Creek Trail (1.2 miles), reputedly one of the park's prettiest hikes, leads along streams and through old redwood stands.

Del Norte Coast Redwoods State Park offers several areas ideal for short hikes. **Coastal Trail** (5.1 miles), located south of the state park, begins at Klamath River Overlook. In addition to ocean vistas, it offers a walk through a spruce and alder forest, plus glimpses of sea lions, whales, and numerous birds.

Damnation Creek Trail (2.5 miles), an ancient Yurok Indian path, winds steeply down from Route 101 to a hidden cove and beach.

Hobbs Wall Trail (3.8 miles) leads through a former lumberjacking region.

Alder Basin Trail (1 mile) meanders along a stream through stands of willow, maple, and alder.

Farther north, **Jedediah Smith Redwoods State Park** has a number of trails to hike.

Stout Grove Trail (.5 mile) highlights several spots along its short course: a 340-foot redwood tree, swimming and fishing holes, plus rhododendron regions.

Hiouchi Trail (2 miles), with its huckleberries, trilliums, and rhododendrons, is equally impressive. This nature trail goes right through a burned-out redwood; it also affords scenic vistas along the Smith River.

Hatton Trail (.3 mile) tours an ancient redwood grove.

Nickerson Ranch Trail (.8 mile) leads through a corridor of ferns and redwoods.

Howland Hill Road (8 miles), now overgrown with salmonberries, was once a vital stagecoach route.

Transportation

CAR

When traveling by car you can choose the ever-winding, spectacular coastal **Route 1**, which provides some of the prettiest scenery this side of Shangri-la. Or take **Route 101**, the faster, more direct freeway that follows an interior route.

AIR

Eureka/Arcata Airport in McKinleyville is served by United Express and Horizon Air. On a bluff above the Pacific, this is one of the most beautiful small fields in California. **Humboldt Transit System** provides hourly service (Monday through Friday) from Eureka and Arcata to the airport. ~ 707-443-0826.

BUS

Greyhound Bus Lines travels the entire stretch of Route 101 between San Francisco and Oregon, including the main route through Redwood Country. ~ 707-442-0370, 800-231-2222.

CAR RENTALS

It's advisable to rent an auto in San Francisco rather than along the North Coast. There are more rental agencies available and prices are lower. At the Eureka/Arcata Airport you can rent from **Avis Rent A Car** (707-839-1576, 800-331-1212), **Hertz Rent A Car** (707-839-2172, 800-654-3131), and **National Interrent** (707-839-3229, 800-227-7368).

PUBLIC TRANSIT

Golden Gate Transit has bus service between San Francisco and Sausalito, then beyond to Point Reyes National Seashore (weekends only). It also covers Route 101 from San Francisco to Santa Rosa. ~ 415-332-6600.

From Santa Rosa you can pick up coastal connections on **Mendocino Transit Authority**, which travels Route 1 from Bodega Bay to Point Arena. There's only one bus a day in either direction. ~ 707-884-3723.

Public transportation from San Francisco to Marin can become a sightseeing adventure when you book passage on a **Golden Gate Transit** ferryboat. ~ 415-453-2100.

Mendocino Stage, a local line, serves Gualala, Point Arena, Mendocino, and Fort Bragg, and travels inland to Ukiah. ~ 707-964-0167.

SIX

Central Coast

If the Central Coast were an oil painting, it would portray a surf-laced shoreline near the bottom of the frame. Pearly beaches and bold promontories would occupy the center, while forested peaks rose in the background. Actually, a mural would be more appropriate to the subject, since the coastline extends 150 miles from San Francisco to Big Sur. The artist would paint two mountain ranges parallel to the shore, then fill the area between with a patchwork of hills, headlands, and farmland.

Even after adding a swath of redwoods along the entire length of the mural, the painter's task would have only begun. The Central Coast will never be captured—on canvas, in print, or in the camera's eye. It is a region of unmatched beauty and extraordinary diversity.

Due south of San Francisco is Half Moon Bay, a timeless farming and fishing community founded by Italians and Portuguese during the 1860s. The oceanside farms are so bountiful that Half Moon Bay dubs itself the pumpkin capital of the world, and Castroville, farther south, claims to be the artichoke capital. While local farmers grow prize vegetables, commercial fishing boats comb the entire coast for salmon, herring, tuna, anchovies, and cod.

In the seaside town of Santa Cruz, on the other hand, you'll encounter a quiet retirement community that has been transformed into a dynamic campus town. When the University of California opened a school here in the 1960s, it created a new role for this ever-changing place. Originally founded as a Spanish mission in 1791, Santa Cruz became a lumber port and manufacturing center when the Americans moved in around 1849. Then in the late 19th century it developed into a tourist resort filled with elaborate Victorian houses.

Like every place on the Central Coast, Santa Cruz is reached from San Francisco along Route 1, the tortuous coast road that twists past sandy coves and granite cliffs. Paralleling it is Route 101, the inland freeway that leads through the warm, dry agricultural regions of the Salinas Valley. Between these two roadways rise the Santa Cruz Mountains, accessible along Routes 35 and 9. Unlike the low-lying coastal and inland farming areas, this range measures 3000 feet in elevation and is filled with redwood, Douglas fir, alder, and madrone.

Different still is the Monterey Peninsula, a fashionable residential area 125 miles south of San Francisco. Including the towns of Monterey, Pacific Grove, and Carmel, this wealthy enclave is a far cry from bohemian Santa Cruz. If Santa Cruz is an espresso coffeehouse, Monterey is a gourmet restaurant or designer boutique.

Farther south lies Big Sur, the most unique area of all. Extending from the Monterey Peninsula for 90 miles along the coast, and backdropped by the steep Santa Lucia Mountains, it is one of America's most magnificent natural areas. Only 1200 residents live in this rugged region of bald crags and flower-choked canyons. None but the most adventurous occupy the nearby Ventana Wilderness, which represents the southernmost realm of the coastal redwoods. Once a nesting place for rare California condors, Ventana is still home to wild boar, black bear, and mountain lion.

The Esselen Indians who once inhabited Big Sur and its mountains have long since vanished. Together with the Costanoans, who occupied the rest of the Central Coast, the Esselen may have been here for 5000 years. By the time the Europeans happened upon California, about 10,000 American Indians lived near the coast between San Francisco and Big Sur. Elk and antelope ranged the region. The American Indians also hunted sea lions, gathered seaweed, and fed on oysters, abalone, clams, and mussels.

Westerners did not settle Big Sur until after 1850, and Route 1 did not open completely until 1937. During the 1950s, novelist Henry Miller became the focus of an artists' colony here. Jack Kerouac trekked through the area, writing about it in several of his novels. Other Beat poets, lured by Big Sur's dizzying sea cliffs and otherworldly vistas, also cut a path through its hills.

Over three hundred years before settlers arrived in Big Sur, Monterey was already making history. As early as 1542, Juan Rodríguez Cabrillo, a Portuguese explorer in Spanish employ, set anchor off nearby Pacific Grove. Then in 1602 Sebastian Vizcaíno came upon the peninsula again and told a whale of a fish story, grandly exaggerating the size and amenities of Monterey Bay.

His account proved so distorted that Gaspar de Portolá, leading an overland expedition in 1769, failed to recognize the harbor. When Father Junípero Serra joined him in a second journey the next year, they realized that this gentle curve was Vizcaíno's deep port. Serra established California's second mission in Monterey, then moved it a few miles in 1771 to create the Carmel Mission. Neither Serra nor Portolá explored the Big Sur coast, but the Spanish were soon building yet another mission in Santa Cruz.

In fact, they found Santa Cruz much easier to control than Monterey. By the 1820s, Yankee merchant ships were plying Monterey waters, trading for hides and tallow. This early American presence, brilliantly described in Richard Henry Dana's classic *Two Years Before the Mast*, climaxed in 1846 during the Mexican War. Commodore John Sloat seized the town for the United States. By 1849, while Big Sur was still the hunting ground of American Indians, the adobe town of Monterey had become the site of California's constitutional convention.

An added incentive for these early adventurers, and modern day visitors as well, was the climate along the Central Coast. The temperature still hovers around 67° in summer and 57° during winter; Santa Cruz continues to boast 300 sunny days a year. Explorers once complained of foggy summers and rainy winters, but like today's travelers, they were rewarded with beautiful spring and fall weather.

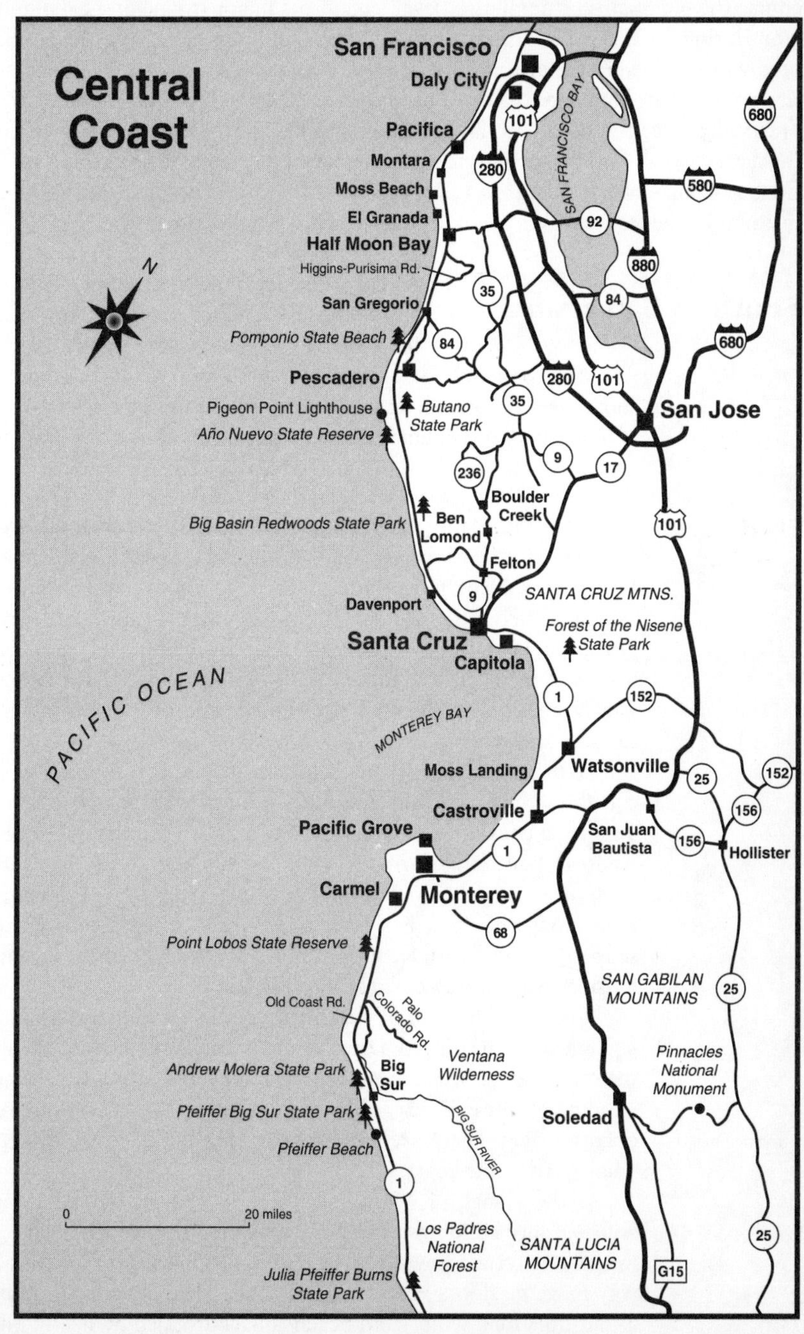
Central Coast
San Francisco
Daly City
Pacifica
Montara
Moss Beach
El Granada
Half Moon Bay
Higgins-Purisima Rd.
San Gregorio
Pomponio State Beach
Pescadero
Pigeon Point Lighthouse
Año Nuevo State Reserve
Butano State Park
Big Basin Redwoods State Park
Ben Lomond
Boulder Creek
Felton
Davenport
Santa Cruz
Capitola
SANTA CRUZ MTNS.
Forest of the Nisene State Park
San Jose
SAN FRANCISCO BAY
PACIFIC OCEAN
MONTEREY BAY
Moss Landing
Watsonville
Castroville
Pacific Grove
San Juan Bautista
Hollister
Carmel
Monterey
Point Lobos State Reserve
Old Coast Rd.
Palo Colorado Rd.
Ventana Wilderness
SAN GABILAN MOUNTAINS
Andrew Molera State Park
Big Sur
Pfeiffer Big Sur State Park
Pfeiffer Beach
Pinnacles National Monument
Soledad
BIG SUR RIVER
Los Padres National Forest
SANTA LUCIA MOUNTAINS
Julia Pfeiffer Burns State Park
0
20 miles
N
101
280
680
580
92
880
35
84
9
17
236
1
152
25
156
68
G15

Perhaps that's why Monterey became a tourist mecca during the 1880s. Of course the old Spanish capital also developed into a major fishing and canning region during the early 20th century. It was then that John Steinbeck, the Salinas-bred writer, added to the already rich history of Monterey with his novels and stories. Much of the landscape that became known as "Steinbeck Country" has changed drastically since the novelist's day, and the entire Central Coast is different from the days of Serra and Sloat. But the most important elements of Monterey and the Central Coast—the foaming ocean, open sky, and wooded heights—are still here, waiting for the traveler with a bold eye and robust imagination.

South of San Francisco

An easy drive from the city, the coast south of San Francisco is full of surprises. You might see a gray whale pod, watch the sea lions at Año Nuevo State Park, or visit one of the rural towns that dot this shoreline. The area along Route 1 between San Francisco and Santa Cruz also sports numerous beaches, bed and breakfast inns, and country roads that lead up into the Santa Cruz Mountains.

SIGHTS

Preceding the beauty, however, is the beast. The road south from San Francisco leads through one of America's ugliest towns. In fact, **Daly City** is the perfect counterpoint to the bay city: it is as hideous as San Francisco is splendid. If Tony Bennett left his heart in San Francisco, he must have discarded a gall bladder in Daly City. This town was memorialized in Malvina Reynolds' song, "Little Boxes," which describes its "ticky tacky" houses and over-developed hillsides.

No matter, this suburban blight soon gives way to Route 1 which cuts through Pacifica and curls into the hills. As the road rises above a swirling coastline you'll be entering a geologic hotspot. The San Andreas fault, villain of the 1906 earthquake, heads back into shore near Pacifica. As the road cuts will reveal, the sedimentary rock along this area has been twisted and warped into bizarre shapes. At **Devil's Slide**, several miles south of Pacifica, unstable hillsides periodically collapse into the sea.

Now that I have totally terrified you, I should add that this is an area not to be missed. Drive carefully and you'll be safe to enjoy the outstanding ocean vistas revealed at every hairpin turn in this winding roadway. Rocky cliffs, pocket beaches, and erupting surf open to view. There are sea stacks offshore and, in winter, gray whales cruise the coast.

At the village of **Montara**, you will pass an old lighthouse whose utility buildings have been converted to a youth hostel. As the road descends toward Moss Beach, precipitous rock faces give way to gentle slopes and placid tidepools. Then in Half Moon Bay a four-mile-long white sand beach is backdropped by neatly tilled farmlands.

Half Moon Bay is what happens when the farm meets the sea. It's a hybrid town, half landlubber and half old-salt. They are as likely to sell artichokes here as fresh fish. The town was named for its crescent beach, but thinks of itself as the pumpkin capital of the world. In October, it hosts the **Pumpkin Festival**, which draws over 300,000 people. At times the furrowed fields seem a geometric continuation of ocean waves, as if the sea lapped across the land and became frozen there. It is Half Moon Bay's peculiar schizophrenia, a double identity that lends an undeniable flair to the community.

From Half Moon Bay, a connecting road leads to Route 35 and Route 9, providing an alternate course to Santa Cruz; this will be covered below, in the "Santa Cruz Mountains" sightseeing section of this chapter. For now, let's stay on Route 1, which continues south, poised between the mountains and the sea.

On the southern outskirts of Half Moon Bay, watch for the **Higgins–Purisima Road**, a country lane that curves for eight miles into the Santa Cruz Mountains, returning to Route 1. This scenic loop passes old farmhouses and sloping pastures, redwood-forested hills and mountain meadows. Immediately upon entering this bumpy road, you'll spy a stately old New England–style house set in a plowed field. That will be the **James Johnston House**, a saltbox structure with sloping roof and white clapboard facade. Dating back to 1853 and built by an original '49er, it is the oldest house along this section of coastline. The house is rarely open to the public; during the summer, it occasionally opens on the third Saturday of the month. ◄HIDDEN

The farming plus fishing spirit of Half Moon Bay prevails as Route 1 continues south. A short distance from the highway, you'll encounter **San Gregorio**, a weather-beaten little town. Once a resort area, today it reveals a quaint collection of sagging roofs and unpainted barns. **Pescadero** represents another timeworn town hid-

✔ CHECK THESE OUT—UNIQUE SIGHTS

- Traverse miles of sand dunes at **Año Nuevo State Reserve**, keeping an eye open for its exotic bird population, sea lions, and in winter, its two-ton mating elephant seals. *page 298*
- Stroll the **Santa Cruz Beach Boardwalk**, and peoplewatch or, better yet, dare to ride the ups-and-downs of the fabled roller coaster. *page 311*
- Spend the day underwater at the **Monterey Bay Aquarium**, with its fabulous marine displays, or touch the bat rays as they swim by you in an open tank. *page 333*
- Wander the trails of **Point Lobos State Reserve** and observe the ghostly Monterey Cypress trees stealing against the wind. *page 344*

den a short way from Route 1. It's a woodframe hamlet of front-porch rocking chairs and white-steeple churches. The name translates as "fisherman," but the Portuguese and Italian residents are farmers, planting artichokes, Brussels sprouts, beans, and lettuce in the patchwork fields surrounding the town.

Be sure to drop by the **San Gregorio General Store**, a classic general store that's been around for over a century. ~ Corner of Stage Road and Route 84, Pescadero; 415-726-0563.

A family-owned farm open to the public, **Phipps Country Store** offers a child-friendly barnyard, a plant nursery, flower and herb gardens, and a market selling dried beans, herbs, and other products grown on the premises. During the summer visitors can pick several varieties of berries. ~ 2700 Pescadero Road, Pescadero; 415-879-0787.

The beacon several miles south is **Pigeon Point Lighthouse**, a 110-foot sentinel that's one of the nation's tallest lighthouses. The point gained a nasty reputation during the 19th century when one ship after another smashed on the rocks. The lighthouse went up in 1872, and originally contained a 1000-piece lens. Doubling as a youth hostel, it now warns sailors while welcoming travelers.

Miles of sand dunes border **Año Nuevo State Reserve**, an enchanting park containing an offshore island where two-ton elephant seals breed in winter. With its tidepools, exotic bird population, sea lions, and harbor seals, the reserve is a natural playground. The Ohlone Indians highly valued the region for its abundant fish and shellfish population. It was here they experienced their first contact with whites in 1769 when Juan Gaspar de Portolá trekked through en route to his discovery of San Francisco Bay. (For further information, see the "Beaches & Parks" section below.) ~ 415-879-2025.

From here to Santa Cruz, the road streams past bold headlands and magnificent seascapes. There are excellent beaches to explore and marvelous vista points along the way. You'll also discover rolling farmlands where giant pumpkins grow at the edge of the sea.

About two miles north of Santa Cruz along Route 1 you'll discover **Wilder Ranch State Park**. This 4000-acre spread has 20 acres that have been designated a "cultural preserve" because of the Ohlone Indian shell mounds and historic houses dotting the property. In addition to an 1839 adobe, the complex features a Greek Revival farmhouse dating to the 1850s and an 1890-era Queen Anne Victorian. You can also tour the outlying barns and workshops portraying life on a turn-of-the-century dairy farm, which this once was. Closed the month of December; only open Friday through Sunday in January; open Wednesday through Sunday from February through November. Admission. ~ 408-426-0505.

LODGING

If there were a hotel on the site of **Hostelling International—Point Montara Lighthouse**, it would easily charge $200 a night.

Set on a bluff overlooking the ocean, on one of those dramatic points always reserved for lighthouses, the hostel charges down-to-earth prices (and requires a morning chore). The daily fee buys you a bunk in a cozy dorm-style room. Couple and family rooms are also available. There are two kitchens, a hot tub, and two common rooms in this old lightkeeper's house. Reservations are strongly recommended. ~ Route 1 at 16th Street, Montara; 415-728-7177. BUDGET.

The Seal Cove Inn, located 30 minutes south of San Francisco and six miles north of Half Moon Bay, is the perfect place to sojourn for one more night before heading farther afield. The decor is decidedly country inn, with flowers, grandfather clocks, antique furnishings, and a fireplace. But the setting is California-style, with seals, whales, long white beaches, and towering cypress trees sharing the surrounding acreage. ~ 221 Cypress Avenue, Moss Beach; 415-728-4114, 800-995-9987, fax 415-728-4116. ULTRA-DELUXE.

The Cape Cod look has become very popular with establishments in the Half Moon Bay area. One of the foremost, **Pillar Point Inn** is a fully modern bed and breakfast cloaked in 19th-century New England disguise. Overlooking the harbor, this 11-room inn combines VCRs, televisions, and refrigerators with traditional amenities like featherbeds, window seats, and fireplaces. Every guest room has a private bath, and there's a deck overlooking the waterfront. Breakfast is a full-course affair. ~ 380 Capistrano Road, Princeton-by-the-Sea; 415-728-7377, 800-400-8281, fax 415-728-8345. ULTRA-DELUXE.

For a touch of the truly magnificent, plant yourself a few blocks inland at **Mill Rose Inn**. This turn-of-the-century inn has been decorated by a master of interior design. There are hand-painted wallpapers, European antiques, and colorful tiles throughout. The grounds resemble an English garden and include a gazebo with hot tub and flagstone patio. Each of the six guest rooms is brilliantly appointed; even the least expensive displays an antique armoire, European featherbed, and marbletop dresser covered with old-style combs and brushes. The sitting room and spacious dining room are equally elegant. This is one of the finest country inns along the entire Central Coast. ~ 615 Mill Street, Half Moon Bay; 415-726-8750, 800-900-7673, fax 415-726-3031. ULTRA-DELUXE.

Among lodgings on this stretch of coastline, **San Benito House** is a personal favorite. Set in a turn-of-the-century building, it's a 12-33room bed-and-breakfast inn with adjoining bar and restaurant. The less expensive rooms are small but quite nice. One room I saw featured a brass light fixture, hanging plants, quilted beds, framed drawings, and wood furniture. There are both shared and private baths. Add a sauna plus a country inn ambience and you have a bargain at the price. ~ 356 Main Street, Half Moon Bay; 415-726-3425. MODERATE.

The blue clapboard home of an early merchant in Half Moon Bay is now a bed-and-breakfast inn called the **Zaballa House.** Within the 1859 structure, the oldest in town, are nine charming rooms, some with fireplaces and large whirlpool tubs. A friendly, unpretentious atmosphere prevails throughout, with guests encouraged to put their feet up in the parlor and relax with a good book. ~ 324 Main Street, Half Moon Bay; 415-726-9123, fax 415-726-3921. MODERATE TO ULTRA-DELUXE.

The **Rancho San Gregorio**, set in the sunny valley of the same name, is a Spanish mission–style bed and breakfast not to be missed if homelike comfort and the orderliness of a five-star hotel suit you. The inn has four spacious rooms, decorated country fashion with exposed beam ceilings. ~ Route 84, five miles inland from Route 1 between the towns of San Gregorio and La Honda; 415-747-0722, fax 415-747-0184. MODERATE TO ULTRA-DELUXE.

Comparable to the low-cost lodging at Montara is **Hostelling International—Pigeon Point Lighthouse.** It has a similarly dramatic windswept setting above the ocean. The rooms are in several shared cottages with kitchens, living rooms, and accommodations for couples. Rates, as in other American Youth Hostels, are budget, and a chore is required. Guests have access to a private, clifftop hot tub for a small fee. Set beneath California's second tallest lighthouse on a beautiful shoreline, the hostel is a charming place to stay. Reservations 48 hours in advance strongly recommended. ~ Route 1, Pescadero; 415-879-0633. BUDGET.

New Davenport Cash Store Bed & Breakfast Inn, located near the coast about ten miles north of Santa Cruz, has a singular appeal. A few rooms here are situated in a historic old house; most are upstairs from a gallery gift shop. The staff is congenial and the accommodations mighty comfortable. All rooms have private baths

✔ CHECK THESE OUT—UNIQUE LODGING

- *Budget:* Witness a lighthouse-keeper's view at **Hostelling International—Point Montara Lighthouse**, an inexpensive coastside lodging. *page 298*
- *Moderate:* Unpack your bags at **Surfside Apartments** and then grab your sunscreen and head to the boardwalk two blocks away. *page 314*
- *Deluxe:* Return to 1889, the year **The Pine Inn** opened in Carmel, and enjoy the Edwardian ambience of this distinct caravansary. *page 345*
- *Ultra-deluxe:* Totally unwind at **Ventana**, where Japanese hot baths, herbal wraps, tile fireplaces, and quilted beds set the tone for this ultimate get-away-from-it-all resort. *page 355*

Budget: under $50 Moderate: $50–$90 Deluxe: $90–$120 Ultra-deluxe: over $120

and are imaginatively decorated with watercolors. In fact, the owners are potters and have adorned some rooms with their handicrafts. You can also look for antique pieces, oak furniture, and wall-to-wall carpeting. ~ 31 Davenport Avenue, Davenport; 408-425-1818, 800-870-1817. MODERATE TO DELUXE.

DINING

Nick's Restaurant has been operated by the same Italian-American family for 69 years and is still pulling in the Pacifica crowds. Wood sculptures of sea life decorate the walls, but the main attraction is the million-dollar view of Rockaway Beach across the street. Nick's is known for its grilled crab sandwiches, sautéed prawns, and fettuccine angelina, and there's music on Friday and Saturday night in the lounge. ~ 100 Rockaway Beach, Pacifica; 415-359-3900. MODERATE.

Tillie's is known for German specialties and Continental dishes. Wienerschnitzel, veal cordon bleu, sauerbraten, cabbage rolls, pork schnitzel, bratwurst, and Hungarian goulash are popular dishes served at tables brightened with checkered linen. Photos of German cities and the owner's family decorate the walls of this brick-faced restaurant. ~ Corner of California Avenue and Route 1, Moss Beach; 415-728-5744. MODERATE.

For dinner overlooking the ocean, there's nothing quite like **Moss Beach Distillery**. The place enjoys a colorful history, dating back to Prohibition days, when this area was notorious for supplying booze to thirsty San Francisco. Today it's a quiet plate-glass restaurant with adjoining bar. The menu includes gulf shrimp, calamari sauté, cioppino, steak, and grilled pork loin medallions with wild mushroom ragoût. The bootleggers are long gone, but those splendid sea views will be here forever. ~ Beach Way and Ocean Boulevard, Moss Beach; 415-728-5595. MODERATE TO DELUXE.

Speaking of seafood, **The Fishtrap** down on Half Moon Bay has some of the lowest prices around. Set in a small woodframe building smack on the bay, this unpretentious eatery features several fresh fish dishes daily. They're liable to be serving ling cod, halibut, and swordfish, as well as shellfish, and steak sandwiches. Friendly, local, inexpensive—and highly recommended. ~ 281 Capistrano Road, Princeton-by-the-Sea; 415-728-7049. MODERATE.

Or try **The Shore Bird**, set in a Cape Cod–style building overlooking the water. This expansive seafood restaurant features a dining room, seafood café, cocktail lounge, garden patio, and more. ~ 390 Capistrano Road, Princeton-by-the-Sea; 415-728-5541. MODERATE TO DELUXE.

The **Village Green** is another local snuggery. Small and cozy, it's an English-style establishment serving "farmhouse breakfasts," "ploughman's lunches," and afternoon teas. If you're in the mood for scones, English sausage, housemade Cornish pasties, or a banger and onion sandwich, this is your only chance for many many miles. Closed Wednesday. ~ 89 Avenue Portola, El Granada; 415-726-3690. BUDGET.

Aficionados of Mexican food often head for **El Perico's**. With its antiqued wood panelling and exposed beam ceiling, the place is rustically fashionable. The menu includes all the south of the border specialties—chile rellenos, tostadas, tacos, burritos, flautas, enchiladas, and so on. ~ 211 San Mateo Road, Half Moon Bay; 415-726-3737. BUDGET TO MODERATE.

For contemporary California cuisine in a country inn setting, there's **San Benito House**. This gourmet restaurant with moderate to deluxe prices incorporates fresh seafood and produce from the surrounding ocean and farm country. On a typical night you might choose Atlantic salmon with mustard vinaigrette, homemade ravioli, or filet of beef with chanterelle mushrooms. The hotel also houses a budget-priced deli (open 11 a.m. to 3:30 p.m.) that serves homemade soup, salad, and bread. ~ 356 Main Street, Half Moon Bay; 415-726-3425. BUDGET TO DELUXE.

Once past Half Moon Bay, restaurants become mighty scarce. Practically anything will do along this lonesome stretch south; but rather than just anything, you can have **Duarte's Tavern**. Open since 1934, this restaurant and tavern has earned a reputation all down the coast for delicious food. There's a menu filled with meat and fish entrées, omelettes, and sandwiches. Personally, I recommend being adventurous by trying the artichoke soup and olallieberry pie. ~ 202 Stage Road, Pescadero; 415-879-0464. MODERATE.

Farther down the coast, the **New Davenport Cash Store Restaurant** offers a countrified atmosphere. It's adjacent to a traditional general store and decorated with colorful wall rugs, handwoven baskets, and fresh flowers. The cuisine at this eatery rambles from chorizo and eggs to tofu and vegetables to mushroom cheese-melt sandwiches to steamed clams. More ordinary fare—omelettes, hamburgers, steak, and seafood—is also on the agenda. They also feature dinner specials such as salmon, scallops, and chicken. ~ 31 Davenport Avenue, Davenport; 408-426-4122. BUDGET TO MODERATE.

NIGHTLIFE

There's jazz and classical music Sunday afternoon at the **Bach Dancing and Dynamite Society**. There's also a classical series on Saturday nights. Situated beachfront off Route 1 about two miles north of the Route 92 intersection, it's renowned for quality sounds. ~ Medio Road, Half Moon Bay; 415-726-4143.

The **New Davenport Cash Store Bar** often features live classical music on the weekends. Listen to harp or guitar in a café setting. ~ 31 Davenport Avenue, Davenport; 408-426-4122.

BEACHES & PARKS

GRAY WHALE COVE This white-sand crescent is a well-known clothing-optional beach. Tucked discreetly beneath steep cliffs, it is also a beautiful spot. The only facilities are toilets; restaurants and groceries are several miles away in Pacifica and Montara. Day-use fee, $5 per person. ~ Located along Route 1 three miles south of Pacifica. Watch for the parking lot on the east side of the highway. Cautiously cross the highway and proceed down the staircase to the beach; 415-728-5336.

MONTARA STATE BEACH Nude sunbathers congregate near the north end of this half-mile-long sand swath; volleyball players and frisbee throwers can be found everywhere. Backdropped by a rocky bluff, it's a very pretty place. Surfers ride the small swells. The only facilities here are toilets; restaurants and groceries are located nearby in Montara. ~ The beach is located along Route 1 seven miles south of Pacifica. There is a trail leading to the beach from Route 1 and 2nd Street in Montara; 415-726-8819.

JAMES V. FITZGERALD MARINE RESERVE Boasting the best facilities among the beaches in the area, this park also has a sandy beach and excellent tidepools. It's a great place to while away the hours watching crabs, sea urchins, and anemones. Since there are houses nearby, this is more of a family beach than the freewheeling areas to the immediate north and south. There are restrooms and a picnic area; restaurants and groceries are available nearby in Moss Beach. ~ Located off Route 1 in Moss Beach about eight miles south of Pacifica; 415-728-3584.

HALF MOON BAY STATE BEACH (OR FRANCIS BEACH) Despite a four-mile-long sand beach, this park receives only a guarded recommendation. Half Moon Bay is a working harbor, so the beach lacks the seclusion and natural qualities of other strands along the coast. Of course, with civilization so near at hand, the facilities here are more complete than elsewhere. Also, Francis Beach is part of a chain of beaches that you can choose from, including Venice Beach, Roosevelt Beach, and Dunes Beach. Personally, I pick the last. Surfing is done at the sandy beach break at Francis Beach and below Half Moon Bay jetty. Restrooms or toilets are available at all four beaches; picnic areas at Francis Beach; restaurants and groceries are located nearby in Half Moon Bay. Day-use fee, $4. ~ All four park segments are located along Route 1 in Half Moon Bay; 415-726-8819.

▲ There are 55 sites for tents and RVs (no hookups) at Francis Beach; $12 to $14 per night. Hiker/biker camp available at Francis. First-come, first-served for all sites.

SAN GREGORIO STATE BEACH There is a white sand beach here framed by sedimentary cliffs and cut by a small creek. Star of the show, though, is the nearby private nude beach (admission) north of the state beach, reputedly the first beach of its type ◄ HIDDEN in California. Among the nicest of the state's nude beaches, it features a narrow sand corridor shielded by high bluffs. There are picnic areas and toilets at the state beach, no facilities at the nude beach; restaurants and groceries are nearby in San Gregorio or Pescadero. Day-use fee, $4. ~ Located along Route 1 about 15 miles south of Half Moon Bay. Entrance to the nude beach is several hundred yards north of the state beach entrance; 415-879-2170.

POMPONIO STATE BEACH Less appealing than its neighbor to the north, this park has a white sand beach that's traversed periodically by a creek. There are headlands on either side of the beach. Facilities include picnic areas and toilets; restaurants and groceries are five miles away in Pescadero. Day-use fee, $4. ~ The beach is located on Route 1 about 16 miles south of Half Moon Bay; 415-879-2170.

PESCADERO STATE BEACH Backed by sand dunes and saltwater ponds, this lovely park also features a wide beach. There are tidepools to the south and a wildlife preserve across the highway. Steelhead run annually in the streams here, while deer, blue herons, and egrets inhabit the nearby marshland. There are picnic areas and toilets; restaurants and groceries are found in nearby Pescadero. Day-use fee, $4. ~ On Route 1 about 19 miles south of Half Moon Bay; 415-879-2170.

BEAN HOLLOW STATE BEACH The small sandy beach here is bounded by rocks, so sunbathers go elsewhere while tidepool watchers drop by. Particularly interesting is nearby Pebble Beach, a coarse-grain strand studded with jasper, serpentine, agates, and carnelians. The stones originate from a quartz reef offshore and attract rockhounds by the pack. But don't take rocks away—it's illegal. Also not to be missed is the blufftop trail between Bean Hollow and Pebble Beach, from which you can espy seals and whales in season. Facilities include a picnic area and toilets; restaurants and groceries are located several miles away in Pescadero. Day-use fee, $4. ~ Located along Route 1 about 21 miles south of Half Moon Bay; Pebble Beach is about a mile north of Bean Hollow; 415-879-2170.

BUTANO STATE PARK This inland park, several miles from the coast, provides a welcome counterpoint to the beach parks. About 2700 acres, it features a deep redwood forest, including stands of virgin trees. Hiking trails traverse the territory. Not as well known as other nearby redwood parks, Butano suffers less human traffic. The park has picnic areas and restrooms; restaurants and groceries are several miles away in Pescadero. Day-use fee, $5. ~ Located 22 miles south of Half Moon Bay. Coming from the north on Route 1, go 20 miles south of Half Moon Bay; turn left (east) on Pescadero Road, and then right on Cloverdale Road about four miles to the park. Or, coming from the south, turn right (east) on Gazos Creek Road (two miles south of Pigeon Point Lighthouse) and then left on Cloverdale Road; 415-879-2040.

▲ There are 39 sites for tents and RVs (no hookups); $12 to $17 per night. Reservations are recommended. Call DESTINET (800-444-7275).

AÑO NUEVO STATE RESERVE Awesome in its beauty, abundant in wildlife, this park is one of the most spectacular on the California coast. It consists of a peninsula heaped with sand dunes. A miniature island lies just offshore. There are tidepools to search and a nature trail for exploring. Seals and sea lions inhabit the area; loons, hawks, pheasants, and albatrosses have been spied here. But most spectacular of all the denizens are the elephant seals, those loveably grotesque creatures who come here between December 15 and March 31 to breed. Reaching two tons and 16 feet, adorned with the bulbous, trunk-like snouts for which they are named, these mammals are unique. Back in 1800, elephant seals numbered in the hundreds of thousands; by the end of the century, they were practically extinct; it's only recently that they have achieved a comeback. When breeding, the bulls stage bloody battles and collect large harems, creating a spectacle that draws crowds every year. During breeding season, docents lead two-and-a-half-hour tours which must be booked eight weeks in advance through DESTINET (800-444-7275). The tours cover seal-breeding areas, which otherwise are closed to the public throughout the breeding season; during the rest of the year the entire park and the seal rookery are open. Be forewarned that it's a three-mile-round-trip walk from the parking lot to the rookery. During the summer there are surf breaks off the end of beach, about ten minutes south of the rookery. The only facilities are toilets; restaurants and groceries are ten miles away in Davenport. Day-use fee, $4. ~ Located off of Route 1, about 22 miles south of Half Moon Bay; 415-879-2025.

GREYHOUND ROCK One of the most secluded strands around, this beach is a beauty. There are startling cliffs in the background and a gigantic boulder—Greyhound Rock—in the foreground; the area is a favorite among those who love to fish. It is also, unfortunately, a favorite for thieves. Keep your valuables with you and lock your car. Bathrooms and picnic areas are the only facilities; restaurants and groceries are seven miles away in Davenport. ~ Located along Route 1 about 30 miles south of Half Moon Bay. From the parking lot at the roadside follow the path down to the beach; 408-462-8333. ◄ HIDDEN

BONNY DOON BEACH This spot ranks among the most popular nude beaches in California. Known up and down the coast, the compact beach is protected on either flank by rugged cliffs. There are dunes at the south end of the beach, caves to the north, plus bevies of barebottomed bathers in between. Keep a close eye on your valuables. This beach has no security nor facilities; restaurants and groceries are located a few miles away in Davenport. ~ Located off Route 1 about eight miles north of Santa Cruz. Watch for the parking lot near the junction with Bonny Doon Road; follow the path across the railroad tracks and down to the beach.

RED, WHITE, AND BLUE BEACH There's a "clothing optional" beach here surrounded by rocky headlands. There are also more RVs than at a Fourth of July picnic. The beach is monitored for safety and no cameras or dogs are allowed. Visitors have to pay upon entry. Of course, the beach does provide facilities and permit camping but somehow the management takes the nature out of bathing au natural. There are picnic areas, restrooms, and hot showers; restaurants and groceries are available in Santa Cruz, seven miles away. Day-use fee, $4 to $7. ~ Located off Route 1, five miles north of Santa Cruz. Watch for the red, white, and blue mailbox at Scaroni Road intersection; follow Scaroni Road a short distance west to the beach; 408-423-6332.

▲ There are 29 sites; $12 to $16 per night.

Santa Cruz Mountains

For a hawk's eye view of the Santa Cruz Mountains and redwood country, leave the coast at Half Moon Bay and catch Route 35 (Skyline Boulevard) south. This rustic highway climbs along a ridgetop, revealing vistas of both the ocean and San Francisco Bay. From the tangled undergrowth on either side of the road, scattered trees, pine and deciduous, stand against open sky.

Then the forest gathers around you as the road tunnels through dense, tall timber. You are entering a land of giants. A gate and small sign, three miles north of the Route 84 turnoff, mark Methuselah, a stately 1800-year-old redwood.

For an interesting detour loop, take Route 84 (La Honda Road) south to La Honda, a knotty-pine town decorated with a bar, a restaurant, and a post office. This forest retreat is novelist Ken Kesey's old stomping ground. During the halcyon days of the '60s, his band of Merry Pranksters, like rebels in the hills, swept down from La Honda through Northern California and beyond. They were mind-guerrillas, set on overthrowing American consciousness with the "Trips Festival," a multimedia extravaganza of rock music, light shows, and street theater, raised to an electric pitch by massive doses of psychedelic drugs.

SIGHTS

Today La Honda has lapsed back into rural consciousness. Rather than tripping out or experiencing heavy life changes, you'll probably just pass through town and pick up Alpine Road, which returns to Route 35. En route you'll encounter **Heritage Grove**, a virgin redwood forest with a creek and hiking trails, and then emerge into rolling hill country marked by broad vistas.

Pick up Route 9 south, the redwood road that will eventually lead to Santa Cruz. Before this winding mountain road descends to the sea, it connects with an even narrower and more sinuous thoroughfare, Route 236, which goes to **Big Basin Redwoods State Park**. One of the area's prettiest parks, it offers nature trails galore, 2000-year-old redwood stands, and complete facilities for picnicking and camping.

Almost as fascinating as the park is the history behind its founding. At the turn of the century, most of these magnificent groves were marked for destruction by lumbermen. But Andrew P. Hill, a local photographer and conservationist, vowed to preserve the giants. Hill had been infuriated and inspired when an arrogant landowner refused him permission to photograph the redwoods because they were private property! Dedicated to "Save the Redwoods," Hill formed the Sempervirens Club, which lobbied for preservation of forests throughout the state.

You can hike to Slippery Rock, opposite a waterfall, where pioneer conservationists made a pact to protect the public's natural heritage.

Rejoining Route 9 in Boulder Creek, you'll find that this town, Ben Lomond, and Felton are central to the area's travel facilities. They house numerous antique stores and crafts shops. In addition to tourists, they also attract a lot of winter rain. In 1982 this became a disaster area: almost two feet of rain fell in just 36 hours, hillsides collapsed, mudslides buried homes, and 21 people died in Santa Cruz County. Outside Ben Lomond, a dozen people are buried in mudslides so deep their bodies have never been recovered.

Now that you're convinced never to go near the region, let me tell you some of its marvelous features—like the **Felton covered bridge** (at the edge of town on Covered Bridge Road). A wood-plank span with sagging shingle roof, the structure dates from 1892. Appropriately, it's set in a secluded spot along the San Lorenzo River. ◄HIDDEN

At nearby **Henry Cowell Redwoods State Park** there are 4000 acres of redwood forest to explore; one trail here leads to the dean of the forest, an ambassadorial, 285-foot tree.

Over at **Roaring Camp Railroad** a vintage steam engine whistles through redwood stands en route to Bear Mountain. Passengers are invited to picnic on the mountain, hike the area, then return on a later train. Admission. ~ Graham Hill Road, Felton; 408-335-4484.

During the summer you can climb aboard the **Santa Cruz, Big Trees and Pacific Railway**, with full-size cars, for a scenic eight-mile journey to the Santa Cruz boardwalk. Admission. ~ Board in the town of Felton or Santa Cruz; 408-335-4484, 408-335-4400.

LODGING

Accommodations in the Santa Cruz Mountains cluster around the towns of Boulder Creek, Ben Lomond, and Felton. They are generally of two types: neon motels and piney lodges. The first are less expensive, the second more inviting.

Tyrolean Inn offers duplex cottages that are small but intimate, with simple decor, wood-paneled walls, wall-to-wall carpeting, a TV, and a stall shower. Some have kitchens as well. Or you can rent a private cottage. Preferable to the duplexes, this unit is warm, bright, and done entirely in knotty pine. ~ 9600 Route 9, Ben Lomond; 408-336-5188, fax 408-336-2804. BUDGET TO MODERATE.

Merrybrook Lodge, set in a redwood grove, has pretty cottages right on a creek. They are one-bedroom structures, with living room, kitchen, and porch. The floors are hardwood, the walls knotty pine, and as a final touch, there's a woodstove. For rustic living high in the mountains, you'll be hard pressed to find a more inviting place. ~ 13420 Big Basin Highway, Boulder Creek; 408-338-6813. MODERATE.

DINING

Located at the only busy intersection for miles around is **Alice's Restaurant**. It sports little more than a counter, a few tables and chairs, and a 12-table outdoor eating area facing Route 35. Alice's is open for breakfast, lunch, and dinner, primarily serving egg dishes, sandwiches, and standard dinner fare like vegetable lasagne. ~ Skyline Boulevard and La Honda Road, Woodside; 415-851-0303. BUDGET TO MODERATE.

Tyrolean Inn, a rustic little restaurant, serves German dishes and specialty sandwiches for lunch. During the dinner hour, they stoke the fires and prepare an array of German dishes. Sauerbraten, wienerschnitzel, and smoked pork chops with sauerkraut are among the European dishes. Served with soup or salad and sourdough or German rye. Closed Monday (and, in winter, Tuesday). ~ 9600 Route 9, Ben Lomond; 408-336-5188. MODERATE.

Around since 1904, **Scopazzi's Inn** can still be trusted for a good meal. The place is perfectly fitted to its mountain environment, with wood-paneled walls, a lofty, exposed-beam ceiling and lots of windows for great views. Add a tile fireplace, a patio, and a lounge for a prize establishment in the heart of Santa Cruz redwood country. The menu is equal to all this: there are numerous dinners—roast beef, filet of sole, veal parmigiana—complete with soup, salad, antipasto, and dessert. At lunch they serve sandwiches, salads, pasta dishes, and several platters including veal cutlet and calamari. Closed Monday and Tuesday. ~ 13300 Big Basin Highway, Boulder Creek; 408-338-6441. MODERATE TO DELUXE.

PARKS

SAN MATEO COUNTY MEMORIAL PARK A 327-acre park, this redwood preserve is covered with hiking trails. There's a creekside swimming hole, a visitors center, and a redwood tree dating back 1500 years. In an area of extraordinary parks, this one's a sleeper, small but beautiful, and a good place to avoid the crowds found at more popular parks. It's also a gateway to 5973-acre **Pescadero Creek County Park**, with a network of trails and hike-in campsites. There's also the very special 60-acre Heritage Grove, an unusual stand of redwoods that are bigger and larger in diameter than others in the park. Facilities include picnic areas, restrooms, showers, and a grocery. Day-use fee, $4. ~ 9500 Pescadero Creek Road about six miles from La Honda; 415-879-0212, 415-879-0238.

▲ There are 132 sites; $14 per night; hike-in sites are free but you need a permit from the park.

PORTOLA REDWOODS STATE PARK With dense stands of redwood, Douglas fir, and tan oak, this natural facility is a great place for exploration. There are 18 miles of hiking trails, including one leading to Tiptoe Falls, a five-foot waterfall. Add to the attributes of this lovely park several creeks filled with steelhead (no fishing, however) and an undergrowth thick with huckleberry. There are picnic areas, restrooms, and showers; restaurants and groceries are several miles away in La Honda or along Route 35. Day-use fee, $5. ~ From Route 35, take Alpine Road west to Portola State Park Road; 415-948-9098.

▲ There are 53 sites plus a backpack camp; $12 to $16 per night.

CASTLE ROCK STATE PARK A hiker's paradise, this 3600-acre semi-wilderness area has no entry roads. To experience the place you'll have to join the many hikers, backpackers, and rock climbers who number this among their favorite parks. The rewards are several: a network of trails, including one that descends 31 miles to the ocean; a waterfall; and the eponymous sandstone boulder which crowns this retreat at 3214 feet. Hike-in campsites feature picnic areas, toilets, and running water; restaurants and groceries are found several miles away in Boulder Creek or Saratoga. Parking fee, $3. ~ The parking lot and trailhead are located on Skyline Boulevard two-and-one-half miles south of the intersection with Route 9; 408-867-2952. ◄ HIDDEN

▲ Permitted at 23 hike-in campsites. For information, contact the park headquarters at 408-338-8860.

BIG BASIN REDWOODS STATE PARK California's oldest state park, this 18,000-acre expanse reaches from the ocean to a 2300-foot elevation. Within that domain are 2000-year-old redwoods, a sandy beach, 88 miles of hiking trails, 20 to 30 miles of mountain-biking trails, and a host of facilities. You'll also find *homo sapiens* in tents, black-tailed deer, coyotes, bobcats, raccoons, and salamanders inhabiting the area, as well as over 250 bird species which either live here or drop by. It's highly recommended that you do also. There are picnic areas, a mini-museum, a snack bar, a grocery, a gift shop, restrooms, and showers. Day-use fee, $5. ~ Located at 21600 Big Basin Way (Route 236), nine miles north of Boulder Creek; Route 9 connects with Route 236, leading to the park; 408-338-8860.

▲ There are 183 designated sites plus several hike-in sites; $14 to $18 per night. Also four-person tent cabins are available for $38 per night; call 800-874-8368 for reservations. (Two especially recommended campsites near park headquarters are the Blooms Creek and Huckleberry campgrounds.)

HENRY COWELL REDWOODS STATE PARK An 1800-acre park on the San Lorenzo River, it features a short nature trail (three-quarter-mile loop) through a redwood forest. One of the goliaths here measures 285 feet; there are also stands of Douglas fir and madrone. With 18 miles of hiking trails, picnic areas, a mini-museum, a bookstore, restrooms, and showers, it's a favorite among locals; restaurants and groceries are nearby in Felton. Day-use fee, $5. ~ Located off Route 9 just south of Felton; 408-335-4598.

▲ There are 113 sites in a campground on Graham Hill Road three miles from the park center; $14 to $17 per night; information, 408-438-2396.

Santa Cruz

One of California's original missions, a University of California campus, a historic railroad, and some of the finest Victorian neighborhoods on the coast are just a few of the pluses in Santa Cruz. This town of 51,000 population is in many respects one big playground. It enjoys spectacular white sand beaches, entertaining nightlife, and an old-style boardwalk amusement park. The city faces south, providing the best weather along the Central Coast. Arts and crafts flourish here, and vintage houses adorn the area.

SIGHTS

Route 1, California's magnificent coastal highway, veers slightly inland upon reaching Santa Cruz, which means it's time to find a different waterfront drive. Not to worry, the best way to begin exploring the place is at the north end of town around **Natural Bridges State Beach**. All but one of the sea arches here have collapsed, leading local wags to dub the spot "Fallen Arches." A pretty spot for a picnic, this is the place to pick up West Cliff Drive, which sweeps the Santa Cruz waterfront. The shoreline is a honeycomb of tiny coves, sea arches, and pocket beaches. From **Lighthouse Point** on a clear day, the entire 40-mile curve of Monterey Bay silhouettes the skyline. Even in foggy weather, sea lions cavort on the rocks offshore, while surfers ride the challenging "Steamer Lane" breaks.

Beach Street continues this coast-hugging route to **Santa Cruz Municipal Pier**, a half-mile-long wharf lined with bait shops, restaurants, and fishing charters. Those early morning folks with the sun-furrowed faces are either fishing or crabbing. They are here everyday with lawn chairs and tackle boxes. When reality overcomes optimism, they have been known to duck into nearby fresh fish stores for the day's catch. The pier is a perfect place to promenade, soak up sun, and seek out local color. It also provides a peaceful counterpoint to the next attraction.

Santa Cruz Beach Boardwalk is Northern California's answer to Coney Island. Pride of the city, it dates back to 1907 and sports several old-fashioned rides. The penny arcade features vintage machines as well as modernistic video games. You'll find shooting galleries and candy stalls, coin-operated fortune tellers and do-it-yourself photo machines. Shops sell everything from baubles to bikinis. Then there are the ultimate entertainments: a slow-circling ferris wheel with chairs suspended high above the beach; the antique merry-go-round, a whirl of mirrors and flashing color; a funicular whose brightly painted cars reflect the sun; rides with names that instantaneously evoke childhood memories—tilt-a-whirl, haunted castle, bumper cars; and that soaring symbol of amusement parks everywhere, the roller coaster. Closed December and most nonsummer weekdays. ~ 400 Beach Street; 408-423-5590.

The **Cocoanut Grove Ballroom**, located on the boardwalk, has hosted Big Band greats like Benny Goodman and the Dorsey brothers, and still sponsors dancing, usually disco or salsa. ~ 400 Beach Street; 408-423-2053.

The playground for shoppers sits several blocks inland along Pacific Avenue. **Pacific Garden Mall** is a tree-lined promenade stretching from Cathcart to Water streets. The entire mall is a study in urban landscaping and planning, beautifully executed. On October 17, 1989, a 7.1 earthquake centered just a few miles from Santa Cruz sent most of the mall tumbling into the street, killing three people. Architects and construction crews have completed rebuilding the mall and the shops are back in business as usual.

SURFER SHRINE

Testament to surfers' talent is the tiny **Santa Cruz Surfing Museum** situated in the lighthouse at Lighthouse Point. Here vintage photos and antique boards re-create the history of the Hawaiian sport that landed on the shores of Santa Cruz early in the century. Closed Tuesday. ~ West Cliff Drive and Lighthouse Point, Santa Cruz; 408-429-3429.

Within walking distance of the mall are several places that merit short visits. The **McPherson Center for Art and History** at 705 Front Street is home to two museums. The **Art Museum of Santa Cruz County** features changing exhibits that focus primarily on California art. Admission. ~ 408-429-1964. The **History Museum of Santa Cruz County** displays exhibits related to the social history of the Santa Cruz area, including photographs and artifacts. Admission. ~ 408-425-7278. Also here is **The Octagon Gallery**, which houses rotating exhibits for the two aforementioned museums within its century-old, eight-sided structure.

And the **Santa Cruz Mission**, a half-scale replica of the 1791 structure, pales by comparison with the missions in Carmel and San Juan Bautista. Closed Monday. ~ Corner of Emmet and High streets; 408-426-5686.

A remarkable piece of restoration, **Santa Cruz Mission State Historic Park** provides a fascinating timeline on California's past. This 1822 home was built for Yokutz Indians who sold the property to Californios (children of Spanish settlers). Later it was bought by Irish immigrants. Various rooms document each of these periods with artifacts excavated on the site. Reflecting the difficulties of early 19th-century interior design, the Californio Room is decorated with mismatched wallpaper sent at different times from the East Coast. Docents lead tours every Saturday at 2 p.m. Cooking demonstrations, candlemaking, and brick-making take place on "Living History Day," held the first Saturday of the month. Closed Monday through Wednesday. Admission. ~ School Street near Mission Plaza; 408-425-5849.

The **Santa Cruz County Conference and Visitors Council** has information to help orient you with the area. ~ 701 Front Street; 408-425-1234.

Santa Cruz's rich history has left a legacy of elegant Victorian houses. Although there are no guided tours, if you set out on your own you won't be disappointed. In the Beach Hill area, not far from the Boardwalk, be sure to see the gem-like home at **1005 Third Street**, counterpoint to the multilevel confection with Queen Anne turret at **311 Main Street**. Near Pacific Garden Mall at 532 Center Street is the Civil War–era **Calvary Episcopal Church**, with its clapboard siding and shingle roof, and the **200 block of Walnut Avenue**, which is practically wall-to-wall Victorians. Located near the Santa Cruz Mission is the white-painted brick **Holy Cross Roman Catholic Church** at 126 High Street. The steeple of this 1889 Gothic Revival beauty is a landmark for miles around. Nearby **Francisco Alviza House** (109 Sylvar Street), vintage 1850s, is the oldest home in town. Around the corner, the **200 block of Mission Street** displays several houses built shortly afterwards. Nearby, at 123 Green Street, is **W. W. Reynolds House**, which was an Episcopal Church in 1850.

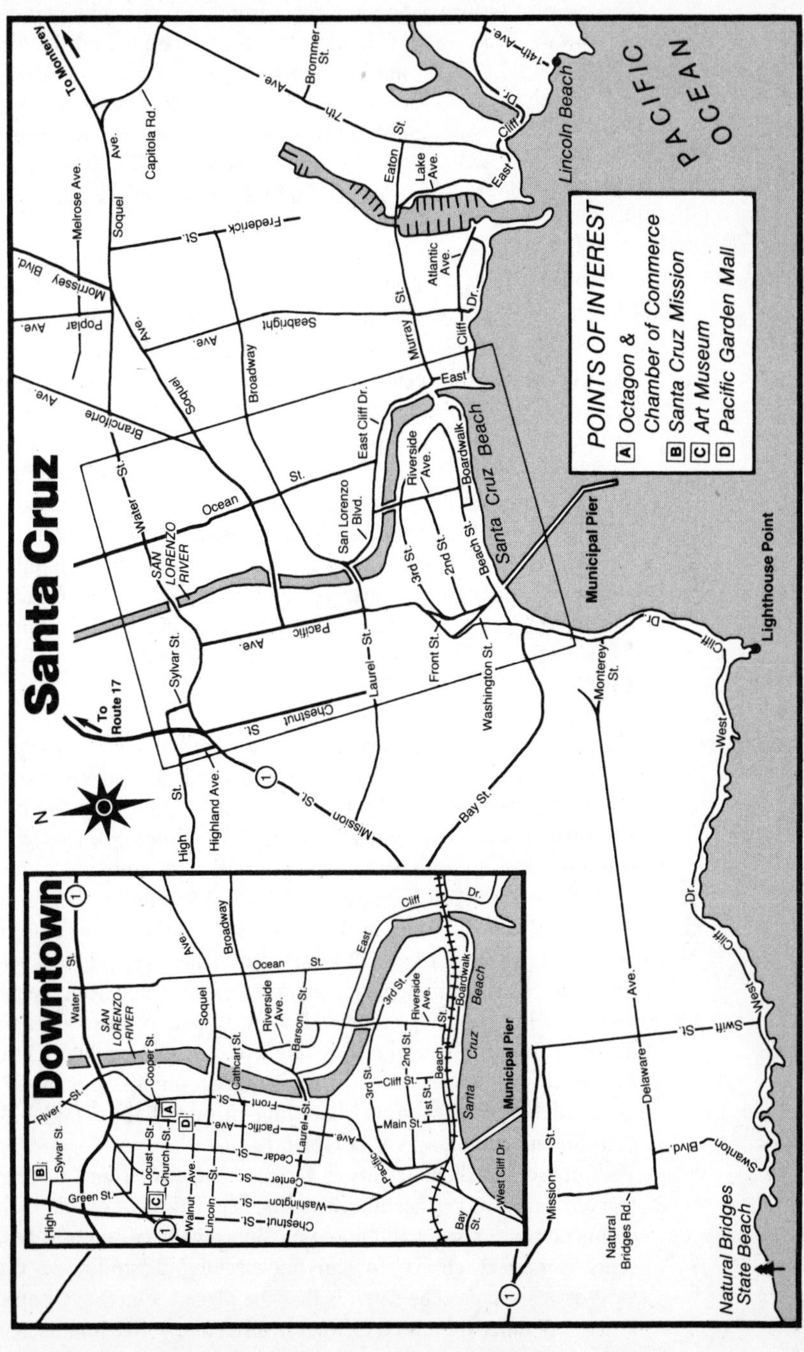
Santa Cruz
Downtown
POINTS OF INTEREST
A Octagon & Chamber of Commerce
B Santa Cruz Mission
C Art Museum
D Pacific Garden Mall
PACIFIC OCEAN
Santa Cruz Beach
Municipal Pier
Lighthouse Point
Lincoln Beach
Natural Bridges State Beach
SAN LORENZO RIVER
To Monterey
To Route 17
Boardwalk
Soquel Ave.
Ocean St.
Water St.
Broadway
Pacific Ave.
Mission St.
West Cliff Dr.
East Cliff Dr.
Delaware Ave.
Swanton Blvd.
Natural Bridges Rd.
Bay St.
Chestnut St.
Laurel St.
Front St.
Washington St.
Beach St.
Riverside Ave.
Seabright Ave.
Murray St.
Eaton St.
7th Ave.
Capitola Rd.
Morrissey Blvd.
Branciforte Ave.
Highland Ave.
Sylvar St.
Cooper St.
Cathcart St.
Center St.
Cedar St.
Lincoln St.
Walnut Ave.
Church St.
Locust St.
Green St.
High St.
River St.

From this last Victorian cluster, High Street leads to the **University of California–Santa Cruz** campus. Turn right at Glenn Coolidge Drive and you'll find an information booth dispensing maps, brochures, and words of wisdom. Those stone ruins and sunbleached buildings nearby are the remains of the old Cowell ranch and limestone quarry from which 2000 of the campus acres were drawn. ~ 408-459-0111.

Of particular interest at UC Santa Cruz are the organic farm as well as the arboretum, with its Mediterranean garden and outstanding collection of Australian and South African plants.

No ivory tower ever enjoyed the view that UC Santa Cruz commands of Monterey Bay. Set on a hillside, with redwood forest and range land all around, the campus possesses incredible beauty. The university itself is divided into eight colleges, insular and self- defined, each marked by a different architectural style. The best way to see this campus is simply to wander: Walk the fields, trek its redwood groves, and explore the different colleges that make it one of the West's most progressive institutions.

The **Joseph M. Long Marine Laboratory**, a University of California research facility located off campus, has a small hands-on aquarium and museum open to the public. This 40-acre facility, overlooking marine terraces, also has other marine life exhibits. Closed Monday. Admission. ~ End of Delaware Avenue; 408-459-4308.

LODGING

When seeking overnight accommodations in Santa Cruz, the place to look is near the beach. That is where you'll want to be and, not surprisingly, where you'll find most hotels and motels. The problem during summer months is the cost. In winter you can have a room for a song, but come June the price tags climb.

The best bargain in town is **Surfside Apartments**. This seven-unit establishment contains several cottages and houses clustered around a flower garden and courtyard. They are truly efficiency units: no television, telephone, parking facilities, or housekeeping services. But they are comfortably furnished, possess a friendly "beach cottage" feel, and feature kitchens. Located two blocks from the Boardwalk, there are one- and two-bedroom apartments. They are available only in summer (late June through Labor Day). ~ 311 Cliff Street; 408-423-5302. MODERATE.

Another excellent facility is **Ocean Echo Motel and Cottages**, located near a quiet neighborhood beach. This 15-unit clapboard complex sits far from the madding Boardwalk crowd and represents a perfect choice for anyone seeking a studio or Cape Cod–style cottage. The catch is that the place is extremely popular and many units are rented to weekly residents. ~ 401 Johans Beach Drive; 408-462-4192, fax 408-475-0265. MODERATE TO DELUXE.

It's big, brash, and blocky, but the **Dream Inn** is also right on the beach. With pool, sauna, jacuzzi, oceanfront restaurants, and lounge, this multitiered establishment extends from a hilltop perch down to a sandy strand. Long on aesthetics it isn't, and it's sometimes noisy on weekends and in the summer, but for location it can't be topped. The boardwalk and fishing pier are a short stroll away. Guest rooms are trimly done with fabric walls and contemporary furnishings; each sports a private balcony and ocean view. The question is whether you'll endure the plastic atmosphere for the sake of proximity to the Pacific. It's your call. (Being lazy myself, I'd book reservations in a minute.) ~ 175 West Cliff Drive; 408-426-4330, 800-662-3838, fax 408-426-4015. DELUXE TO ULTRA-DELUXE.

There is also **Hostelling International—Santa Cruz**, located some distance from the beach. Set in restored Victorian cottages on well-located Beach Hill, it offers 32 dorm-style beds and three private family rooms. The cottages are two blocks from the beach and boardwalk. There are also hot showers, a kitchen, and a common room; bring a sleeping bag, though sheets are available. There's an 11 p.m. curfew and in summer a three-night maximum stay. ~ 321 Main Street; 408-423-8304. BUDGET.

Country inns are rare in Santa Cruz; this California custom is just catching on here. One exception is **Cliff Crest Bed & Breakfast Inn**, a five-bedroom establishment in a historic 1887 Victorian home. Among the features of the house are an outdoor belvedere, a yard landscaped by the designer of San Francisco's Golden Gate Park, and a solarium illuminated through stained-glass windows. Rooms vary in cost from a small room with private bath to the spacious "Rose Room," which has a fireplace. In any case, the decor you're apt to find includes patterned wallpaper, an antique bed, a wicker couch, and a tile bath with a clawfoot tub. ~ 407 Cliff Street; 408-427-2609, 800-427-2609, fax 408-427-2710. DELUXE TO ULTRA-DELUXE.

Another member of this elite club, **Château Victorian**, sits in a vintage home just one block from the Boardwalk. Guests here enjoy two sun decks and a sitting/dining room decorated with antique sideboard and wooden mantel. The entire house has been done by masterful decorators who placed plush carpeting throughout. The place is chockablock with antiques: canopied beds, oak armoires, and so on. Less expensive rooms have carpets and bay window seats and are located in the cottage. Main house rooms are more costly. All rooms have fireplaces and feature tile baths. ~ 118 1st Street; 408-458-9458. DELUXE TO ULTRA-DELUXE.

Less distinguished, but considerably cheaper, is **Harbor Inn** across town. The place sits in a two-story stucco house on a busy street several blocks from the beach. It supports 19 bedrooms, some with kitchens. There are both private and shared baths. All are spacious, attractive, and inexpensively furnished. The staff is helpful and friendly, making this place a fortuitous addition to the local housing scene. ~ 645 7th Avenue; 408-479-9731. MODERATE TO DELUXE.

Santa Cruz also has a string of neon motels within blocks of the Boardwalk. Count on them to provide small rooms with color television, wall-to-wall carpeting, nicked wooden tables, naugahyde chairs, stall showers, etc.; if they have any decorations at all you'll wish they didn't. But what the hell, for a night or two you can call them home. Their rates fluctuate wildly depending on the season and tourist flow. (Generally they charge budget prices in winter; summer prices escalate to the moderate range.) The best of the lot is **St. Charles Court**, which has a pool and is spiffier and quieter than the others. ~ 902 3rd Street; 408-423-2091. BUDGET TO MODERATE.

Located within walking distance of the beach is **Big 6 Motel**. It sits in a two-story stucco building and contains 21 rooms with private baths. ~ 335 Riverside Avenue; 408-423-1651. BUDGET TO MODERATE.

Right next door is the **Super 8 Motel**, which has 23 rooms decorated in a white and burgundy color scheme. Guests here enjoy lounging at the pool. ~ 321 Riverside Avenue; 408-423-9449, 800-800-8000, fax 408-425-5100. BUDGET TO MODERATE.

DINING

Most Santa Cruz restaurants can be found near the Boardwalk or in the downtown area, with a few others scattered around town. Of course, along the Boardwalk the favorite dining style is to eat while you stroll. Stop at **Hodgie's** for a corn dog, Italian sausage sandwich, or fried zucchini; try a slice from the **Big Slice Pizza Bar**; sit down to a bowl of clam chowder or crab salad at the **Fisherman's Galley**; or pause at the **Barbary Coast** for cheeseburgers, baked potatoes, or "chicken nuggets." For dessert there are caramel apples, ice cream, cotton candy, popcorn, and saltwater taffy.

If all this proves a bit much, try one of the budget restaurants on Beach Street, across from the Boardwalk. Foremost is **Beach Street Café**, an attractive little cranny with white tablecloths and potted plants. This café houses the largest U.S. collection of Maxfield Parrish limited-edition prints. Breakfast begins with guacamole omelettes, bagels, croissants, or pancakes. Matter of fact, breakfast continues until late afternoon. Try the "Eggs Sardou" (artichoke bottoms with spinach, poached eggs, and Hollandaise sauce) or the "Eggs Beach Street" (for which they replace the spinach with sautéed shrimp). ~ 399 Beach Street; 408-426-7621. BUDGET.

Nearby **El Paisano Tamales** has the standard selection of tacos, tostadas, enchiladas, and burritos. Closed Monday and Tuesday in winter. ~ 605 Beach Street; 408-426-2382. BUDGET.

Ideal Bar and Grill is a tourist trap with tradition. It's been one since 1917. It also has decent food and a knockout view, especially from the outdoor deck right on the sand. The place is wedged in a corner between the beach and the pier, which means it looks out on everything, from boardwalk to bounding deep. The specialty is seafood—calamari, sand dabs, oysters, lobster, and salmon. Several casseroles, plus a few meat and fowl dishes round out the menu. ~ 106 Beach Street; 408-423-5271. MODERATE TO DELUXE.

Cozy **Casablanca Restaurant**, with its overhead fans and Moroccan flair, is excellent for dinner or Sunday brunch. The place has a wraparound view of the ocean, not to mention a tony decor. The menu includes such gourmet selections as grilled duck, rack of lamb, seafood linguine, and filet mignon with brandy. Casablanca boasts one of the largest selections of wines in Santa Cruz County. ~ 101 Main Street; 408-426-9063. MODERATE TO DELUXE.

Among the many places in the Pacific Garden Mall area, my personal favorite is **The Catalyst.** I don't go there so much to eat as to watch. Not that the food is bad (nor particularly good for that matter), but simply that The Catalyst is a scene. *The* scene in Santa Cruz. At night the place transmogrifies into a club with live music and unfathomable vibrations. By day, it's just itself, a cavernous structure with a glass roof and enough plants to make it an oversized greenhouse. Indeed, some of the clientele seem to have taken root. There are two bars if you're here to people watch. Otherwise meals are cafeteria-style and include a full breakfast menu, deli sandwiches, burgers, and a few dinner selections. ~ 1011 Pacific Avenue; 408-423-1338. BUDGET.

◄ HIDDEN

Join the locals at their favorite Mexican restaurant, **El Palomar**, named the best Mexican restaurant by the readers of *Good Times*, a local entertainment newspaper, for several years running.

✔ CHECK THESE OUT—UNIQUE DINING

- *Budget:* Amble in to **New Davenport Cash Store** and scarf up on the delectable entrées after browsing through the adjacent general store. *page 302*
- *Moderate:* Take an international gourmet journey at **India Joze**, where the creative cuisine is complemented by the local artwork adorning the walls. *page 318*
- *Moderate to deluxe:* Enjoy the coziness of the **Mission Ranch Dining Room**, a turn-of-the-century creamery turned elegant eatery. *page 347*
- *Ultra-deluxe*: Feast on fabulous food and bay views at **Fresh Cream**, where the service is as rarefied as the decor. *page 335*

Budget: under $8 Moderate: $8–$16 Deluxe: $16–$24 Ultra-deluxe: over $24

This leafy Mexican cantina is housed in a beautiful 1930s hotel and sports soaring ceilings and a giant mural of a Mexican woman cooking outdoors. El Palomar serves up such Mexican seafood dishes as prawn burritos and the Jose special—grilled skirt steak, snapper, and prawns. ~ 1336 Pacific Avenue; 408-425-7575. MODERATE.

For Japanese food there's **Benten**, a comfortable restaurant complete with a sushi bar. They serve an array of traditional dishes including *yosenabe*, sashimi, tempura, teriyaki, and a special plate called *kaki* fry (deep-fried breaded oysters). Understated and reliable. Closed Tuesday. ~ 1541 Pacific Avenue, Suite B; 408-425-7079. MODERATE.

Covering the rest of the Far Eastern spectrum is **India Joze**, serving Near to Far East Asian cuisine. Stop by for lunch, dinner, or Sunday brunch and you're bound to enjoy the creative menu. For brunch the staff recommends their *masala dolsa* (an Indian *urad dahl* crêpe filled with spiced new potatoes) served with *dahl*, Joe's yogurt, and chutney. At lunch try dragon calamari (with tangy fresh mint, cilantro glaze, bamboo shoots, and black Asian mushrooms). The dinner menu offers dragon chicken (boneless chicken in a mint cilantro glaze). If you are in town in August stop in for their calamari festival at lunch and dinner. Located in the Santa Cruz Arts Center, India Joze is decorated with artworks by local artisans, illuminated through skylights, and surrounded by pink pastel walls. Don't miss it. ~ 1001 Center Street; 408-427-3554. MODERATE.

Aldo's Harbor Restaurant, a café with patio deck overlooking Santa Cruz Harbor, has seafood dishes, pastas, soups, salads, and sandwiches. Conveniently located near Seabright Beach, this unassuming little place serves breakfast and lunch. ~ 616 Atlantic Avenue; 408-426-3736. BUDGET.

One of the best dining deals anywhere can be found up the hillside on the University of California–Santa Cruz campus. The **Whole Earth Restaurant** not only serves tasty, nutritious meals, it does so at low prices. Limited to breakfast and lunch menus during summer, the restaurant is also open for dinner during the school year. Serving all natural foods, it features pasta and rice dishes with vegetarian sauces in addition to the regular array of sandwiches, soups, salads, and juices. On a typical night, the dinner special will be vegetarian, but occasionally there is also a chicken or a seafood dish. The restaurant itself is neatly tucked into a grove of tall trees and features outdoor dining on a wooden deck. Providing a touch of style at student prices, the facility is far removed from the bustle of busy downtown Santa Cruz. ~ Redwood Building; 408-426-8255. BUDGET.

SHOPPING

The central shopping district in Santa Cruz is along Pacific Garden Mall, a six-block strip of Pacific Avenue converted to a promenade. The section is neatly landscaped with flowering shrubs and potted trees and its sidewalks, widened for window browsers, overflow with people.

You can stop by **Artisans**, which deals in fine handcrafts and gift items by local artists. They feature outstanding pottery, woodwork, glassware, and jewelry. ~ 1364 Pacific Avenue; 408-423-8183. The **Bookshop Santa Cruz** is the finest among this college town's many wonderful bookstores. ~ 1520 Pacific Avenue; 408-423-0900.

Also visit the **Santa Cruz Art Center**. Here the merchandise is fashioned by area craftspeople. There are galleries, gift stores, plus arts and crafts shops. Also, many artisans' studios are located at the center, making it a gathering place for craftspeople as well as a clearinghouse for their wares. ~ 1001 Center Street.

Another short jog from Pacific Avenue places you in **Galleria Santa Cruz**, one of the town's most modern malls. Three tiers of shops comprise this stucco-and-brick enclave. ~ Front and Cooper streets.

NIGHTLIFE

In Santa Cruz, **The Catalyst** is the common denominator. A popular restaurant and hangout by day, it becomes a favored entertainment spot at night. There's live music most weekday evenings in the Atrium, where local groups perform. But on weekends the heavyweights swing into town and The Catalyst lines up big rock performers. Cover charge for live bands. ~ 1011 Pacific Avenue; 408-423-1336.

The unassuming **Kuumba Jazz Center** headlines top-name musicians. Folks under 21 are welcome at this alcohol- and smoke-free club. Cover. ~ 320 Cedar Street; 408-427-2227.

The Jahva House is a funky vegetarian café in an old motor-repair shop. Relax on a couch beneath the hanging plants and soak up the music while sipping a soy espresso drink. ~ 120 Union Street; 408-459-9876.

If you're in the mood to dance to disco or salsa music call the **Cocoanut Ballroom**. Live bands occasionally perform here. Cover. ~ 400 Beach Street; 408-423-2053.

The Crow's Nest offers eclectic entertainment. On any given night they will be headlining jazz, reggae, swing, rock, or, on Sunday night, comedy. Ocean view; cover. ~ 2218 East Cliff Drive; 408-476-4560.

The crowd at **Blue Lagoon** dances to taped and deejay music during the week, and watches go-go dancers on Friday and Saturday night in summer. The club draws "gay boys and girls with a couple straight people thrown in for color." Cover on weekends and Tuesday ('70s disco night). ~ 923 Pacific Avenue; 408-423-7117.

BEACHES & PARKS

NATURAL BRIDGES STATE BEACH Northernmost of the Santa Cruz beaches, this is a small park with a half moon–shaped beach. This is a popular windsurfing spot in the summer. It's quite pretty, though a row of houses flank one side. In the winter, surfers gather on the reef break. This is also an excellent spot to watch monarch butterflies during their annual winter migration (from October through late February). Facilities include picnic areas, a visitors center, a bookstore, and restrooms. No dogs are allowed. Day-use fee, $6. ~ Located at the end of West Cliff Drive near the western edge of Santa Cruz; 408-423-4609.

SANTA CRUZ BEACH Of the three major beaches extending along the Santa Cruz waterfront, this is the most popular, most crowded, and most famous. All for a very simple reason: the Santa Cruz Boardwalk, with its amusement park and restaurants, runs the length of the sand, and the Santa Cruz Municipal Pier anchors one end of the beach. This, then, is the place to come for crowds and excitement. "Steamer Lane" is the Santa Cruz surfing hotspot. A series of reef breaks are located along West Cliff Drive, extending west to Lighthouse Point. Facilities at Santa Cruz Beach include restrooms, showers, seasonal lifeguard, restaurants, and groceries. For rentals of surfboards, boogie boards, wet suits, umbrellas, and beach equipment, contact Santa Cruz Beach Services at 206 Municipal Wharf; 408-429-3460. ~ Located along Beach Street; access from the Municipal Wharf and along the Boardwalk.

SEABRIGHT BEACH Also known as Castle Beach, Seabright is second in Santa Cruz's string of beaches. This beauty extends from the San Lorenzo River mouth to the jetty at Santa Cruz Harbor. It's long, wide, and backdropped by bluffs. The views are as magnificent as from other nearby beaches, and the crowds will be lighter than along the Boardwalk. There are restrooms and a lifeguard; restaurants and groceries are nearby. ~ Access to the beach is along East Cliff Drive at the foot of Mott and Cypress avenues, or at the end of Atlantic Avenue; 408-429-2850.

TWIN LAKES STATE BEACH Just the other side of Santa Cruz Harbor is this odd-shaped beach. Smaller than the two beaches to the north, it is also less crowded. The park is 94 acres, with a lagoon behind the beach and a jetty flanking one side. A very pretty spot. Surfing is sometimes okay in winter or after a storm. A new public swimming pool is slated to open between Swan Lake and 17th Avenue in 1997. As of now there are restrooms and lifeguards in summer; restaurants and groceries are nearby. ~ Along East Cliff Drive, south of Santa Cruz Harbor; 408-429-2850.

LINCOLN BEACH, SUNNY COVE, MORAN LAKE BEACH Located along the eastern end of Santa Cruz, these three sandy beaches are in residential areas. As a result, they draw local people, not tourists; they're also more difficult to get to, and, happily, are less crowded. All are backdropped by bluffs. If you want to buck the crowds, they're worth the trouble. There are restrooms at Lincoln Beach and Moran Lake Beach; otherwise amenities are scarce. Parking is a problem throughout the area (though Moran Lake Beach has a parking lot where you can park all day for a fee during summer and weekends, otherwise free). ~ All three beaches are near East Cliff Drive. Lincoln Beach (part of Twin Lakes State Beach) is at the end of 14th Avenue, Sunny Cove at the end of 17th Avenue, and Moran Lake Beach is near 30th Avenue.

Santa Cruz to Monterey

From Santa Cruz, coastal Route 1 courses south through Capitola, known for its pretty beach and September Begonia Festival, and through Aptos, another bedroom community with equally sparkling beaches.

SIGHTS

Aptos' most popular place these days is a foreboding forest located at latitude 37° 2' and longitude 121° 53'. That precise spot, at the end of a two-mile trail in the Forest of Nisene Marks State Park, is the **1989 earthquake epicenter.** A stake now marks ground zero of the 7.1 shaker that devastated Northern California. To reach the trailhead, follow Aptos Creek Road north from Aptos to the Nisene Marks parking lot. ~ 408-761-1795.

◄ HIDDEN

In nearby Rio del Mar, there's a **rural side trip** that carries you past miles of farmland before rejoining Route 1 near Watsonville. To take this side trip follow San Andreas Road, which tunnels through forest, then opens into rich agricultural acres. Intricately tilled fields roll down to the sea and edge up to the foot of the mountains. At the end of San Andreas Road, follow Beach Street to the ocean. The entire stretch of coastline is flanked by high sand dunes, a wild and exotic counterpoint to the furrowed fields nearby.

Beach Street leads back into Watsonville. Central to the surrounding farm community, Watsonville is the world's strawberry-growing capital. It's also rich in **Victorian houses**, which you can tour with a printed guide available from the **Chamber of Commerce.** ~ 444 Main Street, Watsonville; 408-724-3900.

Back on Route 1, you'll pass Moss Landing, a weather-beaten fishing harbor. With its antique stores, one-lane bridge, bright-painted boats, and unpainted fish market, the town has a warm personality. There is one eyesore, however, a huge power plant with twin smokestacks that stand out like two sentinels of an occupying army. Otherwise the place is enchanting, particularly

HIDDEN ►

nearby **Elkhorn Slough National Estuarine Research Reserve,** a 1400-acre world of salt marshes and tidal flats managed by a federal partnership between the Department of Fish and Game and the National Oceanic and Atmospheric Administration. Within this delicate environment live some 400 species of invertebrates, 80 species of fish and 20 species of birds (among them redshouldered hawks, peregrine falcons, and acorn woodpeckers) as well as harbor seals, oysters, and clams (but don't eat the oysters or clams). To get to the visitors center from Route 1, follow Dolan Road for three miles, go left on Elkhorn Road, and proceed two more miles. Closed Monday and Tuesday. Admission. ~ 1700 Elkhorn Road, Watsonville; 408-728-2822.

Next in this parade of small towns is **Castroville,** "Artichoke Center of the World." Beyond it is a cluster of towns—Marina, Sand City, and Seaside—that probably represent the sand capitals of the world. The entire area rests on a sand dune that measures up to 300 feet in depth, and extends ten miles along the coast and as much as eight miles inland. From here you can trace a course into Monterey along wind-tilled rows of sand.

LODGING

Capitola Venetian Hotel is a mock Italian complex next to Capitola Beach. With its stucco and red tile veneer, ornamental molding, and carved wooden doors, it's a poor cousin to the grand villas of Venice. The 20 guest rooms come equipped with kitchens. There are few wall decorations and the furnishings lack character, but the atmosphere is pleasant. ~ 1500 Wharf Road, Capitola; 408-476-6471, 800-332-2780. MODERATE TO DELUXE.

Harbor Lights Motel, a few steps farther uphill from the beach, is similarly laid out but in a more modern fashion. This ten-unit stucco building has rooms with completely equipped kitchens and ocean views. The accommodations have shag rugs, hokey wall paintings, and bland furniture. Remember, you're paying for what's outside, not inside. ~ 5000 Cliff Drive, Capitola; 408-476-0505. MODERATE TO DELUXE.

Does a trip around the world interest you? If so, the **Inn at Depot Hill** might save you time and money without sacrificing the feel of the trip. This 12-room bed and breakfast, fashioned from a former train station, features internationally decorated rooms with names like "Paris," "Côte d'Azur," and "Portofino." There is a fireplace in each room and most come with a patio and hot tub. Breakfast, hors d'oeuvres with wine, and dessert are included with a night's stay. ~ 250 Monterey Avenue, Capitola; 408-462-3376, 800-572-2632, fax 408-462-3697. ULTRA-DELUXE.

Attention to cozy detail is the forte of the **Blue Spruce Inn**. The rooms come with a variety of decorations ranging from wicker furniture and gas fireplaces to carved oak beds and stained-glass murals. Indeed, this three-building bed and breakfast leaves no quaint stone unturned. In addition to a nightly pillow fluff and turn-down, guests also receive a fresh robe for that long winter's nap. ~ 2815 South Main Street, Soquel; 408-464-1137, 800-559-1137, fax 408-475-0608. DELUXE.

The Pajaro Valley area counts its wealth in strawberries, apples, flowers, and mushrooms.

With two miles of beachfront, **Pajaro Dunes** is ideal for those who want to go down to the sea. Located midway between Santa Cruz and Monterey, this resort colony has 130 condominiums, townhouses, and homes that range from one to five bedrooms. While decorating schemes vary from beach contemporary to brass and glass, all units offer kitchens, fireplaces, decks, and barbecues. The big units are a good bet for large family groups. ~ 2661 Beach Road, Watsonville; 408-722-9201, 800-675-8808. ULTRA-DELUXE.

DINING

The area's foremost dining room is actually outside Santa Cruz in a nearby suburb. True to its name, the multitiered **Shadowbrook Restaurant** sits in a wooded spot through which a creek flows. Food is almost an afterthought at this elaborate affair; upon entering the grounds you descend either via a funicular or a sinuous, fern-draped path. Once inside, you'll encounter a labyrinth of dining levels and rooms, luxuriously decorated with potted plants, stone fireplaces, and candlelit tables. A mature tree grows through the floor and ceiling of one room; in others, vines climb along the walls. When you finally chart the course to a table, you'll be offered a cuisine including prime rib, salmon, and other fresh seafood dishes. Definitely a dining experience. Dinner and Sunday brunch. ~ 1750 Wharf Road, Capitola; 408-475-1511. MODERATE TO DELUXE.

Capitola Beach is wall-to-wall with seafood restaurants. They line the strand, each with a different decorative theme but all seeming to merge into a collection of pit stops for hungry beachgoers. If you're expecting me to recommend one you are asking more than mortal man can do. I say when in doubt, guess. Put your money on **Larry's Surf 'n Turf**. They offer a dining room above the sand, popular bar, and a full-bore beef, pasta, and seafood menu. Lunch, dinner, Sunday brunch. ~ 215 Esplanade, Capitola; 408-475-6215. MODERATE.

Take a seat on the deck at the beachfront **Stockton Bridge Grille**. Seafood specialties include broiled mahimahi and grilled salmon salad. Also on the menu are smoked salmon ravioli, scallops, and scampi. The decor is contemporary Californian with abstract art on the walls. ~ 231 Esplanade, Capitola; 408-462-1350. MODERATE.

Located farther down the highway, try **Skipper's Restaurant**. Specialties include deep-fried oysters, fish stews, and salmon chips, to name a few. The decor at this eatery resembles a New England fish house. ~ Route 1 at Moss Landing Bridge, Moss Landing; 408-633-4453. MODERATE.

Next door is **Maloney's Harbor Inn**. This establishment serves up fresh fish as well as the usual array of meat, chicken, and pasta dishes. Both Skipper's and Maloney's rest on the water overlooking a pretty harbor and an uncommonly ugly power plant. ~ Route 1, Moss Landing; 408-724-9371. MODERATE.

NIGHTLIFE

For a relaxing evening, try **Shadowbrook Restaurant**. Its soft lighting and luxurious surroundings create a sense of well-being, like brandy and a blazing fire. They offer light jazz on Saturday nights. ~ 1750 Wharf Road, Capitola; 408-475-1511.

Several of the restaurant lounges lining Capitola's waterfront have nightly entertainment. Over at **Larry's Surf 'n Turf** the deejay cranks up the victrola on Friday and Saturday and lets fly with dance music. Cover on Friday in summer. ~ 215 Esplanade, Capitola; 408-475-6215. A few doors down at **Zelda's** there's live music ranging from blues and jazz on the weekends to rock Tuesday through Sunday. Cover. ~ 203 Esplanade, Capitola; 408-475-4900.

SHOPPING

Located along Route 1 south of Santa Cruz, the coastal village of Moss Landing is a must for antique hounds. More than 20 shops offer a wide array of treasures from the good old days. Clustered around the intersection of Moss Landing Road and Sand Holt Road are several shops that warrant a close look.

Stepping into **Yesterday's Books** is a bit like discovering a private library filled with antiquarian treasures. ~ 7902 Sand Holt Road, Building E, Moss Landing; 408-633-8033. At **Life in the Past Lane** you'll find art deco designs, antique furniture, slot machines, jukeboxes, and a wide variety of memorabilia. ~ Moss Landing Road, Moss Landing; 408-633-6100. **The Little Red Barn** is the biggest antique store in town. This 3000-square-foot shop sells dolls, china, art glass, furniture, and many other items. ~ 8071 Moss Landing Road, Moss Landing; 408-633-5583.

BEACHES & PARKS

CAPITOLA CITY BEACH Sedimentary cliffs flank a corner of this sand carpet but the rest is heavily developed. Popular with visitors for decades, Capitola is a well-known resort community. However, following a year of heavy storms the beach often disappears under the high tide, and locals claim that there was no beach to speak of in the summer of 1994 and 1995. Seafood restaurants line its shore and boutiques flourish within blocks of the beach. A great place for families because of the adjacent facilities, it trades seclusion for service. The ocean is well protected for water sports and in winter, surfers enjoy the breaks near the jetty, pier, and river mouth. There are restrooms, showers, lifeguards, a fishing pier, and volleyball. ~ Located in the center of Capitola; 408-475-5935.

NEW BRIGHTON STATE BEACH This sandy crescent adjoins Seacliff Beach and enjoys a wide vista of Monterey Bay. Headlands protect the beach for swimmers and beginning surfers; beachcombers frequently find fossils in the cliffs here. Within its mere 94 acres, the park contains hiking trails and a forested bluff. There are picnic areas, restrooms, and showers (for campers only). Day-use fee, $6. ~ Off Route 1 in Capitola, four miles south of Santa Cruz; 408-475-4850.

▲ There are 112 sites for tents and RVs in a wooded area inland from the beach; $16 per night. Hiker/biker camps available ($6 per person). During the summer, reservations are necessary; people book up to seven months in advance. Reserve through DESTINET at 800-444-7275.

SEACLIFF STATE BEACH This two-mile strand is very popular. *Too* popular: during summer, RVs park along its entire length and crowds gather on the waterfront. That's because it provides the safest swimming along this section of coast. There are roving lifeguards on duty during the summer and a protective headland nearby. In summer there are guided walks on Sunday to look at fossils. The beach also sports a pier favored by anglers. It's a pretty place, but oh so busy. There are picnic areas, restrooms, and showers. Day-use fee, $6. ~ Off Route 1 in Aptos, five miles south of Santa Cruz; 408-688-3222.

▲ There are 26 sites for RVs and self-contained vehicles (full hookups); $27 per night. Reservations are required through DESTINET at 800-444-7275.

FOREST OF NISENE MARKS STATE PARK This semi-wilderness expanse, several miles inland, encompasses nearly 10,000 acres. Within its domain are redwood groves, meandering streams, rolling countryside, and dense forest. About 30 miles of hiking trails wind through the preserve. Along them you can explore fossil beds, deserted logger cabins, old trestles, and railroad beds; you can also hike to the epicenter of the 1989 earthquake. The park is a welcome complement to the natural features along the coast. There are no facilities in the park; restaurants and groceries are several miles away in Aptos. Day-use fee, $3. ~ From Route 1 southbound take the Seacliff Beach exit in Aptos, five miles south of Santa Cruz. Take an immediate left on State Park Drive, pass over the highway, and then go right on Soquel Drive. Follow this for a half mile; then head left on Aptos Creek Road. This paved road turns to gravel as it leads into the forest; 408-429-2850.

MANRESA STATE BEACH Here you'll find a strip of white sand bookended by blufftop homes. Popular with surfers, it provides a sweeping view of Monterey Bay. A bit more removed than other nearby beaches, Manresa nevertheless can be quite popular on summer afternoons. Facilities include restrooms, lifeguards, picnic tables, fire pits, and showers; restaurants and groceries are several miles away in Watsonville. Day-use fee, $6. ~ Located 13 miles south of Santa Cruz; from Route 1, take the Larkin Valley Road and San Andreas Road exit, turn right onto San Andreas Road and follow it several miles to the park turnoff; 408-724-1266.

▲ There are 64 walk-in tent sites in Manresa Uplands Campground next to the beach; $14 to $16 per night; information, 408-761-1795.

SUNSET STATE BEACH Over three miles of beach and sand dunes create one of the area's prettiest parks. There are bluffs and meadows behind the beach as well as Monterey pines and cypress trees. This 324-acre park is a popular spot for fishing and clamming. Surfing is also done here but the break is powerful—exercise caution. But remember, there's more fog here and farther south than in the Santa Cruz area. There are picnic areas, restrooms, and showers; restaurants and groceries are several miles away in Watsonville. Day-use fee, $6. ~ Located 16 miles south of Santa Cruz; from Route 1, take the Larkin Valley and San Andreas Road exit, turn right onto San Andreas Road and follow it several miles to the park turnoff; 408-724-1266.

▲ Permitted in 90 sites; $14 to $16 per night; hiker/biker camp available ($6 per person).

ZMUDOWSKI, MOSS LANDING AND SALINAS RIVER STATE BEACHES These three state parks are part of a long stretch of sand dunes. They all contain broad beaches and vistas along Monterey Bay. Though relatively uncrowded, their proximity to Moss Landing's smoke-belching power plant is a severe drawback. Quite suitable anywhere else, they can't compete with their neighbors in this land of beautiful beaches. Surfing is good near the sandbar at Salinas River; great at Moss Landing, which draws locals from Santa Cruz. Each beach has toilet facilities; an equestrian concessionaire at Salinas River offers trail rides; restaurants and groceries are available in Moss Landing. Day-use fee at Moss Landing, $3. ~ All three are located off Route 1 within a few miles of Moss Landing; 408-384-7695.

▲ There's en route camping at Moss Landing for self-contained vehicles (no hookups); $7 per night (maximum one-night stay).

MARINA STATE BEACH The tall, fluffy sand dunes at this 170-acre park are unreal. They're part of a giant dune covering 50 square miles throughout the area. There are marvelous views of Monterey here, plus a chance to fish or sunbathe. It is also the perfect place to try out hang gliding with tandem rides for first-time gliders and hang gliding rentals for the more experienced. The only facilities are restrooms; restaurants and groceries are available in the nearby town of Marina. Regarding surfing, there's a great beach break in summer but it's dangerous in winter. ~ Located along Route 1, nine miles north of Monterey; 408-384-7695.

Monterey

Over two million visitors tour the Monterey area every year. Little wonder. Its rocky coast fringed with cypress forests, its hills dotted with palatial homes—the area is unusually beautiful. The town of Monterey also serves as a gateway to the tumbling region of Big Sur.

For a tour of Monterey Peninsula, begin in Monterey itself. Here are historic homes, an old Spanish presidio, Fisherman's Wharf, and Cannery Row. Set in a natural amphitheater of forested hills, it is also home to one of the richest marine sanctuaries along the entire California coast. Little wonder that this town, with a population that numbers 32,000 people, has served as an inspiration for Robert Louis Stevenson and John Steinbeck. With a downtown district that reflects small town America and a waterfront that once supported a rich fishing and canning industry, Monterey remains one of the most vital spots on the Central Coast.

SIGHTS

History in Monterey is a precious commodity which in most cases has been carefully preserved. Ancient adobe houses and Spanish-style buildings are so commonplace that some have been converted into shops and restaurants. Others are museums or points of interest that can be seen on a walking tour along the **Path of History**. This "Path," carrying through the center of Monterey, measures over two miles if walked in its entirety.

The best place to begin is the **Custom House** at #1 Custom House Plaza across from Fisherman's Wharf. California's earliest government building, the structure dates back to 1827. It was here in 1846 that Commodore Sloat raised the American flag, claiming California for the United States. Today the stone and adobe building houses displays from an 1830-era cargo ship. In Stanton Center you'll find the model ships, old nautical photographs, and a two-story-tall rotating lighthouse lens of the **Monterey Maritime Museum**. Admission. ~ 5 Custom House Plaza; 408-375-2553.

Across the plaza rises **Pacific House**, a two-story balconied adobe with a luxurious courtyard. Constructed in 1847, it was used over the years to house everything from military supplies to a tavern to a courtroom and church. The exhibits inside trace California's history from American Indian days to the advent of Spanish settlers and American pioneers and to the heyday of the canning industry in the 1930s. Today, the building houses the **California Heritage Guide**, which provides maps, brochures, and guided tours. ~ 10 Custom House Plaza; 408-373-6454.

Just behind Pacific House sits **Casa del Oro**, a tiny white adobe which served as Monterey's general store during the 1850s. Today it houses the **Joseph Boston Store**, an old-fashioned mercantile shop selling early American items. Closed Monday, Tuesday, and Wednesday. ~ Olivier and Scott streets; 408-649-3364.

Diagonally across the intersection on Olivier Street sits an office complex behind which is located the **Brick House**, purportedly the first such house in California. Adjacent to this is the **Whaling Station**, an adobe with a balcony from which the early whalers spotted their migrating bounty.

California's First Theater, a block up the street, certainly qualifies as a living museum. It's a landmark building that is still used to stage theatrical performances (mostly 19th-century melodramas, complete with hisses and boos, performed by America's oldest continually operating theater troupe). Performances are held Friday and Saturday (Wednesday through Sunday during July and August). Wander this clapboard and adobe building and you'll encounter almost a century-and-a-half of Monterey's dramatic tradition. ~ Scott and Pacific streets; 408-375-4916.

A left on Pacific Street leads to **Casa Soberanes**, a Monterey-style house with red tile roof and second-story balcony. Completed in the 1840s, this impressive structure was built by a warden at the Custom House. Part of the Monterey State Historic Park, Casa Soberanes can be visited by a guided tour every afternoon except Tuesday and Thursday. Admission. ~ 336 Pacific Street; 408-649-7118.

At 412 Pacific Street, **Casa Serrano**, built in 1843, contains wrought-iron decorations over its narrow windows. Once home to a blind Spanish teacher, it is now open for touring only on weekends. For more information contact the Monterey History and Art Association. ~ 408-372-2608.

Nearby spreads **Friendly Plaza**, a tree-shaded park which serves as a focus for several important places. The **Monterey Peninsula Museum of Art** features works and artifacts by both early and contemporary California artists, as well as special exhibits. Closed Monday and Tuesday. ~ 559 Pacific Street; 408-372-7591.

Pierce Street, running along the upper edge of the plaza, contains a string of historic 19th-century homes. **Colton Hall** is an imposing two-story stone structure with white pillars and classical portico. Site of California's 1849 constitutional convention, it displays memorabilia from that critical event. Given its unique archi-

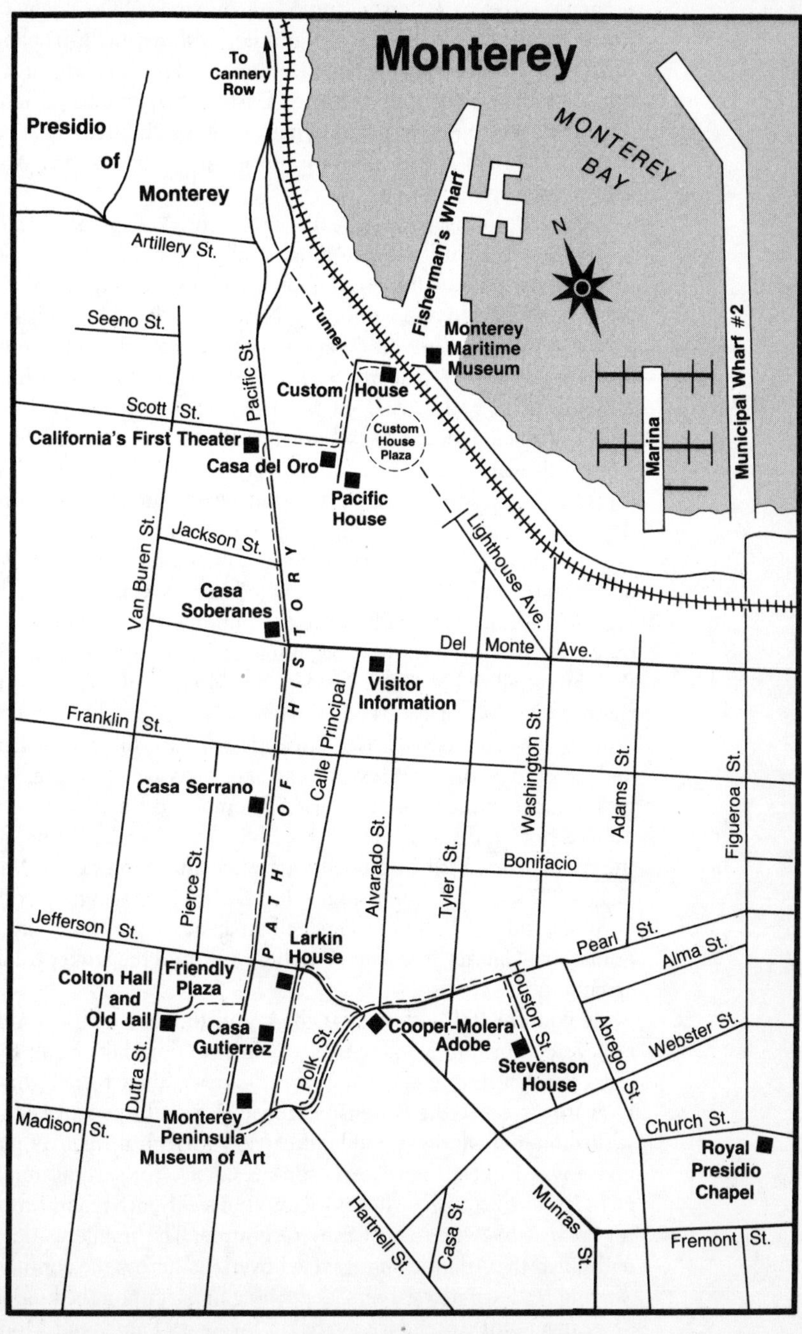
Monterey
To Cannery Row
Presidio of Monterey
MONTEREY BAY
N
Artillery St.
Seeno St.
Tunnel
Fisherman's Wharf
Monterey Maritime Museum
Municipal Wharf #2
Marina
Pacific St.
Custom House
Custom House Plaza
Scott St.
California's First Theater
Casa del Oro
Pacific House
Van Buren St.
Jackson St.
Lighthouse Ave.
Casa Soberanes
PATH OF HISTORY
Del Monte Ave.
Visitor Information
Franklin St.
Calle Principal
Washington St.
Adams St.
Figueroa St.
Casa Serrano
Alvarado St.
Tyler St.
Bonifacio
Pierce St.
Jefferson St.
Larkin House
Pearl St.
Alma St.
Colton Hall and Old Jail
Friendly Plaza
Casa Gutierrez
Cooper-Molera Adobe
Houston St.
Stevenson House
Abrego St.
Webster St.
Dutra St.
Polk St.
Madison St.
Monterey Peninsula Museum of Art
Church St.
Royal Presidio Chapel
Munras St.
Hartnell St.
Casa St.
Fremont St.

tecture and lovely setting, it's one of Monterey's prettiest buildings. ~ Pacific Street at Jefferson and Madison streets. The squat **Old Jail** next door, fashioned from granite, with wrought-iron bars across the windows, dates back to the same era. It creates a startling contrast to its stately neighbor. **Casa Gutierrez,** located across the street, was built by a cavalryman with 15 children. That was back in 1841; its last incarnation (until late 1995) was as a Mexican restaurant.

After exploring the plaza, turn left into Madison Street from Pacific Street, then left again along Calle Principal to one of the town's most famous homes, the **Larkin House**. Designed in 1835 by Thomas Larkin and combining New England and Spanish elements, it's a two-story adobe house with a ground floor veranda and a second-story balcony. Today the antique home is a house museum filled with period pieces. The house is especially important historically because its owner was the only United States Consul to California and a key player in the American takeover. Open for guided tours every afternoon except Tuesday and Thursday. Admission. ~ 510 Calle Principal; 408-649-7118.

A right on Jefferson Street and another quick right on Polk Street takes you past a cluster of revered houses. **Casa Amesti**, dating from 1824, is presently a private club open to the public only on weekends via guided tour beginning at 2 p.m. Admission. ~ 516 Polk Street; 408-372-8173. The **Cooper-Molera Adobe**, across the road at 525 Polk Street, is a sprawling affair that includes a 19th-century museum as well as a "historic garden" filled with herbs and vegetables of the Mexican era. The massive structure, over two decades in the making, housed Thomas Larkin's half-brother, a merchant who sailed the waters of South America, China, and the Pacific isles. Visit by guided tour every afternoon except Monday and Wednesday. Admission. ~ 408-649-7118. Facing each other on either side of Polk and Hartnell streets are two more vintage homes, the **Gabriel de la Torre Adobe**, 1836, and the **Stokes Adobe,** erected in the 1840s.

If you are still with me for the grand finale, backtrack along Polk Street one block to the five-way intersection, take a soft right onto Pearl Street, walk a few short blocks, then turn right on Houston Street to the **Stevenson House**. A grand two-story edifice with shuttered windows and landscaped yard, this former rooming house was Robert Louis Stevenson's residence for several months in 1879. The Scottish writer, vivacious but sickly, arrived in Monterey to visit his wife-to-be Fanny Osbourne. The fragile wanderer had sailed the Atlantic and traveled overland across the continent. Writing for local newspapers, depending in part upon the kindness of strangers for sustenance, he fell in love with Fanny and Monterey both. From the surrounding countryside he drew inspiration for some of his most famous books, including *Treasure Island.* In addition to its period furniture and early California decor, the house features numerous items from Stevenson's life. There are personal belongings, original manuscripts, and first editions, all of which can be viewed on a guided tour every afternoon except Monday and Wednesday. Admission. ~ 530 Houston Street; 408-649-7118.

For information about guided tours of Casa Soberanes, Larkin House, Cooper-Molera Adobe, and Stevenson House contact **Monterey State Historic Park.** You can see all four buildings on a guided 90-minute walking tour that runs three times daily: 10:15, 12:30, and 2:30, year-round. This tour is of the grounds only and does not take you inside the houses. Admission. ~ 408-649-7118.

Two additional places of historical note are located in Monterey but a significant distance from the Path of History. At 550 Church Street, the **Royal Presidio Chapel** is a graceful expression of the 18th-century town. Decorative molding adorns the facade of the old adobe church while the towering belfry, rising along one side, makes the structure asymmetrical. Heavy wooden doors lead to a long, narrow chapel hung with dusty oil paintings. This was the mission that Father Junípero Serra founded in 1770, just before moving his congregation a few miles south to Carmel.

The **Presidio of Monterey** sits on a hill near the northwest corner of town. Established as a fort by the Spanish in 1792, it currently serves as a foreign language institute for the military. There are cannons banked in a hillside, marking the site of Fort Mervine, built by the Americans in 1846. ~ Pacific and Artillery streets; 408-242-5000.

Strangely, Monterey, which elsewhere demonstrates special care in preserving its heritage, has let its wharves and piers fall prey to tinsel-minded developers. **Municipal Wharf #2,** at the foot of Figueroa Street, is a welcome exception. It's actually all that remains from the heyday of Monterey's fishing fleet. Here broad-hulled boats still beat at their moorings, while landlubbing anglers cast from pierside. Gulls perch along the handrails, sea lions bark

A SACRED SPOT

The **Presidio** is also the site of an ancient Costanoan Indian village and burial ground. And a granite monument at the corner of Pacific and Artillery streets marks the spot where in 1602 the Spanish celebrated the first Catholic mass in California. In addition to historic points, the Presidio grounds enjoy marvelous views of Monterey. You can look down upon the town, then scan along the bay's curving horizon.

from beneath the pilings, and pelicans work the waterfront. On one side is the dilapidated warehouse of a long-defunct freezer company. At the end of the dock, fish companies still operate. It's a primal place of cranes and pulleys, forklifts and conveyor belts. There are ice boxes and old packing crates scattered hither-thither, exuding the romance and stench of the industry.

Then there is the parody, much better known than the original. **Fisherman's Wharf**, like its San Francisco namesake, has been transmogrified into what the travel industry thinks tourists think a fishing pier should look like. Something was lost in the translation. Few fishing boats operate from the wharf these days; several charter companies sponsor glass-bottom boat tours and whale-watching expeditions. Otherwise the waterfront haven is just one more mall, a macadam corridor lined on either side with shops. There are ersatz art galleries, shops vending candy apples and personalized mugs, plus a school of seafood restaurants. A few outdoor fish markets still sell live crabs, lobsters, and squid, but the symbol of the place is the hurdy-gurdy man with performing monkey who greets you at the entrance.

Actually this is only the most recent in the wharf's long series of role changes. The dock was built in 1846 to serve cargo schooners dealing in hides. Within a decade the whaling industry took it over, followed finally by Italian fishermen catching salmon, cod, and mackerel. During the Cannery Row era of the '30s, the sardine industry played a vital part in the life of the wharf. Today all that has given way to a bizarre form of public nostalgia.

The same visionary appears responsible for the resurrection of **Cannery Row**. Made famous by John Steinbeck's feisty novels *Cannery Row* and *Sweet Thursday*, this oceanfront strip has been transformed into a neighborhood of wax museums and dainty antique shops. As Steinbeck remarked upon returning to the old sardine canning center, "They fish for tourists now."

The building that housed Doc Rickett's Marine Lab stands at 800 Cannery Row.

Cannery Row of yore was an unappealing collection of corrugated warehouses, dilapidated stores, seedy hotels, and gaudy whorehouses. There were about 30 canneries, 100 fishing boats, and 4000 workers populating the place. The odor was horrible, but for several decades the sardine industry breathed life into the Monterey economy. The business died just before Cannery Row was published in 1945.

Before the entire oceanfront strip was developed in the early 1980s, you could still capture a sense of the old Cannery Row. A few weather-beaten factories remained. Rust stained their ribbed sides, windows were punched, and roofs had settled to an inward curve. In places, the stone pilings of old loading docks still stood, haunted by sea gulls. Now only tourists and memories remain.

At the other end of the Row, Steinbeck aficionados will find a few literary settings. La Ida Café, now an ice cream parlor called **Kalisa's La Ida Café**, still retains its same tumbledown appearance. ~ 851 Cannery Row; 408-372-3621. Wing Chong Market is now **Alicia's Antiques.** ~ 835 Cannery Row; 408-372-1423.

In the middle you'll encounter the scene of the malling of Cannery Row. Old warehouses have been renovated into shopping centers, new buildings have risen, and the entire area has experienced a face lift. Brightest tooth in the new smile is the **Edgewater Packing Company**, a miniature amusement park with a hand-carved vintage-1905 carousel. ~ 640 Wave Street; 408-649-1899.

The most impressive addition is the **Monterey Bay Aquarium**, a state-of-the-art museum that re-creates the natural habitat of local sea life. Monterey Bay is one of the world's biggest submarine canyons, deeper than the Grand Canyon. At the aquarium you'll encounter about 100 display tanks representing the wealth of underwater life that inhabits this mineral-rich valley. For instance, the Monterey Bay Habitat, a 90-foot-long glass enclosure, portrays the local submarine world complete with sharks, brilliant reef fish, and creosote-oozing pilings. A newly opened wing christened the Outer Bay Galleries contains, among other delights, a million-gallon tank filled with all kinds of native Californian species, including green turtles and jellyfish. Another aquarium contains a mature kelp forest crowded with fish. Don't forget the hands-on exhibits where you can pet bat rays and hold crabs, starfish, and sea cucumbers. Also be sure to wander upstairs to where the special exhibits are housed. Together the many displays and exhibitions make it one of the world's great aquariums. Don't miss it. Admission. ~ Cannery Row and David Avenue; 408-648-4888.

LODGING

The problem with lodging on the Monterey Peninsula is the same dilemma plaguing much of the world—money. It takes a lot of it to stay here, especially when visiting one of the area's vaunted bed and breakfasts. These country inns are concentrated in Pacific Grove and Carmel, towns neighboring on Monterey.

The town of Monterey features a few such inns as well as a string of moderately priced motels. Budget travelers will do well to check into the latter and also to consult several of the Carmel listings below. Monterey's motel row lies along Munras Avenue, a buzzing thoroughfare that leads from downtown to Route 1. Motels are also found along Fremont Street in the adjacent town of Seaside. These are cheaper, drabber, and not as conveniently situated as the Munras hostelries.

Since overnight facilities fill rapidly around Monterey, particularly on weekends and during summer, it's wise to reserve in advance. Contact **Resort To Me**, a reservation agency for the Monterey Peninsula. ~ 408-646-9250, 800-757-5646, fax 408-372-2529. Or try **Carmel's Tourist Information Room Finders,** who might prove useful in securing that elusive room. ~ Mission Street between 5th and 6th streets in the Mission Patio, Carmel; 408-624-1711, 800-847-8066.

Among the moderately priced motels lining Munras Avenue, **El Adobe Inn** is closest to downtown Monterey. This 26-unit establishment offers standard motel accommodations. The rooms are clean, carpeted, and comfortable, but far from cozy. They come equipped with television, telephone, and table. There's hokey art on the walls, and the environment generally is safe but sterile. Continental breakfast and use of the motel's hot tub are included. ~ 936 Munras Avenue; 408-372-5409, 800-433-4732, fax 408-624-2967. MODERATE TO DELUXE.

Located five blocks from downtown, the **Days Inn Monterey** features 35 rooms with private baths. ~ 1288 Munras Avenue; 408-375-2168, fax 408-375-0368. MODERATE TO DELUXE.

At the **Driftwood Motel,** you'll find 14 standard units decorated in soft pastel hues. ~ 2362 North Fremont Street; 408-372-5059. MODERATE.

For good cheer and homespun atmosphere, the **Old Monterey Inn** provides a final word. Before innkeepers Ann and Gene Swett decided to open their Tudor-style house to guests, they raised six children here. Now they raise rhododendrons and roses in the garden while hosting visitors in their ten-room bed and breakfast. The house rests on a quiet street yet is located within a few blocks of downtown Monterey. Among the trimly appointed rooms are several with feather beds, tile fireplaces, wicker furnishings, and delicate wallhangings. There are spacious dining and drawing rooms downstairs and the landscaped grounds are studded with oak and redwood. You'll find this friendly little inn a perfect spot for an evening fire and glass of sherry. ~ 500 Martin Street; 408-375-8284, 800-350-2344, fax 408-375-6730. ULTRA-DELUXE.

Located in the downtown district, **Merritt House** is not only an overnight resting place but also a stopping point along Monterey's "Path of History." Part of this 25-room inn rests in a vintage 1830 adobe home. Accommodations in the old house and the adjoining modern quarters are furnished with hardwood period pieces and feature vaulted ceilings, fireplaces, and balconies. The garden abounds with magnolia, fig, pepper, and olive trees. Continental breakfast is served. ~ 386 Pacific Street; 408-646-9686, 800-541-5599, fax 408-646-5392. DELUXE TO ULTRA-DELUXE.

Oceanfront on Cannery Row stands the **Spindrift Inn,** an elegant 42-room hotel. The lobby is fashionably laid out with skylight and sculptures and there is a rooftop solarium overlooking the waterfront. Guest rooms carry out the award-winning architectural motif with bay windows, hardwood floors, wood-burning fireplaces, and built-in armoires. ~ 652 Cannery Row; 408-646-8900, 800-841-1879, fax 408-646-5342. ULTRA-DELUXE.

A standard issue motel, the **Westerner Motel** is just ten minutes from downtown. There is a swimming pool and 22 carpeted rooms with double beds, off-white wallpaper, and contemporary furniture. ~ 2041 Fremont Street; 408-373-2911, 800-350-6685, fax 408-655-3450. BUDGET TO MODERATE.

Catering to a mixed gay and straight clientele is the **Monterey Fireside Lodge**, a 24-room hostelry. In addition to comfortable accommodations there is a jacuzzi and patio. Continental breakfast included. ~ 1131 10th Street; 408-373-4172, 800-722-2624, fax 408-655-5640. MODERATE.

DINING

Few restaurants can compete with **Stokes Adobe** for ambience. Housed in an 1840 California adobe with stucco walls, artwork by local artists, and European antiques, this restaurant serves new American cuisine with Mediterranean influences. ~ 500 Hartnell Street; 408-373-1110. MODERATE.

◄ HIDDEN

Franklin Street Bar & Grill is very popular with Monterey folk. A lot of them just come here to drink and carouse. They bend an elbow at the bar, chuck a few darts, or play a game of pool. Others are here to eat. The reason is quite simple: few tourists wander into this midtown establishment. Pity, because the prices are easy on the purse and the food quite good. The fare includes appetizers and light snacks like calamari, squid and chips, and buffalo wings. ~ 150 West Franklin Street; 408-375-1005. BUDGET.

Eating at **Gianni's Pizza** is a guaranteed good time. You can feel it when you walk in the door of this casual restaurant. The tables sport red-and-white-checked tablecloths, there are bottles of wine and pictures of Italy on the walls, and on weekends banjo and accordion players serenade diners with lively tunes. You can order fresh pastas, hand-tossed, thick-crusted pizza, or oven-baked sandwiches from various stations, and they are prepared and delivered to your table. There's also a bar, an espresso counter, and wonderful gelato for dessert. ~ 725 Lighthouse Avenue; 408-649-1500. BUDGET.

Though it's not on the water, the **Clock Garden Restaurant** features more fresh fish than Cannery Row ever dreamed of. On an average night they'll have prawn fettuccine, snapper, salmon, and shrimp salad. Not interested? How about spare ribs or chicken teriyaki? There's a patio outside; they also serve lunch and Sunday brunch; the bar mixes potent drinks—who could ask for more? ~ 565 Abrego Street; 408-375-6100. MODERATE.

Small and personalized with an understated elegance is the most fitting way to describe **Fresh Cream**. Its light green and gray walls are decorated with French prints and leaded glass. One wall is floor-to-ceiling windows that provide a great view of the bay. Service is excellent and the menu, printed daily, numbers among the finest on the Central Coast. Only dinner is served at this gourmet retreat; on a given night you might choose from beef tournedos in Madeira sauce, sautéed veal loin, blackened ahi tuna, duckling in black currant sauce, and rack of lamb. That's not even mentioning the appetizers, which are outstanding, or the desserts, which should be outlawed. Four stars. ~ Heritage Harbor, Pacific and Scott streets; 408-375-9798. ULTRA-DELUXE.

One of Monterey Bay's most abundant seafood products is squid, the inky creature that often turns up on local restaurant menus as the more palatable-sounding calamari. Under any name, the best place to enjoy it is **Abalonetti**, a casual wharfside restaurant overlooking the bay. The menu presents calamari in an array of guises, including deep-fried, sautéed with wine and garlic, and baked with eggplant. ~ 57 Fisherman's Wharf; 408-375-5941. MODERATE.

SHOPPING

In Monterey, there are stores throughout the downtown area and malls galore over on **Cannery Row**. Every year another shopping complex seems to rise along the Row. Already the area features cheese and wine stores, clothiers, a fudge factory, and a gourmet supply store. There's also a collector's comic book store, the inevitable T-shirt shop, knickknack stores, and galleries selling artworks that are like Muzak on canvas.

NIGHTLIFE

The classiest spot around is **McGarrett's**. Entertainment changes nightly, with two different rooms—one for DJs spinning dance tunes, the other for live music on Friday and Saturday night. Cover. ~ 321-D Alvarado Street; 408-646-9244.

Viva Monterey has been called the "Cheers of Monterey" and appeals to the twentysomething crowd. A popular local hangout with four pool tables, the club has nightly music: On weekdays a songwriters showcase gives musicians the chance to play original compositions, and on weekends singalongs encourage audience participation. ~ 414 Alvarado Street; 408-646-1415.

There are also several nightspots over by Cannery Row. **Kalisa's**, a funky restaurant and ice-cream parlor in a building that dates to the Steinbeck era, offers belly dancing on some weekends. This is also the home of John Steinbeck's birthday party every February 27, now a recognized town holiday. ~ 851 Cannery Row; 408-372-3621.

Doc Rickett's Lab has live music (reggae, blues, rock) and dancing nightly. Cover. ~ 95 Prescott Avenue; 408-649-4241.

The **Club House** caters to an older, 30s-and-40s crowd in an old Victorian hardwood-floored building. You can spend the evening upstairs in a nonsmoking environment, listening and dancing to reggae, jazz, or blues. Or you can stay downstairs and observe the scene upstairs on a big-screen TV, hear jazz Monday through Wednesday, and not only smoke but purchase a cigar at the cigar bar. ~ 638 Wave Street; 408-372-7200.

For dancing to deejay rock, the gay crowd heads to **After Dark**. With two bars and a high-tech design motif, the place is decorated with handsome lithographs. There's also a patio. Open Thursday through Sunday. Cover after 10 p.m. ~ 214 Lighthouse Avenue; 408-373-7828.

Pacific Grove

Projecting out from the northern tip of Monterey Peninsula is the diminutive town of Pacific Grove. Covering just 1700 acres, it is reached from Monterey along Lighthouse Avenue. Better yet, pick up Ocean View Boulevard near Cannery Row and follow as it winds along Pacific Grove's surf-washed shores. A quiet town with a lightly developed waterfront, Pacific Grove offers paths that lead for miles along a rock-crusted shore.

Costanoan Indians once dove for abalone in these waters. By the 19th century, Pacific Grove had become a religious retreat. Methodist Episcopal ministers pitched a tent city and decreed that "bathing suits shall be provided with double crotches or with skirts of ample size to cover the buttocks." The town was dry until 1969. Given the fish canneries in Monterey and teetotalers in this nearby town, local folks called the area "Carmel-by-the-Sea, Monterey-by-the-Smell, and Pacific Grove-by-God."

SIGHTS

Today Pacific Grove is a sleepy residential area decorated with Victorians, brown-shingle houses, and clapboard ocean cottages. The waterfront drive goes past rocky beaches to **Point Pinos Lighthouse**. When this beacon first flashed in 1855, it burned sperm oil. Little has changed except the introduction of electricity; this is the only early lighthouse along the entire California coast to be preserved in its original condition. The U.S. Coast Guard still uses it to guide ships; it is the oldest continually operating lighthouse on the West Coast. Two rooms have been restored to look as they did in Victorian times, and there's a short history of Emily Fish, the woman who ran the lighthouse in the 19th century. Open for self-guided tours from Thursday through Sunday. ~ North of Lighthouse Avenue; 408-648-3116.

Sunset Drive continues along the sea to **Asilomar State Beach**. Here sand dunes mantled with ice plant front a wave-lashed shore. There are tidepools galore, plus beaches for picnics, and trails leading through the rolling dunes.

Pacific Grove's major claim to fame lies in an area several blocks inland: around George Washington Park on Melrose Street and in a grove at 1073 Lighthouse Avenue. This otherwise unassuming municipality is known as "Butterfly Town, U.S.A." Every mid-October, brilliant orange-and-black **monarch butterflies** migrate here, remaining until mid-March. Some arrive from several hundred miles away to breed amid the cypress and oak trees. At night they cling to one another, curtaining the branches in clusters that sometimes number over a thousand. Then, at first light, they come to life, fluttering around the groves in a frenzy of wings and color.

Also of interest are the **Pacific Grove Museum of Natural History,** an excellent small museum. Closed Monday. ~ Central and Forest avenues; 408-648-3116. The **ivy-cloaked cottage** at 147 11th Street is where John Steinbeck lived and wrote *Tortilla Flat*, *In Dubious Battle*, and *Of Mice and Men*. (Not open to the public.) **Gosby House Inn** is a century-old Victorian mansion decorated in period antiques. ~ 643 Lighthouse Avenue. Next door, the **Hart Mansion,** now Gernot's Victoria House Restaurant, is an elaborate old Victorian house. ~ 649 Lighthouse Avenue; 408-646-1477.

17 MILE DRIVE From Pacific Grove, 17 Mile Drive leads to Pebble Beach, one of America's most lavish communities. This place is so exclusive that the rich charge $6.75 per vehicle to anyone wishing to drive around admiring their homes. No wonder they're rich.

Galling as the gate fee might be, this is an extraordinary region that must not be missed. The road winds through pine groves down to a wind-combed beach. There are miles of rolling dunes tufted with sea vegetation. (The oceanfront can be as cool and damp as it is beautiful, so carry a sweater or jacket, or better yet, both.)

Among the first spots you'll encounter is **Spanish Bay,** where Juan Gaspar de Portolá camped during his 1769 expedition up the California coast. (The picnic area here is a choice place to spread a feast.) At **Point Joe,** converging ocean currents create a wild frothing sea that has drawn several ships to their doom.

Seal Rock and **Bird Rock,** true to their nomenclature, are carpeted with sea lions, harbor and leopard seals, cormorants, brown pelicans, and gulls. Throughout this thriving 17 Mile Drive area are black-tail deer, sooty shearwaters, sea otters, and, during migration periods, California gray whales.

There are crescent beaches and granite headlands as well as vista points for scanning the coast. You'll also pass the **Lone Cypress,** the solitary tree on a rocky point that has become as symbolic of Northern California as perhaps the Golden Gate Bridge.

The **private homes** en route are mansions, exquisite affairs fashioned from marble and fine hardwoods. Some appear like stone fortresses, others seem made solely of glass. They range from American Colonial to futuristic and were designed by noted architects like Bernard Maybeck, Julia Morgan, and Willis Polk.

This is also home to several of the world's most renowned **golf courses**—Pebble Beach, Spyglass Hill, and Cypress Point—where the AT&T National Pro-Am Championship takes place each year. More than the designer homes and their celebrity residents, these courses have made Pebble Beach a place fabled for wealth and beauty.

The best part of the drive lies along the coast between the Pacific Grove and Carmel gates. Along the backside of 17 Mile Drive, where it loops up into Del Monte Forest, there are marvelous views of Monterey Bay and the San Gabilan Mountains. Here also is **Huckleberry Hill**, a forest of Monterey and Bishop pine freckled with bushes.

LODGING

Asilomar Conference Center provides one of the area's best housing arrangements. Set in a state park, it's surrounded by 120 acres of sand dunes and pine forests. The beach is a stroll away from any of the center's 17 hotel lodges. There's a dining hall on the premises as well as meeting rooms and recreational facilities (pool and volleyball court). Catering primarily to groups, Asilomar does provide accommodations (depending on availability) for independent travelers. Rooms in the "rustic buildings" are small and spartan but adequate (*and* designed by Julia Morgan). They lack carpeting

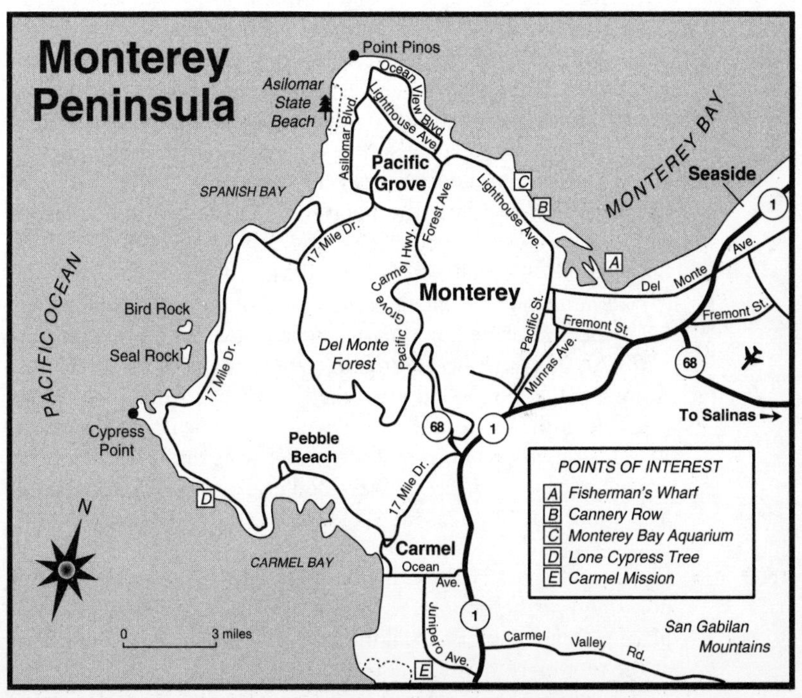

on the hardwood floors and include little decoration. The "deluxe building" rooms are nicely appointed with wallhangings, study desks, and comfortable furnishings. Fireplaces are also available. Every lodge includes a spacious lounge area with stone fireplace. No doubt about it, Asilomar is a splendid place at a relaxing price. ~ 800 Asilomar Boulevard; 408-372-8016, fax 408-372-7227. MODERATE.

Monterey cypresses grow nowhere in the world except along Carmel Bay.

One of Monterey Peninsula's less expensive bed and breakfasts is nearby. **Gosby House Inn**, a century-old Victorian mansion, includes 22 refurbished rooms. Each is different, and all have been decorated with special attention to detail. In any one you are liable to discover an antique armoire, brass lighting fixtures, stained glass, a Tiffany lamp, or a clawfoot bathtub. The two rooms in the carriage house have jacuzzi tubs. They are all small after the Victorian fashion, which sacrifices space for coziness. The afternoon wine and hors d'oeuvres and nightly turn-down service add to the homey feeling. ~ 643 Lighthouse Avenue; 408-375-1287, 800-527-8827, fax 408-655-9621. DELUXE TO ULTRA-DELUXE.

Green Gables Inn represents one of the region's most impressive bed and breakfasts. The house, a Queen Anne–style Victorian, dates from 1888. Adorned with step-gables, stained glass, and bay windows, it rests in a storybook setting overlooking Monterey Bay. Five bedrooms upstairs and a suite below have been fastidiously decorated with lavish antiques. Most rooms share a pair of bathrooms and rent at deluxe price; the suite, with sitting room and private bath, is ultra-deluxe. Set in a town filled with old Victorian homes, this oceanside residence is an ideal representation of Pacific Grove. There are also five separate units in a building adjacent to the main house. These are suites with private bath and fireplace; full breakfast, afternoon wine and cheese, and access to the main house are included. ~ 104 5th Street; 408-375-2095, 800-722-1774, fax 408-375-5437. ULTRA-DELUXE.

Commanding a front and center view of the spectacular waterfront is the **Martine Inn**, a pastel stucco Mediterranean-style villa with 20 individually decorated rooms, many with fireplaces. Among the accommodations is the Edith Head Room, which has 1920s furnishings from the Hollywood costume designer's estate. A full sitdown breakfast and afternoon wine and hors d'oeuvres are included. ~ 255 Ocean View Boulevard; 408-373-3388, 800-852-5588, fax 408-373-3896. DELUXE TO ULTRA-DELUXE.

DINING

For inexpensive snacks on the beach in Pacific Grove, try the **hot dog stand** at the bottom of the steps in Lover's Point Park. The place is something of a local institution. ~ Ocean View Boulevard at the foot of 16th Street. BUDGET.

Nearby at **The Tinnery** you'll find an American-style restaurant serving breakfast, lunch, and dinner. The restaurant overlooks the water. ~ 631 Ocean View Boulevard; 408-646-1040. MODERATE.

Or step up and over to the **Old Bath House Restaurant**, a luxurious building decorated in etched glass and sporting a Victorian-style bar. The Continental/California cuisine includes duckling, lamb, lobster, steak, and seafood dishes. Open for dinner only. ~ 620 Ocean View Boulevard; 408-375-5195. MODERATE TO ULTRA-DELUXE.

Peppers Mexicali Cafe pays homage to the red chile and has attracted an incredible number of devotees, as witnessed by the sometimes lengthy wait for a table. Chile posters and pepper prints by local artists decorate the walls, and the food is Tex-Mex. Among the offerings are grilled prawns with fresh lime and cilantro dressing, chicken *mole*, snapper Veracruz, and more mundane dishes such as tacos, burritos, and enchiladas. ~ 170 Forest Avenue; 408-373-6892. MODERATE.

SHOPPING

The main area for window browsing in town can be found along Lighthouse Avenue. Just above this busy thoroughfare, on 17th Street, artisans have renovated a row of small beach cottages. In each is a creatively named shop. There's **Reincarnation Vintage Clothing**, which sells vintage clothing, jewelry, and accessories. ~ 214 17th Street; 408-649-0689. At **Mum's Place**, there's high-quality oak, maple, cherry, and pine furniture. ~ 246 Forest Avenue; 408-372-6250.

From designer fashions to gourmet cookware, the 50 shops at **American Tin Cannery Factory Outlets** are a shopper's paradise. A good place to look for luggage, books, shoes, housewares, and cosmetics, this renovated two-story complex has a variety of outlet stores. If you're looking for bargains in the Monterey area, don't miss this gem. ~ 125 Ocean View Boulevard; 408-372-1442.

NIGHTLIFE

The Tinnery, an attractive complex on the waterfront in Pacific Grove, spotlights local entertainers every night, usually a soloist playing contemporary music. ~ 631 Ocean View Boulevard; 408-646-1040.

BEACHES & PARKS

ASILOMAR STATE BEACH This oceanfront facility features over 100 acres of snowy white sand dunes, tidepools, and beach. It's a perfect place for daytripping and exploring. The best surfing here is just off the main sandy beach. Since northern and southern currents run together here, the waters are teeming with marine life. If you're into algae, you'll want to know that over 200 species congregate in the ocean here. Another species—Homo sapiens—gathers at the park's multifaceted conference center (overnight accommodations are described in "Lodging" above). ~ Located along Sunset Drive in Pacific Grove; 408-372-4076.

Carmel

The first law of real estate should be this: The best land is always occupied by the military, bohemians, or the rich. Think about it. The principle holds for many of the world's prettiest spots. Generally the military arrives first, on an exploratory mission or as an occupying force. It takes strategic ground, which happens to be the beaches, headlands, and mountaintops. The bohemians select beautiful locales because they possess good taste. When the rich discover where the artists have settled, they start moving in, driving up the rents, and forcing the displaced bohemians to discover new homes, which will then be taken by another wave of the wealthy.

The Monterey Peninsula is no exception. In Carmel the military established an early beachhead when Spanish soldiers occupied a barracks in the old Catholic mission. Later the bohemians arrived in numbers. Poet George Sterling came in 1905, followed by Mary Austin, the novelist. Eventually such luminaries as Upton Sinclair, Lincoln Steffens, and Sinclair Lewis, writers all, settled for varying periods. Jack London and Ambrose Bierce visited. Later, photographers Ansel Adams and Edward Weston relocated here.

The figure most closely associated with this "seacoast of Bohemia" was Robinson Jeffers, a poet who came seeking solitude in 1914. Quarrying rock from the shoreline, he built the Tor House and Hawk Tower, where he lived and wrote haunting poems and epics about the coast.

Then like death and tax collectors, the rich inevitably moved in. As John Steinbeck noted when he later returned to this artists' colony, "If Carmel's founders should return, they could not afford to live there. . . . They would instantly be picked up as suspicious characters and deported over the city line."

It's doubtful many would want to remain anyway. Today Carmel is so cute it cloys. The tiny town is cluttered with over four dozen inns, about six dozen restaurants, and more than 300 shops. Ocean Avenue, the main street, is wall-to-wall with merchants. Shopping malls have replaced artists' garrets, and there are traffic jams where there was once solitude.

SIGHTS

Typifying the town is the **Tuck Box**, a gingerbread-style building on Dolores Street between Ocean and 7th avenues (there are no street numbers in Carmel), or the fairy tale-like Hansel-and-Gretel cottages on Torres Street between 5th and 6th avenues.

Still, reasons remain to visit Carmel, which is reached from Monterey via Route 1 or from the Carmel gate along 17 Mile Drive. The window shopping is good and several galleries are outstanding. Some of the town's quaint characteristics have appeal. There are no traffic lights or parking meters, and at night few street lights. Drive around the side streets and you will encounter an architectural mixture of log cabins, adobe structures, board-and-batten cottages, and Spanish villas.

A secret that local residents have long withheld from visitors is **Mission Trail Park.** No signs will direct you here, so watch for an entrance at the corner of Mountain View and Crespi avenues. Within this forest preserve are miles of hiking trails. They wind across footbridges, through redwood groves, and past meadows of wildflowers en route to Carmel Mission. There are ocean vistas, deer grazing the hillsides, and an arboretum seeded with native California plants. ◄HIDDEN

Carmel's most alluring feature is the one which early drew the bohemians—the Pacific. At the foot of Ocean Avenue rests Carmel Beach, a snowy strand shadowed by cypress trees. From here, Scenic Road hugs the coast, winding above rocky outcroppings.

Just beyond stretches **Carmel River State Beach**, a sandy corridor at the foot of Carmel Bay. For additional information, see the "Beaches & Parks" section below.

Even for the non-religious, a visit to **Carmel Mission** becomes a pilgrimage. If the holiness holds no appeal, there's the aesthetic sense of the place. Dating back to 1793, its Old World beauty captivates and confounds. The courtyards are alive with flowers and birds. The adobe buildings surrounding have been dusted with

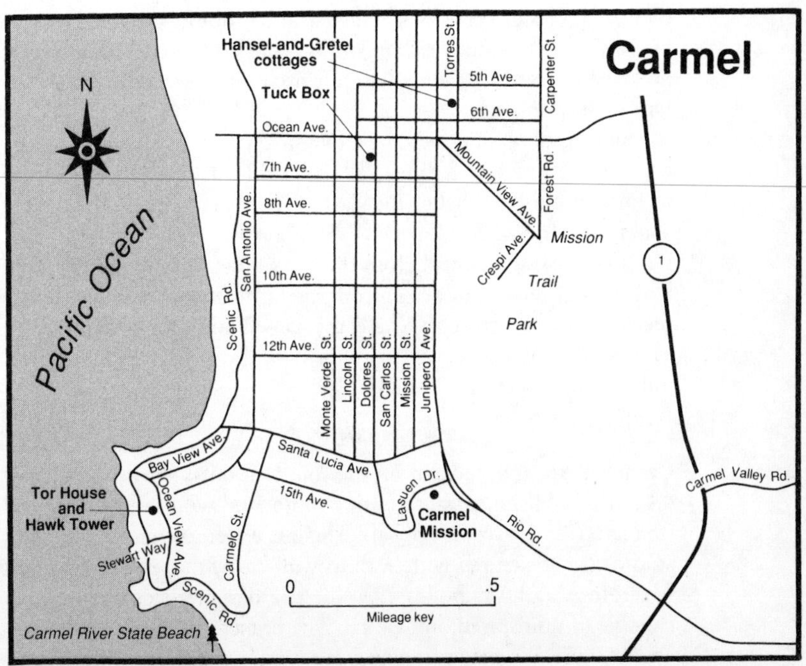

time—their eaves are hunchbacked, the tile roofs coated in moss. ~ Located on Rio Road just off Route 1; 408-624-3600.

Established by Father Junípero Serra, this mission is one of California's most remarkable. The basilica is a vaulted-ceiling affair adorned with old oil paintings and wooden statues of Christ; its walls are lime plaster made from burnt seashells. The exterior is topped with a Moorish tower and 11 bells.

Junípero Serra lies buried in the sanctuary, his grave marked with a stone plaque. There are also museum rooms demonstrating early California life—a kitchen with stone hearth and rudimentary tools, the state's first library (complete with waterstained bibles), and the cell where Father Serra died, its bed a slab of wood with a single blanket and no mattress. Close by, in the cemetery beside the basilica, several thousand American Indians are also buried.

Just two miles south of Carmel lies **Point Lobos State Reserve,** an incomparable natural area of rocky headlands and placid coves. The park features hillside crow's nests from which to gaze out along Carmel Bay. Before Westerners arrived, the American Indians gathered mussels and abalone here. Later Point Lobos was a whaling station and an abalone cannery. Today it's a park intended primarily for nature hikers. You can explore pine forests and cypress groves, a jagged shoreline of granite promontories, and wave-lapped coves. Every tidepool is a miniature aquarium pulsing with color and sea life. The water is clear as sky. Offshore rise sea stacks, their rocky bases ringed with mussels, their domes crowned by sea birds. This region, also rich in wildlife and underwater life, should not be bypassed; for complete information, see the "Beaches & Parks" section below.

As if its shoreline was not enough, Carmel also boasts an extraordinary interior. Carmel Valley Road leads from Route 1 into the distant hills, paralleling the Carmel River in its circuitous course. The lower end of the Carmel Valley promises fruit orchards and fields of grazing horses before the road ascends into the wooded heights that separate Carmel from the farmlands of Salinas. Along the way you can stop by **Château Julien Winery** for a tasting and tour (at 10 a.m. and 2 p.m. daily). ~ 8940 Carmel Valley Road, five miles from Route 1; 408-624-2600.

LODGING

Carmel River Inn, located on the southern outskirts of town, is a 43-unit establishment with both a motel and woodframe cottages (the latter have greater appeal). The less expensive guest units are studio-size structures with wall-to-wall carpeting, televisions, refrigerators, and telephones; their interior designer was obviously a capable, if uninspired, individual. The pricier cottages vary in size and facilities, but may contain extra rooms, a fireplace, or a kitchen.

~ Route 1 at Carmel River Bridge; 408-624-1575, 800-882-8142, fax 408-624-0290. MODERATE TO DELUXE.

Carmel's most closely kept secret is a hideaway resort set on 21 acres and overlooking the ocean at a distance. Scattered about the tree-shaded grounds at the **Mission Ranch** are triplex cottages and a quadraplex unit, in addition to the older white clapboard farmhouse. There are tennis courts, trim lawns, and ancient cypress trees. With mountains in the background, the views extend across a broad lagoon and out along sandy beachfront. The ranch dining room is favored by local people. A rare find indeed with continental breakfast included. ~ 26270 Dolores Street; 408-624-6436, 800-538-8221, fax 408-626-4163. DELUXE TO ULTRA-DELUXE.

The Homestead is also one of the area's better housing arrangements. Set in a maroon house with shiplap siding, its 12 rooms each have a private bath. This is not a bed and breakfast, so it lacks the community atmosphere of other country inns, though a touch of the intimacy lingers. The rooms are carpeted and equipped with televisions; the furniture is functional more than fashionable. Also available are four studio cottages with kitchenettes. ~ Lincoln Street and 8th Avenue; 408-624-4119. MODERATE.

The Pine Inn is not only Carmel's oldest hostelry, but also another of the town's more reasonably priced places. This 49-room hotel dates back to 1889 and still possesses the charm that has drawn visitors for decades. The lobby is a fashionable affair with red brocade settees, marbletop tables, and a brick fireplace. The less expensive accommodations are smaller but do have the antique furnishings, private baths, televisions, and phones common to all the rooms. Each one has been designed in Edwardian style and is likely to feature patterned wallpaper and ornamental wall-

STONE POEM

Just before the intersection with Stewart Way, gaze uphill toward those two stone edifices. Poet Robinson Jeffers' **Tor House and Hawk Tower** seem drawn from another place and time, perhaps a Scottish headland in the 19th century. In fact, the poet modeled the house after an English-style barn and built the 40-foot high garret with walls six feet thick in the fashion of an Irish tower. Completed during the 1920s, the structures are granite and include porthole windows that Jeffers salvaged from a shipwreck. Tours of the house and tower are conducted on Friday and Saturday by reservation. Admission. ~ 26304 Ocean View Avenue; for information, call 408-624-1813.

hangings. Rather than a country inn, this is a full-service hotel with restaurant and bar downstairs as well as room service for the guests. ~ Ocean Avenue between Lincoln and Monte Verde streets; 408-624-3851, 800-228-3851, fax 408-624-3030. DELUXE.

You may want to follow the trails that lead from the Carmel River through meadows to a 2000-foot peak in 5000-acre Garland Ranch Regional Park. ~ Carmel Valley Road, nine miles from Route 1; 408-659-4488.

Holiday House is a six-room bed and breakfast located several blocks from the beach. Set in a brown-shingle house, it features a parlor with stone fireplace and a nicely tended garden. The rooms are small, neat, and prim; though attractively furnished, they lack the lavish antiques found in more expensive country inns. The outdoor decoration should adequately substitute—ask for a room with an ocean view. ~ Camino Real between Ocean and 7th avenues; 408-624-6267. DELUXE.

Highlands Inn is one of those raw-wood-and-polished-stone places that evoke the muted elegance of the California coast. Ultramodern in execution, it features a stone lodge surrounded by wood shingle buildings. The lodge houses two restaurants and an oceanview lounge while the neighboring structures contain countless guest rooms, each a warren of blond woods and pastel tiles. All the rooms have fireplaces and most have patios. Parked on a hillside overlooking an awesome sweep of ocean, the inn is the ultimate in Carmel chic. ~ Route 1 about four miles south of Carmel; 408-624-3801, 800-682-4811, fax 408-626-1574. ULTRA-DELUXE.

DINING

In Carmel, the thing to do is drop by the **Tuck Box** for afternoon tea. The establishment sits in a dollhouselike creation with a swirl roof and curved chimney. The prim and tiny dining room also serves breakfast and lunch. During the noon meal there are omelettes, sandwiches, shrimp salad, and Welsh rarebit. Closed Monday and Tuesday. ~ Dolores Street between Ocean and 7th avenues; 408-624-6365. BUDGET TO MODERATE.

Join the line in front of **Mondo's Trattoria** for good times and fabulous food. As you step through the door you might think you're in Italy: Wine bottles, cooking utensils, and strings of garlic adorn the walls, and the staff is very friendly, often breaking into song for impromptu celebrations. If that isn't enough, the food is *motte bene*. You can't go wrong with a fresh pasta dish such as the San Remo (sundried tomatoes and goat cheese in cream sauce) or la mafiosa (calamari, prawns, and scallops in a spicy tomato sauce). Dinner specials include veal, seafood, fish, and chicken entrées and at lunch sandwiches are added to the menu. Save room for the desserts, especially the tiramisu! ~ Dolores Street between Ocean and 7th avenues; 408-624-8977. MODERATE.

Then there's **Hog's Breath Inn**, a name so outrageous it begins to have appeal. If owner Clint Eastwood adds a hotel facility, he can call it The Innsomnia. Actually Carmel could use a few more doses of humor like this; the town takes itself so dreadfully seriously. Anyway, back to Hog's Breath. Quite nice, it is laid out in a courtyard arrangement with a flagstone dining patio flanked on one side by a pub and on the other by the dining room. At lunchtime, you can eat outdoors or inside next to a stone fireplace. A boar's head adorns one wall and the menu, as you may have guessed, runs heavy on meat. Dinner entrées include pork chops, filet mignon, prime rib, and chicken in whiskey; there is also a catch of the day. Lunch includes sandwiches and salads. ~ San Carlos Street between 5th and 6th avenues; 408-625-1044. MODERATE TO DELUXE.

Reasonably priced, casual, and contemporary. Who could ask more than what they're offering at **Rio Grill**? The cuisine at this popular dining room is American grill with a Southwestern touch. Smoked chicken and artichokes and calf's liver with sweet potato pancake are among the entrées. Critically acclaimed. ~ Crossroads Shopping Center, Route 1 and Rio Road; 408-625-5436. MODERATE.

Located in a cute rural-themed shopping center, **Michael's at The Barnyard** is owned and operated by Bradley Jones, one of the Monterey Peninsula's celebrity chefs. The ambience is casual Southwestern, with lots of palms and other plants, ceiling fans, and white wooden shutters. Chef Bradley prepares regional American cuisine with Mediterranean accents, which can be seen in such dishes as pancetta-wrapped artichoke quarters, pistachio-crusted rack of lamb, and roast duckling with orange pulp. ~ 3690 The Barnyard; 408-622-5200. MODERATE.

The **Thunderbird Bookshop Café** combines two of the world's most pleasurable activities, eating and reading. You can browse the bookstore, then dine in the dining room or out on the patio. ~ 3600 The Barnyard; 408-624-9414. BUDGET.

Patisserie Boissière belongs to that endangered species—the moderately priced French restaurant. The simple French country dining room adjoins a small bakery. In addition to outrageous pastries for breakfast, they offer weekend lunch and nightly dinner with such entrées as coquilles St. Jacques, salmon in parchment paper, and braised rabbit. Baked brie and French onion soup are also on the bill of fare. A bargain hunter's delight in dear Carmel. Lunch only on Monday and Tuesday. ~ Mission Street between Ocean and 7th avenues; 408-624-5008. MODERATE. ◄ HIDDEN

Old time Carmel residents will tell you about the **Mission Ranch Dining Room**. How it dates back over a century to the days when it was a creamery. Today it's just a warm, homey old building with a stone fireplace plus a view of a sheep pasture and a neighboring ocean. The menu is a combination of fresh seafood and all-American fare: steak, fish, chicken, that sort of thing. Dinner, Saturday lunch, and Sunday brunch. ~ 26270 Dolores Street; 408-625-9040. MODERATE TO DELUXE.

Text continued on page 350.

The Old Spanish Mission Town

Time permitting, there's one overland excursion that must be added to your itinerary—a visit to the **Mission at San Juan Bautista**. While this graceful mission town, located 90 miles south of San Francisco, is easily reached from Route 101, the most inspiring route is via Route 156 from the Monterey Peninsula.

Anyone who has read Frank Norris's muckraking novel about the railroads, *The Octopus*, will recognize this placid village with its thick, cool adobe church. And anyone who remembers the climax to Hitchcock's *Vertigo* will instantly picture the mission—even though the bell tower that Jimmy Stewart struggled to climb was a Hollywood addition that you won't see at the real San Juan Bautista. Founded in 1797, the mission was completed in 1812. Today it numbers among California's most enchanting locales. With its colonnade and sagging crossbeams, the mission has about it the musty scent of history. The old monastery and church consist of a low-slung building roofed in Spanish tile and topped with a belfry. ~ 408-623-4528.

My favorite spot in this most favored town is **Mission Cemetery**, a small plot bounded by a stone fence and overlooking valley and mountains. It's difficult to believe that over 4300 American Indians are buried here in unmarked graves. The few recognizable resting places are memorialized with wooden crosses and circling enclosures of stone. Shade trees cool the yard. Just below the cemetery, symbolic perhaps of change and mortality, are the old Spanish Road (*El Camino Real*) and the San Andreas Fault.

The mission rests on a grassy square facing **Plaza Hall**. Originally a dormitory for unwed American Indian women, this structure was rebuilt in 1868 and used as a meeting place and private residence. Peek inside its shuttered windows or tour the building and encounter a child's room cluttered with old dolls, a sitting room dominated by a baby grand piano, and other rooms containing period furniture.

Behind the hall sits a **blacksmith shop**, filled now with wagon wheels, oxen yokes, and the "San Juan Eagle," a hook-and-ladder wagon drawn by a ten-man firefighting crew back in 1869. Nearby **Plaza Stable** houses an impressive collection of buggies and carriages.

The **Plaza Hotel** lines another side of the square. Consisting of several adobe structures, the earliest built in 1814, the place once served as a stagecoach stop. Today its myriad rooms contain historic exhibits and 1860s-era furnishings. Admission. Similarly, the **Castro-Breen Adobe** next door is decorated with Spanish-style pieces. Owned by a Mexican general and later by Donner Party survivors, it is a window on California frontier life. Nearby are **San Juan Jail**, an oversized outhouse constructed in 1870, and the **settler's cabin**, a rough log cabin built by East Coast pioneers in the 1830s or 1840s.

All are part of the **state historic park** which comprises San Juan Bautista. Like the plaza, 3rd Street is lined with 19th-century stores and houses. Here amid porticoed haciendas and crumbling adobe are antique stores, a bakery, restaurants, and other shops. Admission. ~ 408-623-4881.

A block away is **El Teatro Campesino**, an excellent resident theater group. This Latino company originated *Zoot Suit*, an important and provocative play that was eventually filmed as a movie. With a penetrating sense of Mexican-American history and an unsettling awareness of contemporary Latino social roles, they are a modern expression of the vigor and spirit of this old Spanish town. From May to June summer productions are held in their theater; the Christmas show is staged in Mission San Juan Bautista. ~ 705 4th Street; 408-623-2444.

Accommodations are scarce in San Juan Bautista, but **Posada de San Juan** offers comfortable (yet somewhat sterile) rooms within walking distance of the mission and 3rd Street's shops and restaurants. The 34 rooms are equipped with minibars, oversized bathtubs, and gas fireplaces. Decorated in a hacienda style, this inn reflects the distinctly Mexican flavor of San Juan Bautista. ~ 310 4th Street; 408-623-4030, fax 408-623-2378. DELUXE.

Also in the area is **Bed & Breakfast San Juan**, fittingly placed in a 1858 house. Located along a busy highway, the house is slightly rickety, but possesses solid charm. Rooms are a shade less expensive than most bed and breakfasts, which offsets the establishment's vaguely rundown state. ~ 315 The Alameda; 408-623-4101. MODERATE.

As for restaurants, **La Casa Rosa** sits in an 1858 house. Open for lunch only, this family-run eatery features an "old California casserole," a "new California casserole," and a chicken soufflé dish. The first entrée is made with cheese, meat sauce, and a corn base; the second dish features green chiles. La Casa Rosa is charming and intimate. Closed Tuesday. ~ 107 3rd Street; 408-623-4563. MODERATE.

In the same block, **Jardines de San Juan** is recommended as much for its garden as its food. In addition to the usual tacos, burritos, and flautas, weekend specials get fancy: Veracruz-style red snapper served with *crema* on a bed of rice, or *pollos borrachos* cooked in sherry with ham and sausage. ~ 115 3rd Street; 408-623-4466. MODERATE.

Of course the ultimate dining place is **The Covey at Quail Lodge**, up in Carmel Valley. Set in one of the region's most prestigious hotels, The Covey is a contemporary European restaurant with a California influence, serving, for example, grilled salmon on prawn and artichoke hash. Richly decorated, it overlooks the lodge's lake and grounds. Dinner jackets and reservations, please. Dinner only. ~ 8205 Valley Greens Drive; 408-624-1581. DELUXE TO ULTRA-DELUXE.

SHOPPING

In Carmel, shopping seems to be the raison d'être. If ever an entire town was dressed to look like a boutique, this is the one. Its shops are stylish and expensive.

The major shopping strip is along Ocean Avenue between Mission and Monte Verde streets, but the best stores generally are situated on the side streets. The **Doud Arcade** is a mall featuring artisan shops. Here you'll find leather merchants, potters, and jewelers. ~ Ocean Avenue between San Carlos and Dolores streets.

Most of the artists who made Carmel famous have long since departed, but the city still maintains a wealth of art galleries. While many are not even worth browsing, others are outstanding. The **Carmel Bay Company** features posters by contemporary artists. ~ Lincoln Street and Ocean Avenue; 408-624-3868. The **Carmel Art Association Galleries**, owned and operated by artists, offers paintings and sculpture by local figures. ~ Dolores Street between 5th and 6th avenues; 408-624-6176. Also of note is the **Beaches Gallery**, which features local artists as well. ~ 7th Avenue between Mission and San Carlos streets; 408-624-1985.

Carmel is recognized as an international center for photographers. Two of the nation's most famous—Ansel Adams and Edward Weston—lived here. **The Weston Gallery** displays prints by both men, as well as works by other 19th- and 20th-century photographers. ~ 6th Avenue between Dolores and Lincoln streets; 408-624-4453. At **Photography West Gallery** Weston and Adams are represented, as are Imogen Cunningham and Brett Weston. ~ Dolores Street between Ocean and 7th avenues; 408-625-1587.

Carmel's prettiest shopping plaza is **The Barnyard**, an innovative mall housing 47 shops and restaurants. Set amid flowering gardens is a series of raw wood structures reminiscent of old farm buildings. ~ Route 1 and Carmel Valley Road; 408-624-8886. Browse the boutiques and gift shops, then follow those brick pathways to the **Thunderbird Bookshop & Café**. With a marvelous collection of hardbacks and paperbacks, it is one of the finest bookstores along the Central Coast. Better still, they have an adjoining café and a nearby book-and-toy store for children. ~ 408-624-1803, 408-624-4995.

NIGHTLIFE

For the warm conviviality of an English pub consider **Bully III.** ~ Dolores Street and 8th Avenue; 408-625-1750. Another restaurant-cum-bar is **The Forge in the Forest** with its copper walls, hand-carved bar, and open fire. ~ Junipero Street and 5th Avenue; 408-624-2233.

Possibly the prettiest place you'll ever indulge the spirits in is the **Lobos Lounge** at Highlands Inn. An entire wall of this leather-armchair-and-marble-table establishment is plate glass. And the picture on the other side of those panes is classic Carmel—rocky shoreline fringed with cypress trees and lashed by passionate waves. If that's not entertainment enough, there's a piano bar during the week and a three-piece combo on weekends. ~ Route 1 about four miles south of Carmel; 408-624-3801.

BEACHES & PARKS

CARMEL RIVER STATE BEACH This beach would be more attractive were it not upstaged by Point Lobos, its remarkable neighbor to the south. Nevertheless, there's a sandy beach here as well as a view of the surrounding hills. The chief feature is the bird refuge along the river. The marshes offer willets, sandpipers, pelicans, hawks, and kingfishers, plus an occasional Canadian snow goose. The beach has restrooms; restaurants and groceries are nearby in Carmel. ~ Located at the end of Carmelo Road in Carmel (take Rio Road exit off Route 1); 408-624-4909.

POINT LOBOS STATE RESERVE In a region packed with uncommonly beautiful scenery, this park stands out as something special. A 1225-acre reserve, only 456 acres of which are above water, it contains over 300 species of plants and more than 250 species of animals and birds. This is a perfect place to study sea otters, harbor seals, and sea lions. During migrating season in mid-winter and mid-spring, gray whales cruise the coast. Along with Pebble Beach, Point Lobos is the only spot in the world where Monterey cypresses, those ghostly, wind-gnarled coastal trees, still survive. There are 80-foot-high kelp forests offshore, popular with scuba divers who know the reserve as one of the most fascinating places on the coast. Reservations to dive must be made three weeks in advance by phone or e-mail. Facilities include picnic areas and restrooms; restaurants and groceries nearby in Carmel. Day-use fee, $6. ~ On Route 1 about three miles south of Carmel; 408-624-4909, e-mail ptlobos@mbay.com.

PINNACLES NATIONAL MONUMENT Set far inland amid the softly rolling San Gabilan Mountains are the sharp, dramatic volcanic peaks that centerpiece this unusual park. Sheer spires and solitary minarets vault 1200 feet from the canyon floor. Comprising the weathered remains of a 23-million-year-old volcano, these towering peaks challenge day hikers and technical rock climbers alike. Rockclimbing is a major activity here in spring and fall (it's too hot in summer). There are caves to explore, and more than 30 miles of trails leading through the remnants of the volcano. Coyote, gray fox, and bobcat roam the region, while golden eagles and redshouldered hawks work the skies above. Since the cliffs are accessible only by trail, visitors should be prepared to hike. Bring water, durable shoes, loose clothing, and a flashlight for cave exploring. The best time to visit is spring, when the wildflowers bloom, or autumn; summer brings stifling heat to the area and winter carries rain. The east side of the park has an information center, picnic areas, and restrooms. The west side offers a ranger station, picnic areas, and restrooms. There's a grocery on the east side, but restaurants are 36 miles away in Hollister. From the west side, restaurants and groceries are 13 miles away in Soledad. Day-use fee, $4. ~ No road traverses the park. You must enter either on the east side, by following Route 25 south from Hollister for 32 miles, then proceeding four miles west on Route 146; or on the west side along Route 146, about 13 miles east from Soledad (which is just off Route 101); 408-389-4485.

▲ **Pinnacles Campground**, a private facility with 125 sites (some with partial RV hookups), sits astride the park's east side; fees are $6 per person nightly or $24 for a group of up to six people. ~ 2400 Route 146, Paicines; 408-389-4462. On the west side of the park, 18 walk-in campsites are located in the park; $10 nightly fee per site.

Big Sur

From Point Lobos, the highway hugs the coastline as it snakes south toward Big Sur. Like Route 1 north of San Francisco, this is one of America's great stretches of roadway. Situated between the Santa Lucia Mountains and the Pacific, Route 1 courses about 30 miles from Carmel to Big Sur, then spirals farther south along the coast toward San Luis Obispo and Los Angeles.

The Big Sur district is where the Santa Lucia Mountains encounter the Pacific. Backed by the challenging Ventana Wilderness, the region is marked by sharp coastal cliffs and unbelievable scenery. Though it's hard to conceive, Big Sur may be even more beautiful than the other sections of the Central Coast.

Along Route 1, each turnout provides another glimpse into a magic-lantern world. Here the glass pictures a beach crusted with rocks, there a wave-wracked cliff or pocket of tidepools. The canyons are narrow and precipitous, while the headlands are so close to the surf they seem like beached whales. Trees are broken and blasted before the wind. The houses, though millionaire affairs, appear inconsequential against the backdrop of ocean and stone.

SIGHTS

At **Soberanes Point**, eight miles south of Carmel, hiking trails lead out along the headlands. Here you can stand on a rock shelf directly above the ocean and gaze back at the encroaching hills.

◀ HIDDEN

For an intriguing excursion into those hills, head about six miles up **Palo Colorado Road**, which intersects with Route 1 a couple of miles south of Garrapata Creek. Though paved, this country road is one lane. The corridor tunnels through an arcade of redwoods past log cabins and rustic homes. If you're feeling adventurous, follow the twisting eight-mile road to its terminus at Los Padres National Forest.

Back on Route 1 you'll traverse **Bixby Creek Bridge**, which stretches from one cliff to another across an infernal chasm. Local legend cites it incorrectly as the world's longest concrete arch span. With fluted hills in the background and a fluffy beach below, it may, however, be the world's prettiest.

◀ HIDDEN

For another incredible side trip, you can follow **Coast Road** for about 11 miles up into the Santa Lucia Mountains. Climbing along narrow ledges, then corkscrewing deep into overgrown canyons, the road carries you past exquisite views of forests and mountain ridges. There are hawk's-eye vistas of the Pacific, the rolling Big Sur countryside, and Pico Blanco, a 3709-foot lime-rich peak. This is the old coast road, the principal thoroughfare before Route 1 was completed in the 1930s. Take heed: It is so curvy it makes Route 1 seem a desert straightaway; it is also entirely unpaved, narrow, rutted, and impassable in wet weather. But oh those views!

Coast Road begins at Bixby Bridge and rejoins Route 1 at Andrew Molera State Park. If instead of detouring you stay on Route 1, it will climb along **Hurricane Point**, a promontory blessed with sweeping views and cursed by lashing winds, and descend toward **Little Sur Beach**. This sandy crescent is bounded by a shallow lagoon. There are dunes and lofty hills all around, as well as shore birds. Another lengthy beach leads to **Point Sur Light Station**, set on a volcanic headland. This solitary sentinel dates back to 1889. The only way to visit this lighthouse is by a guided tour. Tours run

HENRY MILLER LITE

There's not much to the **Henry Miller Library**, but somehow the unassuming nature of the place befits its candid subject. Occupying a small woodframe house donated by Miller's friend Emil White, the museum contains volumes from the novelist's library as well as his evocative artworks. Closed Monday. ~ Route 1 about a mile south of Ventana Inn; 408-667-2574.

Saturday at 10 a.m. and 2 p.m., Sunday at 10 a.m. and Wednesday (April through October only) at 10 a.m. and 2 p.m. Admission. ~ 408-625-4419.

Then the road enters the six-mile-long Big Sur River Valley. **Big Sur**, a rural community of about 1200 people, stretches the length of the valley. Lacking a town center, it consists of houses and a few stores dotted along the Big Sur River. The place received its name from early Spanish settlers, who called the wilderness south of Carmel *El País Grande del Sur*, "the big country to the south."

Later it became a rural retreat and an artists' colony. Henry Miller lived here from 1947 until 1964, writing *Big Sur and the Oranges of Hieronymus Bosch*, *Plexus*, and *Nexus* during his residence. Today the artists are being displaced by soaring land values, while the region is gaining increased popularity among visitors. It's not difficult to understand why as you cruise along its knife-edge cliffs and timbered mountainsides. You can drive for miles past eye-boggling vistas, then turn back on Route 1 to the Monterey Peninsula, or continue on to a strange and exotic land called Southern California.

LODGING

For a variety of accommodations, consider **Big Sur Campground and Cabins**. Set in a redwood grove along the Big Sur River, this 13-acre facility has campsites, tent cabins, and A-frames. Camping out on the grounds costs $24 for two people and includes access to hot showers, a laundry, a store, basketball and volleyball courts, and a playground. The tent cabins, $44 per night, consist of wood-frame skeletons with canvas roofs. They come with beds, bedding and towels and share a bath house. The tent cabins are closed during the rainy season. The "cabins" along the river are actually mobile homes, neatly furnished but rather sterile. More intimate are the A-frame cabins with Franklin stoves and sleeping lofts. The newer modular units include pine floors with bedrooms as well as a kitchen and a private bath. ~ Route 1; 408-667-2322. DELUXE TO ULTRA-DELUXE.

Ripplewood Resort has 16 cabins. The least expensive is a small, basic duplex unit with redwood walls, a gas heater, and carpeting. It has a bath but lacks a kitchen. The more expensive units are larger, with kitchens, sitting rooms, and decks, and are located above the river. My advice? Compromise with one of the riverfront cabins. They feature kitchens, decks, and spacious bedrooms. (No extra charge for the river tumbling past your doorstep.) ~ Route 1; 408-667-2242. MODERATE.

Located within Pfeiffer Big Sur State Park is **Big Sur Lodge**, a complex containing 20 cottages with two to six units per cottage. The "lodge" represents a full-facility establishment complete with conference center, restaurant, gift shop, grocery, laundromat, and heated pool in the summer. It's very convenient, if undistinguished. The cottages are frame houses with wood-shingle roofs. They are simple in design, yet have a kitchen and a fireplace. The interiors are pine and feature wall-to-wall carpeting and high beam ceilings; each cottage features a porch or a deck. ~ Route 1; 408-667-2171, 800-424-4787, fax 408-667-3110. DELUXE TO ULTRA-DELUXE.

Big Sur has long been associated with bohemian values and an easy lifestyle. Today landed gentry and wealthy speculators have taken over many of the old haunts, but a few still remain. One such is **Deetjen's Big Sur Inn**, a 20-unit slapdash affair where formality is an inconvenience. The place consists of a hodgepodge collection of clapboard buildings. The outer walls are unpainted and the doors have no locks, lending the residence a tumbledown charm. Rooms are roughhewn, poorly insulated, and funky. Throw rugs are scattered about, the furniture is traditional, and local art pieces along the wall serve as decoration. If all this is beginning to discourage you, you're getting older than you think; after all, this offbeat hideaway does possess an enchanting quality. ~ Route 1; 408-667-2377. DELUXE TO ULTRA-DELUXE. ◄ HIDDEN

If, on the other hand, you spell Big Sur with a capital $, there are two places to consider. The first option is **Ventana**. Set along 243 mountainside acres overlooking the Pacific Ocean, this fabled resort is the *ne plus ultra* of refined rusticity. Buildings are fashioned from raw wood and most guest rooms are equipped with tile or marble fireplaces. There are cedar walls and quilt beds. With Japanese hot baths, saunas, two pools, a fitness room, and a clothing-optional sun deck, the place exudes an air of languor. Guests enjoy a continental breakfast and afternoon wine and cheese, hike nearby trails, and congratulate themselves for having discovered a secluded resort where doing nothing is a way of life. ~ Route 1; 408-667-2331, 800-628-6500, fax 408-667-2419. ULTRA-DELUXE.

The second is **The Post Ranch Inn**, located just across the highway. Defying description, this cliff-edge hotel is a testimony to rustic perfection. Consisting of 30 separate units and designed to fit the surrounding landscape, the hotel features some rooms that are built into the hillside and covered by grass and others that are perched on stilts high above the forest floor. Each room is decorated by wood and stone, has a king-size bed, and, best of all, offers an open view of the Pacific Ocean or tree-covered hillside. ~ Route 16; 408-667-2200, 800-527-2200, fax 408-667-2824. ULTRA-DELUXE.

The ultimate resting place in this corner of the world is the **Tassajara Zen Center**. Set deep in the Santa Lucia Mountains along a meandering country road, Tassajara has been a hot springs resort since the 1880s. Before that its salubrious waters were known to American Indians and the Spanish. When the Zen Center pur- ◄ HIDDEN chased the place in 1967, they converted it into a meditation center. There are only a few telephones and electrical outlets in the entire complex, making it ideal for people seeking serenity. Every year from May until September, the Zen Center welcomes day-visitors and overnight guests. The hosts provide three vegetarian meals daily plus lodging in the private rooms and cabins dotted about the grounds. Day-visitors are charged a $12 admission, $15 on weekends; lodging facilities with shared bath and meals included begin from $80 per person weekdays and $90 on weekends (cabins with private baths are $95 and $110, respectively); shuttle service into the resort is available from Jamesburg, south of the Carmel Valley. Be sure to make your reservations far in advance, since this unique place is very popular. ~ For information, contact the Zen Center, 300 Page Street, San Francisco, CA 94102; 415-863-3136; for reservations, call 415-431-3771.

South from Big Sur about 20 miles, on the edge of an ocean cliff, sits **Lucia Lodge.** Perched 500 feet above a cobalt blue bay are ten cozy rooms offering otherworldly views along a curving sweep of shoreline. All of the accommodations are rustic and sufficiently removed from the highway to create a sense of natural living in this extraordinary landscape. An adjacent restaurant and store make it a convenient hideaway. ~ Route 1, Lucia; 408-667-2391. MODERATE TO ULTRA-DELUXE.

DINING

For a gourmet dinner, **Glen Oaks Restaurant** is the prime location along Big Sur. Redwood tables, oil lamps, and lots of plants create an intimate atmosphere at this small establishment. Add to these a series of attractive oil paintings along the walls and a copper-sheathed fireplace in one corner. The cuisine ranges broadly: there are such dishes as mushroom stroganoff, scampi, steak, and a selection of seafood that includes salmon, rock cod, and mahimahi. Closed Tuesday. Dinner only. ~ Route 1; 408-667-2264. MODERATE TO DELUXE.

Nearby **Fernwood,** a combination restaurant-bar-store, has hamburgers, sandwiches, barbecued chicken, homemade soup, and chili. This local gathering spot is your best bet for an inexpensive lunch or dinner. ~ Route 1; 408-667-2422. BUDGET.

Ventana Restaurant, part of the extraordinary complex which includes a prestigious inn, is one of the region's most elegant dining places. Resting on a hillside overlooking the mountains and sea, it's a perfect spot for a special meal. At lunch you'll be served salad, steak sandwiches, or fresh pasta, either inside the wood-paneled dining room, or alfresco on a sweeping veranda. For dinner you can start with oysters on the half shell or steamed artichoke, then proceed to such entrées as roast duckling, rack of lamb, salmon, filet mignon, or fresh fish grilled over oak. ~ Route 1; 408-667-2331. DELUXE TO ULTRA-DELUXE.

Whether or not you're staying at the Post Ranch Inn, you'll hardly want to miss dinner at the resort's signature restaurant, **Sierra Mar.** The magnificent views of the ocean and surf 1100 feet below become tenfold more dramatic at dinnertime when the sun drops behind the Pacific. The menu features California cuisine and changes daily. Among the limited menu selections are lean beef, seafood, and poultry dishes seasoned and accompanied by fresh produce from the hotel's own garden. Dinner only; bar serves light snacks the rest of the day. ~ Route 1, Big Sur; 408-667-2800. ULTRA-DELUXE.

Another bird's eye-view is offered at **Nepenthe.** Perched on a cliff overlooking the Pacific, this fabled dining spot has plenty of personality. People come across the continent to line its curving bar or dine along the open-air patio. It's a gathering place for locals, tourists, and everyone in between. There are sandwiches, quiches, and salads for lunch. At dinner the menu includes fresh fish, broiled chicken, and steak. If you're not hungry, stop in for a drink—the scene is a must. ~ Route 1; 408-667-2345. DELUXE.

For breakfast or lunch, try the outdoor **Café Kevah,** located downstairs. Personally, I think it's a much better deal than Nepenthe. Closed in January and February. ~ 408-667-2344. MODERATE TO DELUXE.

Watch whales swim by while enjoying a spinach salad, pizza, or sandwich at the **Coast Gallery Cafe.** There's a deck outside for that perfect unobstructed view. The gallery in which the café is located was constructed out of giant redwood water tanks, giving it a rather unique layout. Open for early dinner only. ~ Route 1; 408-667-2301. BUDGET.

SHOPPING

Set in a circular wooden structure resembling an oversized wine cask (and made from old water tanks) is one of Big Sur's best known art centers. The **Coast Gallery** is justifiably famous for its displays of arts and crafts by local artists. There are lithographs by novelist Henry Miller as well as paintings, sculptures, ceramics, woodwork, handmade candles, and blown glass by Northern California craftspeople. An adjoining shop features a wide selection of Miller's books. ~ Route 1; 408-667-2301.

NIGHTLIFE

Down in Big Sur the lights go out early. There is one place, **Big Sur River Inn,** that has a wood-paneled bar overlooking the Big Sur River and keeps a candle burning. During the week the bar is open until the wee hours; on Saturday night and Sunday afternoon, music ranges from Dixieland bands to string quartets. ~ Route 1; 408-667-2700.

BEACHES & PARKS

GARRAPATA STATE BEACH This broad swath of white sand is particularly favored by local people, some of whom use it as a nude beach. Easily accessible, it's nevertheless off the beaten tourist path, making an ideal hideaway for picnicking and skinny dipping. There are no facilities; restaurants and groceries are located about eight miles away in Carmel. ~ It's along Route 1 about 12 miles south of Carmel. Watch for the curving beach from the highway; stop at the parking lot just north of the Garrapata Creek bridge. From here a path leads down to the beach; 408-667-2315.

ANDREW MOLERA STATE PARK An adventurer's hideaway, this 4800-acre park rises from the sea to a 3455-foot elevation. It features three miles of beach and over 16 miles of hiking trails. The forests range from cottonwood to oak to redwood, while the wildlife includes mule deer, bobcat, harbor seals, and gray whales. Big Sur River rumbles through the landscape and surfers try the breaks on the beach. The only thing missing is a road: this is a hiker's oasis, its natural areas accessible only by heel and toe. The wilderness rewards are well worth the shoe leather. This is the only place in Big Sur where you can ride a horse; you can hire a horse from a concessionaire and check out Captain Cooper's Cabin, a 100-year-old pioneer log cabin. Toilets are the only facilities; restaurants and groceries are a few miles away in Big Sur. Day-use fee, $6. ~ It's along Route 1 about three miles north of Big Sur; 408-667-2315.

▲ There are hike-in sites (tents only); $3 per person per night.

PFEIFFER BIG SUR STATE PARK One of California's southernmost redwood parks, this 800-acre facility is very popular, particularly in summer. With cottages, restaurant, grocery, gift shop, picnic areas, restrooms, showers, and laundromat on the premises, it's quite developed. However, nature still retains a toehold in these parts: the Big Sur River overflows with trout and salmon (fishing is prohibited, however), Pfeiffer Falls tumbles through a fern-banked canyon, and the park serves as the major trailhead leading to Ventana Wilderness. Day-use fee, $6. ~ Located along Route 1 in Big Sur; 408-667-2315.

▲ There are 218 sites for both tents and RVs (no hookups); $18 to $19 per night.

PFEIFFER BEACH Of Big Sur's many wonders, this may be the most exotic. It's a sandy beach littered with boulders and bisected by a meandering stream. Behind the strand rise high bluffs which mark the terminus of a narrow gorge. Just offshore loom rock formations into which the sea has carved tunnels and arches. Little wonder poet Robinson Jeffers chose this haunting spot for his primal poem "Give Your Heart to the Hawks." Since we're dropping names, it's interesting to remember that Richard Burton and Elizabeth Taylor filmed *The Sandpiper* here. The only facilities are toilets; restaurants and groceries are several miles away in Big Sur. ~ Follow Route 1 for about a mile south past the entrance to Pfeiffer Big Sur State Park. Turn right onto Sycamore Canyon Road, which leads downhill two miles to the beach; 408-667-2423.

JULIA PFEIFFER BURNS STATE PARK This 3580-acre extravaganza extends from the ocean to about 1500 feet elevation and is bisected by Route 1. The central park area sits in a redwood canyon with a stream that feeds through a steep defile into the ocean. Backdropped by sharp hills in a kind of natural amphitheater, it's an enchanting glade. A path leads beneath the highway to a spectacular vista point where 80-foot-high McWay Waterfall plunges into the ocean. Another path, one-and-eight-tenths miles north of the park entrance, descends from the highway to an isolated beach near Partington Cove that has been declared an underwater park (permit required). There are picnic areas, restrooms; restaurants and groceries are about 11 miles away in Big Sur. Day-use fee, $6. ~ Located on Route 1 about 11 miles south of Pfeiffer Big Sur State Park; 408-667-2315.

▲ There are two hike-in sites for tents only; $18 to $19 per night with an eight-person maximum. Reservations are required.

VENTANA WILDERNESS Part of the Los Padres National Forest, this magnificent 216,500-acre preserve parallels Route 1 a few miles inland. It covers a broad swath of the Santa Lucia Mountains with elevations ranging from 600 feet to 5800 feet. Within its rugged confines are 237 miles of hiking trails. Wild boars and turkeys, mountain lions, and deer roam its slopes. Bald eagles soar the skies. The only facilities are ranger stations; restaurants and groceries are along Route 1 in Big Sur. Parking fee, $2. ~ From Route 1 in the Big Sur area, there are two entry points. The ranger station, where maps and fire permits can be acquired, is just south of Pfeiffer Big Sur State Park. For information and permits, contact the U.S. Forest Service (Monterey District, 406 South Mildred Avenue, King City, CA 93930; 408-385-5434).

▲ There are 55 primitive, hike-in sites, all of which are free.

Outdoor Adventures

SPORTFISHING

The Central Coast is renowned for its open-sea fishing. Charter boats comb the waters for rock cod, salmon, and albacore.

SOUTH OF SAN FRANCISCO If you want to test your skill, or luck, contact **Captain John's Fishing Trips**. They operate 4 boats, ranging from 55 to 65 feet. ~ 111 Pillar Point Harbor, Princeton-by-the-Sea; 415-726-2913.

SANTA CRUZ To take a charter from Santa Cruz in search of salmon call **Shamrock Charters**. ~ 2210 East Cliff Drive at the Santa Cruz Yacht Harbor; 408-476-2648. For do-it-yourself adventures,

Santa Cruz Boat Rentals provides outboards and fishing gear. ~ Santa Cruz Municipal Pier; 408-423-1739.

MONTEREY **Monterey Sport Fishing & Whalewatching** has three boats, ranging from 50 to 75 feet. Charter trips last about eight hours. ~ 96 Old Fisherman's Wharf #1; 408-372-2203. Or you can spend the day with **Randy's Fishing Trips.** ~ 66 Old Fisherman's Wharf; 408-372-7440.

BALLOON RIDES & HANG GLIDING

If you want to leave terra firma behind and see the beauty of the Central Coast from on high, consider a balloon ride or a hang-gliding excursion.

SANTA CRUZ TO MONTEREY If your preference is to soar through the air, hang-gliding lessons at Marina Beach are the way to fly. Call **Western Hang Gliders** for more information. ~ Reservation Road and Route 1, Marina; 408-384-2622. Or, for a hot air balloon ride, try **Balloons By the Sea,** which also offers skydiving. ~ Marina Municipal Airport, Marina; 800-464-6420.

WHALE WATCHING & NATURE CRUISES

To see the whales during their annual migration from December to April, head for whale-watching lookouts at Pillar Point in Half Moon Bay, the coast around Davenport, Point Pinos in Pacific Grove, or Cypress Point in Point Lobos State Reserve. (See the "Whale Watching" section in Chapter Five.) The summer whale-watching season typically runs from mid-June through September while the winter migration is viewable from mid-December through mid-March.

MONTEREY If you'd prefer a close look at these migrating mammals and other marine life—sea lions, seals, otters, sea birds—head to Fisherman's Wharf in Monterey and catch a cruise with **Randy's Fishing Trips.** ~ 408-372-7440. To catch glimpses of blue whales, humpbacks, and dolphins, hop on board a 65-foot vessel with **Monterey Sport Fishing and Whalewatching.** ~ 96 Old Fisherman's Wharf #1; 408-372-2203. **Sam's Fishing Fleet** offers cruises that last anywhere from two to six hours. ~ 84 Old Fisherman's Wharf; 408-372-0577. **Twin Otter Dive Charters** offers dive cruises from Wharf #2. ~ P.O. Box 8744, Monterey, CA 93943.

SEA KAYAKING

Whether you are young or old, experienced or a novice, the Central Coast awaits discovery by sea kayak.

MONTEREY Explore Monterey Bay and Elkhorn Slough, or paddle your way along the coastal waters with **Monterey Bay Kayaks.** They also offer naturalist-led tours around the Monterey aquarium, where you'll see a wide variety of marine life. ~ 693 Del Monte Avenue, Monterey; 408-373-5357. To experience the thrill of sea kayaking, call **Adventures by the Sea.** They have 120 double and single kayaks for rent. ~ 299 Cannery Row; 408-372-1807.

DIVING

The Central Coast offers premiere diving in Northern California. Although coastal waters are quite frigid, the unique kelp forests, wide array of fish, spotted harbor seals, and other fascinating marine life make for unforgettable diving.

SANTA CRUZ For adventures underwater, contact **Adventure Sports.** ~ 303 Potrero Street #15, Santa Cruz; 408-458-3648. To explore the magical world of the deep, contact **Ocean Odyssey Dive Center**, a full-service dive shop with rentals and gear. ~ 2345 South Rodeo Gulch Road, Santa Cruz; 408-475-3483.

MONTEREY **Aquarius Dive Shop** offers instruction and rentals. ~ 2040 Del Monte Avenue, Monterey; 408-375-1933.

CARMEL **Point Lobos State Reserve** has some of the finest diving opportunities on the Pacific Coast. Reservations are a must. ~ Route 1; 408-624-4909.

SURFING & WIND-SURFING

Catching a wave when the surf's up near Lighthouse Point north of Santa Cruz is a surfer's dream. Known as "Steamer Lane," this stretch of coastline hosts many international surfing competitions. On the east side, Pleasure Point is a popular surf spot with several reef breaks. Surfboards and wet suits (the water is always cold) are available at **Arrow Surf 'n Sport.** ~ 2324 Mission Street, Santa Cruz; 408-423-8286. On the east side, surfboards and wet suits can be rented from **Freeline Design.** ~ 821 41st Avenue, Santa Cruz; 408-476-2950. In Capitola, try **O'Neill's Surf Shop.** ~ 1149 41st Avenue, Capitola; 408-475-4151. Or catch the wind on a windsurfing board. Rentals and lessons are available at **Club Ed Surfing and Windurfing**, as are regular surfing lessons and equipment. ~ Cowell Beach next to the Santa Cruz wharf; 408-459-9283.

RIDING STABLES

Exploring the coast and inland trails astride a galloping horse is one way to enjoy a visit to the Central Coast.

SOUTH OF SAN FRANCISCO With its four-mile white sand beach and surrounding farm country, Half Moon Bay is a choice region for riding. **Seahorse Ranch and Friendly Acres Ranch**, located on the coast, rents over 2000 horses. They also have pony rides for kids. No reservations are necessary, and you can ride without a guide if you like. ~ 2150 Route 1, Half Moon Bay; 415-726-8550.

PACIFIC GROVE There are escorted tours along 20 miles of trails at the **Pebble Beach Equestrian Center**. Call ahead to reserve a horse. ~ Portola Road and Alva Lane, Pebble Beach; 408-624-2756.

GOLF

For golfers, visiting the Monterey Peninsula is tantamount to arriving in heaven. Pebble Beach is home to the annual AT&T National Pro-Am Golf Championship. Several courses rank among the top in the nation. With stunning views of the rugged coastline,

Pebble Beach Golf Course is the most renowned. ~ 17 Mile Drive, Pebble Beach; 408-624-3811. Or you might want to tee off at **Spyglass Hill Golf Course.** ~ Stevenson Road, Pebble Beach; 408-624-3811. Be prepared: Green fees at these courses are steep! Set on a century-old property, **Old Del Monte Golf Course** is a relatively flat course studded with ancient trees. ~ 1300 Sylvan Road, Monterey; 408-373-2436. **Pacific Grove Golf Course** overlooks Monterey Bay and the Pacific Ocean. It has a pro shop and driving range. ~ 77 Asilomar Boulevard, Pacific Grove; 408-648-3177.

BIKING

The **Pacific Coast Bikecentennial Route** follows Route 1 through the entire Central Coast area to Big Sur and beyond. There are camping sites along the way. The ocean views and rolling pastures make this an ideal course to peddle, if you are experienced and careful.

For scenic and historical bike tours of Carmel, check with **Bay Bike Rentals.** They lead tours of 17 Mile Drive, the Carmel Coast down to Point Lobos, and a Big Sur downhill ride from the Old Coast Ridge through Andrew Molera State Park. ~ 408-625-2453.

Both Santa Cruz and Monterey have bike paths for beginners and skilled riders alike. Especially good for touring are **17 Mile Drive**, the bike trail along the bayshore from **Seaside to Marina**, the trail from **Seaside to Lover's Point** (via Cannery Row), and the roads in **Point Lobos State Reserve.**

Bike Rentals For bicycle rentals in Santa Cruz, go to the **Bicycle Rental Center.** ~ 415 Pacific Avenue; 408-426-8687. In Monterey, try **Bay Bike Rentals.** ~ 640 Wave Street; 408-646-9090. For maps, brochures, and rentals, contact **Freewheeling Cycles.** ~ 188 Webster Street, Monterey; 408-373-3855.

HIKING

To fully capture the beauty and serenity of the region's woodlands, chaparral country, and beaches, explore its hiking trails. The Santa Cruz and Santa Lucia mountains offer several hundred miles of trails through fir, madrone, and redwood forests. Getting lost, so to speak, among these stands of ancient trees is a splendid way to vacation. Or hike the inland hills with their caves and rock spires. Down at the sea's edge you'll discover more caves, as well as tidepools, sand dunes, and a world of marine life.

SOUTH OF SAN FRANCISCO If you have an urge to see elephant seals breeding, take the three-mile guided walk led by docents at **Año Nuevo State Reserve.** To protect these mammoth mammals, the preserve is open during breeding season only to those on the guided tours. They are scheduled from December through March and require reservations ten days in advance; call 800-444-7275. To explore this area after mating season, you can hike on your own past sand dunes, tidepools, and sea caves. Follow **Año Nuevo Trail** (2.5 miles), beginning at the west end of the parking lot, to Año Nuevo Point.

SANTA CRUZ MOUNTAINS For hikers and beginning rock climbers, **Castle Rock State Park** offers a chance to try out skills and enjoy magnificent views. **Castle Rock Trail** (3 miles) is a moderate hike through oak and madrone woodlands. The trail starts at the south side of the Skyline Boulevard parking lot. Castle Rock is about a half-mile from the trailhead. Continue along the Castle Rock Trail, then pick up the **Saratoga Gap Trail** (2.8 miles), which leads to Castle Rock Trail Camp.

For a backpacking trip over the Santa Cruz Mountains, take the magnificent **Skyline-to-the-Sea-Trail** (28.4 miles). The trail begins at Saratoga Gap (Skyline Boulevard and Route 9) or Castle Rock State Park (adding three miles to the trek) and climaxes on the Pacific shore. Campgrounds at Waterman Gap, Big Basin, and along Waddell Creek provide resting places for hikers traveling this heavily forested path. Be sure to make reservations for campsites; information, 408-338-8860.

There are hikes for everyone along the 60 miles of trails in **Big Basin Redwoods State Park,** the oldest of California's state parks. Covering 18,000 acres, Big Basin has spectacular trails leading to waterfalls and redwood groves. **Redwood Trail** (.6 mile) is a self-guiding nature trail easy enough for the entire family. Take the trail that begins west of the parking lot and stroll past a grove of giants.

Berry Creek–Sunset Loop Trail (10 miles) is an arduous trek through the most beautiful scenery in the park. Follow Redwood Trail, then pick up Skyline-to-the-Sea Trail, which will run into Berry Creek Trail. The trek climaxes at Lower and Upper Berry Creek Falls, which tumble more than 50 feet over sandstone cliffs. A return on the Sunset Trail completes the journey; allow about six hours.

The **Howard King Trail** (3 miles) begins at the Middle Range Fire Road and ascends gradually to Mt. McAbee overlook. En route you'll encounter meadows, old-growth redwoods, and views of the Pacific.

✔ CHECK THESE OUT—UNIQUE OUTDOOR ADVENTURES

- Paddle your way around playful sea otters and boisterous sea lions as you kayak **Monterey Bay.** *page 360*
- Pick and choose between world-class golf courses and tee off at **Spyglass Hill** or **Pebble Beach Golf Course.** *page 362*
- Shoot the curl at **Steamer Lane,** where international surfing competitions are often taking place. *page 361*
- Explore the depths of 80-foot-high kelp forests and other underwater mysteries at **Point Lobos State Reserve.** *page 360*

MONTEREY AREA One of California's most beautiful spots is the six-mile shoreline at **Point Lobos State Reserve.** The park is laced with trails leading to tidepools, sandy coves, and whale-watching vistas.

Cypress Grove Trail (.8 mile), one of the most popular (and populated) in the park, leads through a stand of Monterey cypress trees and offers cliff-top views of the ocean.

Bird Island Trail (.8 mile) takes you through coastal shrubbery to two exquisite white sand beaches—China Cove and Gibson Beach. The path also overlooks Bird Island, a refuge for cormorants and brown pelicans.

Pine Ridge Trail (.7 mile), beginning near Piney Woods, goes inland through forests of Monterey pines and Coast live oak. Deer, squirrel, and such birds as pygmy nuthatches and chestnut-backed chickadees make this a tranquil nature hike.

South Shore Trail (1 mile), an oceanside walk between Sea Lion Point and the Bird Rock parking area, allows close looks at tidepool life and shore birds. You can also play amateur geologist, examining multicolored patterns in sedimentary rocks.

For rock climbers and hikers alike, **Pinnacles National Monument** offers great sport. Because of the summer heat and winter weather, it's recommended that you come in spring or fall to explore the park's rock spires, talus caves, and covered canyons. At any time of year, bring plenty of water.

Hiking along the narrow ledges of **High Peaks Trail** (5.4 miles), you'll find splendid views of the entire park. The steep trail begins across from the Chalone Creek picnic area, travels up through the High Peaks and ends up at the Moses Spring parking lot. Allow at least three to four hours.

Old Pinnacles Trail (2.3 miles) begins at Chalone Creek picnic area and goes along relatively level terrain near the west fork of the creek to Balconies Caves.

Juniper Canyon Trail (1.8 miles) starts near the west end of the park at the Chaparral ranger station and climbs 760 feet to connect with the park's east side High Peaks Trail. It's the steepest trail in the monument.

BIG SUR Over 216,500 acres of rugged mountain terrain comprise the **Ventana Wilderness** of Los Padres National Forest. About 200 miles of hiking trails make it easy to explore the Santa Lucia Mountains while escaping the trappings of civilization. Several roads off Route 1 will take you onto the preserve. Big Sur Station and Bottchers Gap Station are the only staffed coastal entrances.

Bottchers Gap–Devils Peak Trail (4 miles) is a steep hike through coniferous forests to spectacular vistas overlooking the northern section of the Ventana Wilderness.

Kirk Creek–Vicente Flat Trail (5.1 miles) winds along ridgelines that afford mountain views.

Pine Ridge Trail (40.7 miles) begins at Big Sur Station and carries two miles to the park boundary before heading into the Ventana Wilderness. First stop is Ventana Camp, near the Big Sur River. Then the trail leads past several campgrounds and ends at China Camp.

Transportation

CAR

From San Francisco, coastal highway **Route 1** is the most scenic way to explore the Central Coast. In the Santa Cruz Mountains, **Routes 35** and **9** lead through redwood forests and rural towns. **Route 101**, which runs inland parallel to the coast is the fastest route. Numerous side roads lead from this highway to points along the Central Coast.

AIR

Several airlines fly regular schedules to the **Monterey Peninsula Airport**. American Eagle Airlines, Sky West, United, United Express, USAir, and USAir Express service this area from San Francisco and other departure points. ~ 408-648-7000.

BUS

Greyhound Bus Lines has continual service to Santa Cruz (425 Front Street; 408-423-1800) and Monterey (1042 Del Monte Avenue at the Exxon station; 408-373-4735) from San Francisco and Los Angeles. ~ 800-231-2222.

TRAIN

For railroad buffs, **Amtrak** offers daily service on the "Coast Starlight." The train runs from Seattle to Los Angeles with stops in Oakland, San Jose, and Salinas (11 Station Place). Once in Salinas, passengers can transfer to a Greyhound or Monterey–Salinas Transit bus. ~ 800-872-7245.

CAR RENTALS

If flying directly into Monterey, you can rent a car at the airport from **Avis Rent A Car** (408-373-3327, 800-331-1212), **Budget Rent A Car** (408-373-1899, 800-527-0700), **Hertz Rent A Car** (408-373-3318, 800-654-3131), or **National Interrent** (408-373-4181, 800-328-4567). Additional rental agencies are located in town. Try **American International Rent A Car** (800-392-8724).

PUBLIC TRANSIT

Peerless Stages connects with Greyhound Bus Lines in San Jose and Oakland and travels to Santa Cruz. ~ 408-423-1800.

San Mateo County Transit, or **Sam Trans**, departing from the Daly City and Colma BART stations, has local bus service to Pacifica, Montara, Moss Beach, and Half Moon Bay. Bus service is also available between Año Nuevo and San Mateo and Half Moon Bay during seal season (January through March). Reservations are required (through Sam Trans). ~ 800-660-4287.

From Waddell Creek in northern Santa Cruz County, the **Santa Cruz County Transit System** covers Route 1 as far south as Watsonville. (On weekends and holidays during the summer, shuttle service is provided to the beach from downtown Santa Cruz.) ~ 408-425-8600.

From Watsonville, connections can be made to Monterey and Big Sur via the **Monterey–Salinas Transit Company**. These buses carry passengers to many points of interest including Cannery Row, Point Lobos, and Andrew Molera and Pfeiffer Big Sur State Parks. Buses from Monterey to Big Sur run twice daily from May through early September. ~ 408-899-2555.

SEVEN

Gold Country & High Sierra

Setting out from a flat, warm, agricultural region several hundred feet above sea level, this chapter ends far past timberline amid snow-domed peaks 13,000 feet high. The rivers that irrigate the farmland begin high in the Sierra Nevada. These whitewater currents slice through the mountains, carving canyons and dumping rich minerals along the riverbanks. Among the precious metals is one that altered the course of California history. It also gave its name to the foothill region that lies between the heights and the lowlands—the Gold Country.

Sacramento rests at the heart of California's Central Valley, the richest farming area in the world. Sacramento's other business is politics; this city of 400,000 is the state capital. Originally, however, its business was gold. No yellow metal was ever found along Sacramento streets. Sacramento made its fortune supplying the gold fields, providing men and materials for the nearby strikes.

The man who founded the town was also directly responsible for the original discovery of gold. John Sutter created Sacramento in 1839 when he built a fort to protect the huge land grant that the Spanish government bestowed upon him. Using American Indians as serfs, he set out to create an inland empire, New Helvetia. With Sacramento as headquarters, his domain spread to the nearby Sierra foothills.

Then occurred an event of historic import, which should have secured his power and fortune. Instead, it destroyed him. Gold was discovered on John Sutter's land. That was January, 1848. By the next year, machinists and farm hands, scoundrels and preachers, filled with hope and a hunger for gold, began descending in mobs. Over 40,000 miners arrived in 1849; three years later there were 100,000. They came to John Sutter's land. His workers quit to join the miners, farmland fell fallow, projects went unfinished, buildings were stripped for firewood. By 1852, Sutter was bankrupt.

His town, however, boomed. In 1854, Sacramento became the capital. By 1856 it boasted California's first railroad, and in 1860 the city was a center for the Pony

Express. The transcontinental railroad was conceived in Sacramento, and by the turn of the century, this river town was adorned with the beautiful Victorian homes it still displays.

The precious metal that built Sacramento was found throughout the Gold Country east of the capital. There a rich vein of quartz and gold, the Mother Lode, parallels the Sierra Nevada range for several hundred miles.

The Gold Country became a land of dreams, but its gold fields were often a nightmare. Eventually two *billion* dollars worth of yellow metal was mined, yet for many argonauts, prospecting meant coming up empty-handed and then facing inflated prices for provisions. Little wonder that most of the towns which mushroomed in the wilderness have long since vanished. The towns remaining go by names such as Mariposa, Sonora, Coloma, and Nevada City. Still maintaining antique buildings and old mining scars, they are located along a 300-mile stretch of Route 49.

If time and territory can possibly be compared, perhaps the historic importance of the Gold Rush is equal to the grandeur of the mountains which forged the gold. The Sierra Nevada is the largest single mountain range in the country. It's a solitary block of earth, tilted and uplifted, 430 miles long and 80 miles wide. A mere child in the long count of geologic history, it rose from the earth's surface a few million years back and did not reach its present form until 750,000 years ago. During the Pleistocene epoch, glaciers spread across the land, grinding and cutting at the mountains. They carved river valleys and deep canyons, and sculpted bald domes, fluted cliffs, and stone towers.

The glaciers left a landscape dominated by ragged peaks where lakes number in the hundreds and canyons plunge 5000 feet. There are cliffs sheer as glass that compete with the sky for dominance. It is, as an early pioneer described it, a "land of fire and ice."

To the pioneers, however, the beauty of the place was of little consequence compared to its magnitude. The Sierra Nevada was a hellish gateway to the promised land, the final obstacle before entering California. The first to cross it was Jedediah Smith, a mountain man who followed the Stanislaus River in 1827. Then, in 1841, the Bidwell-Bartleson party became the first emigrant wagon train to trek the Sierra. By 1845, the mountain migration route was opening as 250 settlers crossed; twice that number traveled the "California Trail" the next year. Present-day hikers can explore a network of old emigrant trails throughout the mountains. Trees still living near timberline bear blazes left by pioneers back in the 1850s.

Before the settlers, Maidu and Miwok peoples hunted the western slopes, while Washoes and Paiutes stalked the eastern heights of Nevada. Today much of the land is preserved in a series of state parks and national forests. There's Calaveras Big Trees with its solitary trails through dense sequoia stands; Mono Lake, a prehistoric sea adorned with rock statues; and the High Sierra wilderness, domain of backpackers and golden eagles.

The hot spot of the Sierras is Lake Tahoe, an alpine resort that goes year round. Tahoe enjoys 300 sunny days annually, but also manages to receive 18 feet of snow. Skiers challenge its slopes at Squaw Valley, Alpine Meadows, Sugar Bowl, and a dozen other runs. Spring and fall carry crisp weather to Tahoe; since summers are warm, anglers, boaters, and waterskiers replace snow lovers.

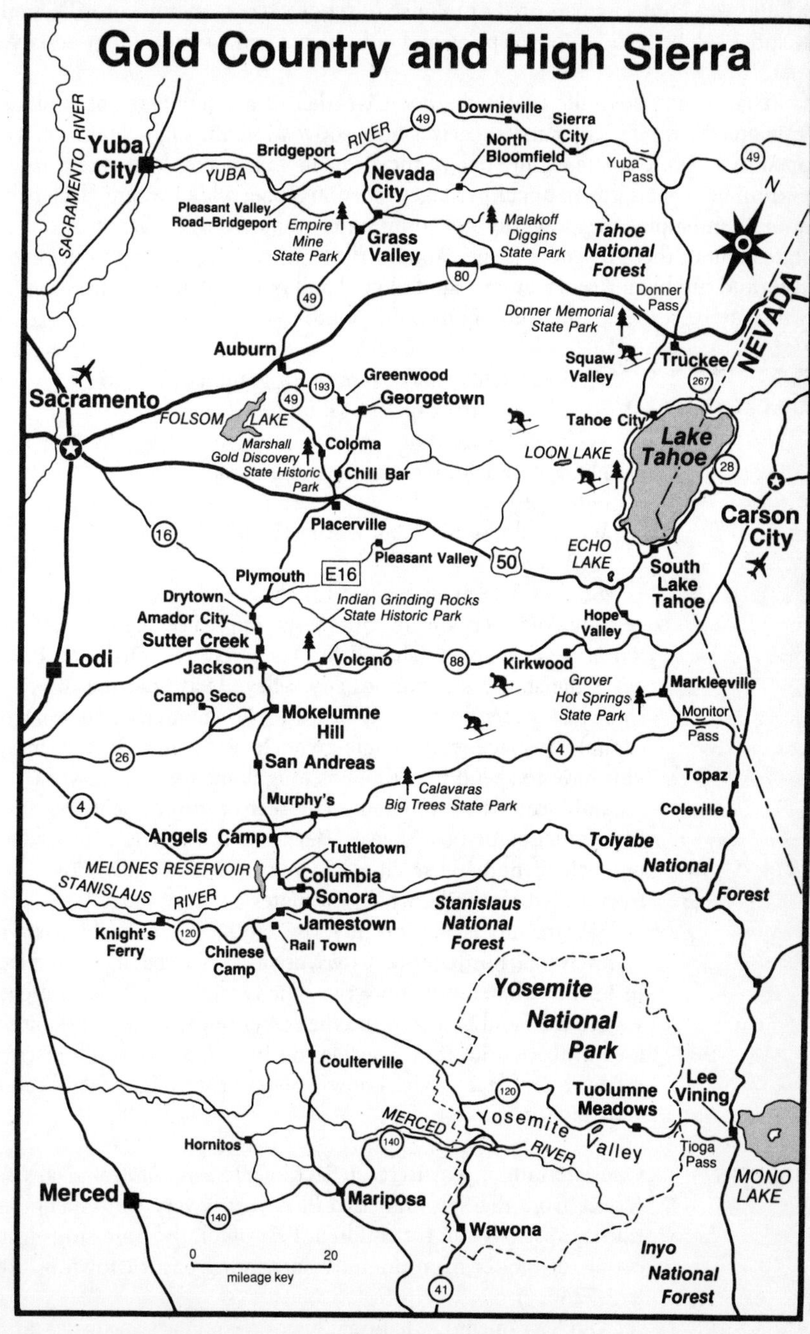
Gold Country and High Sierra
Sacramento River
Yuba City
Yuba
Bridgeport
River
Downieville
Sierra City
North Bloomfield
Yuba Pass
Nevada City
Pleasant Valley Road–Bridgeport
Empire Mine State Park
Grass Valley
Malakoff Diggins State Park
Tahoe National Forest
Donner Pass
Donner Memorial State Park
Nevada
Auburn
Squaw Valley
Truckee
Sacramento
Greenwood
Georgetown
Folsom Lake
Tahoe City
Marshall Gold Discovery State Historic Park
Coloma
Chili Bar
Loon Lake
Lake Tahoe
Carson City
Placerville
Pleasant Valley
Echo Lake
South Lake Tahoe
Plymouth
E16
Drytown
Amador City
Sutter Creek
Indian Grinding Rocks State Historic Park
Hope Valley
Lodi
Jackson
Volcano
Kirkwood
Grover Hot Springs State Park
Markleeville
Campo Seco
Mokelumne Hill
Monitor Pass
San Andreas
Topaz
Murphy's
Calavaras Big Trees State Park
Coleville
Angels Camp
Tuttletown
Toiyabe National Forest
Melones Reservoir
Stanislaus River
Columbia
Sonora
Jamestown
Rail Town
Stanislaus National Forest
Knight's Ferry
Chinese Camp
Yosemite National Park
Coulterville
Lee Vining
Tuolumne Meadows
Merced River
Yosemite Valley
Hornitos
Tioga Pass
Mono Lake
Merced
Mariposa
Wawona
0 20
mileage key
Inyo National Forest

In the Gold Country, winter usually brings rain, spring covers the hillsides with wildflowers, and summers are hot. Not so hot, however, as Sacramento. There the weather can be torrid, though spring and fall are cool and winter is foggy and overcast.

That means Yosemite enjoys the finest weather of all: summers are mild, and in winter Yosemite Valley itself receives little snow while the high country is wide open to skiers. Climate is only one of the elements that makes Yosemite a special place. The Park is our national heritage etched in stone; a land where glaciers, sequoias, and alpine meadows are ringed by stately mountains. If Sacramento is the state capital, then Yosemite is the capital of the Sierra, representing in its angled cliffs and tumbling rivers a unique land of gold and granite. Since businesses in the area may be seasonal, travelers should call ahead.

Sacramento

Remember those quizzes in grammar school?
What's the capital of Illinois?
—*Chicago.*

No, Springfield. How about New York?
—*Brooklyn.*
Wrong, dodo, it's Albany. And Florida?
—*Orlando.*
No, not Miami either, but Tallahassee.

I flunked every one of those tests simply because the state capital is never where it should be. It's rarely obvious, and almost never the state's big, famous city. They always put the capital in some backwater no one ever heard of, hoping that because it's the capital the place will become great. It never does. It only means kids have to spend four times as long doing their homework.

California is no different. The seat of government should be San Francisco or Los Angeles. But instead it's Sacramento, which is north of both those cities. Sacramento is actually closer to a town called Vacaville, which translates as "cow town."

Sacramento is not my favorite city. (Neither is Harrisburg, Pennsylvania, nor Jefferson City, Missouri.) Not that it's a bad place. In fact, Sacramento is more than the capital city: it's also a gateway to the Gold Country and the center of the richest agricultural area in the world. If you decide to tour the town, you'll discover it has several faces. Who knows? Sacramento might even become your favorite capital.

SIGHTS

One entertaining way to reach Sacramento is by **Amtrak**. Daily rail service from the San Francisco Bay Area is very convenient. The ride is especially fun for children. Best of all, the train stops just a couple of blocks from the most interesting part of town. ~ 800-872-7245.

Old Sacramento, a national historic landmark, provides a perfect introduction to the Gold Country. Lined with wooden sidewalks and heavy-masonry storefronts, its streets date to Sacramento's gilded era. Once considered the city's skid-row section, Old Sacramento today is a 28-acre historic park comprising more than 100 restored and re-created buildings. The neighborhood, situated between the Sacramento River and roaring interstate Route 5, can easily be seen in the course of a short walking tour.

For complete details, begin by stopping at the **Old Sacramento Tourist Information Center.** ~ 1104 Front Street; 916-442-7644. Then head over to the **B. F. Hastings Building** at 2nd and J streets. Behind the iron doors of this 1852 structure is a museum commemorating the western headquarters of the Pony Express.

It's just one block to the **California State Railroad Museum.** The highpoint of any visit to Old Sacramento, this showplace challenges all the senses. The sights, sounds, and smells of the railroads are here in a series of evocative displays. Trains hoot, station-yard dogs bark, and steam engines hiss as you wander past antique locomotives and narrow gauge passenger trains. There's a full-scale diorama portraying the construction of the intercontinental railroad in the High Sierra during the 1860s. If the re-creation is not enough for you, take a six-mile train ride on a historic locomotive from the museum's Central Pacific Depot (every weekend during summer, the first weekend of the month during winter). Admission. ~ 2nd and I streets; 916-323-9280.

A walking tour will also carry you past the **Eagle Theatre,** an 1849 playhouse where Gold Rush–era plays and dramas are still presented. ~ 925 Front Street; 916-446-6761.

You'll also pass the **Globe** (foot of K Street), a replica of a brig that sailed around Cape Horn in 1849. At Front and L streets, the **Old Sacramento Schoolhouse,** with its bolted desks and wood stoves, evokes the days when stern taskmasters wielded cane rods. Then continue past the balconied buildings and brick warehouses that create a sense of nostalgia throughout this antique enclave.

✔ CHECK THESE OUT—UNIQUE SIGHTS

- Hop aboard the exhibits at the **California State Railroad Museum** and take in all the sights and sounds—and even smells—of the rail yards depicted in provocative displays. *page 371*
- Wander the streets of **Columbia State Historic Park** for a view of life as it was during the rowdy California Gold Rush. *page 380*
- Stop at **Mono Lake,** where eerie bone-white rock formations rise from turquoise waters in what is left of a prehistoric sea. *page 411*
- Look down on Yosemite Valley from **Glacier Point,** and watch Yosemite Falls tumble thousands of feet below. *page 418*

From Old Sacramento, follow Capitol Mall, a tree-lined boulevard, to the **State Capitol Building**. Set in a gracefully landscaped park, adorned with statuary and lofty pillars, it's an impressive sight. Looking like capitols everywhere, the Roman Corinthian structure is capped with a golden dome and dominated by a grand rotunda. What makes this building different from others is that many rooms have been renovated and opened to the public. The old governor's office has been furnished with period pieces, equipped with a coal-burning pot-bellied stove, and returned to its 1906 glory. The state treasurer's office has been converted to a historical condominium—half re-creating 1906 and the other half portraying the Depression era. Guided tours are available.

Wander up to the third floor when the legislature is in session and you can sit in the gallery watching the solons battle it out. Both the **Assembly** and **Senate galleries** are often open to visitors. Like the rooms downstairs, they feature antique furnishings and traditional decor, but the chambers also incorporate such newfangled devices as automatic vote counters and electronic sound systems. ~ 10th Street between L and N streets; 916-324-0333.

Having listened to the legislators ramble on, you'll be ready to adjourn to **Capitol Park**. Surrounding the Capitol Building, this urban oasis includes a trout pond, cactus and rose gardens, and a grove of trees transplanted from southern battlefields to memorialize the Civil War dead. From the east end of the park, Capitol Avenue leads to **Sutter's Fort**. It was back in 1839 when John Sutter founded Sacramento, building an adobe fort near the American River. Having received a 76-square-mile land grant from the Spanish, he named the domain "New Helvetia" after his native Switzerland. The fort became a cultural and strategic center for all Northern California. Donner Party survivors sought refuge here, Captain John Fremont and Kit Carson visited, and in 1846, during the Mexican War, a key Spanish leader was imprisoned and the American flag raised over the fort.

When strolling through Capitol Park, look for the memorial to Californians lost in the Vietnam War.

The original fortress has long since dissolved to dust and a re-created version raised in its stead. Lacking the feel of authenticity, it nevertheless possesses some interesting displays. There are weaving rooms with large but primitive looms, plus living quarters complete with rusty utensils and the most uncomfortable beds imaginable. You'll see a cooper shop where buckets and barrels were fashioned, museum cases portraying early California life, and a room hung with traps and animal skins. Admission. ~ 2701 L Street; 916-445-4422.

Then from the adjacent **California State Indian Museum**, you'll gather an idea of California before the advent of Sutter and his Spanish benefactors. Admission. ~ 2618 K Street; 916-324-0971.

The capital city features several other points of interest. Contact the **Sacramento Convention and Visitors Bureau** for maps, brochures, and information. Closed Saturday and Sunday. ~ 1421 K Street; 916-264-7777.

The **Crocker Art Museum** provides a grand example of form overwhelming content. There are paintings by renowned American artists and sculpture and decorative arts from Europe. But the entire collection is dominated by the building it is housed in. With its parquet floors and repoussé ceilings, the Edwin Bryant Crocker mansion represents the ultimate artwork. Browsing the museum means wandering through a grand ballroom, along sweeping staircases, and past walls carved by hand. If you can overcome the impact of the interior, there are many interesting art- works to study. Or you can adjourn to the glass-walled pavilion, which houses part of the museum's contemporary California art collection. Children will enjoy the museum's Discovery Gallery, which features student artwork and craft activities. Closed Monday and Tuesday. Admission. ~ 216 O Street; 916-264-5423.

Then there's the **Governor's Mansion** that houses no governors. Not any longer, that is. It did serve as home to 13 state leaders from 1877, when it was built, until 1966, when Ronald Reagan and wife Nancy refused to live there. The rest of the story is typical of California's wacky history. Reagan decided to build a new mansion, which wasn't ready until he left the governorship and went on to other things. The place was completed in time for Jerry Brown to occupy. But it looked more like an architectural testimonial to Reagan than a house. Brown refused to take up residence, preferring to slap a mattress on an apartment house floor and call it home. Which he did—for eight years. The next governor finally decided he'd like to move in, but the legislature, controlled by the opposition party, refused to let him have the place.

Anyway, that's the tale of the "new" governor's mansion. The 30-room old mansion became a museum open to tours. It's a Victorian-Empire structure that looks like a woodframe wedding cake. Within its 15 rooms are antiques and artifacts from the early 20th century. Admission. ~ 16th and H streets; 916-323-3047.

The largest collection of antique, vintage, and classic Fords in the world is not in Dearborn, Michigan. It's at **Towe Ford Museum**. Here 225 vehicles span the period from 1896 to the middle of the century. Included are classic Model-Ts, Mustangs, Thunderbirds, Edsels, and Skyliners. A decidedly ecumenical place, the showplace also includes former California Governor Jerry Brown's blue Plymouth and former Chief Justice Earl Warren's black Cadillac. Be sure to check out the library, which houses an extensive automotive collection of manuals and brochures. Admission. ~ 2200 Front Street; 916-442-6802.

A tribute to the men and women of California who have served in the U.S. Armed Forces since the Civil War, the **California Citizen Soldier Museum** exhibits weapons, uniforms, and artifacts. In addition to profiling the California National Guard's role in the country's major wars, the museum looks at peacetime relief work such as the rescue efforts following the 1906 earthquake. Closed Monday. Admission. ~ 1119 2nd Street; 916-442-2883.

HIDDEN ►

For a taste of country life right here in the city, you can pick your own fruits and vegetables at one of Sacramento's **farms**. Many of the region's farmers allow visitors to wander the fields, plucking produce right from the tree. The seasons are summer and autumn, but it's best to call ahead to find out what's ripe; costs for picking are minimal. For a list of farms in the Sacramento area and elsewhere, call the Small Farm Center at University of California—Davis at 916-752-8136.

LODGING

Every city has its motel row, a single street illuminated in neon and offering dozens of overnight possibilities. In Sacramento it's West Capitol Avenue, a busy highway extending out from the city's freeway nexus. As you buzz along this boulevard, the motels fly past in furious fashion, becoming a blur along the periphery of vision.

For inexpensive accommodations near the downtown area, it's hard to compete with the **Mansion View Lodge**. Nothing special—just a 41-room neon motel—but at a budget price you were hoping maybe for the Ritz? There is wall-to-wall carpeting, a television, and a phone in every unit. So if you aren't expecting to spend a lot of time in the room anyway, give it a try. ~ 711 16th Street; 916-443-6631, 800-409-9595, fax 916-442-7251. BUDGET.

The **Sterling Hotel** doesn't have to be as pretty as it is to succeed. A typical room has a four-poster bed, armoire, Henredon furniture, fine art, an elegant chandelier, and a jacuzzi in the marble-tiled bathroom. When this 1894 mansion was remodeled, 12 accommodations were arranged on the three upper floors and the cellar was converted into a restaurant. ~ 1300 H Street; 916-448-1300, 800-365-9595. DELUXE TO ULTRA-DELUXE.

Bed-and-breakfast inns, many of which are in the fine old mansions that were built in Sacramento during the early part of the century, are providing a welcome alternative to motels and faceless business hotels. One of these is **Hartley House Bed and Breakfast Inn**, on a residential street lined with majestic elms and conveniently close to the Capitol and Old Sacramento. Attracting both gay and straight guests, the inn offers five period-decorated rooms with private baths and such old-fashioned, homelike touches as a porch swing, cozy parlor, and well-stocked cookie jar. ~ 700 22nd Street; 916-447-7829, 800-831-5806, fax 916-447-1820. MODERATE TO DELUXE.

In the same pleasant neighborhood is **Amber House,** which features a 1905 Craftsman's-style main house and an adjacent Mediterranean-style house built in 1913. Each of the eight guest rooms is named for a painter or poet. Among the amenities are marble bathrooms with jacuzzis, canopy beds, and antique washstands. ~ 1315 22nd Street; 916-444-8085, 800-755-6526, fax 916-552-6529. DELUXE TO ULTRA-DELUXE.

Another gracious hostelry in the midtown area is **Abigail's Bed & Breakfast,** which is in a 1912 Colonial Revival house with five guest rooms. One of the rooms has a mahogany four-poster bed high enough to require its own built-in step ladder. Another has an ivy-leaf-patterned canopy bed festooned with flowers and ribbons. All are furnished with antiques or period reproductions. The rates include a full breakfast and access to a spacious living room and secluded garden with jacuzzi. ~ 2120 G Street; 916-441-5007, 800-858-1568, fax 916-441-0621. DELUXE TO ULTRA-DELUXE.

DINING

The **Whistle Stop Café** is good for just that—a whistle-stop meal. With a railroad mural, train trinkets, and railway posters, the place has what's called a unifying decorative theme. Meals are what you would expect in a train station—bland and cheap, but plenty filling. Open for breakfast and lunch daily, the Whistle Stop features egg dishes, sandwiches, soups, and salads. ~ 1115 Front Street between K and L streets; 916-446-4445. BUDGET.

Also situated in Old Sacramento, the city's antique neighborhood, **Fulton's Prime Rib** conveys a sense of the 19th century. The setting is an 1860s building with brick-and-wood paneled interior, and the waitresses are dressed in the fashion of the period. True to the name, the menu specializes in beef dishes, but also includes such seafood selections as halibut, rainbow trout, sole, and swordfish. Lunch likewise is a surf-and-turf affair with several entrées as well as sandwiches. ~ 900 2nd Street; 916-444-9641. DELUXE.

For inexpensive Asian food, there's only one **New Lu-Shan.** The all-you-can-eat Chinese buffet is perfect for wallet-conscious diners. There's also a menu with over 130 dishes. Since the restaurant is located in the Chinese Cultural Center, you can tour the Asian enclave after dining. ~ 403 J Street; 916-444-2543. BUDGET.

◄ HIDDEN

Located away from the downtown district, **Restaurant Taki** is a small and casual Japanese café, popular among local folks. Among the selections are teriyaki, yakitori, tempura, and donburi dishes. With its bamboo-lined walls and Asian decor, Taki's is a choice spot for a simple meal. Closed Sunday. ~ 1925 J Street; 916-446-1943. BUDGET.

Sacramento's capital restaurant is **The Firehouse,** a plush Victorian-style dining room set in an 1850s-era fire station. The cuisine at this jacket-and-tie establishment is California Continental, as in roasted duck, swordfish, rabbit, and rack of lamb. During summer months you can dine outdoors in a brick courtyard. Open for lunch Monday through Friday, dinner Tuesday through Saturday; closed Sunday. ~ 1112 2nd Street; 916-442-4772. DELUXE TO ULTRA-DELUXE.

At **Biba**, Italian specialties include lasagna, veal scallopine, marinated lamb chops with polenta, and duck in a red currant and brandy sauce. Among the featured pasta dishes are a fresh seafood linguine and angelhair pasta with sundried and fresh tomatoes. The mirrored, off-white dining room features both modern and neon art. Open for lunch Mondy through Friday, dinner Monday through Saturday. ~ 2801 Capitol Avenue; 916-455-2422. DELUXE.

A vaulted ceiling, Tuscan murals, and a display kitchen make **Tavola Trattoria** a popular spot for northern Italian dining. There's an antipasto bar lined with marble and a dining area that offers a choice between banquettes and open tables. The restaurant specializes in rotisserie items like lamb, veal, pork, duck, and rabbit. Also on the menu are gourmet pizzas and seafood specials like sea bass and swordfish. ~ 2627 Town and Country Place; 916-973-1800. MODERATE.

Or climb aboard the **Delta King**, a five-decked riverboat that serves as a floating restaurant, hotel, and cultural curiosity. ~ Foot of K Street; 916-444-5464. DELUXE.

SHOPPING

There are two prime sections for shoppers in the capital city. First is **Old Sacramento**, a warren of 19th-century buildings that have been renovated and converted into shops and malls. Within the course of a few short blocks are knickknack stores, antique shops, and clothiers. The **California State Railroad Museum Shop** has books, hats, T-shirts, and children's toys. ~ 125 I Street; 916-324-4950.

Artists' Collaborative is an excellent place to pick up locally wrought items. The crafts here include acrylics, woodwork, stained glass, jewelry, metal sculpture, ceramics, and watercolors. ~ 2nd Street between J and K streets; 916-444-3764.

The other shopping district lies along **K Street**, a 14-block pedestrian walkway. Extending from Old Sacramento past the Capitol Building to 14th Street, this street-cum-shopping mall is lined with stores. There are major department stores, small shops, and fashionable restaurants along the strip. Also, the mall has been attractively landscaped with fountains and flowering trees, lending a natural feel to this consumer park.

NIGHTLIFE

After sundown in the state capital, there are two places to look for entertainment. Old Sacramento, the city's historic sector, has several saloons and dancehalls. Better yet, head for the downtown area, where you'll find an array of nightclubs and watering holes.

Without doubt the weirdest spot in Old Sacramento is **Fanny Ann's Saloon**, a multitiered bar and restaurant. The staircase rises past an endless series of rooms, each decorated in high tack fashion with old boots, wagon wheels, dangling bicycles, and striped barber poles. The main action occurs along the ground floor bar where drinkers line up elbow to elbow. ~ 1023 2nd Street; 916-441-0505.

Music that ranges from alternative to progressive to retro brings a lot of diversity to **The Rage**. A state-of-the-art laser and light system, a four-level dancefloor, mirrored walls, and two bars are just a few of the added attractions. Closed Monday. Cover. ~ 1890 Arden Way; 916-929-3720.

With room for 556 guests, **Faces** is Sacramento's largest gay nightclub. There's dancing to disco music in the dance annex and a chance to relax on the patio or at an attractive bar. Weekend cover. ~ 2000 K Street; 916-448-7798.

For karaoke on weekends as well as pool and video games, there's the **Town House**. This gay nightspot, restaurant, and bar features live shows. ~ 1517 21st Street; 916-441-5122.

PARKS

AMERICAN RIVER PARKWAY This chain of parks stretches for 23 miles along the American River, providing access for anglers, bikers, hikers, and picnickers. The parkway leads from Discovery Park in Sacramento to Nimbus Dam near Lake Folsom. Unfortunately, access roads do not follow the river too closely, so to reach the water you must use a series of side roads. The parkway provides opportunities to explore the riverbanks and engage in the area's numerous watersports. There are also miles of equestrian and bike trails. Within the park are picnic areas and restrooms; restaurants and groceries are located in nearby towns. Day-use fee, $4. ~ The three major parks lie along this strip—Discovery Park, C. M. Goethe Park, and Ancil Hoffman Park. To reach C. M. Goethe Park (916-366-2061), follow Route 50 east from Sacramento for several miles to the Watt Avenue exit. Take Watt Avenue to La Riviera Drive. La Riviera Drive and Folsom Boulevard parallel the river parkway for most of its length. From Folsom Boulevard, Rod Beaudry Road leads to C. M. Goethe Park. To reach Ancil Hoffman Park from Route 50 east take the Watt Avenue exit. Turn right on Fair Oak Boulevard, then right on Van Alstine Avenue. Turn left on California Avenue, then right on Tarshes Drive. This will take you through the main gate of the park.

Southern Gold Country

Extending from Mariposa to the restored Gold Rush town of Columbia, the southern Mother Lode consists of gentle, rolling foothill country laced by rivers that pour down from the Sierra Nevada. Sparsely populated, it is dotted with small towns, covered bridges, a steam railroad, and numerous monuments to the region's 19th-century heyday. Sonora is the region's hub, a good base for excursions into the Gold Country's emerald forests.

SIGHTS

A likely place to start is the town of **Mariposa**. The mine here was discovered in 1849 by the famous scout Kit Carson and became part of the 45,000-acre tract owned by his colleague, Colonel John C. Fremont. The **Mariposa Museum** displays a collection of artifacts from that era ranging from children's boots to Indian baskets to mining tools. Open every day from March through October; open weekends only in November, December, and February; and closed in January. ~ 5119 Jessie Street, Mariposa; 209-966-2924.

Along Bullion Street, on a hill overlooking town, the **old jail** and **St. Joseph's Catholic Church** still stand. A study in contrast, the jail is a squat granite building with formidable iron door, while the church is tall and slender with a lofty steeple. Most impressive of these period structures is the **Mariposa County Courthouse**. The state's oldest court of law, it was built back in 1854 with wooden pegs and square-cut nails. Still in use, the courtroom contains a wood stove, kerosene lanterns, and original wooden benches.

HIDDEN ►

North of Mariposa, there's a memorable side trip to the ghost town of **Hornitos**. Just pick up Old Toll Road in Mt. Bullion, then catch Hornitos Road; on the way back take Bear Valley Road. All are paved country roads leading through tree-studded hills on this 25-mile round-trip detour.

A Mexican-style village centered around a plaza, Hornitos was a hideout for the notorious bandito Joaquin Murieta. According to legend, this Robin Hood figure, a semi-mythical hero to the Spanish miners, used a secret tunnel in the fandango hall to escape the law.

The Anglos in this rowdy mining town also claimed a famous citizen. Domingo Ghirardelli, the San Francisco chocolate manufacturer, built one of his earliest stores here in 1859. Several walls still remain, as do many of the town's old buildings. There's also an old jail, measuring little more than the size of a cell but possessing granite walls two feet thick.

The community contains something more than ruins of brick and stone. Because of its removal in time and space, Hornitos reflects the old days more fully than surrounding towns. There are windmills and range fences, grazing cows and crowing roosters. The tiny population goes about its business with an intensity not unlike that of the 15,000 who once lived here. And up on a hill, at a point closer to heaven than the rest of town, the old stone-and-wood church gazes down on the scene.

The region between Mariposa and Jamestown represents the least developed section of the Gold Country. It's a perfect place to capture a pure sense of the past. Particularly picturesque is the stretch from Mariposa to Coulterville, where Route 49 weaves wildly through the Merced River valley. The sharp slopes and hairpin turns provide grand vistas of the surrounding mountains.

Nestling beneath forested slopes, **Coulterville** is an architectural hodgepodge that includes several historic buildings. The **Northern Mariposa County History Center** sits astride a sturdy stone-and-iron structure, the former home of Wells Fargo. Open Tuesday through Saturday during summer and weekends only during winter; closed January. ~ Coulterville; 209-878-3015.

In **Chinese Camp**, another falsefront town with a gilded past, are ruins of the Wells Fargo building, a 19th-century store, plus an old church and cemetery. Once home to 5000 Chinese miners, this placid area was the scene of a violent tong war. About 2000 members of the Yan Wo and Sam Yap fraternities settled a mining dispute in 1856 with pikes, tridents, and axes.

North of Chinese Camp, Route 49 leads to **Jamestown**. More commercially developed than mining centers to the south, this town has been ambitiously gentrified. Its restored hotels, attractive restaurants, and antique shops are a prelude to the new, improved Gold Country awaiting you. *High Noon* and *Butch Cassidy and the Sundance Kid* were filmed here.

During the summer months, **Railtown State Historic Park**, the old Sierra Railroad, is open. There's a roundhouse museum with blacksmith shop, turntables, and historic locomotives. You can also ride several miles to nearby mining towns aboard an 80-year-old locomotive. ~ 5th Avenue and Reservoir Street, Jamestown; 209-984-3115.

Sonora marks the center of the southern Gold Rush region. The seat of Tuolumne County and one of the largest towns in the

THE BRIDGE OF STANISLAUS COUNTY

The gold town of **Knight's Ferry**, located on the Stanislaus River, features a rare California sight—a covered bridge. Built on a stone foundation, the wood-plank span adds an air of New England to the old mining center. The local general store has been operating over a century. Among the many Gold Rush–era buildings still standing is the unmarked **Dent House**, owned by relatives of former President Ulysses S. Grant, and visited by Grant himself in 1854. ~ Route 120.

Mother Lode, it has been preeminent almost since its founding in 1848. Settled by Mexicans, Sonora gained an early reputation both for its lawlessness and commercial potential. When rich strikes were discovered here, racist Americans pushed the Mexicans out of the action. They levied a $20-a-month residence tax on "foreigners," which they soon repealed when local merchants complained that the emigration of Mexican miners was hurting business!

Much of the history is written in the town's architecture. The best way to explore is with a walking tour brochure available from the **Tuolumne County Museum and Historical Society**. With about 20 points of interest, the tour will carry you through the historic and geographic heart of the old "Queen of the Southern Mines." ~ 158 West Bradford Avenue, Sonora; 209-532-1317.

Of the countless gold towns strung along Route 49, Columbia is not to be missed. Much of the old mining center has been preserved as **Columbia State Historic Park**. Here is a window on 19th-century life in the Sierra foothills. The refurbished buildings and rare artifacts create a picture that will help make sense of the random ruins found elsewhere in the Mother Lode.

Wandering the several streets that comprise this time-capsule town, you'll pass the old newspaper office, miners' boarding house, livery stable, and schoolhouse. There are hook-and-ladders so ancient they resemble Roman chariots, and a dentist's office containing fiendish-looking tools. Former Chinese residents are represented by a temple and herb shop, while the nearby apothecary remains stocked with Western-style potions and nostrums.

The old justice court serves the legal system no longer. It does, however, serve the public as it is open for touring. Over at the blacksmith shop are tools that bear an unsettling resemblance to those in the dentist's office. Like the four dozen buildings in this outdoor museum, it presents a perfect reconstruction of an imperfect era. ~ Route 49, Columbia; 209-532-4301.

LODGING

Jamestown features several historic hotels that have been refurbished. Least expensive is the **Royal Hotel**, a 15-room hostelry with a small lobby. Neither so grand nor so old as the town's other lodges, it attracts visitors with reasonable prices. Accommodations are small but freshly decorated. You'll find wall-to-wall carpeting, patterned wallpaper, and furnishings that range from pockmarked dressers to appealing brass beds. Ask for a room facing north, since the other side abuts another building, or rent one of the prim cottages out back. Continental breakfast is served on weekends and holidays. ~ 18239 Main Street, Jamestown; 209-984-5271. MODERATE.

The **Jamestown Hotel** is one of the best-restored hostelries in the Gold Country. An attractive two-story brick building with a balconied falsefront, it blends modern comforts such as a deck and solarium with old-fashioned Victorian decor, including floral wallpaper, brass beds, patchwork quilts, and wicker settees. A continental breakfast is served. ~ 18153 Main Street, Jamestown; 209-984-3902, 800-205-4901, fax 209-984-4149. MODERATE TO DELUXE.

Set in a sprawling Spanish-style structure, the **Sonora Inn** has 64 rooms. This is a full-service hotel complete with restaurant, lounge, and swimming pool. Rather than a rustic-inn decor, the hotel is done in more modern, less imaginative fashion. You'll encounter simulated-wood desks and naugahyde chairs, telephones, and televisions. The rooms are small and tidy, and equipped with lovely tile showers. ~ 160 South Washington Street, Sonora; 209-532-7468, 800-580-4667, fax 209-532-4942. MODERATE.

Staying at the **City Hotel** is almost a civic responsibility. Situated in Columbia State Historic Park, this charming establishment is a nonprofit organization and a training ground for hospitality management students from nearby Columbia Junior College. The ten-room hotel, dating from 1856, has been nicely restored and furnished with period pieces. There's a dining room and saloon downstairs. The guest rooms feature rugs across refinished pine floors, patterned wallpaper, and wall sconces. All include half-baths, with shared showers down the hall. "Balcony rooms" include patios overlooking the town's quiet Main Street. ~ Main Street, Columbia; 209-532-1479. MODERATE TO DELUXE.

Just across from Columbia State Historic Park, **Touch of Country** is of modern construction but furnished with antiques. Each of the four guest rooms has its own theme and has been decorated accordingly with a very personal touch. The furniture in Grandma's Room, for example, belonged to the owner's great grandmother. ~ 11250 Pacific Street, Columbia; 209-533-8269. MODERATE.

✔ CHECK THESE OUT—UNIQUE LODGING

- *Budget to moderate:* Retire to the caravansary where presidents Hoover and Garfield once hung their hats—the **National Hotel**. *page 388*
- *Moderate to deluxe:* Check in at the **City Hotel**, where the service ought to be great—it's a training ground for hospitality managers. *page 381*
- *Moderate to ultra-deluxe:* Retreat to the High Sierras at **Sorensen's**, with cabins offering views of rugged granite heights all around. *page 412*
- *Ultra-deluxe:* Slumber in a hotel almost as grand and dramatic as its setting in Yosemite Valley, the **Ahwahnee Hotel**, decorated in intricate American Indian designs. *page 420*

Budget: under $50   Moderate: $50–$90   Deluxe: $90–$120   Ultra-deluxe: over $120

The **Harlan House**, one of Columbia's finest homes at the turn of the century, sits on a hill across from the old schoolhouse. You'll sleep among Victorian and other American antiques, and relax on a shady front porch. ~ 22890 School House Street, Columbia; 209-533-4862. MODERATE.

DINING

Some evening when Mexican food sounds appealing, consider the **Café Smoke**. It's a friendly, upbeat place decorated with local artwork, Mexican tile floors, and potted cacti. The menu features the full gamut of Mexican-style dishes and the adjoining saloon cooks up some mean margaritas. Dinner only. Closed Monday. ~ Main Street, Jamestown; 209-984-3733. MODERATE.

Good Heavens, A Restaurant serves quiche dishes and salads during lunch hour. There are also open-face sandwiches like turkey and cranberry, ham and pineapple, or beef with green chiles. The entrée menu might feature tarragon shrimp pasta or shrimp and broccoli crêpes. This homemade restaurant is a diner's dream (and reasonably priced besides!). Lunch and Sunday brunch only. ~ 49 North Washington Street, Sonora; 209-532-3663. MODERATE.

For gourmet dining in a Gold Rush–era atmosphere, try **The City Hotel**. Built in 1856, the hotel is part of Columbia State Historic Park. The dining room is appointed in period with brass chandeliers, high-back chairs, and gold-framed oil paintings. Dinner is an extravaganza featuring poached salmon with pink-peppercorn hollandaise, roasted leg of lamb, veal loin chop with an herbed crust, and swordfish fillets. Sunday champagne brunch is also served. The food is delicious here and highly recommended. Closed Monday. ~ Main Street, Columbia; 209-532-1479. DELUXE.

SHOPPING

Jamestown has almost as many antique stores as saloons. Dotted along falsefront Main Street are shops selling pieces that date back almost as far as the stores themselves. Matter of fact, other than an occasional pharmacy, hardware store, and knickknack shop, that's pretty much all you'll find here.

Up in **Sonora**, you'll encounter a full-blown shopping scene. This is the commercial center for Southern Gold Country. Washington Street is lined with stores along its entire length. Since the shops cater to local residents, many are service outlets of little interest to travelers. But you will find clothiers, camera stores, jewelers, art galleries, bookshops, and antique stores.

NIGHTLIFE

Jamestown is one place that remembers its past. Main Street in this 19th-century community is still decorated with a string of drinking spots. For casual drinking in an easy setting, the hotel bars, such as the one in the **National Hotel**, are best. ~ 77 Main Street, Jamestown; 209-984-3446.

The Rawhide Saloon is another get-down country bar complete with pool tables, jukebox, dancefloor, and wide-screen TV. Every Friday and Saturday night, a country band cranks up and wails into the wee hours. There's karaoke every Tuesday, Thursday, and Sunday. ~ Route 108, Jamestown; 209-984-5113.

In Columbia, the **Columbia Actors Repertory** performs dramas, musicals, and comedies at the Fallon House Theatre. ~ Columbia State Historic Park; 209-532-4644.

PARKS

COLUMBIA STATE HISTORIC PARK A fully reconstructed Gold Rush town, this park represents an extraordinary outdoor museum. It stretches across many acres and provides a graphic representation of life in mid-19th century California. Facilities include restrooms, picnic areas, restaurants, groceries, hotels, a museum, and much more. ~ It's off Route 49 about five miles north of Sonora; 209-532-4301.

▲ There is no camping in the park, but two private campgrounds for tents and RVs lie adjacent to the park. **'49er Trailer Ranch** (209-532-9898) charges $22.50 double nightly for tent camping; full hookups and cable available. **Marble Quarry RV Park** (209-532-9539) collects $22.50 for partial hookups, $25 for full hookups and cable. Both feature picnic areas, hot showers, and other facilities. My vote goes to Marble Quarry RV Resort, where the folks are particularly friendly.

NEW MELONES LAKE TUTTLETOWN RECREATION AREA AND NEW MELONES LAKE GLORYHOLE RECREATION AREA Set on the shores of spacious Melones Reservoir, these areas are popular with boaters and anglers. The entire lake is surrounded by oak trees and rolling hills, making it a pretty place to picnic. It was even more beautiful, conservationists claim, before the reservoir was created by the controversial Melones Dam, which flooded the historic Stanislaus River Valley. There are toilets and showers; restaurants and groceries are several miles away in Sonora, Columbia, and Angels Camp. ~ Tuttletown and Acorn are off Route 49 about ten miles north of Sonora; Gloryhole is about 16 miles north of Sonora; 209-536-9094.

▲ There are 144 sites (including hike-ins) at Gloryhole Campground; $14 per night; two-week limit; first-come, first-served. Tuttletown Campground features 95 sites with a few spaces big enough for RVs; there are also 65 sites at Acorn Campground; $14 per night.

STANISLAUS NATIONAL FOREST Rising along the western slope of the Sierra Nevada, this rugged region extends from the Gold Country to Yosemite National Park. Elevations range from 1100 to over 11,000 feet, and there are hiking trails through much of the forest's 1700 square miles. Since it parallels Route 49 and represents the nearest high country to San Francisco, Stanislaus is quite popular. Among its attractions are the Merced, Tuolumne, Clavey, Stanislaus, and Mokelumne rivers, which have cut deep canyons through the forest. There are also ponderosa pine, incense cedar, cottonwood, and willows. Grouse, quail, black bear, and blacktail deer inhabit the mountains and wildflowers grow in brilliant profusion throughout the spring. Within the forest are picnic areas and restrooms; ranger stations are dotted around the area; restaurants and groceries are available in towns scattered along the roads through the forest. ~ From Route 49 you can take Route 120, Route 108, or Route 4 east through the forest; 209-532-3671.

▲ There are 47 campgrounds, including Pine Crest Campground, which has 200 sites; $13.50 per night; and Frazer Flat Campground, which has 30 sites; $9 per night.

Central Gold Country

Mark Twain and Bret Harte helped immortalize it. Birthplace of the California Gold Rush and a good place to visit American Indian landmarks, the central Mother Lode is also home to giant sequoias and wineries, a famous frog jumping contest, white water rafting, and some favorite hiking trails. Spread out along Route 49 between Angels Camp and Placerville, this area is a great escape.

SIGHTS

About nine miles north of Sonora, a side road leads from Route 49 to the reconstructed **Mark Twain Cabin**, where the fledgling writer lived for five months during the 1860s. It was Twain's Gold Country story, "The Celebrated Jumping Frog of Calaveras County," that first propelled him to fame.

The annual jumping frog contest takes place every May up in **Angels Camp**, an old mining town which Twain visited during his California sojourn. The community boasts several antique buildings and a museum, but its chief notoriety is literary; it hosted not only the creator of Huckleberry Finn, but also Bret Harte, who probably used the mining center as a model in his story, "The Luck of Roaring Camp."

From Angels Camp, Route 4 leaves Route 49 and heads east toward the High Sierra. On the way it passes several points of interest including limestone caverns, the town of Murphys, and Calaveras Big Trees State Park. **Moaning Cavern** and **Mercer Caverns** are extraordinary limestone formations descending hundreds of feet underground. Guided tours lead into these subterranean cathedrals where rock formations are twisted into bizarre figures. Entering them is like descending into an ice palace filled with sparkling creations. Despite the tourist trappings, either of these caverns warrants a visit. Mercer Caverns is open weekends only in winter. Admission at both. ~ Moaning Cavern: 209-736-2708. Mercer Caverns: 209-728-2101. If you prefer a full-bore spelunking tour in another nearby cavern, call 209-736-2708.

Murphys is an attractive little town, established by two enterprising Irishmen in 1848. Among the historic buildings fronting its tree-lined streets is **Murphys Historic Hotel**. Built in 1856, it has housed an impressive assemblage of guests, among them Bret Harte, Jacob Astor, Jr., Count Von Rothschild, and Ulysses S. Grant. ~ 457 Main Street, Murphys; 209-728-3444.

Many of the 19th-century luminaries signing the Murphys Hotel guest book were en route to the "Big Trees," which had been recently discovered and were fast becoming a world famous tourist destination. Today **Calaveras Big Trees State Park** preserves these "Monarchs of the Forest." Located along Route 4 about 25 miles east of Angels Camp, the park rests at 4000 to 5000 feet elevation. Admission. ~ 209-795-2334.

Within it are two groves of giant sequoias, the largest living things on earth. Closely related to coastal redwoods, these trees trace their ancestry back to the age of dinosaurs. One tree in the park stands 320 feet high, another measures 27 feet in diameter. Like their coastal cousins, they create a hushed sense of awe which cannot be described, but must be experienced as you stand amidst these mountain goliaths.

The spirit of '49 remains alive and well on Route 49 as it continues north from Angels Camp. There are buildings of note in **San Andreas**. The argonaut community of **Mokelumne Hill** contains a Main Street lined with old-time buildings, including an **IOOF hall** that represents the Gold Country's first three-story structure.

Two **country tours** in this region will carry you past ancient mining claims tucked in the mountains. Little evidence remains of the '49ers, but the routes lead through pretty places away from civilization. First is an alternative 25-mile route from Angels Camp to San Andreas via Dogtown, Calvaritas, and Mountain Ranch roads. These country lanes wind past rolling ranchlands and mountain streams. Second is a westward course 11 miles each way to Campo Seco. From Mokelumne Hill take Route 26 to Paloma Road to Campo Seco Road. Settled by Mexicans in 1849, **Campo Seco** reveals its gilded past in a series of stone ruins lining the road. ◄ HIDDEN

If you haven't tired of walking tours, pick up a map of **Jackson** at the Amador County Chamber of Commerce. Closed Saturday and Sunday. ~ 125 Peak Street, Suite B, Jackson; 209-223-0350.

In addition to a balconied Main Street, this county seat features the **Amador County Museum**. One of the region's best museums, it honors the Chinese with displays of abacuses, Chinese drums, and coolie hats. There are also tours of the Kennedy Mine Model display, geologic showcases, and a photograph collection featuring the dourest-looking people imaginable. Closed Monday and Tuesday. ~ 225 Church Street, Jackson; 209-223-6386.

The next town along Route 49 is named for the man on whose land gold was first discovered, John Sutter. **Sutter Creek** warrants a walking tour, too. Within a few blocks along Main and Spanish streets are dozens of buildings and homes rich with history.

Volcano is another well-preserved mining center. Located on Sutter Creek Road about 12 miles east of the town of Sutter Creek, Volcano was a booming town of 5000 back in the days of the argonauts. In addition to a Masonic hall, express office, and three-story hotel, the community sports another relic—"Old Abe." According to local folks, this cannon was used during the Civil War to warn off Confederate sympathizers who sought to divert the town's gold to the Rebel cause.

On the same road two miles from Volcano is **Indian Grinding Rocks State Historic Park.** Here along a limestone outcropping the Miwok Indians gathered to collect acorns and grind seeds, berries, and nuts. Using the limestone bedrock as a natural mortar, they eventually ground over a thousand cavities in the rock. These unusual mortar holes, together with several hundred petroglyphs, can be toured along a self-guided trail. You'll also pass facsimile displays of ceremonial roundhouses, bark houses, granaries, and a Miwok playing field. Admission. ~ Pine Grove–Volcano Road; 209-296-7488.

North from Sutter Creek, Route 49 bisects **Amador City**. The focus of a quartz mining operation, this pretty community still contains many of its original brick and woodframe buildings. It was the creek, not the miners, that was dry in neighboring **Drytown.** Matter of fact, the place contained about 25 saloons during its golden youth.

HIDDEN ►

From Plymouth, take a side trip up Shenandoah Road (county road E16) to the **Shenandoah Valley wine-growing region.** Vineyards have prospered here since Gold Rush days and at present almost two dozen wineries dot the area. Many are clustered along a ten-mile stretch of Shenandoah Road.

Foremost is **Sobon Estate**, which dates from 1856. Enjoy the tasting room or take a self-guided tour through the original cellar. This rock-walled enclosure still contains the old handmade oak casks and hewn wooden beams. Specializing in zinfandel, Sobon also produces fumé blanc, French syrah, and viognier. While this winery is open daily, others have limited schedules and often require reservations. ~ 14430 Shenandoah Road, Plymouth; 209-245-6554.

It's wise to pick up a free winetasting brochure from the **El Dorado County Chamber of Commerce.** Closed Saturday afternoon and Sunday. ~ 542 Main Street, Placerville; 916-621-5885.

If visiting between September and December during the apple harvest, ask at the Chamber of Commerce for information about **Apple Hill**. Located on a mountain ridge east of Placerville, this area is crowded with orchards where for a modest fee you can pick your own apples. Many of the orchards lie just off Route 50 on Carson Road.

HIDDEN

Placerville, one of the largest towns in the Mother Lode, has been heavily developed and lacks the charm of neighboring villages. There are a few historic places remaining, however, such as the **Gold Bug Mine**, where you can step between the timbers and explore a narrow stone tunnel that leads deep into the earth. One of the few mines open to the public, Gold Bug also features a weatherbeaten stamp press mill used to grind gold from bedrock. ~ Gold Bug Lane, off Bedford Avenue, one mile from downtown Placerville.

Placerville also served as a supply center for other mining towns, including several that can be visited via a **side trip** along Route 193. Just north of town you can pick up this mountain road and follow it in a 28-mile semi-circle, rejoining Route 49 a few miles south of Auburn. In the course of its arc, the road curls along the sides of the mountains as it curves up from the American River Valley. There are open views of pine-fringed peaks and dark green canyons. Among the old mining communities are **Chili Bar**, perched astride the American River, **Georgetown** with its antique buildings lining a boulevard-wide Main Street, and the one-street town of **Greenwood**.

Limestone caves where secret orders of Masons once held meetings lie just outside the town of Volcano along Pine Grove–Volcano Road.

This country detour is recommended only if you plan to cover the Placerville to Auburn span along Route 49 as well. Otherwise you'll miss **Marshall Gold Discovery State Historic Park**. Like Columbia, this park features a reconstructed Gold Rush town—Coloma. It also happens to be the place where it all began. Here on January 24, 1848, James Marshall found shining metal in a sawmill owned by John Sutter. "Boys," Marshall exclaimed, "I believe I have found a gold mine." The history of California and the West was changed forever. Within the park, a self-guiding trail leads past a reconstruction of Sutter's mill and to the discovery site on the banks of the American River. With the skeletal-looking mill on one hand and a foaming river on the other, it's an eerie sensation standing on the spot that once lured tens of thousands across a continent. Admission. ~ Route 49, Coloma; 916-622-3470.

There's also a museum with display cases portraying the days of '49 and a miner's cabin complete with long johns and animal pelts hanging from the rafters. In all, this 265-acre park features two dozen points of interest and is second only to Columbia in its ability to evoke California's glittery past.

LODGING

If anything, **Murphys Historic Hotel** is historic. The place dates to 1856 and numbers among its previous guests Ulysses S. Grant, Mark Twain, Black Bart, and William Randolph Hearst. Stay here and your dreams might even carry you back to those roughhewn days. The nine rooms are still maintained much as they were back when, with oak wardrobes, antique dressers, and patterned wallpaper. Each room has the name of a famous guest painted on the door. All the rooms share baths. For a historic splurge, book the presidential suite, containing the same bed on which Grant slept. (There's also an adjoining motel with 20 rooms, but staying there contradicts the reason for coming to Murphys.) ~ 457 Main Street, Murphys; 209-728-3444, 800-532-7684, fax 209-728-1590. MODERATE.

In a nice switch from the usual "store-bought" furnishings of most bed-and-breakfast inns, **The Heirloom** is filled with the lifelong possessions of the two innkeepers. The accommodations in this scaled-down antebellum house are so different from one another that it's hard to believe they share the same premises. Antique bedframes, handmade quilts, and fresh flowers decorate the four main-house rooms. An additional adobe cottage features two rooms with open-beam ceilings, skylights, and wood-burning stoves. Exquisite breakfasts are included. ~ 214 Shakeley Lane, Ione; 209-274-4468. MODERATE TO DELUXE.

The best bargain in all the Gold Country is found at the **National Hotel**. This hulking 30-room hotel claims every California governor since 1862 (until 1960) as a guest, not to mention Presidents Garfield and Hoover. Happily, it hasn't gone to the hotelkeeper's head. He still rents suites and rooms with private baths for affordable rates. Standard rooms are small, furnished with antiques, but mismatched in decor (the carpeting doesn't quite go with the wallpaper). There's a restaurant and Western-style saloon downstairs. ~ 2 Water Street, Jackson; 209-223-0500. BUDGET TO MODERATE.

If the National Hotel has the cheapest lodging, **Sutter Creek Inn** provides the most commodious. Innkeeper Jane Way has been running this 18-room facility since 1966 and doing so with special flair. Among her trademarks are four rooms with swinging beds, a complete country-style breakfast, and a spacious lawn with shade trees and hammocks for lounging guests. Some of the guest rooms are located in the main house, a New England–style home built of redwood in 1859; others are located in the cottages which dot the grounds. Each room is individual in size, decor, and furnishings, but all feature private baths. There's also a library where guests can cozy up with a good book. ~ 75 Main Street, Sutter Creek; 209-267-5606, fax 209-267-9287. MODERATE TO DELUXE

HIDDEN ►

The **Mine House Inn** represents the region's most intriguing hostelry. It's located in the former office building of the Old Keystone Consolidated Mining Company. Millions of dollars worth of gold was assayed and smelted in this century-old building. As a result, the place is built of brick with walls thirteen inches thick. Each of the eight guest rooms was once an individual office, so if you check into the "Vault Room" be prepared to share the space with a ceiling-high iron vault. The "Keystone Room" was fashioned from the dumbwaiter shaft used to transport bullion, and the "Retort Room" features a keystone arch built to support the vault. An inn since 1955, the Mine House is creatively furnished with period pieces and has a swimming pool on the premises. ~ 14125 Route 49, Amador City; 209-267-5900, 800-646-3473. MODERATE TO DELUXE.

A gay resort located along the Cosumnes River, **Rancho Cicada Retreat** offers rustic accommodations in two comfortably furnished cabins and 22 tents set on platforms and equipped with mattresses. Although catering primarily to men, the resort also welcomes women. The grounds include rock gardens, lawns, strolling peacocks, and places for sunbathing, volleyball, croquet, and swimming. ~ P.O. Box 225, Plymouth; 209-245-4841. DELUXE.

DINING

A 19th-century hostelry, **Murphys Historic Hotel** features an informal dining room. Though there are antiques dotted about, the restaurant lacks the charm of the hotel. The Continental menu features a full breakfast, lunch, and an array of dinnertime spreads. ~ 457 Main Street, Murphys; 209-728-3444. MODERATE.

The Upstairs is a small second-story affair decorated with plenty of greenery and attractive prints on the walls. It's popular among residents and visitors alike. The menu features California-cuisine dishes such as New Zealand lamb in a zinfandel and gorgonzola sauce and grilled salmon with a citrus-dill sauce. Midday

✔ CHECK THESE OUT—UNIQUE DINING

- *Budget*: Hang out with the local gentry at **Old Post Office Coffee Shop**, where homemade cookin' is done with downhome skill. *page 404*
- *Moderate:* Sidle up to the polished bar at **Ron and Nancy's Palace**, once a saloon in the 19th century, and now a restaurant serving Continental cuisine. *page 390*
- *Deluxe:* Test your epicurean taste buds at **Wolfdale's**, a noted eatery serving such delicacies as quail, broiled sturgeon, and squab. *page 405*
- *Deluxe to ultra-deluxe:* Join the Sacramento pols at **The Firehouse**, a fire-station-turned-gourmet-dining establishment. *page 375*

Budget: under $8 Moderate: $8–$16 Deluxe: $16–$24 Ultra-deluxe: over $24

offerings include a variety of gourmet sandwiches and salads. Closed Monday. ~ 164 Main Street, Jackson; 209-223-3342. MODERATE TO DELUXE.

Set in a vintage 1884 building, **Ron and Nancy's Palace** served as a saloon back in the 19th century. Today this fashionable restaurant boasts three dining rooms, a polished bar, and a decor highlighted by stained-glass windows. The Continental cuisine includes prime rib, chicken, and fresh seafood dishes. ~ 76 Main Street, Sutter Creek; 209-267-1355. MODERATE.

Zachary Jacque, a provincial French restaurant, is trimly appointed with paintings and decorative china plates. Wood paneling and a cozy fireplace add to its warm appeal. Among the evening entrées, you can choose from rack of lamb, beef Wellington, duck with ginger and lavender, and fresh fish. Closed Monday and Tuesday. ~ 1821 Pleasant Valley Road, Placerville; 916-626-8045. MODERATE TO DELUXE.

SHOPPING

There are several arts and crafts shops in **Angels Camp, Murphys, Jackson**, and **Volcano**. Then, proceeding north, you'll encounter a pair of towns with antique buildings that have been remodeled into charming shops. Foremost is **Sutter Creek**. Along the 19th-century Main Street are shops like **Old Hotel Antiques**. It boasts Depression glass, old Coca-Cola advertisements, and antique jewelry. ~ 68 Main Street, Sutter Creek; 209-267-5901.

Within a couple of blocks are no fewer than a dozen antique shops. Of course in this historic town, the stores as well as their contents are antiques: even the local plumbing company is situated in an 1869 building.

Amador City has been renovated in like fashion. Route 49 barrels through the center of this aged town, past handicrafts shops, art galleries, and those places that seem more plentiful than restaurants—antique stores.

Placerville serves as a regional shopping area for the Central Gold Country, with stores of all sizes.

NIGHTLIFE

There are nondescript bars in Angels Camp, San Andreas, and Mokelumne Hill. Up at the old **Murphys Historic Hotel** there's an old-time miners' saloon. The crowd here is drawn not only by the nightlife, but also because of the fame of this hostelry. There's occasional live music. ~ 457 Main Street, Murphys; 209-728-3444.

There's a Western-style saloon in the historic old **National Hotel**. The place is complete with bright red wallpaper, gilded mirrors, and glittery chandeliers. On weekends the piano player will probably have a beer resting alongside the ivories and a garter belt holding up one sleeve. ~ 2 Water Street, Jackson; 209-223-0500.

Sports Bar and Grill, just outside Placerville, hosts country bands every Friday and Saturday night. Other evenings you can play shuffleboard, shoot pool, or watch sports on big-screen televisions. ~ 5641 Mother Lode Drive, El Dorado; 916-626-0336.

The **Coloma Club**, just north of historic Coloma, features rock-and-roll or country bands every weekend. It's a down-home bar complete with pool table and dancefloor as well as karaoke and open-mike nights. ~ Route 49, Coloma; 916-626-6390.

High culture is also part of the Gold Country tradition. If visiting during a weekend in summer, you might take in a show by one of the region's many repertory groups. Several feature traditional drama, though most present light melodramas.

Theater El Dorado performs six to eight plays each year in a 200-seat theater on the Placerville County fairgrounds. The theater covers the whole spectrum of stage performances: musicals, comedies, classics, and dramas. ~ 100 Placerville Drive, Placerville; 916-626-5193.

Out in Volcano, the **Volcano Pioneers Community Theatre Group** headlines at the Cobblestone Theatre. ~ Volcano; 209-223-4663. The **Coloma Crescent Players** are featured at the Coloma Theatre. ~ Coloma; 916-626-5282.

PARKS

CALAVERAS BIG TREES STATE PARK Straddling the north fork of the Stanislaus River, this magnificent park covers almost 6000 acres of mountainous terrain. Its 18 miles of hiking trails lead along deep canyons and riverside beaches. The chief attractions, however, are the two groves of giant sequoias. Of particular interest is the South Grove, explored along a three-mile trail, which still possesses a sense of the primeval. Facilities in the park include an information center, museum, picnic areas, and restrooms; restaurants and groceries are nearby in towns along Route 4. Day-use fee, $5. ~ The park is located along Route 4 about 25 miles east of Angels Camp; 209-795-2334.

▲ There are 74 sites at Northgrove Campground and 55 sites at Oak Hollow Campground; both campgrounds have showers; $13 to $16 per night.

INDIAN GRINDING ROCKS STATE HISTORIC PARK Set at about 2400-feet elevation, this facility features interesting American Indian displays in the Regional Native American Museum. There is a reconstructed Miwok village complete with dwellings, petroglyphs, and bedrock mortars. Surrounding meadows are brilliant with wildflowers in spring and the forest is filled with manzanita and ponderosa pine, as well as black oak trees from which the Miwok gathered acorns. Facilities include picnic areas, restrooms, and showers; restaurants and groceries are two miles away in Volcano. Day-use fee, $5. ~ About 12 miles east of Jackson; from Route 49 in Jackson take Route 88 east to Pine Grove, then follow Pine Grove–Volcano Road to the park. Or from Volcano take Pine Grove–Volcano Road two miles to the park; 209-296-7488.

▲ There are 23 sites; $12 to $16 per night.

MARSHALL GOLD DISCOVERY STATE HISTORIC PARK This re-created Gold Rush town was the site of the original strike. The primary interest is historic and the park is fully described in the "Central Gold County" section above. Facilities include an information center and museum, historical buildings and displays, picnic areas, and restrooms; groceries and restaurants are nearby. Day-use fee, $5. ~ Located along Route 49 in Coloma; 916-622-3470.

▲ Camping is not permitted within the park, but there are campgrounds located nearby. The closest is **Coloma Resort,** with 100 campsites; $26.50 to $28.50 per night (showers and grocery store are available). ~ Route 49, Coloma; 916-621-2267.

Adjacent to the park is **American River Resort,** with riverside sites for $28 per night (showers, restaurant, grocery, and swimming pool on the premises). ~ Route 49, Coloma; 916-642-9600.

Camp Lotus, a few miles from Coloma, also has riverbank camping and is very popular with river rafters (fees are $4 per person during the week or $6 on Friday and Saturday; $7 minimum per party during the week and $10 minimum on weekends). In addition to 115 campsites, there are five cottages and two cabins available. ~ Bassi Road, Lotus; 916-622-8672.

Northern Gold Country

This forested region features colorful pinnacles, covered bridges, mining museums, and some of the state's more notable Victorians. The fastest growing part of the Gold Country, it also offers cross-country skiing, inviting river swimming holes, ghost towns, and 19th-century hotels that are a journey back in time. Extending from Auburn to Sierra City, the northern section of the Mother Lode is traversed by the historic transcontinental railroad.

SIGHTS

Auburn, like Placerville, has grown too large to enjoy the rural charm of other Mother Lode communities. The only section of note is "Old Town," built near the American River in the 19th century. There's an interesting walking tour through this brick-and-woodframe neighborhood, which you should take after obtaining an Old Town map from the **Auburn Area Chamber of Commerce.** ~ 601 Lincoln Way, Auburn; 916-885-5616. Among the sights are a trim three-story firehouse capped with a bell tower, an old town antique shopping center, and a maze of falsefront streets.

The mines to the north along Route 49 were a far cry from the simple mining claims that started the Gold Rush. Prominent during the latter half of the 19th century, these big buck operations were heavily industrialized. **Grass Valley,** for instance, has 367 miles of tunnels running beneath its streets. The town's **North Star**

Mining Museum displays the sophisticated machinery that replaced the gold pan and rocker. Closed during winter and early spring. ~ End of Mill Street on Allison Ranch Road, Grass Valley; 916-273-4255.

Be sure to see the art deco Courthouse on Church Street and City Hall at 317 Broad Street in Nevada City. They're welcome anomalies amid the Gold Country's masonry-and-iron-door architecture.

At nearby **Empire Mine State Historic Park** you can view the engineering office and machine shops of the richest hardrock gold mine in California. Walk about 50 feet into the black entranceway of a shaft that leads more than a mile down and wander through the many buildings comprising this multimillion dollar venture. With its tailing piles and eroded hillsides, the surrounding area presents a graphic illustration of how mining destroyed the landscape. It's ironic that the rich mine owners, whose opulent homes you can view here, chose to build their estates in neighborhoods they were turning to rubble heaps. Admission. ~ 10791 East Empire Street, Grass Valley; 916-273-8522.

Despite the scars, Grass Valley still reveals several pretty sections. Along Mill and Main streets, the gas lamps, awnings, balconies, and brick facades remain from the gold era. A replica of the Lola Montez House contains the **Nevada County Chamber of Commerce** where you can obtain brochures and walking maps. Together with Lotta Crabtree, Lola represents Grass Valley's early days of glory. After rising in Europe as a dancer and the mistress of King Ludwig of Bavaria, Lola settled in Grass Valley in 1852. Her seven-year-old protégée, Lotta Crabtree, eventually became a nationally renowned theatrical entertainer. ~ 248 Mill Street, Grass Valley; 916-273-4667.

Nevada City was once the third largest city in California. Still grand by local standards, it nevertheless has a country village charm. There are gaslights, turreted houses, and balconied stores along Broad Street. Much of the Victorian elegance remains amid the widow's walks, church steeples, and gingerbread facades. A walking map of the town, available from the **Nevada City Chamber of Commerce**, will guide you through the historic heart of town. ~ 132 Main Street, Nevada City; 916-265-2692.

◄ HIDDEN

For an adventurous side trip from town, head to **Malakoff Diggins State Park**. While it is a fully developed park, this area is so remote it represents a good example of "hidden California." You reach it from Nevada City on North Bloomfield–Graniteville Road, a 17-mile journey that will carry you over the Yuba River. The last half of the road is unpaved and parts of it are quite steep and sinuous. But the scenery is startling and the seclusion splendid.

The park includes the rustic town of North Bloomfield, built during the 1860s as a hydraulic mining center. There's a livery stable filled with wagons, plus a whitewashed church and old general store, all neatly preserved. The immediate area has been heavily eroded by hydraulic mining, which involves washing away hillsides with hoses, then sifting gold from the mud. Bald cliffs and a miniature lake remain as evidence of these destructive techniques. But the rest of the region is wild and untouched, wide open for exploration. Admission. ~ North Bloomfield–Graniteville Road; 916-265-2740.

To delve deeper into the mountains, continue north from Nevada City on Route 49. Towns are few and far in this region of tall pines and deep river valleys. About 13 miles from town you can take a 14-mile (round-trip) detour along Pleasant Valley Road to the

HIDDEN ►

Bridgeport covered bridge. Stretching 230 feet, it is reputedly the West's longest single-span covered bridge.

Route 49 follows a serpentine course along the Yuba River as it climbs to **Downieville**, an enchanting town cradled in a canyon. The crooked streets and tin-roof houses of this 1849 settlement are completely encircled by mountains. The town gallows and many picturesque buildings still stand in this natural amphitheater.

Higher still is **Sierra City**, built in the shadow of the Sierra Buttes. The highway streams past fruit orchards and alpine meadows en route to this avalanche-plagued town, then climbs 6700-foot Yuba Pass and heads for the High Sierra.

LODGING

Country Squire Inn is a 1970s time warp with 80 units spread across three buildings. Rooms and suites offer king- and queen-sized beds, vanities, and small tables convenient for workaholics and families that like to dine in. There's a swimming pool and whirlpool on the premises. ~ 13480 Lincoln Way, Auburn; 916-885-7025, fax 916-885-9503. BUDGET.

Anchoring the center of Nevada City, the **National Hotel** claims to be the oldest continuously operating hotel west of the Rockies. With its bar, dining room, and Victorian decor, the place has served travelers since the 1850s. Accommodations vary from rooms that are plain but comfortable to suites that feature love-seats, canopy beds, and 19th-century frills. ~ 211 Broad Street, Nevada City; 916-265-4551. BUDGET TO MODERATE.

For a true living-history experience, delve into the secret treasures of

HIDDEN ►

The Parsonage Bed & Breakfast. Each of the six guest bedrooms honors a Dane family pioneer who settled in the Gold Country in the 1850s. The house is decorated with authentic period pieces and attention to detail is a way of life. You'll sleep on line-dried and hand-pressed linens. Breakfast includes fresh baked muffins and croissants, and homemade jams and fresh fruit, all served on Haviland china. ~ 427 Broad Street, Nevada City; 916-265-9478, fax 916-265-8147. MODERATE TO DELUXE.

DINING

Several good restaurants cluster around the "Old Town" section of Auburn. Among them is **Shanghai Restaurant**, a Chinese eatery that has been around since 1912. This high-ceilinged establishment features a standard array of Cantonese dishes. Closed Tuesday. ~ 289 Washington Street, Auburn; 916-823-2613. BUDGET.

At **Friar Tuck's** you can dine in a cozy back room or in a livelier dining area next to the bar. With its brick walls, exposed beams, and heavy posts, the restaurant is reminiscent of an old gold mine. But potted plants, private booths, and a guitarist performing through dinner add warmth to one of the region's most popular restaurants. Fresh fish is a specialty here. Mahimahi, ahi, and salmon are standard menu items; and you can also order teriyaki steak or pasta primavera. Dinner only. ~ 111 North Pine Street, Nevada City; 916-265-9093. MODERATE.

For that special occasion, try **Potager at Selayas**, a restaurant with a gourmet menu that features delicacies like beef Wellington, salmon, and roast stuffed chicken. There are appeteasers like escargots and wild-mushroom gratin, and for dessert there are fresh-made selections daily. The decor is lace-and-brass Victorian and the mood very inviting. Downstairs in the "diggin's" you'll discover an entirely different ambience—a mine shaft with brick walls and wooden beams. Dinner only. Closed Monday. ~ 320 Broad Street, Nevada City; 916-265-5697. MODERATE.

SHOPPING

Auburn contain expansive shopping sections and serves as a regional center for folks throughout the central Mother Lode. Window browsing Auburn's "Old Town" section is tantamount to a historic adventure. Most of the 19th-century buildings have been converted to shops. The Empire Livery Stable is now a mini-mall, the old Hop Sing Laundry and Chinese Joss Houses are antique stores. Located along Sacramento, Washington, and Commercial streets are other new shops in old clothing.

Grass Valley and **Nevada City** are the chief shopping destinations in the northern Mother Lode area. The better of the two is Nevada City, where early stores have received a face-lift. You'll find a jewelry shop beside the family barber, a T-shirt store near an old saloon, and an oriental rug shop next door to a historic hotel. The best places to browse are along Broad, Commercial, and North Pine streets. Happy hunting!

NIGHTLIFE

Nevada City has two varied nightspots within a few doors of one another. **McGee's** is a posh brick-walled drinking emporium with overhead fans and stained-glass decoration that's good for a quiet cocktail. ~ 315 Broad Street, Nevada City; 916-265-3205. **Cirino's** is neither so formal nor as neatly decorated. ~ 309 Broad Street, Nevada City; 916-265-2246.

PARKS

AUBURN STATE RECREATION AREA This sprawling facility covers over 30,000 acres and includes Lake Clementine, a small reservoir. Long and narrow in its configuration, the park follows the American River basin for about 30 miles. There are opportunities to hike, swim, and fish in this former placer mining region. No facilities; restaurants and groceries are available in Auburn. ~ The ranger station is located along Route 49 about one mile south of Auburn; 916-885-4527.

▲ Permitted in 100 primitive sites; $7 to $10 per night.

FOLSOM LAKE STATE RECREATION AREA One of California's most popular parks, this mammoth facility completely encircles Folsom Lake's 75-mile shoreline. Visitors come to boat, waterski, ride horseback, picnic, swim, and camp. Anglers try for trout, bass, perch, and sturgeon. There are also 65 miles of hiking trails around the lake. Quite crowded in summer, the park is best visited during the week. Facilities include an information center, marinas, picnic areas, restrooms, and showers; restaurants and groceries are located in Auburn and Folsom. Day-use fee, $6. ~ Located along Folsom–Auburn Road between Auburn and Folsom; 916-988-0205.

▲ There are 175 sites in three campgrounds; $14 per night.

MALAKOFF DIGGINS STATE HISTORIC PARK Remote and beautiful, this 3000-acre facility includes a well preserved Gold Rush town. The park rests near the Yuba River, where anglers catch rainbow and brook trout; there are also black bass and bluegill in nearby Blair Reservoir. The park's slopes, climbing from 2200 to 4200 feet, are open to hikers. Swimming is good in the reservoir. The park has an information center and museum, picnic areas, and restrooms; restaurants and groceries are located 17 miles away in Nevada City. Day-use fee, $5. ~ From Nevada City, take Highway 49 north for 11 miles and make a right onto Tyler Foote Crossing Road. Follow the paved road 17 miles to Derbec Road, which leads to the park. The last half of the road is unpaved; 916-265-2740.

▲ Permitted in 30 sites; $7 to $10 per night. There are also three rustic cabins for rent; $20 per night.

PLUMAS-EUREKA STATE PARK Set deep in the Sierra, this 6600-acre spread contains waterfalls, creeks, and two small lakes. The park rises from 4000 feet to 7447-foot Eureka Peak and is home to the pileated woodpecker, the largest woodpecker in North America, and the caliope hummingbird, the smallest of its kind on the continent. The park is also home to golden eagles, great blue herons, deer, and beaver. This area is also a pioneer ski region, which hosts winter sports events. Displays in the museum (admission) focus on the hard-rock mining of the area. Other facilities include an information center, picnic areas, restrooms, and showers; restaurants and groceries are in nearby towns. ~ From Route 49 north of Sierra City take Gold Lake Road to Greagle, then go five miles west on County Road A14, which begins near the intersections of Routes 89 and 70; 916-836-2380.

▲ Permitted in 67 sites (including 14 walk-in) from approximately May 15 to October 15; $14 per night.

Lake Tahoe Area

There aren't many places in America where you can waterski from one state to another. Nor can I think of many spots perfect for wilderness hiking during the day and shooting craps at night. And how many lakes can you name that are so clear you can see objects 200 feet below the surface? One of the West's most unique areas, the Lake Tahoe region is a remarkable blend of nature and kitsch.

In addition to its raw beauty and Nevada gambling, Lake Tahoe is also very popular simply because it is so easily accessible. From Route 49 in the Gold Country, numerous highways lead east into the Sierra and on toward Tahoe. The main road from San Francisco is Route 80, a fast, efficient freeway that bisects Sacramento and traverses the Sierra about twelve miles north of Lake Tahoe.

SIGHTS

It was not always so simple. During the terrible winter of 1846–47, a party of stalwart pioneers, unable to cross the Sierra because of drifting snow, camped for the winter. Many perished from exposure and hunger, others went insane, and some resorted to cannibalism. Today the **Emigrant Trail Museum** at **Donner Memorial State Park** commemorates their passing. There is also a monument on the grounds. Its base stands 22 feet high—the depth of the snow that winter. Today Route 80, the transcontinental interstate, passes within yards of the Donner Party's tragic resting place. Admission. ~ Donner Pass Road, Truckee; 916-582-7892.

For a more hospitable sense of the Old West, truck on over to **Truckee**, two miles east on Route 80. This 19th-century town sits astride a mountain pass high in the Sierra. Framed by forested slopes, Truckee is a woodframe town overlooking an old railroad yard and depot. The main street, Commercial Row, is lined with falsefront buildings. Clapboard warehouses and meeting halls with second-story balconies remain from the town's old lumbering and railroad days. Then as now, Truckee was a gateway. Today it leads to the gambling palaces and ski resorts of Tahoe.

To tour one of the most famous of the ski resorts, head south from Truckee toward Lake Tahoe on Route 89, and follow the signs to **Squaw Valley**. The 1960 Winter Olympics put this vale on the map, and ski bums have been making the pilgrimage ever since. Ringed by 8200-foot-high mountains, and sprinkled with lodges and condos, it's a favored jet-set landing ground.

As soon as the highway from Squaw Valley rises to meet **Lake Tahoe**, it becomes evident why the region's rivers run fast and pure. This lake, situated 6225 feet above sea level, contains water so clear that objects 200 feet below the surface are visible. With depths reaching an incredible 1645 feet, it is the biggest alpine lake of such purity in all North America. Tahoe is 22 miles long and measures 72 miles around. The entire lake is framed by 10,000-foot mountain peaks, a translucent gem set in a granite ring.

Unlike nearby lakes of glacial origin, Tahoe formed by faulting. About 150 million years ago the basin was created when the Carson Range rose to the east while the Sierra Nevada grew to the west, leaving a giant trough between. When volcanoes dammed the end of the basin, rain and snow filled the natural bowl to brimming. Washoe Indians eventually inhabited the lakeshore regions, and enjoyed uninterrupted predominance until 1844 when Captain John Fremont and Kit Carson, searching a mountain pass into California, "discovered" the lake. By the 1870s, with the advent of the railroad, Tahoe emerged as a popular resort area.

Today the tourist scene along this alpine jewel centers around the "North Shore" and the "South Shore." The former includes a series of small towns, each featuring resort facilities, restaurants, and various attractions. The latter highlights South Lake Tahoe, the region's most populous town.

On either shore, crossing the border between California and Nevada is like passing from one country to another. The reason is simple—gambling. It's legal in Nevada, and is not in California. Within a few steps of the border rise the casinos of Incline Village and Stateline, with their brilliant lights and promise of quick and easy wealth.

Mark Twain visited the lake over a century ago, long before the gaming palaces, and was overwhelmed. "As it lay there with the shadows of the mountains brilliantly photographed upon its still surface," he remarked in *Roughing It*, "I thought it must surely be the fairest picture the whole earth affords."

Tahoe. The word still carries power. But in recent decades it has become a riddle, an oxymoron. To some it conjures images of dark casinos and fateful gaming tables. To others it evokes pristine thoughts of trackless wilderness and oceanic depths. Never the twain shall meet: Tahoe is an environmental battleground. Developers, wedded to tomorrow's dollar, struggle against environmentalists committed to yesterday's beauty. Every fight the conservationists lose results in more structures along the lake, greater erosion, and another cloud across that glassy water.

The resource they seek to protect is a magical place. To see Tahoe fully, you should circle the entire lake, beginning perhaps on the North Shore, swinging down the California side, then returning along the Nevada lakefront. Routes 28, 89, and 50 comprise this loop. Within its course, the road cuts through dense conifer forests, then passes dramatic outcroppings of granite. Intermit-

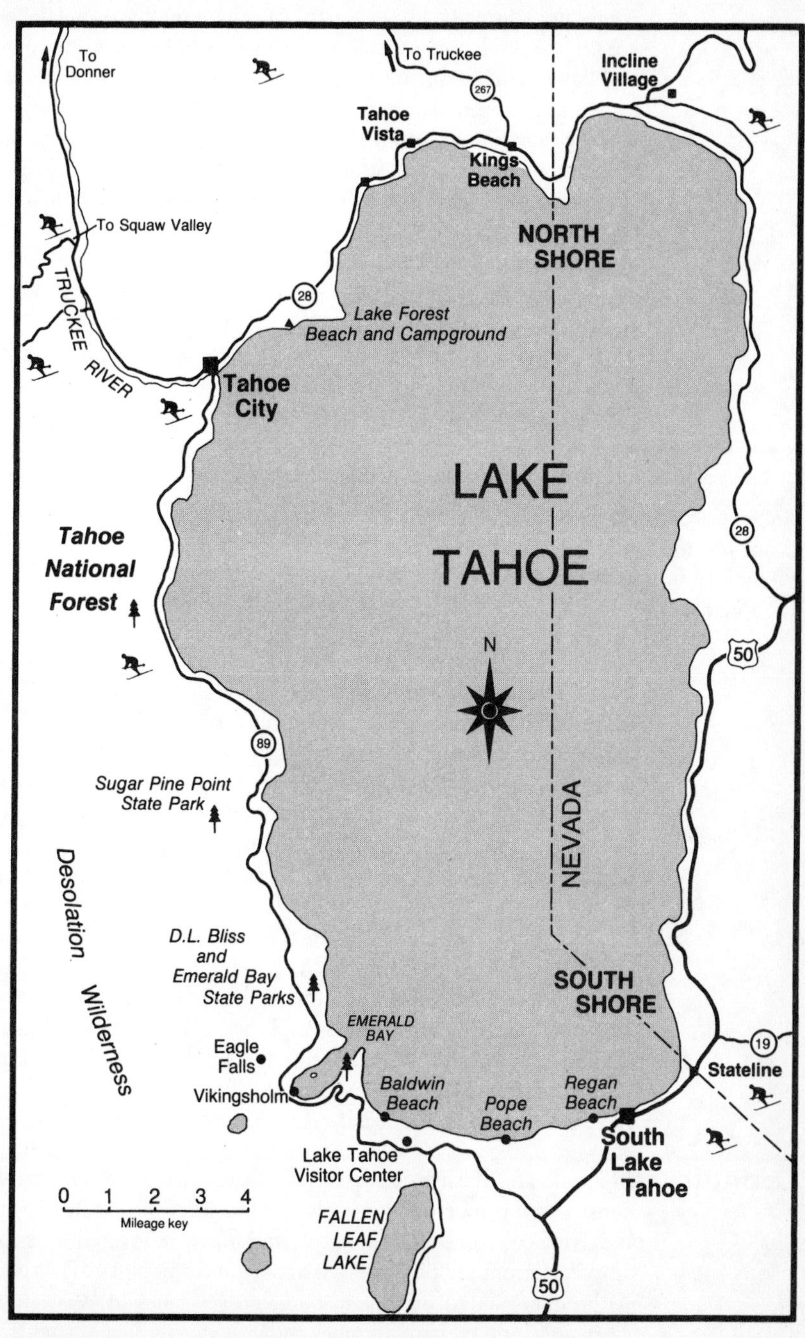

To Donner
To Truckee
267
Incline Village
Tahoe Vista
Kings Beach
To Squaw Valley
NORTH SHORE
TRUCKEE RIVER
28
Lake Forest Beach and Campground
Tahoe City
LAKE TAHOE
Tahoe National Forest
28
N
50
89
Sugar Pine Point State Park
NEVADA
Desolation Wilderness
D.L. Bliss and Emerald Bay State Parks
SOUTH SHORE
EMERALD BAY
19
Eagle Falls
Stateline
Vikingsholm
Baldwin Beach
Pope Beach
Regan Beach
South Lake Tahoe
Lake Tahoe Visitor Center
0 1 2 3 4
Mileage key
FALLEN LEAF LAKE
50

tently the highway opens onto broad lake vistas, swept by westerly winds and adorned with the sails of careening sloops. Along the way are private residences worthy of a prince; magnificent stone edifices with lawns rolling down to the lip of the lake. These are mansions, leaded-glass affairs that appear drawn from *The Great Gatsby*.

The best known of all is **Vikingsholm**, a 38-room castle situated a few miles west of South Lake Tahoe. Open for tours in the summer, this unusual structure was designed on the lines of a 9th-century Norse fortress. It's built of granite and hand-hewn timbers and marked by a series of towers. Admission. ~ 916-525-7277.

Anchored offshore, near Vikingsholm, is tiny **Fanette Island**, where a stone teahouse built to similar specifications sits.

As if this extraordinary stonework were not enough, the castle rests beside two-mile-long **Emerald Bay**. From the vista point located along Route 89, this spectacular cove, guarded by lofty conifers, presents the most picturesque site along the entire lake. At the far end, poised between two peninsulas, is a slender opening into the lake; at the near edge, cascading along granite steps, is **Eagle Falls**. A short path leads from the vista point to a wooden footbridge below the falls, or you can hike one mile down from the vista point to Vikingsholm.

Lake Tahoe is named for an American Indian word meaning "big water" or "water in high place."

Along the western outskirts of South Lake Tahoe, between Baldwin Beach and Pope Beach, are the **Tallac Historic Site Estates**, comprising more of Tahoe's fabulous old mansions. Here you can stroll through the woods on a path strewn with pine needles. You'll pass a cluster of old brown-shingle buildings, a log cabin, and the fabled estates. These include the Pope house, built in 1884; Valhalla, a brown-shingle beauty; and the McGonagle estate, a prestigious house designed ironically in the fashion of a log cabin. Closed during winter.

The estate trail lies between the **Lake Tahoe Visitors Center** (916-573-2600) and Camp Richardson, along Route 89. Closed during winter. Other helpful information centers are located at the Chamber of Commerce offices in Tahoe City ~ 245 North Lake Boulevard, 916-581-6900; South Lake Tahoe ~ 3066 Lake Tahoe Boulevard, 916-541-5255; and the U.S. Forest Service ~ 870 Emerald Bay Road, Suite 1, South Lake Tahoe, CA 96150; 916-573-2600.

LODGING

In a chic and flashy area like Lake Tahoe, where everything was constructed tomorrow, it's a pleasure to discover a place such as the **Truckee Hotel**. Built in 1868, and nicely renovated, this four-story falsefront building sprawls across an entire block. The rooms, with either shared or private bath, possess an Old West charm. They are cluttered with antiques and crowded with character. Even if you don't plan on staying there, the hotel is well worth the visit.

~ Corner of Bridge Street and Commercial Row, Truckee; 916-587-4444, 800-659-6921, 916-587-1599. MODERATE TO DELUXE.

For lakefront lodgings on the North Shore, try **Sun and Sand Lodge.** This knotty-pine motel has 26 units near the water. There's a sandy beach along one edge of the property and a sunny smile at the front desk. ~ 8308 North Lake Boulevard, Kings Beach; 916-546-2515, 800-547-2515, fax 916-546-0112. MODERATE.

How can anyone go wrong at a place named **Tatami Rustic Cottage Resort**? With 18 cottages clustered across the street from the lake, this charming complex offers a clapboard alternative to the chic lodges hereabouts. The houses are neatly furnished and feature knotty-pine interiors; all are tucked under an awning of pine trees. Some units have kitchens and fireplaces. It's a cute and cozy place. ~ 7449 North Lake Boulevard, Tahoe Vista; phone/fax 916-546-3523. MODERATE TO DELUXE. ◄HIDDEN

Another great lakefront facility is **Beesley's Cottages Resort**, a collection of pine-frame houses fronting a private sand beach. Set in a grove of lodgepole pines, this homey establishment has cottage rooms and individual cottages. The latter are spacious affairs with full kitchen and living room. They are neatly furnished, paneled in that ever-present knotty pine and carpeted wall-to-wall. Closed during winter. ~ 6674 North Lake Boulevard, Tahoe Vista; 916-546-2448, 415-854-2823. MODERATE TO ULTRA-DELUXE.

You could get lost in the enormous suites at beachfront **Tahoe Vista Inn & Marina.** Five of the six accommodations in this multilevel, wood-shingled inn offer sweeping lake views. They each have bedrooms, as well as a living room, stone fireplace, full kitchen, and private porch. A few of the suites have jacuzzis. Sun pours through windows into rooms lightened even more by soft grays and off-white modern decor. Worth the price. ~ 7220 North Lake Boulevard, Tahoe Vista; 916-546-7662, 800-662-3433, fax 916-546-7963. ULTRA-DELUXE.

Mountain lodge meets high-class resort at the redwood, multi-gabled **Sunnyside Restaurants and Lodge.** Nestled in pine woods and sitting before its own marina, the lodge features a cozy country lobby with river rock fireplace adorned with hunting trophies. Ducks and decoys are everywhere in the 23 lakefront or lakeview accommodations, simply furnished in wicker and wood and featuring individual touches like an old sea chest or armoire. Many have fireplaces and wet bars. ~ 1850 West Lake Boulevard, Tahoe City; 916-583-7200, 800-822-2754, fax 916-583-2551. DELUXE TO ULTRA-DELUXE.

Mayfield House, a six-room bed and breakfast set in a 1930s-era house, is one block from the lake and within walking distance of shopping areas. In addition to cozy guest accommodations there is a living room with stone fireplace. Some rooms have private baths. ~ 236 Grove Street, Tahoe City; 916-583-1001. MODERATE TO DELUXE.

The **Resort at Squaw Creek** lures guests with an extravagant 405-room hotel that is showcased by a stream and waterfall which plunge 250 feet through the property. Situated a half-mile from Squaw Valley's vaunted ski slopes, the resort is a summer destination as well as winter hideaway. For warm weather enthusiasts there are eight tennis courts, an 18-hole golf course, bike paths, miles of equestrian and hiking trails in the surrounding mountains, and an aquatic center with three pools and a water slide. In winter it provides ice skating facilities and easy access to the ski slopes. ~ 400 Squaw Creek Road, Olympic Valley; 916-583-6300. ULTRA-DELUXE.

Camp Richardson Resort, a multifaceted facility, sits along a pretty beach on the western outskirts of South Lake Tahoe. In addition to a spacious lodge, this switch-hitting establishment has cabins for rent as well as a multitude of campsites. The lodge is a classic mountain retreat. It offers a cozy lobby with knotty-pine walls, log beams, and a stone fireplace. The rooms are neatly if unimaginatively furnished. The cabins are rustic in appearance, but furnished in comfortable fashion. Woodframe in construction, they are set around the resort's wooded acres not far from the lake, with some located right on the water's edge. The cabins include complete kitchen facilities. In summer the resort prefers to rent cabins by the week. ~ 1900 Jameson Beach Road, South Lake Tahoe; 916-541-1801, 800-544-1801, fax 916-541-1802. MODERATE TO DELUXE.

Sky Lake Lodge is a 23-unit motel located on the South Shore's main drag. The guest rooms here are nicely furnished and decorated with flair. Some have been shingled along the interior; all have phones, carpets, color televisions, and stall showers. Ask for a room away from the highway. ~ 2644 Lake Tahoe Boulevard, South Lake Tahoe; 916-544-0770. MODERATE.

Tahoe travelers who just have to be where the action is will find refined charm amid the chaos along Route 50 at the stone-and-shingle **Inn by the Lake**. The 100 accommodations, set back from

BEACH BLANKET MOTEL

Positively the best lodging bargain in hectic South Lake Tahoe is **Sail In Motel Apartments**. Not only is the place away from the busy section of town, it's also located right on a beach. The rooms are few, which might be why the owners have taken such care in furnishing them. The interior decoration shows imagination. And the exterior? Step outside and you'll find a knockout view of Lake Tahoe. ~ 861 Lakeview Avenue, South Lake Tahoe; 916-544-8615. MODERATE.

the highway on landscaped grounds, feature blond woods and lush pastel bedspreads and wallhangings. Many view the lake across the street; suites have full kitchens. There's also a pool, sauna, and bi-level hot tub. ~ 3300 Lake Tahoe Boulevard, South Lake Tahoe; 916-542-0330, 800-877-1466, fax 916-541-6596. DELUXE TO ULTRA-DELUXE.

Another recommended spot is **Hansen's Resort**, on the road to Heavenly Valley ski area. A collection of cabins tucked beneath arching pines, this facility is splendidly situated. It's a short stroll to the center of South Lake Tahoe or to the ski region. For a quiet but convenient retreat, the place is ideal. There's an individual cabin (with bedroom, living room, and kitchen) as well as two single-room motel units. All facilities are pine-paneled, very well-furnished, and immaculately clean. Cool and spiffy. ~ 1360 Ski Run Boulevard, South Lake Tahoe; 916-544-3361. MODERATE TO DELUXE. ◄HIDDEN

At the very edge of South Lake Tahoe, near the gambling casinos and Nevada border, are countless motels. These are all within walking distance of the gaming tables and cater mainly to gamblers. Because of competitive rates, they can also be attractive to travelers. The problem is they're often crowded and their rates fluctuate wildly. Count on paying more during the summer and on weekends. Even the rates quoted below constitute little more than an estimate. I'll list three of the area's motels; it's advisable to shop among others nearby for the best deal.

First choice is the **King Franklin Motel**, a 20-unit facility, located one block from a private beach. ~ 3988 Pine Boulevard, South Lake Tahoe; 916-544-4281. BUDGET TO MODERATE.

Just two blocks from a private beach, **Seven Seas Motel** is a 17-unit establishment with a hot tub. ~ 4145 Manzanita Avenue, South Lake Tahoe; 916-544-7031, 800-800-7327. BUDGET TO MODERATE.

The nearby **Blue Jay Lodge** is a sprawling 65-unit hostelry. ~ 4133 Cedar Avenue, South Lake Tahoe; 916-544-5232, 800-258-3529, fax 916-544-0453. BUDGET TO MODERATE.

The next best thing to your own house on a lake is **Lakeside B 'n B Tahoe**, which literally has Lake Tahoe in its backyard. The inn features spectacular views from each of its three guest rooms, one of which has its own jacuzzi and steam room. Attracting a gay and lesbian clientele, the simply but comfortably furnished hostelry offers a lakeside deck, library, grand piano, fireplace, and gourmet breakfast. ~ 550 Gonowabie Road, Crystal Bay, Nevada; 702-831-8281, fax 702-831-7329. MODERATE TO ULTRA-DELUXE.

DINING

The Passage is a fine Truckee dining spot. Located downstairs in the century-old Truckee Hotel, the place has a vintage ambience. The bar is an old pine structure with brass footrests. The restaurant is small and comfortable with overhead fans and kerosene lanterns, plus a patio out back. At dinner, the menu ranges from fresh fish to pepper steak to pasta. They also feature sandwiches, salads, and hamburgers at lunch, plus a brunch menu with specialties like seafood quiche and eggs Benedict. ~ Corner of Bridge Street and Commercial Row, Truckee; 916-587-7619. MODERATE.

Col. Clair's is the ideal spot for that special meal. It's chic but comfortable, fashionable but informal. Specializing in Cajun and Creole dishes, the Colonel provides entrées like mixed shellfish fettuccine, jambalaya, Cajun prime rib, and blackened fish. The interior is paneled in knotty pine, with such decorative touches as stained glass, hooded lamps over each table, an antique sideboard, and stone fireplace. ~ 6873 North Lake Boulevard, Tahoe Vista; 916-546-7358. DELUXE.

Dark woods, white linens, a stone fireplace, and windows brimming with plants create romance at **Captain Jon's**. The European menu changes daily and favors fresh fish entrées such as lobster whiskey, scallops shiitake, and salmon en croûte. There's also a waterside lounge. Extensive wine list. Closed Monday and three weeks in November. ~ 7220 North Lake Boulevard, Tahoe Vista; 916-546-4819. MODERATE TO DELUXE.

French-country dining to the max, **Le Petit Pier** greets guests with blue awnings outside and a partially glass-enclosed, candlelit dining room highlighted by white linens, and walls covered with culinary awards. A horde of black-tie waiters serve entrées such as pheasant *souvaroff*, grilled châteaubriand, and *filet sauté au poivre vert*. Closed Tuesday. ~ 7252 North Lake Boulevard, Tahoe Vista; 916-546-4464. DELUXE TO ULTRA-DELUXE.

The folks at the **Old Post Office Coffee Shop** only serve breakfast and lunch, but they do it with country flair. Popular with local people, the restaurant offers pancakes, waffles, and omelettes from the early hours. By lunchtime, the griddle is blazing with a variety of chicken breast sandwiches and the cook is ladling out homemade soup and chili. ~ 5245 North Lake Boulevard, Carnelian Bay; 916-546-3205. BUDGET.

Bacchi's Inn has been owned and operated by the same family for three generations. Famed for its minestrone soup, this Italian eatery serves family-style meals. The dining room, open for dinner only, is decorated with traditional red-checkered tablecloths and lantern candles. ~ 2905 Lake Forest Road, Tahoe City; 916-583-3324. MODERATE.

Tahoe House, another dinner-only establishment, is owned by a Swiss family. The decor is Swiss country and the cuisine is a mix of Swiss, German, French, Italian, and Californian. Specialties include veal dishes, homemade pasta, fresh-baked bread, and lavish desserts with Swiss chocolate. ~ Route 89, Tahoe City; 916-583-1377. MODERATE.

Rosie's Café is one of those laid-back eating spots California is famous for harboring. Just across the street from the lake, the place is bizarrely decorated with old sleds, bicycles, skis, and wall mirrors. It's open all day and into the night, featuring imaginative cuisine. At breakfast there are bagels and eggs "benecado" (with guacamole and hollandaise sauce). Lunch carries salads, sandwiches, tostadas, and more. Come dinner, the menu expands to include pasta, vegetarian and stir-fry dishes, roast duckling, chicken scallopine, steak, and seafood. Tasty and popular. ~ 571 North Lake Boulevard, Tahoe City; 916-583-8504. MODERATE.

Wolfdale's, located on Tahoe's north shore, touts itself as a "cuisine unique restaurant." It's well known and critically acclaimed. The menu is regularly changing but may feature delicacies like fresh swordfish, quail, broiled sturgeon, seafood pasta pesto, and squab. It's well worth a taste test. Dinner only. Closed Tuesday. ~ 640 North Lake Boulevard, Tahoe City; 916-583-5700. DELUXE.

With a wraparound glass dining room, the chalet-style **Christy Hill** commands great lake views that complement its modern, minimalist decor. This California-cuisine eating spot is highly regarded by guests and locals. Fresh food in light sauces are Christy Hill's hallmark, with entrées such as Hawaiian *ono* in mango, ginger, and lime sauce. Closed Monday. ~ 115 Grove Street, Tahoe City; 916-583-8551. DELUXE.

A lovely little Tahoe cottage houses **Evan's American Gourmet Café**, where the menu ranges from Continental to Asian to American regional. Soft lighting, large original watercolors, and mauve and blue decor set off an appealing room of only 11 tables. The far-ranging menu might include entrées such as venison with caramelized apples in calvados sauce. Killer homemade desserts. Closed Sunday. ~ 536 Emerald Bay Road, South Lake Tahoe; 916-542-1990. MODERATE TO DELUXE.

For a taste of the Far East, try **Siam Restaurant**. It's an informal establishment with a few rows of booths inside. The menu runs the gamut of Thai dishes: coconut soup, squid, red snapper, spicy roast duck, etc. Closed Tuesday. ~ 2180 Lake Tahoe Boulevard, South Lake Tahoe; 916-544-0370. BUDGET.

The European-style **Christiania Inn** is a shingled restaurant with lots of lace and antiques, a large fireplace, and two wine cellars. Dinner choices include beef Wellington, fresh seafood platters, and a variety of Continental dishes that change seasonally. Also offered is the après-ski special, a four-course meal available for a reasonable price. Desserts range from tableside flambées to baked Alaska. ~ 3819 Saddle Road, South Lake Tahoe; 916-544-7337. MODERATE TO DELUXE.

The Dory's Oar is a unique and fashionable establishment. The place sits in a red Cape Cod–style cottage with green shutters. In keeping with the architecture, the bill of fare includes Eastern clams and oysters, plus live Maine lobsters. These last can be personally selected from a display tank. For the timid, there are Chesapeake

Bay soft-shelled crabs, steak dinners, and stuffed baby salmon. Choice place for a special occasion. ~ 1041 Fremont Avenue, South Lake Tahoe; 916-541-6603. MODERATE TO DELUXE.

The **Horizon Casino Resort** provides an incredible spread that on a typical night will include roast beef, veal tips, filet of snapper, roast pork, chicken, rigatoni, and a salad bar. ~ Route 50, Stateline, Nevada; 702-588-6211. MODERATE.

Over at **Harvey's Resort Hotel**, there's often a similar deal at the Garden Buffet. ~ Route 50, Stateline, Nevada; 702-588-2411. MODERATE.

Harrah's Lake Tahoe Resort has a Forest Buffet up on the 18th floor where you can enjoy an array of dishes as well as a panoramic view. Typical specialties include pork chops, veal parmigiana, prime rib, roast ham, and baked turkey. The prices are quite affordable and children under six dine for free. The catch, of course, is that you must escape from the casino before gambling away the money you just saved on dinner. ~ Route 50, Stateline, Nevada; 702-588-6611. MODERATE.

NIGHTLIFE

For a get-down, stomping good time, the place to head is Truckee. This Old West town, 12 miles north of Lake Tahoe, has as many saloons as any self-respectin' frontier outpost. Lining the falsefront main drag are places like **O. B.'s Pub & Restaurant.** ~ 10046 Commercial Row, Truckee; 916-587-4164. At **Bar of America** there's live music every Friday and Saturday. Cover on weekends. ~ Commercial Row at Bridge Street, Truckee; 916-587-3110.

There are other saloons that wail through the weekend with live music. All of them are hat brim to hat brim with ten-gallon locals. This is a Wild West town that knows how to party.

There are waterfront lounges and other nightspots around Lake Tahoe, particularly along the North Shore and in South Lake Tahoe. The real action, though, lies across the line in Nevada. Here legalized gambling has resulted in miles of neon casinos.

These garish, enticing establishments offer slot machines, roulette wheels, keno, and sports betting as well as gaming tables for poker, twenty-one, and other pastimes. The clubs also have plush lounges featuring top-name entertainers. As a result, the shows are extravaganzas complete with dance troupes and orchestras.

POKER AND PASTA

Among the cheapest places to eat on the South Shore are the casino hotels just across the border in Stateline, Nevada. All of them feature "gambler's specials" of one sort or another: breakfast for a buck or perhaps a full-course meal in a good restaurant at budget prices.

On the North Shore, the scene centers around Incline Village. Down along the South Shore everyone gravitates over to Stateline, Nevada. Here a string of casinos lines a Vegas-like strip. One top club is the **Horizon Hotel and Casino,** which offers a string of slot machines and gambling tables. ~ Route 50, Stateline, Nevada; 702-588-6211. Be sure to check out the scene at **Harvey's Resort Hotel.** ~ Route 50, Stateline, Nevada; 702-588-2411. At **Caesar's Tahoe** there are 76 table games and 1060 slot machines. ~ Route 50, Stateline, Nevada; 702-588-3515. Good luck!

PARKS

DONNER MEMORIAL STATE PARK Set in a pine-and-fir forest astride three-mile-long Donner Lake, this facility lies north of Lake Tahoe. It was here in the winter of 1846–47 that the ill-starred Donner party, trapped in heavy snow, was confronted with cannibalism or death. Today the accommodations are more commodious. There are campgrounds, a museum, and a resident population of porcupines, beaver, raccoons, and bears (plus perhaps the ghosts of several hungry pioneers). In addition to an information center and museum, the park now features picnic area, restrooms, and showers; restaurants and groceries are available two miles away in Truckee. Open from Memorial Day until the end of September. Day-use fee, $5. ~ Located just off Route 80, two miles west of Truckee; 916-582-7892.

▲ Permitted during the summer in 154 sites; $14 per night.

TAHOE NATIONAL FOREST Rising from the Gold Country to the Sierra crest, this mammoth forest covers over 800,000 acres. Its scenic beauty and recreation facilities make it very popular year-round. Swimming and horseback riding opportunities are available during warm months, with skiers taking over in winter. Hunters, anglers, and gold panners also frequent the area. Within the forest are picnic areas and restrooms; restaurants and groceries are in towns scattered along the highways. ~ Located northwest of Lake Tahoe, the region is traversed by Routes 49, 80, and 89. The Tahoe National Forest Headquarters is located at Route 49 and Coyote Street, Nevada City; 916-265-4531.

▲ Permitted in 68 campgrounds throughout the forest; $8 to $24 per night. Located at Sugar Pine Reservoir, Giant Gap Campground has 30 sites; $8 to $24 per night. At Jackson Meadow Reservoir, you'll find Pass Creek Campground, which has 30 sites; $11 per night.

KINGS BEACH STATE RECREATION AREA A tiny eight-acre plot, this facility is important because it's one of the few public beaches near Nevada on the North Shore. Anticipate a small sandy beach plus a picnic area and restrooms. Restaurants and groceries are nearby in Kings Beach. ~ Located in

Kings Beach along Route 28 about 12 miles east of Tahoe City; 916-546-7248.

LAKE FOREST BEACH AND CAMPGROUND These are two discrete units situated within walking distance of one another. The beach consists of a stretch of sand bordered by aspen trees. There are picnic areas and toilets. The campground, which is inland from the lake, features sites near a grove of trees. It's equipped with picnic areas and restrooms. Restaurants and groceries are located two miles away in Tahoe City. Parking fee, $5. ~ Located off Route 28 along Lake Forest Road about two miles east of Tahoe City; 916-583-3796.

▲ There are 20 sites; $10 per night; 916-525-7232.

TAHOE STATE RECREATION AREA Little more than a pocket park, this 62-acre facility possesses a small patch of lakefront property. The beach is unattractive, but the area behind it is studded with shady conifer trees. Facilities include picnic area and restrooms; restaurants and groceries are nearby in Tahoe City. Open only from Memorial Day to Labor Day. Day-use fee, $5. ~ Located on Route 28 just east of Tahoe City; 916-525-7232.

▲ There are 39 sites; $14 per night.

SUGAR PINE POINT STATE PARK One of the Tahoe region's most precious jewels, this magnificent park extends along almost two miles of lakefront. Inland it runs nearly four miles. Within that expanse is a forest of Jeffrey and sugar pines. The lakefront is dotted with sandy beaches, and the park possesses several historic structures, among them a pioneer log cabin and an old mansion that's been converted to a museum. There are also hiking trails, a tennis court, picnic areas, restrooms, and showers. Restaurants and groceries within a few miles in either direction. ~ On Route 89 about ten miles south of Tahoe City; 916-525-7232.

▲ Permitted in 175 forested sites; $14 per night.

D. L. BLISS AND EMERALD BAY STATE PARKS These contiguous beauties curve along six miles of lakefront. Within their borders lie some of the area's most picturesque sites. Emerald Bay, a narrow cove bounded all around by dense forest, is a shimmering body of water. A spectacular waterfall feeds the cove. The forest which dominates both parks includes Jeffrey and ponderosa pines, incense cedar, quaking aspen, mountain dogwood, and willows. Wildflowers and berries flourish throughout the area. Tours of Vikingsholm Mansion (916-541-3030) are daily. There are picnic areas, restrooms, and showers in both parks. Day-use fee, $5. ~ Both parks are along Route 89; D. L. Bliss is 17 miles south of Tahoe City, Emerald Bay is 22 miles south; 916-525-7232.

▲ There are 168 sites at D. L. Bliss. At Emerald Bay there are 100 sites plus 20 boat-in sites; $14 per night.

DESOLATION WILDERNESS This preserve, extending across 63,475 acres of alpine terrain, is a favorite among outdoor adventurers. With elevations ranging from 6500 to 10,000 feet, the domain encompasses about 130 lakes. Juniper, fir, and pine grow along the streams that tumble through the mountains, but large stretches, stripped by glacial action, are devoid of trees and appear like a moonscape. Because of heavy snowfall, the best time to explore is summer. Other than 15 miles of hiking trails, there are no facilities here; the closest restaurants and groceries are along Lake Tahoe. A wilderness permit is necessary to enter. Contact the U.S. Forest Service at 870 Emerald Bay Road, South Lake Tahoe, CA 96150; 916-573-2674. ~ Located a few miles southwest of Lake Tahoe; accessible from Route 89 or Route 50.

▲ Camping is hike-in only. Because of heavy summer use, a reservation and quota system has been instituted. Some wilderness permits can be reserved up to 90 days in advance; others are available on a first-come, first-served basis.

LAKE TAHOE BASIN MANAGEMENT UNIT This bureaucratic sounding region is actually an extremely beautiful part of Tahoe National Forest, concentrated around the south shore of Lake Tahoe. Its 148,800 acres include some of Tahoe's prettiest beaches (see listing below), several campgrounds, picnic areas, plus ski and horseback riding opportunities; restrooms throughout. Day-use fee at several locations. ~ Located along Route 89 around the lake's south shore. For more information contact the Lake Tahoe Visitors Center on Route 89 along the western outskirts of South Lake Tahoe, near Fallen Leaf Lake; 916-573-2674.

▲ Permitted at several campgrounds along the southern part of Lake Tahoe. My favorite is Meeks Bay, located on a pretty white sand beach; there are 40 sites; $14 per night. Information, 916-573-2674. There are also campsites in another part of Tahoe National Forest north of Lake Tahoe; these are located along Route 89 between Truckee and Tahoe City. Information, 916-587-3558. Elsewhere in the national forest, camping is allowed without a permit, but a fire permit is required.

SOUTH SHORE BEACHES Located within a few miles of South Lake Tahoe are several of the region's loveliest beaches. Matter of fact, the stretch from Baldwin Beach, near Emerald Bay, to the edge of South Lake Tahoe, is a golden swath of sandy beach. Edged by trees and vegetation, backdropped by mountains, it's an idyllic site overlooking the entire lake. The sandy skein begins with Baldwin Beach and includes Kiva and Pope beaches. There are picnic areas, restrooms, and an information center at Kiva Beach; restaurants and groceries a few miles away in South Lake Tahoe. ~ Located along Route 89 west of South Lake Tahoe; 916-573-2674.

CAMP RICHARDSON RESORT This lakefront facility includes a campground among its many features. Situated in piney woods within strolling distance of the beach, this private campground is part of a full-facility complex that includes access to a marina, lawn sports, riding stable, and bike rentals. There are also picnic areas, restrooms, and showers; grocery nearby. ~ Located on Route 89 near the western outskirts of South Lake Tahoe; 916-541-1801.

▲ There are more than 250 sites, some with RV hookups. Fees are $17 for tent sites; $19 for water and electric hookups; $22 for water, electric, and sewage hookups.

REGAN BEACH Not really a beach, this is an open picnic area along the waterfront. Nevertheless, it's nicely landscaped with a lawn and shade trees. Central to South Lake Tahoe, the park is still off the main thoroughfare. Facilities include picnic tables, barbecue grills, sand volleyball courts, and restrooms; restaurants and groceries are available nearby. ~ Located five blocks from Route 50 on Lakeview Avenue at Sacramento Street in South Lake Tahoe.

EL DORADO BEACH This pocket park, with its patch of sand, commands a sweeping view of the lake. Unfortunately, it's located right on a busy highway. Things can become rather schizophrenic with pristine nature extending out before you and civilization rumbling along behind. But its location in the center of South Lake Tahoe makes it popular nonetheless. The only facilities are picnic tables; restaurants and groceries nearby. ~ Located in South Lake Tahoe along Route 50 near the intersection with Lakeview Avenue.

EL DORADO NATIONAL FOREST Rising from 1620 to 10,380 feet, this 668,000-acre facility extends from the Gold Country to the High Sierra. Within its domain are numerous lakes, plus over 600 miles of fishing streams. Anglers try for brown, rainbow, and eastern brook trout; birdwatchers search out golden and bald eagles, grouse, quail, and several owl species; hunters stalk deer and bear. There are also 350 miles of hiking trails. There are picnic areas and restrooms within the forest; restaurants and groceries are available in towns scattered along the highways. ~ Located southwest of Lake Tahoe, the region is traversed by Routes 50 and 88. The information center is located at 3070 Camino Heights Drive, Camino; 916-644-6048.

▲ Permitted in 43 campgrounds, including the beautiful Silver Lake and Caples Lake campgrounds along Route 88; $8 to $10 per night.

Lake Tahoe to Yosemite

There are few better ways to experience High Sierra country than by following the mountain roads leading from Lake Tahoe to Yosemite. Route 89 heads from South Lake Tahoe and intersects with Route 395, which in turn links with Route 120, the back road into Yosemite.

Along the way are views of bald-domed mountains, lofty and elegant, backdropped by even taller ranges. The road courses just below the ridge of the world, where jagged peaks dominate the sky, with valleys spread below, flat and broad. There are alpine meadows wild with flowers and aspen trees palsied in the wind.

SIGHTS

The route cuts through **Monitor Pass**, an 8300-foot plateau across which early pioneers and gold seekers once trekked. Today it is unchanged, tufted with grass, like an elevated prairie. Then the highway dives into boulder-strewn defiles, along rumbling rivers with white water like lace. There are tiny towns along the way—Topaz, Coleville, and Bridgeport—plus an occasional rest area.

◄ HIDDEN

Seven miles south of Bridgeport and 13 miles east (three of which are along a pothole-studded dirt road), **Bodie State Historic Park** rests like a kind of woodframe time capsule in a high-desert setting. One of the West's finest ghost towns, this 1880 boom center, once home to 10,000 people, is now an outdoor museum complete with the houses, taverns, stores, and churches of a bygone era. Because of unmaintained roads, the park is usually inaccessible during winter. Admission. ~ 619-647-6445.

In the mountains high above Yosemite, Route 395 arrives at **Mono Lake**, one of California's strangest and most controversial spots. Located along the western edge of the Great Basin, it's a saline-alkaline body of water, the remnant of a prehistoric inland sea. At first glance it seems eerie and forbidding, an alien place with weird stalagmite-like formations that resemble a moonscape.

Actually, those spire-shaped figures are "tufa" towers, composed of calcite and formed by the confluence of fresh-water springs and salt water. Many have taken the form of delicate statuary, rising like minarets and rock candy mountains from the surface. They create a provocative landscape of bone-white rock against turquoise water.

The reason these underwater fossils are presently above the lake surface is the key to a bitter environmental controversy. For over five decades the distant city of Los Angeles has been draining water from streams feeding the lake. Together with natural evaporation, that action dropped the lake level about 40 feet and doubled salinity.

Since Mono Lake breeds brine shrimp and brine flies, favored food for gulls, it is home to the state's largest nesting gull population. Grebes and phalaropes also gather in great numbers. Their habitat has been threatened because the drain-off has killed the brine shrimp. In 1994, the State Water Board intervened, declaring that water diversion must decrease. As a result, the water level is steadily rising for the first time in 50 years. Thirsty Los Angeles will continue to divert a small amount of water but hopefully Mono Lake will reach a stabilization level in 20 to 30 years. However, the future of this surreal and beautiful lake still hangs in the balance since the Water Board's decision could be appealed. ~ Route 395; 619-647-3044.

The Mono Craters, south of the lake, represent the youngest mountain range in North America.

Just beyond Mono Lake, Route 395 meets Route 120, along the backside of Yosemite. Before entering the Park, the road cuts through **Inyo National Forest**, where jagged peaks angle upwards so sharply they seem like fortress walls. Below the road, other cliffs dive into gorges of granite and swirling water. The waterfalls cutting into these rockfaces have worked at the granite for thousands of years, barely chiseling a bed.

The road spirals up through **Tioga Pass** (9941 feet) and streams past **Ellery Lake**, an alpine crystal set at 9523 feet. Then it begins a steady descent into one of the country's prettiest parks—Yosemite.

LODGING

Set high in the Sierras, just off a highway, there is a perfect mountain facility called **Sorensen's**. The 29 cabins (including eight log cabins) are scattered among a grove of aspen trees and look out upon rugged granite heights. Most are efficiency units, complete with kitchen facilities and everything you need for a few secluded days in the hills. Nicely remodeled and decorated with wallhangings, they have a rustic charm. Two cabins feature fireplaces and private decks, and one has a hot tub. This is also an excellent locale for hiking and cross-country skiing. ~ Route 88, Hope Valley; 916-694-2203, 800-423-9949. MODERATE TO ULTRA-DELUXE.

Caples Lake Resort is another alpine jewel. Set on a sparkling lake at 7800 feet, it features a lodge with a restaurant and seven individual cabins. There are fishing and boating facilities available, and the resort is also favored by skiers. Rooms in the lodge are somewhat plain, but they are neat and clean. And the views of lake and mountains are extraordinary. The cabins are much nicer: they lack wall decorations, but are adequately furnished and have complete kitchen units (plus those oh so outrageous views). ~ Route 88, Kirkwood; 209-258-8888, fax 209-258-8898. MODERATE TO DELUXE.

Deep in the mountains seems hardly the place to find a historic hotel. But there it is, **Bridgeport Inn**, contained in a century-old white-shingle building. Add a valley setting surrounded by snowy peaks and it becomes an even more remarkable establishment.

Downstairs there is a white-linen dining room, as well as a parlor with chandelier and granddaddy wood stove. For some unfortunate and inexplicable reason, the guest rooms, rather than being upstairs in this vintage structure, are located in an adjacent motel-type unit. As a result the accommodations are sterile and disappointing. The hotel is open from March 1 to January 1. ~ 205 Main Street, Bridgeport; 619-932-7380. MODERATE.

Situated at 9600 feet, directly above Yosemite National Park, is **Tioga Pass Resort.** With ten log cabins, four motel rooms, a restaurant, and other facilities, this is a perfect jumping-off place for the adventure-minded. The resort is surrounded by Inyo National Forest, providing ample opportunity for trout fishing, hiking, boating, and cross-country skiing during the winter. The cabins come complete with kitchens and are rented on a weekly basis. There are also motel units that are rented nightly. This resort's proximity to Yosemite makes it extremely popular, so book your reservations early. Open from mid-May to mid-October. ~ P.O. Box 7, Route 120, Lee Vining; 209-372-4471. BUDGET TO MODERATE.

DINING

High in the Sierras, out in the no man's land between Lake Tahoe and Yosemite, there's a waterfront restaurant at **Caples Lakes Resort.** Serving dinner Thursday through Sunday, this eatery is a favorite among mountain-bound adventurers. The menu ranges from steak to seafood to daily specials. ~ Route 88, Kirkwood; 209-258-8888. MODERATE.

◄ HIDDEN

Restaurants are rare and far between along Route 395. There is a homey café en route, **Meadowcliff.** The folks hereabouts serve hamburgers and chili at lunch. Dinner features an array of Mexican dishes, and breakfast is available too. The food's good, which is mighty fortunate, since this is the only game around. ~ Route 395, Coleville; 916-495-2180. BUDGET TO MODERATE.

Bridgeport Inn, set in a century-old house, contains a very attractive dining room. With its ceiling fans and antique wall fixtures, the place radiates a congenial atmosphere. The dinner menu, offering prime rib, veal chops, lobster, and catch-of-the-day, is deluxe in price, but breakfasts and lunches here are fairly inexpensive. Closed January and February. ~ Main Street, Bridgeport; 619-932-7380. DELUXE.

Way up behind Yosemite, more than 5000 feet above the valley, there's a friendly restaurant at **Tioga Pass Resort.** Serving three meals daily, this mountain retreat features a menu ranging from sandwiches to homemade chili to hearty full-course dinners with delicious homemade desserts. It's particularly welcome for travelers heading from the High Sierra down to Yosemite. ~ Route 120, Lee Vining; 209-372-4471. BUDGET.

PARKS

TOIYABE NATIONAL FOREST This is the biggest national forest in the lower 48 states. Its 600,000 High Sierra acres reach from Lake Tahoe to Mono Lake and extend across the California border into Nevada. Routes 89 and 395, the main High Sierra roads between Lake Tahoe and Yosemite, traverse the heart of Toiyabe. In addition to alpine meadows and rugged mountain peaks, it contains coniferous forests inhabited by deer, black bear, porcupine, and mountain lion. There are numerous hiking trails and trout streams. Skiing, canoeing, and rafting are also popular here. Permits are required for backpacking. Facilities include picnic areas and restrooms; restaurants and groceries are available in towns scattered along the highways. ~ The easiest access is along Routes 89 and 395, south of Lake Tahoe. For information, contact the Bridgeport Ranger District at Route 395, Bridgeport; 619-932-7070.

▲ There are 38 campgrounds; $7 to $8 per night.

GROVER HOT SPRINGS STATE PARK Set in a mountain meadow and backdropped by 8000-foot peaks, this 650-acre park is a lovely sight. The Toiyabe National Forest and Carson Iceberg Wilderness Area completely surround it; hiking trails lead from the park to lakes and other points throughout the forest. There is fishing for rainbow and cutthroat trout. The central attractions, however, are the springs. Water from underground springs bubbles up at 148° and is cooled to an inviting 101° to 104° for the park's hot bath. This, together with a swimming pool, is situated in the meadow and open to the public. If you long for an outdoor hot tub in an alpine setting, this is the ticket. Other facilities include picnic areas, restrooms, and showers. Day-use fee, $5. ~ Located off Route 89, about four miles from Markleeville; 916-694-2248.

▲ There are 76 sites (20 winter sites) in two campgrounds within walking distance of the pools. Campgrounds require reservations from about May 15 to Labor Day; during the rest of the year sites are on a first-come, first-served basis; $14 per night.

INYO NATIONAL FOREST Part of this sprawling facility lies along both Route 395, near Mono Lake, and Route 120, directly above Yosemite. Within this section of Inyo are several excellent campgrounds that have picnic areas and restrooms. There are also lakes and streams for fishing. ~ Easiest access is along Routes 395 and 120. For information, contact the Lee Vining Ranger District at Route 120, Lee Vining; 619-647-3000.

▲ Permitted in 90 campgrounds. Particularly recommended are Tioga Lake Campground and Ellery Lake Campground, both are along Route 120 directly above Yosemite. They're situated on lovely alpine lakes; $8 a night.

Yosemite National Park

It is a national institution, one of America's foremost playgrounds, a spectacular park climbing across the Sierra Nevada from 2000 feet elevation to a dizzying 13,000 feet—Yosemite. Within its domain is a valley whose sheer granite cliffs have been carved by the cold blade of a glacier. It's a region of bald domes, sunshot waterfalls, and stately sequoias. At the lower elevations are broad mountain meadows browsed by deer. During summer the place riots with wildflowers; in winter it's cloaked in snow.

SIGHTS

Center of this natural wonderland is **Yosemite Valley**. Formed about two million years ago, this Sierra canyon has a flat meadow floor surrounded by vertical precipices. It seems that glacial action tore away softer sections of granite, leaving the more durable rocks like El Capitan and Half Dome.

For thousands of years, the Ahwahneechee and other Indians inhabited the valley. After its "discovery" by whites in the 19th century, the region became a curiosity point for tourists. To protect the place, President Lincoln in 1864 declared Yosemite Valley and the Mariposa Grove to be public parks. Several years later, John Muir, a Scottish naturalist, moved to Yosemite and began a campaign to further protect the natural environment by having it declared a national park. In 1890 his efforts succeeded.

The valley which Muir saved must be experienced; it cannot adequately be described. It was once a massive lake fed by the glaciers that created the surrounding cliffs. Erosion and stream sediment eventually filled it, creating fields rich in vegetation.

Above the valley bed, vertical cliffs extend on either side to the limit of sight. In the far distance rises **Clouds Rest**, at 9926 feet the highest mountain visible from the valley. In front of that stands **Half Dome**, a monstrous rock which appears to have been cleft in two by the hand of God, leaving a sheer wall 2200 feet straight up. There is **Mirror Meadow Lake**, a mountain jewel named for the peaks reflected in its gleaming waters, and **Royal Arches**, granite shells that have been formed into great arcs by time and glaciation.

Before them looms **Sentinel Rock**, last remnant of a mammoth block of granite, the rest of which has been cracked and dumped into the valley. It's named for its resemblance to a watchtower, while **Leaning Tower** gains its name from the rock's disconcerting tilt.

There are the **Cathedral Spires**, granite shafts rising about 2000 feet above the floor; **Three Brothers**, imposing forms honoring the three sons of Yosemite's greatest Indian chief; and **Yosemite Falls**, among the world's tallest waterfalls, tumbling 2425 feet in three dramatic cascades.

King of Kings among these grand geologic formations is **El Capitan**. It might well be the largest exposed monolith on earth, for this hard granite giant measures twice the size of the Rock of

Gibraltar. Composed of several types of granite, its sheer cliff rises over 3000 feet from the valley floor. Solitary and unshakable, it seems to peer down upon the human antics occurring far below.

For Yosemite Valley is generally a beehive of activity. The busiest spot of all is **Yosemite Village**, a cluster of buildings and shops along the northern wall of the valley. The visitors center keystones the complex. In addition to an information desk, the center hosts a photographic display of the valley and a regionally oriented bookstore. ~ 209-372-0299.

Next door is the building housing the **Indian Cultural Museum** with exhibits illustrating the cultures of the Miwok and Paiute peoples who once inhabited the area. The museum gallery has rotating exhibits on Yosemite Valley. Directly behind the museum spreads a mock village complete with bark dwellings called *umachas* and earth-covered houses.

Also within Yosemite Village is a shop selling prints by the great photographer Ansel Adams, whose shots of the valley are renowned for their beauty and mystery. There's an art center nearby, as well as a post office, gift shop, grocery, and restaurants.

Summer, holidays, and weekends are particularly crowded in Yosemite Valley. In recent years the place has sometimes assumed the quality of a human zoo, with traffic jams and long lines. If possible, it's best to visit during the week or in the off-season. Also consider walking, bicycling, or using the free shuttle service around the valley; it will save you a headache and help cut down on the traffic flow.

Something else to remember: Yosemite Valley covers seven square miles, and everyone seems intent on crowding into its confines. For good reason—the valley is an extraordinary sight and must not be missed. But there are 1200 square miles of Yosemite National Park, many of them hardly touched by visitors. These outer reaches also possess singular beauty and should be part of your itinerary.

Plan to visit the High Sierra country above the valley by following Route 120, Tioga Road, in its eastward climb toward the top of the mountain range. This road is closed during snowy months, but in periods of warm weather it leads past splendid alpine regions with meadows, lakes, and stark peaks.

At about 7000 feet, it passes a virgin stand of red fir, then continues up to **White Wolf**. The lodge here provides cabins, a campground, and a restaurant. Past this enclave a spectacular view of the **Clark Range** is revealed; then the road passes a grove of quaking aspen.

Olmstead Point has a short trail leading to a granite dome which looks down toward the north side of Half Dome and up to

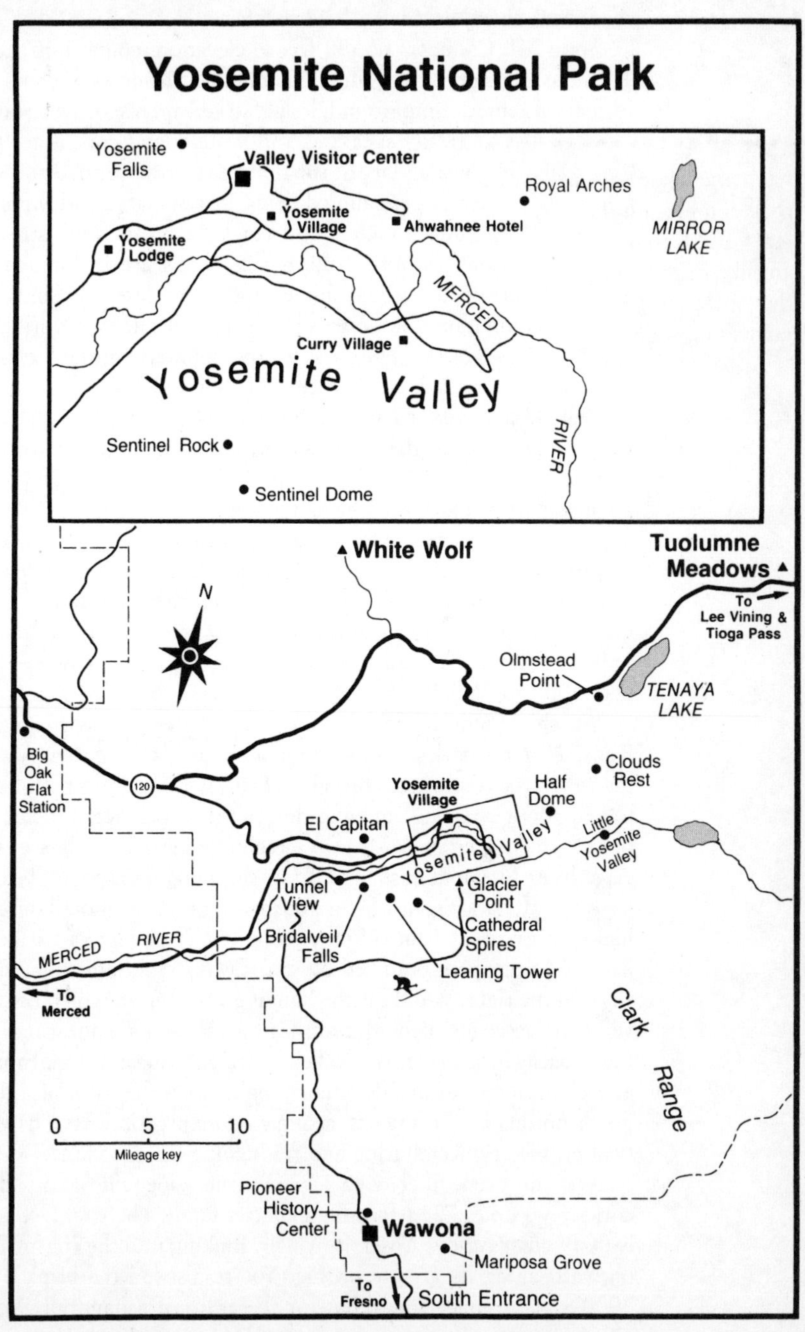
Yosemite National Park
Yosemite Falls
Valley Visitor Center
Royal Arches
Yosemite Village
Ahwahnee Hotel
MIRROR LAKE
Yosemite Lodge
MERCED
Curry Village
Yosemite Valley
RIVER
Sentinel Rock
Sentinel Dome
White Wolf
Tuolumne Meadows
To Lee Vining & Tioga Pass
N
Olmstead Point
TENAYA LAKE
Big Oak Flat Station
120
Clouds Rest
Yosemite Village
Half Dome
El Capitan
Little Yosemite Valley
Yosemite Valley
Tunnel View
Glacier Point
Cathedral Spires
Bridalveil Falls
MERCED RIVER
Leaning Tower
To Merced
Clark Range
0 5 10
Mileage key
Pioneer History Center
Wawona
Mariposa Grove
To Fresno
South Entrance

Tenaya Lake. This long, slender body of water, set at 8149 feet, is shadowed on either side by bald rockfaces.

Soon **Mt. Conness,** 12,590 feet in elevation, comes into view. Then the highlight of the journey, **Tuolumne Meadows,** with its information center, campground, lodge, store, and restaurant. Statistically speaking, this wonderland constitutes the Sierra's largest subalpine meadow. Located at 8600 feet, its sunglinted fields are populated with smooth granite boulders and cut by a meandering stream. Conifers border the meadow and are in turn backdropped by bald domes and sharp faces. In summer, mountain wildflowers carpet the hillsides with brilliant shades of red, blue, and yellow, counterpointing the hard gray rocks with gentle forms and soft colors.

Keep a keen eye open for rock climbers on the face of El Capitan—ant-like in proportion, they inch along its unyielding walls.

Beyond is **Lembert Dome,** a lopsided peak carved by glaciers. Glittering patches of glacial polish can still be seen along the dome surface. **Mount Dana** (13,053 feet) and **Mount Gibbs** (12,764 feet) are also part of this incredible landscape.

Then the road rises into **Tioga Pass.** Constructed at 9941 feet, this roadway marks the highest automobile pass in California. It is also the gateway to Mono Lake, and to other mountain roads. On these you can travel north to Oregon, south toward Death Valley, or turn around and return to that extraordinary valley now over 5000 feet below.

Another interesting trip from Yosemite Valley carries you along Route 41 to the park's southwestern boundary. Shortly after leaving the valley, the road passes **Bridalveil Falls,** where a short path leads to a 620-foot cascade. Tumbling along a sharp rockface, buffeted by breezes, the waterfall twists into intaglio designs. The edges of the cascade are blown to mist and fall like soft rain on the people below.

Soon afterwards, just before burrowing into the mountain, the highway arrives at **Tunnel View.** From here, Yosemite Valley looks like God's playpen, bounded by sharp walls and domed in azure sky. On the right, you'll see the hanging valley from which Bridalveil Falls descends. Behind it are Cathedral Rocks, appearing like hunchbacks bent to meet the valley. Sentinel Dome is a stone rapier, and Half Dome, from this unique angle, takes the form of a dolphin's bottlenose. To the left, a single figure predominates, its vertical profile at once alluring and frightening—El Capitan.

For an even finer view, follow the long side road that corkscrews up to 7214-foot-high **Glacier Point.** The vital fact here is that you are *above* Yosemite Valley, looking into the chasm and outward along its granite profile. You're also on the brink of a 3000-foot precipice (there but for the grace of a handrail go we all). Gaze out and you'll see that Half Dome now has transformed into a bird's head. Across the valley a two-tiered cascade, Upper and Lower Yosemite Falls, tumbles thousands of feet. This is the most spectacular of all Yosemite viewpoints, with the High Sierra stretching along a limitless series of snowcapped peaks. Below, the Merced River meanders past camps and hotels deep in Yosemite Valley. Glacier Point is open only during the summer.

The main road continues through miles of tall, cool forest to Wawona, a small settlement in the park's southwest corner. Here, just past an old covered bridge, is the **Pioneer Yosemite History Center**. There are log cabins and houses dating back well into the 19th century, plus a blacksmith shop and Wells Fargo Office. This intriguing outdoor museum also features a collection of wagons and buckboards.

Beyond, near the park's south entrance, rises **Mariposa Grove**. Most impressive of Yosemite's three giant sequoia groves, it can be reached by tram or along a two-and-a-half mile trail. Within the grove stands Grizzly Giant, a 2700-year-old forest denizen. Giant sequoias, the world's largest living things, often weigh more than two million pounds. Within this grove are about 200 trees measuring over ten feet in diameter. Unlike redwoods, which hug the cool, moist coastal areas, sequoias flourish between 5000 and 8000 feet in sunny climates. Here in the cathedral silence of the grove, these forest giants number not only among the earth's biggest life forms, but its most regal as well.

LODGING

Accommodations in Yosemite are varied, plentiful, and, paradoxically, difficult to reserve. About three million people a year pour through the Park's granite arches, many in search of a place to rest their wonder-struck heads. As a result, the park provides several locations with facilities ranging from canvas tents to cabins to cottages to hotel rooms to deluxe suites.

Still it is not enough. Particularly during the summer months, facilities are booked far in advance. Matter of fact, it's not a bad idea to make reservations the year before your arrival. During the colder months the situation eases: even then, however, weekends, holidays, or good skiing snow can draw summer-size crowds back to the park. To make your reservations, contact **Yosemite Reservations, Yosemite Concession Services.** ~ 5410 East Home Avenue, Fresno, CA 93727; 209-252-4848.

Most facilities are located right in the valley—at the Yosemite Lodge, Curry Village, and the Ahwahnee Hotel. Others—Tuolumne Meadows, White Wolf, and Wawona—are situated in distant parts of the park and offer retreats from the crowds in the valley. Prices quoted below are summer rates; during the week in winter, rates are sometimes significantly lower.

Yosemite Lodge hosts several styles of accommodations. Foremost are the lodge rooms; these are motel-type affairs in a series of low-slung buildings near the central lodge facility. One I stayed in was nicely furnished in oak, modern in design, spacious, and quite comfortable. It had a telephone but no television, and enjoyed a private patio looking out upon a pine grove. Deer browsed 20 feet from the window. There are also cabins available, small but cozy duplex units with private bath. These lack wall decorations, but are adequately furnished and carpeted wall-to-wall. The "cottage rooms," contained in multi-unit buildings nearby, are more spacious and slightly upscale. ~ MODERATE TO DELUXE.

Over at **Curry Village**, in a nearby section of the valley, cabins are available at the same prices. Hotel rooms here have natural wood furnishings and stall showers. The wall decorations are tastefully selected and some rooms have lofts providing extra sleeping areas. The village also contains "canvas tent cabins," which provide an excellent means to visit Yosemite at an inexpensive price. They're wall tents on raised wooden platforms, with mosquito nets, windows, and canvas flaps for privacy. Furnishings include beds with complete bedding, plus time-battered shelves; basic but sufficient. People staying in any Curry facility have access to the sitting room, swimming pool, shops, and restaurants on the premises. ~ BUDGET TO MODERATE.

Yosemite provides the opportunity to bivouac in a flowering meadow, sleep in a pine forest, or rest yards away from the world's greatest geologic wonders. Nowhere, though, are the accommodations as grand and dramatic as at the **Ahwahnee Hotel**. Built in 1927, the place is an architectural marvel, a multitiered building of wood and stone back-dropped by rain-fluted cliffs. Its manicured lawns and natural arbors place it among world-class hotels. The high-ceilinged interior is decorated after American Indian designs with intricate rugs and patterned glass. There are grand fireplaces large enough to stand inside and chandeliers that belong in a castle. Befitting the rest of the hotel, the bedrooms are spacious affairs decorated in the same motif. Even if you decide not to stay here at least plan to tour the hotel. It's a singular feature in an extraordinary park. ~ 209-372-1489, fax 209-372-1463. ULTRA-DELUXE.

Tuolumne Meadows Lodge, nestled along Route 120 at 8600 feet, has tent cabins available. These are similar to the facilities in

A SHOT OF SOUTHERN COMFORT

In Yosemite National Park's southwest corner is the **Wawona Hotel**. Its rolling lawn and white-pillared building make this century-old establishment a vision of the Old South. Indeed, the pace here is much slower, and the living easier, than in Yosemite Valley. There's a nine-hole golf course, tennis court, inviting swimming pool, and a covey of ivy-clad cottages. Rooms in this glorious old place often contain brass beds. Several share a bath (clawfoot tubs, as a matter of fact). ~ 209-375-6556. MODERATE.

the valley, consisting of a bed, complete bedding, sparse furnishings, and, to warm those chilly mountain nights, a wood stove. The experience here is somewhere between hotel living and camping; bathrooms and showers are shared. The nearby lodge contains a dining room and lobby available to tent sleepers. The entire complex sits in a beautiful meadow bounded by thick forest. Idyllic and easy. Closed during winter and early spring. ~ BUDGET.

White Wolf Lodge, located midway between Yosemite Valley and Tuolumne Meadows at 7700 feet, also has tent cabins as well as wood cabins with private baths. With its dining room, stables, and nearby hiking trails, it makes a great escape hatch. Closed during winter and early spring. ~ BUDGET TO MODERATE.

Or try the nearby **Redwoods Cottages**, a privately owned facility within the park. Here are cabins set in the woods just off a side road. Accommodations range from one- to six-bedroom facilities and feature living rooms, fireplaces, and patios. ~ Box 2085, Wawona Station; 209-375-6666, fax 209-375-6400. MODERATE TO ULTRA-DELUXE.

One of the great frustrations of visiting Yosemite National Park is landing a reservation at the often sold-out Ahwahnee Hotel. Now **Tenaya Lodge at Yosemite** offers 242 rooms near the park's southern entrance. The hotel has a spacious lobby decorated with American Indian art, nicely landscaped grounds, indoor and outdoor pools with jacuzzis, and a variety of recreational programs centered around the park. The resort-style lodge also offers a bar and lounge and an exercise room. The only drawback is the 45-minute trip down to the Yosemite Valley floor. ~ 1122 Route 41, Fish Camp; 209-683-6555, 800-635-5807, fax 209-683-6147. ULTRA-DELUXE.

DINING

Yosemite Village, at the northern edge of the valley, provides three dining possibilities. In addition to **Degnen's Delicatessen** and a **pizzeria** (both, by definition, budget-priced), there's an informal dining room called **Degnen's Pasta Place.** Dominated by a mammoth fireplace, this restaurant boasts a daily buffet with an assortment of fresh pasta. The lunchtime menu includes hamburgers and sandwiches, soups and salads. Closed during winter. ~ BUDGET.

Over at Yosemite Lodge there are three more restaurants, providing a fuller array of dining possibilities. It doesn't take much imagination to picture the **cafeteria**, serving steam-tray food at low, low prices. Though the meals sometimes sit too long above the steam, and the dining hall is cavernous and impersonal, this is a place for anyone who believes that a full stomach shouldn't mean an empty wallet. ~ BUDGET.

The nearby **Four Seasons Restaurant** provides a step upscale to a large but comfortable dining room. An exposed-beam ceiling adds a touch of class to the surroundings, where both breakfast and dinner are served. Breakfast dishes are pretty standard; at dinner the Four Seasons features chicken hunter stew, Pacific red snapper, and roast pork loin, as well as less expensive items such as vegetarian stir-fry and barbecue chicken. ~ MODERATE.

The **Mountain Broiler** is yet another step heavenward. Smaller and more intimate than its neighbors, this dining room also hosts an outdoor patio. The interior is dominated by a striking photo of a rock climber dangling upside down from a granite cliff. At the tables outside, the scene is highlighted by the actual rockfaces that draw such climbers from around the world. All of which is enough to make you forget the menu. To refresh your memory, they serve steak, steak, and steak—as in sirloin, prime rib, filet mignon, and New York cut. Or try the broiled salmon, rainbow trout, and breast of chicken. Sorry, dinner only. ~ DELUXE.

Curry Village features two dining places, a hamburger stand called the **Meadow Deck** and **Curry Dining Pavilion**. The latter, open for breakfast and dinner, is another of the park's best restaurant bargains. It's large, impersonal, and cafeteria-style, but dinners here—like beef stew, ham steak, lasagna, or rainbow trout—are cheap. Closed during winter. ~ BUDGET.

For special occasions, or just a personal indulgence, there's the **Ahwahnee Dining Room**. An entire wing of this grand old hotel is dedicated to the fine art of dining. Part of the experience simply involves sitting in the dining room, a high-ceilinged affair with exposed-log beams. The interior is fashioned of stone and glass, with wood-paneled sections painted in American Indian designs. Service is impeccable. The breakfast menu is standard; lunch includes entrées like chicken pot pie, eggplant marinara, pork cutlet, and fish. There are also omelettes, salads, and sandwiches. Dinner is the hotel's premier meal. Appetizers alone range from chilled artichoke to creamed herring to Dungeness crab cake. Entrées include duck à l'orange, prime rib, veal marsala, poached salmon, and grilled lamb, to name a few. Dining here is an experience unto itself. Reservations required; dress code. ~ 209-372-1489. DELUXE.

Scattered around the various corners of this expansive park are several other restaurants. Outside the valley, up on Route 120, there's a dining facility at **White Wolf Lodge**. Further up the highway, you'll encounter **Tuolumne Meadows Lodge**, a mountain hideaway with a surprisingly sophisticated cuisine. The dining room features mountain brook trout, Cajun steak, a vegetarian plate, liver, pasta, and prime rib. They also serve hearty breakfasts, but no lunch. Reservations required for dinner. ~ MODERATE.

Then over at Wawona, located in the park's southwest corner, is the **Wawona Hotel**. An old establishment in the style of the deep South, this splendid place contains a white-linen dining room that overlooks manicured lawns. Decorated with antique photos of Yosemite and illuminated by hooded lamps, it's a regal affair. In addition to breakfast, they feature a lunch buffet. Dinner presents baked polenta, trout, roast loin of pork with plum sauce, baked scallops, or filet mignon. Such good food and elegant surroundings are hard to match out here deep in the forest. ~ 209-375-6556. MODERATE.

NIGHTLIFE

In Yosemite National Park, the **Mountain Room Bar** at Yosemite Lodge is a spacious, oak-paneled lounge complete with fireplace. The perfect spot for a late-night brandy, the room is walled-in glass and looks out toward Yosemite Falls. Over at the beautiful Ahwahnee Hotel, you'll encounter the intimate **Indian Room Bar**, a plushly appointed drinking place.

PARKS

YOSEMITE NATIONAL PARK One of the country's most extraordinary and renowned parks, this 748,000-acre giant offers every activity from sightseeing a spectacular glacial valley to skiing alpine meadows. About 90 percent of the park has been targeted for wilderness status. Its domain spreads from 2000 to 13,000 feet, climbing from the foothills to the roof of the Sierra. Since its features are so extensive, Yosemite is discussed at length in most other sections of this chapter, so consult them for details. Among the many facilities in Yosemite are hotels, restaurants, stores, museums, shuttle service, organized nature programs, information centers, picnic areas, restrooms, showers, a ski area, almost 800 miles of hiking trails, stables, and more than 600 miles of riding trails. Day-use fee, $5. ~ Located along Routes 120, 140, and 41 about 200 miles southeast of San Francisco; 209-372-0299. For information on weather, road conditions, and campground status, call 209-372-0200.

▲ Permitted in campgrounds in Yosemite Valley and throughout the park ($14 fee in Yosemite Valley). There is a seven-day limit in the valley during the summer, fourteen days in other areas. Reservations are a must during the summer, since the park's 2161 sites are in great demand. At other times of the year, campsites are on a first-come, first-served basis (though in Yosemite Valley reservations are necessary year round). Reservations can be made with DESTINET; 800-436-7275. Wilderness permits are required for back country camping; these are available at the Yosemite Valley visitors center, and in Big Oak Flat, Yosemite Valley Wilderness Center, Tuolumne Meadows, and Wawona.

There are also five High Sierra camps with dormitory tents and dining facilities. Spaced about seven miles apart and open during the summer, these are ideal for hikers exploring the high country. Fees are about $58 per person daily for two meals, lodging, and use of showers; or $24 for meals only. Contact High Sierra Reservations, Yosemite Concession Services, 5410 East Home Avenue, Fresno, CA 93727; 209-252-4848.

Outdoor Adventures

Pick almost any lake or river in the Gold Country and High Sierra, bait a hook, and you're bound to come up with trout for dinner.

SPORT-FISHING

SACRAMENTO In Sacramento, contact **Sacramento Sport Fishing Guides.** ~ 1531 Wyant Way, Sacramento; 916-487-3392.

LAKE TAHOE AREA One of Lake Tahoe area's best bets is **Tahoe Sport Fishing.** ~ 900 Ski Run Boulevard, South Lake Tahoe; 916-541-5448.

WATER SPORTS

From rafting and waterskiing on the American and Sacramento rivers to sailing and windsurfing on Lake Tahoe, the Gold Country and High Sierra are prime places for watersports.

SACRAMENTO For sailboards, kayaks, and rafts, contact **American River Rafting.** ~ 11257 South Bridge Street, Rancho Cordova, 95670.

LAKE TAHOE *The* place for recreational boating, including sailing, canoeing, ski boating, and board sailing, is Lake Tahoe. For boat rentals, contact **Richardson's Resort Marina.** ~ Jameson Beach Road, Camp Richardson; 916-542-6570. For boat, jetski, and waterski rentals, call **High Sierra Marina.** ~ 1850 West Lake Boulevard, Tahoe City; 916-581-2628.

WHITE-WATER RAFTING

Another river sport combines spectacular scenery with high adventure —whitewater rafting.

SACRAMENTO In the Sacramento area, check out **American River Recreation**, which offers runs on the American, Klamath, and Merced rivers. ~ 11257 South Bridge Street, Rancho Cordova; 916-622-6802.

CENTRAL GOLD COUNTRY In the Gold Country, contact **Chili Bar Outdoor Center** for a full swinging outdoor adventure on the American River. ~ P.O. Box 554, Coloma, CA 95613; 916-621-1236. **ABLE and Beyond Limits Adventure Tours** provides one- and two-day trips on various rivers throughout the region. ~ P.O. Box 215, Riverbank, CA 95367; 916-626-6208. **Zephyr River Expeditions** offers guided tours of the Tuolumne, Stanislaus, Kings, Merced, and American rivers. ~ P.O. Box 510, Columbia, CA 95310; 209-532-6249.

LAKE TAHOE AREA Call **Mountain Air Sports** for a family ride on the gentle Truckee River. ~ 205 River Road, Tahoe City; 916-583-5606.

ROCK CLIMBING

Ready to scale a sheer granite cliff? Then Yosemite National Park is your playground. Lessons and guides are available at **Yosemite Mountaineering and Cross-Country Ski School.** ~ Badger Pass, Yosemite National Park; 209-372-1244.

BALLOON RIDES

A hot air balloon may not get you there sooner, but it will carry you higher while offering spectacular views of Sacramento's rich farm country.

SACRAMENTO Just contact **Mountain Air Balloon Adventures.** ~ 1147 Brunswick Way, Sacramento; 916-348-8778.

LAKE TAHOE AREA For a flight above the Sierra and Lake Tahoe areas, call **Mountain High Balloons.** ~ Truckee; 916-587-6922.

GOLD PANNING

If sifting dirt along cold mountain streams sounds like fun, try your luck panning for gold. You may not strike it rich, but then again, who knows?

SOUTHERN GOLD COUNTRY **Gold Prospecting Expeditions** will take you to their own private 1849 gold mining camp. You'll find Mark Twain's cabin and Sutter's mill as well as original pistols, lanterns, and flumes used during that serendipitous era. ~ 18170 Main Street, Jamestown; 209-984-4653.

CENTRAL GOLD COUNTRY **Roaring Camp Mining Co.** is the place to contact for daily guided tours along the Mokelumne River. They also have cabins where you can vacation while seeking out your fortune. ~ P.O. Box 278, Pine Grove, CA 95665; 209-296-4100. **Gold Country Prospecting** provides equipment and lessons. ~ 3119 Turner Street, Placerville; 916-622-2484.

SKIING

You don't have to be an Olympic medal winner to ski the Sierra, but you might run into one on the slopes.

LAKE TAHOE AREA **Alpine Meadows** is a skiers paradise with 12 skilifts and more than 100 runs. ~ 2600 Alpine Meadows Road, Tahoe City; 916-583-4232.

With 8 chairlifts and 55 ski runs, **Sugar Bowl** has 1100 acres of skiable terrain. ~ Norden; 916-426-3651.

Nestled in the High Sierra amidst 8000 acres of wilderness preserve, **Squaw Valley** boasts 34 chairlifts, 6 mountain peaks, and a 2850-foot vertical drop. ~ Olympic Valley; 916-583-6985.

Located six miles south of Tahoe City, **Ski Homewood** features 8 chairlifts, 57 runs, and a 1650-foot vertical drop. ~ 5145 West Lake Boulevard, Homewood; 916-525-2992.

For 4800 acres of pure white powder, head on over to **Heavenly Ski Resort**, where hotels, restaurants, and day lodges round out the amenities. ~ Corner of Wildwood and Saddle, South Lake Tahoe; 916-541-1330.

Located in a lovely alpine valley, **Kirkwood Ski Resort** sports 2300 acres of skiable terrain along with a 2000-foot vertical drop. ~ 1501 Kirkwood Meadows Drive, Kirkwood; 209-258-6000.

Cross-country skiers can contact **Royal Gorge**, which encompasses 9172 acres of skiable terrain. ~ 9411 Pahatsi Road, Soda

Text continued on page 428.

Ski California

As a travel destination, California offers everything. Even during winter, when rain spatters the coast and fog invades the valleys, the Golden State has one more treat in its bottomless bag—snow.

No sooner has the white powder settled than skiers from around the world beeline to the region's high altitude resort areas. They come to schuss through fir forests in the Cascades, challenge the runs above Lake Tahoe, and breathe the beauty of Yosemite at Christmas.

The season begins in late fall and sometimes lasts until May. During those frosty months dozens of ski areas offer both downhill and cross-country skiing. In the Far North, the **Shasta Cascade Wonderland Association** provides information on facilities. Here, 14,162-foot Mt. Shasta and 10,457-foot Mt. Lassen feature downhill skiing as well as miles of trackless wilderness. ~ 14250 Holiday Road, Redding, CA 96003; 916-275-5555.

The center of California skiing lies in the Sierra, where large resorts surround Lake Tahoe and extend south toward Yosemite National Park and beyond. Squaw Valley played host to the 1960 Winter Olympics and numerous other resorts have won plaudits from world-class skiers. With temperatures hovering between 20 and 40 and snowfall measuring 200 to 400 inches, the region is ideal for winter sports. The **California Ski Industry Association** has full information. ~ 74 New Montgomery Street, Suite 750, San Francisco, CA 94105; 415-543-7036.

Many resorts focus on downhill and alpine-style skiing and provide complete facilities for their athletic guests. Some, like **Squaw Valley**, are self-contained villages offering every facility imaginable. Such "G-rated" resorts often feature boutiques, galleries, pools, tennis courts, groceries, restaurants, and *après-ski* spots. There are instructors for beginners and intermediate skiers alike, snow school for children, and enough diversions to keep even a non-skier content. ~ Olympic Valley, CA 96146; 916-583-6985.

The more demanding nordic style of cross-country skiing is gaining increased popularity around the state. This is the adventurer's way to explore the slopes—fill a daypack, strap on skis, and take off across the mountains. In the pack are extra clothes, food, water, flashlight, knife, map, compass, blanket, matches, equipment repair tools, and a first-aid kit.

Unrestricted by ski lifts and marked runs, cross-country skiers venture everywhere that geography and gravity permit. Their sport is tantamount to hiking on skis, with the entire expanse of the Sierra Nevada their domain. Some skiers disappear into the wilderness for days on end, emerging only when supplies run low. Particularly favored by these explorers is Desolation Wilderness, a stark, glaciated region just west of Lake Tahoe.

If you prefer a base of operations from which to experience the wild, more than a dozen nordic ski centers operate extensive trail systems in the Tahoe region. **Royal Gorge Wilderness Lodge**, for instance, houses guests in a 60-year-old building formerly used by hunters. The thirty private rooms share baths and offer modern conveniences like heat, electricity, a sauna, and an outdoor hot tub. The lodge's chef specializes in French country cuisine.

Royal Gorge Lodge sits amid the largest network of cross-country trails in the nation. About 200 miles of groomed track and 83 trails extend in every direction, leading through forests of fir and lodgepole pine. There are frozen lakes to explore, extraordinary mountain vistas, and secluded warming huts where you can enjoy afternoon tea. ~ 9411 Pahatsi Road, Soda Springs, CA 95728; 916-426-3871.

Other nordic lodges offer moonlight tours through alpine meadows, overnight trips to backwoods cabins, cross-country races, and guided tours of the High Sierra. There are workshops in snow survival and winter photography. Or maybe you're ready for the Tahoe-version triathlon—six miles cross-country skiing, followed by twelve miles bicycling, six miles running, and finished off with a mere five miles kayaking along the Truckee River. What better time than winter to work up a sweat.

Springs; 916-426-3871. Or you can try the **Tahoe Nordic Ski Center.** ~ Tahoe City; 916-583-9353.

YOSEMITE NATIONAL PARK Located 22 miles from Yosemite Valley, **Badger Pass Ski Area** features three chairlifts, nine runs, and an 800-foot vertical drop. ~ Glacier Point Road, Yosemite National Park; 209-372-8430. For nordic skiing, contact the **Yosemite Mountaineering and Cross-Country Ski School.** ~ Badger Pass, Yosemite National Park; 209-372-1244.

For further information on both downhill and cross-country skiing, see the "Ski California" section in this chapter.

RIDING STABLES

Cantering through the parks of Sacramento or packing in to the Sierra wilderness . . . nothing brings you closer to the Old West than horseback riding.

SACRAMENTO For one- and two-hour trail rides through an oak-filled meadow near the American River, contact **Shadow Glen Riding Stables.** ~ 4854 Main Avenue, Fair Oaks; 916-989-1826.

CENTRAL GOLD COUNTRY In the Gold Country, try **Camanche North Shore Resort.** ~ Ione; 209-763-5295.

LAKE TAHOE AREA Around Lake Tahoe, call **Camp Richardson's Corral.** Their guided trips pass aspen, pine, and fir trees en route to Fallen Leaf Lake. ~ Emerald Bay Road, Camp Richardson; 916-541-3113. In the spring, **Alpine Meadows Stable** will take you on a ride through wildflower-filled meadows. ~ Alpine Meadows, Tahoe City; 916-583-3905.

YOSEMITE NATIONAL PARK **Yosemite National Park** has stables in the Valley, and at Wawona, and Tuolumne Meadows. Most of the Yosemite stables are closed during winter. ~ 209-372-1000.

LLAMA TREKS

For expeditions of another kind, consider **Sierra Llama Company.** This group provides tours of Tahoe National Forest, Yosemite, and other points of interest using traditional pack animals of Peru. ~ 13325 Peninsula Drive, Auburn; 916-269-2204.

BIKING

Exploring the Gold Country and High Sierra by bicycle can be an exhilarating experience. It's an area best toured by physically fit folks on ten-speed bikes. Almost all roads are open for bicycles, but heavy traffic, steep grades, and the high altitude make for an arduous journey. To enjoy touring this area, cyclists should plan their trips carefully, if possible scouting out the routes in advance.

SACRAMENTO The **Jedediah Smith Memorial Bicycle Trail** runs along the American River Parkway for 30 miles and is ideal for a family outing.

GOLD COUNTRY Auburn State Recreation Area offers over 100 miles of mountain bike trails. The two-mile **Stagecoach Trail** runs from Russell Road in Auburn to the old Foresthill Bridge on the north fork of the American River. For nine miles the **Old Lake Clementine Road** meanders along the American River. To ride past a creek through oak-and-pine-filled meadows, try the ten-mile **Olmstead Loop Trail.**

LAKE TAHOE When it comes to mountain biking few places can beat the Sierra Nevada. Some of the best off-road trails are found in **Tahoe National Forest.** At the park office you can pick up information on mountain biking trails throughout the region. ~ 631 Coyote Street, Nevada City; 916-265-4531.

Other trails in the area that are not in the national forest include the **Flume Trail** off Spooner Summit at the junction of Routes 50 and 28. It offers challenging rides of 10 to 30 miles. **Angora Lakes Trail** (12 miles) in the Fallen Leaf Lake area is another possibility. For more information contact **Tahoe Bike Shop.** Closed during winter. ~ 2277 Lake Tahoe Boulevard; 916-544-8060.

Another good bet is **Kirkwood Ski Area** 30 miles south of Lake Tahoe. This resort offers a mountain biking program in the summer months. There are 50 miles of trails within the Kirkwood property. Spring wildflower and fall foliage trips are highly recommended. ~ Route 88, Kirkwood; 209-258-6000. In addition the resort provides easy access to hundreds of miles of trails in the **El Dorado National Forest.** The easy **Kirkwood Meadow Loop** (6 miles) is a good way to get acclimated. If you're in great shape and feeling ambitious take the grueling **Mr. Toad's Wild Ride** off Luther Pass. This 35-mile trip runs from Kirkwood through Hope Valley to the Tahoe basin. Alternatively ride from Kirkwood to Hope Valley up Old Luther Pass Road to the Grass Lake area (40 miles). **Schneider Camp** (7 miles) is another enjoyable ride offering great views of Caples Lake. Remember, it takes a few days to adjust to the high altitude; also plan on drinking plenty of fluids.

YOSEMITE NATIONAL PARK There is a paved **loop trail** (8 miles), which circles the valley floor and takes you as far as Mirror Lake.

Bike Rentals For bike rentals and information in Sacramento, contact **American River Bicycle Center.** ~ 9203 Folsom Boulevard, Sacramento; 916-363-6271. In Auburn, try **Auburn Bike and Hike Shop** for rentals and repairs. ~ 1440 Canal Street; 916-885-3861. In Tahoe City, be sure to check out **Cycle Path Mountain Bikes.** Closed Monday and Tuesday. ~ 1785 West Lake Boulevard; 916-581-1171. At **Yosemite National Park,** try the bike shop at **Curry Village.** ~ 209-372-1200. There are also rentals available at the **Yosemite Lodge Bike Stand.** ~ 209-372-1208.

HIKING

The Gold Country and High Sierra represent two of nature's most magnificent contributions to Northern California. In the old mining territory you'll find groves of giant sequoias to explore. Then in the High Sierra, Lake Tahoe and Yosemite National Park offer networks of trails and Desolation Wilderness provides the closest wilderness area to San Francisco.

Little wonder that the **Pacific Crest Trail**, a 2600-mile path from Canada to Mexico, passes through the heart of this area. Traversing the Desolation Wilderness, it continues south to Yosemite, then follows the mountains past Mount Whitney into Southern California. While it's doubtful you'll be making the entire international trek, you might want to hike a short distance along this amazing trail.

CENTRAL GOLD COUNTRY Two trails wind through **Calaveras Big Trees State Park**'s ancient forest of giant sequoias. **North Grove Trail** (1 mile) is a gentle loop through a stand of sequoia, ponderosa, and sugar pine. Included along the way is **Three Senses Trail** (600 feet) where you can touch, smell, and hear the forest around you. **South Grove Trail** (3 miles), more remote and primitive, winds up Big Trees Creek past nearly one thousand giant sequoias.

NORTHERN GOLD COUNTRY Though formerly the site of one of the world's largest hydraulic mining operations, **Malakoff Diggins State Historic Park** has been partially healed by nature. About 15 miles of trails lead past mining era ruins, colorful pinnacles, minarets, and lakes created by the miners. **Blair Trail** (1.5 miles) is an easy hike on a tree-shaded path that ends at an old-time swimming hole. **Rim Trail** (3 miles), beginning at Shoot Hill Campground, leads to a vista point above the pond at the site of the diggings.

LAKE TAHOE AREA Donner Summit offers **Summit Lake Trail** (2 miles), located off Route 80 near the Donner Summit rest stop. It is an easy hike to Summit Lake through a conifer forest and flowering meadows.

Sandridge Lake Trail (6 miles) begins on the Pacific Crest Trail near Donner Summit and carries through pine and fir forests. It passes two alpine meadows en route to a small lake.

Because of its easy accessibility, **Desolation Wilderness** is extremely popular with daytrippers and campers alike. The number of backpackers is therefore held to a quota from June 15th to Labor Day, and a wilderness permit is required year-round of all who enter (for further information, consult Chapter One).

Mt. Tallac via Gilmore Lake Trail (5.7 miles) starts near Glen Alpine Creek and ends at Mt. Tallac Summit. From the summit, you'll have one of the region's most dramatic views of Lake Tahoe.

Pacific Crest Trail to Lake Aloha (3 miles) begins with a ride in a water taxi operated by Echo Lake Resort (information, 916-659-7207). The trail, one of the most heavily traveled in Desolation Wilderness, leads to sparkling mountain lakes.

Tahoe–Yosemite Trail to Rubicon Lake (7 miles) starts near Meeks Bay Resort and follows the northern part of lengthy Tahoe–Yosemite Trail to glimmering Rubicon Lake.

Bay View Trail to Velma Lake (5 miles) offers some stunning views of Lake Tahoe.

Glen Alpine to Lake Aloha Trail (5.8 miles) starts near Glen Alpine Creek, and winds up at Lake Aloha, the most popular lake in Desolation Valley.

Fallen Leaf Trail (5 miles) is an easy walk through alpine forest and along the shores of a picturebook lake.

Eagle Falls–Eagle Lake Trail (2 miles) begins at the Eagle Falls picnic area and traverses the cascade along a wooden footbridge. Then it crosses a blocky talus slope which offers beautiful views of the Tahoe Basin, and finally arrives at Eagle Lake.

Lake Tahoe has numerous hiking adventures. **Five Lakes Trail** (3 miles) begins on Alpine Meadows Road off Route 89. This fairly steep trail goes past beautiful alpine scenery to a group of small, cold mountain lakes.

Shirley Lake Trail (2.5 miles) traverses spectacular Squaw Valley and passes stunning waterfalls. If you're so inclined, take the tram up and then hike down.

Rubicon–Emerald Point Trail (3.1 miles) carries past Lake Tahoe's only lighthouse and offers wonderful views of Emerald Bay.

Loon Lake Trail (4.5 miles), beginning at Loon Lake Campground, is an easy hike through a wild area. The trail crosses seasonal creeks as well as fir and pine groves en route to Spider Lake.

YOSEMITE NATIONAL PARK Called the "Incomparable Valley," Yosemite is *the* place for hikers to seek the solitude, excitement, and grandeur of the wilderness. More than 100 hiking trails, both within and outside Yosemite Valley, lace the park. Remember, multiday hikes require a wilderness permit. In July 1996, a 400-foot piece of granite slide 2500 feet down a mountain near Happy Isles in Yosemite. The destructive rock plowed down over 2000 trees and left nothing but granite dust in its path. Mist Trail and John Muir Trail are among the many trails in the area closed until further notice. Call ahead before planning your hike.

✔ CHECK THESE OUT—UNIQUE OUTDOOR ADVENTURES

- Strike it rich, or maybe just have fun, as you test your luck panning for gold in the Gold Country's **mountain streams.** *page 425*
- Take in the majestic scenery as you shoot the rapids while whitewater rafting the **Stanislaus River.** *page 424*
- Pitch a tent within walking distance of inviting hot baths featuring 101° to 104° water at **Grover Hot Springs State Park.** *page 414*
- Hike **Half Dome Trail** for a dizzying view of Yosemite Valley, but please stand back if you're acrophobic. *page 432*

Valley Floor–West Loop Trail (6.9 miles) carries past Bridalveil Falls, Cathedral Rocks, and El Capitan.

Valley Floor–Yosemite Village Loop Trail (2 miles) offers views of Yosemite Falls, Half Dome, and Royal Arches.

Valley Floor–Mirror Lake Loop Trail (3 miles) carries past Mirror Lake and Half Dome along a tree-shaded route. It also features views of treacherous Tenaya Canyon.

Yosemite Falls Trail (7.2 miles), a strenuous half-day hike, climbs to the top of Upper Yosemite Falls.

Sentinel Dome Trail (1.2 miles) one of the most-traveled paths in the park, carries across bedrock to the summit of Sentinel Dome. At the top are views of El Capitan, Yosemite Falls, Half Dome, and the lone Jeffrey pine that crowns this peak.

Vernal–Nevada Falls Loop Trail (7.8 miles) is one of the most scenic hikes in the valley. Initially it follows Mist Trail, where you'll be sprayed with rain from Vernal Falls (bring rain gear, or in summer a bathing suit). After enjoying the views from Clark Point, pick up John Muir Trail for the climb to Nevada Falls.

Little Yosemite Valley Trail (7.9 miles) is a semi-loop trail that is best hiked in two days. This trail is a major starting point for backpackers heading deep into Yosemite. Watch out for bears!

Half Dome Trail (8.2 miles) is a strenuous mountain climb that ends at the most spectacular summit in the park. Not a hike for acrophobics.

Lembert Dome–Dog Lake Loop Trail (4.2 miles) begins in the Tuolumne Meadows parking lot and leads to the top of Lembert Dome. It continues to Dog Lake with views of Mt. Dana, Mt. Gibbs, and Mt. Lewis.

Harden Lake Trail (3 miles) is an easy hike from White Wolf Campground to one of the area's warmest lakes.

Alder Creek Trail to Bishop Creek (3.5 miles) is a moderate half-day trek in the Wawona area. Hard to find but very beautiful, this trail is best hiked in springtime when the creeks flow and the temperature is moderate. One of the most outstanding features is the flowering plant life, including mountain misery, a lightly scented shrub.

Glacier Point to Yosemite Valley via Nevada and Vernal Falls Trail (8.5 miles) is one of the more scenic routes into the valley. It begins at the Glacier Point parking lot and gives startling views of Tenaya Canyon, Half Dome, Illilouette Fall, Clouds Rest, Nevada and Vernal Falls—to name just a few!

Transportation

CAR

The large section of the state covered in this chapter is serviced by numerous highways. From San Francisco, **Route 80** travels northeast directly to Sacramento, then bisects the Gold Country, and continues into the High Sierra, passing within ten miles of Lake Tahoe's North Shore. The quickest way to the South Shore is via **Route 50** from Sacramento. To reach Yosemite, follow the freeways leading east from San Francisco, then pick up either **Route 120** or **Route 140** into the park. The Gold Country can be toured along **Route 49.**

AIR

Several major airlines fly into **Sacramento International Airport.** These include Alaska Airlines, American Airlines, America West, Delta Air Lines, Horizon Air, Northwest Airlines, Southwest Airlines, United Airlines, and USAir.

The city of South Lake Tahoe has the lake's only commercial airport, **South Lake Tahoe Airport,** located just south of the city on Route 50. Boone Air flies directly into the airport while most other airlines fly into Reno and are shuttled by Tahoe Casino Express.

Airlines with flights into **Reno–Cannon International Airport** include Alaska Airlines, America West, American Airlines, Delta Air Lines, Reno Air, Southwest Airlines, and United Airlines.

BUS

Greyhound Bus Lines provides service to Sacramento and Lake Tahoe. ~ 800-231-2222.

TRAIN

Train aficionados can climb aboard **Amtrak** for an excursion to Sacramento, Lake Tahoe, or Yosemite. From Oakland, the "Coast Starlight" provides service from Tuesday through Saturday to Sacramento, while the "Zephyr" carries passengers to Truckee in the Tahoe area. ~ 800-872-7245.

Those traveling to Yosemite from Oakland or Los Angeles can take Amtrak's "San Joaquin" to Merced, where **Yosemite Via Busline** provides connecting bus service into Yosemite Valley. ~ 209-722-0366.

CAR RENTALS

The following agencies are at Sacramento Metropolitan Airport: **Avis Rent A Car** (916-922-5601, 800-331-1212), **Budget Rent A Car** (916-922-7316, 800-527-0700), and **Hertz Rent A Car** (916-927-3882, 800-654-3131). Other agencies offer airport pick-up service, including **Thrifty Car Rental** (916-447-2847, 800-367-2277). Check the Yellow Pages for agencies in town.

At South Lake Tahoe Airport, cars are available through **Avis Rent A Car** (916-542-5638), **Budget Rent A Car** (916-541-5777, 800-331-1212), or **Hertz Rent A Car** (916-544-2327, 800-654-3131). Rentals are also available in the towns of Truckee, Incline Village, and South Lake Tahoe.

PUBLIC TRANSIT

To get around Sacramento by bus, call **Sacramento Regional Transit** (916-321-2877). **Tahoe Area Regional Transit** (916-581-6365), or TART, services North Lake Tahoe and offers a shuttle service between Tahoe City and Truckee. In South Lake Tahoe, **South Tahoe Area Ground Express** (916-573-2080), or STAGE, provides transportation around the South Shore and from one end of Tahoe City to the other. In Yosemite Valley, a free **shuttle bus** (209-372-1240) ferries folks between various points of interest.

TOURS

A unique way to travel from San Francisco to Sacramento is to board a modern river boat and cruise several hours upriver to the state capital. For information, contact **Delta Travel.** Tours begin in mid-May and continue through mid-October. ~ P.O. Box 813, West Sacramento, CA 95691; 916-372-3690.

To travel between the south and north shores of Lake Tahoe in winter, try **Lake Tahoe Cruises.** ~ 916-541-3364. **North Tahoe Cruises** explores the west shore of the lake and Emerald Bay from May through November. ~ 850 North Lake Boulevard, Tahoe City; 916-583-0141.

EIGHT

Far North

California's best-kept secret is a sprawling, thinly populated area full of history and incredible natural beauty. Much of the sector's lush terrain is virtually untouched. Reaching from Redding to Oregon and from the Coast Range to Nevada, the Far North encompasses a huge swath of California. Siskiyou, Modoc, Shasta, and Lassen counties are part of this tumbling block of territory.

A wilderness of alpine lakes and granite heights, its mountains include the Klamath, Marble, Salmon, Trinity, and Warner ranges. Foremost is the Cascade Range, extending south from Washington and Oregon. Mt. Shasta, rising over 14,000 feet, is lord of the land, a white-domed figure brooding above a forested realm. Lassen Peak, its infernal cousin, is an active volcano which last erupted in 1921.

Sprinkled along the region's panoramic byways are tiny hamlets where traffic lights are nonexistent. Virtually every town with more than a gas station has a museum showcasing its early history, but the most revealing glimpses are in the countryside, where small farms keep in step with an ancient drummer.

The Far North represents "hidden California" in its truly pristine state. Thousands of lakes and rivers make it a paradise for whitewater rafting. Chinook run 50 pounds and the fishing is excellent for trout and bass as well. Most of the region is preserved in a series of national forests, making it a retreat for hikers and campers.

The wilderness here has given birth to all sorts of things—rare species, trophy fish, and big game animals. The most prized find of all may not even exist. For over a century, people have been sighting an elusive creature, kin perhaps to the abominable snowman, named Bigfoot. Said to range in height up to 14 feet, he weighs as much as 800 pounds. His skin is dark and tough as leather; hair covers his entire body. Bigfoot has a flat nose, short ears, human-like features, and walks with a ten foot stride. He inhabits deep river valleys and thick forests, leaving huge footprints in the untrammeled wilderness.

In addition to a rich mythology, the countryside boasts a history that dates back millions of years when volcanic activity created the Cascade Range and other geologic forces formed neighboring mountains. Modoc, Paiute, Pit River, and Shoshone peoples originally inhabited the Far North, fishing its endless waterways and hunting the surrounding forests. The region was not opened to Europeans until 1817 when Captain Luis Arguello, a Spanish adventurer, probed the wilds. By the 1840s, American wagon trains were rolling through the territory. When gold was discovered around the end of the decade, prospectors began panning the rivers.

The original inhabitants, pushed from their lands by settlers and gold-seekers, struck back in the "Modoc War." During the tragic climax in 1873, the U.S. Army fought a pitched battle in the Lava Beds area against a group of Modocs led by Chief Kientpoos, also known as Captain Jack. "Nobody will ever want these rocks," the American Indian leader pleaded. "Give me a home here."

Except for a handful of descendants, the American Indians have disappeared, but cowboys continue to ride the range, thanks in part to a thriving cattle business. With ranches everywhere, particularly around Alturas, the Far North ranks as the largest beef-producing region in the state. Since practically any place that's not a granite mountain or alpine lake is covered with forest, the lumber industry is also an important factor in the economy.

Tourism reigns as the biggest source of local revenue. Despite a major chemical spill along the Sacramento River in 1991, the Far North remains a year-round vacation zone. The spill, which resulted from a train derailment north of Dunsmuir, was contained, though a ban on fishing remains in effect along a 43-mile stretch of the river.

Everywhere else in the Far North aquatic enthusiasts arrive in ever-increasing numbers during the warm summer months and skiers pile in during the winter. Many facilities shut down during the cold season, and many roads are closed, so sightseers are advised to visit between late spring and early fall. Mid-summer brings large crowds, so if touring then, plan ahead, make reservations well in advance.

Regardless of the season, the Far North rarely disappoints the adventurous traveler. A land of giant dams and endless waterways, it is a wonderland for outdoor sports and a place of exquisite beauty.

Redding

Route 5 runs like a spine through this rural region, moving north and south from Sacramento to Oregon. Redding, capital of the "Inland Empire," is the closest facsimile around to a buzzing metropolis. This town of 70,000 folks is also the major jumping-off point for sightseers.

From here, it's less than an hour along Route 299 to Whiskeytown, Shasta, and Trinity lakes, as well as the history-book towns of Shasta and French Gulch. Further north on Route 5 are the ski slopes of Mt. Shasta and the antique town of Yreka. Route 44 leads from Redding to Lassen Volcanic National Park, and Route 395 winds into the far northeast corner of California.

SIGHTS

No matter where you plan to visit, the first stop should be the **Shasta-Cascade Wonderland Association**. The friendly staff here will provide enough maps and brochures to stuff an extra suitcase. ~ 14250 Holiday Road; 916-275-5555, 800-474-2782.

Caldwell Park features a municipal pool and picnic areas. More important, it houses the **Redding Museum of Art and History** with its fascinating revolving historical displays. There are usually displays re-creating local pioneer and American Indian life as well as a contemporary selection. Admission. ~ 56 Quartz Hill Road; 916-243-8801.

Best known for its colony of native animals, the **Carter House Natural Science Museum** is the place to get up close and personal with a great horned owl, opossum, or northern flying squirrel. At the hourly animal discovery time, two or three animals are brought out from their indoor cages for a show and tell session. Visitors are welcome to touch these injured animals who can not be safely returned to their native habitats. Special exhibits cover a wide range of natural science topics, and hands-on exhibits include computers, microscopes, and puzzles. There's an observation beehive on the

premises and you're welcome to take natural history walks. Admission. ~ 48 Quartz Hill Road; 916-243-5457.

LODGING

For a last, luxurious taste of civilization before heading into the hills, try **La Quinta Inn**. This stylish establishment features positively huge rooms with plush wall-to-wall carpeting. The furnishings have a cherrywood finish with pastel upholstery and the decor is quite inviting. Despite the proximity to Route 5, this is an extremely quiet inn. ~ 2180 Hilltop Drive; 916-221-8200, 800-531-5900, fax 916-223-4727. MODERATE.

On a bluff overlooking the Sacramento River, **Palisades Paradise** is a contemporary bed-and-breakfast inn. The spacious Sunset Suite, with its mix of contemporary and antique furnishings, features an outdoor spa and 50-foot long patio. The inn's other guest room, the "Cozy Retreat," offers queen-size beds and a muted color scheme. A continental breakfast is served throughout the week. Weekend breakfast is even more substantial and includes specialties such as oven pancakes with fresh fruit. ~ 1200 Palisades Avenue; 916-223-5305, 800-382-4649. MODERATE.

Less lavish yet still quite comfortable, the **Best Western Hospitality House** is located in the heart of Redding's neon motel strip. Biggest and best of the bunch, it boasts 61 clean but sterile rooms. Amenities include color cable television in your room and a swimming pool on the grounds. ~ 532 North Market Street; 916-241-6464, 800-700-3019, fax 916-244-1998. BUDGET TO MODERATE.

Bargain hunters take note: You'll find numerous inexpensive motels along this strip, each proudly displaying its nightly rates as part of a local price war. The **Thriftlodge–Casa Blanca Motel** features rooms with Spanish-tile kitchenettes. ~ 413 North Market Street; 916-241-3010, 800-525-9055, fax 916-241-9029. BUDGET.

Just as economical is the **Economy Inn**, which features standard amenities. ~ 525 Market Street; 916-246-9803. The **Cedar Lodge Motel** will certainly get you through the night, though not exactly in style. ~ 513 Market Street; 916-244-3251.

DINING

It's tough to bust your budget while dining in Redding. With surroundings as pleasant as those at **El Papagayo Mexican Restaurant**, there's no reason to even stretch it. This restaurant is decorated with colorful posters, stained glass, and murals. And then there's the food, there's an extensive menu that includes everything from a chile relleno, taco, and enchilada combination to guacamole omelettes. ~ 460 North Market Street; 916-243-2493. BUDGET TO MODERATE.

It looks like a typical roadside restaurant, complete with flashing neon sign and naugahyde booths, but **Lim's Cafe** offers a large selection of Chinese and American dishes. The Asian dinners include a combination plate that consists of chicken noodle soup, pork chow mein, sweet and sour pork, and fried shrimp. For those with an American palate there are chicken dishes, sandwiches, and steaks. ~ 592 North Market Street; 916-241-9747. BUDGET.

Even before you step inside **Andy's Cow Patty Palace**, it's obvious that the place is going to be a little different. After all, it takes a sense of humor to advertise your wares with a sign that reads "TSAFKAERB, HCNUL, DLOC SKNIRD." Translation: "Breakfast, Lunch, Cold Drinks." The craziness doesn't stop there. The head waiter and chef are one person, a stand-up comic named Andy Berwind. Between turns at the griddle, this former Hollywood actor cracks jokes, sings, and spouts poetry that's long on rhyme and short on reason. He's serious about his cooking, though; all of the chowders, soups, chili dishes, pies, and biscuits are homemade. A great place for a light breakfast or lunch. Closed Sunday. ~ 2105 Hilltop Drive; 916-221-7422. BUDGET.

SHOPPING

If you're in the market for locally produced arts and crafts, the **Redding Museum of Art and History** has jewelry, handcrafted pottery, baskets, and woodcarvings. Postcards and booklets describing the area's history are also available. ~ 56 Quartz Hill Road; 916-243-8801.

NIGHTLIFE

At **Misty's,** live bands and trios play rock, pop, oldies, and a wide variety of special requests. Located at the Red Lion Inn, this lounge also offers karaoke on Sunday night. A contemporary room with highback furniture, easy chairs, and couches, Misty's has a small dancefloor. ~ 1830 Hilltop Drive; 916-221-8700.

The gigantic dancefloor at **The Derringer** packs in the country-and-western crowd with live music on weekends and dance lessons five nights a week. The decor is rustic country with one wall made out of old barn wood. Besides dancin' and drinkin', you can shoot pool, throw darts, and play air hockey and pinball. ~ 2655 Bechelli Lane; 916-221-2727.

Redding to Weaverville

Rising up from the Central Valley the road from Redding to Weaverville leads west toward the gateway to one of Northern California's premier recreational destinations. While best known for water sports, this area is also the place to find old mining towns, historic commercial districts, and American Indian landmarks.

From Redding, Route 299 leads west for a few miles to the late, great gold mining outpost of **Shasta**. This brickfront ghost town was the region's "Queen City" back in the 1850s, producing over $100,000 in gold dust every week. A trail leads along a row of old ruins.

SIGHTS

At **Shasta State Historic Park**, you'll find a restored county courthouse, American Indian artifacts, antique photos, wanted posters, yellowed newspapers, and paintings by California artists. Closed Monday and Tuesday in summer, and Monday to Thursday from November through February. Admission. ~ Route 299W, Shasta; 916-243-8194.

Five miles farther west along Route 299 lies **Whiskeytown Lake**, one of California's best boating, fishing, camping, and swimming spots. With 36 miles of shoreline, green rolling hills, tiny wooded islands, and dense stands of ponderosa pine, it's a paradise for backcountry explorers.

HIDDEN ►

The historic mining town of **French Gulch**, settled in 1849, is situated off Route 299 along Trinity Mountain Road. Once an important way station on the Old Oregon Pacific Trail, it's a place where time has refused to budge for the last 100 years. The townsfolk still take family walks down Main Street, paint their picket fences white, and rarely lock their bikes. Among the municipal heirlooms there is **St. Rose's Church**, a picturesque wood-frame structure.

From here, Route 299 winds past beautiful mountain vistas en route to **Weaverville**, a country-style Victorian town shaded by honey locusts. In addition to its small-town charm, Weaverville has a colorful past worth exploring.

At the **Jake Jackson Memorial Museum**, displays re-create the tragedy and romance of the Gold Rush days. There's a complete blacksmith's shop, as well as early mining tools (including a stamp mill used for obtaining gold from ore), archaic medical supplies, and a fascinating display of Chinese weapons, gowns, and money. From December through February, only open on Tuesday afternoon. ~ 508 Main Street, Weaverville; 916-623-5211.

One block away sits **Joss House State Historic Park**, known as the "Temple Amongst the Forest Beneath the Clouds." Here Chinese Taoists have worshipped since 1853. Nestled in a grove of trees near a wooded footbridge, this shrine is a tribute to the Chinese miners whose hard labor brought them neither riches nor acceptance in the Old West. Closed Tuesday and Wednesday from October to May, and Monday through Thursday from November to April. Admission. ~ Main and Oregon streets, Weaverville; 916-623-5284.

LODGING

At the gateway to the Trinity Alps lies the **Weaverville Hotel**, which first opened its doors in 1861. Although all seven rooms are plainly furnished with inexpensive carpets, tables, and dressers, the hotel is quiet and clean. Life is casual here; as a matter of fact, you'll check in to the hotel at Brady's Sport Shop next door. ~ 201 Main Street, Weaverville; 916-623-3121. BUDGET.

Tucked away in a woodsy corner, the **Red Hill Motel** delivers comfortable rooms and cabins. All of the accommodations feature knotty-pine walls and include color cable television, but the best deals are the individual cabins. These include full kitchenettes, afford ample privacy, and cost a few dollars more. They also offer knockout views of the Trinity Alps through the pines. ~ Red Hill Road, Weaverville; 916-623-4331. BUDGET.

DINING

In the time-machine town of Weaverville, you'll find the **Pacific Brewery Café**. Erected in 1853, this sturdy brick building was originally home of the Meckel brothers' beer distillery. It now operates as a restaurant where you can immerse yourself in local history while enjoying breakfast, lunch, or dinner in rustic surroundings. Pull up a tree stump at the bar and you'll be encircled by artifacts from Weaverville's colorful past: old gas lanterns, hand saws, street signs, gold pans, and rifles. On the walls are faded photographs and maps of the surrounding mountain country. The food here ranges from sandwiches and salads to steaks and chicken to homemade biscuits and sweet rolls. ~ 401 South Main Street, Weaverville; 916-623-3000. BUDGET TO MODERATE.

Just across the street is **The Mustard Seed**. This café sits on the upper part of a two-story flat and provides an excellent vantage point for studying the town's street life. Mornings, sample homemade waffles, hash browns, or an omelette. At lunch, you'll find vegetarian sandwiches, quiche, spicy tacos, and cool fruit smoothies. On warm days, you can eat outdoors on the deck. ~ 252 South Main Street, Weaverville; 916-623-2922. BUDGET.

Weaverville to Yreka

The best path between Weaverville and Yreka is Route 3, a sinuous track plagued with fast-moving lumberjacks on wheels, but offering extraordinary mountain vistas. It parallels Trinity (Clair Engle) Lake and the Trinity Alps on its 105-mile journey back to civilization at Yreka.

If you're feeling even more adventurous, you can travel west from Weaverville on Route 299 into Humboldt County, connect with Route 96, and head north into Salmon River country. This

FAR NORTH EXPERIENCES

- Delve into the history of Chinese laborers at the **Joss House State Historic Park**, better known as the "Temple Amongst the Forest Beneath the Clouds." *page 440*
- Rest under the stars on Shasta Lake as you float about on a houseboat rented from **Antlers Resort**. *page 447*
- Dine at the **Grand Cafe**, an old-style eatery where even the prices seem stuck in the past. *page 453*
- Trek through **Lava Beds National Monument** and explore the lava tubes caves of an active volcano. *page 451*

winding roadway passes Six Rivers National Forest and approaches whitewater stretches of the mighty Klamath River. Slow but scenic, it's the long way home to Yreka, doubling the distance to 213 miles, and leading along poorly maintained roads.

SIGHTS

If you opt for Route 3, watch for the Buckeye Creek Road turnoff about seven miles from Weaverville. Turn right and you'll discover some striking panoramas of **Trinity (Clair Engle) Lake**, a 16,500-acre expanse.

At **Scott Museum** you'll see displays representing the pioneer days, everything from Indian baskets to snowshoes for horses. It also boasts one of the country's largest collections of barbed wire—nearly 500 different samples. Open May to September. ~ Scott Road, Trinity Center.

To explore the **Trinity Alps Wilderness Area**, or for a closer look at the mountains, go eight miles past Trinity Center and turn left on Coffee Creek Road. It carries past waterfalls and rushing rivers, through deep forest and dark canyons. Just past the North Fork Coffee Creek Bridge lies the wilderness area, with its granite peaks and glacial lakes.

Back on Route 3, continue north into the placid Scott Valley region. **Callahan**, once an important trade center, still sports boardwalks and 19th-century buildings along its one-block commercial strip. Other small towns along the way—Etna, Greenview, and Fort Jones—also feature antique buildings.

In **Yreka**, you'll find a reconstructed mining town, as well as hiking trails and a fishing lake in **Greenhorn Park**, located on Greenhorn Road. At the **Siskiyou County Museum** are displays of American Indian artifacts, as well as pioneer-era musical instruments, dolls, dresses, and hats. There are also vintage photographs, hand-colored panoramic images of Yreka and vicinity in the 1920s. The Davis Cabin, part of this excellent facility, was built in 1856. Admission. ~ 910 South Main Street, Yreka; 916-842-3836.

Be sure to visit **Miner Street**, a timeworn commercial row where most of the buildings have been standing since the late 19th century, and explore the town's **Victorian home district** (bounded by 3rd, West Lennox, Gold, and Lane streets). Some of the wealth that built these grand homes is displayed at the **Siskiyou County Court House**. Here, behind a glass case, rests a king's ransom in gold nuggets from neighboring mines. ~ 311 4th Street, Yreka.

Railroad fans won't want to miss **The Blue Goose**, a historic Baldwin steam locomotive that departs from the turn-of-the-century Yreka depot. You can ride on an open flatcar or in one of the art deco coach cars. The eight-mile ride heads up the Shasta Valley to Montague, where you'll have plenty of time for a picnic before returning south. With luck your run will be raided by "bandits" who frequently entertain passengers with their dastardly deeds. Trains run June through October. Admission. ~ 300 East Miner Street, Yreka; 916-842-4146.

LODGING

"A complete 90-acre vacation village on Trinity (Clair Engle) Lake" is the way **Wyntoon Resort** bills itself. This multifaceted enclave consists of 20 fully equipped cottages, a trailer park, 80 campsites, a marina with rental boats, supermarket, gas station, and more. Although the pseudo-rusticity characterizing the cabins is disillusioning, the location provides a base for exploring the nearby Trinity Alps. The cottages house up to four people; there are two- and three-day minimums on weekends and holidays, respectively. ~ Route 3, Trinity Center; 916-266-3337, 800-715-3337, fax 916-266-3820. MODERATE.

Route 3 is the old California–Oregon Wagon Road.

You won't find much in the way of exotic rentals up in Siskiyou County, but the 44-unit **Thunderbird Lodge** does have a few extras to make it stand out from the rest. Like the exceptionally spotless rooms, color televisions, and a heated pool. The accommodations at this neon motel are comfortably but unimaginatively furnished. ~ 526 South Main Street, Yreka; 916-842-4404, fax 916-841-0439. BUDGET.

If the Thunderbird is already booked, try the **Best Western Miner's Inn**. With 134 rooms, it has two swimming pools and a coffee shop nearby. ~ 122 East Miner Street, Yreka; 916-842-4355, fax 916-842-4480. BUDGET.

DINING

Chinese dishes, teriyaki steak, seafood, and a full bar featuring Hawaiian cocktails are the main attractions at **Ming's Cocktail Lounge and Restaurant**. The soft lighting, thatched furnishings, and tropical fish aquarium create an island atmosphere. The menu follows a similar theme with Alaskan king crab, mandarin duck, and several different combination plates. For a delightful dessert treat, try the Hawaiian coconut ice cream. Closed Monday. ~ 210 West Miner Street, Yreka; 916-842-3888. BUDGET TO MODERATE.

The Peasantry features superb sourdough pancakes, as well as omelettes and other breakfast fare from 7 a.m. to 2:30 p.m. Located in a historic brick building built in 1856, the restaurant also serves lunch, with avocado sandwiches as the specialty. Closed Sunday and Monday. ~ 322 West Miner Street, Yreka; 916-842-5418. BUDGET.

SHOPPING

Antique stores are one of Yreka's strongest attractions. **James Place** is reputedly the largest single-owner shop of its type in the Pacific Northwest, and has been doing business for over 27 years. Here you'll find vintage clothing, quilts, miniatures, and folk art. There's also a large variety of antique toys, including dolls, stuffed bears, and carousel animals. ~ 216 3rd Street, Yreka; 916-842-5454.

It's About Time sells a bit of everything in the way of antiques. There's furniture, glass, china, perfume bottles, Franciscan ware, watercolors, framed crate labels, and old *Life* and *Saturday Evening Post* magazines. The store is located in the heart of Yreka's original shopping district, where most of the buildings date back to the 19th century. ~ 216 West Miner Street, Yreka; 916-842-1714.

PARKS

SHASTA-TRINITY NATIONAL FOREST Whiskeytown, Shasta, and Trinity (Clair Engle) lakes are just three of the 131 natural lakes found in this seemingly unending paradise. It's visited by more than 5 million people each year, but there's still plenty of room to spare within the park's 2,159,001 acres. About 3100 miles of hiking trails, including part of the Pacific Crest Trail, wind through the forest. Towering Mt. Shasta, the region's most prominent peak, overlooks nearly 2000 miles of tributaries and streams. Wildlife includes bald eagles, ospreys, great blue herons, black bears, mule deer, striped skunks, gray fox, and golden-mantled squirrels. There are numerous visitors centers, restrooms, and picnic areas throughout the park; restaurants and groceries are available in the nearby towns. ~ The forest is located northeast, south, and west of Redding. Principal access is from Routes 3, 5, 89, and 299. For Whiskeytown, Shasta, and Trinity (Clair Engle) lakes, and for Trinity Alps Wilderness Area and Mt. Shasta, see listings below. Park headquarters is located at 2400 Washington Avenue, Redding; 916-246-5222.

▲ Permitted in more than 100 campgrounds; $6 to $14 per night depending on the site. Some free campsites (without facilities) are scattered throughout the forest, and with a wilderness permit and a campfire permit you can camp anywhere in the forest.

WHISKEYTOWN-SHASTA-TRINITY NATIONAL RECREATION AREA This area, established by Congress in 1865, offers numerous recreational activities. With environments that vary from coniferous forest to mountain lake, hiking, horseback riding, swimming, and boating are just a few of the sports available here. Bear, mountain lion, raccoon, and deer are plentiful throughout the area and bald eagles and osprey are often spotted soaring in the sky.

Whiskeytown Unit The main event here is Whiskeytown Lake, a 3220-acre body of water that's ideal for swimming, canoeing, and sailing. There are beaches at Brandy Creek and Oak Bottom; the fishing for bass, kokanee salmon, and brown and rainbow trout is good. There are picnic areas, restrooms, food service, an information center, and canoe rentals. ~ Located along Route 299 around eight miles west of Redding; 916-246-1225.

▲ There are 37 free RV sites (no hookups) at Brandy Creek, while Oak Bottom is run by DESTINET (make reservations by calling 800-365-2267) and offers 50 RV sites and 100 tent sites; $12 to $14 per night. There are also seven primitive campgrounds (permit required).

Shasta Unit California's largest artificial lake, Shasta Lake boasts more than 370 miles of shoreline. The lake's water temperature during the summer months averages 72°, making it ideal for houseboating, swimming, windsurfing (although winds are tame), and waterskiing. Fishing is excellent year-round, with bass, trout, bluegill, and sturgeon among the most frequent catches. There are restrooms, picnic areas, and boat ramps; restaurants, groceries, boat rentals, and hotel facilities are located near the lake. ~ The lake is off Route 5 about 20 miles north of Redding; 916-275-1589.

▲ Permitted in 24 forest service campgrounds, including several reached only by boat; free to $14 per night depending on the campsite.

Trinity (Clair Engle) Unit Sitting in the shadow of the Trinity Alps, Trinity (Clair Engle) Lake measures 150 miles of shoreline. Popular for swimming, sailing, waterskiing, and houseboating, it's also recommended for trout and smallmouth bass fishing. There are picnic areas and restrooms; restaurants, groceries, boat rentals, and hotel facilities are located near the lake. ~ The lake parallels Route 3 just a few miles north of Weaverville; 916-623-2121.

▲ There are ten forest service campgrounds (some located on sandy beaches); $6 to $10 per night depending on the site.

TRINITY ALPS WILDERNESS AREA A high, sharp mountain range, the Trinity Alps vault from glacial canyons to 9000-foot heights. In addition to startling granite peaks, the region contains alpine lakes, pristine streams, and giant talus boulders. There are no facilities here. A wilderness permit is required, as is a free fire permit during fire season. ~ Located west of Redding, the area is accessible from Routes 299 and 3; 916-246-5222, 916-623-2121, or 916-623-6106.

▲ Permitted for backpacking campers; no fee. Motorized vehicles are not allowed within the wilderness area.

SIX RIVERS NATIONAL FOREST Stretching from the Oregon border almost into Mendocino County, this 980,285-acre playground is the home of six major waterways—the Smith, Klamath, Trinity, Mad, Van Duzen, and Eel rivers. Although there are 203 miles of hiking trails, fishing is the most popular sport, followed by river rafting. There are picnic areas and restrooms; restaurants and groceries are available in nearby towns. ~ Extending 140 miles along the western perimeter of the Far North, this facility is accessible from Routes 101 (via Routes 36, 299, and 199); 707-442-1721.

▲ Permitted in 15 specified campgrounds and in other areas throughout the forest; $6 to $8 per night. Fire permits are often required May through October. For more information call any of the national forest's ranger districts: Smith River National Recreation Area (Gasquet; 707-457-3131), Orleans Ranger District (Orleans; 916-627-3291), Lower Trinity Ranger District (Willow Creek; 916-629-2118), or Mad River Ranger District (Mad River; 707-574-6233).

Redding to Mt. Shasta

A cross between Valhalla and Shangri-la, Mt. Shasta is the quintessential Cascade mountain backdrop. Driving north from Redding toward this volcanic peak, you'll pass manmade and natural attractions alike before ascending this magic mountain.

SIGHTS

Due north along Route 5, you'll encounter **Shasta Lake**, an extremely popular recreation area which is a paradise for naturalists and statisticians alike. Why the strange combination of interests? Because Shasta Lake, with its 370-mile shoreline and 30,000-acre expanse, is the largest manmade lake in the state. Its four arms stretch into the Sacramento, McCloud, and Pit rivers, as well as Squaw Creek. It boasts 17 types of game fish, a colony of houseboats, hiking trails, and every other possible outdoor diversion imaginable.

Then there's **Shasta Dam**, located along Shasta Dam Boulevard five miles west of Route 5. Three times taller than Niagara Falls, it measures 602 feet, making it the second highest dam in the United States. Nearly seven years labor and six-and-a-half million cubic yards of concrete went into its completion. If those superlatives are insufficient, continue north on Route 5 a few miles and you'll cross **Pit River Bridge**, the world's highest double-deck bridge.

From the nearby town of O'Brien (population 2), you can visit **Lake Shasta Caverns**. Guides will take you on a 15-minute ride across the lake by boat, then along a picturesque road by bus, to this mazework of limestone caves. Within are strangely shaped stalactites and awesome stalagmites, dating back perhaps 250 million years. This natural statuary comes in the form of spires and minarets, stone curtains and Disneyesque figures. Within these tunnels, temperatures average 58°, so you may want to bring a sweater. Admission. ~ Shasta Caverns Road, O'Brien; 916-238-2341.

Castle Crags State Park, farther north along Route 5 in Castella, is a land of granite domes and startling landscapes. From vista points, you can gaze out upon the Cascade Range. ~ Castella; 916-235-2684.

Foremost among these majestic peaks is awesome **Mount Shasta**, a 14,162-foot giant which carries five glaciers along its flanks. Dominating the skyline, it consists of two volcanic cones and features alpine lakes, flower-choked meadows, and deep forests. For a closer look at this sacred mountain, follow Route A10 through Mt. Shasta Recreation Area. The road winds to an elevation of 6800 feet and offers a different view at every hairpin turn.

Near the foot of Mt. Shasta, along Route 89, rests the gas-lamp town of **McCloud**. A 19th-century lumber center, it still contains much of its early architecture. The **McCloud Chamber of Commerce** provides free maps and brochures. ~ 205 Quincy Avenue, McCloud; 916-964-3113. ◄ HIDDEN

LODGING

Idyllically situated in the Sacramento Arm of Shasta Lake, **Tsasdi Resort** is the perfect place to get away from it all without leaving all the conveniences behind. It offers 20 cabins that come complete with kitchens, patio decks, picnic tables, and barbecues. Fairly plush by rustic standards, they have knotty-pine interiors and sit in a black-oak forest overlooking Shasta Lake. The facilities also include a heated swimming pool, private dock, recreation room, and small convenience store. During the summer, most cabins are rented by the week only. ~ 19990 Lakeshore Drive, Lakehead; phone/fax 916-238-2575, 800-995-0291. MODERATE TO DELUXE.

Neighboring **Antlers Resort** rents both houseboats and cabins. Many folks claim the only way to experience Shasta Lake is by houseboat, but the thrill doesn't come cheap. Prices for the smallest seagoing accommodations *start* in the ultra-deluxe range, with a three-day minimum (seven-night minimum for late-June through August). You can make the costs quite reasonable by bringing along a few friends. The comforts of home include a complete kitchen, bathroom, and even a cassette music system. Landlubbers may find the housekeeping cabins more to their liking, with rates starting lower than the houseboats. Rustic but well appointed, half have wood stoves and all include open porches. These are among the most comfortable cabins on the lake. ~ Antlers Road at Shasta Lake, Lakehead; 916-238-2553, 800-238-3924, fax 916-238-2340. DELUXE TO ULTRA-DELUXE.

Farther south is **Holiday Flotels**, a houseboat haven. The houseboats are well maintained and come complete with kitchen, barbecue, and stereo system. All you need to add is food, linens, pillows, and gasoline. Each of the three available houseboats sleeps 10 to 12 people. There's a four-day minimum during off-season and a one-week minimum from early June until early September. Closed October through April. ~ Packers Bay Marina at Shasta Lake; phone/fax 916-275-5570. DELUXE TO ULTRA-DELUXE.

Town living is combined with a touch of rusticity at **Bavaria Lodge**. Here eight log cabins sit along the edge of town. Nothing fancy, mind you; each is decorated with a few paintings along raw-wood walls and all but two are equipped with a kitchenette. The entire complex is nestled in the trees. ~ 4601 Dunsmuir Road, Dunsmuir; 916-235-4707. BUDGET.

Since the town of Mount Shasta doesn't offer much in the way of nightlife, it's important to pick a hotel that features more than just a bed and hot shower. **Mountain Air Lodge** covers more than the basics and does so with flair. There is one jacuzzi, a community kitchen, and a recreation room. The suites themselves are spacious, carpeted wall-to-wall, and decorated with attractive wood furnishings. Some rooms have kitchenettes. ~ 1121 South Mount Shasta Boulevard, Mount Shasta; 916-926-3411. BUDGET TO MODERATE.

A two-story Bavarian-style lodge, the **Alpenrose Cottage Hostel** is an ideal youth hostel retreat. Panoramic views of Mount Shasta and proximity to skiing, hiking, rafting, and cycling make this retreat a great vacation base. On warm nights you can sleep outside on the deck. There's a complete kitchen and a charming garden. ~ 204 East Hinckley Street, Mount Shasta; 916-926-6724. BUDGET.

DINING

For an incredible view of 4000-foot granite spires and a nostalgic trip back to the time when the railroad was king, climb aboard the **Railroad Park Restaurant and Lounge**. You'll discover two restored dining cars—decorated with antique hand tools, steam gauges, and plush pile carpeting—which brilliantly re-create the romance of the rails. The dinners, priced a bit steep by local standards, include chicken dishes, seafood entrées, or prime rib dinners. Dinner only. Always closed Tuesday; closed Monday through Wednesday October through May. ~ 100 Railroad Park Road, Dunsmuir; 916-235-4611. MODERATE TO DELUXE.

"Welcome back to homemade food—eat and enjoy" is the rule at **Michael's**. This downtown restaurant offers seafood, pasta, sandwiches, and a long list of wine and beers priced in the moderate range. At lunchtime, try the pasta alfredo; linguine with white clam sauce and Russian ravioli top the dinner listings. A large window provides a breathtaking view of Mt. Shasta from the dining room. Closed Sunday and Monday. ~ 313 North Mount Shasta Boulevard, Mount Shasta; 916-926-5288. MODERATE.

The **Black Bear Diner** has taken the diner one step further with a themed restaurant specializing in bears. Pictures of black bears

ALL ABOARD THE CABOOSE MOTEL

One of the most unusual and imaginative resting places in the Far North is the **Railroad Park Caboose Motel**. Part of the Railroad Park Resort, this historic hostelry features 23 cabooses, each converted into a sleeping unit. The facility also offers four cabins, three with kitchens. The adjacent restaurant is housed in old railroad cars. Amenities at the resort include a swimming pool and jacuzzi. ~ 100 Railroad Park Road, Dunsmuir; 916-235-4440, fax 916-235-4470. MODERATE.

and old-time shots of Mt. Shasta decorate the walls, and you can chow down on sandwiches and burgers with names like Papa Bear. Just in case you're interested, the Papa Bear is a half-pound of ground beef on a grilled French roll with Swiss cheese, bacon, tomato, and lettuce, with a mountain of fries on the side. ~ 401 East Lake Street, Mount Shasta; 916-926-4669. BUDGET TO MODERATE.

For an elegant dining experience, try **The Mount Shasta Golf Resort Restaurant** five minutes outside town. Part of a 50-chalet exclusive resort, the restaurant offers stunning vistas of Mt. Shasta and the golf course amidst a wine-colored atmosphere of teal green carpets and burgundy tabletops. The chef creates an array of pasta, chicken, beef, seafood, and vegetarian entrées that include shrimp and scallop sauté pasta, chicken cordon bleu, shrimp scampi, and châteaubriand. ~ 1000 Siskiyou Lake Boulevard, Mount Shasta; 916-926-3030. MODERATE.

SHOPPING

Even if you're not planning to take a run down the nearby slopes, the **Fifth Season** warrants a walk-through. This sports trading post provides ski equipment, mountaineering and bicycling gear, and a complete line of all-weather clothing. ~ 426 North Mount Shasta Boulevard, Mount Shasta; 916-926-3606.

◄ HIDDEN

The **Golden Bough Bookstore** caters to the many spiritual seekers who look to nearby Mt. Shasta for magical power. For books about local folklore, or for a dash of friendly conversation, drop by. ~ 219 North Mount Shasta Boulevard, Mount Shasta; 916-926-3228.

PARKS

CASTLE CRAGS STATE PARK They might look like the work of an avant-garde sculptor, but the granite spires highlighting this 4000-acre facility were created more than 200 million years ago. In addition to the hiking on these 4000-foot statues, the park features canoeing along the Sacramento River. Because of a 1991 chemical spill in this area fishing is limited to catch and release. The park has picnic areas, restrooms, and showers; restaurants and groceries are located in nearby towns. ~ Located six miles south of Dunsmuir, just west of Route 5; 916-235-2684.

▲ There are 64 sites; $12 to $14 per night.

MT. SHASTA RECREATIONAL AREA Dominated by 14,162-foot Mt. Shasta, this facility is favored by sightseers and climbers alike. Here you can explore living glaciers, whitewater canyons, and pristine lakes. A park road rises to 7800-feet elevation and hiking trails crisscross the mountain. Facilities include picnic areas and restrooms; restaurants and groceries are available in the nearby town of Mount Shasta. ~ Located about 55 miles north of Redding off Route 5; turn east on Everitt Memorial Highway (Route A10); 916-926-4596.

▲ Permitted in six campgrounds, including two on the side of the mountain; $5 to $8 per night, depending on the campground.

KLAMATH NATIONAL FOREST Fishing and river rafting are popular sports in this remote park. Covering parts of six different mountain ranges, it extends from Oregon across most of Siskiyou County. The Klamath, Scott, and Salmon rivers are explored here by many commercial outfitters, while fishing lodges have sprouted up near Happy Camp. Also within the forest is **Marble Mountain Wilderness Area**, a 213,363-acre preserve crowded with wildlife and sport fish. There are picnic areas, restrooms, and showers; restaurants and groceries are in nearby towns. ~ Accessible along Routes 96 and 97; 916-842-6131.

▲ There are 31 campgrounds with 381 sites; free to $8 per night. For more information contact any of the six ranger districts: Oak Knoll (Klamath River; 916-465-2241), Happy Camp (Happy Camp; 916-493-2243), Ukonom (Orleans; 916-627-3291), Scott River (Fort Jones; 916-468-5351); Salmon River (Etna; 916-467-5757), or Goosenest (Macdoel; 916-398-4391).

Northeast Loop

The best way to explore California's hidden northeastern corner is along a 400-plus mile odyssey from Redding. Heading east to Lassen Peak and beyond, it will carry you past mountain lakes and one-street towns. Then turning north, you'll skirt the Warner Mountains, detour to Lava Beds National Monument, and return to Redding via lonely Route 299.

SIGHTS

First stop on this wilderness expedition is **Lassen Volcanic National Park**, located about 50 miles from Redding off Route 44. Lassen Peak, a 10,457-foot volcano, is the highlight and highpoint of this extraordinary region. This is part of the same mountain chain which brought you the Mt. St. Helens catastrophe. Lassen's last eruptions were between 1914 and 1921. Spewing fumes and ash 20,000 feet in the air, one explosion tore away an entire side of the mountain and flicked 20-ton boulders down the hillside. Today it's still a semi-active volcano, and the surrounding area is filled with steam vents, mud pots, and moonscape features.

Route 89 curves along three sides of the volcano, reaching an elevation of 8512 feet. Along this magnificent roadway are startling views of Lassen Peak, which still reveals scars from its furious eruptions. Also be sure to see Bumpass Hell, near the southern park boundary; it's a roaring region of boiling springs, mud volcanoes, and pools colored gold and turquoise. (Although this 106,000-acre park is open year-round, Route 89 is closed from the end of October until early June. If you're traveling during the ski season, consider taking Route 36 east from Red Bluff to the park's southwest entrance.) ~ 916-595-4444.

From Lassen, Route 36 heads east to **Lake Almanor,** a crystal blue expanse which mirrors the surrounding mountains. Measuring 52 square miles and bounded by evergreen forests, it's a prime place for swimming, boating, and waterskiing. Among the sport fish here are brown and rainbow trout as well as bass. Over 50 other lakes dot this pristine region and 500 miles of streams tumble through the area.

There are restaurants and lodgings in Chester, Susanville, and other small towns along the way. The **Lassen County Chamber of Commerce** can help you get your bearings in this sparsely populated region. ~ 84 North Lassen Street, Susanville; 916-257-4323.

Leading into the state's vast, empty northeastern corner, Route 395 proceeds north through high desert country. Sage brush hills and whistling winds are your sole companions. You'll pass Standish (population 100), Litchfield (population 65), Termo (population 50), and Madeline (population 100) en route to the grand metropolis of **Alturas** (population 3500).

The **Modoc County Museum** has an extensive collection of Paiute and Modoc artifacts and the counter from a turn-of-the-century general store with its inventory of corsets, high button shoes, and other period pieces. There's also an entire wall of weaponry, a rock and gem collection, and an intriguing exhibit on the region's bird life. Another display tells the story of Fort Bidwell, the pioneer military headquarters for this region. Here you'll learn about some of California's last Indian battles. Closed November through May. ~ 600 South Main Street, Alturas; 916-233-2944.

The **Alturas Chamber of Commerce** can provide information and direct you to local attractions. ~ 522 South Main Street, Alturas; 916-233-4434. One recommended stop is **Lava Beds National Monument.** This amazing park is a land of cinder cones, craters, and 30,000-year-old lava flows. It also features one of the world's finest series of lava tube caves, many open to exploration (the total number is about 330 caves). Once occupied by the Modoc people, this volcanic area contains numerous petroglyphs and pictographs. ~ Along Routes 299 and 139; 916-667-2283.

Nearby **Klamath Basin National Wildlife Refuge** is a migration point for one of the greatest concentrations of waterfowl on the continent. Together with neighboring areas, it draws two million birds during the spring and fall, including mallards, pintails, and snow geese. ~ Off Route 139, Tulelake; 916-667-2231. ◄ HIDDEN

From this remote preserve you can return to civilization, following Route 139 and then Route 299 as it cuts an alpine path back to Redding. Before leaving the wilderness entirely, stop at **McArthur–Burney Falls Memorial State Park.** Located midway between Mount Shasta and Lassen Park, it features two spectacular waterfalls, fed by springs, which cascade over a 129-foot cliff. Ornamented with rainbows and an emerald pool, the twin falls were reputedly deemed the eighth wonder of the world by President Theodore Roosevelt. They are a fitting climax to this long, lonely loop into California's most secluded realm. ~ 916-335-2777.

LODGING Modern amenities can be found at the **Lassen Mineral Lodge.** Here the rooms are conventionally styled with wood paneling and wall-to-wall carpeting. Rooms with kitchenettes are available. ~ Route 36, Mineral; 916-595-4422. BUDGET TO MODERATE.

Tucked between Mount Lassen and Lake Almanor you'll find **Cedar Lodge.** More of a motel than rural lodge, its cedar walls surround rather bland furnishings—secondhand store bedroom sets—but in such technicolor territory, your eyes probably need a rest. Some rooms come equipped with kitchenettes. ~ Junction of Routes 36 and 89, Chester; 916-258-2904. BUDGET.

Further east, set among towering pines, is the **Timber House Lodge.** Rooms here are plain but comfortable, with large beds, shower-tub combinations, color televisions, and wood furnishings. There's also a restaurant. ~ Route 36 and 1st Street, Chester; 916-258-2729. BUDGET.

Since most of its 34 rooms are filled by permanent residents, the **St. Francis Hotel** provides a glimpse into small town hotel living. Little has changed since the hotel opened its doors back in 1914. The modestly decorated rooms feature furniture from early in the century and the entire place has the aura of a bygone era. Despite its location in Historic Uptown Susanville, the hotel is exceptionally quiet. Reservations must be made in person. ~ 830 Main Street, Susanville; 916-257-3317. BUDGET.

HIDDEN ► The ultimate home-on-the-range experience out here in California big-sky country is at **Spanish Springs**, a 70,000-acre dude ranch where you can join cattle and horse drives. For eight days and seven nights, leave the commotion and clatter of everyday behind, pitch a tent under the stars, and let the cows lull you to sleep. At the main ranch, guests stay in cabins, suites, and duplexes decorated in Wild West fashion. Here you can join trail rides, swim

NATURAL BOUNTY

Outside Susanville, a 28-mile (roundtrip) detour on County Road A1 leads to **Eagle Lake**, one of the state's biggest natural lakes. The high alkaline content of this 22,000-acre body of water has created an environment which supports an incredible variety of animal life. In addition to the native Eagle Lake trout, there are antelope, porcupine, deer, white pelicans, and a rare species of osprey along its shores.

in the pool, play tennis, fish, or practice archery. For a true sense of life on the plains, you can even rent a 19th-century homestead. ~ Route 395, Ravendale; 916-234-2050, fax 916-234-2041. ULTRA-DELUXE.

Located within half a mile of the Niles Saloon and Modoc County Museum, the **Super 8** has 49 rooms plus a restaurant. It's a typical generic motel with the usual dresser-desk combination and dime store paintings; the staff is friendly, though, and it happens to be the nicest place in town. ~ 511 North Main Street, Alturas; 916-233-3545, fax 916-233-3305. BUDGET TO MODERATE.

DINING

After a busy day on the slopes of nearby Mt. Lassen, you can take your mountain-sized appetite to the **Timber House Restaurant** where you'll be treated to superb meals in a unique setting. Sam Herreld spent over three years as a one-man construction crew to assemble this architectural wonder from what he calls "the debris of the forest." Using a chain saw to carve 500-pound blocks of wood, Herreld put together a structure so solid that he claims the building will stand for at least 300 years. As you might expect, the bar, dining tables, and other furniture are all hand cut, giving the Timber House an earthy yet elegant look. The culinary delights include a seafood omelette plus a sampling of sandwiches. But it's around dinnertime that the chef really struts his stuff—sweet and sour baby back ribs, brochettes of beef, shrimp, and lobster, in addition to four different types of steak. This is without a doubt one of the Far North's most memorable meals. ~ Route 36 and 1st Street, Chester; 916-258-2729. DELUXE.

The **Kopper Kettle Cafe** has the formica-counter-and-metal-chair appearance of a typical coffee shop, but the food is great. Just ask any of the local residents who crowd into this gathering spot. For a hearty breakfast, try the pork chops and eggs, which come with hash browns, toast, and applesauce. Then for lunch there are giant hamburgers and fries. If you're on a budget, it's a good place to chow down. No dinner. ~ Route 36 and Myrtle Street, Chester; 916-258-2698. BUDGET.

"Time paid a visit to the Grand Cafe around 1935," a roving reporter once noted, "and it hasn't been back since." Everything about the **Grand Cafe** is at least 60 years old. This humble eatery is an uncrowded place where old-timers congregate to sip coffee and swap tales. Probably the most striking features in the Grand Cafe are the 30-foot-long formica counter and the wooden swivel chairs with hat clips. You'll also find art deco wooden booths, a wooden refrigerator, and seven deer heads mounted on the walls. Even the prices seem like something out of the past. In addition to standard breakfast and lunch coffee shop offerings, there are also homemade soups and breads. Closed Sunday. ~ 730 Main Street, Susanville; 916-257-4713. BUDGET.

◄ HIDDEN

The **Niles Hotel's High Grade Room** is a dining place and museum "where the West still lives." In addition to serving the best New York steak, filet mignon, and prime rib around, this elegant café houses a thriving saloon and an incredible array of antiques. There are several vintage Wurlitzer's, and hundreds of sepia-toned photographs. The frosted-glass doors, brass lighting fixtures, and hardwood floors have been beautifully restored. In winter, closed Sunday through Tuesday. Dinner only. ~ 304 South Main Street, Alturas; 916-233-3261. MODERATE TO DELUXE.

SHOPPING

Stover Landing is a treasure trove of books, locally crafted jewelry, unusual gifts, and coffee beans. ~ 118 Watson Road, Chester; 916-258-3779.

You'll find some unusual gifts at **Country Victorian Charm**, an elegant boutique that sells handmade Victorian dolls created by local artists, handcrafted furniture, pewter picture frames, Victorian angels, and everlasting floral arrangements. ~ 718 Main Street, Susanville; 916-257-8392.

NIGHTLIFE

The **Niles Saloon** is by far the best of the Far North's cowboy watering holes. Since 1908, this site has been synonymous with Saturday night for the area's cow-punchers. The drinks are Texas-sized concoctions, mounted trophy animals hang from every wall, and the decor consists of a collection of retired one-armed bandits. This down-home, goodtime atmosphere is accented by the sounds of a jukebox and leather boot heels across a hardwood floor. ~ 304 South Main Street, Alturas; 916-233-3261.

Other than these nightspots, you'll find restaurant bars and local saloons in small towns throughout the Far North. Many are short on entertainment, but provide a glimpse into this rough-hewn, backwoods region.

PARKS

LASSEN NATIONAL FOREST Sprawling across 1,100,000 acres, this giant facility fronts numerous lakes, including the popular Lake Almanor and Eagle Lake. It also contains Thousand Lake Wilderness, with its glacier-carved valley and 9000-foot peaks; **Caribou Wilderness**, a pine-forested plateau area featuring numerous lakes; and **Ishi Wilderness**, a 41,000-acre oak brushland with pine-covered plateaus. Facilities include picnic areas and restrooms; restaurants and groceries are available in nearby towns. ~ Accessible from Routes 44, 36, and 89; 916-257-2151.

▲ Permitted in 39 campgrounds; $6 to $12 per night for standard sites.

LASSEN VOLCANIC NATIONAL PARK Lassen Peak, a 10,457-foot plug dome volcano, tops the horizon in this 106,000-acre coniferous forest. The park's 50 lakes and numerous streams provide limited catch-and-release flyfishing. This area is popular with sightseers, cross-country skiers, and hikers (there are 150 miles of hiking trails). Motorized boats are prohibited. The park has picnic areas, restrooms, and a snack bar; restaurants and groceries are nearby. ~ Route 89 bisects the park, which is located about 50 miles east of Redding; 916-595-4444.

▲ Permitted in six campgrounds; $6 to $10 per night. The Manzanita Lake and Summit Lake campgrounds are the most popular, right off Route 89.

MCARTHUR–BURNEY FALLS MEMORIAL STATE PARK The chief attraction at this 853-acre facility is the twin, 129-foot waterfall; but the park also features a ponderosa forest, lake and stream fishing, and a bird population which includes bald eagles, Canada geese, owls, and grebes. Within the park are picnic areas and restrooms; restaurants and groceries are located nearby. Day-use fee, $5. ~ Located off Route 89 about 11 miles northeast of Burney; 916-335-2777.

▲ There are 128 campsites; $14 per night. Reservations are required Memorial Day through Labor Day; call DESTINET (800-444-7275).

LAVA BEDS NATIONAL MONUMENT Known primarily for its extensive network of lava tube caves, this amazing place features an active volcano, high desert plateaus, and large wilderness area. There are 25 miles of hiking trails. The visitors center provides free flashlights, which are essential for exploring, and sells headgear ($3.25), which is required for entering the caves. (A bicycle helmet is acceptable as headgear.) A visitors center and restrooms are the only facilities; restaurants and groceries are available 22 miles away in Tulelake. Day-use fee, $4. ~ Located off Route 139, 26 miles northwest of Canby; 916-667-2283.

▲ There are 44 designated campsites; $6 to $10 per night.

MODOC NATIONAL FOREST Nestled in the remote northeastern corner of California, this 1,654,392-acre facility is infrequently visited. Nevertheless, its features include obsidian cliffs, lava tubes, volcanic craters, open rangeland, basalt-domed plateaus, and mountain meadows. There are 118 miles of trails, plus numerous lakes and streams with fishing for trout and bass. The Warner Mountains and South Warner Wilderness are part of the forest. Toilets are the only facilities; restaurants and groceries available in nearby towns. ~ Located both east and west of Alturas, this noncontiguous facility is accessible from Route 395; 916-233-5811.

▲ There are 26 campgrounds; $5 to $7 per night for sites with tested water and garbage facilities; free for campsites without these amenities.

Outdoor Adventures

SPORT-FISHING

Some of the best year-round fishing in the American West is found right here in the Far North. Steelhead, salmon, and sturgeon run the region's countless rivers and trout and bass inhabit the mountain lakes. For an unforgettable adventure, check with one of the many outfitters offering fishing expeditions.

WEAVERVILLE TO YREKA Try **Kutzkey's Yreka** for a serendipitous catch. ~ Yreka; 916-842-4360. **Klamath River Outfitters** can lead you to the region's great fishing holes. ~ Somes Bar; 916-469-3349. **Trinity Alps Angling Experiences** arranges fishing charters on the Sacramento River and Trinity Lake. ~ Lewiston; 916-623-6757.

BOATING

Whether you prefer gliding across a crystal-blue lake in a rowboat, on waterskis, or paddling a canoe, the Far North resorts will cater to every desire.

REDDING To spend your days idling away on the water, contact **Bridge Bay Resort.** They rent houseboats and other kinds of motor boats. ~ Redding; 916-275-3021.

REDDING TO WEAVERVILLE Nestled in a valley surrounded by trees and water, **Oak Bottom Marina** rents several kinds of recreational boats. For those of you who like to sail, there are small sailboats. ~ Whiskeytown; 916-359-2269.

REDDING TO MT. SHASTA For fishing, waterskiing and houseboating, be sure to try **Antlers Resorts Marina.** ~ Lakehead; 916-238-2553. Located on the Sacramento arm of Lake Shasta is **Shasta Marina Resort.** ~ O'Brien; 916-238-2284.

WEAVERVILLE TO YREKA Situated in the lovely Trinity Alps, **Cedar Stock Marina** is the perfect spot to rent a houseboat. ~ Trinity Lake; 916-286-2225.

GLIDING

For a hawk's-eye view of Shasta Valley and Southern Oregon consider taking a sailplane ride with **Montague Aviation.** Basic rides average 15 to 20 minutes. You can also ride in a motor-powered airplane to see Mt. Ashland, Lassen Peak, Mt. Shasta, and the Klamath National Forest. ~ 1471 Airport Way, Montague; 916-459-3456.

SKIING

Ski enthusiasts can explore the Far North's winter wonderland on both downhill runs and cross-country treks. The skiing is particularly popular around Mt. Shasta and Lassen Peak. The **Shasta–Cascade Wonderland Association** will provide general information. ~ Redding; 916-275-5555.

REDDING TO MT. SHASTA Located at the foot of beautiful Mt. Shasta, **Mt. Shasta Ski Park** features four chairlifts and a 1350-foot vertical drop. You can also cross-country ski here. ~ Mount Shasta; 916-926-8686.

NORTHEAST LOOP For cross-country skiing call **Lassen Park Ski Area.** Lassen's most popular nordic trails begin at the Lassen Chalet (near Mineral on the park's south side) and lead to such enticing spots as Forest Lake. On the north side of Lassen, there's a nice beginner trail around Manzanita Lake (1.6 miles) and a popular medium-difficulty trail up the drainage of Manzanita Creek (10 miles). No rentals are available in the park. ~ Mineral; 916-595-4444.

PACK TRIPS

For the ultimate Western-style vacation, consider a horseback expedition through the Far North's mountainous wilderness. Experienced guides offer pack trips deep into this region of lost mountains and alpine rivers.

WEAVERVILLE TO YREKA To explore new frontiers, call **Six Pak Packers** for an exciting trip through the wilderness. ~ Weaverville; 916-623-6314.

REDDING TO MT. SHASTA If saddling a llama sounds more adventuresome, contact **Shasta Llamas.** ~ Mount Shasta; 916-926-1146.

BIKING

Bike riding in the Far North is a challenge which is rewarded with spectacular mountain scenery. It's a region for cyclists with experience: The climbs are often steep and the narrow-shouldered roadways are traveled by lumber trucks and RVS. But there are several highways well worth exploring.

WEAVERVILLE TO YREKA **Route 3** passes Trinity (Clair Engle) Lake and the historic town of Callahan on a lengthy journey from Weaverville to Yreka.

REDDING TO WEAVERVILLE For a ride through Shasta State Historic Park and along Whiskeytown Lake, try **Route 299** outside Redding. Be careful; it's a popular road with moderate traffic.

NORTHEAST LOOP **Route 89** from Mt. Shasta to McArthur–Burney Falls State Park rolls from 2000 to 4500 feet elevation while passing pristine countryside and tiny towns. **Route 44** between Lassen Volcanic National Park and Susanville traverses unspoiled timber country.

Bike Rentals For rentals and repairs in Redding, contact **Bikes Etcetera.** ~ Corner of Athens and Locust streets; 916-244-1954. In Yreka, try **Mt. Shasta Valley Bikes.** ~ 299 West Miner Street; 916-842-7701.

HIKING

More than any other part of the state, the Far North earns the description "Hidden California." Inhabited by black bears, coyotes, black-tailed deer, and an occasional bald eagle, the land offers hikers a glimpse of nature in its unspoiled state. The Trinity Alps feature more than 500 miles of trails for exploring glacial lakes, cool forests, and silent meadows. Mt. Shasta's snow-domed summit rewards mountaineers with other-worldly views, and Lassen Peak reveals the explosive side of this highly volcanic countryside.

WEAVERVILLE TO YREKA **Trinity Alps Wilderness Area** is an extraordinary haven for backpackers. Less crowded than other California wilderness areas, it possesses knife-edge peaks, deep pine forests, and lakes crowded with trout. You can camp anywhere in the forest with a wilderness permit (and a campfire permit, if you plan to build a fire).

Tangle Blue Lake Trail (4 miles) begins off Route 3 and leads through a flowering meadow to a lake rimmed by jagged peaks.

The Trinity Alps section of the **Pacific Crest Trail** (17 miles) starts at Scott Mountain Campground. It's one of the most scenic trails in the wilderness area, carrying past alpine lakes, meadows, and forests.

There's a choice to make when hiking the **Caribou Basin and Sawtooth Ridge Trail** (9.6 miles). You can follow a 100-year-old trail across Caribou Mountain, or take a newer trail that's easier to trek, more crowded, and measures two miles longer. In either case, the hike leads past mountain lakes and affords singular views from Sawtooth Ridge.

Stuart Fork to Emerald, Sapphire, and Mirror Lakes Trail (14.5 miles) is one of the most popular hikes in the Trinity Alps. It's one of Northern California's most picturesque hikes, resembling the Alps. It traverses an area teeming with wildlife en route to three subalpine lakes.

Beginning at Coffee Creek Road, the **Adams Lake Trail** (2.3 miles) leads to a tiny lake shadowed by a 7500-foot granite mountain.

For a journey to three excellent fishing lakes, take **Big Bear Lake Trail** (4.7 miles) located off Route 3. This steep path climbs through fir and cedar forests and past thickets of willow and alder. An added treat is the 200-foot Bear Creek waterfall. En route, beware of rattlesnakes basking in the sun.

Mavis Lake–Fox Creek Lake Trail (4.7 miles) leads to another group of lakes. Beginning seven miles from Callahan, it climbs through heavy timber country to four trout lakes.

A lake covered with lilypads and a desolate canyon populated by coyotes, deer, and black bears are the destinations along **Boulder Lake to Poison Canyon and Lilypad Lake Trail** (4 miles). A steep ridge makes this a hike for the hearty.

REDDING TO MT. SHASTA Unparalleled adventure awaits skilled mountaineers in **Mt. Shasta Recreation Area.** The 14,162-foot Mt. Shasta is accessed via three routes: **Horse Camp to Avalanche Gulch Trail, Mt. Shasta Ski Bowl Lodge Trail,** and **Horse Camp to Shastina Trail.**

Roller Coaster River Rides

If your favorite carnival ride is the roller coaster, you're ready for the adrenalin-pumping, spine-chilling thrill of whitewater river rafting. At one time it was strictly a sport for daredevils, but more and more vacationing adventurers are taking to the rapids. As a result, over 60 professional guide services in Northern California now combine expertise and equipment in a variety of tour packages.

Whether you're looking for a true test of nerve, or prefer excitement in smaller doses, these knowledgeable river pilots can provide an enjoyable whitewater experience. You're liable to wind up in the drink at least once, especially if you choose one of the more challenging runs. But getting wet is part of the intoxicating rush created by a fast-moving stretch of river. There's also the serenity of paddling past untracked forests and bald mountains. In spite of river rafting's increasing popularity, the Far North's endless river system makes it a solitary wilderness activity.

Tours vary in length from one to seven days, and generally include food and all the equipment necessary except sleeping bags. Camping is usually the rule, but lodge trips are also available.

River rafting is primarily a summertime sport, centered in the Klamath, Shasta, Trinity, and Six Rivers National Forests. The most frequently explored routes include Hell's Corner Gorge in the Upper Klamath River, the Salmon River, and Upper Sacramento River. For whitewater pioneers, Burnt Ranch Gorge in the south fork of the Trinity River, the Scott River, and Lower McCloud River Canyon offer unmatched challenges.

For rates, reservations, and more information contact **Friends of the River**. ~ 128 J Street, 2nd floor, Sacramento; 916-448-3820. **William McGinnis' Whitewater Voyages** offers an array of river trips including one- and two-day trips as well as extended expeditions. ~ P. O. Box 20400, El Sobrante, CA 94820; 510-222-5994. To experience the thrill of a river run, contact **Wilderness Adventures**. Besides that, they'll point out plenty of wildlife—eagles, deer, hawks, beavers, and otters. ~ 108 Ski Village Drive, Mount Shasta, CA 96067; 916-926-6282.

Climbers should obtain information and equipment in the town Mount Shasta and register (if ascending higher than 6000 feet) on the east side of the Forest Service office (204 West Alma Street; 916-926-4511) before ascending the mountain.

NORTHEAST LOOP **Lassen Volcanic National Park** offers 150 miles of hiking trails leading past lava flows, volcanic craters, and boiling mud pots.

Starting from the park's southwest entrance station, the **Forest Lake and Brokeoff Mountain Trail** (3.8 miles) carries past open meadows and thick forest. Offering scenic views of Mt. Shasta, it's also an excellent route for flower-gazing and birdwatching.

For a hike to a 75-foot waterfall, follow **Mill Creek Falls Trail** (2.3 miles) along its scenic course.

The **Ridge Lakes Trail** (1.1 miles) cuts through fir and pine forests and arrives at two jewel-like lakes (which become a single lake when the water level rises). There's a 1000-foot elevation change on this climb.

The largest hydrothermal area in Lassen lies along **Bumpass Hell Trail** (1.5 miles). One of the region's most dramatic hikes, the trail passes hot springs, steam vents, and mud pots.

Still, the finest hike in the park is **Lassen Peak Trail** (2.5 miles). Leading to the summit, it provides 360 views of the surrounding countryside and reveals evidence of recent volcanic activity. Hikers should be in good physical condition, bring water and jackets, and turn back in case of thunderstorms.

Devastated Area Trail (.3 mile) is an easy way to see a variety of rock formations and park panoramas. Highlights of this walk are volcanic formations from the May 1915 eruption and lava flow. Wheelchair accessible.

Chaos Crags and Crags Lake Trail (1.8 miles) begins near the Loomis Museum parking lot. Along this relatively easy walk are half a dozen immense crags, as well as wildflowers and a variety of geologic formations. During wet years a small lake forms in a "recently" (300 year-old) collapsed dome at the top of the trail.

Terrace, Shadow, and Cliff Lakes Trail (1.7 miles) begins at a high elevation and carries along a flower-banked path to three lakes.

The best spot for summer wildflowers is **Paradise Meadows Trail** (1.5 miles). Beginning at the Hat Lake parking area, the trail climbs for a mile before reaching the meadows.

Crystal Lake Trail (.4 mile) begins on the east side of Juniper Lake and goes through forests and meadows to one of the park's most beautiful lakes.

For views of Lassen and other nearby peaks, climb **Inspiration Point Trail** (.8 mile). It tracks through western white pine and red fir forests and offers unforgettable vistas.

Cinder Cone Nature Trail (2 miles) travels up one of the nation's most perfectly formed cinder cones. The trail begins at Butte Lake Campground. High-top boots are recommended.

Beginning at Badger Flat, the Lassen Park section of the **Pacific Crest Trail** (19.2 miles) carries past Soap Lake, Fairfield Peak, Lower Twin Lake, Swan Lake, Pilot Mountain, Boiling Springs Lake, and Red Mountain to Little Willow Lake. In this area, the trail (which in its entirety extends from Canada to Mexico) is fairly level and can be hiked in two days at a comfortable pace.

Transportation

CAR

From San Francisco, **Route 80** connects with **Route 5**, which leads through the heart of the Far North. It passes through Redding, Dunsmuir, Mount Shasta, and Yreka en route to Oregon.

AIR

For those traveling by air, Horizon Air, Sierra Expressway, and United Express fly into **Redding Municipal Airport**.

BUS

Greyhound Bus Lines travels Route 5, stopping in Redding, Dunsmuir, Mount Shasta, and Yreka. ~ 800-231-2222.

TRAIN

Amtrak provides daily service on their "Coast Starlight" to Redding and Dunsmuir. ~ 800-872-7245.

CAR RENTALS

Avis Rent A Car (916-221-4620, 800-331-1212) and **Hertz Rent A Car** (916-221-2855, 800-654-3131) have facilities at Redding Municipal Airport.

Lodging Index

Dining Index

Index

HIDDEN GUIDES

Adventure travel or a relaxing vacation?—"Hidden" guidebooks are the only travel books in the business to provide detailed information on both. Aimed at environmentally aware travelers, our motto is "Adventure Travel Plus." These books combine details on unique hotels, restaurants and sightseeing with information on camping, sports and hiking for the outdoor enthusiast.

THE NEW KEY GUIDES

Based on the concept of ecotourism, The New Key Guides are dedicated to the preservation of Central America's rare and endangered species, architecture and archaeology. Filled with helpful tips, they give travelers everything they need to know about these exotic destinations.

ULTIMATE FAMILY GUIDES

These innovative guides present the best and most unique features of a family destination. Quality is the keynote. In addition to thoroughly covering each destination, they feature short articles and one-line "teasers" that are both fun and informative.

Order Form

Ulysses Press books are available at bookstores everywhere. If any of the following titles are unavailable at your local bookstore, ask the bookseller to order them. Or you can order them directly from Ulysses Press (P.O. Box 3440, Berkeley, CA 94703; 510-601-8301, 800-377-2542).

HIDDEN GUIDEBOOKS

___ Hidden Boston and Cape Cod, $9.95
___ Hidden Carolinas, $15.95
___ Hidden Coast of California, $15.95
___ Hidden Colorado, $13.95
___ Hidden Florida, $15.95
___ Hidden Florida Keys and Everglades, $9.95
___ Hidden Hawaii, $15.95
___ Hidden Idaho, $13.95
___ Hidden Maui, $12.95
___ Hidden Montana, $12.95
___ Hidden New England, $16.95
___ Hidden Oregon, $12.95
___ Hidden Pacific Northwest, $16.95
___ Hidden Rockies, $16.95
___ Hidden San Francisco and Northern California, $15.95
___ Hidden Southern California, $15.95
___ Hidden Southwest, $16.95
___ Hidden Tahiti $15.95
___ Hidden Wyoming $12.95

THE NEW KEY GUIDEBOOKS

___ The New Key to Belize, $14.95
___ The New Key to Cancún and the Yucatán, $13.95
___ The New Key to Costa Rica, $15.95
___ The New Key to Ecuador and the Galápagos, $15.95
___ The New Key to Guatemala, $14.95

ULTIMATE FAMILY GUIDEBOOKS

___ Disneyland and Beyond, $12.95
___ Disney World and Beyond, $12.95

Mark the book(s) you're ordering and enter the total cost here ☞ [ ]

California residents add 8% sales tax here ☞ [ ]

Shipping, check box for your preferred method and enter cost here ☞ [ ]

❑ BOOK RATE **FREE! FREE! FREE!**
❑ PRIORITY MAIL $3.00 First book, $1.00/each additional book
❑ UPS 2-DAY AIR $7.00 First book, $1.00/each additional book

Billing, enter total amount due here and check method of payment ☞ [ ]

❑ CHECK ❑ MONEY ORDER
❑ VISA/MASTERCARD________________________ EXP. DATE ________

NAME ______________________________ PHONE ______________
ADDRESS ____
____
CITY ________________________ STATE ______ ZIP ____________

MONEY-BACK GUARANTEE ON DIRECT ORDERS PLACED THROUGH ULYSSES PRESS.

ABOUT THE AUTHOR

RAY RIEGERT is the author of seven travel books, including *Hidden Southern California*. His most popular work, *Hidden Hawaii*, won the coveted Lowell Thomas Travel Journalism Award for Best Guidebook. In addition to his role as publisher of Ulysses Press, he has written for the *Chicago Tribune*, *Saturday Evening Post*, *San Francisco Examiner and Chronicle*, and *Travel & Leisure*. A member of the Society of American Travel Writers, he lives in the San Francisco Bay area with his wife, co-publisher Leslie Henriques, and their son Keith and daughter Alice.

ABOUT THE UPDATE AUTHOR

JUDY JACOBS is an inveterate world traveler whose journeys have taken her to more than 25 countries. Her articles, which number over 1000, have appeared in more than 50 magazines and newspapers including *Business Travel News*, *The Christian Science Monitor*, *Hemispheres*, *Ms.*, and *San Francisco Focus*. She writes for children as well and is the author of *Indonesia, A Nation of Islands*.